The *Denbigh's* Civilian Imports

Customs Records of a Civil War Blockade Runner between Mobile and Havana

Dated July 29, 1864, Thomas C. Healy's portrait of the blockade-runner *Denbigh* shows the ship as configured in '64 and '65. Here the *Denbigh* departs Mobile with a full load of cotton bales a week before Admiral Farragut's West Gulf Blockading Squadron ended that port's use by runners. *Peery Southern Maritime Collection, South Carolina Historical Society, Charleston, South Carolina.*

The *Denbigh's* Civilian Imports

Customs Records of a Civil War Blockade Runner between Mobile and Havana

J. Barto Arnold III
Institute of Nautical Archaeology
Texas A&M University
College Station, Texas

Denbigh Shipwreck Project
Publication 5

INSTITUTE OF
NAUTICAL ARCHAEOLOGY

THE *DENBIGH'S* CIVILIAN IMPORTS:
CUSTOMS RECORDS OF A CIVIL WAR BLOCKADE RUNNER
BETWEEN MOBILE AND HAVANA

Library of Congress Control Number 2011913266
ISBN 978-0-9795874-2-9

Institute of Nautical Archaeology
P.O. Drawer HG, College Station, Texas 77841
http://ina.tamu.edu/

Printed in the United States of America

Contents

Figures

Introduction to the *Denbigh*

and Her Mobile Customs Documents

As the Civil War commenced, the newly formed Confederacy found itself short of cash and manufactured goods, and soon its sellable agricultural products were for the most part blockaded. So the South turned largely to Great Britain and a few other European powers as sources of weapons, clothing, tools, and medicines that could be paid for with bales of cotton. Importing goods to and from the Confederate States of America (C.S.A.) was not easy, however, since Southern financial factors first had to establish themselves abroad. Then too, blockade-running ships and crews had to be purchased or otherwise acquired for transporting cotton to nearby neutral ports and merchandise to Dixie.

The present tome considers merchandise brought through the Union cordon by one successful and famous blockade runner, the British steamer *Denbigh.* It discusses the goods involved in the Mobile blockade-running trade by publishing fascinating ships' invoices as well as customs records. These raw descriptions reveal much about life in a blockaded southern city and the mechanics of the trade intended for the civilian population. The route between Mobile and Havana in the Gulf of Mexico region is stressed. This was the first operating area of the blockade-runner *Denbigh*, whose wreck we excavated in 1998–2002.

Without doubt the description of the financial side of blockade running, plus the details of the imported goods and their handling, furnishes insights into the economic woes of the Confederate States. Yet such troubles were often mitigated by blockade-running successes at home and the work of dedicated representatives of the Confederate government abroad.

It is my recommendation that this and the other books of the *Denbigh* Project Series produced by the Institute of Nautical Archaeology (INA) be examined by the reader, for they document the career and demise of a single blockade runner. Blockade running was clearly vital to the South's war effort, but for financiers and crew was a dangerous way to earn one's daily bread.

Background on the *Denbigh* Shipwreck Project

This book presents a large number of Civil War documents, some quoted in full including all of the *Denbigh's*, and some synopsized. The customs records and correspondence were selected to elucidate blockade running in the Gulf of Mexico region. Publishing this data facilitates access and promotes future analysis. Mobile and Galveston were the Confederacy's ports of call for the blockade-runner *Denbigh* (pronounced "Den-bee"). Most of the documents reference the *Denbigh* herself and the rest help explain the activities of this ship and her sisters in the runner's trade. The *Denbigh* documents can easily be compared and contrasted to the prewar and early-war examples in this book.

We collected documents of the Confederate States Customs House at Mobile consisting of import customs forms (manifests[1]) and accompanying detailed invoices. Throughout the book were added notes and footnotes containing comments relevant to the *Denbigh* Project. Also included were a few documents that show the *Denbigh's* cotton cargoes outbound from Mobile. The ship's voyages on the Havana–Mobile–Havana route dated January–August 1864. The cargoes continued in processing until December of that year when the *Denbigh's* final customs forms were filed. The *Denbigh* was the last runner out of Mobile when the Union Navy captured the forts at the mouth of Mobile Bay in early August 1864.

In the Gulf, the purpose of steam vessels such as the *Denbigh* was to bring in army supplies and manufactured goods, mainly from Havana. The ships then returned through the blockade to Cuba carrying

---

[1] A list or invoice of a ship's cargo, specifying the marks, numbers, contents, shipper, consignee, etc. of each package of goods, to be exhibited at the customs house.

cotton (Figure 1). Smaller and more numerous sailing vessels did much the same, but put ashore at secondary and shallower ports, bays, and bayous. The purpose of the Union Navy's blockading squadron was to prevent this trade by destroying or (preferably) capturing blockade runners.

The utility of this book for the *Denbigh* Project was as follows. The most basic context for the *Denbigh* was the 1864–1865 activities of the blockade runners going to and from Mobile and Galveston and other western Gulf ports. One important question was what goods were imported for civilians. The present book provided the required information in surprising detail, even to the level of individual families. Military imports were well understood, but civilian imports have had little attention. The result was important both to those generally interested in the Civil War and especially to those interested in the history and nautical archaeology of blockade runners.

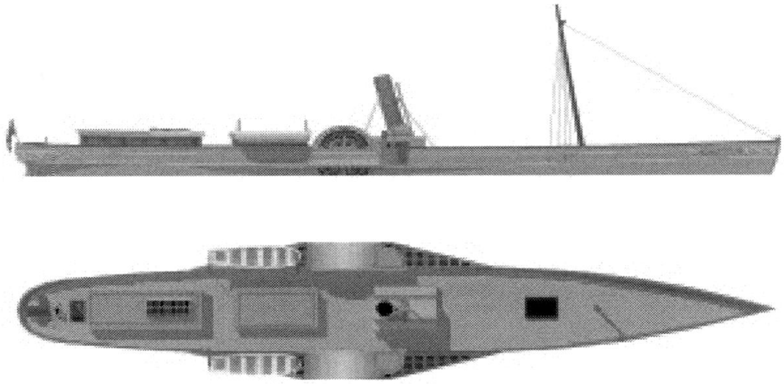

Figure 1. The *Denbigh* based on a contemporary portrait. *Illustration by Andrew W. Hall, INA.*

Table 1. The *Denbigh* at a Glance.

Launched:	August 1860
Built:	Laird, Sons & Co., Birkenhead
Length:	182 feet (55.5 meters) b.p., ~195 feet o.a.
Beam:	22 feet (6.7 meters), excluding paddle wheels
Depth of Hold:	8.7 feet (2.65 meters)
Register Tons:	162.69
Sustained Speed:	13.7 knots (15.75 miles per hour)
Cost to Build:	£ 110,250 (approximately $ 1 million today)
Port of Registry:	Liverpool, England
Trips as Runner:	13 successful round trips
Cargo Capacity:	Approx. 500 bales (225,000 pounds) cotton
Crew:	21 officers and men

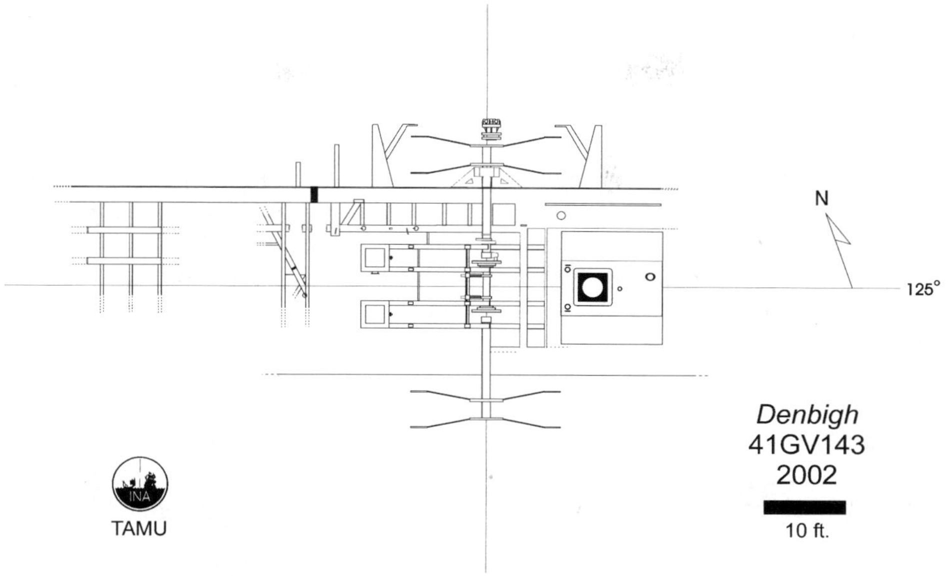

Figure 2. The *Denbigh's* deck level site plan. *INA*.

The archival documents herein were from the National Archives, Southeast Regional Center in Atlanta (NARA–Atlanta). They were Confederate customs house of Mobile, Alabama's records, including a large number of customs forms and invoices, detailed records essential for studying civilian imports. The documents pertained to the *Denbigh* herself. All placed the ship in the context of the increasingly desperate last years of the Civil War. Many revealed the thoughts and attitudes of the people involved in fascinating personal ways. These extractions from the archives provided vital information concerning the *Denbigh* and imported supplies for the citizens of Mobile.

Imported munitions and other, often surprising, strategic material meant life or death for the Confederate States of America. Goods for civilians have received much less attention. The records of civilian trade herein revealed fascinating insights of daily life for the blockaded population of Mobile and neighboring areas. Studying the *Denbigh* and her place in the blockade-running supply system was enlightening. It became clear that the issue was not only what supplies were brought in and why, but also that the system that evolved contrasted sharply with the prewar period in ways clearly shown by the civilian customs records.

The Customs Records Described

The *Denbigh* served Mobile and then Galveston from late 1863 through May 24, 1865. The side-paddler grounded entering Galveston and was burned by the Union Navy about the time of the Trans-Mississippi Department's last gasp. Until the Battle of Mobile closed the port in early Aug. 1864, the *Denbigh* made the Havana–Mobile run seven times and became a great favorite of the Alabama townspeople. Her stealthy and persistent ways led to several frustrated comments in dispatches from Adm. Farragut, and the British-flagged ship acquired "the Packet" as nickname due to her clockwork-like reliability.

The main function of the blockade runners was to bring in military supplies for the Confederate armed forces and to take out cotton to pay for these goods. The merchandise brought in for the civilian population was a secondary matter in the government's view. The *Denbigh* Project included, as a complement to the archaeology, historical research to find the scattered trail of documents about the ship. Recently INA's research led to customs records for Mobile located at the NARA–Atlanta. The *Denbigh*'s import files revealed surprising and numerous invoices showing small individual family purchases from Havana stores. Prior to the war, large merchant orders had predominated. There were some less numerous, medium-sized merchant orders during the *Denbigh's* time as well, and some of these were matched to newspaper advertisements offering goods for sale.

A constant question for the *Denbigh* Project staff concerned the daily life implications that might be provided by the archaeological remains in combination with the historical records. What were the owners, crew, and customers up to, and why did they do things the way they did? Getting to the level of daily life for individuals and small groups was often the most elusive and yet exciting goal. Here was a treasure trove of such detail concerning the citizens of Mobile and surrounding areas. Due to peculiarities of the *Denbigh*'s operations, the customs records showed exactly what individual families ordered after about three years of war and shortages and the amount of cash they felt they could risk in an uncertain and dangerous trade.

Part I of the present book shows transcripts of all the *Denbigh*'s documents in Mobile's customs house files (Jan. 1864–Dec. 1864).[2] In Part II we present the whole file of customs documents from Nov. 1860 for purposes of prewar comparison. Also included are a sample of other prewar customs documents from the fall of 1860 and early war documents of general interest. The same section includes a few records for other blockade runners probably owned by the same company that owned the *Denbigh*, the European Trading Company (E.T.C.). These last provide an idea of that company's larger activities. We also include a chapter with the customs export forms for the *Denbigh*'s cotton cargoes and a customs derived list of blockade runners trading at Mobile.

There were merchant orders among the *Denbigh* files, but they were much smaller (in merchandise quantity and total price) than prewar merchant orders. The wartime merchant orders were filled in Havana contrasting with prewar shipments mostly direct from Great Britain. The merchants seemingly drew in their horns during the blockade, not risking large amounts of capital like the investments required for large prewar cargoes.

Interestingly, items from some of the *Denbigh*-carried merchant shipments could be traced directly to Mobile newspaper ads for auction sales. We included advertisement examples with the relevant customs records. These showed merchants importing desirable civilian merchandise on speculation, no doubt expecting substantial profit at auction as opposed to goods on order for individuals. There would doubtless be great cost savings, even paying a small commission for the service plus customs duties, for the family that could make a small order directly to a Havana merchant. The difference was who took the risk of loss inherent in running the blockade, the merchant or the ordering family. The *Denbigh*'s record of successful runs gave confidence to those who chose to forgo the middleman. This ship's success may have stemmed in part from the *Denbigh* Capt. Abner M. Godfrey's knowledge of local waters gained as a bayman (sailor in the bay trade) before the war (personal communication from a direct descendant).

From other, non-customs documents we knew that the *Denbigh* took C.S. government munitions through the blockade to Mobile. These shipments for the government did not appear with the civilian cargoes detailed in customs records. War-like goods (e.g. gun powder) occasionally appeared as cargo items in the customs documents, but they were privately owned and for sale in Mobile to either civilian or military.

The *Denbigh*'s Capt. Godfrey was associated as facilitator on most of the invoices for small orders. A typical invoice indicated that Godfrey bought from a given merchant, on behalf of a named person, presumably residing in Mobile, a brief list of articles in listed quantities at specified prices. A handful of the invoices bore the name of Peter Skuse, an officer of the *Denbigh*. The author received the impression that these items were for Skuse's private trade. The custom of, presumably limited, side trade by officers and crew was known. The large number of invoices by Godfrey made one wonder if his deals were private on his own account or on the ship's account, i.e. for the profit of the ship's owners. One document pointed toward this being Godfrey's personal trade.

Godfrey lived in Mobile both before and after the war. Perhaps the small orders and all the work involved began as an accommodation for friends and relations. It appeared to have grown quickly. This kind of customs invoice for family orders dating either before or during the war was not observed in the other ships' customs records from the same NARA–Atlanta files. Presumably normal peacetime trade mechanisms were not functioning, and this kind of trade, arranged by Capt. Godfrey, took their place as a makeshift.

Similarly, what about ship's hold space for the extra civilian goods above and beyond the government cargo? One might speculate that the military goods probably tended to be high weight, low volume like cases of rifles. That might well have left plenty of excess cargo capacity for packages with low weight, high volume civilian goods like fabric for new clothes and a few pairs of shoes, which were among the most frequently

---

[2] NARA–Atlanta, RG 36 Bureau of Customs, Mobile, Alabama, Entry of Merchandise 1820–1905; 1864–1866; Box 21 & 22, Entry 1564c.

appearing items. Can't you just hear it? "It's been a while–Momma wants a new dress! *And* the kids have outgrown their shoes." Added to the short list was often a treat for Dad such as Cuban cigars and maybe something special for the whole family like fancy preserves, fine tea, or coffee. The small orders were mostly for basic necessities and a few "luxury" items and typically totaled $50–75. This was an amount a modestly well-to-do family could risk losing should the ship be captured by a blockading Union ship.

The customs records herein allowed informed speculation about daily life in Civil War Mobile and environs, even down to the family level. The shipwreck archaeologist is part anthropologist, part historian, striving for the rare glimpses of such details. How did they live back then? How and why did they do things a particular way? The *Denbigh*'s import records yielded some thoughts along these lines in ways not always available from archaeological findings alone. Researchers may find additional insights in this data. Making convenient access to the customs forms and their data was an important reason to publish this book.

Although not all sets were complete, it seemed proper customs import documentation for a shipment consisted of a preprinted form for calculating duties accompanied by foreign merchant's invoice with purchase price of the merchandise. Signatures of seller, buyer, buyer's agent, and customs officer attested to accuracy and conformance to regulations. Interestingly, the government customs collector's signature very rarely appeared in its allotted space on the war-time forms. The prewar forms were much more complete with signatures dates present in the appropriate blanks. Was this an attempt to hide identities and responsibility if the war was lost? Was it simple prudence by the government's agents or perhaps an assessment of the Confederacy's prospects?

The preprinted customs form was an oversized sheet of paper folded to about the size of a business envelope (4⅛ in. x 9½ in. or 10.5 cm x 24.1 cm). When folded with invoices inside, the form functioned like a file folder, holding the related documents together. In addition to the parties discussed above, the following information was supposed to be provided on the form: name of ship transporting the goods, captain's name, suppliers and facilitators in the foreign port, commissions and charges, abstract of types of goods in the shipment (rate of duty varied by type of goods), date ship entered port, and date the import duties paid and cargo released by customs house (termed "merchandise entered"). The form was folded in such a way as to show on the outside an abstract block with the most important data.

Expected in prewar sets but usually missing from the wartime examples were a consul's certificate and bill of lading. The (importing country's) consul's certificate was obtained in the foreign port where the voyage originated, testified to the legitimacy of the shipment, and provided invoice costs of the goods. The issuing consul was a diplomatic representative of the country to which the cargo was bound. The bill of lading was issued by the ship's captain acknowledging receipt of the cargo in good condition, parties involved, costs of shipping, terms of storage aboard, and method of unloading in the port of delivery. The consul's certificate and the bill of lading were important components of the "ship's papers," without which the legality of the voyage might be in question. If a suspicious ship ditched her papers to hide the circumstances of the voyage, this alone was enough evidence under international law for a prize court to condemn the ship as a blockade runner and to award the proceeds of sale of ship and cargo to the captors.[3]

Often the invoices provided the most interesting details and varied from formal printed forms including the merchant's letterhead to mere scraps of paper hastily scribbled in pencil. The latter type were hurriedly prepared as the cargo lot was processed in the customs house and import duties calculated just prior to delivery to the buyer. The examples quickly prepared on a scrap of paper provided a fig leaf to cover the regulation requiring an invoice document with proper calculation and payment of import duties. Many of the invoices and not nearly as interesting customs forms are illustrated in this book. Prewar files usually contained a more detailed and formal invoice than did the wartime files.

In some instances the folded forms contained no invoices, leaving one to wonder if the usual contents had been lost over time or if requirements for complete documentation were sometimes flouted. Maybe the answer was both of the above. At any rate the customs documentation business was *a lot* of tedious work. Fortunately for us, really interesting details of daily life often worked their way into the listings of merchandise. The author called such details to the reader's attention with notes and footnotes and interesting cargo items in the transcripts were highlighted with boldfaced type.

[3] The *Denbigh* Project has a book on prize law in preparation for publication.

The NARA–Atlanta's folders containing the documents were mostly arranged by the months in which the duty was paid and the cargo therefore cleared for delivery from the customs house. On a single voyage there were numerous cargo lots, each lot containing numerous items bought by one owner or firm. It usually took more than one month for all of a ship's cargo lots to clear customs, so lots carried by the *Denbigh* on a single voyage were scattered over several NARA monthly file folders. It would have been ideal to arrange the *Denbigh's* documents in this book by the voyage on which the cargo traveled. Unfortunately, many of the customs forms were not filled out completely, lacking the critical ship's arrival date by which to be sorted. This necessitated the monthly file based approach adopted here.

Context for Blockade Runners at Mobile

The author scanned the *Mobile Register and Advertiser* newspaper for information about the blockade runners in articles and advertisements. We concentrated on the period when the *Denbigh* was active in Mobile, reading Dec. 1863 through mid-June 1864, the period that could be obtained on microfilm. Dates for the rest of the time through early August were not available. The matching of customs documents to auction sale advertisements was interesting. In the process the author noted the following articles and ads concerning blockade runner stock for sale (Figures 3–7), and an actual receipt for an investor (Figure 8) was found in a history of Mobile examined during research in that city (Delaney 1971:155).

Also noted were Mobile commodity and stock prices reported in each Sunday edition of the *Mobile Advertiser and Register* that included listings for blockade-runner stock (Table 2). The price listings seemed confusing to the modern reader. For example, the Sunday May 1, 1864 paper showed the price for *Donegal* stock as 400@500. Did it mean $400 bid and $500 asked? Or did it mean shares of $400 face value were selling for $500? Readers back then were expected to already know how the system worked. The terms "settled" and "nominal" were fairly clear. The investments "settled" probably indicated successful completion of a voyage or a fixed time period and then repayment to investors of capitol and profits. "Nominal" and "par." seemed to mean shares were selling at face value. "Captured" was self-evident and meant loss of the ship and investment. In the price listing tables a series of blanks seemed to indicate the vessel was no longer running or at least no stock price was quoted. In mid-April 1864, the newspaper changed its reporting format, dropping some vessel listings and adding others. The *Denbigh* stock listing appeared at that point.

The table of stock prices was interesting in itself and the data were presented here to make it easily available. Many questions remain about how the investor aspect of blockade running was conducted. The author welcomes contact from those who might have a more complete interpretation of the stock listings.

Blockade Stocks.

STEAMERS.	
Donegal	400@500
Phœnix	nominal
Mary	nominal
Denbigh	nominal
Mary Virginia	200@250
Breckinridge	60@ 64
Fanny	50@ 60
Lizzie Davis	200@250
Alabama Steamship Company	125@150
Alabama	100@125
SCHOONERS.	
Phantom	200@250
Thistle	100@110
Judson	100@110
Cecilia	100@110
J. C. Gwinn	200@250
Badger	nominal
Mischief	nominal

Figure 3. Example of weekly stock quotes (*Mobile Advertiser and Register* May 1, 1864).

Table 2. Mobile, Alabama blockade stock prices.[4]

Steamers	**1/3/64**	**1/11/64**	**1/17/64**	**1/24/64**	**1/31/64**	**2/7/64**	**2/14/64**
Warrior	100@125	125@150	125@150	150@200	300@325	300@325	200@225
Crescent	100@125	125@150	100@125	125@150	200@225	200@225	200@225
Fanny	75@125	75@100	75@100	100@125	100@125	100@125	100@125
W. H. Smith	125@150	125@150	250@300	200@250	250@300	200@250	150@200
Lizzie Davis	175@225	200@250	200@250	200@250	250@300	250@300	250@300
AE&DT Co.[5]	135@150	125@135	125@135	100@125	125@135	125@130	120@150
Alabama	40@50	100@125	75@100	125@150	100@125	150@200	150@200
Alabama SS Co.[6]	125@150	125@150	125@150	125@150	125@150	125@150	125@150
Alice Vivian	400@450	400@450	400@450	400@450	400@450	400@450	400@450
Breckinridge	100@110	100@110	100@110	100@110	100@110	100@110	100@110
Mary Virginia	100@110	100@110	100@125	100@110	100@125	100@125	100@125
Alice	no rate	no rate	no rate	no rate	no rate	no rate	no rate
Schooners							
Alert	Rept captrd	captured	captured	captured	captured	captured	captured
Magnolia	100@110	100@110	100@110	100@110	100@110	100@110	100@110
Clementine	100@110	100@110	100@110	100@110	100@110	25@50	25@50
Badger	100@110	100@110	100@110	100@110	100@110	100@110	100@110
Mischief	100@110	100@110	100@110	100@110	100@110	100@110	100@110
J. C. Gwinn	100@100	100@110	100@110	150@200	150@200	200@250	250@300
Star	400@500	400@450	400@500	300@400	300@400	400@450	400@450
Maria				100@150	150@200	150@200	150@200

2/21/64	**2/28/64**	**3/6/64**	**3/13/64**	**3/20/64**	**3/27/64**	**4/4/64**	**4/10/64**	**Steamers**
300@350	400@450	300@350	250@300	300@350	settled	settled	settled	*Warrior*
150@200	250@300	200@250	125@150	150@300	settled	settled	settled	*Crescent*
100@125	100@125	50@60	50@60	50@60	50@60	50@60	60@75	*Fanny*
200@250	250@300	200@250	250@300	300@350	400@450	400@450	400@430	*W. H. Smith*
250@300	300@350	300@350	250@300	250@300	250@300	250@300	200@250	*Lizzie Davis*
125@135	125@150	150@175	125@150	125@150	125@150	125@150	125@150	AE&DT Co.
150@200	150@200	150@200	125@150	settled up	100@125	100@125	100@125	*Alabama*
125@150	150@200	150@200	125@150	125@150	125@150	125@150	125@150	Al SS Co.
400@450	450@500	400@450	350@400	400@450	settled	settled	settled	*Alice Vivian*
100@110	100@110	100@110	100@110	100@110	100@110	100@110	100@110	*Breckinridge*
100@125	100@125	100@125	100@125	100@125	100@125	100@125	100@125	*Mary Virginia*
no rate	no rate	no rate	no rate	no rate	no rate	no rate	no rate	*Alice*
								Schooners
captured	captured	captured	captured	captured	captured	captured	captured	*Alert*
75@100	75@100	25@50	50@75	25@50	captured	captured	captured	*Magnolia*
25@50	25@50	25@50	25@50	25@50	settled	settled	settled	*Clementine*
100@110	100@110	100@110	100@110	100@110	100@110	100@110	100@110	*Badger*
100@110	100@110	100@110	100@110	100@110	100@110	100@110	100@110	*Mischief*
250@2?0	400@500	350@400	450@500	400@450	350@400	400@450	400@450	*J. C. Gwinn*
400@450	450@500	400@450	350@400	400@450	350@400	400@450	400@450	*Star*
150@200	150@200	150@200	150@200	captured	captured	captured	captured	*Maria*

[4] Table of weekly prices constructed as one large table presented in three segments due to spacing.
[5] Alabama Exporting & Direct Trade Co.
[6] Alabama Steamship Co.

Steamers	**4/19/64**	**4/24/64**	**5/1/64**	**5/8/64**	**5/15/64**	**5/22/64**
Warrior						
Crescent						
Fanny	40@50	50@60	50@60	50@60	70@80	70@80
W. H. Smith	467@533					
Lizzie Davis	187@200	200@250	200@250	200@250	200@250	200@250
AE&DT Co.	83@100					
Alabama	67@83	75@100	100@125	125@150	100@125	100@125
Alabama SS Co.	83@100	100@125	125@150	125@150	125@150	125@150
Alice Vivian						
Breckinridge	67@78	50@60	50@60	50@60	50@60	50@60
Mary Virginia	133@187	200@250	200@250	200@250	125@150	125@150
Alice						
Donegal		nominal	400@500	500@550	500@600	500@600
Mary		nominal	nominal	nominal	nominal	nominal
Denbigh		nominal	nominal	nominal	nominal	nominal
Phoenix			nominal	nominal	par.	par.
Schooners						
Alert						
Magnolia						
Clementine						
Badger	nominal	nominal	nominal	nominal	nominal	nominal
Mischief	nominal	nominal	nominal	nominal	nominal	nominal
J. C. Gwinn		200@250	300@350	300@350	200@300	
Star						
Maria						
Phantom		200@250	200@250	200@250	200@250	200@250
Thistle		100@110	100@110	100@110	100@110	100@110
Judson		100@110	100@110	captured	captured	captured
Cecelia		100@110	100@110	100@110	100@110	100@110

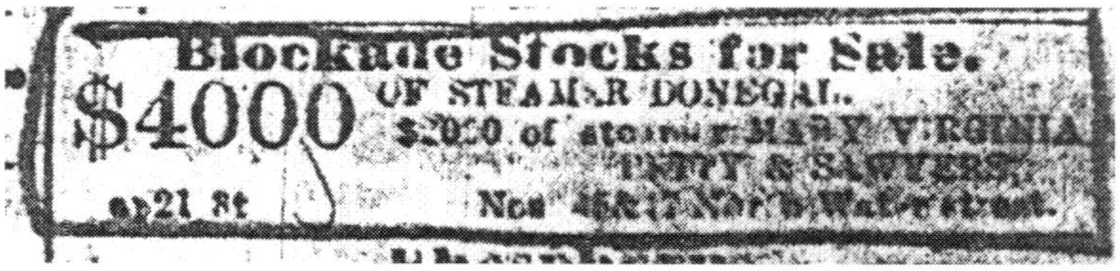
Blockade Stocks for Sale.
$4000 OF STEAMER DONEGAL.
ap21 3t

Figure 4. Ad for stock in *Donegal* and *Mary Virginia* (*Mobile Advertiser and Register* April 21, 1864).

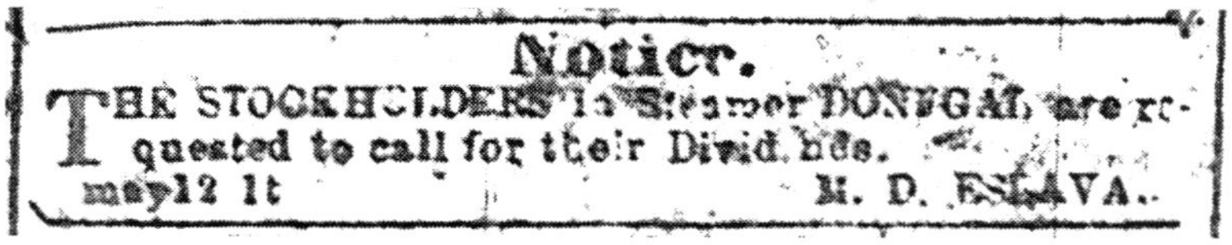
Notice.
THE STOCKHOLDERS in Steamer DONEGAL are requested to call for their Dividends.
may12 1t M. D. ESLAVA.

Figure 5. Dividend notice for stockholders of the *Donegal* (*Mobile Advertiser and Register* May 12, 1864).

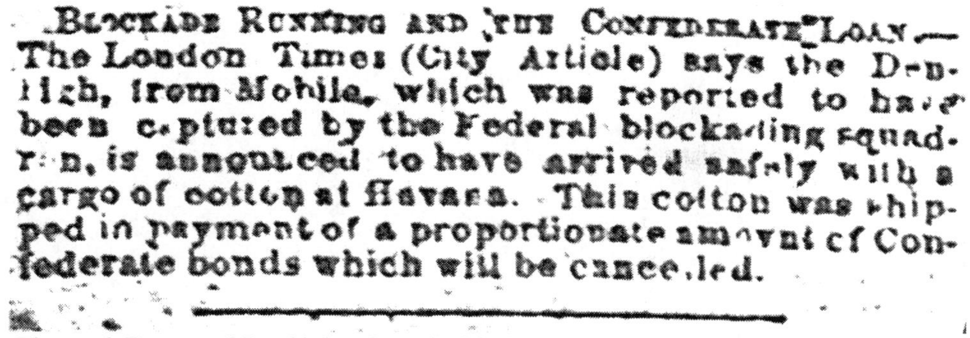

BLOCKADE RUNNING AND THE CONFEDERATE LOAN.— The London Times (City Article) says the Denbigh, from Mobile, which was reported to have been captured by the Federal blockading squadron, is announced to have arrived safely with a cargo of cotton at Havana. This cotton was shipped in payment of a proportionate amount of Confederate bonds which will be cancelled.

Figure 6. Report of *Denbigh* safe arrival in Havana with a load of cotton purchased with Erlanger bonds (*Mobile Advertiser and Register* April 26, 1864).

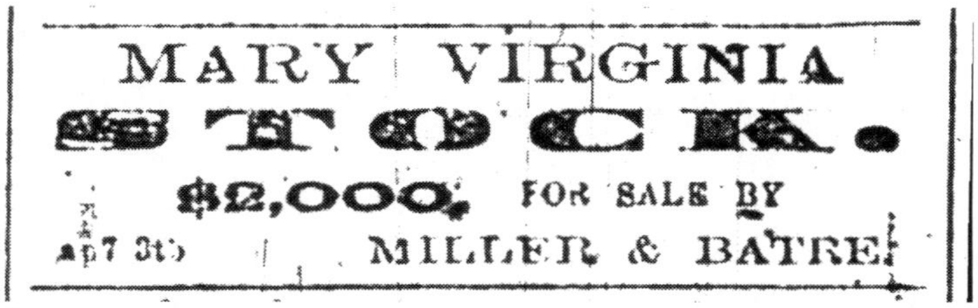

MARY VIRGINIA
STOCK.
$2,000, FOR SALE BY
ap7 3t MILLER & BATRE

Figure 7. Ad regarding sale of stock in the runner *Mary Virginia* (*Mobile Advertiser and Register* April 7, 1864).

No ... Mobile, ... 186...

Received from ... Dollars, in Steamer ... venture hence to Havana, or other Foreign port, and back to Mobile or this Confederacy. Transferable ~~on Books at office of L. Baron & Son. Mobile. to his order~~ on surrender of this Certificate.

Agent

Figure 8. Receipt for sale of blockade runner *Phoenix* stock (Delaney 1971: 155).

Figure 8 showed the receipt of a $1,000 investment in the *Phoenix* for a voyage in May 1864. Wording made clear that the investment was for a share of one voyage from Mobile to Havana and return to Mobile or other Confederate port. The investor prospectively would have profited from the outbound cargo and the inbound cargo. Presumably the thousand dollars invested would be part of the money spent in Mobile to buy the cotton bales to export. Part of the cotton's proceeds would fund purchase of the cargo for the return voyage to Mobile. Total profits of a successful two-way trip would be split among ship's owners and investors according to a formula not specified on the receipt.

Denbigh Cotton Cargoes Outbound from Mobile to Havana

This section shows information on the *Denbigh's* cargoes of cotton outbound from Mobile to Havana. The figures in Table 3 were extracted from the export customs forms[7] transcribed and shown in Chapter 13. The export duty paid, based on ⅛¢ per lb., allowed the calculation of the Mobile market price per pound of cotton shown in the table. The Mobile market price of cotton was used to calculate the immediate profit on the cotton (shown in the last row of the table) as it sat in Mobile given that the cotton was acquired from the government using Erlanger cotton bonds. The cotton bonds by the terms of the bonds could be exchanged in a Confederate port at the rate of 6 pence/lb. (about 12¢/lb.).

Table 3. The *Denbigh's* cotton cargo for the Mobile to Havana leg of her voyages.

Voyage	1	2	3	4	5	6
Date 1864	16 Jan	16 Mar	16 Apr	4 May	26 May	14 June
Captain	McNevin	McNevin	Godfrey	Godfrey	Godfrey	Godfrey
Agent	Benj. Donaldson	Benj. Donaldson	Benj. Donaldson	A. I. Ingersol	Benj. Donaldson	Benj. Donaldson
Company	H. O. Brewer & Co.	H. O. Brewer & Co.	H. O. Brewer & Co.	H. O. Brewer & Co.	H. O. Brewer & Co.	H.O. Brewer & Co. 346 b/c, John Scott 75 b/c
# Bales	500	424	476	445	442	421
Weight in Lbs.	249,658	201,600	212,760	210,992	224,544	218,890
Value in $[8]	$ 124,729	$ 151,111	$ 153,365	$ 105,496	$ 112,272	$ 124,764
Export Duty $ @	311.82	252.00	266.00	263.74	280.68	223.68
Local Market Value per lb.	50¢	75¢	72¢	50¢	50¢	57¢
Purchase price $ @ 6 pence/lb. (12¢/lb.)	$ 29,959	$ 24,192	$ 25,531	$ 25,319	$ 26,945	$ 26,267
Profit in Mobile at purchase	416%	625%	600%	416%	416%	475%

The *Denbigh* operators exchanged Erlanger bonds for cotton. Under the terms of the bonds, the C.S. government was obliged to provide the bales for the price of 6 pence/lb. (about 12¢/lb.). This represented a substantial built-in profit versus the Mobile market price, if the ship successfully ran through the blockade. At a 400–600% profit in Mobile, it is no wonder there was a gold-rush atmosphere in the blockade running trade. The cotton price delivered in England was probably even higher than the Mobile market price, providing profits piled higher and higher.

Only voyages 4 and 5 carried any cargo aside from bales of cotton. On each of those voyages there were also 20 bbls. of rosin. On voyage 5 the entry for 442 bales bore an extra note explaining the packaging, "442 Bales Cotton in 450 Packages." Fitting the maximum cargo below decks likely involved splitting a few bales into smaller packages in order to fit in nooks and crannies of the hold.

The NARA–Atlanta files for the *Denbigh* contained three export documents composing a set for each voyage and entitled:[9]

1. Entry of Cotton, which showed export duty and signed by the shipper's representative.

---

[7] NARA–Atlanta, RG 36, Bureau of Customs, Mobile, Box 98, NC-154 Entry 1557, Manifests 1820–1904, 1863–65.

[8] Duty paid based on local market price, not purchase price set by bond contract at 6 pence/lb. (12¢/lb.).

[9] NARA–Atlanta RG 36, Bur. of Customs, Mobile, Manifests 1820–1904; 1863–65, Box 98, NC-154 Entry 1557.

2. General Manifest–Report and Manifest, which provided particulars of ship and cargo, signed by the captain.
3. Special Manifest–Outward, a double size page with particulars of ship and cargo and signed by the shipper's representative.

These forms constituted part of a ship's papers demonstrating a legitimate voyage appropriately recorded at the departure port's customs house. We presented here the relevant data in Table 3. For transcripts of the export documents see Chapter 13.

Notable Importers and Import Documents

The customs forms transcribed below included some very interesting names. Several of the Confederate Army commanders stationed at Mobile imported personal supplies for their families including Gen. Maury, Gen. Higgins, and other officers. People prominently associated with the *Denbigh* appeared, including J. H. Schroder, the international banker and ship co-owner. Another was Thomas Healy, the ship's portrait painter who ordered artist supplies that might well have been the very canvas and paints for the *Denbigh's* likeness. There was a shipment for Lehman Brothers, who started business in the 1850s in Montgomery, Alabama. The wife of Confederate Senator Louis Wigfall of Texas had an order. President F. Gautrelet imported a box of books for Spring Hill College of Mobile, a Catholic college still in operation today. Interestingly, many of the names from the manifests produced hits when searched on the Internet. Some of the footnotes herein include details found that way.

The customs records presented in this book provide to the careful reader many insights into daily life in Civil War Mobile. Many researchers can profit from this data, and the author strongly encourages the careful perusal of these documents.

Acknowledgments for *Denbigh* Project Funding

The *Denbigh* Project works under the aegis of the Institute of Nautical Archaeology at Texas A&M University, a nonprofit scientific and educational organization. J. Barto Arnold III is project director and principal investigator; Thomas J. Oertling and Andrew W. Hall were co-principal investigators for archaeology and history, respectively. The *Denbigh* Project appreciates the kind financial support of the Anchorage Foundation; the Albert & Ethel Herzstein Charitable Foundation of Houston; the Brown Foundation, Houston; the Communities Foundation of Texas; the Dana and Myriam McGinnis Charitable Fund of the San Antonio Area Foundation; the Ed Rachal Foundation of Corpus Christi; the Institute of Nautical Archaeology Foundation; the Hillcrest Foundation of Dallas, founded by Mrs. W. W. Caruth, Sr.; the Horlock Foundation, Houston; the Houston Endowment; the Strake Foundation of Houston; the Summerfield G. Roberts Foundation of Dallas; the Summerlee Foundation of Dallas; the Joseph Ballard Archeology Fund of the Texas Historical Foundation of Austin; the Trull Foundation of Palacios; and many individual donors. Finally, the *Denbigh* Project acknowledges its debt to Texas A&M University, Galveston, for generous assistance throughout the course of the project.

Bibliography

Arnold, J. B. III
1987 Marine magnetometer survey of archaeological materials near Galveston Texas. *Historical Archaeology* 21:18–47.

Arnold, J. B. III, Oertling, T. J., and Hall, A. W.
1999 The *Denbigh* Project: Initial observations on a Civil War blockade runner and its wreck-site. *International Journal of Nautical Archaeology* 28:126–144.
2001a The *Denbigh* Project: Excavation of a Civil War blockade runner. *International Journal of Nautical Archaeology* 30:231–249.

2001b The *Denbigh* Project: Test excavations at the wreck of an American Civil War blockade runner. *World Archaeology* 32:405–417.

2003 The *Denbigh* Project 2002: Excavation of a Civil War blockade runner. *Bulletin of the Texas Archeological Society* 74:131–140.

Block, W. T.

2007 *Schooner Sail to Starboard: The US Navy vs. Blockade Runners in the Western Gulf of Mexico. Denbigh* Shipwreck Project Publication Series No. 3. Institute of Nautical Archaeology, College Station, Texas.

Davis, C. S.

2008 Colin J. McRae: Confederate Financial Agent; Blockade Running in the Trans-Mississippi South as Affected by the Confederate Government's Direct European Procurement of Goods. *Denbigh* Shipwreck Project Publication Series No. 4. Institute of Nautical Archaeology, College Station, Texas.

Delaney, C.

1971 *Confederate Mobile: A Pictorial History.* Mobile: The Haunted Book Shop.

Nichols, J. L.

2006 *The Confederate Quartermaster in the Trans-Mississippi: The Blockade Runners Texas Connection. Denbigh* Shipwreck Project Publication Series No. 2. Percheron Press.

Watson, W.

1892 *The Adventures of a Blockade Runner.* London: T. F. Unwin. (Reprinted as *The Civil War Adventures of a Blockade Runner, Denbigh* Shipwreck Project Publication Series No. 1. [College Station: Texas A & M University Press, 2001]).

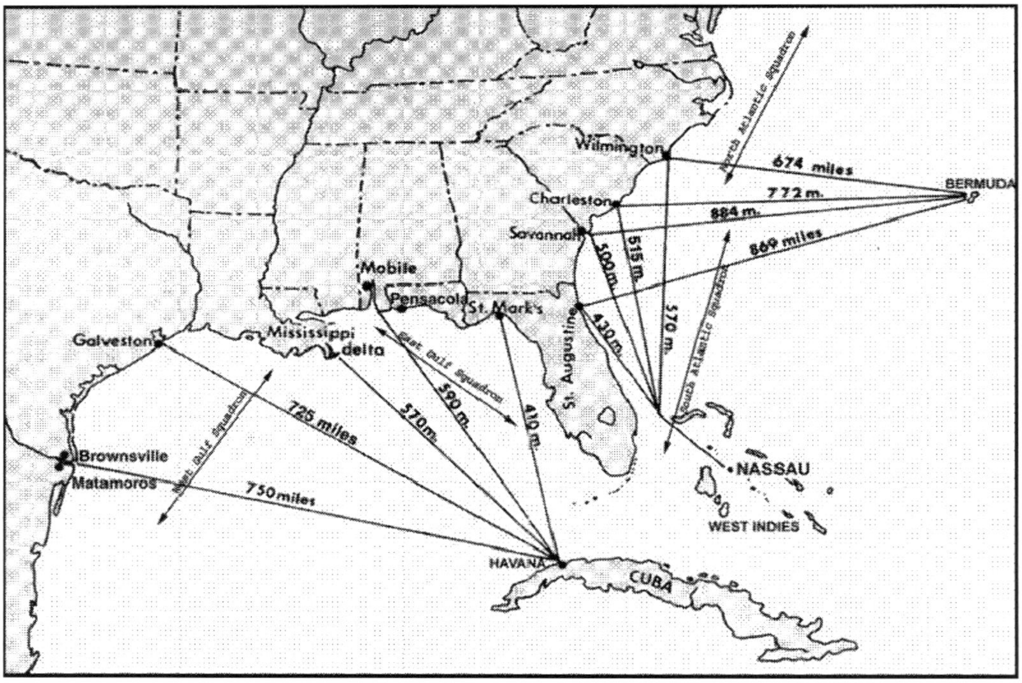

Figure 9. The Confederate coast. *Naval Historical Center.*

Part I

The *Denbigh's* Mobile Imports

1

Denbigh Customs Manifests, Jan. 1864, Transcripts

Denbigh Voyage No. 1, Havana-Mobile-Havana.[10]
Havana, last date on document prepared there was 6 Jan 1864 so the ship sailed soon thereafter.
Mobile, date ship entered (port and reported arrival to C.S. Customs) was 9 Jan 1864.
Mobile departure, cotton export manifests dated 16 Jan 1864 so ship sailed soon thereafter. (500 bales cotton, 249,658 lbs., $ 124,729, 50¢ per lb.)

1029-1033 (Frame numbers of camera used recording documents at the National Archives Regional Facility in Atlanta (NARA–Atlanta).)
Preprinted Customs Form

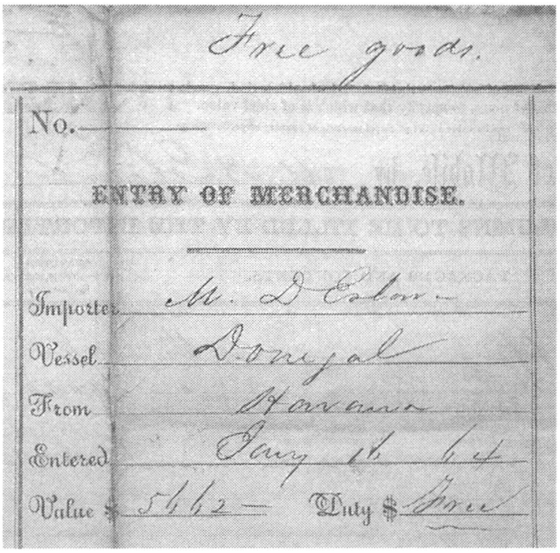

Free goods.

No.

ENTRY OF MERCHANDISE.

Importer M. D Eslon

Vessel Donegal

From Havana

Entered Jany 11 64

Value $ 5662— Duty $ Free

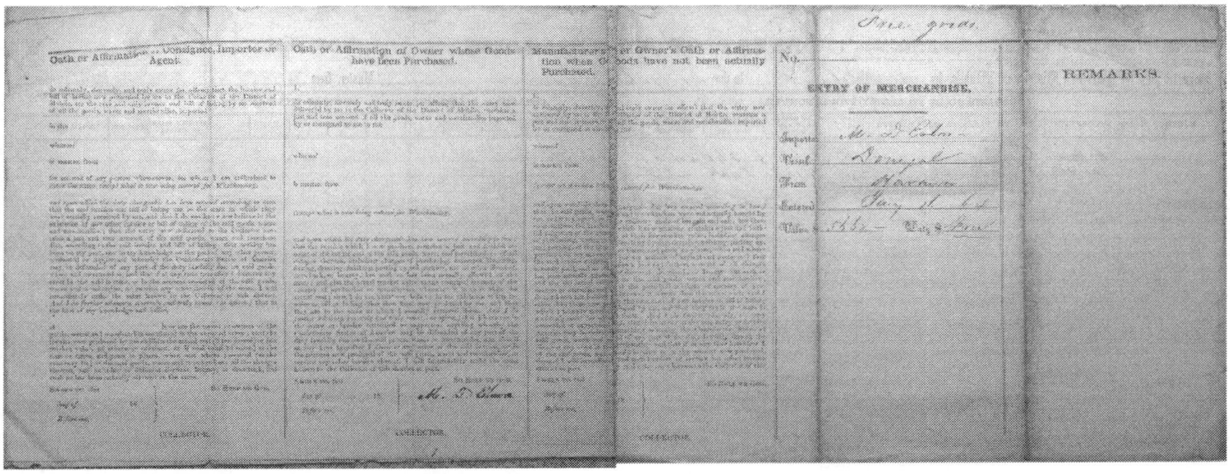

Oath or Affirmation of Consignee, Importer or Agent.

Oath or Affirmation of Owner whose Goods have been Purchased.

Manufacturer's or Owner's Oath or Affirmation when Goods have not been actually Purchased.

REMARKS.

10 NARA–Atlanta RG 36, Bur. of Customs, Mobile, AL, Entry of Merchandise 1820–1905; 1864–1866; Boxes 21–22, E 1564c.

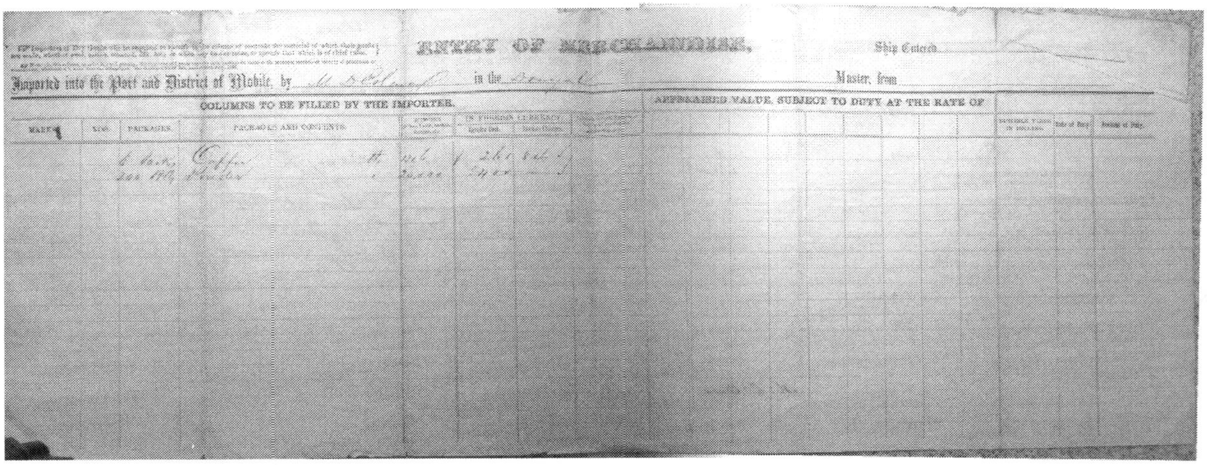
ENTRY OF MERCHANDISE.

Ship Entered

Imported into the Port and District of Mobile, by M D Eslava in the Donegal Master, from

COLUMNS TO BE FILLED BY THE IMPORTER.

APPRAISED VALUE, SUBJECT TO DUTY AT THE RATE OF

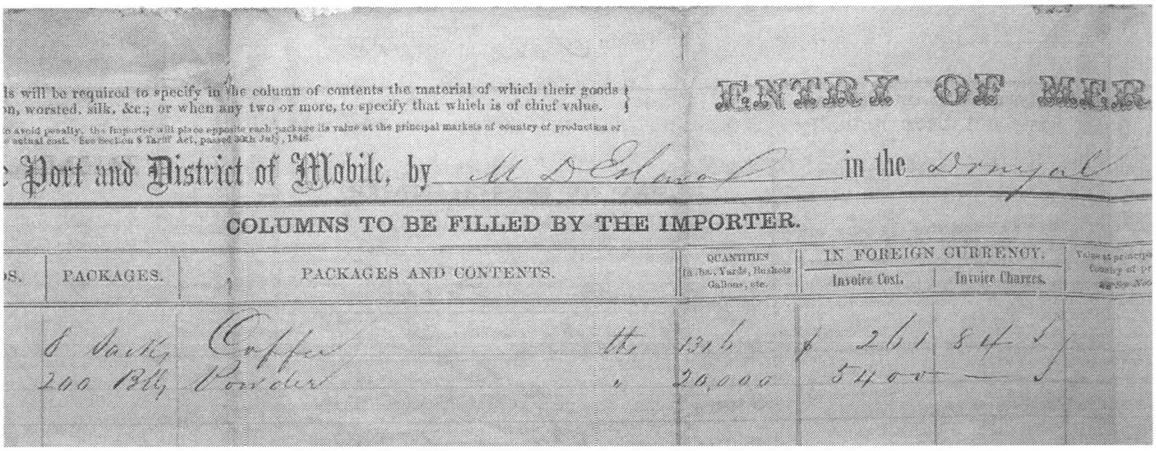
...ls will be required to specify in the column of contents the material of which their goods ...n, worsted, silk, &c.; or when any two or more, to specify that which is of chief value.

ENTRY OF MER...

...Port and District of Mobile, by M D Eslava in the Donegal

COLUMNS TO BE FILLED BY THE IMPORTER.

PACKAGES.	PACKAGES AND CONTENTS.		QUANTITIES.	IN FOREIGN CURRENCY. Invoice Cost.	Invoice Charges.
8 Sacks	Coffee	lbs	1216	$ 261	84
200 Blls	Powder	"	20,000	5400	—

Figure 10. Views of preprinted customs form. Outside above, inside below.

Free Goods
Entry of Merchandise
No. ______
Importer M. D. Eslava
Vessel *Donegal*
From Havana
Entered Jany 16 64
Value $ 5662 Duty $ Free

Oath of Owner whose Goods have been Purchased
(signed) M. D. Eslava

Ship Entered ___________

Imported into the Port and District of Mobile, by M D Eslava in the *Donegal* ________Master, from ___________ (Many times blanks were left empty. Punctuation was randomly used or omitted.)

Packages	Packages and Contents	In Foreign Currency Invoice Value	Appraised Value, Duty Rate			Duty
			10	15	20	
8 Sacks	Coffee lbs 1216	$ 262.84				
200 blls (barrels)	Powder " 20,000	5400.00				

1034
Invoice

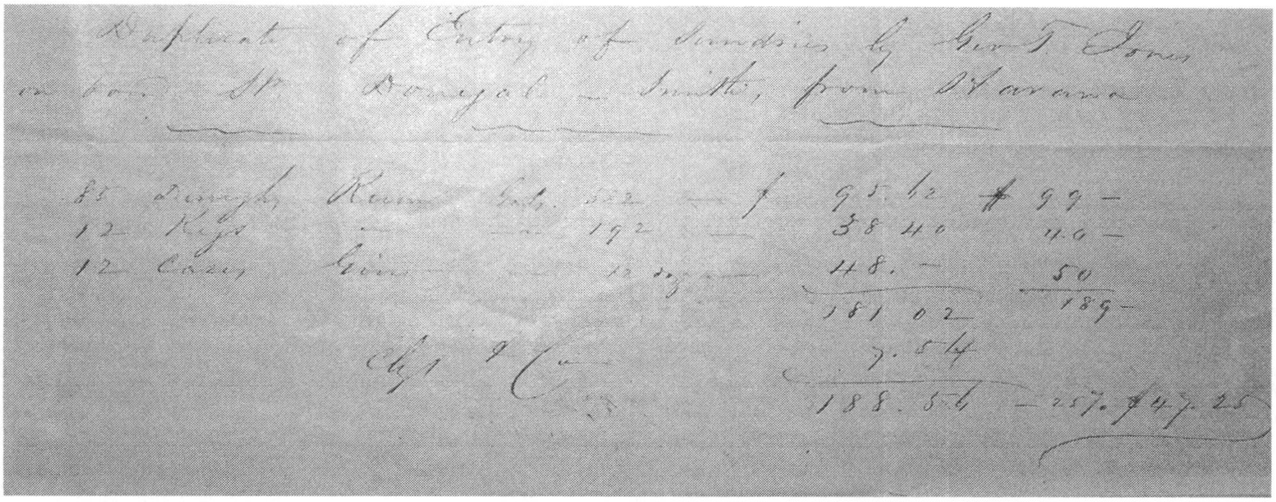

Figure 11. Invoice for alcohol on the *Donegal*.

Duplicate of Entry of Sundries by Geo T. Jones on board Str (Steamer) *Donegal* – Smith (Master), from Havana

85 Demijohns[11]	Rum	Gals 382	$ 95.62	$ 99
12 Kegs	"	" 192	38.40	40
12 Cases	Gin	12 dozen	48.00	50
			181.02	189
	Chgs & Com (Charges & Commission)		7.54	
			188.56	25% $ 47.25 (duty)

1035-1038
Preprinted Customs Form

Entry of Merchandise
No. 13
Importer Danl McNeill
Vessel *Denbigh*
From Havana
Entered Jany 14 '64
Value $ 76 Duty $ 10.00

[11] Demijohn – Large glass bottle usually covered in wicker, normally about 15 gallons or 54 liters, but here 382/85= around 4.5 gallons or 17 liters each. Fragments of a demijohn including the neck with wicker cover were excavated from the *Denbigh's* engine room near the port engine.

Ship Entered_____.

Imported into the Port and District of Mobile, by Danl McNeill in the Br. St. (British Steamer) *Denbigh*
McNevin ________Master, from Havana

Marks	Packages	Packages and Contents	In Foreign Currency Invoice Value	Appraised Value, Duty Rate			Duty
				10	15	20	
D. M.	One Chest	Tea 46 lbs	£ 5. 7. 4	28			$ 2.80
"	Two Boxes	Starch 122 "	2. 17. 8		15		2.25
"	One "	Boots 6 prs (pairs)	6. 7. 6		33		4.95
			14. 12. 6	28	48		10.00
		Chgs & Com	19. 6				
			15. 12. 0	or	$ 75.50		

1039
Invoice

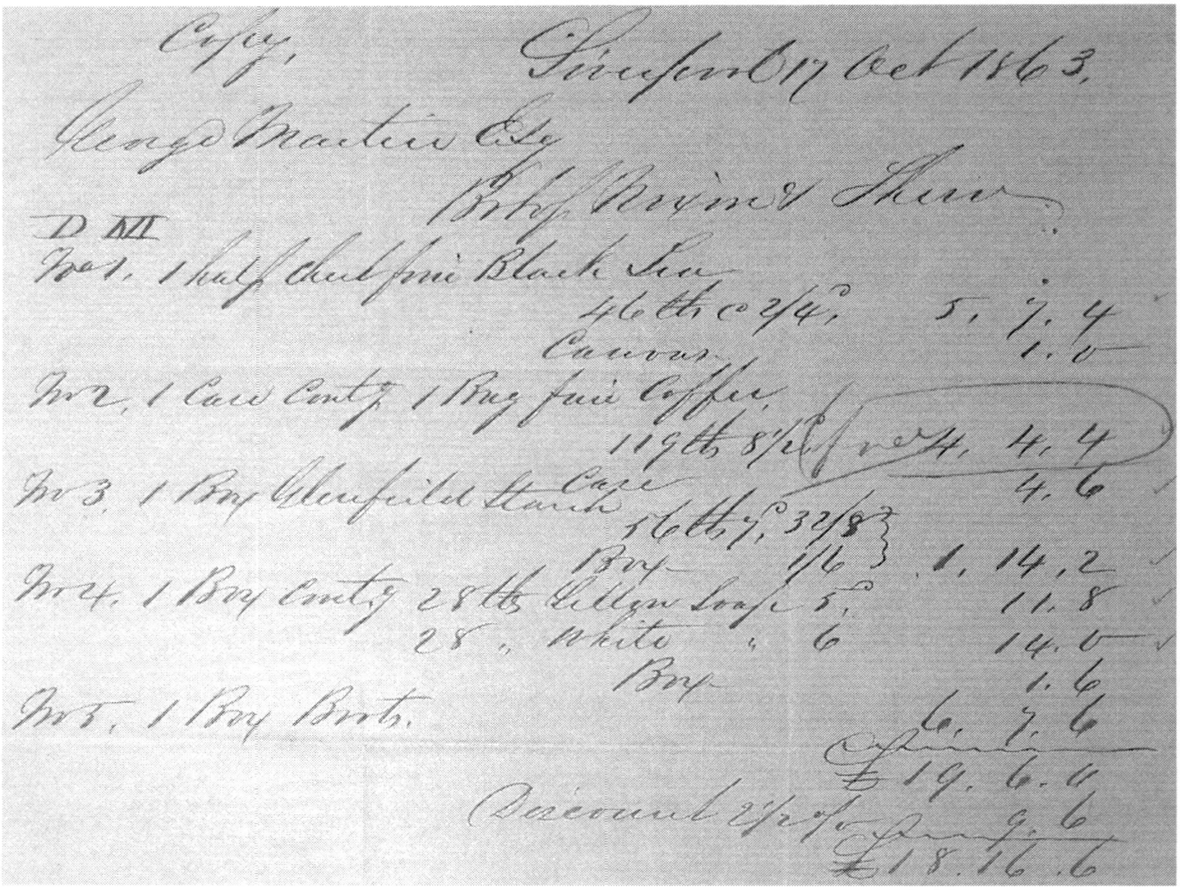
Copy,
Liverpool 17 Oct 1863,
George Martin Esq
Bot of [illegible]
D M
No 1. 1 half chest fine Black Tea
46 lbs @ 2/4d 5. 7. 4
Canvas 1. 0
No 2, 1 Case Contg 1 Bag fine Coffee,
119 lbs 8½d 4. 4. 4
Case 4. 6
No 3. 1 Box Glenfield Starch
16 lbs @ 32/8 }
Box 1/6 } 1. 14. 2
No 4. 1 Box Contg 28 lbs Yellow Soap 5d 11. 8
28 " White " 6 14. 0
Box 1. 6
No 5. 1 Box Boots 6. 7. 6
£19. 6. 4
Discount 2½% 9. 6
£18. 16. 6

Figure 12. Invoice of goods for George Martin.

Figure 13. Glenfield starch label.

Copy Liverpool 17 Oct 1863
George Martin Esq.

Bishop Nixon & Shaw

DM				
No 1	1 half chest	fine Black Tea	46 lbs @ 2/4¢ (2 shillings/4 pence)	5. 7. 4
			Canvas	1. 0
No 2	1 Case Contg (Containing)	1 Bag fine Coffee	119 lbs 8½¢ free	4. 4. 4
			Case	4. 6
No 3	1 Box	**Glenfield Starch**[12]	56 lbs 7¢ 32/8	
			Box 1/6	1.14. 2
No 4	1 Box Contg	Yellow **Soap**[13]	28 lbs 5¢	11. 8
		White "	28 lbs 6¢	14. 0
			Box	1. 6
No 5	1 Box	Boots		6. 7. 6
				£19. 6. 6
			Discount 2½%	9. 6
				£18. 6. 6

[12] Famous British brand of high quality starch.
[13] The author used bold font herein for interesting or noteworthy cargo items.

1040
Preprinted Customs Form

Entry of Merchandise
No. 14
Importer Boykin & McRae[14]
Vessel *Denbigh*
From Havana
Entered Jany 15
Value $ 411 Duty $ 54.60

Oath of Consignee, Importer or Agent
In the Br. St. ~~*Donegal*~~ *Denbigh*
Sworn 15th day of Jany 1864
(signed) S. L. Lockweed

Ship Entered Jany 9 1864

Imported into the Port and District of Mobile, by Boykin & McRae in the Br. St. *Denbigh* McNevin Master, from Havana

Marks	Packages	Packages and Contents	In Foreign Currency Invoice Value	Appraised Value, Duty Rate			
				10	15	20	Duty
	10 Pkgs	**Gold Leaf**	$ 135.00	141			$ 14.10
	65 oz	**Quinine** oz 65	260.00		270		40.50
			395.00	141	270		$ 54.60
		Chgs & Com	15.80				
			410.80				

1044a
Invoice

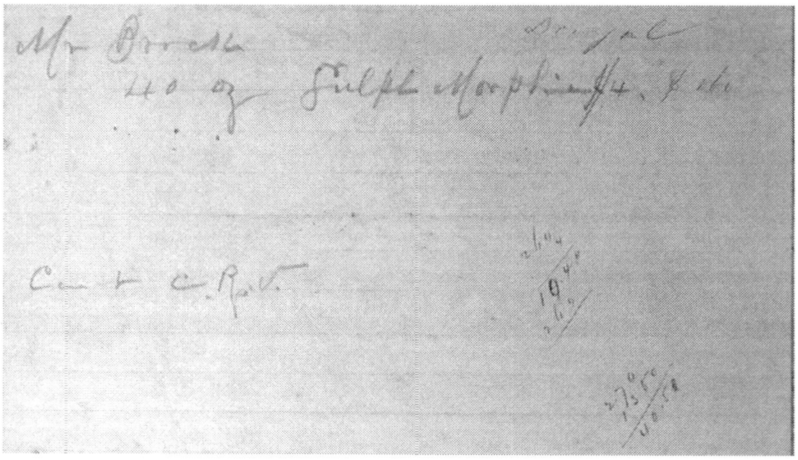

Figure 14. Invoice for morphine. The bottom margins of invoices were often used to calculate duties.

[14] Collin McRae became lead C.S. financial agent in Europe. (See *Collin McRae* by Davis, *Denbigh* Shipwreck Project Publication No. 4.)

Mr. Brock (Boykin?) *Donegal*

40 oz Sulph **Morphine** $ 4 $ 1.60

1044b
Invoice

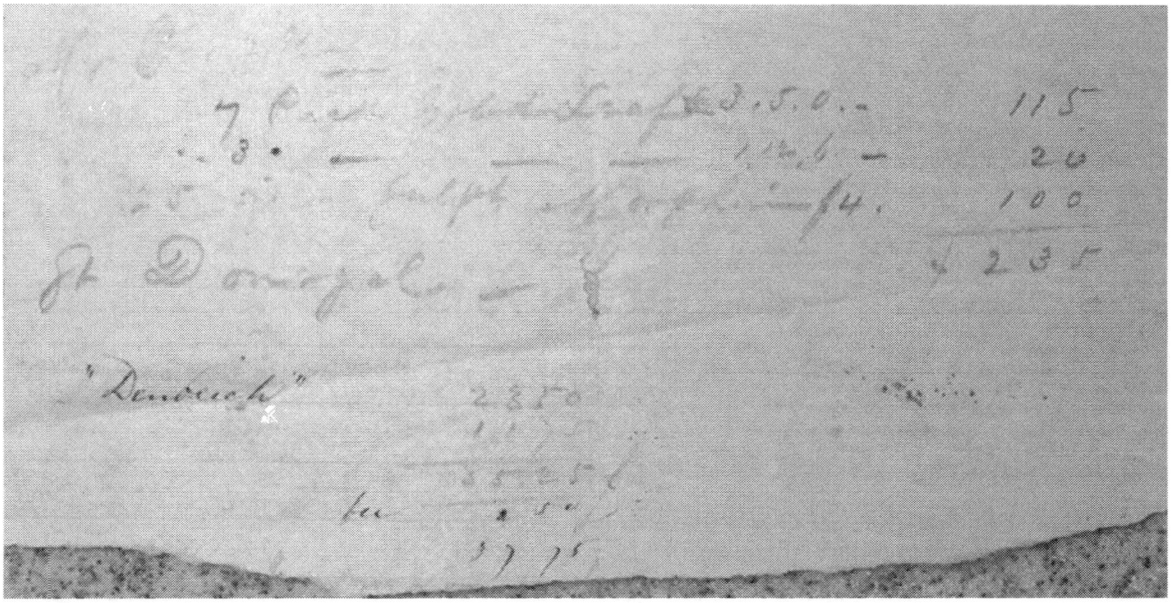

Figure 15. Invoice for gold leaf and morphine.

Note: Many of the invoices were quickly scribbled on informal scraps of paper along with calculations of monetary conversion and amount of duty. The transporting ship's name was corrected from *Donegal* to *Denbigh*. The possible switching of cargo from one ship to the other was the reason for including a few *Donegal* documents.

Mr. Brock (?[15])

	7 Packs	Gold Leaf	£ 3. 5. 0	115
	3 "	" "	1. 12. 6	20
	25 oz	Sulph **Morphine** $ 4		100
St *Donegal*				$ 235

Denbigh		35.35 (duty?)
	fee	2.50
		37.75

---

[15] Question marks were used herein to indicate unclear or illegible words.

1045-1050
Preprinted Customs Form

Entry of Merchandise
No. 15
Importer H O Brewer & Co
Vessel Brit. St. *Denbigh*
From Havana
Entered Jany 16 '64
Value $ 5753 Duty $ 773.60

Oath of Consignee, Importer or Agent
Benj. Donaldson

Ship Entered _______

Imported into the Port and District of Mobile, by H. O. Brewer & Co in the Br. St. *Denbigh* McNevin Master, from Havana

Marks	Packages	Packages and Contents	In Foreign Currency Invoice Value	Appraised Value, Duty Rate			Duty
				10	15	20	
G	10 Cases	Silk mfs (manufactures)	£ 120. 2. 6		600		
		Cotton " Prints	460. 4. 0		2298		
		Wool "	236.10. 9		1182		
		Hosiery	48. 3. 5		242		
		Buttons	16. 4. 2		82		
		Flax mfs	84. 2. 6		421		
		Clothing (ready made) Shirts	57. 2. 5		284		
		Combs	6. 1. 3		31		
		Tooth Brushes	2. 11. 3			13	
			£ 1031. 3. 1		5140	13	
		Chgs & Com	33. 9. 2				
			£ 1064. 2. 8	or	5152.72		$773.60

1051
Invoice

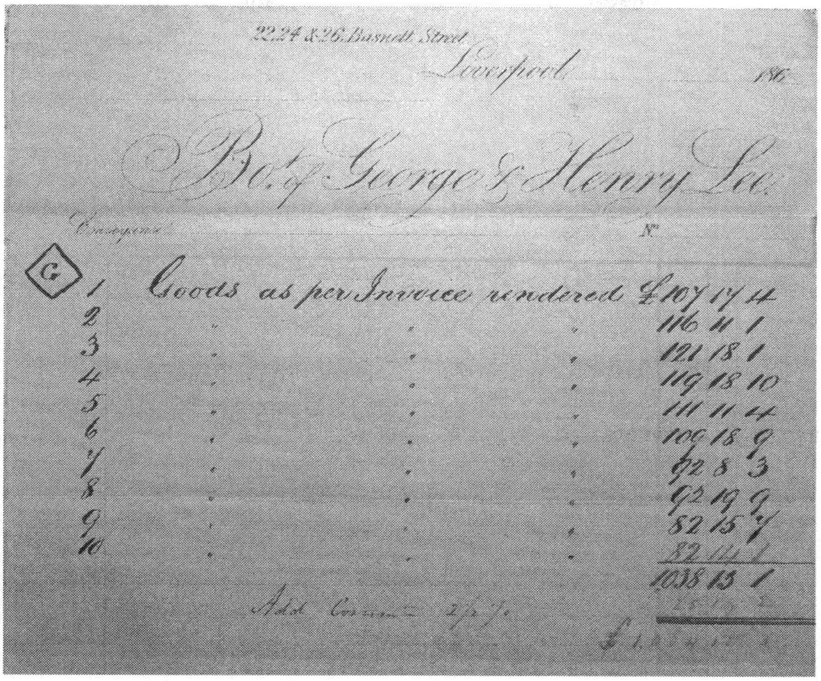

Figure 16. Invoice from George & Henry Lee, Liverpool merchants.

22 24 & 26 Basnett Street
Liverpool _______186__
Bot (Bought) of George & Henry Lee

G 1	Goods as per Invoice rendered	£ 107	17	4
2	"	116	11	1
3	"	121	18	1
4	"	119	18	1
5	"	111	11	4
6	"	100	18	10
7	"	92	8	3
8	"	92	19	9
9	"	82	15	7
10	"	82	14	1
		1038	13	1
	Add Comm = 2½%	25	19	2
		£ 1064	12	2

1053-1056
Preprinted Customs Form

Entry of Merchandise
No. 16
Importer H. O. Brewer & Co

Vessel *Denbigh*
From Havana
Entered Jany 18 '64
Value $ 4214 Duty $ 632.10

Oath of consignee, Importer or Agent
18 day of Jan 1864

Ship Entered Jany 1864.

Imported into the Port and District of Mobile, by H. O. Brewer & Co in the Str. ~~*A. Vivian*~~ *Denbigh*
McNevin Master, from Havana

Marks	Packages	Packages and Contents	In Foreign Currency Invoice Value	Appraised Value, Duty Rate			
				10	15	20	Duty
~~M F~~	~~1 Box~~	~~Playing Cards~~	~~$ 719.80~~				
	~~18 Bags~~	~~Black pepper~~					
	~~50~~						
	500 Bdls	Hoop iron	$ 719.80		749		$112.35
H.O.B.	1 Case	Smoking pipes	334.80		348		52.20
00/SI	1/3 3 "	Quinine oz 999	2997.00		3117		467.55
			4051.60		$ 4214		632.10
		Chgs & Com	162.06				
			$ 4213.66				

Note: This form was begun for one ship, crossed out, and used for a different ship. Perhaps this was an indication of forms in short supply. These documents sometimes included strikeouts which herein were so indicated.

1057a
Invoice

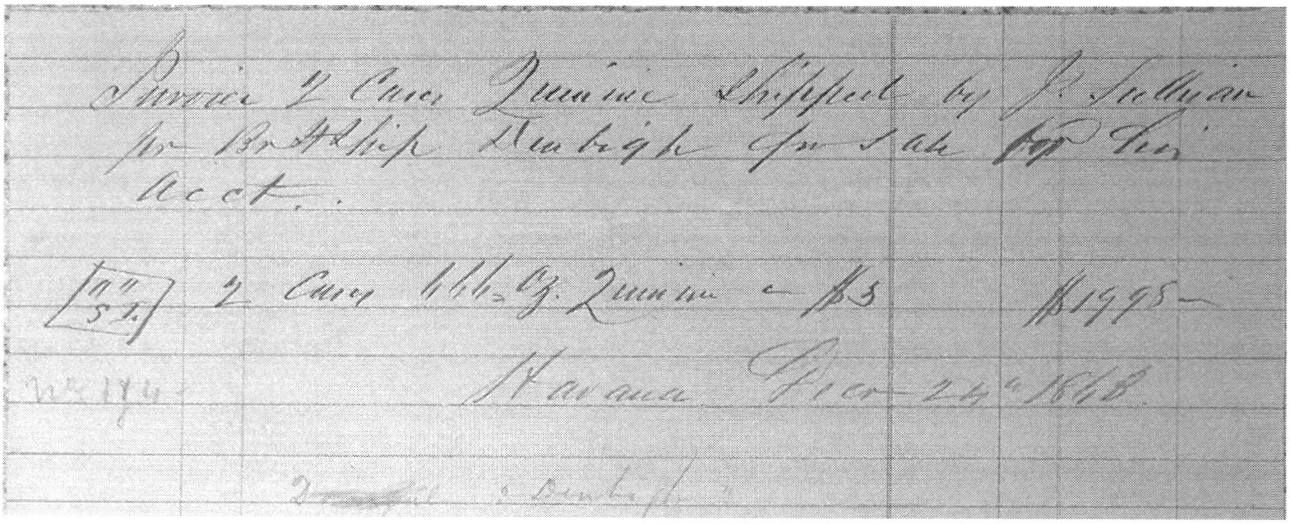
Invoice 2 Cases Quinine Shipped by J. Sullivan
for Br Ship Denbigh for sale for their
Acct.
2 Cases 666 Oz. Quinine @ $3 $1998
No 174
Havana Dec 24th 1863

Figure 17. Invoice for 666 oz. of quinine.

Invoice 2 Cases Quinine Shipped by J. Sullivan pr (per) Br (British) St (Steam) Ship *Denbigh* for sale for his Acct. (Account).

00/SL (mark)	2 Cases 666 Oz. Quinine		@ $ 5	$ 1995.00

Havana Decm 24th 1863

1057b
Invoice

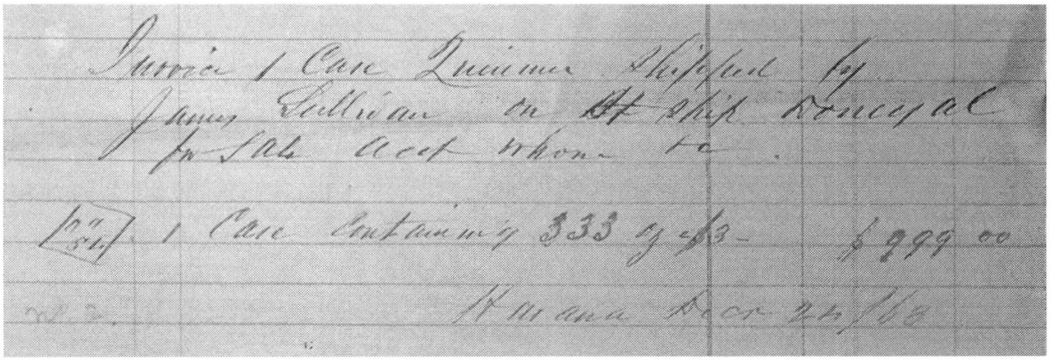

Figure 18. Invoice for 333 oz. of quinine.

Invoice 1 Case Quinine Shipped by James Sullivan on St Ship *Donegal* for sale Acct whom &c.

00/SL (mark)	1 Case	Containing 333 oz	@ $ 3	$ 999.00

Havana Decm 24/63

1059
Invoice

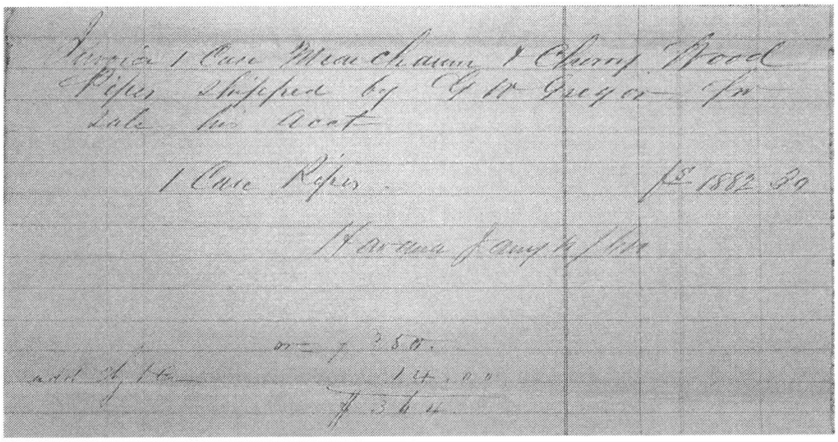

Figure 19. Invoice for Meerschaum pipes and cherry wood pipes.

Invoice 1 Case **Meerschaum & Cherry Wood Pipes** Shipped by G. W. Gregor for sale his Acct

	1 Case	Pipes	fs (franks) 1882.30
			Havana Jany 6/64
Add Chg & Com		or $ 350.00	
		14.00	
		$ 364.00	

1060
Invoice

Note: Originally shipped from Liverpool 17 April 1861 for New Orleans. The cargo was delayed and probably held at Havana maybe due to the outbreak of war. Finally made it to Mobile in Jan. 1863. The cargo was bundles of iron hoops including 400 "Chilln Hoops" (Children's hoops, a toy?); shipped by Fraser Trenholm & Co. by order of H. O. Brewer & Co. for Givins & Co., the customer who was perhaps a wholesale or retail merchant. Interestingly there was insurance against delay of the shipment and a credit for this was applied to the total.

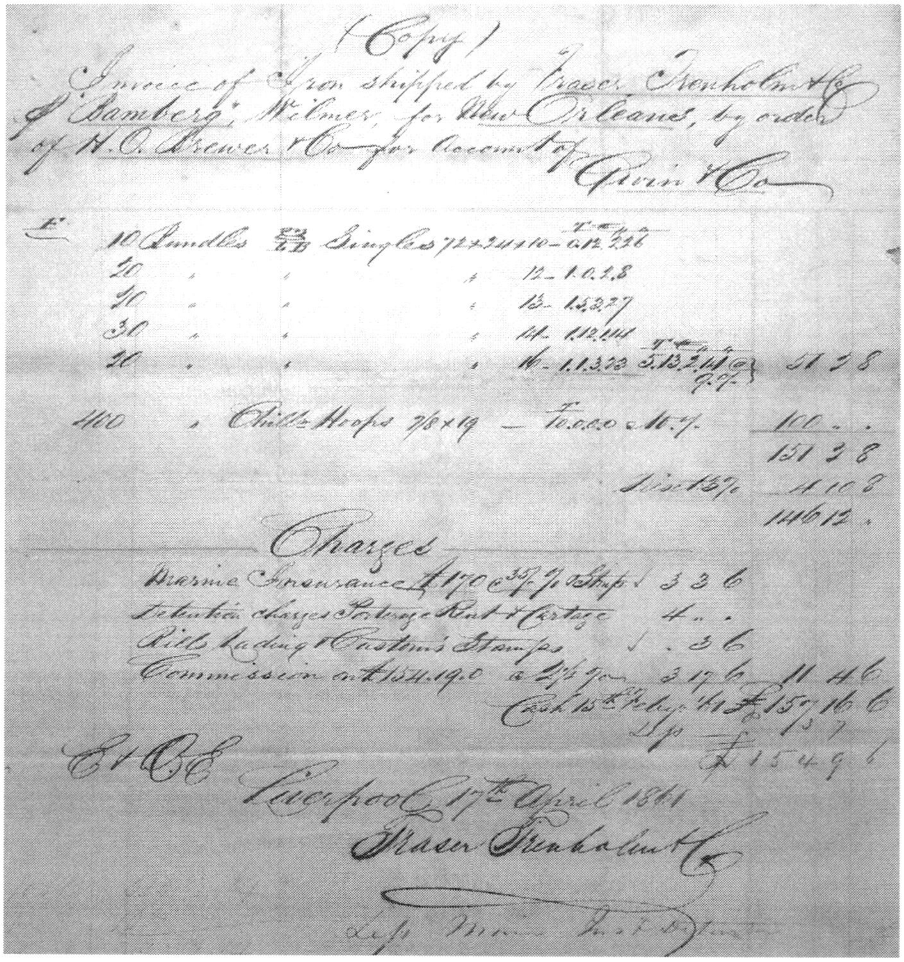
(Copy)
Invoice of Iron shipped by Fraser Trenholm & Co
p Bamberg, Wilmer, for New Orleans, by order
of H. O. Brewer & Co for Account of
Givin & Co

£ 10 Bundles Singles 72 x 24 x 10 – 0.12.2.26			
20 " " " 12 – 1.0.2.8			
40 " " " 13 – 1.5.2.27			
30 " " " 14 – 1.12.1.14			
20 " " " 16 – 1.1.3.23	5.13.2.14 @ 9.7		51 2 8
400 " Chilln Hoops 7/8 x 19 – 10.0.0.0 @ 10.7			100 . .
			151 2 8
		Disc 13%	4 10 8
			146 12 .

Charges

Marine Insurance £170 @ 35/- % Ship	3 3 6	
Detention charges Portage Rent & Cartage	4 . .	
Bills Lading & Customs Stamps	1 . 3 6	
Commission on £154.19.0 @ 2½ %	3 17 6	11 4 6
Cash 15th Feby '61		£157 16 6
		1 3 7
		£154 9 1

E & O E
Liverpool 17th April 1861
Fraser Trenholm & Co

Figure 20. Invoice for cargo of iron.

(Copy)

Invoice of Iron shipped by Fraser Trenholm & Co. per *Bamberg*, Wilmer (master), for New Orleans, by order of H. O. Brewer & Co for Account of Givin & Co.

F				T # " " (weight)		
	10 Bundles	??/LB	Singles 72x24x10	0.12.2.26		
	20 "	"	" 12	1.0.2.8		
	20 "	"	" 13	1.5.3.27		
	30 "	"	" 14	1.12.1.14	T??	
	20 "	"	" 16	1.1.3.23	5.13.2.14 @	51 2 8
					9.%	
				T		
	400	"	Chilln Hoops 7/8x19	10.0.0.0	10.%	100 0 0
						151 2 8
				Disct	(discount) 3%	4 10 8
						146 12 0
			Charges			
			Marine Insurance ??	170@35/"% Ship	3 3 6	
			Detention charges Portage Rent & Cartage		4 0 0	
			Bills Lading & Customs Stamps		3 17 6	11 4 6
			Cash 15th Feby '61	?? 15%		157 16 6
				??		3 7 0
		E&OE		??		154 9 6
			Liverpool 17th April 1861			
			Fraser Trenholm & Co			
	(notes)		Less Main Ins ???			
	16 9 4		Detention on $ 747.66			

Note: Weights given in English notation (tons, cwt., qrs., and lbs.).

1061-1062
Preprinted Customs Form

Summary: This example showed a typical small order for goods that went into Mobile on the *Denbigh*, perhaps a single family's order. Contrast this with the order just shown that was likely a merchant's large scale order.

Entry of Merchandise
No. 17
Importer D Campbell
Vessel *Denbigh*
From Havana
Entered Jany 22 '64
Value $ 137 Duty $ 20.55

Oath of Owner whose Goods have been Purchased
I, Douglas Campbell
12 day of Jany 1864
(signature crossed out)

Ship Entered_____
Imported into the Port and District of Mobile, by D Campbell in the Br. St. *Denbigh* McNevin Master, from Havana

Packages	Packages and Contents	In Foreign Currency Invoice Value	Appraised Value, Duty Rate			
			10	15	20	Duty
1 Pkg	Wool mfs	$ 80.00		83		
(package)	Cotton mfs Prints & Clothg	52.00		54		
		132.00		137	15%	$ 20.55
	Chgs & Com	5.28				
		$ 137.28				

2

Denbigh Customs Manifests, March–April 1864, Transcripts

Denbigh Voyage No. 2, Havana-Mobile-Havana
Havana, last date document prepared there, 9 Mar 1864 so the ship sailed soon thereafter.
Mobile, date ship entered (port and reported arrival to C.S. Customs) was 14 Mar 1864.
Mobile departure, cotton export manifests dated 16 Mar 1864 so ship sailed soon thereafter. (424 bales cotton, 201,600 lbs., $ 151,111, 75¢ per lb.)

Denbigh Voyage No. 3, Havana-Mobile-Havana.
Havana, last date document prepared there, 8 Apr 1864 so the ship sailed soon thereafter.
Mobile, date ship entered (port and reported arrival to C.S. Customs) was 14 Apr 1864.
Mobile departure, cotton export manifests dated 16 Apr 1864 so ship sailed soon thereafter. (476 bales cotton, 212,760 lbs., $ 153,365, 72¢ per lb.)

Two voyages were mixed in this and subsequent files as indicated by "Ship Entered" dates.

Note: The listing of small orders for individually identified people showed how the city profited by the local connections of the *Denbigh*, particularly the good offices of H. O. Brewer, an important Mobile cotton broker and merchant and A. M. Godfrey, a Mobile resident before the war. Brewer was one of the ship's owners and Godfrey began as supercargo and became ship's captain. The customs files of most other ships in the period 1861 until the end of August, 1864, when Union Admiral Farragut captured the forts at the bay mouth, did not contain documents on small individual orders to the extent of the *Denbigh's* records. What was not clear was the extent to which the small orders were on the ship's account (that is official company business of the ship owners) or the private trade of the *Denbigh's* officers on their own account. Both practices were commonplace. All the private trade was a relatively minor matter compared to the ship's main business of carrying in military supplies for the government and carrying out cotton on both public and private accounts to pay for those manufactured goods.

1068-1071
Preprinted Customs Form

Entry of Merchandise
No. 3
Entry of Merchandise
Importer Chs. E. Forstall
Vessel *Denbigh*
From Havana
Entered March 16, 64
Value $ 116 Duty $ 17.75

Owner's signature
C. E. Forstall

Ship Entered March 14 64

Imported into the Port and District of Mobile, by Chs. E. Forstall in the Br. Str. *Denbigh* Mac Nevin Master, from Havana

Marks	Packages	Packages and Contents	Quantities	In Foreign Currency Invoice Value	Appraised Value, Duty Rate			Duty
					10	15	20	
J. C. Davis	1 Box	Cassimere[16]		$ 72		75		$ 11.25
		Tea	8 lbs	12.20	13			
		Gold Lace		10.20			10	
	1 Box	Sugar	100 lbs	9.45			10	
	1 "	Soap	60	8.00		8		
				$ 111.65				
		Chgs & Com		3.89				
				115.54				

1073a
Invoice

Note: These two invoices were clearly preorders by people in Mobile. Perhaps these small orders were for family and friends of the crew and were arranged on the *Denbigh*'s first voyage to Mobile for delivery on her second voyage. The *Denbigh* was popular with the people of Mobile as indicated by newspaper accounts of her doings. She came to be called "The Packet" which we first thought to reference her clockwork like schedule of runs. Packet service was a term that implied a ship was committed to runs on a given route so as to be reliable for passengers and cargo. It seems that the term "packet" in packet service perhaps had a larger and more literal meaning. It seems from the *Denbigh* records that those running the ship made her available to facilitate the individual person's purchase orders to the stores in Havana, handling transportation and arrangements that might be involved. With large merchant orders limited due to high risk and local stores nearly bare of goods, it was little wonder the *Denbigh* excited favorable attention in Mobile.

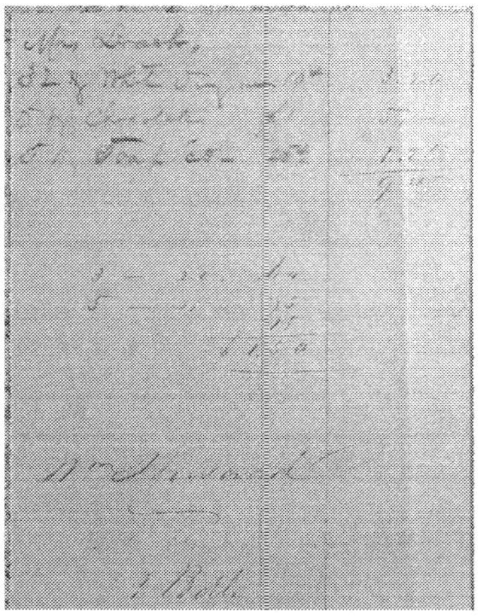

Figure 21. Invoice to Mrs. Leach for soap and chocolate.

[16] Cashmere. The variable spellings that appeared on the documents were transcribed as written.

Mrs. Leach

32 lbs	White Soap	10¢	3.20
5 lbs	**Chocolate**	$ 1	5.00
5 lbs	Soap cst	25¢	1.25
			9.45
	3 --- 20	.60	
	5 --- 15	75	
		15	
		$ 1.50	
	Wm Howard		
	1 Bdle (Bundle)		

1073b
Invoice

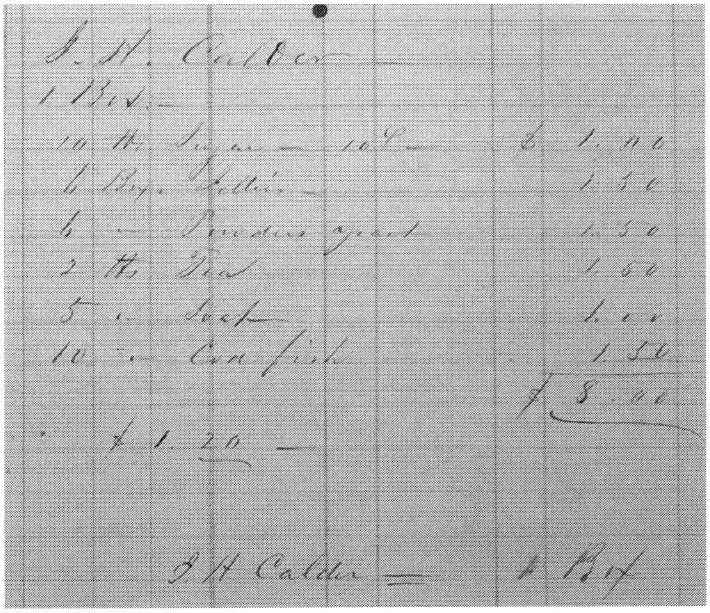

Figure 22. Invoice to J. H. Calder for one box of goods.

J. H. Calder
1 Box

10 lbs	Sugar 10¢	$ 1.00
6 Box	Jellies	1.50
6 "	Powdered Yeast	1.50
2 lbs	Tea	1.50
5 "	Soap	1.00
10 "	Cod fish	1.50
		$ 8.00
	$ 1.20 (duty)	
	J. H. Calder	1 Box

1075-1078
Preprinted Customs Form

Entry of Merchandise
No. 8
Importer J M Reid Jr
Vessel *Denbigh*
From Havana
Entered March 18 64
Value $ 199 Duty $ 40.75

Owner's Signature
John Reid Jr.

Ship Entered March 14
Imported into the Port and District of Mobile, by John Reid in the Br. St *Denbigh* MacNevin Master, from Havana

Marks	Packages	Packages and Contents	Quantities	In Foreign Currency Invoice Value	Appraised Value, Duty Rate			
					10	15	25	Duty
J Reid Jr	1 Box	Comfits		$ 34.75			36	$9.00
	1 "	**Segars** (Cigars)	700	76.50			80	20.00
	1 Bdle	Hosiery		14.50		15		2.25
		Tea	5 lbs	10.00	10			1.00
M Haywood	1 Trunk	Ready made clothes		55.90		58		8.70
				101.65	10	73	116	$ 40.95
		Chgs & C		7.84				
				199.49				

1079
Invoice

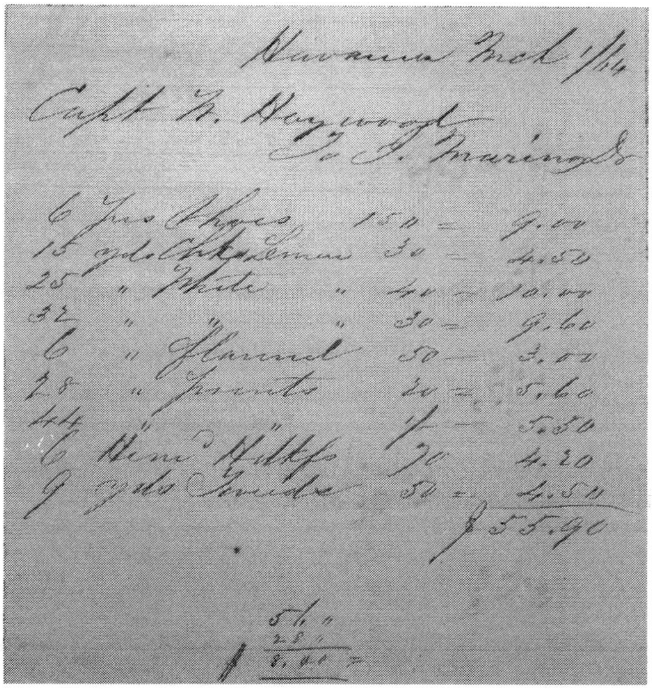
Havana Mch 1/64
Capt N. Haywood
To J. Muring Dr
6 prs Shoes 150 = 9.00
15 yds Chk Linen 30 = 4.50
25 " White " 40 = 10.00
32 " " " 30 = 9.60
6 " flannel 50 = 3.00
28 " prints 20 = 5.60
44 " " 1/ = 5.50
6 Hem^d Hdkfs 70 4.20
9 yds Tweeds 50 = 4.50
$55.90
5%
28
$ 8.40

Figure 23. Invoice for fabric and shoes.

Havana Mch 1, 64

Capt. N. Haywood

To J. Muring (Waring?) Dr. (Debit)

6 prs	Shoes	150	$ 9.00
15 yds (yards)	Chk (Checked) Linen	30	4.50
25 "	White "	40	10.00
32 "	" "	30	9.60
6 "	flannel	50	3.00
28 "	prints	20	5.60
44 "	"	1/	5.50
6	Hemd (Hemmed) Hdkfs (Handkerchiefs)	70	4.20
9 yds	Tweeds	50	4.50
			$ 55.90
	$ 8.40 (duty)		

1080
Invoice

Note: Mr. Ramsay sent several small items to friends or associates, perhaps in response to letters that went to Havana on the *Denbigh* when she returned from the first trip.

Invoice of Stores shipped by C G Ramsay on board Steamer *Denbigh* bound for Mobile for account of whom it may concern reassigned to John Reid Jr. Esq.

Marks					
John Reid	1 Box containing	3 Doz (Dozen) Boxes	Sugar Candy	@4.25	12.75
El Vapor *Denbigh*[17]		4½ " "	Jelly & Marmalade	" 4 $	18.00
		2 " half "	" "	" 2 $	4.00
	did not this amt.	20 lbs	Chocolate Walsh	" 1 $	20.00
Steamer *Denbigh*					
John Reid Esq	1 Box "	2 M	1st Londres (London) (cigar name)		
JW (Later correction)	did not (ship) 300 Sigars		Cubanas 300 for Mr. Walsh	" 45	90.00
John Reid Esq Mobile	1 Bundle "	5 Varas[18]	marked to H C Lehoveder		5.87
		1	**Penknife**[19]		2.13
		2 Pairs	Gloves in a paper marked Henry Meyers		2.50
		1 Doz Pairs	Ladies Stockings in a package marked Mr A Westfield		4.00
		5 lbs	Tea Black marked to Mrs C J Hallete		10.00
John Reid Esq	1 Bag	180 lbs	Coffee $ 36 free		
					$ 169.25
			Charges		
			Boxes	1.00	
			Drayage[20] & Lighterage[21]	2.00	3.00
					$ 172.25
			Export duty	1.50	
			Havana March 5th 1864		
			C G Ramsay		

1082-1085
Preprinted Customs Form
Note: Large quantities probably indicated commercial orders.

Entry of Merchandise
No. 12

[17] The Steamer *Denbigh*
[18] A Spanish measure of length that varied at times from 32 to 43 inches (81 to 109 cm), abbreviated va.
[19] The *Denbigh* shipwreck excavation produced a pocketknife, probably either cargo or a crew possession.
[20] Charge for hauling and delivery of cargo while on dry land in port.
[21] Charge for delivery of cargo by boat between land and ship at anchor in a harbor or offshore.

Importer **F. J. Hilton**
Vessel *Denbigh*
From Havana
Entered March 22 64
Value $ 690 Duty $ 148.85

Owner's Signature
Fredr J. Hilton

Ship Entered March 14 64
Imported into the Port and District of Mobile, by F. J. Hilton in the Br. Str. *Denbigh* MacNevin Master, from Havana

Packages	Packages and Contents	Quantities	In Foreign Currency Invoice Value	Appraised Value, Duty Rate			
				10	15	25	Duty
1 Bdl	**Sigaritos** (Paper Cigars)		$ 51.20			53	
2 Kegs	Whiskey	16 Gals	35.00			36	
1 Box	**Chocolate**	168 lbs	92.40		96		
1 "	Sausages	21 lbs	21.00		22		
2 Pkgs	Buttons	122 each	55.30	57			$ 5.70
1 Box	Sardines in oil		20.00			21	22.65
2 Kegs	Herrings		15.50		17		120.50
1 Box	Mustard	5 doz	15.00		16		$ 148.85
12 "	Claret	12 "	111.00			115	
11 "	Champagne	11 "	121.00			126	
12 Cases	Gin 16 in ea	16 doz	96.00			100	
~~12~~	~~Rum~~		not on board			31	
12 Demijohns	Rum Jamaican	38 Gals	30.00	57	151	482	
			663.40				
	Chgs & Com		26.76				
			690.16				

1087
Scratch sheet for calculating duty and correcting list of cargo.

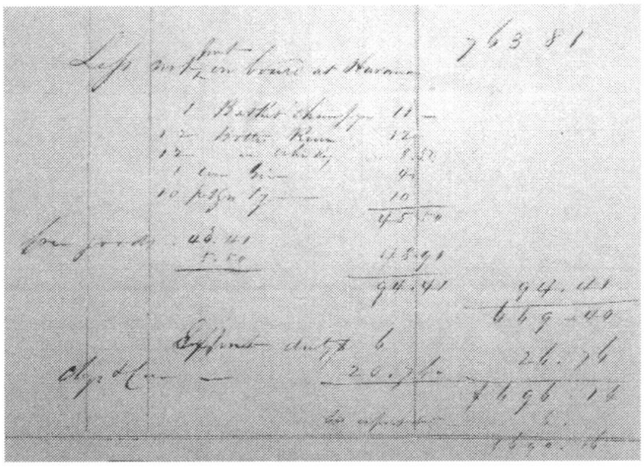

Figure 24. Scratch sheet for duties.

			763.81
Less	not put on board at Havana		
	1 Basket Champagne	11.00	
	12 Bottles Rum	12.00	
	12 " Whiskey	8.50	
	1 case Gin	4.00	
	10 Pkgs[22] ???	10.00	
free	goods 43.41		
	5.50	48.91	
		94.41	94.41
			669.40
	Export duty	6.00	
	Chgs & Com	20.76	26.76
			$ 696.76
	less import duty		6.00
			$ 690.16

1088
Invoice

Note: Perhaps the *Denbigh*'s captain was trading on his own behalf. It would probably have been easy to sell these items while in port at Mobile. At any rate, as attested at the bottom of the invoice, McNevin paid this bill to O. A. Schneider & Co. This cargo could have been trade on the ship's account (i.e. owners' account) but probably was not supplies for consumption by the crew on board since customs duty would not have been paid in that case.

Havana March 9th 1864

Capt. McNevin

To O. A. Schneider & Co Dr (Debit. i.e. a bill payable to S & Co)

1 Barrel	paper Cigars 2048	@ 40 for ¢	51.20
	Export duty on 2 Barrels of same		6.00

22 Packages.

1 Keg	Bourbon whiskey	10 gals 2 $	20.00
1 "	Brandy	6½ gals	15.00
12 Cases	Chocolate	168 lbs 53¢	92.40
1 Bag	Coffee (duty) free[23]	193 21¢	40.53
2	hams (duty) free	16 lbs 18¢	2.88
14	Sausages Bologna	21 lbs 1 $	21.00
4	Round Cheese	$1.25	5.00
1 Barrel	Butter	112 lbs Nett 40¢	44.80
1 Box	Liverwurst (?)		6.50
1 Box	Sardines	100/4 tins	20.00
2 Cases	Soda Crackers	$ 2.75	5.50
2 "	Butter "	$ 2.75	5.50
12 Boxes	Sauterne wine	$ 9.25	111.00
6 Kitts	herrings	$ 1.50	9.00
12 Boxes	Champagne 11 Boxes only	11 $ 121.00	132.00
12 large cases	Gin	8 $	96.00
12 Demij(ohns)	Rum	$ 2.50	30.00
12 Bottles	Jamaica Rum	not on board	12.00
12 "	Whiskey	"	8.50
1 Small Case	Gin	"	4.00
1 Box	Mustard	3 ?? 5 $	15.00
10 packages	paper cigars	not on board	10.00
	Rec ???	Net	$ 763.81
	O A Schneider & Co.		

1093-1096
Preprinted Customs Form

Entry of Merchandise
No. 3
Importer Boykin & McRae
Vessel *Denbigh*
From Havana
Entered April 6 64
Value $ 419 Duty $ 63.15

Signature of Consignee, Importer or Agent
S L Lockwood

Ship Entered March 64

Imported into the Port and District of Mobile, by Boykin & McRae in the Br. Str. *Denbigh* MacNevin Master, from Havana

Marks	Packages	Packages and Contents	In Foreign Currency Invoice Value	Appraised Value, Duty Rate			
				10	15	20	Duty
EMM	1 Case	Cotton goods Hose &c	£ 6. 17. 8		35		

[23] Duty free items were always carefully noted in these documents.

		Wool mfs Flannels	24. 10. 10		122		
		Muslins	34. 10. 11		172		
		Medicinal preparations	1. 9. 6		7		
		Shoes & Combs	13. 15. 9		71		
		Cotton & Wool cards[24]	1. 3. 1		6		
		Brushes	1. 3. 0			6	
			83. 18. 6		413	6	$ 63.15
		Chgs on 3 Boxes 12/1	2. 14. 7				
		Comm 2/2/1	£ 86. 13. 1				
			or $ 419.41				

1097
Invoice

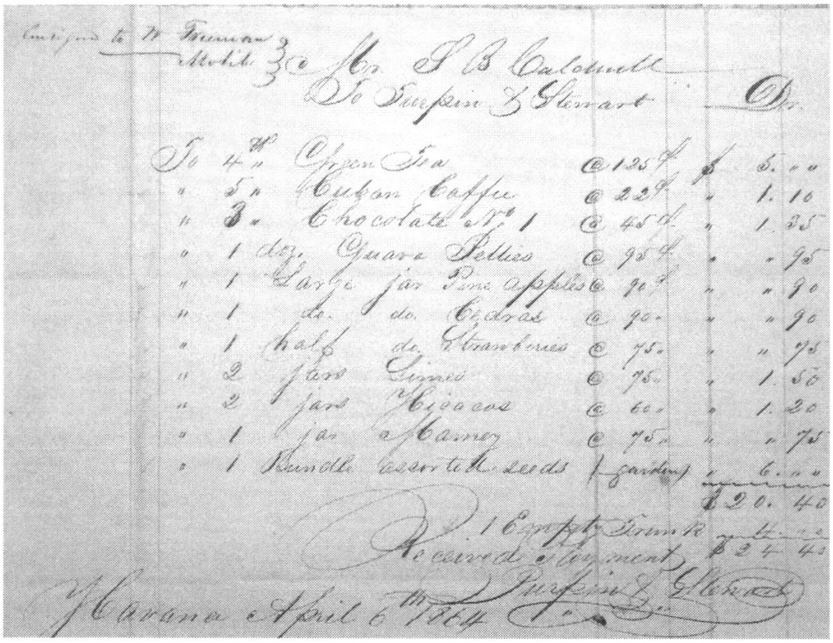
Consigned to W. Freeman Mobile } Mr. S B Caldwell
To Turpin & Stewart Dr.

To 4 lb	Green Tea	@ 125¢	$	5.00
" 5 "	Cuban Coffee	@ 22¢	"	1.10
" 3 "	Chocolate No 1	@ 45¢	"	1.35
" 1 doz.	Guava Jellies	@ 95¢	"	.95
" 1	Large jar Pine apples	@ 90¢	"	.90
" 1	do. do. Cidras	@ 90	"	.90
" 1	half do. Strawberries	@ 75	"	.75
" 2	jars Limes	@ 75	"	1.50
" 2	jars Hicacos	@ 60	"	1.20
" 1	jar Mameys	@ 75	"	.75
" 1	Bundle assorted seeds (garden)		"	6.00
				$ 20.40
	1 Export Permit			4.00
				$ 24.40

Received payment
Turpin & Stewart
Havana April 6th 1864

Figure 25. Invoice for tea, coffee, jelly, and other treats.

Consigned to W. Freeman, Mobile (for delivery to buyer)
Mr. S. B. Caldwell[25]
To Turpin & Stewart Dr.

To 4 lb	Green Tea	@ 125¢	$ 5.00
" 5 "	Cuban Coffee	@ 22¢	1.10
" 3 "	Chocolate No 1	@ 45¢	1.25
" 1 doz	Guava Jellies	@ 95¢	.95
" 1 Large Jar	Pine Apples	@ 90¢	.90

---

[24] Tools for preparing fibers for spinning. Shortages of these cards retarded home production of cloth.

[25] Likely this was the Lt. Samuel. B. Caldwell who helped the Confederates seize the Revenue Cutter *Robert McClelland* in New Orleans at the beginning of the Civil War.

" 1 do (ditto) do	Cedras[26]	@ 90"	.90
" 1 half do	Strawberries	@ 75"	.75
" 2 jars	Limes	@ 75"	1.50
" 2 jars	Hicacos[27]	@ 60"	1.20
" 1 jar	Mamey[28]	@ 75"	.75
" 1 Bundle	**assorted seeds garden**		6.00
			$ 20.40
	1 Empty Trunk		4.00
	Received Payment		$ 24.40
	Turpin & Stewart		
	Havana April 6th 1864		

1100
Invoice

Note: In many cases the small orders like this one seemed to represent things the lady of the house might need or want after a period of shortages. Also such items might be bought in Havana for considerably less money than would be changed in a store in Mobile, if available at all. This was a good example of an order that might have been made for a single household.

Sam B. Caldwell Consigned to W. Freeman
Bought from the Florida Store

1 pc	White Linen	$ 17.00
2½ doz	Spool Thread	4.05
30 papers	Needles	3.00
14 "	Pins	.50
5 pck	Hair Pins	.30
5 "	Darning Cotton	2.50
1	**Hoop Skirt**	3.00
1 doz	ladies Handkerchiefs	2.25
1 "	" "	1.50
2	Embroidered "	8.00
2	**Corsets**	4.75
12 Yds	colored linen @ .25	3.00
1½ doz	ladies Hose	6.00
½ "	" "	5.00
2 pr	Shoes	3.50
1	Shall	4.25
1	Comb	.40
1 p	Scissors	1.25
		$ 76.25
	Havana Apl 6/64	

---

[26] Cedras de America (Cedars of America) in Spanish referring to a tree on Barbados.
[27] A species of cactus.
[28] Mamey (Spanish) – American mammee tree. Its fruit was used for medicine and oil. In this case the fruit appears in a list of jars of jelly and fruit clearly intended for eating.

1101-1102
Substitute for Preprinted Customs Form

Note: Trade by Peter Skuse, one of the *Denbigh's* officers. This document seemed to be a hand written substitute for the preprinted customs form. Perhaps there was a shortage of the forms. The outside of a sheet of blue paper when folded to serve as a file folder presented the abstract of the shipment. The main side of paper showed details of the shipment.

Figure 26. When a printed customs form was not available, a substitute of uniform type was used showing the most important data.

No. 9
P Skuse
Denbigh
Havana
April 16 64
$ 83 $ 20.75

Figure 27. Substitute for preprinted customs form for cargo of rum.

Copy of Entry of Merchse. Made by P(eter). Skuse per Str. *Denbigh* from Havana

S	6 Bbls	Rum Gals 180	$ 50
	10 Demijohns	do " 40	30
			80
			3
			83
	Spirits $ 83	-- 25 -- $ 20.75 (duty)	

1098
Invoice

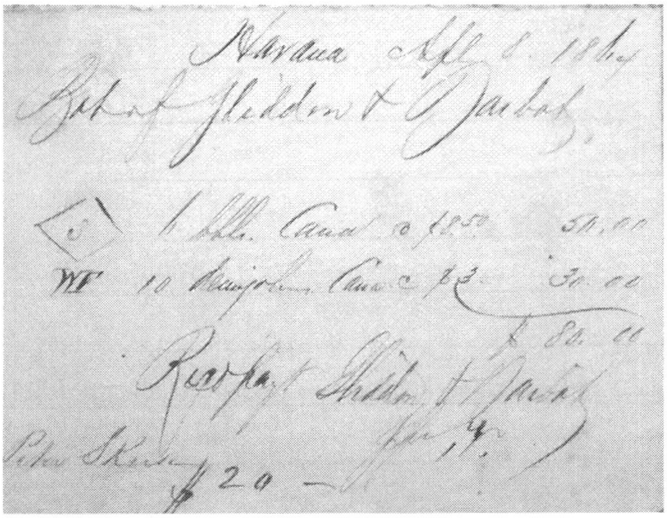

Figure 28. Invoice for cana (rum).

Havana Apl 8 1864
Bot of Glidden & Narbat (?)

S	6 bbls (barrels)	Cana (Spanish for rum)	@ $ 8.50	50.00
WF	10 demijohns	Cana	@ $ 3	30.00

				$ 80.00
		Rcd Payt Glidden & Narbat		
		Peter Skuse $ 20 (duty)		

Note: A subsequent invoice shows that in this case "Cana" meant rum in Cuban Spanish. See below. Perhaps referring to cane as in sugar cane of which rum is a product. Peter Skuse was an officer on the *Denbigh* so this might have been his private trade.

1103
Invoice

Consigned to T. Langdon

A Ferman (?)
Bot (Bought) on 7th April of Mr. Slater at Havana
1 Bbl Rum ~~$ 7.50~~ $ 8.50 8.50

Thos Brenan
Bot on 7th of April at Havana of Mr. Slater
1 Bbl Rum ~~$ 7.50~~ $ 8.50 8.50

Pat Cain
Bot on 7th of April of Mr. Slater at Havana
1 Bbl Rum ~~$ 7.50~~ $ 8.50 8.50

25.50

Note: One wonders if maybe these men were crew or passengers with limited means who nevertheless wished to profit from taking a barrel of rum to Mobile were it might easily sell at a profit. Or on the other hand, the men might have stayed in Alabama and sent an order for rum with the ship when she returned to Havana from her prior run.

1105-1106
Substitute for Preprinted Customs Form

Note: For clarity herein this kind of document will have the data headings included although just the data from the blanks of the printed forms was written on the outside of the substitute. See example 1101-1102 above.

(Entry of Merchandise)
No. 8
(Importer) Thos. Langdon
(Vessel) *Denbigh*
(From) Havana
(Entered) April 16 1864
(Value) $ 28 (Duty) $ 7.00

Copy of Entry made by Thos Langdon of goods received per *Denbigh* from Havana

3 Bbls Rum Gals 90 $ 27.50

Spirits $ 28 --- @ 25 --- $ 7.00 (duty)

1107-1108
Substitute for Preprinted Customs Form

Entry of Merchandise
No. 12
Importer W. Freeman
Vessel *Denbigh*
From Havana
Entered April 16 1864
Value $ 97 Duty $ 15.30

Copy of Entry of goods made by W. Freeman per *Denbigh* from Havana

S. Caldwell					
1 Trunk	Flax mfs	$ 17.00	$ 18	15	2.70
	Cotton "	55.55	60	"	9.00
	Needles, pins &c	4.05	4	"	.60
	Tea 4 lbs	5.00	5	10	.50
	Jellies & preserved fruit	8.30	10	25	2.50
		89.90	107		
	Chgs & Com	6.70			
		96.60			

1109-1111
Preprinted Customs Form

No. 4
Entry of Merchandise
Importer H O Brewer & Co
Vessel *Denbigh*
From Havana
Entered April 12 '64
Value $ 660 Duty $ 134.40

(note: H O B & Co deposit $300)
Owner's signature: Benj Donaldson

Ship Entered March 64

Imported into the Port and District of Mobile, by H O Brewer & Co. in the Br. Str. *Denbigh* MacNevin Master, from Havana

Marks	Packages	Packages and Contents	Quantities	In Foreign Currency Invoice Value	Appraised Value, Duty Rate				
					10	15	20	25	Duty
Yeoman	12 Cases	Wine Madeira	Gals 112	$ 249.25				259	$ 64.75
& Co.	12 "	Brandy		54.18				56	14.00
	1 "	Sardines in oil		19.43				20	5.00
	9 "	Preserved meats & vegetables		100.24			104		20.80
		Sperm oil	Gals 40	80.53		84			12.60
	2 "	Salted fish		16.92		17			2.55
	Box	Soap	56 lbs	9.30		10			1.50
	2 Bbls	White Sugar	lbs 212	21.22			22		4.40
	2 Chests	Tea	lbs 60	83.50	88				8.80
				634.51	88	111	126	335	$ 124.40
		Chgs & Com		25.36					
				659.93					

Note: This high dollar and large quantity order appeared to be a merchant's order rather than an individual family order. The mark probably was that of the merchant whose shipment this was.

1114
Invoice

Claret	$ 100.80		$ 100.80
Brandy	43.25	Less Short 19.45	23.80
S. Whisky	30.80	" " 6.45	24.35
Old Tom	17.75	" " 11.72	6.00
Madeira	121.20	" " 25.25	95.95
Sherry	70.00	" " 17.50	52.50
	383.80	$ 80.37	303.43
Tea	62.20		
Sugar	21.22		
Cheese	21.30		
Soap	9.30		
Candles & oil	80.53		331.14
Fish salted	16.92	dutiable	$ 634.57
" in oil	19.43	2½% Cm	15.87
preserved meat & ??	100.24	Total	$ 650.44
	714.94		
Free	106.56		
	821.50		
Less Shortage	80.87		
	741.13		
free	106.50		
	634.57		

1115 and 1117
Invoice

Havana March 7th 1864

Shipment of Goods per Steamer *Denbigh*
By E. Yeomans & Son

H.Y. E 3 1/??					
No 1	1 Hhd.[29]	Claret			100.80
2/6	5 Doz	**Hennessey's Brandy**	8/??		43.25
		5 Cases			
7/14	8 "	Scotch Whiskey	3/85		30.80
		8 Cases			
15/17	5 "	Old Tom	3/35		17.75
		3 Cases			
18/25	8 "	Madeira	15/15		121.20
		8 Cases			
26/30	5 "	Brown Sherry	14/-		70.00
		5 Cases			
31	1 - ½ Chest	Fine Congou[30] Tea	45 lb @ /60		27.35
		Canvas /35			
32	1 - ½ Chest	Hylou	46 lb @ /75		34.85
		Canvas /35			
33/34	2 Barrs.	Crushed Sugar	2. 0. 12 9/60		21.22
		2 Casks 1/-			
35/36	2 Bags	Fine Coffee	534 lb 19/20		38.40
37	3 2 Doz tins	Yarmouth Bloaters[31]	@ /60	1.80	
	72 ½ Boxes	Sardines	2/88	17.28	
		1 Case		.35	19.43
38	12 2 lb tins	**Scotch Salmon**	24 lb @ /34	8.16	
	12 1 " "	Yarmouth Bloaters		2.88	
	12 1 " "	Mackerel		2.88	
	12 1 " "	Codfish		2.40	
		Case		.60	16.92
39	12 2 lb tins	Green Peas	24 lb	2.88	
	12 2 " "	Carrots	24 "	4.30	
	12 1 " "	**Artichokes**	12 "	2.40	
	12 1 " "	French Haricot[32]		2.40	
		1 Case		.60	13.80

[29] Hogshead.
[30] Fine grade of Chinese black tea.
[31] Fish cured by soaking and smoking; a large herring that has been soaked in brine and smoked.
[32] White bean.

	12 2 lb tins	Roast Beef	24 lb -/28	6.72	
	12 2 lb "	Cured Briskets (?)	24 " -/24	5.76	
	12 2 lb "	Roast Mutton	" -/28	6.72	
	12 2 lb "	Boiled do	" -/24	5.76	
		1 Case		.60	25.56
			Carried over		580.61

			Brought over		580.61
No 41	12 2 lb tins	Roast veal	24 lb @ -/28	6.72	
	12 " "	Curried "	" " "	6.72	
	12 " "	Mutton Chops	" " "	6.72	
	12 " "	Rump Steaks	" " " -/30	7.20	
	12 " "	Roast Lamb	" " " -/32	7.68	
			1 Case	. 85	35.89
42/44	6 Doz	Tart Fruits assorted	2/52	15.12	
			3 Cases	1.44	16.56
45	12	**Pale York Hams**	182¾ lb 24/	39.16	
			Canvas Cask & Salt	3.48	42.64
46/47	16	**Bellies Wiltshire Bacon**	2. 0. 5	21.60	
			2 Cases Canvas & Salt	3.92	25.52
48	24 1 lb Bottles	Assorted Candies	-/36	8.64	
			1 Case	.51	9.15
49	1	**Cheshire Cheese**	0. 3. 14 @ 20/20	17.57	
			Bladders & Case	1.00	18.57
50	1	Cheddar Cheese	11½ lb	2.45	
			Bladders & Case	.30	2.75
51	2 5lb tins	Cracknels[33]	1/44	2.88	
	1 " "	Abernethy's		1.20	
	1 " "	Mixed		1.20	
	1 lb "	Cinnamon		1.00	
	1 " "	Nutmegs		1.80	
	1 " "	Cloves		.60	
	1 " "	Allspice		.36	
	1 " "	Ginger		.50	
	1 " "	Mace		.85	
			1 Case	.36	10.03
52	24 Jars	Table Salt		2.88	

[33] A hard brittle biscuit.

			1 Case	.52	3.40
53/54	5 Sacks	**Liverpool Salt**	10- pc 8	4.80	
			5 Double Bags	.60	5.40
55/59	50 lb	Sperm (whale oil) Candles	-/24	12.00	
				.50	12.50
60/63	100 lb	?? Candles	4/-	32.00	
				1.00	33.00
64/65	10 Galls	fine Lamp oil	1/44	14.40	
			2 Iron Kegs	1.80	16.20
66	14 lb	Toilet Soap	-/3. 9	4.20	
	6 Cakes	Shaving Soap		1.44	
	6 Bars	Yellow " 18 lbs		1.76	
	1 Box	Bryant imayi **matches**		1.44	
			1 Case	.46	9.30
		E&OE			$ 821.52
		(Note added later)	Add Com		

Note: These appeared to be high-quality luxury goods, many from Great Britain.

1118
Invoice

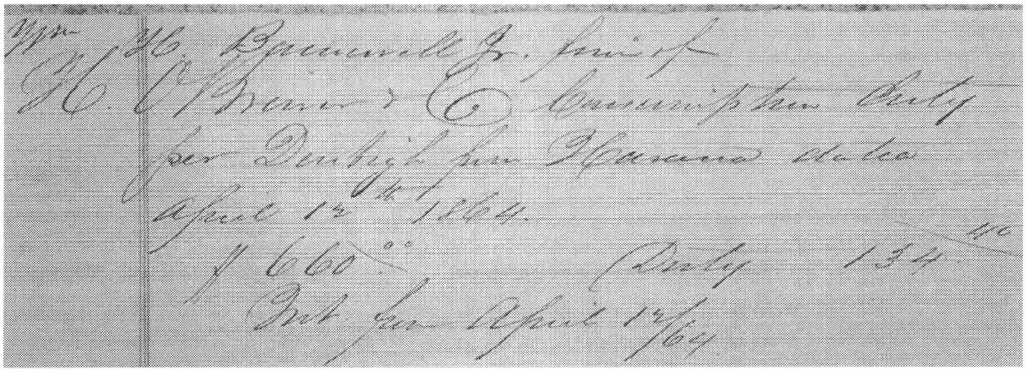
Wm H. Barnwell Jr. firm of
H. O Brewer & Co Consumption Duty
per Denbigh from Havana dated
April 12th 1864.
$ 660.00 (Duty 134.40
Int from April 12/64

Figure 29. Invoice for consumption duty.

Wm. H. Barnwell Jr. firm of
H O Brewer & Co. Consumption duty[34]
Per *Denbigh* from Havana dated

[34] Type of customs fee.

April 12th 1864
$ 660.00 Duty 134.40
Ent(ry?) from April 12/64

1119
Preprinted Customs Form

Entry of Merchandise
No. 6
Importer H O Brewer & Co
Vessel *Denbigh*
From Havana
Entered April 6, 64
Value $ 268 Duty $ 40.20

Consignee, Importer or Agent signature:
Benj. Donaldson

Ship Entered March 64

Imported into the Port and District of Mobile, by H. O. Brewer & Co. in the Br. Str. *Denbigh* MacNevin Master, from Havana

Marks	Packages	Packages and Contents	Quantities	In Foreign Currency Invoice Value	Appraised Value, Duty Rate				
						15	20	25	Duty
G. Tolson	1 Trunk	Ready Made Clothing		$ 205.36					
		Charges, Trunk & Comm		25.50					
				230.86		231			34.65
G. B. Emtis	1 Box	Woolen shirts &c & chg		37.00		37			5.55
				267.86		268			$ 40.20
			268 @24%	$ 64.52					

1123a
Invoice

Note: On this invoice there was a calculation of customs duty added to the bottom. Such figures appeared frequently in the customs documents, but were omitted herein. The preprinted customs forms show the duty amounts and the calculation by which they were derived.

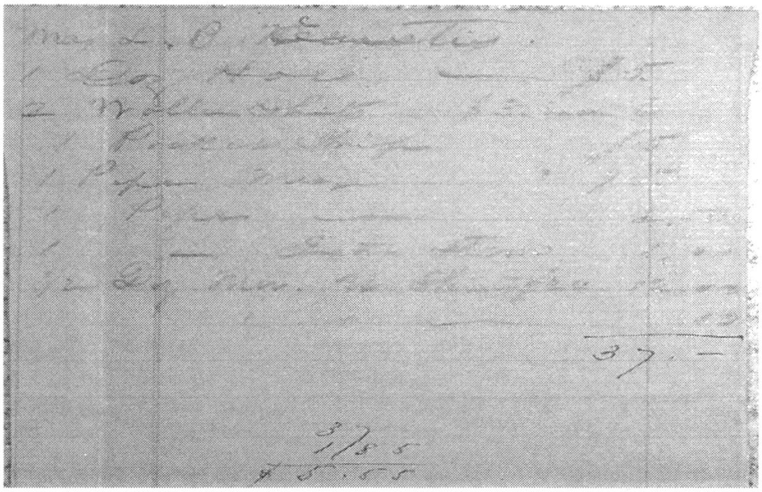

Figure 30. Invoice for Maj. L. B. Custis.

Maj. L. B. Custis (?)

1 Doz	Hoes	$ 5
2	Woolen Shirts $3 each	6
1	Pocket Knife	5
1	Pipe Mrs (Meerschaum?)	5
1	Pipe	2.50
1	___ Extra Item	1.00
½ Doz	Mr. N. Shirts ??	12.00
	1 Box	.50
		37.00
	$5.55 (duty)	

1123b
Invoice

Mr. H. Barnwell Jr. firm of
H O Brewer & Co Consumption duty per
Br Str *Denbigh* from Havana Cuba
Duties April 6th 1864
Value $ 268 @ 24% $ 64.52
Interest from 6th April /64

1125-1126
Invoice

Mr. George Folsom Debit
To Gutierrez Bros & Co.

2 pieces of	White Cotton Cloth	28 vs each @ 7$	14.00
1 " "	" linen Cloth	32 yds @ 12 $	12.00
1 " "	" fine White linen Cloth	7 vs @ 2.50	2.50
10 varas	White Flannel "	@ 65¢	6.50
13 "	Worsted cloth for dresses	@ 50¢	6.50
8 "	Checked flannel	@ 60 "	4.80
4 "	Colored Cotton Cloth	@ 50 "	2.00
20 "	colored Linen for dresses	@ 37½ "	7.50
8 "	Cachimir (cashmere)	@ 75 "	6.00
2	Dresses of Muslin with	24 varas @ 31 "	7.44
4	do do "	50 varas @ 25 "	12.50
1	do do "	15 " @ 15 "	2.25
1	do do "	for	1.75
7	do Colored Calico with	84 varas @ 31 "	26.04
2	Remnants with	4 varas	.80
4	**Turkish Towels**		2.00
1	dozen Ladies Stockings		7.50
2	do Children's Socks		6.00
1	dozen Linen Handkerchiefs		2.75
			$ 130.83
	Havana 6 March 1864		
	Received		
	Gutierrez Herm. Y Ca[35]		
	List of goods in same trunk •	continued	
16 yards	braid 4¢ - 11 yds **Ribbon** 50¢		6.14
5½ "	Ribbon 62¢ - .3 Ladies **Belts** 1.50		7.94
	Pins, hooks & Eyes & White cord		.80
	Thread & Tape		1.15
2 Doz	Spool Cotton	1.75	3.50
5 "	Buttons	12¢	.60
2	Bottles **olive oil**	75¢	1.50
		over	152.46
	Amt brot (brought) over		152.46
2	Bottles **Castor oil**	80¢	1.60
6	Combs .66 ½¢ 4--[36] 2 packs Rice powder 25¢ 50¢		4.50
3 pr	Ladies Shoes	1.25	3.75
4 "	Children's " 75¢ 2 toy books 30¢ ea		3.60
1	Bottle Brandy 2-- 2 lbs Castile soap 20¢		2.40
2	Calf Skins 2.75 18 papers needles 10¢		7.30
3	Tooth brushes 30¢ 1 pr scissors 1--		1.90
2	Bottles Cough Syrup	1.75	2.50
8 lbs	Coffee 25¢ 6 lbs Chocolate 25¢		3.50
2	Boxes Jelly	75¢	1.50

[35] Gutierrez Brothers & Co.

[36] In these invoices 00 was sometimes expressed by a dash as: 4.00 and 4--. In most cases for clarity the author used 00 in place of --.

1½ lbs	Tea			3.75
25 lbs	Sugar 10¢ 5 lbs Salt 5¢			2.75
2 Boxes	**Night tapers**			.50
12 lbs	Candles		33 1/3¢	4.00
1	**Fan** 10¢ 2 packs hair pins 10¢			.30
10 yards	White Flannel		60¢	6.00
	Candies & Toys			1.25
	Cosmetique			.60
	Trunks & Straps & Charges			25.50
				$ 230.86

1127-1130
Preprinted Customs Form

No. 7
Entry of Merchandise
Importer Geo H Gardner
Vessel *Denbigh*
From Havana
Entered April 12, 64
Value $ 262 Duty $ 39.30

Consignee, Importer or Agent signature:
John Johnson

Ship Entered _____
Imported into the Port and District of Mobile, by Geo H Gardner. in the Br. Str. *Denbigh* MacNevin Master, from Havana

Marks	Packages	Packages and Contents	In Foreign Currency Invoice Value	Appraised Value, Duty Rate				
				10	15	20	25	Duty
GHG/S	2 Boxes	Cotton mfs	£ 16. 9. 6		83			
1/2		Wool "	32. 4. 0		161			
		Shoes	3. 11. 0		18			
			52. 4. 6		262	15%		$39.30
		Charges & Comm	1. 17. 2					
			£ 54. 1. 8					
			$ 261.76					

1131
Invoice

Capt McRae (?)

3	Straw Hats	1.25	3.75
10 yds	???	50¢	5.00
6	Silk ???	50¢	3.00
1	???	75¢	7.50
2	??? ???	$ 2.00 ea	4.00
6	???	40¢ ea	2.40
27	??? check	75¢	19.75
15	" "	1.25	18.75
2 Pair	Shoes	1.50 ea	3.00
1 doz	Soap	$ 2	2.00
			69.15
	10.55 (duty)		
	~~Paid~~		

Note: Document nearly illegible.

1133
Letter

Note: Occasionally the customs documents yielded related items such as the following letters. The correspondence showed how people who lived at a distance from Mobile managed to order things from forwarding merchants through a factor located in the port city. The letter arranged for a friend, business associate, or forwarding agent to handle a shipment. It seemed to be a routine thing to do. In this case the boxes were likely sent from England by Colin McRae, an important Confederate official in England.

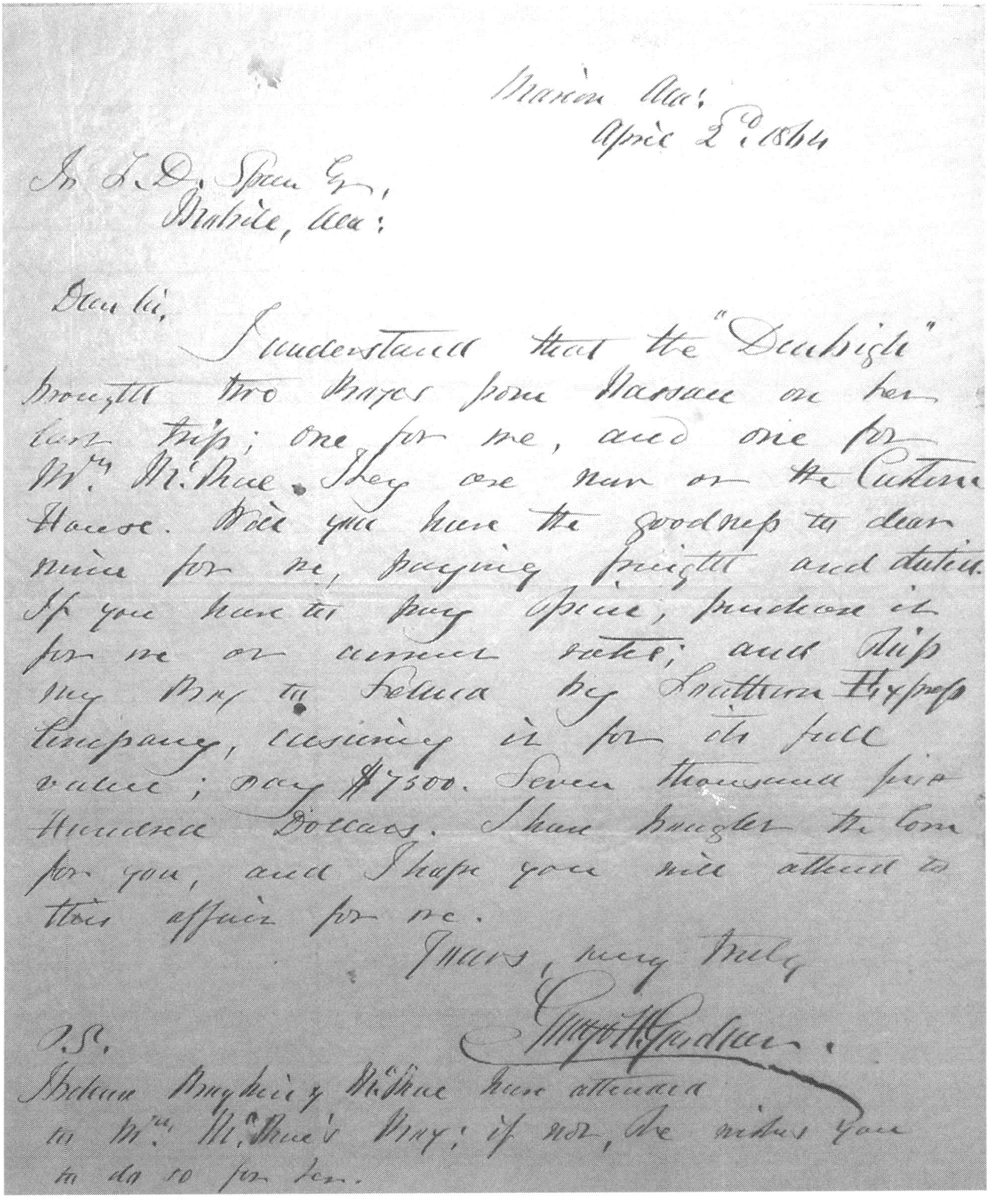

Marion Ala:
April 2d 1864

Mr. J. D. Spear Esq.,
Mobile, Ala:

Dear Sir,

I understand that the "Denbigh" brought two Boxes from Nassau on her last trip; one for me, and one for Mrs. McRae. They are now in the Custom House. Will you have the goodness to clear mine for me, paying freight and duties. If you have to pay Specie, purchase it for me at current rates; and ship my Box to Selma by Southern Express Company, insuring it for its full value; say $7500. Seven thousand five Hundred Dollars. I have brought the Com for you, and I hope you will attend to this affair for me.

Yours, very truly
Geo. H. Gardner.

P.S.
Unless Messrs Bayley & McRae have attended to Mrs. McRae's Box; if not, she wishes you to do so for her.

Figure 31. Letter making arrangements for cargo belonging to George H. Gardner and Mrs. McRae.

Marion Ala.
April 2nd, 1864

To L. D. Spencer (?) Esq.
Mobile, Ala.

Dear Sir,

I understand that the *Denbigh* brought two boxes from Nassau on her last trip; one for me, and one for Mrs. McRae. They are at the Custom House. Will you have the goodness to clear mine for me, paying freight and duties. If you have to pay specie, purchase it for me at the current rate; and ship my box to Selma by Southern Express Company, insuring it for its full value; say $7,500, seven thousand five hundred dollars. I have bought the Corn (?) for you, and I hope you will attend to this affair for me.

Yours, very truly
George H. Gardner

PS
I believe Boykin & McRae have attended to Mrs. McRae's box; if not, she asks you to do it for her.

1134
Letter

Note: This letter showed the commercial complications brought about by the devaluation of C.S. currency and issuance of new paper money in the south.

Selma April 8th 1864

John Johnson Esqr
Mobile

Dear Sir:

This letter from Mr. G. H. Gardner explains itself. He called on me so soon as I returned. I advised him to write to Genl Butler which he did in my office. Mr. G is the gentleman that purchased the com (?) I write you about. He says he has purchased it payable in the New Currency payable on the first of May if not paid then, the ?? to pay interest in the amount. He can take it anytime but the roads are too bad to haul now. Will you please to enquire at the Custom House for Mr. Gardner's goods & ship them. He has the gold & silver to pay duties &c. He knows the amount. Mesrs (?) Goodman & Rubin at the ?? firm here wish me to enquire if there can be purchased in Mobile a Tyler and Duval cotton press. Knowing that you are acquainted with Mr. Hammond & the Cotton Press, may I take the liberty of asking you to please enquire & let me know the particulars. We are all well. It has been raining 2 days & raining a gale. I have here some of the new currency today.

Yours truly J. D. Spencer (?)

1135
Invoice

Note: Occasionally invoices were written on preprinted forms with attractive engraved letter head. (See examples herein.) Also of interest on invoices from Great Britain were tax stamps affixed at the bottom of the invoices.

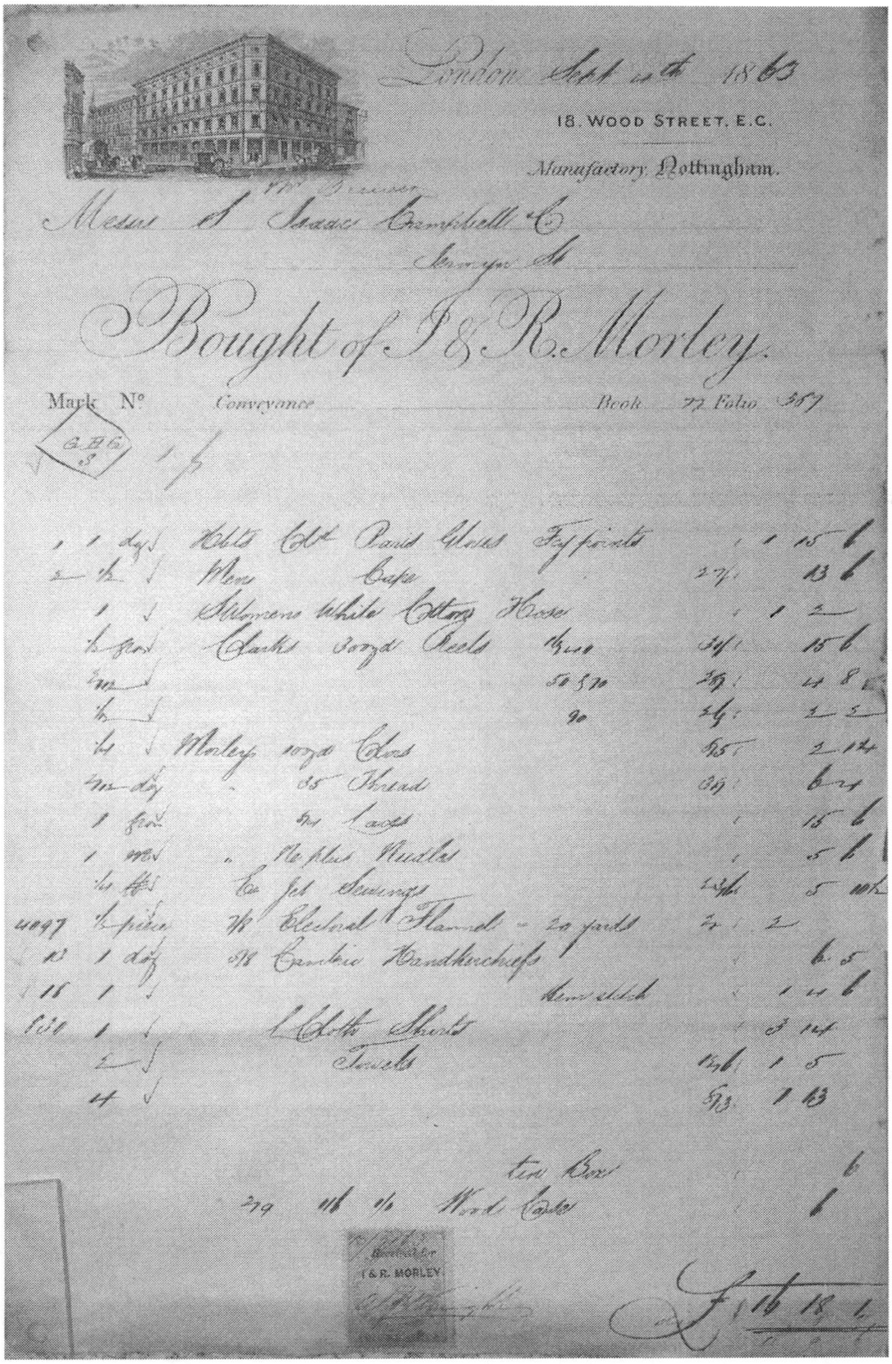

Figure 32. Invoice to H. O. Brewer for goods shipped home from England.

London Sept 4th 1863
18. Wood Street, E.C.
Manufactory, Nottingham.

Mr. Brewer (added note)
Messrs S Isaac Campbell & Co
Iermyn St

Bought of I & R. Morley

Mark No. Conveyance ______________ Book 77 Folio 387
GHG/S 1/2

1	1 dz	Hbts (?) Cold Paris **Gloves** Faj (?) points		1 15 6
2	½	Men's Cape	27/	13 6
	1	S Women's White Cotton Hose		1 2 0
	½ gros	Clarks 300 yd Reels 16 40	31/	15 6
	½	50 370	28/	4 8
	½	90	26/	2 2
	¼	Morley 10 yds Colors	8/5	2 14
	2/12 dz	" 35 Thread	3/9	6 4
	1 ??	8/4 Laces (?)		15 6
	1 ~~M~~	" Ne plus Needles		5 6
	¼ lb	Ex (?) Jet Sewings	23/6	5 10½
4097	½ piece	7/8 Electoral Flannel[37] = 20 yards	2/	2 0 0
10	1 doz	5/8 Cambric Handkerchiefs		6 5
18	1	Hem stitch		1 4 6
830	1	L Cloth Shirts		3 14 0
	2	Towels	1&6	1 5 0
	4		8/3	1 13 0
		tin Box		6
		2/9 1/6 1/1 Wood Case		6 0
		Inland Revenue one penny stamp over-signed		£ 16 18 1
		10/9/63 W R Wright (discount)	dis	8 7
				16 9 6

Note: It seemed H. O. Brewer sent this shipment to George H. Gardner, a friend or associate, when the *Denbigh* crossed the Atlantic from Liverpool to start running the blockade. It made good sense to take advantage of the *Denbigh*'s trans-Atlantic crossing to send packages home. The early Sept. 1863 dates conformed to this idea since the ship sailed from England not long thereafter.

1140
Invoice

[37] Very fine, picked wool from the Electoral of Saxony (Germany) used in manufacturing gentlemen's superfine cloth.

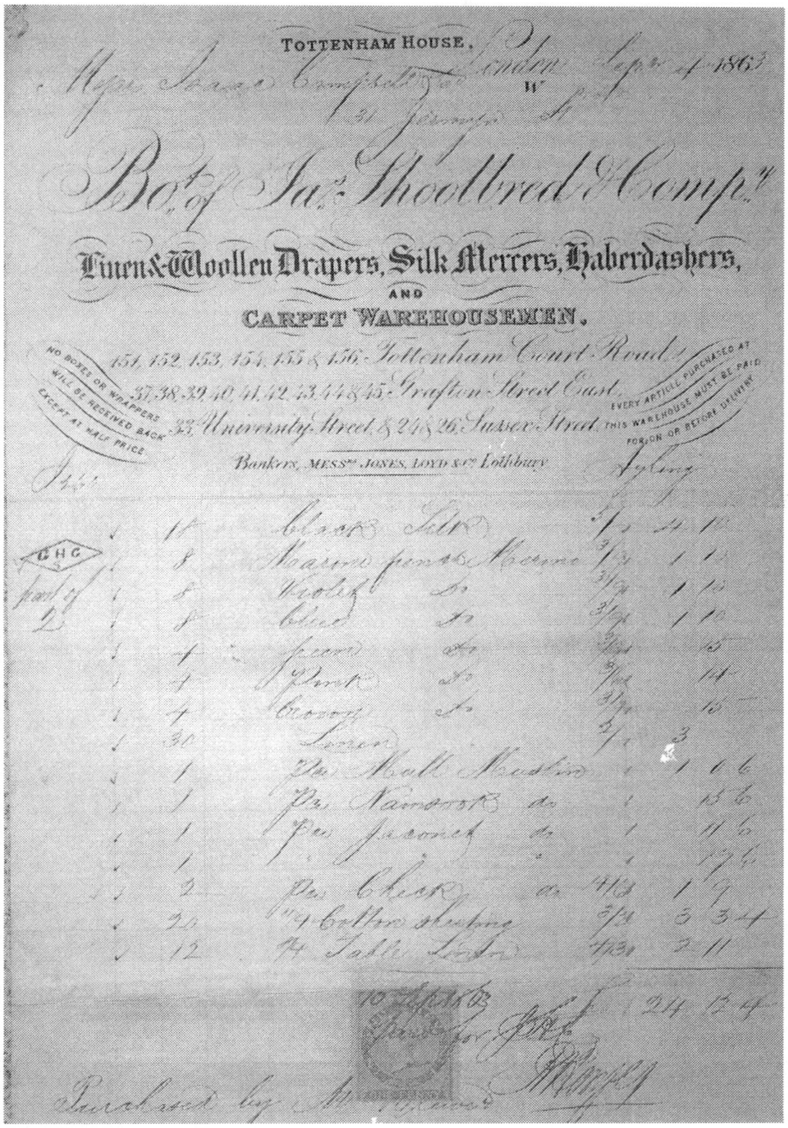

Figure 33. Invoice for fabric bought in London.

Tottenham House

Messrs Isaac Campbell & Co — London Septr 4 1863

31 Jermyn St

Bot of Jas Shoolbred & Compy

Linen & Woollen Drapers, Silk Mercers, Haberdashers,

And

Carpet Warehousemen.

<table>
<tr><td colspan="2">No boxes or wrappers will be received back except at half price.</td><td>151, 152, 153, 154, 155 & 156 Tottenham Court Road, 37, 38, 39, 40, 41, 42, 43, 44 & 45 Grafton Street East, 33, University Street & 24 & 26, Sussex Street</td><td colspan="2">Every article purchased at this warehouse must be paid for on or before delivery</td></tr>
<tr><td colspan="2">I & Co</td><td>Bankers, Messrs. Jones, Loyd & Co. Lothbury</td><td colspan="2">Ayling</td></tr>
<tr><td>GHG/S</td><td>18</td><td>black Silk</td><td>5/</td><td>4 10 0</td></tr>
</table>

	8	Marine French Merino	5/9	1 10 0
	8	Violet Do	3/9	1 10 0
	8	blue Do	3/9	1 10 0
	4	green Do	3/9	15 0
	4	Pink Do	3/6	14 0
	4	brown Do	3/9	15 0
	30	Linen	2/	3 0 0
	1 pec (piece)	Mull Muslin		1 0 6
	1 pec	Namsook[38] do		15 6
	1 pec	Jaconet do		11 6
	1 "	" "		17 6
	2 pec	Check do	14/6	1 9 0
	20	11/4 Cotton sheeting	3/2	3 3 4
	12	8/4 Table Linen	4/3	2 11 0
				£ 124 12 4
		Inland Revenue Stamp over written		
		10 Sept 1863 paid for JHC R Henry (?)		
		Purchased by Mr. Brewer		

1143
Invoice

St. Paul's Ch. Yd.
London. Sept 9 1863
E.C.

Messrs Isaac Campbell & Co Jermyn St
Bot. of Cook, Son & Compy
Wrappers & Boxes not returnable

(marked) GHG/S part of 2 JO.3bygz
Terms 2½ Cash.[39] FO.

	2		
Cp	39½ = 79 36 Long cloth	914	3 0 11
	2½		1 6
			2 19 5
	10/9/63 Inland Revenue stamp over printed "Received for Cook, Son & Co." over-written F Hawthorn		

---

[38] Nansook: a lightweight, plain weave, cotton cloth often used in lingerie and dresses. This fabric dated back to 17th century India, and the Hindi derived word had a variety of spellings in English usage.
[39] From the calculation of total bill this note meant "discount of 2½% for payment in cash."

1145
Invoice

40 Pall Mall

London, Sept 3rd 1863
S.W.

Brewer Esq.
To Saul Isaac Esq

To Goody & Jones,
Tailors,
To his Grace the Archbishop of Canterbury,
And Bishop of London.
Habit and Court Dresses. Army & Navy Outfitters
Accoutrements of Every Description. Interest Charged on Credit, 6 Months after Date of Invoice
(Marked) GHG/S part of 2

3 yds	Grey Doeskin[40]	8/	1 4 0
9 "	Shp'ds (Shepard's) Plaid[41]	5/9	2 11 9
1	Fancy Waistcoating Check	6/6	6 6
1	" " "	6/6	6 6
1 dozen	White Pearl Buttons	1/	1 0
21 & 18	Trou___ ___tons[42]	1/	1 0
	One Penny Inland Revenue stamp		£ 4 10 9
	(overwritten) Pd by cash		
	G ? Goody 10/9/63		

1146
Invoice

[40] A fine, soft, smooth woolen cloth with a slight nap, used for suits, sportswear, etc.
[41] Border tartan, sometimes known as Northumbrian tartan, Shepherds' Plaid or Border Drab, or Border check is a design used in woven fabrics historically associated with the Anglo-Scottish Border, including the Scottish Borders and Northumberland.
[42] Words covered by revenue stamp, perhaps trouser buttons.

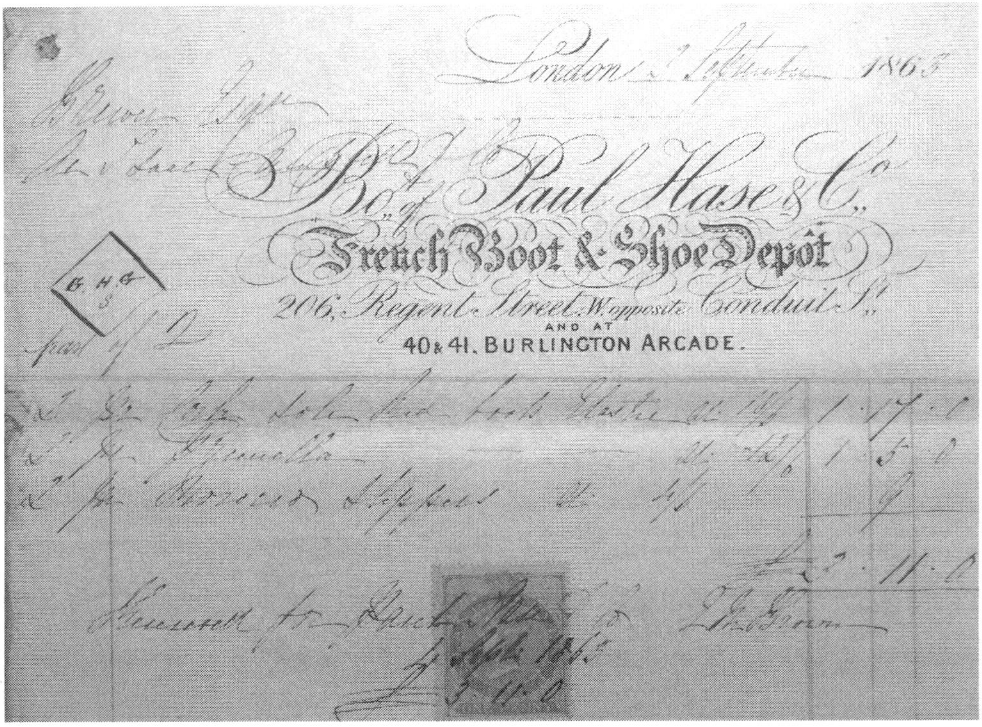
London 1863
Bo.t of Paul Hase & Co.
French Boot & Shoe Depot
206, Regent Street W. opposite Conduit St.
AND AT
40 & 41. BURLINGTON ARCADE.

Figure 34. Invoice for footwear bought in London.

London 3 September 1863

Brewer Esqre
To Isaac Campbell & Co

Bot of Paul Hase & Co
French Boot & Shoe Depot
206 Regent Street W. opposite Conduit St
and at
40 & 41 Burlington Arcade

(marked) GHG/S part of 2

2 pr	Cork Sole Kid boots Elastic at	18/6	1 17 0
2 pr	prunella " " at	12/6	1 5 0
2 pr	Worsted Slippers at	4/6	9 0
	(revenue stamp overwritten)		£ 3 11 0
	Received for Paul Hase & Co		
	E M Brown 4 Sept 1863		
	£ 3 11 0		

1147
Invoice

Note: It appeared that H. O. Brewer himself arranged for the shipment via the *Denbigh* of these first-class goods, perhaps as a favor to Collin McRae or another friend or associate in Mobile. McRae arrived in England May 13, 1863 to assume his duties as agent for the Erlanger loan. McRae also encouraged the formation of blockade running enterprises like the European Trading Company started by Brewer, Schroder, and Erlanger. The E.T.C. owned the *Denbigh* and several other runners.

Per *Denbigh* for a/c of Boykin & McRae from Havana.

GHG/S	1	Goods as per J. & R. Morley's Invoice	16 9 6
	2	" " " J. Shoolbreds "	24 12 4
	"	" " " Cook Son & Co "	2 19 5
	"	" " " Goody & Jones "	4 10 9
	"	" " " Paul Hase & Co "	3 11 0
		Packing Case lined Tin	9 6
			£ 52 12 6
		Com = 2½ 1 17 2	

1149
Invoice

Appraised value of goods for a/c of Mr. Gladney

6 yds	linen	@ $ 1	x	~~6~~
7	dress Pattern	" 6		42
1	Crape Shawl	" 25		25
1	Lace Do	" 20		20
2	Veils	" 2	x	4
1	Silk Duster	" 20		20
1	Range (?) Dress	" 6	x	~~6~~
1 Lot	buttons, pins &c	" 30		30
2	under shirts	@ 2	x	4
2 yds	Silk	@ .50	x	~~1~~
2	Fans	@ 2.50	x	~~5~~
1	?? pins	@ 30		30
1	Pin Cushion	1	x	~~1~~
				$ 194
		$173		

1151-1152
Substitute for Preprinted Customs Form

Entry of Merchandise
No. 16
Importer J Buttner
Vessel *Denbigh*
From Havana
Entered April 16 1864
Value $ 53 Duty $ 13.25

Copy of Entry of goods made by J Buttner recd per *Denbigh* from Havana

1 Cask Claret	$ 30	32	25%	$ 8.00
500 Segars	20	21	"	5.25
	50	53		$ 13.25
Chg & Com	3			
	53			

1153
Substitute Preprinted Customs Form

No. 15
Entry of Merchandise
Importer G. E. Williamson
Vessel *Denbigh*
From Havana
Entered April 16 '64
Value $ 93 Duty $ 13.95

Entry of Merchandise made by G. E. Williamson per *Denbigh* from Havana
1 Box ready made clothing & cottons, prints with all chgs $ 93 15% $ 13.95

1155
Invoice

Mr W Thasom (?)

9	Calico Dress	$ 4	$ 36.00
1 Doz	??	$ 6	6.00
1 "	Cotton ??	$ 1	1.00
1 "	?? ??	$12	?? 8.00
30 yds	**Mos(quito) Netting**	30¢	9.00
2	Hats	$ 5 ea	10.00
3	?? ??	25¢ ea	.75
3 Pair	Shoes (?)	$ 1.25	3.75
1 "	Shoes	$ 1.25	1.25
1 Lot	Taper	$ 1	1.00
10 yds	Check (?)	50¢	5.00
1	?? ??	$ 5	5.00
1 Doz	Silk Bolt	$ 6	6.00
			64.75
			32.00
			96.75
	?? ??		7.00
			89.75

Note: Difficult invoice to decipher.

1156-1157
Substitute for Preprinted Customs Form

Entry of Merchandise
No 2
Importer J. B. Gladney
Vessel *Denbigh*
From Havana
Entered April 4 1864
Value $ 179 Duty $ 26.85

Duplicate of Entry made by J B Gladney of goods recd pr Str *Denbigh* form Havana March '64

J. B. Gladney	Clothing	173		
	chgs & Com	6		
		179	15%	$ 26.85

1158
Invoice

Mr. Bube (?)

9	?	25 ¢	$ 1.25
4	?	@ $ 4 ea	16.00
4	?		1.00
2	?	$ 2	4.00
1	?	$ 5	5.00
3	?	1.25	3.75
4	?	$ 1	4.00
1	?	$ 8	8.00
1	?	$ 5	5.00
1	?	1.25	1.25
1	?	$ 5	5.00
4	?? Coffee	$ 4	16.00
			$ 71.25
	Mr. Coleman (?)		
	71	15	$ 10.65 (duty)

Note: This invoice written in pencil and mostly illegible.

1159-1160
Substitute for Preprinted Customs Form

Entry of Merchandise
No 14
Importer Mr. J Bube (?)
Vessel *Denbigh*
From Havana
Entered April 16 '64
Value $ 74 Duty $ 11.10

Copy of Entry made by Mr. J. Bube of goods received by him pr *Denbigh* from Havana

1 Case	Clothing	$ 58.25	60		
	Shoes & Boots 2 pr	13.00	14		
		71.25	74	15%	$ 11.10
	Chgs & Com	3.00			
		74.00			

1161
Invoice

Sugar	50 lbs	12½[43]	$ 6.25
Tea	12½ "		15.75
			22.00
	$ 23	F David.	
	20		
	4.60		
		16	1.60
		6	1.20
			$ 2.80
	26		
	16		
	6.24		

1163-1164
Substitute for Preprinted Customs Form

No 20
Importer F. David
Vessel *Denbigh*
From Havana
Entered April 18 '64
Value $ 22 Duty $ 2.80

Entry of goods entered by Frank David importer pr *Denbigh* from Havana

[43] Spanish coinage in Cuban usage had 8 reales to the peso or 12½¢ per real. Hence the odd prices in multiples of 12½ reflect conversion of reales to cents.

1 Package	Tea	12 lbs	$ 15.00	16	10%	$ 1.60
	Sugar	50 "	6.25	16	20%	1.20
			21.25			$ 2.80
			1.00			
			$ 22.25			

1165-1169
Preprinted Customs Form

Note: Change of the *Denbigh's* captain. For the first two voyages, McNevin was captain and Godfrey was supercargo.

No. 10
Entry of Merchandise
Importer L. F. Zantzinger
Vessel *Denbigh*
From Havana
Entered April 16 1864
Value $ 206 Duty $ 50.90

Oath of Owner whose Goods have been Purchased
(signed) L. F. Zantzinger, Purser

Ship Entered April 14 1864
Imported into the Port and District of Mobile, by L. F. Zantzinger in the Br. Str. *Denbigh* **Godfrey** Master, from Havana

Packages	Packages and Contents	Quantities	In Foreign Currency Invoice Value	Appraised Value, Duty Rate				
				10	15	20	25	Duty
58 Demijohns	Rum Gals	232	$ 107.00				116	$ 29.00
?? Blls & Kegs		240	77.75				84	21.00
2 Boxes	Macaroni		6.00		6			.90
			190.75		6		200	$ 50.90
	Shipg Chgs	& Com	15.20					
	(Shipping)		$ 205.95					

1170a
Invoice

Copy Havana April 2d 1864
L. F. Zantzinger
Bot of H Gliddon

58 Demijohn	Rum	232 gals	$ 107
4 Kegs	Do		
5 Blls	Do	240 Gals	77.75
Demijohns	Gin		
2 Boxes	Macaroni		6.00

1170b
Invoice

Simms (?) Havana Apl 8, 1864
Bot of Gliddon
7 Demijohns @ 1.25 $ 8.75
Rich. Gliddon
(duty) $ 2.25 Paid

1171a
Invoice

John Hutchison Havana Apl. 8 1864
Bot of Gliddon
5 Demijohns Cana (Cana = Rum) @ 1.75 $ 8.75
Rcpd Glidden
Bearer has no Specie

1171b
Invoice
Danl Thompson Havana Apl 8, 1864
Bot of Gliddon
5 Demijohns Cana $ 1.75 $ 8.75
Rcd Glidden
(duty) 2.25

1172 a
Invoice
John Cassar Havana Apl. 8 1864
Bot of Gliddon
5 Demijohns Cana $ 1.75 $ 8.75
Rcpt Gliddon
$2.25 (duty) Paid

1172b
Invoice

Tymin (?) Havana Apl. 8 1864

Bot of Gliddon
4 Demijohns Cana $ 2.00 $ 8.00
Rcpt Gliddon
$1.20 (duty) Paid

1174a
Invoice

Note: This invoice was particularly informal. The reverse side showed that the scrap of paper had been a report form for the lighthouse service. It seemed that since an invoice was expected and required as part of customs documentation, this type of informal invoice was prepared in Mobile not in Havana.

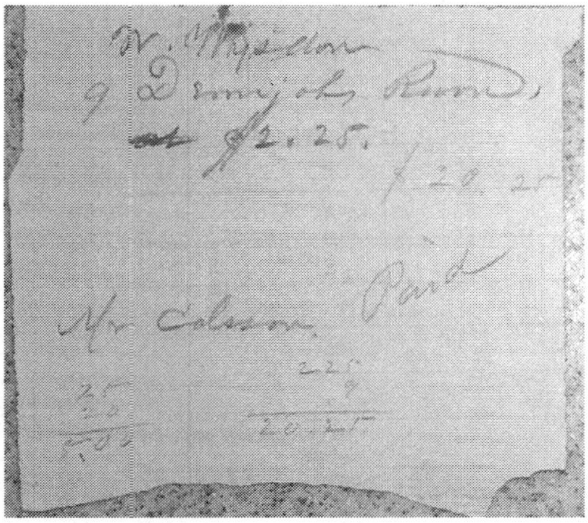

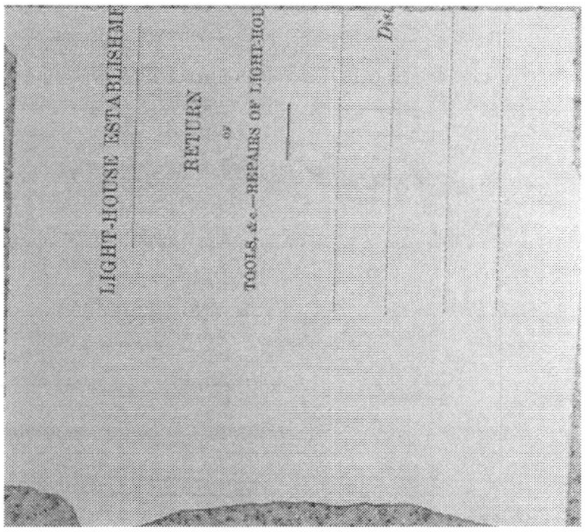

Figure 35. Makeshift invoice for rum prepared, probably at the customs house, on a scrap of an old Lighthouse Service form.

W. Wysdom
9 Demijohns Rum
@ $ 2.25
$ 20.25
Mr. Colsson Paid
5.00 (duty)

1174b
Invoice

Andrea Dansovick (?) Compdo de Gonzales & Co
A (mark) 1 Bl de 30 Galones Aquaardiente $ 8.50
Dia 10 Aprile 1864 Ignazio Gonzales

1174c
Invoice

Havana Apl 8, 1864

T. Harney

Bot of Glidden

1 bbl	Cana	$ 8.50
1 Keg	"	4.25
2 boxes	**Macaroni**	6.00
		$ 18.75
Paid		
	Rcd Glidden	
	$ 4.15 (duty)	

1174d
Invoice

Havana April 8, 1864

Bought of Glidden & Barbot (?)

AI	2 Kegs	Cana		
I	2 Kegs	do		
JI	1 bbl	do	= 3 bbl $ 8½	$ 25.50
	1 box	Cod fish		8.00
				$ 33.50
		Paid	Glidden & ??	
			?? 15%	

1176a
Invoice

John Nash Havana Apl 8 1864

Bot of Glidden

1 bbl Cana 30 gal $ 8.50

Recd Glidden

$ 2.25 Paid (duty)

1176b
Invoice

Geo Turner Havana Apl 8, 1864

Bot of Glidden & Barbot (?)

Black ball 5 demijohns Cana $ 8.75
In paint Recd payt
(mark) Glidden & Barbot
$ 2.25 Paid (duty)

1176c
Invoice

Edw Wright Havana Apl 8 1864
Bot of Glidden
5 demijohns Cana $ 1.75 $ 8.75
Recpt Glidden
$ 2.25 Paid (duty)

1177a
Invoice

John Woolcott Havana Apl. 8 1864
Bot of Gliddon
5 Demijohns Cana $ 1.75 $ 8.75
Rcpt Gliddon
Paid $2.25 (duty)

1177b
Invoice

Deliver Havana Apl. 8 1864
McNevin
Bot of Gliddon
5 Demijohns Cana $ 1.75 $ 8.75
Rcpt Gliddon
Paid S2.25 (duty)

1177c
Invoice

J Took Havana Apl. 8 1864
Bot of Gliddon
5 Demijohns Cana $ 1.75 $ 8.75
Rcpt Gliddon
$2.25 (duty) Paid

1178
Invoice

Collins
Bbl Rum $ 8.50
Mr. Coleson
Paid 2.25 (duty)

1179-1181
Preprinted Customs Form

No. ____
Entry of Merchandise
Importer G. G. Garner
Vessel *Denbigh*
From Havana
Entered April 18 64
Value $ 40 Duty $ 7.60

Ship Entered________

Imported into the Port and District of Mobile, by Geo G Garner in the Br. Str. *Denbigh* Godfrey Master, from Havana

Packages	Packages and Contents	In Foreign Currency Invoice Value	Appraised Value, Duty Rate				
			10	15	20	25	Duty
1 Pkg	Sugar	$ 9.00			9		$ 1.80
	Sweet oil	14.00		15			2.25
	Tea	3.00	3				.30
1 Keg	Wine Sherry	13.00				13	3.25
		39.00					$ 7.60
	Com & chgs	1.35					
		40.35					

1183-1185
Preprinted Customs Form

No. ___
Entry of Merchandise
Importer J. R. Edwards
Vessel *Denbigh*
From Havana
Entered April 18, 64
Value $ 497 Duty $ 74.55

Oath of Owner whose Goods have been Purchased
18 day of April 1864 J R Edwards

Ship Entered April 14 1864

Imported into the Port and District of Mobile, by J. R. Edwards in the Br. Str. *Denbigh* Godfrey Master, from Havana

Packages	Packages and Contents	Quantities	In Foreign Currency Invoice Value	Appraised Value, Duty Rate				
				10	15	20	25	Duty
1 Case	Containing							
	Shoes	Pairs 21	£ 11. 10. 6		59			
	Cotton mfs		24. 3. 5		124			
	Wool		25. 4. 4		128			
	Clothing ready made		16. 4. 0		82			
	Hosiery Cotton		5. 5. 0		27			
	Flax		14. 18. 4		77			
			£ 97. 5. 7		497	@	15%	$ 74.55
	Shippg Chg & Com		5. 7. 0					
	or	$ 496.73	102. 12. 7					

1188
Invoice

Invoice of Goods shipped to you through Mr. R. Perez Havana pr. Royal Mail Co. via Southampton
(Marked)
R H 5x1
99 2x3
N D 1x8

1	3 Pr.	of Ladies Booties No 5	9/6	£ 1. 8. 6
2	5 "	" " " " 2	9/6	2. 7. 6
3	4 "	" " " 9x6	4/7	1. 10. 0
4	2 "	Boys Oxford Shoes	9/6	19. 0
5	2 "	Small	8/1	16. 0
6	2 "	Stout Balmoral	19	1. 18. 0
7	2 "	Fine Prince George	23	2. 6. 0
8	1 Paper	Shoe thread	5/6	5. 6
	3 Pcs	9/8 prints 155 Yds.	9d	5. 16. 3
	1 "	36 Calico 86½ "	9½	3. 8. 10
	12 Yds	blk. (black) Winter Cashmire	12/6	7. 10. 0
	4 "	Pilot[44]	10/0	2. 0. 0
	4 Pcs	7/8 fine linen 10 9½ yards	2/1	11. 8. 2
5014	2 "	White flannel 46 ea 97 y	2/2	9. 19. 4
5/26	1 "	Scarlet do " 46 "	2/6	5. 15. 0
	4/12 Gross	sewing reels	15/0	5. 0
	¼ Gross	Pearl Buttons	28/0	7. 0
	¼ "	" " large	32	8. 0
	¼ "	" " bone	8/0	2. 0
	½ "	Flat silk laces	15/0	7. 6
	1 lb	Lit (?) sewing silk	36	1. 16. 0
	1/12 doz	marshall thread	56/0	4. 8

[44] A thick blue cloth used to make overcoats and coats for sailors etc.

	2 "	Boys cotton ½ Hose	11/0	1. 2. 0
	2 "	Men's ½ do	15/0	1. 10. 0
3	1 "	White do	8/0	8. 0
A	2 "	do do	10/0	1. 0. 0
B	2	women's do	12/6	1. 5. 0
12	2	7/8 Handkerchiefs	15/0	1. 10. 0
550	2 doz	men's lin.(linen) Shirts	118/0	11. 16. 0
5787	1 "	Batist[45] Handkerchiefs	30/0	1. 10. 0
		Including charges & Com over		£ 80. 19. 3
		Amount brought forward		£ 80. 19. 3
5915	1 doz	Batis Handkerchiefs	28/0	1. 8. 0
	12 Yds	Stout drill (?)	1/11d	16. 0
	3 Rs	Prime Eng. Butts 92 lbs	3/2d	14. 11. 4
	6	French Calfskins 17d	4/1	3. 8. 0
		Case, tin case, Hooping, papering & packing		1. 10. 0
				£ 102. 12. 7
		London January 2d 1864		
		(signed) J Lowenthal		

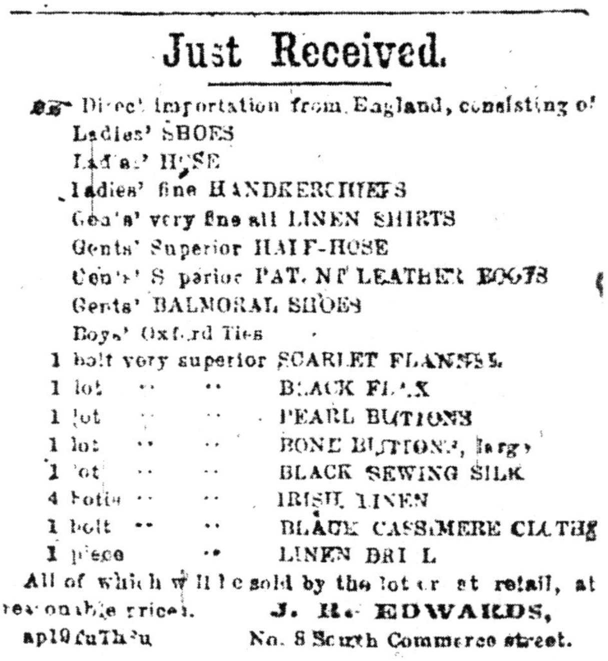

Just Received.

Direct importation from England, consisting of
Ladies' SHOES
Ladies' HOSE
Ladies' fine HANDKERCHIEFS
Gent's very fine all LINEN SHIRTS
Gents' Superior HALF-HOSE
Gents' Superior PAT. NT LEATHER BOOTS
Gents' BALMORAL SHOES
Boys' Oxford Ties
1 bolt very superior SCARLET FLANNEL
1 lot .. .. BLACK FLAX
1 lot .. .. PEARL BUTTONS
1 lot .. .. BONE BUTTONS, large
1 lot .. .. BLACK SEWING SILK
4 bolts .. .. IRISH LINEN
1 bolt .. .. BLACK CASSIMERE CLOTH
1 piece .. LINEN DRILL
All of which will be sold by the lot or at retail, at reasonable prices.
J. R. EDWARDS,
No. 8 South Commerce street.
ap19 TuThu

Figure 36. Ad for sale of goods by J. R. Edwards.

Ad for rare sale of a cargo shipped from England and transshipped in Havana (*Mobile Advertiser and Register* April 19, 1864). The cargo left London shortly after the Jan. 2, 1864 date of the invoice and arrived in Mobile on April 14, 1864, just a little more than three months in transit. Not bad considering the blockade.

[45] The term *batiste* is a French word that refers to a fine quality lightweight cloth, similar to cotton lawn, but a thicker fabric. Cotton batiste is commonly used to make women's lingerie, dressy blouses, and handkerchiefs. Cotton batiste can be used as an underlining for dresses and nightgowns as well.

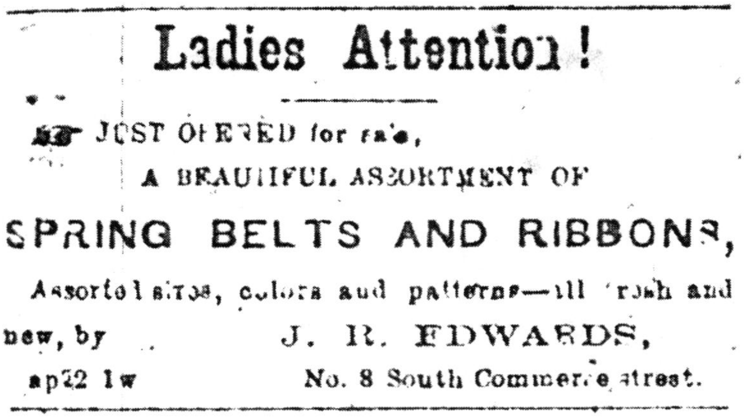
Ladies Attention!
JUST OFFERED for sale,
A BEAUTIFUL ASSORTMENT OF
SPRING BELTS AND RIBBONS,
Assorted sizes, colors and patterns—all fresh and new, by
J. R. EDWARDS,
ap22 1w No. 8 South Commerce street.

Figure 37. Ad for sale of lady's belts and ribbons.

Edwards ad for belts and ribbons, items not specifically mentioned in the invoice above (*Mobile Advertiser and Register* April 22, 1864).

1190-1194
Preprinted Customs Form

No. 25
Entry of Merchandise
Importer H. M. Blair
Vessel *Denbigh*
From Havana
Entered April 20, 64
Value $ 69 Duty $ 10.55

Oath of Owner whose Goods have been Purchased
20 day of April 1864 C. H. M. Blair

Ship Entered April 14 64
Imported into the Port and District of Mobile, by C. H. M. Blair in the Br. Str. *Denbigh* Godfrey Master, from Havana

Packages	Packages and Contents	In Foreign Currency Invoice Value	Appraised Value, Duty Rate			
			10	15	20	Duty
one Box	Wool mfs	$ 38.50		40		$ 6.00
	Wearing Apparel	23.65		25		3.76
	Soap & tooth Brushes	4.00			4	.80
	Chg & Com	3.00		65	4	$ 10.55
		69.15				

1195-1198
Preprinted Customs Form

No. 23
Entry of Merchandise
Importer Wm. Leighton
Vessel *Denbigh*
From Havana
Entered April 18, 64
Value $ 86 Duty $ 21.50

Oath of Owner whose Goods have been Purchased
Wm Leighton

Ship Entered April 14 64
Imported into the Port and District of Mobile, by C. H. M. Blair in the Br. Str. *Denbigh* Godfrey Master, from Havana

Packages	Packages and Contents	In Foreign Currency Invoice Value	Appraised Value, Duty Rate			
			10	15	25	Duty
2 Kegs	Rum 30 Gals	$ 9.00				
40 Demijohns	Do 160 "	72.00				
		81.00				
Chg & Com		5.15				
		$ 86.15			86	$ 21.50

1199-1202
Preprinted Customs Form

No. 24
Entry of Merchandise
Importer H. O. Brewer & Co
Vessel *Denbigh*
From Havana
Entered April 18, 64
Value $ 1081 Duty $ 211.15

Oath of Consignee, Importer of Agent
18 day of April 1864 Benj Donaldson

Ship Entered April 14 64
Imported into the Port and District of Mobile, by H O Brewer & Co in the Br. Str. *Denbigh* Godfrey Master, from Havana

Marks	Packages	Packages and Contents	Foreign Currency Invoice Value	Appraised Value, Duty Rate		Duty
				15	25	
AM Godfrey	1 Case	Morphine oz 100	$ 350.00	368		$ 55.20

" " "	1 Case	Castor oil Gals 21	36.75	39		5.85
" " "	1 Case	Quinine oz. 100	170.00	179		26.85
	20 Demijohn	Gin Gals 80	90.00		94	23.50
	24 Boxes	Gin Doz 24	60.00		63	15.75
	2 Pipes	Rum ~~white~~ aquardiente Gals 240	64.00		67	16.75
Zantzinger	1 Bll (barrel)	Do " 30	8.50		9	2.35
Do	2 Cases	Whiskey Scotch Dz 2	20.00		21	5.25
Do		**Watch Springs**	4.80	5		.75
			804.05			
AM Godfrey		Brandy Gals 200	225.00		236	
			1029.05	591	499	211.15
		Chgs & Com	51.45			
			1080.50			
		Medicines &c	$ 591.00	@15%		$ 88.65
		Gin Brandy Whiskey	490.00	@30%		147.00
			$ 1081			$ 235.65

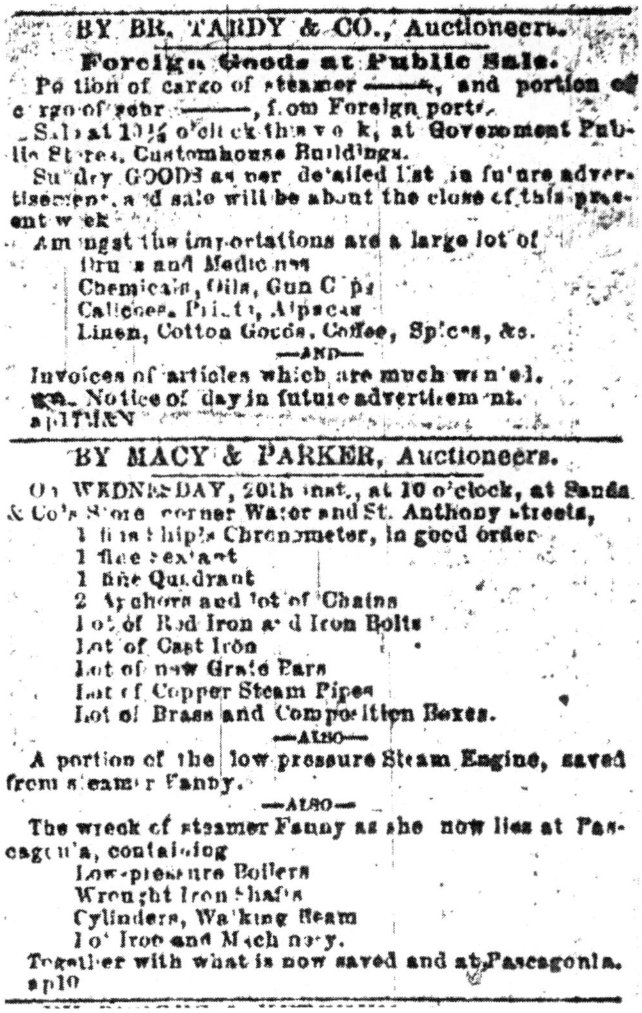

BY BR. TARDY & CO., Auctioneers.

Foreign Goods at Public Sale.

Portion of cargo of steamer ——, and portion of cargo of schr ——, from Foreign ports.

Sale at 10½ o'clock this week, at Government Public Stores, Customhouse Buildings.

Sundry GOODS as per detailed list in future advertisement, and sale will be about the close of this present week.

Amongst the importations are a large lot of

Drugs and Medicines
Chemicals, Oils, Gun Caps
Calicoes, Prints, Alpacas
Linen, Cotton Goods, Coffee, Spices, &c.

—AND—

Invoices of articles which are much wanted.

Notice of day in future advertisement.

ap17tf&N

BY MACY & PARKER, Auctioneers.

On WEDNESDAY, 20th inst., at 10 o'clock, at Sands & Co's Store corner Water and St. Anthony streets,

1 first Ship's Chronometer, in good order
1 fine Sextant
1 fine Quadrant
2 Anchors and lot of Chains
Lot of Rod Iron and Iron Bolts
Lot of Cast Iron
Lot of new Grate Bars
Lot of Copper Steam Pipes
Lot of Brass and Composition Boxes.

—ALSO—

A portion of the low pressure Steam Engine, saved from steamer Fanny.

—ALSO—

The wreck of steamer Fanny as she now lies at Pascagoula, containing

Low-pressure Boilers
Wrought Iron Shafts
Cylinders, Walking Beam
Lot Iron and Machinery.

Together with what is now saved and at Pascagoula.

ap10

Figure 38. Two ads for sale of blockade-runner goods including *Denbigh* cargo.

Two ads giving notice of blockade runner sales were shown in Figure 38. Above was a preliminary notice of sale of two ships' cargoes probably including that of the *Denbigh* which had entered port April 14, 1864. Below was notice of a salvage sale for the runner *Fanny* wrecked at Pascagoula. The *Fanny* may have been a sister E.T.C. ship of the *Denbigh* (*Mobile Advertiser and Register* April 17, 1864).

1203a
Invoice

Note: Possibly private trade.

A. M. Godfrey

1 Large Box	Gin	add/3.25	4.75
5 Small "	do	@ 75¢ 2.25	11.25
6 Boxes	Brandy	6.00	36.00
3 Bots	Bokess Biltus (?)	1.25	3.75
3 Sacks	Coffee	506 lbs 20.20 free	103.75
1 Bbl	41.20 Galls Whiskey	1.25	51.87
800	Cigars	@ $20 pr ~~M~~ (thousand)	16.00
1 Box	Candles	25 lbs w.74	6.75
5 Boxes	Brandy	6.00	30.00
20 Blls	**Kerosene**	?? 8/0	20.00
10 doz	Jellies		10.00
2 Cases	Clacas (?)	3.50	7.00
			301.12
	Chg & Cm		12.00
			313.00
	less 3 Sacks Coffee & Com		103.75
			209.25
	$ 49.45 (duty)		

(Note on reverse side) Goods at Custom House

1203b
Invoice

Mr. H. Barnwell Jr from (?)
H. O. Brewer & Co Consumption Duty per
Denbigh from Havana Cuba
Dated April 6th 1864
Value $ 209.00 Duty $ 57.95
Amt From April 6/64

1205-1206
Substitute for Preprinted Customs Form

No 5
Entry of Merchandise
Importer H O Brewer & Co
From Havana
Entered April 6 1864
Value $ 209 Duty $ 49.45

Duplicate Entry made by H. O. Brewer & Co for act of A. M. Godfrey Str *Denbigh* from Havana

A.M.G.	2 Cases	Ker(osene) Oil	Gals 20	$ 26.75	$ 28 15%	$ 4.20
	1 Box	Comfits		10.00	11 25%	
	11 Boxes	Brandy	Doz 11	69.75	74 "	
	6 "	Gin		23.00	24 "	
	800	Sigars		16.00	17 "	
	1 Keg	Whiskey	41 Gals	51.87	55 "	45.25
				197.37	209	$ 49.45
		Chgs & Com		12.00		
				209.37		
		Ker Oil	$ 28 @ 15%	4.20		
		Comfits	11 @ 25%	2.75		
		Brandy & Gin	98 @ 30%	29.40		
		Sigars	17 @ 30%	5.10		
		Whiskey	55 @ 30%	16.50		
			$ 209	67.95		

Note: The tabulation at bottom was done in pencil at a later time than the top of the invoice and corrected mistakes in the calculation of duties.

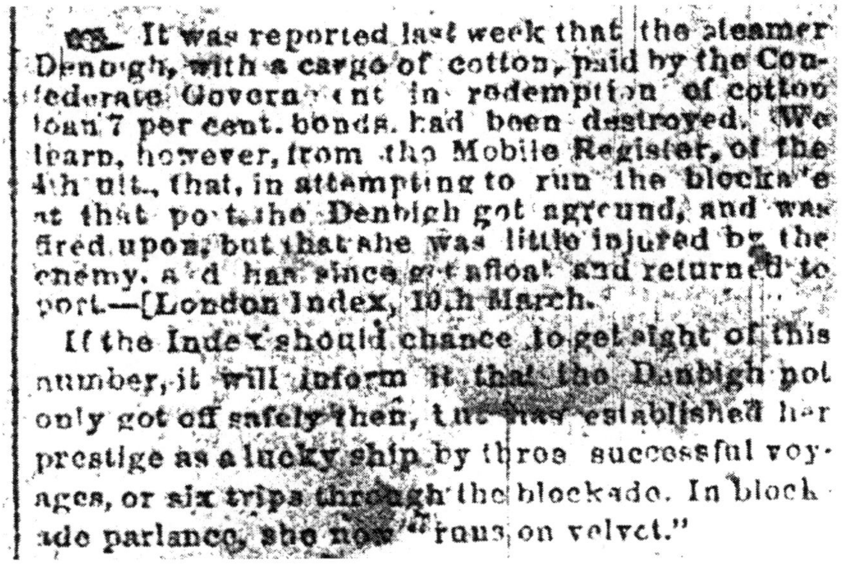
It was reported last week that the steamer Denbigh, with a cargo of cotton, paid by the Confederate Government in redemption of cotton loan 7 per cent. bonds, had been destroyed. We learn, however, from the Mobile Register, of the 4th ult., that, in attempting to run the blockade at that port the Denbigh got aground, and was fired upon; but that she was little injured by the enemy, and has since got afloat and returned to port.—[London Index, 10th March.

If the Index should chance to get sight of this number, it will inform it that the Denbigh not only got off safely then, but has established her prestige as a lucky ship by three successful voyages, or six trips through the blockade. In blockade parlance, she now "runs on velvet."

Figure 39. Article on the *Denbigh's* safe run with cargo of cotton (*Mobile Advertiser and Register* April 20, 1864).

This story (Figure 39) referred to the *Denbigh's* first outbound voyage when she went aground near Fort Morgan (Mobile Advertiser and Register April 20, 1864). She was erroneously reported lost as quoted in the London Index in the first paragraph, The Mobile paper informed that the *Denbigh* "not only got off safely then, but has established her prestige as a lucky ship by three successful voyages, or six trips through the blockade. In blockade parlance, she now 'runs on velvet.'"

3

Denbigh Customs Manifests, May 1864 1 of 2, Transcripts

Denbigh Voyage No. 4, Havana-Mobile-Havana.
Havana, last date on document prepared there was 26 Apr 1864 so the ship sailed soon thereafter.
Mobile, date ship entered (port and reported arrival to C.S. Customs) was 30 Apr 1864.
Mobile departure, cotton export manifests dated 4 May 1864 so ship sailed soon thereafter. (445 bales cotton, 210,992 lbs., $ 105,496, 50¢ per lb. plus 20-blls. rosin, $ 100.)

Denbigh Voyage No. 5, Havana-Mobile-Havana.
Havana, last date on document prepared there was 13 May 1864 so the ship sailed soon thereafter.
Mobile, date ship entered (port and reported arrival to C.S. Customs) was 18 May 1864.
Mobile departure, cotton export manifests dated 26 May 1864 so ship sailed soon thereafter. (442 bales cotton, 224,544 lbs., $ 112,272, 50¢ per lb., plus 20-blls. rosin, $ 200.)

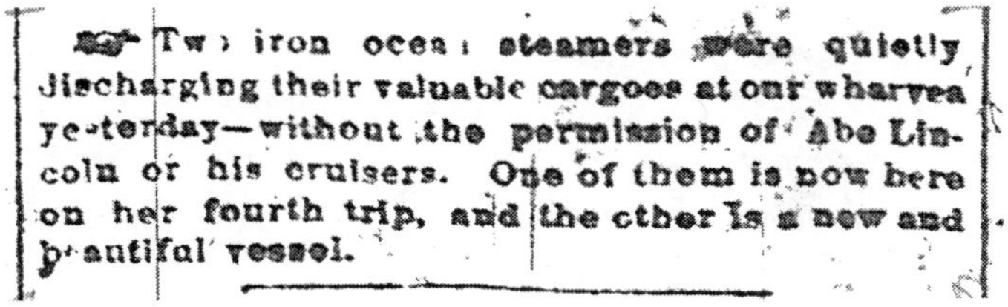

Two iron ocean steamers were quietly discharging their valuable cargoes at our wharves yesterday—without the permission of Abe Lincoln or his cruisers. One of them is now here on her fourth trip, and the other is a new and beautiful vessel.

Figure 40. Article reporting two runners at Mobile wharves (*Mobile Advertise and Register* May 3, 1864).

The *Denbigh* probably was one of the ships at the Mobile wharves (Figure 40). She arrived on April 30 and departed again for Havana on May 7, 1864.

468-472
Preprinted Customs Form

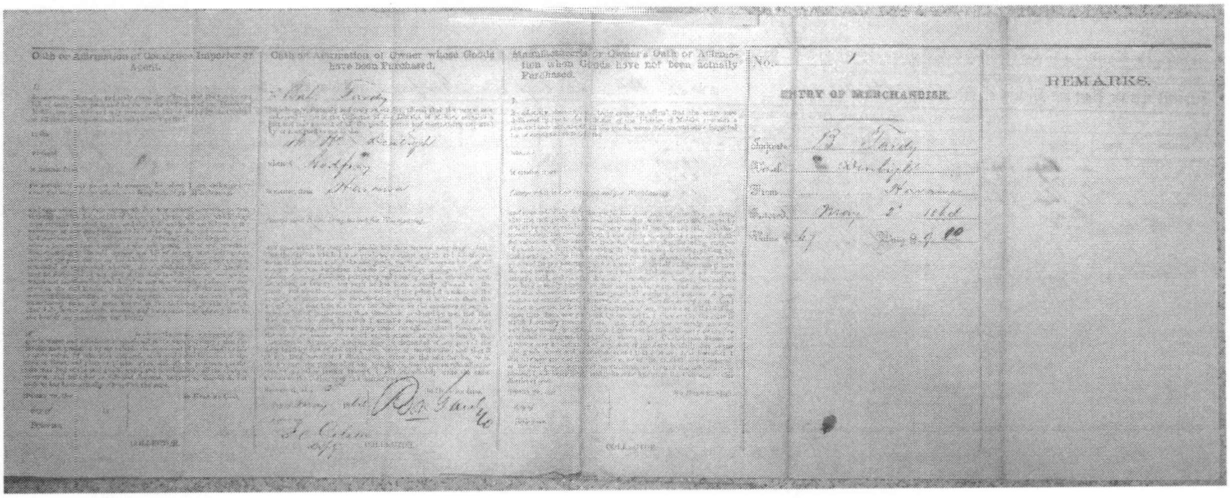

No. 1

ENTRY OF MERCHANDISE.

REMARKS.

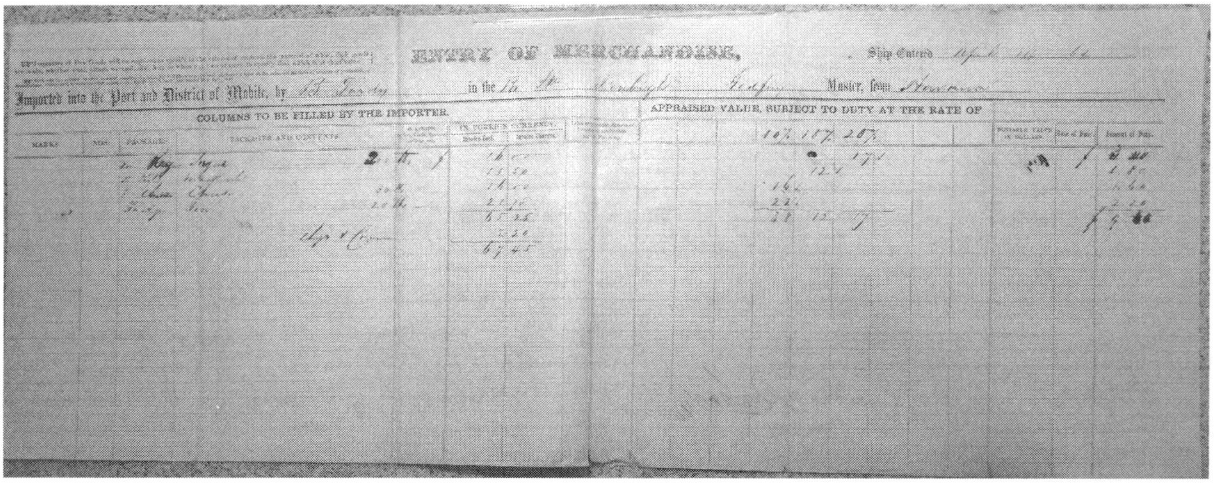
ENTRY OF MERCHANDISE, Ship Entered

Imported into the Port and District of Mobile, by

COLUMNS TO BE FILLED BY THE IMPORTER.

APPRAISED VALUE, SUBJECT TO DUTY AT THE RATE OF

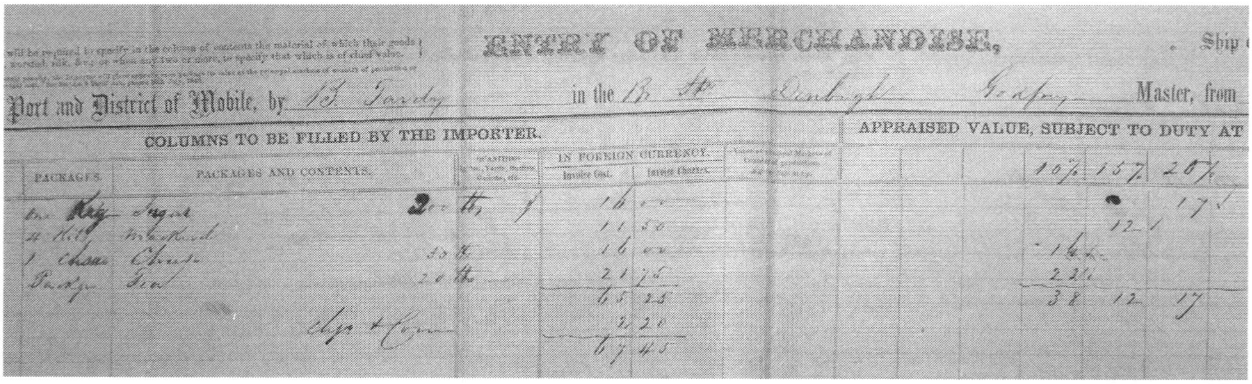
ENTRY OF MERCHANDISE, Ship

Port and District of Mobile, by in the Master, from

COLUMNS TO BE FILLED BY THE IMPORTER.

APPRAISED VALUE, SUBJECT TO DUTY AT

PACKAGES | PACKAGES AND CONTENTS. | IN FOREIGN CURRENCY. Invoice Cost. Invoice Charges.

Figure 41. Preprinted customs form dated April 14, 1864.

No. 1
Entry of Merchandise
Importer Bal. Tardy
Vessel *Denbigh*
From Havana
Entered May 2d 1864[46]
Value \$ 67 Duty \$ 9.00

(signed) Owner (Illegible)
Sworn before me 2d day of May 1864
(signed) J. C. Colson, Depty (Deputy) Collector

Ship Entered April 14 64

Imported into the Port and District of Mobile, by B. Tardy in the Br. Str. *Denbigh* Godfrey Master, from Havana

Packages	Contents	Quantities	Invoice Cost	10%	15%	20%	Amount of Duty
one Keg	Sugar	200 lbs	\$ 16.00			17	\$ 3.40

[46] Date this parcel of ship's cargo was cleared through customs and duty paid. It took up to a few weeks for all the cargo to be inspected, assessed, and duty paid. The invoices commonly had extra notations and calculations added at the bottom or on the reverse dealing with this processing.

4 Kits[47]	Mackerel		11.50		12		1.80
1 Cheese	Cheese	30 lbs	16.00	16			1.60
Package	Tea	20 lbs	21.75	22			2.20
			65.25	38	12	17	$ 9.00
		Chgs & Com (?)	2.20				
			67.45				

475
Form for additional Oath of Importers or Agents

Note: These forms were scattered throughout the documents from this file onward. There was a change in the language of the customs regulations not reflected in the preprinted forms as seen above. In the present manuscript, these forms were mostly omitted.

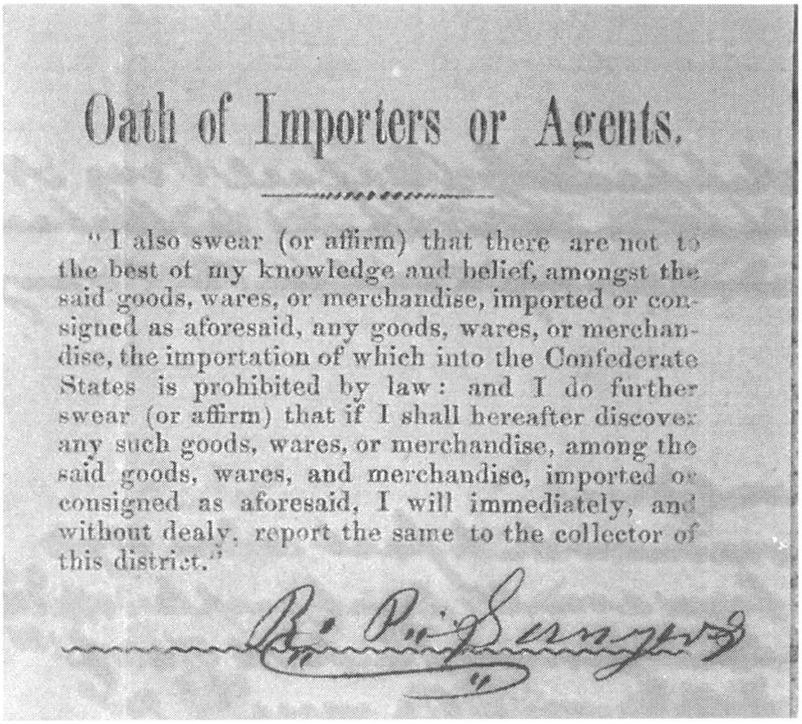

Oath of Importers or Agents.

"I also swear (or affirm) that there are not to the best of my knowledge and belief, amongst the said goods, wares, or merchandise, imported or consigned as aforesaid, any goods, wares, or merchandise, the importation of which into the Confederate States is prohibited by law: and I do further swear (or affirm) that if I shall hereafter discover any such goods, wares, or merchandise, among the said goods, wares, and merchandise, imported or consigned as aforesaid, I will immediately, and without dealy, report the same to the collector of this district."

Figure 42. Short form for revised Importer's Oath.

476-477
Substitute for Preprinted Customs Form

---

[47] Kit – small tub.

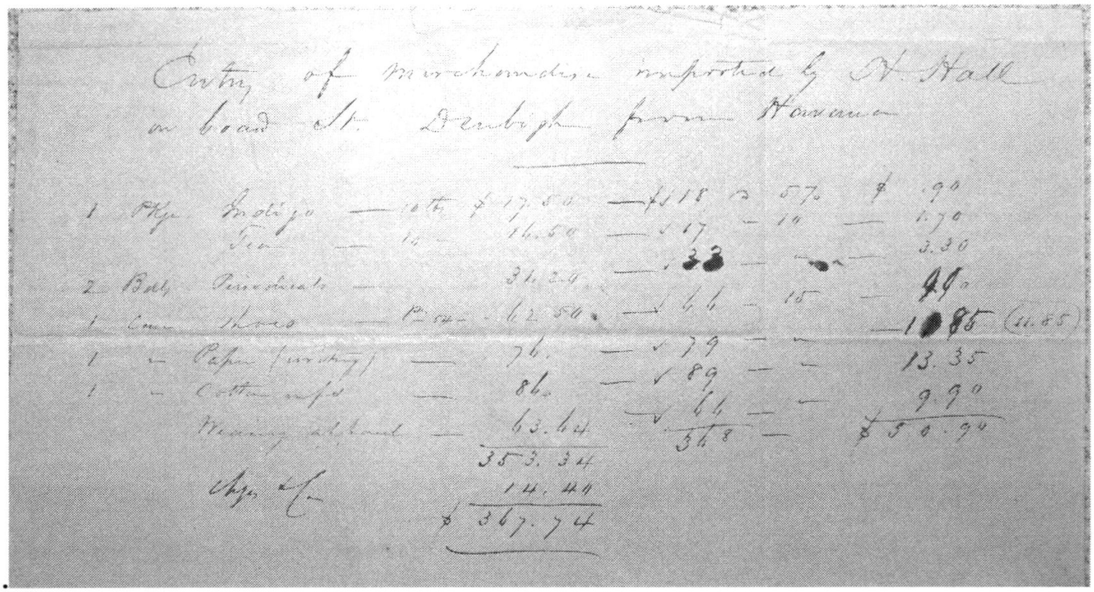
Entry of merchandise imported by H. Hall
on board St. Denbigh from Havana
353.34
14.40
$ 367.74

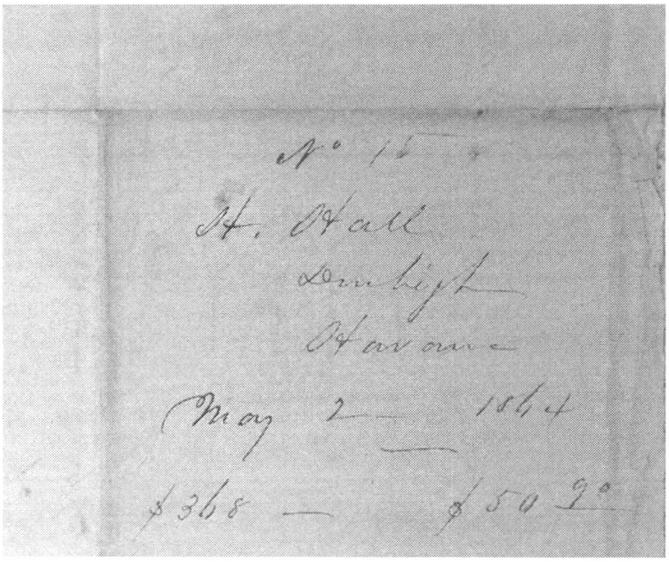
No 15
H. Hall
Denbigh
Havana
May 2 1864
$368 — $50.90

Figure 43. Substitute for preprinted form including periodicals and 54 pairs of shoes.

No. 15
Entry of Merchandise
Importer H. Hall
Vessel *Denbigh*
From Havana
Entered May 2 1864
Value $ 368 Duty $ 50.90

Entry of merchandise imported by H. Hall on board St. *Denbigh* from Havana.

1 Pkge	Indigo[48]	10 lbs	$ 17.50	$ 18	@ % 5	$ .90
	Tea	10 lbs	16.50	17	10	1.70

[48] Blue dye.

2 Bdls	**Periodicals**		31.20	33		3.30
1 Case	Shoes	pr 54	62.50	66	15	9.90
1 -	Paper (writing)		76.00	79		11.85
1 -	Cotton mfs[49]		86.00	89		13.35
	Wearing apparel		63.64	66		9.90
			353.34	368		$ 50.90
	Chgs & Comm[50]		14.40			
			$ 367.74			

478-479
Substitute for Preprinted Customs Form

No. 12
Entry of Merchandise
Importer J B Fellows
Vessel *Denbigh*
From Havana
Entered May 2 1864
Value $ 293 Duty $ 43.30

Entry of Merchandise imported by J. B. Fellows on board Str. *Denbigh* – from Havana Apl 30, 64

Trunk	Shoes pair	15 $	26.07	$ 27.00	15%	$ 4.05
	Flax mfs &c		91.60	95		14.25
	Cottons, Hosiery &c		152.10	158		23.70
	Tea lbs	10	12.50	13	10%	1.30
			282.27	293		43.30
	Comm		10.59			
			292.86			

480-481
Invoice

Capt. H. Hall[51]

Dr.[52] to F. X. Barbot

1864				
Ap.	10 doz	children's cop. toed shoes	@ $ 8	$ 80.00
	1 "	do cloth bootees[53]		10.50

[49] Abbreviation for "manufactures," meaning items of a manufactured rather than raw material nature.
[50] Abbreviation for Charges and Commission.
[51] Henry Hall was First Officer or Chief Mate of the *Denbigh.* It seemed likely that most of this invoice was for merchandise he purchased from F. X. Barbot in Havana and brought to Mobile for sale on his own speculation. It also included at least two small orders for named customers.
[52] Dr. on invoices was the abbreviation for debit.
[53] A boot for women and children, esp. an ankle-length one.

	1 "	do Morocco "		10.00
	1 "	do Goat "		9.00
	½ "	Superior "		10.00
	2 "	Morocco,	11 @ 12, @ 12.50	25.00
	2 prs	Gents' Shoes,	@ 4.25	8.50
	10 reams	Letter paper,	@ $ 2	20.00
	10 "	Fools cap	@ 2.50	25.00
	10 "	Note	@ 1.35	13.50
	5 ~~M~~	Envelops 2¼ / 2½ ~~M~~	2 / 2½ ~~M~~	10.62½
	10 gross	Sup. Pens	@ 50	5.00
	10 ~~M~~	Needles, 000. 00. 0.	@ 1.25/	12.50
	10 "	" 1. 2. 3.	1 / 2½ /	11.25
	10 gross	bone Buttons	1.75 /	17.50
	10 "	China do.	1	10.00
	10 "	do " large	2.75	27.50
	10 lbs.	Manila Indigo	1.75	17.50
	10 "	Black Tea	1.65 /	16.50
	~~2 demij.~~	~~Gin~~	not rendered[54] ~~$ 5~~	~~10.00~~
	8 doz.	N.Y. papers	2.40 /	19.20
	5 "	do	2.40 /	12.00
	2 pr	Swiss Muslin	$ 5	10.00
	2 "	Jaconet[55]	5.50/	11.00
	1 doz.	black Belts	25¢ /	3.00
	1 "	col'd[56] do	25¢ /	3.00
	6	silk HdKf[57]	@ 50¢ /	3.00
	1	" Cravat		1.25
			card for'd (carried forward)	$ 413.32½
			Less	100.50
				312.82
			Bro't for'd	$ 312.82
	1 piece	linen check		10.50
	1 box	Raisins	X	~~4.00~~
	3 "	Figs	X	~~3.75~~
	25 lbs	Almonds	X	~~5.50~~
	2	Dutch Cheeses		2.00
	1 box	Claret	X	~~4.75~~
		Candy		~~1.00~~
			325.32	$ ~~444.82~~
Mrs.	Bell			
	25 lbs.	Loaf Sugar		$ 3.00
	25 "	Castile Soap		3.00
	2 prs[58]	Ladies Shoes	@ 3$	6.00

[54] By this date the luxury import and liquor prohibition law must have been in effect.
[55] A lightweight cotton cloth with a smooth and slightly stiff finish; used for clothing and bandages.
[56] Abbreviation for colored.
[57] Handkerchief was abbreviated in several ways in the invoices.
[58] Pairs.

	1 string	Garlic	($ 13.00)	1.00
Mrs.	Rose			
	3	print Dresses	36 yds @ 20¢ /	7.20
	12	Flannel, red	70¢ / ($ 15.40)	8.20
	2	Trunks		8.50
	5	Boxes		1.00
		Drayage, cartage, & C/H		5.00
				$ 487.72½
			By Cash	~~200.00~~
				~~$ 287.72½~~
			Less shoes	$ 90
		Recd. payt by due bill[59]		
		A. M. Godfrey	(signed) Gleddon	

483
Packing Slip

Contents of Packages. Recapitulation

W. H. 1. Raisins
Box 2. Garlic and Soap for Mrs. Bell
" 3. Claret
" 4. Cheese, figs, & ~~sugar~~ almonds
" 5. Sugar for Mrs. Bell
" 6. Tea
Trunk 7. Paper, steel pens & buttons of all kinds & needles
" 8. Envelopes, plaids & flannel **for Mrs. Rouse**
~~9.~~ Sundry shoes, indigo & candy; also 2 pr. Shoes **for Mrs. Bell**
Handkerchiefs, Cravat, Belts & all the newspapers
1 Box W H No.9 Contains some sugar, Coffee, Jelly, & Chocolate **for Dr. Diruslyer** (?) at
Dr. J. C. Notts. Mrs. Delsecco (?) will deliver my letter to Diruslyer.

I solemnly swear that eleven dozen children shoes and cloth booties which are herein invoiced were not put on board of the Str. *Denbigh*, but remained in Havana.
Mobile May 3, 1864.

(signed) H Hall

	477.72
	18.00
	460.72
Less shoes	90.50
Total	370.22

---

[59] A written acknowledgment of indebtedness to a particular party but not payable to the party's order or transferable by endorsement. It was not clear whether the business was being done by Hall, First Mate, and Godfrey, Captain, on the ship's behalf or on their personal account as a side deal. Some of the invoices were marked in such a way that identified who in Mobile or environs ordered the merchandise. In this case part of the list was specified for Mrs. Bell and another part for Mrs. Rose.

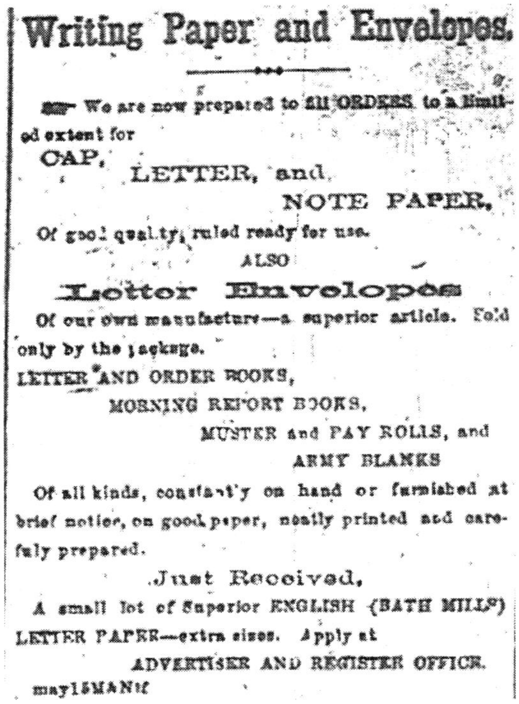

Writing Paper and Envelopes.

We are now prepared to fill ORDERS to a limited extent for

CAP, LETTER, and NOTE PAPER,

Of good quality, ruled ready for use.

ALSO

Letter Envelopes

Of our own manufacture—a superior article. Sold only by the package.

LETTER AND ORDER BOOKS,
MORNING REPORT BOOKS,
MUSTER and PAY ROLLS, and
ARMY BLANKS

Of all kinds, constantly on hand or furnished at brief notice, on good paper, neatly printed and carefully prepared.

Just Received,

A small lot of Superior ENGLISH (BATH MILLS) LETTER PAPER—extra sizes. Apply at

ADVERTISER AND REGISTER OFFICE.

may15MANtf

Figure 44. Ad for goods carried by the *Denbigh*. The "Just Received" section likely refers to stationery listed in the above *Denbigh* manifests. (*Mobile Advertiser and Register* May 15, 1864).

484
Invoice

Captain A. M. Godfrey to J. W. Dover Dr for Jno C. Hodges

22 Varas	Calico	25	$ 5.50
11 "	Blue Muslin	37½	4.13
2	white Corsets	3.75	7.50
4½ Varas	White Muslin	50	2.25
4 "	Jaconet Edging		2.50
1 Doz	Spools thread		1.75
2 prs	Black Mits (mittens ?)	75	1.50
2 prs	Black Silk		2.00
6 Oz	single Zepher[60]		3.30
3 "	" " Black		1.65
4 "	" " White		2.20
2 "	" " Blue		1.10
½ papers	pins		1.25
2 Boxes	hair pins		.50
3 prs	Men's Gaiters	4	12.00
1 lb	Young Dyson (?) Tea		1.25
1"	Black do		1.25
	Loan Ch		.50
	Com 2½		1.29
			$ 53.42

[60] Zephyr – gauzy jersey.

487a-d
Invoices

J. B. Caldwell
To Wm. Smith Dr.

15 Yds	English Crape	@ 25	$ 3.75
28 "	Linen for Dress	@ 25	7.00
14 "	" " "	@ 30	4.20
1 piece	" " "		7.00
1 piece	Cambrick		3.50
2 pr	Ladies Shoes	1.75	3.50
1 Doz	Towels	2.50	2.50
1	**Coffee Pot**		1.50
	Sewing Silk		.75
	Received Payment		$ 33.70
	(signed) Wm Smith		

J B Caldwell
To Wm Smith Dr.

1Doz	Linen Handkerchiefs		1.00
2 pr	Children's Shoes		2.75
			$ 3.75
	Received Payment		
	Wm Smith		

J. B. Caldwell
To Wm Smith Dr.

2 lb	Tea	@ 2½	$?.25
1 Doz	Shoe ?		.37½
	Shoe String		.10
			$ 4.12½
	Received Payment		
	Wm Smith		

J. B. Caldwell
To Wm Smith Dr.

2 pr	Shoes (Children's)	50¢	1.00
2 "	" "	37½	.75
			$ 1.75
	Received Payment		
	Wm Smith		

488-489
Substitute for Preprinted Customs Form

No. 14
Entry of Merchandise
Importer J C Hodges
Vessel *Denbigh*
From Havana
Entered May 2 1864
Value $ 53 Duty $ 7.80

Entry of merchandise imported by J. C. Hodges per *Denbigh* from Havana.

1 Box	Tea	2 lbs	$ 2.50	$ 3 @ 10%	$ .30
	Shoes	3 prs	12.00	12 @ 15	1.80
	Cotton mfs		37.13	38 " "	5.70
			51.63	$ 53	7.80
	Chs & Com		1.79		
			53.42		

491-492
Substitute for Preprinted Customs Form

No. 13
Entry of Merchandise
Importer W. Freeman for J. B. Caldwell
Vessel *Denbigh*
From Havana
Entered May 2d 1864
Value $ 50 Duty $ 7.50

Entry of Merchse. Imported by Wd. Freeman by St. *Denbigh* from Havana.

SBC	1 Box	Candy &c	$ 7.48	$ 7		
	1 Pkg.	Clothing &c	32.42	33		
		Shoes	8.50	10		
			48.40	50	15%	$ 7.50
			2.00			
			$ 50.40			

493-494
Invoice

Capt. A. M. Godfrey

To J. W. Dever Dr

	J. B. Fellows		
1 Piece	Bleached domestic		$ 7.25
1 do	do do fine		7.25
1 do	Nansook muslin 22 vs	35¢	7.70
1 do	Irish linen 38 Varas	@ 37½	14.25
½ do	do do fine 19 "	" 40¢	7.60
26 Varas	check linen	" 45¢	11.70
6	**Patterns** 2¼ vs each 13½ vs		
	figured linen for children	50	6.75
26 Varas	" Cambric	@ 40¢	10.40
44 do	Printed Jaconet	" 37½	16.50
66 do	finest French calico	30¢	19.80
1 Piece	28 yds Common do		4.75
1 dozen	Gents linen Hdkfs		4.50
1 do	Ladies " " fine		5.50
3	do Children " "	3.25	9.75
1 Piece	white bird eye Diaper 30 yds	@ 40	14.00
1 Dozen	tape assorted		3.75
1 do	fine Eng. Cotton hose No. 9		7.50
1	Fine French calfskin		3.50
1¾ (?) Yds	Scarlet cloth	@ 4.25	7.44
1 Dozen	Eng. Cotton hose No. 8		5.50
1 do	do do do " 7		5.50
1 do	do do ½ do " 10½		4. "
1 do	do do " " 6½		4. "
1 do	do do " " 4		4. "
8 do	Spool Cotton	@ 1.75	14.00
6 do	Pearl buttons		
12 do	" "		
6 do	" "		
6 do	" "		
6 do	" "		
6 do	" " assorted		7.00
15 Papers	needles 1 to 12		2.00
1 Dozen	papers pins 3 sizes		4.25
1 do	Hooks & Eyes		1.25
2 Prs	Ladies Gaiters No. 5	@ 2.75	5.50
	Amt (Amount) forward		$ 225.59

	Amt bt (brought) forward		$ 225.59	
1 Pair	Ladies thick sole Gaiters		1.37	
2 "	Girls' shoes	@ 1.37½	2.75	
1 "	" Gaiters		3.75	
2 "	shoes & Gaiters		6.25	
3 "	boys' do	@ 1.25	3.75	
3 "	" do small	" 90¢	2.70	
1 Dozen	skeins black silk		3.00	
1	Fine soft felt hat No. 7¼		4.75	
10 Lbs	black Tea	1.25	12.50	
25 "	Coffee	@ 22¢	~~5.50~~ free	

1 Pr	patent leather boy's Gaiters		2.75	
	Launch, package, labor, drayage		4.25	
	Commn. 2½%		7.00	$ 287.16
	26 Varas Brown Russi Crash	40¢	10.40	10.40
	E&OE			$ 297.56
	Habana April 26, 1864			
	Error in extension of			
	26 Varas Linen			1.30
				$ 298.86
	Less Coffee			5.50
	(signed) J. W. Dever			293.36

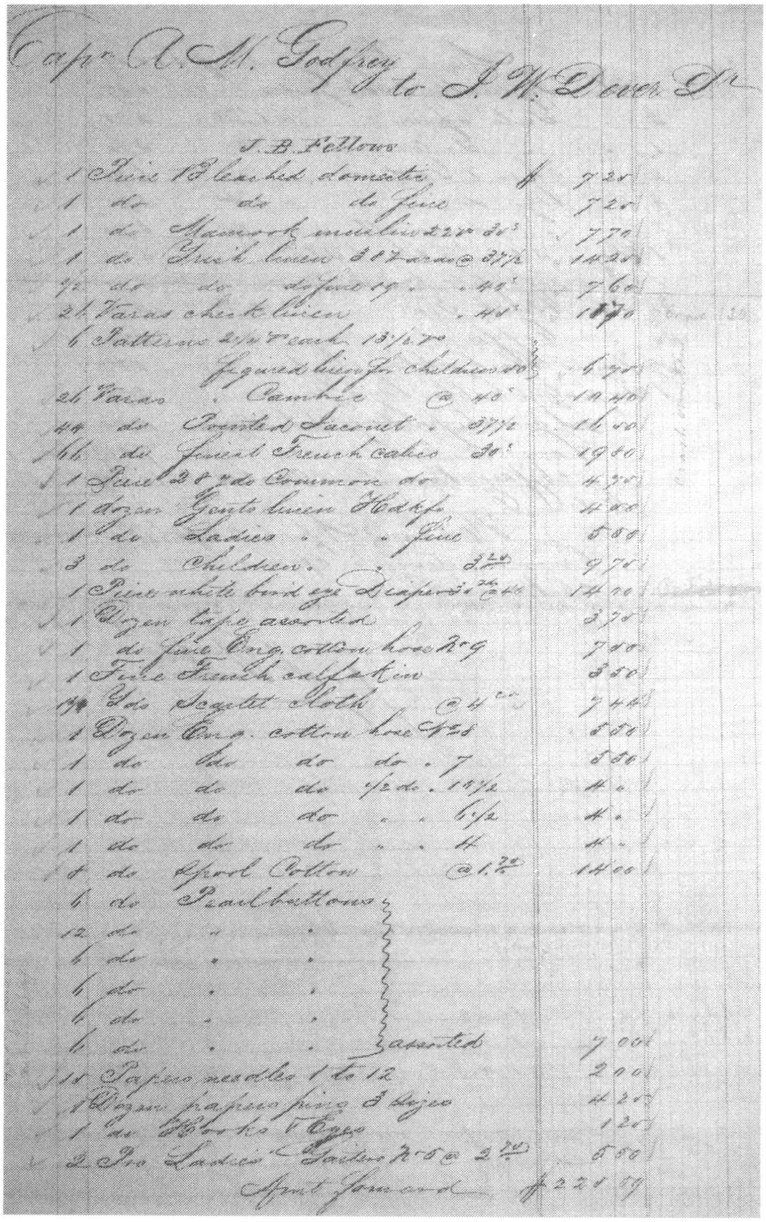
Capt A. M. Godfrey
to J. W. Dever Dr
J. B. Fellows

Figure 45. Large invoice of sundries for J. B. Fellows.

495
Invoice

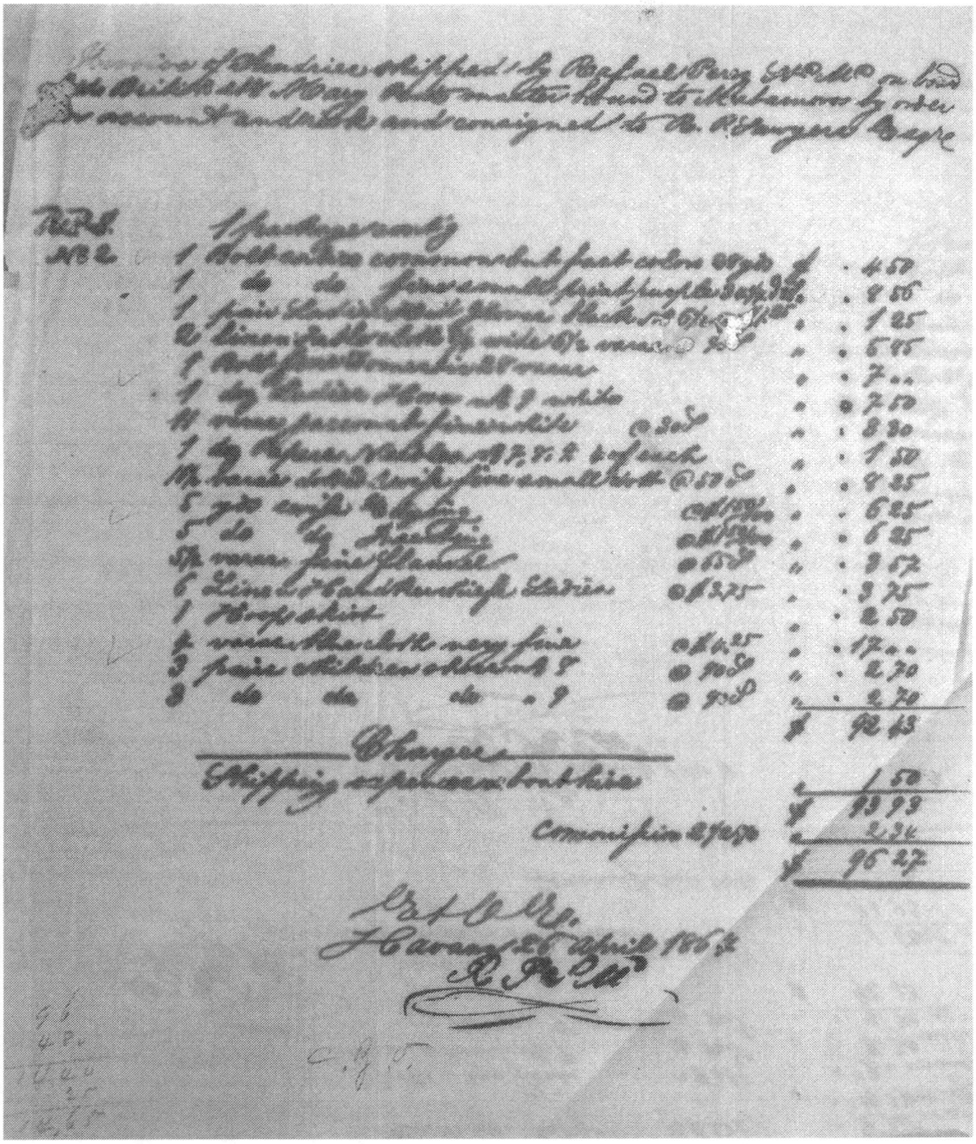

Figure 46. Invoice of sundries perhaps for one family.

Invoice of Sundries shipped 1 by Rafael Perez Sta Ma (Santa Maria) on board the British Str *Mary*[61] ??? (indicates illegible word) Master bound to Matamoros[62] by order & for account and ??? consigned to R. P. Sawyer Esqre.

[61] This document was written on an onion skin paper and the ink was blurry so reading this page was difficult. The shipment was either changed from *Mary* to the *Denbigh*, not an unusual happening, or perhaps misfiled in the archives. The former was perhaps the more likely.

RPS		Package cont'g		
Ma	1 Bolt	calico common but fast colors 28 yds		4.50
	1 do	do fine small print purple 34½ ???		8.56
	1 pair	Ladies small gloves black ?? 6½ ??	?1.25	1.25
	2	linen ??? cloth ?? wide 6½ varas	???	5.85
	1 Bolt	fine domestic 28 varas		7.00
	1 doz	Ladies Hose no. 9 white		7.50
	11 varas	??? fine white		8.30
	1 doz	Papers Needles no. 7, 8, 9 4 of each	@ 30¢	1.50
	16½ varas	dotted Swiss fine small ???	@ 50	8.25
	5 yds	Swiss ???	@ $ 1.50/1.00	6.25
	5 do	do ???	@ $ 1.50/1.00	6.25
	5½ varas	fine flannel	@ 65¢	3.57
	6	Linen Handkerchiefs Ladies	@ $ 3.75	3.75
	1	**Hoop skirt**		2.50
	4 varas	blue cloth very fine	@ $ 4.25	17.00
	3 pairs	children shoes no. 8[63]	@ 90¢	2.70
	3	do do do " 9	@ 90¢	2.70
				$ 92.43
		Charges		
		Shipping expenses: boat hire		1.50
				$ 93.93
		Commission 2½%		2.34
		(signed) ???		$ 95.27
		Havana 26 April 1864		
		R Pe S Ma		

496-497
Substitute for Preprinted Customs Form

No. 9
Entry of Merchandise
Importer R L Sawyer
Vessel *Mary* (An E.T.C. ship like the *Denbigh.* Some *Mary* documents included herein for comparison.)
From Havana
Entered May 3 1864
Value $ 96 Duty $14.40

Entry of Merchandise received by R. L. Sawyer on board Str. *Mary* – Sent from Havana – Apl 30, 64

1 PKge	Calicoes, Cottons, gloves, needles &c	$ 51.96	$ 54		
	Wool mfs.	28.82	30		
	Flax "	6.25	7		
	Shoes	5.40	5		

[62] False destination at a neutral port, a fairly transparent attempt to make the voyage legal. If a captured runner's papers showed she was bound to a blockaded port like those of the Confederacy, that would constitute important evidence to condemn the ship as a valid capture in a prize court proceeding.
[63] The two orders for children's shoes in specific sizes made this seem a shipment for a specific family in Mobile.

	Chgs & Com	3.84	96	15%	$ 14.40
		96.27			

498
Invoice

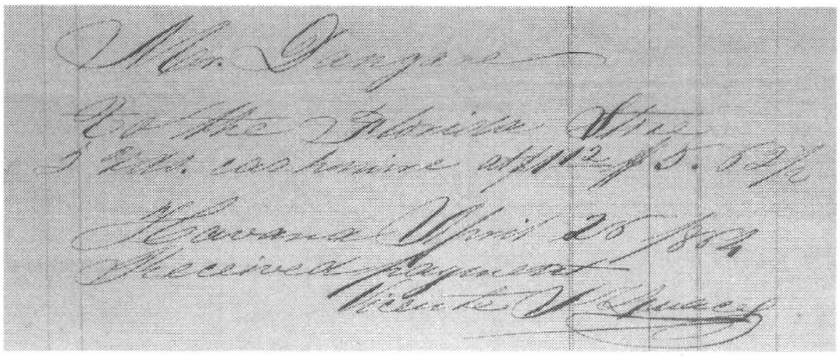

Figure 47. Invoice for cashmere.

Mr. Dargane (?)
To the Florida Store
5 Yds. Cashmere at $ 1.12 $5.62½
Havana April 26 1864
Received payment
(signed) Vicente V ????

499
Invoice

M		From the Florida Store		
	12 Yds.	Suiz (Swiss) muslin	at 30¢	3.60
	2	ladies belts		50
	17 Yds.	Linen Cambric	at 32	5.44
	½ doz	cotton hose		2.00
	15 Yds.	Linen inserting	at 60¢	9.00
	1 pc.	White linen Lawn		8.50
				$ 29.04
		Havana April 26 1864		
		Received payment		
		(signed) Vicente H ???		
		Mitten 4.60		

502
Invoice

Mr. Geo. T. Pane
To the Florida Store Dr.

1 pc	brown linen at		$ 9.00
1 pc.	Nansook		5.00
8 Yds.	Linen Cambric	at 32	2.56
3 pr.	Ladies Gatrs (Gaiters)	at 40¢	1.20
1 lb	black thread		1.20
1 do	White thread		1.50
12 doz.	Buttons		1.00
15 Yds.	Linen colord	at 31¢	4.65
4	ladies belts	at 25 "	1.00
2	do	" 40	.80
20 Yds.	of poplin	at 70	14.00
7	Whaled Crins (Crinolines ?)	at 20¢	1.40
1	trunk		3.00
1	suit of linen Drillen		12.00
1 pc.	Linen blue checks		10.50
1 pc.	White cotton		7.00
5 Yds.	of linen lining	at 25¢	1.25
18 Yds.	Linen Cambric	a 25 "	4.50
5½ Yds	Dress silk		6.50
2 doz.	Cords.		.50
3 pair	ladies mits		1.50
20 Yds	. White flannel	at 50¢	10.00
1 doz	ladies hose		4.00
9 pairs	Miss cotton hose		2.75
2	hoop Skirts		4.00
			$ 110.86
	Havana April 26 1864		
	Received payment		
	(signed) Vicente H. ???		

503
Substitute for Preprinted Customs Form

No. 2
Entry of Merchandise
Importer J. Forsyth
Vessel *Denbigh*
From Havana
Entered May 2 1864
Value $ 37 Duty $ 4.40

J. Forsythe importer per *Denbigh* April 14, 64
Entered 2 May

1 pKge	Tea	29	10%	$ 2.90
1 "	Shoes	2	15 "	.30
1 "	Sugar	6	20 "	1.20
		37.00		4.40

505
Invoice

John Forsyth
To H. O. Brewer & Co.

50 lbs	Sugar	$ 6.24
12 "	Tea	15.62
1 pr	Slippers	1.50
10 lbs	Tin	12.50
		$ 35.87

Havana April 14, 1864
John Forsyth

507-508
Substitute for Preprinted Customs Form

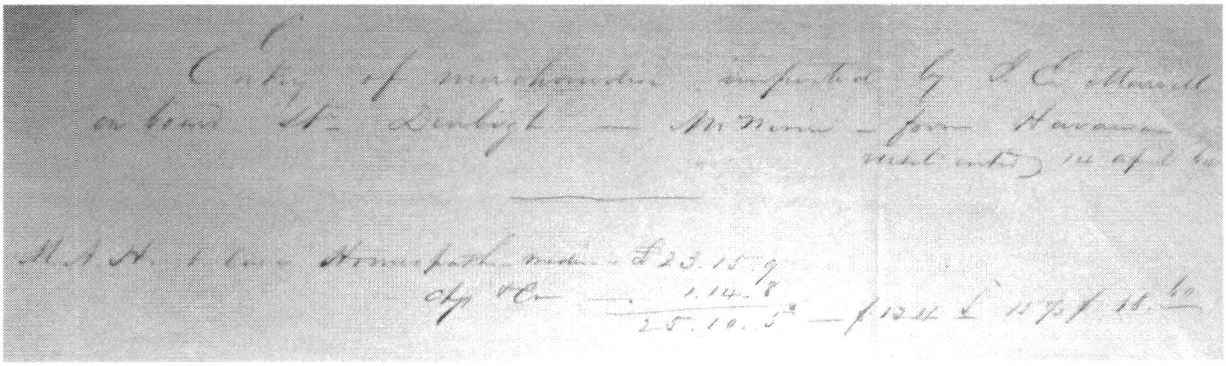

Figure 48. Substitute for customs form for homeopathic medicine.

No. 3
Entry of Merchandise
Importer J. E. Morrell
Vessel *Denbigh*
From Havana
Entered May 2d 1864
Value $ 124 Duty $ 18.60

Entry of Merchandise imported by J. E. Morrell on board Str. *Denbigh* – McNevin – from Havana, vessel entered 14 April '64.

M. A. H.	1 Case **Homeopathic medicine**		£ 23.15.9			
		Chgs & Cm	1.14.8			
			25.10.5 -	$ 124	15%	$ 18.60

509-510
Substitute for Preprinted Customs Form

No. 4
Entry of Merchandise
Importer N H Brown
Vessel *Denbigh*
From Havana
Entered May 2 64
Value $ 17 Duty $ 2.55

Entry of goods by N. H. Brown per *Denbigh* from Havana, April 14 '64.
1 PKg Shoes with chgs & Com $ 17 15% $ 2.55

511-512
Substitute for Preprinted Customs Form

No. 5
Entry of Merchandise
Importer R. W. Hallett
Vessel *Denbigh*
From Havana
Entered May 2 1864
Value $ 110 Duty $ 16.50

Entry of goods imported by R. W. Hallett on board Str. *Denbigh* from Havana April 14/ '64.

J. H. Hammond	1 Box	Flax mfs	$ 28.30	29		
		Cotton "	42.10	45		
		Wool "	28.82	29		
	1 Box	Soap	6.00	7		
			105.22	$ 110	15%	$ 16.50
			5.10			
			$ 110.32			

513
Invoice

Havana Apl 6, 1864
T. H. Stanash (?)

	Bot of J. W. Dever	Dr.	
1 pc	18 yds. Blk & White Silk	1.25	22.50
1 Bolt	bird Eye Diaper 20 yds.	45	9.00
24 yds	plaid flannel	62½	15.00
6 papers	White pins		17½
6 papers	Black pins		17½
1 doz	Spools Cotton		1.87½
3 "	" Black		6.00
12 Skeins	blk Silk		7.00
2 Bolts	Linen 35 yds	$ 13	26.00
1 Bolt	Shirting Linen		12.00
2 Prs	Blk Kid Gloves		
2 "	Calic' (?) do		7.00
1 doz	Silk Buttons black		50
6 yds	trimming for dress		2.00
	Recpt.		99.22
	(overwritten note) $ 14.85 Paid[64]		

515
Substitute for Preprinted Customs Form

No. 6
Entry of Merchandise
Importer Bal. Tardy
Vessel *Denbigh*
From Havana
Entered May 2 64
Value $ 249 Duty $ 37.35

Entry of Merchandise by Geo. T. Jones, per Str. *Mary*, from Havana.

Case	Medicinal preparations	$ 74.67	$ 77		
	Quinine	25.00	26		
Bld	Flax mfs	29.04	30		
Trunk	Flax mfs	54.96	57		
	Cotton "	42.90	44		
	Flannels	14.62	15		
		241.19	249	15%	37.35
	Chgs & Com	8.25			
		$ 249.44			

---

[64] Possibly a note regarding duty paid.

517
Invoice

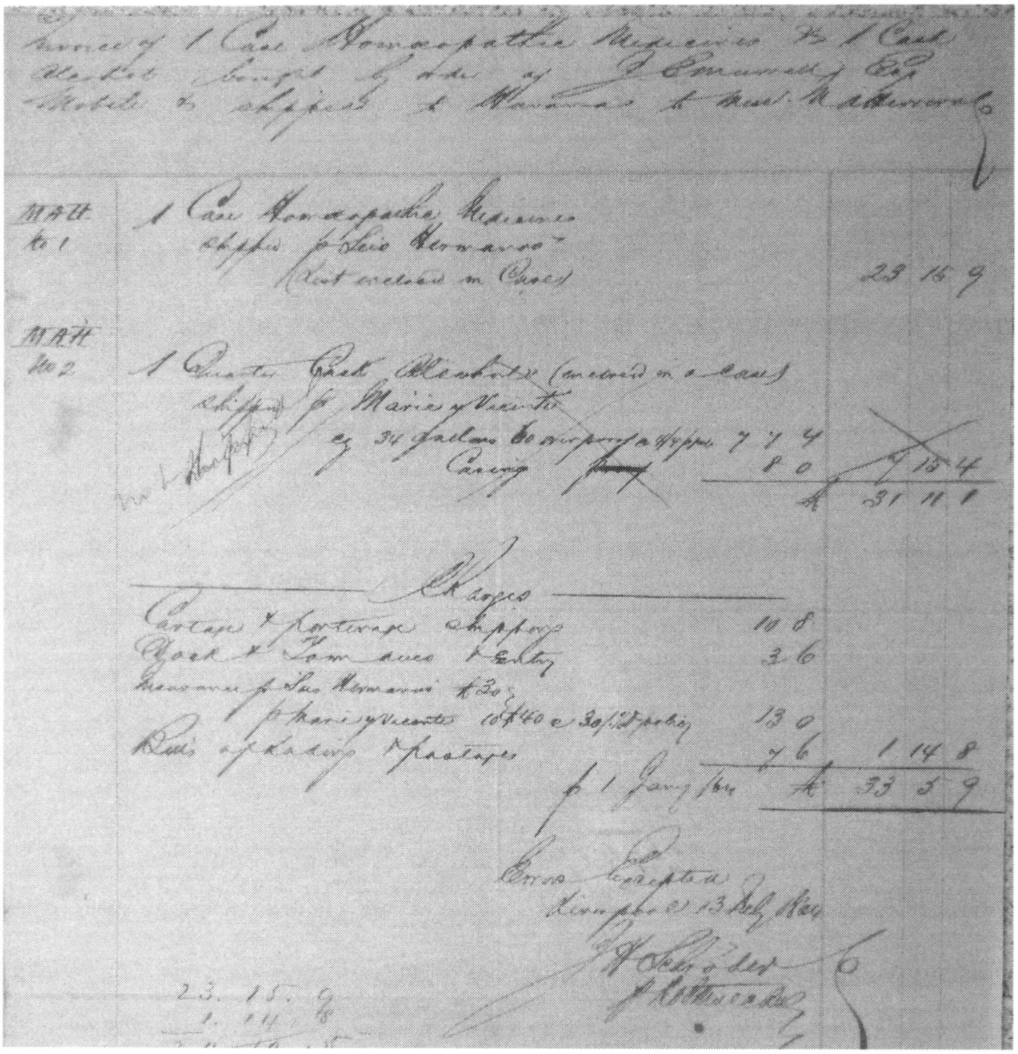

Figure 49. Invoice for medicine and alcohol lamps sent from Liverpool by J. H. Schroder.

Invoice 1 Case Homeopathic Medicines & 1 Case Alcohol lamps by order of J. Emunds (?) Esq. Mobile & shipped to Havana to Miss. Madison.

MAH	1 Case Homeopathic Medicines		
No. 1	shipped pr Luis Hermanas		
	(List enclosed in Case)		23.15.9
MAH	1 Quarter Cask Alcohol (enclosed in a case)		
No. 2	shipped pr Marie Vicente		
	?? 34 gallons 60 over proof @ 4/4 sh/d	7.7.4	
		0.8.0	7.15.4
	(later note: not shipped)		£ 31.11.1

	Charges		
	Cartage & porterage shipping	10/8	
	Dock & Town dues & Entry	3/6	
	Insurance ?? Luis Hermanas £ 30		
	?? Marie Vicente 10 ?? 40 @ 30/0/0d policy	13/0	
	Dues appraising (?) & postages	7/6	1.14.8
	?? 1 Jany /64		£ 33.5.9
	Errors Excepted		
	Liverpool 13 Feb 1864		
	(signed) **J. H. Schroder**[65]		
	(signed) ????????		

520–521
Invoice

[65] Prominent merchant banker, U.K. agent for the Erlanger bond sales, and co-owner of the *Denbigh*.

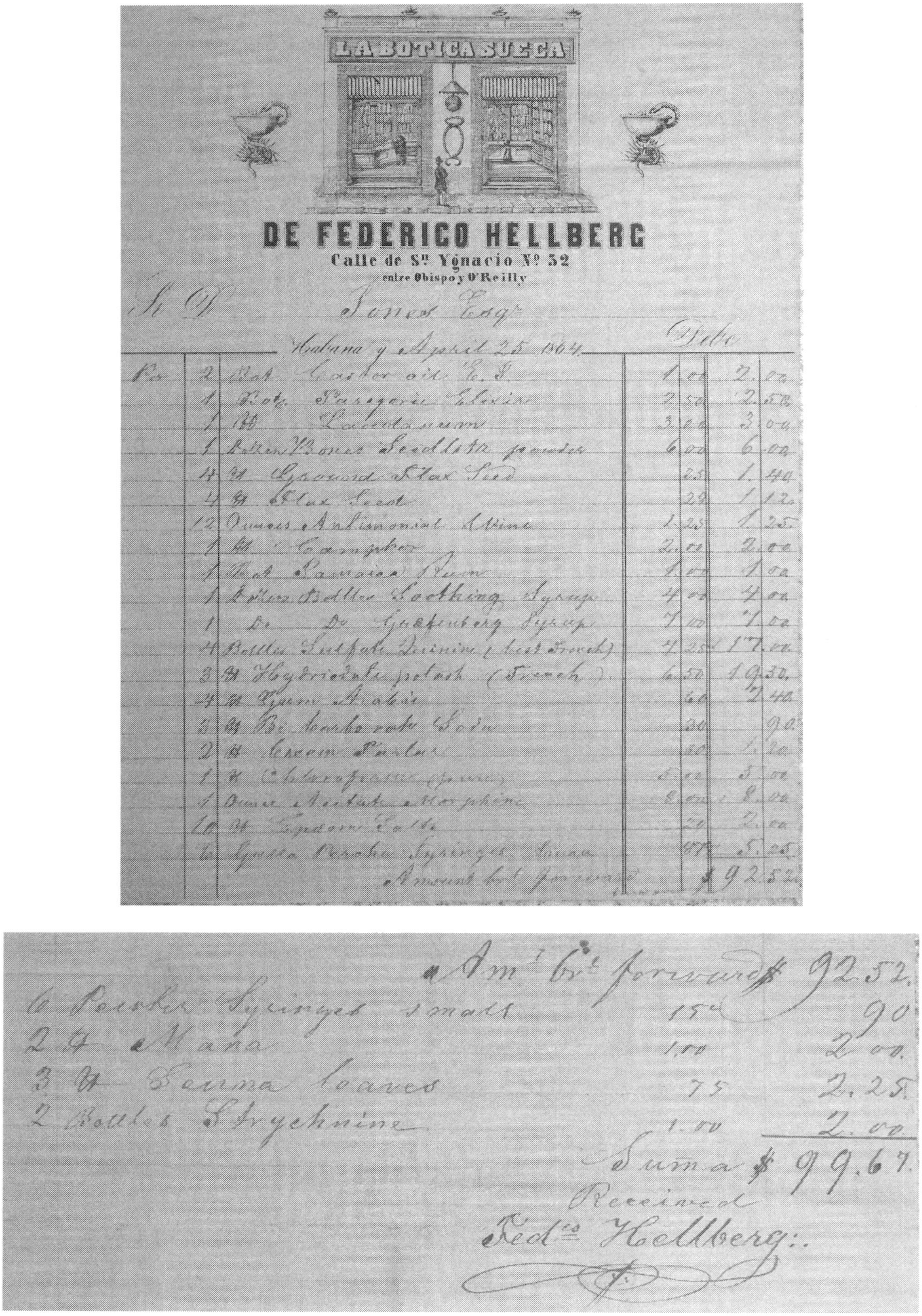

LA BOTICA SUECA

DE FEDERICO HELLBERG

Calle de Sn Ygnacio No 52

entre Obispo y O'Reilly

Sr D. Jones Esqr

Habana y April 25 1864

Debe

Pa	2	Bot Castor oil E. I.	1.00	2.00
	1	Bots Paregoric Elixir	2.50	2.50
	1	lb Laudanum	3.00	3.00
	1	Dozen Boxes Seidlitz powder	6.00	6.00
	4	lb Ground Flax Seed	.25	1.40
	4	lb Flax Seed	.28	1.12
	12	Ounces Antimonial Wine	1.25	1.25
	1	lb Camphor	2.00	2.00
	1	Bot Jamaica Rum	1.00	1.00
	1	Dozen Bottles Soothing Syrup	4.00	4.00
	1	Do Do Gaefenberg Syrup	7.00	7.00
	4	Bottles Sulfate Quinine (best French)	4.25	17.00
	3	lb Hydriodate potash (French)	6.50	19.50
	4	lb Gum Arabic	.60	2.40
	3	lb Bi carbonate Soda	.30	.90
	2	lb Cream Tartar	.80	1.60
	1	lb Chloroform (pure)	5.00	5.00
	1	Ounce Acetate Morphine	8.00	8.00
	10	lb Epsom Salts	.20	2.00
	6	Gutta Percha Syringes large	.87½	5.25
		Amount brt forward		$ 92.52

	Amt brt forward		$ 92.52
6	Percha Syringes small	15c	.90
2 lb	Mana	1.00	2.00
3 lb	Senna leaves	.75	2.25
2	Bottles Strychnine	1.00	2.00
	Suma		$ 99.67

Received

Fedco Hellberg

Figure 50. Invoice for medical supplies.

La Botica Sueca de Federico Hellberg, Calle de Sn. Ygnacio No. 32, entre Obispo y O'Reilly.
Sr D Jones Esqr

Havana y April 25 1864 Debe

2 Bot(tle ?)	Castor oil E. P.	1.00	2.00
1 Bot	Paregoric Elixir	2.50	2.50
1 lb (?)	Laudanum	3.00	3.00
1 Dozen	Boxes Leidliz powder	6.00	6.00
4 lb (?)	Ground Flax Seed	.35	1.40
12 Ounces	Antimonial Wine	1.25	1.25
1 lb (?)	Camphor	2.00	2.00
1 Bot	Jamaica Rum	7.00	7.00
1 Dozen Bottles	Soothing Syrup	4.00	4.00
1 Do Do	Grafenberg Syrup	7.00	7.00
4 Bottles	Sulfate Quinine (best French)	4.25	17.00
3 lb	Hydriadate potash (French)	6.50	6.50
4 lb	Gum Arabic	.60	2.40
3 lb	Bi Carbonate Soda	.30	.90
2 lb	Cream Tartar	.60	1.20
1 lb	Chloroform (French)	5.00	5.00
1 Ounce	Acetate Morphine	8.00	8.00
10 lb	Epsom Salts	.20	2.00
6	Gutta Percha Syringes Small	.87	5.25
	Amount brt forward		$ 92.52
	turn over		
	Amt brt forward		$ 99.67
6	Percha Syringes small	.15	.90
2 lb	Mana	1.00	2.00
3 lb	Seirna leaves	.75	2.25
2 Bottles	Strychnine	1.00	2.00
	Suma		$ 99.67
	Received		
	Fedco. Hellberg		

522-527
Preprinted Customs Form

Note: At this point it seemed that the supply of preprinted customs forms was renewed. The present form was interesting as an unusual example including cargoes from two ships instead of one ship only. The rare examples showing two ships on one form shown previously were unclear as to why the dual listing came about.

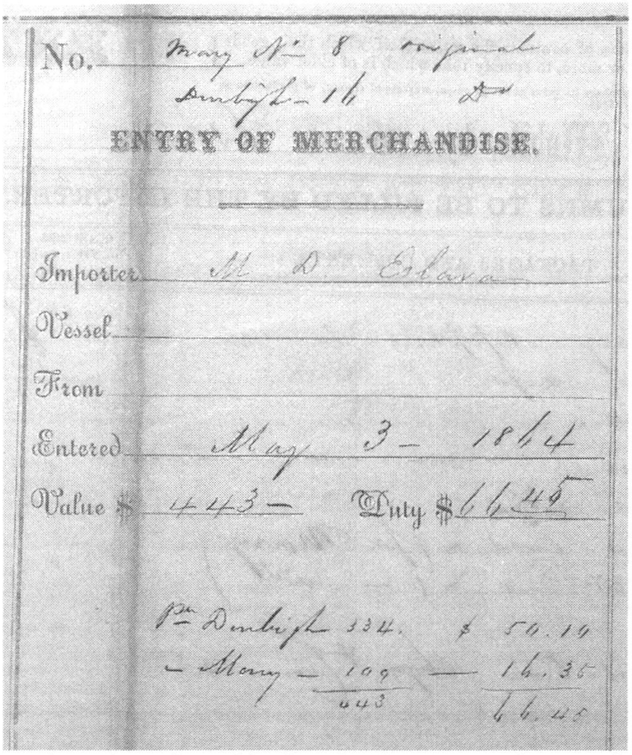

No. Mary No. 8 original
Denbigh 16 Do

ENTRY OF MERCHANDISE.

Importer M. D. Eslava

Vessel

From

Entered May 3 – 1864

Value $ 443 – Duty $ 66.45

Pr Denbigh 334. $ 50.10
– Mary – 109 – 16.35
443 66.45

(enlarged section of outside showing important abstracted data)

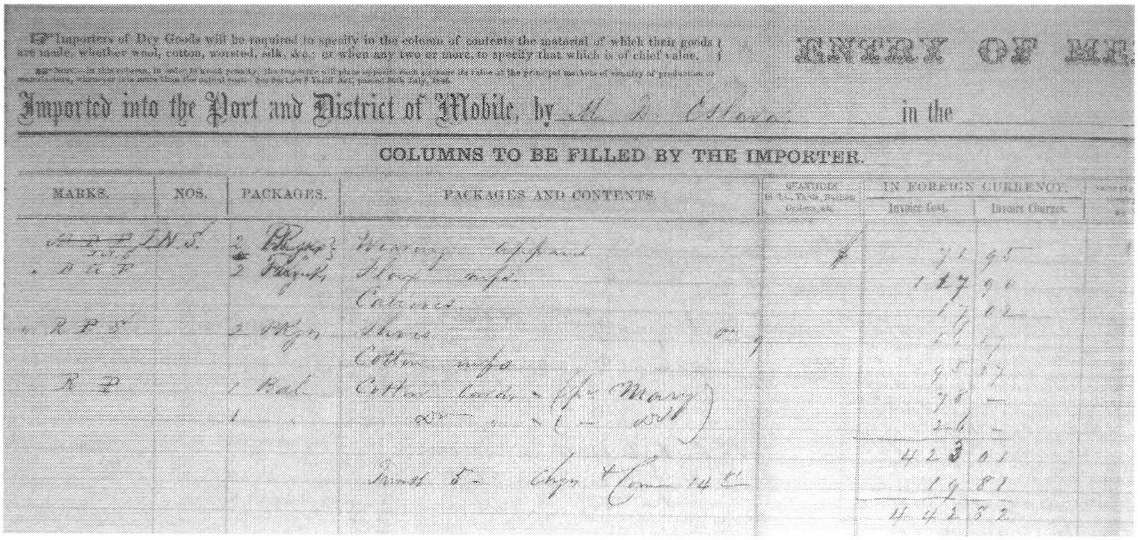

☞ Importers of Dry Goods will be required to specify in the column of contents the material of which their goods are made, whether wool, cotton, worsted, silk, &c.; or when any two or more, to specify that which is of chief value.

ENTRY OF ME

Imported into the Port and District of Mobile, by M. D. Eslava in the

COLUMNS TO BE FILLED BY THE IMPORTER.

MARKS.	NOS.	PACKAGES.	PACKAGES AND CONTENTS.	QUANTITIES	IN FOREIGN CURRENCY. Invoice Cost.	Invoice Charges.
			Wearing apparel		71	95
			Cotton cards – (pr Mary)		78	–
					423	01
					19	81
					442	52

(inside enlarged, left part)

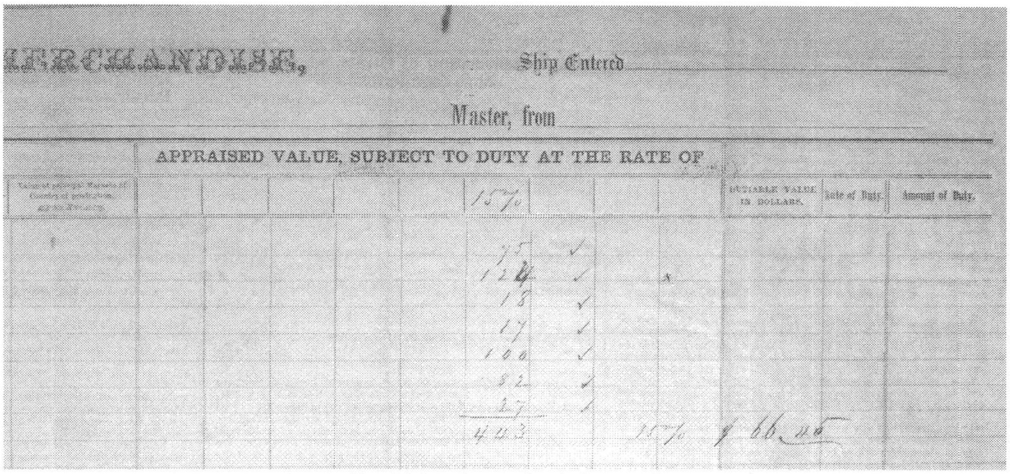
MERCHANDISE, Ship Entered

Master, from

APPRAISED VALUE, SUBJECT TO DUTY AT THE RATE OF

DUTIABLE VALUE IN DOLLARS. | Rate of Duty. | Amount of Duty.

15%

75, 124, 18, 17, 100, 82, 27

443 15% $ 66.45

(inside enlarged, right part)

Figure 51. Unusual customs form citing shipments on two ships.

No.__*Mary*__No. 8 original
Denbigh " 16 Do[66]
Entry of Merchandise.
Importer__M. D. Eslava
Entered__May 3, 1864
Value $__443 Duty $ 66.45

Per *Denbigh*	334.	$ 50.10
" *Mary*	109	16.35
	443	66.45

Oath of Owner
(signed) M. D. Eslava

Imported into the Port and District of Mobile, by M. D. Eslava in the __________ Ship Entered ______ Master, from

Marks	Packages	Packages and Contents	In Foreign Currency.	Appraised Value Rate 15%	Duty
J.N.S.	2 PKgs	Wearing apparel	$ 71.95	75	
D G F	2 PKgs	Flax mfs.	117.90	124	
		Calicoes	17.02	18	
R P S	2 PKgs	Shoes per 9	16.27	17	
		Cotton mfs	95.87	100	
R. P.	1 Bdl.	Cotton Cards (pr *Mary*)	78.00	82	
	1 "	Do " (" Do)	26.00	27	
			423.01	443	$ 66.45
		Trunk 5 Chgs & Com 14.81	19.81		
			442.82		

[66] Perhaps this document indicated a merger of a shipment at first intended for the *Mary*, but actually sent on the *Denbigh*. Maybe the *Mary* and *Denbigh* came into Mobile together and the cargoes were clearing customs together, an indication that the *Mary* in question was the one owned by the European Trading Company (E.T.C.), owner of the *Denbigh*.

528
Invoice

Invoice of Sundries shipped by Rafael Perez Sta Ma on board of the British Str *Denbigh* Godfrey master bound to Matamoros by order for account & risk and consigned to M. D. Eslava Esq

MDE		1 case cont'd		$ .50
	2 pieces	English Burge (?) 16½ varas	@ 31 ?	23.71
	2 do	Muslins small figured fast colors		23.60
	1 do	fine white liner Muslin 15 yds		7.25
	6	black lace shawls	@ $ 15	90.00
	6	**bouquets artificial flowers for bonnets**	@ $ 2 1/8	12.75
	1 doz	Gents pocket handkerchiefs		8.50
	1 doz	Ladies do do		7.50
	6 pieces	wide silk ribbon asst'd (assorted) colors	@ $ 4¼	25.50
	6 do	French calico fast colors 259 ?/100 ?	@ 30 ?	77.84
		1 trunk (charged to S. G. Gaston ?) cont'g		
		1 bundle with		
	6 gross	fishing lines assorted sizes	@ 4 $ 24.00	
	6 do	**fish tackle** do do	@ 22.50	46.50
				$ 324.65
		Charges		
		Shipping expenses & boat Ride		2.50
				$ 326.15
		(signed) ??????		
		Havana 25 April 1864		
		Copy Rcd S M		
		(note added in pencil)		
	1 Bundle	Black Jersey (?) Silk $ 20		
	1 "	contg Ladies waiste ???? 18		
		$ 38		
		Delivered		

529
Invoice

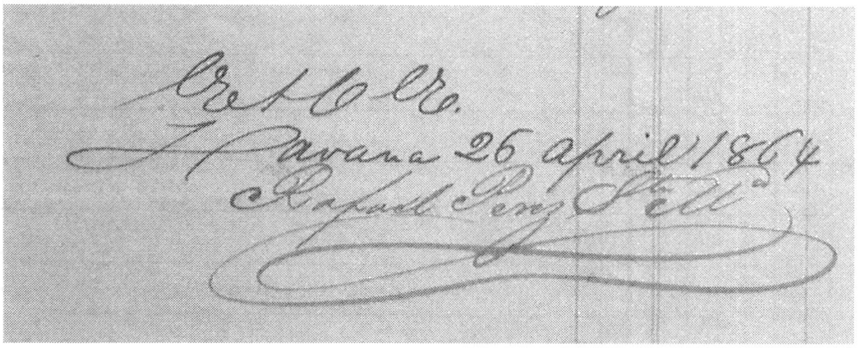

(signature block, enlarged)

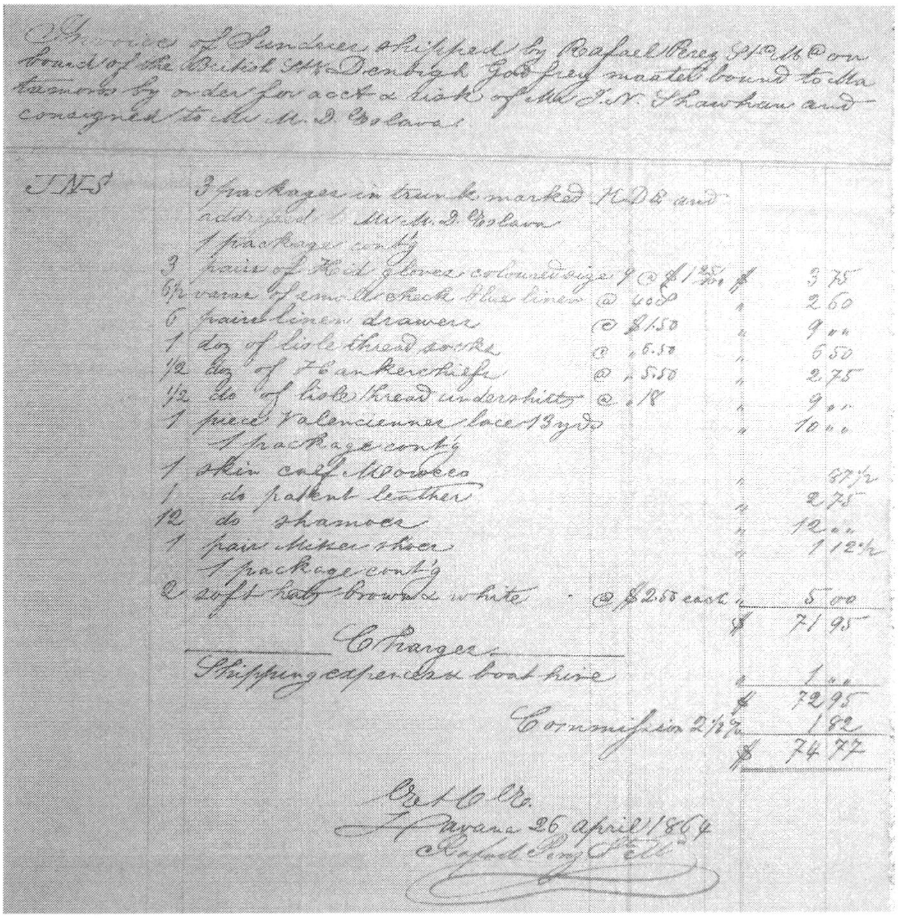

Figure 52. Invoice showing false destination, the neutral port of Matamoros.

Invoice of Sundries shipped by Rafael Perez Sta M on board of the British Str *Denbigh* Godfrey master bound to Matamoros by order for acct & risk of Mr. J. N. Shawhan and consigned to Mr. M. D. Eslava.

JNS		3 packages in trunk marked MDE and		
		addressed to Mr. M. D. Eslava		
		1 package cont'g		
	3 pairs	of Kid gloves colored size 9	@ $ 1 25/100	$ 3.75
	6½ varas	of small check blue linen	@ 40¢	2.60
	6 pairs	linen drawers	@ $ 1.50	9.00

	1 doz	of lisle thread socks	@ " 6.50	6.50
	½ doz	of Handkerchiefs	@ " 5.50	2.75
	1 piece	Valenciennes lace 13 yds		10.00
		1 package cont'g		
	1	skin calf Morocco		.87½
	1	do patent leather		2.75
	12	do shamoes		12.00
	1 pair	Misses shoes		1.12½
		1 package cont'g		
	2	soft hats brown & white	@ $ 2.50 each	5.00
				$ 71.95
		Charges		
		Shipping expenses & boat hire		1.00
				$ 72.95
		Commission	2½%	1.82
		???????		$ 74.77
		Havana 26 April 1864		
		Rafael Perez Sta Ma (?)		

530
Invoice

Invoice of Sundries shipped by Rafael Perez Sta Ma on board of the British Str *Denbigh* Godfrey master bound to Matamoros by order for account and risk of Mr. D. G. Fulton and consigned to Mr. M. D. Eslava.

DGF		2 packages in trunk marked MDE and		
		addressed to M. D. Eslava, cost of trunk		$ 5.00
	6	French calf skins	@ $ 30 doz	15.00
		1 package cont'g		
	1 piece	brown linen Drill 36 yds	@ 40¢	14.40
	2 do	striped & checked linen Drill	46¢ @ 75¢	34.50
	1 do	Irish Linen 35 yds	@ $ 13	13.00
	1 do	Linen sheeting 10/ 25 varas	@ $ 1	25.00
	1 do	Domestic bleached 40 yds	@ " 7	7.00
	2 doz	Spool cotton thread 500 yards	@ $ 1.25	3.50
	1 lb	Flax thread black	@ $ 1.75	3.50
	1 doz pairs	Ladies Hose		4.25
	2 pieces	calico fast colors 68 10 varas	@ 25¢	17.02
				$ 139.92
		Charges		
		Shipping expenses & boat hire		1.08
				141.00
		Commission	2½%	3.52
		????????		$ 144.52
		Havana 26 April 1864		
		Rafael Perez Sta Ma		

531
Invoice

RPS		2 packages in trunk marked MDE and		
		addressed to M. D. Eslava.		
No. 1		1 package cont'g		
	1 Bolt	bleached domestic fine 34 yds		7.00
	1 do	calico fine small print pink 50½ yds (?)	@ 25¢	12.62
	1 piece	white Swiss fine 16 yards		7.25
	1 Bolt	Card Muslin fine small checks 12 yds		4.75
	1 do	Linen diaper small figure 21 ?	@ 40¢	8.40
	1 do	Irish linen fine 32 yds		15.00
	1 do	blue check linen fine 40 ?	@ 40¢	16.00
	1 do	lawn fine small print 40 yds	@ 40¢	16.00
	1 doz	Spool thread ? Machine	@ 125/100	1.25
	5½ varas	fine blue flannel	@ 70¢ vara	3.85
	6	linen handkerchiefs for gents		2.75
		1 package cont'g		
	1 pair	Ladies Gaiters No. 3		1.12½
	3 do	children shoes " 8	@ 90¢	2.70
	3 do	" " " 9	@ 90¢	2.70
	1 do	Boys boots " 18		3.00
	1 do	do do " 2		3.00
	1 do	Men's do " 7		3.75
				$ 112.14½
		Charges		
		Shipping expenses & boat hire		1.07½
				$ 113.22
		Commission	2½%	2.83
		(signed) ????		$ 116.05
		Havana 26 April 1864		
		Copy --- R P S Ma		

532
Invoice

Invoice of Cotton cards shipped by Rafael Perez Sta Ma on board of the British Steamer *Mary* Peats Master bound to Nassau by order for account and risk of Mr. Wiebel and consigned to M D Eslava Esqre.

R P	1	Bundle with three boxes contg. Each 2 dozens		
		No. 10 Cotton Cards Super fine – together		
		6 dozens	@ $ 13 doz	$ 78.00
		Charges		
		Export duty in bond out on 6 doz Cotton Cards @		

		$ 9 doz $ 54.00 @ 1¼%	$ .68	
		Rec'g & Delv'y & drayage to the wharf & boat hire	2.10	
		Entry & permit in the Custom House	.50	
		Freight paid here as per agreement	40.00	43.28
				$ 121.28
		Commission	2½%	3.03
				$ 124.31
		E & O E		
		Havana 26 April 1864		
		The bundle contains four boxes one of which is		
		for Mr. Reid for a/c of Mr. C G Ramsay.		
		Rafael Perez Sta Ma		
		(note added) 2 Doz Cotton Cards. J. R??? $ 13		

533-537
Preprinted Customs Form

No. 17
Entry of Merchandise.
Importer L. F. Zantzinger
Vessel *Denbigh*
From Havana
Entered May 3d 64
Value $ 292 Duty $ 43.80

Oath of Owner
(signed) L. F. Zantzinger

Ship Entered _________

Imported into the Port and District of Mobile, by L. F. Zantzinger in the Br. Str. *Denbigh* Godfrey Master, from Havana

Marks	Packages	Packages and Contents	Quantities	In Foreign Currency	Appraised Value, Subject to Duty 15%	Duty
L F Z	1 PKge	Sul. Morphine	2¾ oz	$ 19.25	20	
Woodruff	1 "	Crouther (?) over coat		12.00	12	
J. Hessen (?)	1 "	Silk mfs		8.25	8	
W B Gaude (?)	1 "	Clothing, 1 Hat		47.00	49	
McDowell	? "	Linen mfs		3.35	3	
Do	4 "	Flax mfs		46.37	49	
Do		Flannels		15.94	16	
D. W. Goodman	3 PKgs	Cotton mfs, Hose, Silk lawn		49.09	52	
T. McConaughy	1 "	Clothing, ready made		29.75	31	
A. T. Mullany	1 "	Cotton mfs		43.67	45	

Do		Shoes	4 prs	6.75	7	
				281.42	292	$43.80
		Chgs & Com	2½%	10.20		
				291.62		

538
Invoice

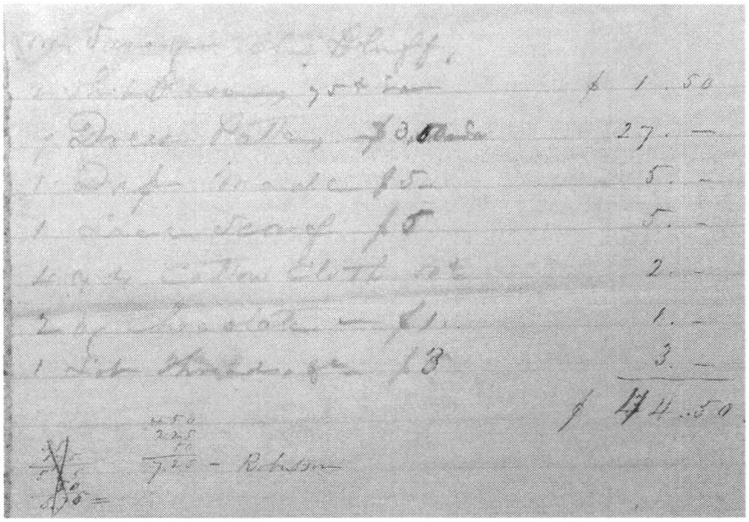
$ 1.50
27. —
5. —
5. —
2. —
1. —
3. —
$ 44.50

Figure 53. Invoice for sundries including dress patterns.

Mr. Tamage (?) Elm Bluff

2	White ????	75¢ & ??	$ 1.50
9	**Dress Patterns**	$ 3.00 ??	27.00
1	Dress Made	$ 5	5.00
1	Lace Scarf	$ 5	5.00
4 yds	Cotton Cloth	50¢	2.00
2 oz (?)	chocolate	$ 1	1.00
1 Lot	Thread, &c	$ 3	3.00
			$ 44.50

540
Invoice

(Noted on side) Mr. Layton
Settled for Freight
H. O. Brewer & Co.
Mr. Benj. Donaldson

	Wm. Layton					
2 ½ Bbls	Rum 30 Gals.	30 ???	9			

10 Galls	Ker.(osene ?) Oil	$ 1	10		
2 Demijohns	Gin	$ 4.50 Ea	9		
1 "	Wine	$ 4 Ea	4		
~~1 dmjo~~	~~??? Champaign~~		32		
	Send to Wm House				
	Sanford Examine				
				5.50	
				1.50	
				.50	Paid
				7.50	

Faint pencil note on back: Capt. Murry (?). I send you by dray the ?? other last ?? Send for Inspection.
A. Stokes, C.S.

542
Invoice

Mr. Brennan Havana 6 Mach /64
Bot. of Slater & Co.

6 Bbl	Liquor 15 Gals each	$ 45.00
22 Demijohn	Liquor	33.00
2 Cases	Gin	5.00
1 Jar	S. Oil & Ker oil 105-	11.00
1 Box	Soap	3.50
		$ 97.50
	Rec Payment	
	Slater & Co.	
	Ch & Com 1.36 (?)	

544-555
Invoice

Mr. Bunker

1 Box				
R.S.B.	5 Yds	Flannel	$ 1.50	7.50
	1	Hat	4.00	4.00
	6 pr	Socks ??	.50	3.00
	1 Pr	gloves	5.00	5.00
	1	Box		.50
		with Chgs & Com		60.00
		Shirts 13		
		Cigars 25		38.00

		6.00		
		3.00		
		$ 9.25 over		

(reverse side)
Mr. Westfeld
20 Yds - Trans ship
Duty paid
20
10
3.00

546
Invoice

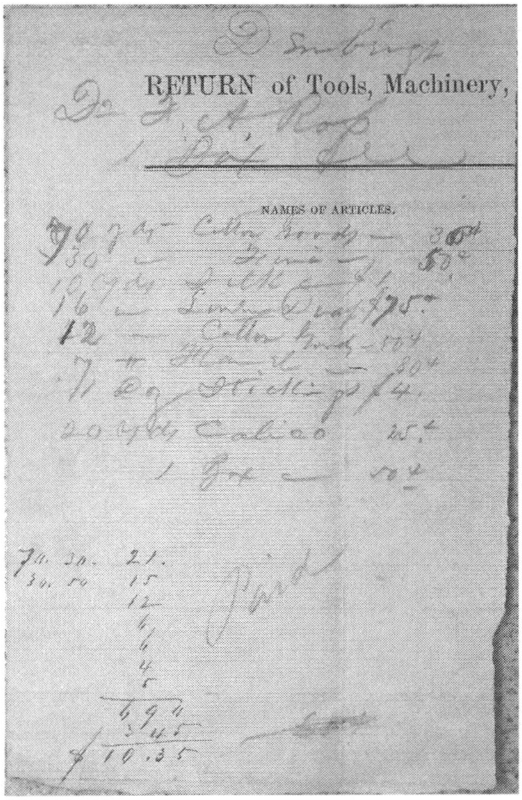

Figure 54. Invoice for fabric prepared on reused scrap of printed form.

Denbigh
Return of Tools, Machinery,
Dr. T. A. Rap
1 Box

	Names of Articles.	
70 Yds	Cotton Goods	.30

30	"	.50
10 Yds	Silk	1.00
16 "	Linen Diap.(er)	.75
12 "	Cotton Goods	.50
7 "	Flannel	.80
20 Yds	Calico	.25
	1 Box	.50
	70. 30.	21
	30. 50	15
		12
		6
	Paid	6
		4
		5
		6.90
		3.45
		$ 10.35

547
Invoice

Thomas St. John Havana
Bot. of Douglass & Co.

2 pr	Ladies Corsetts	2.50
1 pr	Shoes	3.00
1 dozen	Ladies Hose	5.50
1/I (?)	Sewing thread	2.00
1 dejn	Ane Lacrs (?)	.50
		$ 13.50
	(signed) Thomas St. John	
	Duty Paid H. O. B. & Co.	

548
Receipt

Commission ??? duty per Str *Denbigh* from Havana
April 16th 1864
Thos St. John $107 @ 24% $ 25.68

550
Invoice

Note: These were perhaps personal supplies for the Colonel Garner's kitchen.

Memorandum of Articles shipped by C. G. Ramsay per Steamer *Denbigh* to Col G. G. Garner Mobile[67]

Mark				
G. G. Garner	1	Bbl cntg		
	12 Bottles	French Mustard		~~4.25~~
	12 Bottles	Yeast Powder		6.00
	12 Bottles	Pickles		8.50
	1	Cheese 22 lbs	30¢	6.60
	8 Bottles	essences		8.25
	5 lbs	whole pepper		~~1.25~~
	5 "	ground "		~~2.50~~
	6	??? 64 lbs	20¢	~~12.80~~
	1 Can	Soda Crackers		1.75
	2 lbs	Indigo		~~4.00~~
	1 Box	Soap 60 lbs	12½¢	7.50
	1 "	Macaroni		3.75
	1 Kit	Mackerel		3.00
				$ 70.15

551-552
Invoice

(reverse side)
W. J. Delano
Denbigh
May 3 '64

(front side) (Dr.)

L. Lay To F. X. Barbot, Dr.

1864				
Apr	1 gross	Soap (toilet)		$ 9.00
	1 "	Penholders		2.75
	½ "	Tooth Brushes	@ 15 $	7.50
	½ "	Dressing Combs	@ 13 $	6.50
	2 doz	Penknives	@ 5.50	11.00
	1 "	boxes steel pens		6.00
	6 packs	Pins	@ 4	3.00
	2~~M~~	**Mourning Envelopes**	@ 3.25	6.50
	6 reams	Letter Paper	@ 2 $	12.00
	9 doz	files (handsaw)	@ 8	9.00
	1 "	Soft Hats		15.00
	2 demijs	**Best Gin (Bell brand)**		~~10.00~~

[67] Col. G. G. Garner was Chief of Staff, HQ, Dist. of the Gulf, Mobile.

	1 gr.	Hair Pins (½ Buffalo, & ½ gat. per.)		4.00
	1½ doz	Sardines, without bones	@ 3¼	4.87
	1½ "	" with bones	@ 2.12	3.16
	3 lbs	Sup. Black Tea	@ 1.50	4.50
		Drayage		.50
				$ 115.30
				19.03
		Chec Pay's (?)		96.27
		(signed) F. X. Barbot		

555
Invoice

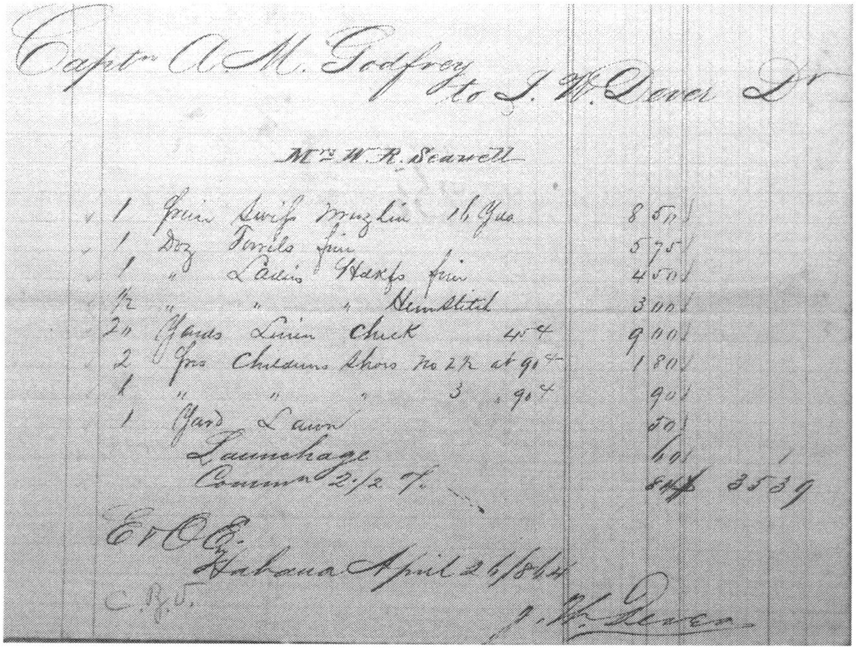
Captn A. M. Godfrey to J. W. Dever Dr
Mrs W. R. Seawell
1 piece Swiss Muzlin 16 Yds 8.50
1 Doz Towels fine 5.75
1 " Ladies Hdkfs fine 4.50
½ " " " Hemstitch 3.00
20 Yards Linen check 45¢ 9.00
2 prs Childrens Shoes No 2½ at 90¢ 1.80
1 " " " 3 " 90¢ .90
1 Yard Lawn .50
Launchage .60
Commn 2½% .84 $ 35.39
E & O E
Habana April 26/864
C. R. S.
J. W. Dever

Figure 55. Invoice of sundries for Mrs. W. R. Seawell.

Captn. A. M. Godfrey

To J. W. Dever Dr.

	Mrs. W. R. Seawell			
1 piece	Swiss Muzlin 16 Yds.		8.50	
1 Doz	Towels fine		5.75	
1 "	Ladies Hdkfs fine		4.50	
½ "	" " Hemstitch		3.00	
20 Yards	Linen check	45¢	9.00	
2 prs	Children's Shoes No 2½	at 90¢	1.80	
1 "	" " 3	" 90¢	.90	
1 Yard	Lawn		.50	
	Launchage		.60	
	Commn	2½%	.84	$ 35.39

	E&OE			
	Habana April 26 1864			
	(signed) J. W. Dever			

556
Invoice (one of a few written in Spanish)

Comprado a la Flor de la Havana

5 varas	nle de reca	a 8 ??	$?.00
1 pra	cambray ancho	a	4.50
1 pra	escocia de cuantico		3.50
1 Yd	Jacona liso	a	3.75
1 Yd	olan basita ch escocia		10.00
1 Yd	nansis	a	5.00
1	Sna pensas ch seca		4.50
			$ 36.25
	Abril 25 de 1864		
	Rs. Felipe Vegaz ??		

557
Invoice

Note the pencil notations added later to the rather informal invoice providing name of purchaser and translation of "seda" – silk in English.

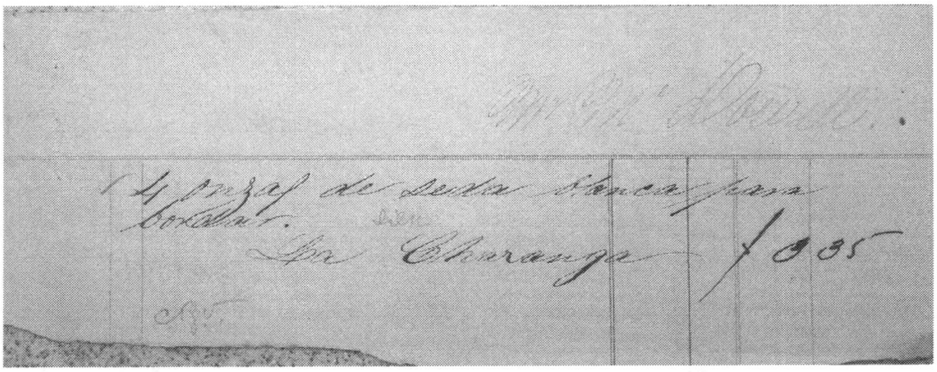

Figure 56. Informal invoice for silk to Mr. McDowell.

Mr. McDowell
4 onzas de seda Blanca para
bondar silk
La Charanga $ 3.35

558
Invoice

Mr. McDowell
To the Ninfas Debt.

11	varas Marsellaise	a 70 cts	7.70
4½	vs. check flannel	a 75 cts	3.37
6½	vs. plain blue flannel	a 75 cts	4.87
			$ 15.94
	Havana 25th of April 1864		
	Ramon Gutierrez Sta Ma		

559
Invoice

Compra ala Sederia la Esquina
3 onzas seda swissa (?) $ 3.37½
Habana Y Abril 26 1864
Rvs. Ramon Victoreo (?) Beule (?)

8 Yards White Flannel $ 4.50
The finest that could be found.
(Penciled translation added to invoice at some time after original writing.)

560
Invoice

Mr. Adams McDowell
a La Diema Debe
Por 4½ vs Olan (?) Calico ??? $ 6.75
Haba. (Habana) Abril 25 1864
(signed) ??????

561
Invoice

Mrs. Adams (then, later added in pencil) N. B. Gause
To the Florida Store

½ doz.	linen Shirts	$ 25.00
½ doz.	linen drawers	9.00
½ doz.	Under Shirts	7.50

		$ 41.50
	Havana April 26 1864	
	Received payment	
	(signed) Vicente A. ????	
2	black hats	5.50
		$ 47.00

562
Invoice

Mr. ????
To the Ninfas Debe
5½ vs. of colored Silk a 1.50 $ 8.25
Havana 25th of April '64
(signed) Rmos. Gutierrez ??? ???

563
Invoice

Mr. D. N. Goodman
To the Ninfas Debt

1	Embroidered Handkerchief		$ 10.00
½ doz.	white linen Handkerchiefs		4.00
2 pairs of	Corsets	a 3 $	6.00
10½ vs. of	plain silk lace	a 1.25	13.14
1 dozen of	Ladies hose	a 9 $	9.00
2 boxes of	hair pins	a 10 cts	.20
			$ 42.34
	Havana 25th of April 1864		
	(signed) Rmos Gutierrez ?? ??		

564
Invoice

Mr. Adams (added in pencil) D. N. G.
A La Diana Debe
Por 4½ vs. Encage imitn. Ynglaterra a 12 sh $ 6.75
Haba. Abril 25 1864
(signed) Knos. Enelles y ????

565
Invoice

Mr. T. McConaughey
To the Florida Store

6	linen Shirts	$ 21.00
½ doz.	handkfs.	3.75
		$ 24.75
	Havana April 24 1864	
	Received payment	
	(signed) Vicente A. ????	
1	**Photographic Album**	$ 5.00

567
Invoice

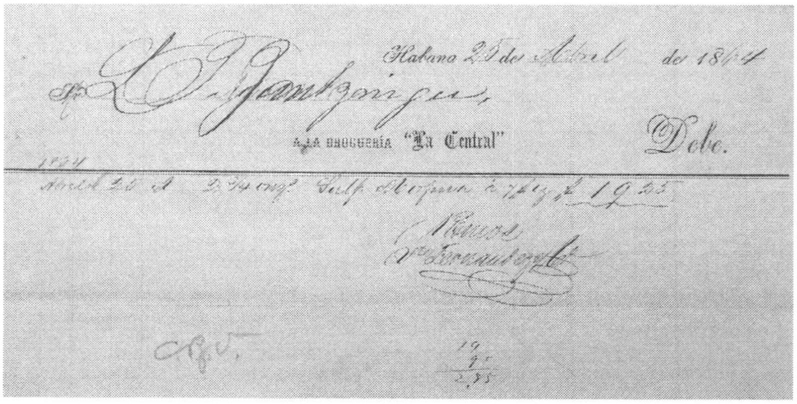

Figure 57. Invoice for morphine.

Sr. L. Zantzinger Habana 25 de Abril de 1864
A La Drogueria "La Central" Debe.
1864
Abril 25 A 2¾ onzs. Sulf. Morfina a 7 $ oz $ 19.25
(signed) Ramos
Vte. Fernandez y Ca.

568
Invoice

Mr. V. T. Mullaney
To the Florida Store

1 pc.	Suiz (Swiss) Muslin		5.50
1 doz.	Socks		3.50

1 doz.	Ladies cotton hose		5.00
26 Yds.	P(rint?) calico	at 22¢	5.72
26 do.	do	20	5.20
2 pcs	White cotton		14.00
2 pairs	ladies Gaitrs.		4.75
2 do	do Miss		4.75
1	ladies corset		2.50
			$ 50.42
	Havana April 24 1864		
	Received payment		
	(signed) Vicente ? ?????		
1	Doz Mustard		$ 4.50
			54.92

569
Invoice

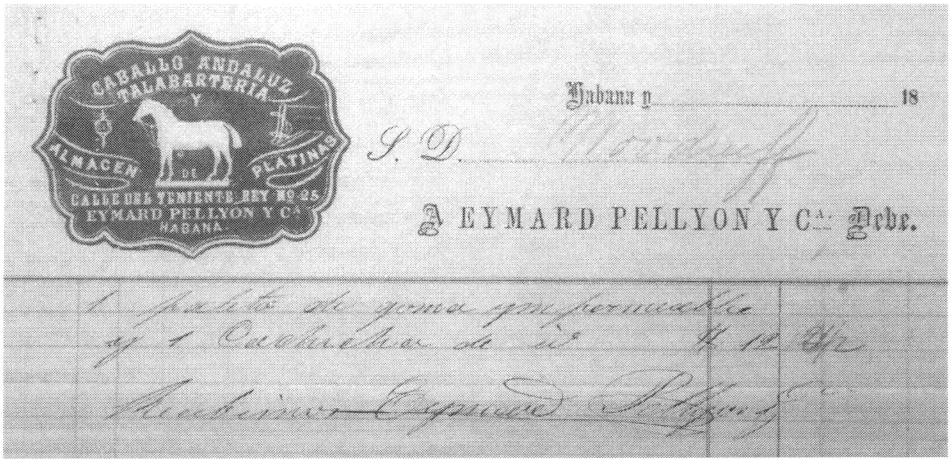

Figure 58. Spanish invoice with interesting letterhead.

Habana

S. D. Woodruff

A Eymard Pellyon Y Ca. Debe.

1 paleta de goma ympermiable y 1 Cachucha de ?? $ 12.12½

Recebimos Eymard Pellyon y Ca.

572

Invoice

Mr. Thomas Henry

A la Flor de la Habana

1	shawl	for	3.00
4 pieces	each 14.14.19. & 8. varas calico	@ 20 cs (cents)	11.00
1	Hoop skirt	for	2.50
26 varas	crape	@ 4 sh (shillings)	13.00
3 pairs	children's hose	for	0.75
10 skeins	black silk	"	1.42
1 piece	domestic	"	7.00
1 do	do	"	7.00
1 dozen	stockings	"	4.50
1 do	Linen handkfs.	"	3.00
1 pair	corsets	"	3.00
	E. & O. E.		$ 56.17
	Habana March 5 1864		
	(signed) RS Felipe Vega y Ca.		

573

Record of Charges

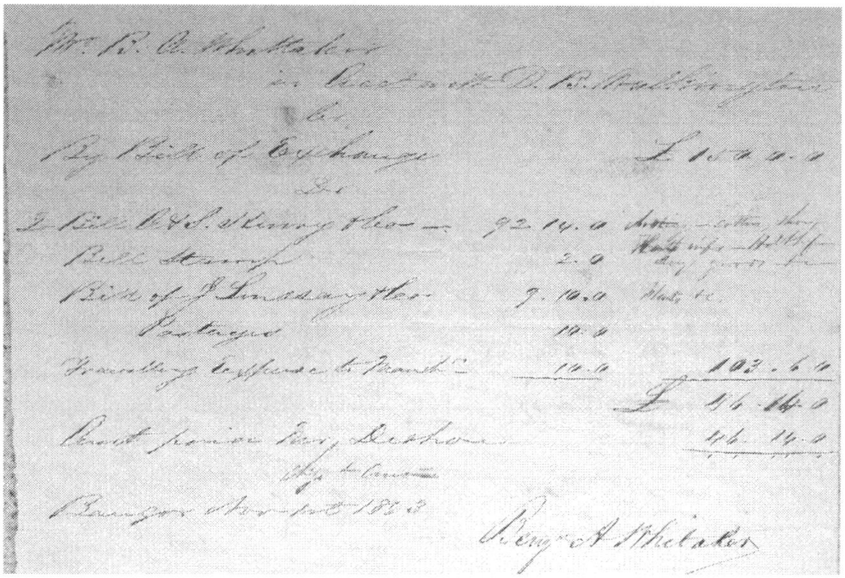

Figure 59. Record of charges by bill of exchange.

Mr. B. A. Whittaker

In Acct. with D. B. Malkington ??

By Bill of Exchange £ 150. 0. 0

Dr

To	Bill A & S Henry & Co.	92. 14. 0	Shirting (?) – cotton, ??? ?? inf – Hd Wrs (?)
	Bill Stenson (?)	2. 0	dry goods &c.
	Bill of J Lindsay & Co	9. 10. 0	Hats &c.
	Postages (?)	10. 0	
	Traveling Expenses to March	10. 0	103. 60
			£ 46. 14. 0
	Acct. ???? Mr. Deshon		46. 14. 0
	Chg & Com		
	Bangor (?) Nov. 1st 1863		
	Benj A. Whitaker		

573
Invoice

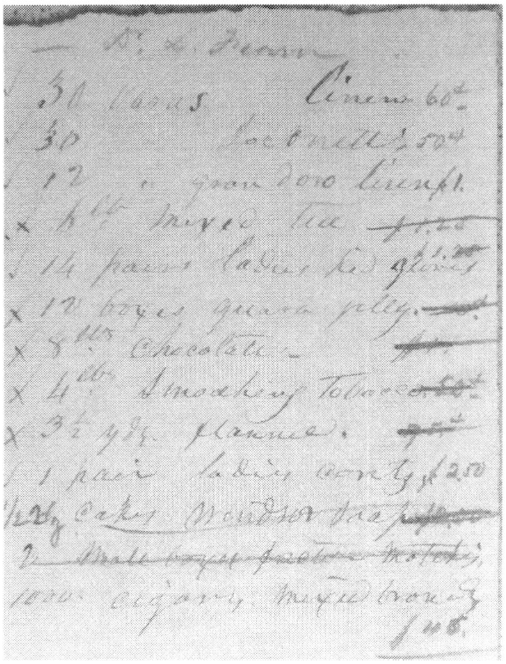

Figure 60. Invoice for sundries to Dr. L. Pearson.

Dr. L. Pearson[68]

30 varas	Linen	60¢
30 "	Joconett	50¢
12 "	gran doro linen	$ 1.00
6 lb	Mixed tea	$ 1.25
14 pairs	ladies Kid gloves	$ 1.25
12 boxes	guaro jelly	50¢
8 lbs	chocolate	$ 1.00 (?)
4 lbs	Smoking tobacco	50¢
3½ yds.	Flannel	75¢
1 pair	ladies corset	$ 2.50
½ dz	cakes Windsor Soap	$ 2.00
2 Small boxes	**friction Matches**	
1000	cigars Mexico bond	
		$ 46.00

575-576
Invoice

Capn. A. M. Godfrey

To J. W. Dever Dr.

	(penciled note added) Preble			
	Geo. R. Suttly			

[68] This invoice difficult to decipher with many strike troughs and informal abbreviations.

30 Yds	blk Silk	1.75	52.50	
22 "	Organdy Muslin	45¢	9.90	
6½ "	" " Swale	.45	2.92	
9 "	Eng barge (?)	40¢	3.60	
1 piece	dimity – 34 Yds.		7.25	
1 dz pr	Stockings No. 8		4.75	
1 " "	" " 9		4.75	
2	Corsets 22 & 21	at 4.00	8.00	
2 dz	fine Hdkfs	at 5.50	11.00	
11 Yds.	Eng. Muzlin	37½	4.12	
1 piece	bright green Ribbon		4.75	
1 "	White " "		4.75	
	Artificial flowers for bonnet		3.00	
2 dz Spools	White thread	1.75	3.50	
1 " papers	Needles		1.50	
	Amt forward		$ 126.29	
	Amt brot. over		$ 126.29	
12½ lbs.	Tea ~~Green~~ & blk	1.25	~~15~~.63	
100 "	Coffee	22¢	22.00	
1 piece	Calico		4.75	
5 Lbs	Green Tea	@ 1.25	6.25	
	Export Launch, cartage &c		2.00	
	Commn 2½%		4.37	$ 181.29
	Coffee	from		22.00
	E & OE			$ 159.29
	Habana April 26th 1864			
	(signed) J. W. Devers			

578
Invoice

Captn. A. M. Godfrey
to J. W. Dever Dr.

	~~Julius Keiser~~ for M. Waring			
22 Varas	black Grenadine	@ 1.00	$ 22.00	
1 Pair	do mits		.75	
1 doz skeins	black silk		2.00	
	Launch		.50	
	Commn 2½%		.60	$ 25.86
	(signed) J. W. Dever			
	(pencil note added) We will			
	pay the duty.			
	H. O. Brewer & Co.			

	by B. D.			
	C. R. V. (added later)			3.90[69]

579
Invoice

To _______

From the Florida Store

41 Yds.	French calico	at 22¢	$ 9.20
1 doz	ladies cotton hose		2.50
1 pc	French muslin		11.00
1 doz.	Spool thread		1.62½
1 pc	of ribbon		4.25
	pins		.50
1000	needles		1.00
			$ 29.89½
	Havana March 4 1864		
	Vicente H. (?) Luace (?)		
3 Pr	child shoes		$ 1.25
1 "	Do.		2.00
1 ?	Tea		1.25
2	**Dolls**		1.00
		paid	

580
Invoice

Peter Mechiovich (?)

3 Blls	Cayna (?)	90 gals @ 25%	24.50
10 Demijohns	Do	$ 2.00	20.00
1 Can	**Kerosene Oil**	5 Gallon	6.25
			$ 50.75
	Green print	3 Blls ???	9.00
20 Doz	pine apples		$ 20.00
			29.00

[69] Penciled notes at bottom were common, perhaps showing the calculation of duty. The faint initials C. R. V. appeared on each one.

581
Invoice

Mr. Baker Havana 7 March /64
La Schiender & Co.

To 135 Galls	Rum	8 Pkges	$ 38.25
18 Demijohns	Gin	@ $ 5.50	63.00
			$ 101.25

582
Invoice

Mr. Skuse[70] Havana 7 Mar
To Schiender & Co.

To 4 Blls	Rum ea 20 gals.	@ $ 8.50	$ 66.00
" 5 Demijohns	Gin	@ 3.50	17.50
" 2 do	Rum	@ 2.50	5.00
			$ 88.50
		has error	32.00
			56.50

583
Invoice

1 Trunk

One piece	Linen	$ 24.00
" "	Do	22.00
1 doz pair	Silk Hose	30.00
1	Cotton do	3.00
1	Ribbon	2.12
3	Corsetts	12.75
7 pair	Slippers & Gaiters	14.50
2 Pr	Kid Gloves	2.50
¼	Silk thread	2.50
One	Mantilla cotton	25.50
4 pr	Shoes	5.50
6 "	Gloves	7.50
2 "	Shoes	8.00
4 "	"	6.00
2 "	"	5.00
1 Doz	Kid Gloves	16.00
		$ 186.87

---

[70] *Denbigh* crewman.

584
Letter of instructions to agent in Mobile from an out of town buyer.

Macon Geo. March 19 – 64

Charles Fonda Esq
Mobile Ala. Dear Sir,

I Telegraphed you today as per Enclosed Copy. Since Landing off the *Dispatch*, I find it is a Trunk instead of a Box, on board the *Denbigh*. I Enclose Copy of the Invoice, Cost of the Country. When you ascertain & pay the Expenses on the Trunk. Please include your Commission and Send Mr. Toby your Check on me for the amt.

Truly yours,
(signed) ???? Scott

585
Invoice

Capt. Gardner

6	Shirts	$ 4 ea.	24.00
7 yds	Blk cloth	$ 5	35.00
13	Linen drill	75¢	9.75
18	Cotton ???	50¢	9.00
1 Doz	Linen Hdfs		6.00 (?)
2 "	Socks	3.50	7.00
1	Vest Pattern	1.50	1.50
1	Silk Hdf	$ 2	2.00
1	" Scarf	$ 5	5.00
1 Doz	Linen Hdfs	$ 10	10.00
4	Dress Patterns	$ 5 ea	20.00
2	Fine Ki??	$ 3.50 ea	7.00
6	silk Neck Ties	50¢ ea	3.00
6	Linen Fancy Shirts	$ 3.00	18.00
1	Trunk	$ 1.50	1.50
2 pr	Shoes	$ 1.75 ea	3.50
1 "	Gaiters	$ 3.50	3.50
2	Calf Skin	$ 3.00 ea	6.00
1	**opium** g (?) Bott.	7.50	7.50
	including chgs & Com		$ 178.25
	$ 26.70 (duty)		

586
Substitute for Preprinted Customs Form

Entry of goods per Str. *Denbigh* – made by G. Balurdo

8	Kegs Rum				
25	Demijohns Rum	240 Gals	. $ 78.00	81	$ 20.25
2½	Cases Gin	2 doz.	5.00	5	1.25
2	Lamp oil	10 Gals.	11.00	11	1.65
1	Box Soap	56 lb	3.50	4	.60
			97.50	101	$ 23.75
	Chgs & Com		3.88		
			$ 101.38		

587
Invoice

Mr. Evans Havana Apl 8 1864
Dbt of J. W. Dever

6 doz.	Pearl Buttons	@ 37½	2.25
1 pr	Swiss Muslin		8.50
2 prs	Corsets	$ 4.25 (?)	8.50
1 pr.	W. Linen 3 35 yds	40¢	14.00
1	**gold pen**		3.50
	2½% Comn.	.92	
	Charges	.50	1.40
			$ 38.15

588-589
Substitute for Preprinted Customs Form

No. 21
Entry of Merchandise
Importer Matt. R Evans
Vessel *Denbigh*
From Havana
Entered April 18, '64
Value $ 39 Duty $ 5.90

Entry made by Matt. R. Evans of goods imported per *Denbigh* from Havana.

Bdle	Cottons	$ 19.25	20	15%	$ 3.00
	Linens	14.00	14	"	2.10
	1 Gold Pen	3.50	4	20	.80
		36.75			5.90
	comm.	1.50			
		$ 38.25			

590-591
Substitute for Preprinted Customs Form

No. 17
Entry of Merchandise
Importer A V Gardner
Vessel *Denbigh*
From Havana
Entered April 18 64
Value $ 178 Duty $ 26.70

Entry of goods made by A. V. Gardner, imported per St. *Denbigh* form Havana. (No. 17, April 18, 64)

1 Trunk	Shoes 3 pairs	$ 18.00	
	Clothing	40.00	
	Wool mfs	40.00	
	Flax "	20.00	
	Cotton	51.00	
		178.00	@ 15% $ 26.70

592-593
Substitute for Preprinted Customs Form

No. 11
Entry of Merchandise
Importer T. St. John
Vessel *Denbigh*
From Havana
Entered April 16 1864
Value $ 107 Duty $ 16.05

Copy of Entry made by T. St. John of goods per Br. St. *Denbigh* from Havana.

T. S. J.	1 Bundle	Wearing apparel	$ 13.50	$ 14		
Dr. F. A. Ross	1 Box	Cottons, Calicoes &c	69.00	72		
C. Westfeldt	1 Bdle	Muslins	20.00	21	@ 15%	$ 16.05
			102.50	107		
		Chgs & Com	4.00			
			106.50			
		(pencil note added)		$ 107	@ 30%	$ 32.10

594-595
Substitute for Preprinted Customs Form

No. 11
Entry of Merchandise
Importer Peter Michiarich
Vessel *Denbigh*
From Havana
Entered March 22 64
Value $ 85 Duty $ 15.90

Entry made by Peter Michiarich (?) of Sundries per Str. *Denbigh* from Havana.

3 Bbls	Rum	90 Gals	$ 24.50	$ 26	@ 25%	$ 6.50
10 Demijohns	Rum	40 "	20.00	21	" "	5.25
1 Can	Kn. (?) Oil	5 "	6.25	7	" 15	1.05
	Green print		29.00	31	" 10	3.10
			79.75			$ 15.90
	Chg & Com		4.50			
			84.25			

596-597
Substitute for Preprinted Customs Form

Note: Since three people paid the duty, one might assume that each of them ordered a part of the merchandise.

No. 1
Entry of Merchandise
Importer J. Robertson
Vessel *Denbigh*
From Havana
Entered March 16 64
Value $ 89 Duty $ 15.00

Entry made by J. Roberson, goods import in Str. *Denbigh*. (No. 1, March 16, 64)

1 Box	**Figs**	$ 1.25	1	20%	$ .20
3 "	Ready made clothing	29.89	31	15	4.65
1 Sack	Sugar 25 lbs	6.00	6	20	1.20
3 Demijohn	Rum 12 Gals	6.00	6	25	1.50
2 Bdle	Calicos	36.00	38	15	5.76
1 Box	Comfits	6.00	7	25	1.75
		85.14			$ 15.00
	Chgs & Com	3.80			
		88.94			
	Robertson	$ 2.25			
	Mr. Gage	5.75			
	Mr. Paraje	7.00			
		15.00			

598-599
Substitute for Preprinted Customs Form

No. 4
Entry of Merchandise
Importer Benj. Whitaker
Vessel *Denbigh*
From Havana
Entered March 16 64
Value $ 510 Duty $ 76.50

Entry of goods per Str. *Denbigh* made by Benj. A. Whitaker, March 16, '64.

Box	Clothing	$ 252.50	263	15%	
	Shoes	52.75	55	"	
	Cotton mfs	102.77	107	"	
	Flax mfs	64.00	66	"	
	Stats	17.95	19	"	
		489.97	510	"	$ 76.50
		19.56			
		509.53			

600-601
Substitute for Preprinted Customs Form

No. 9
Entry of Merchandise
Importer T. Henry & Co.
Vessel *Denbigh*
From Havana
Entered March 18 1864
Value $ 59 Duty $ 8.85

Entry of Merchandise made by T. Henry & Co. Per Str. *Denbigh* form Havana.

1 Trunk	Cotton mfs	$ 39.75	41		
	Silk "	17.42	18		
		57.17	59	15%	$ 8.85
	Chgs & Com	2.28			
		59.45			

602-603
Substitute for Preprinted Customs Form

No. 10
Entry of Merchandise

Importer R. L. Fiarn
Vessel *Denbigh*
From Havana
Entered March 19 1864
Value $ 104 Duty $ 19.60

Duplicate Entry of goods per Str. *Denbigh* imported by R. L. Fiarn (?).

Trunk	Flax mfs	$ 30	15%	4.50
	Cotton "	20	"	3.00
	Gloves "	14	"	2.10
	Sigars	40	25%	10.00
		$ 104		$ 19.60

604-605
Substitute for Preprinted Customs Form

No. 7
Entry of Merchandise
Importer A Baker
Vessel *Denbigh*
From Havana
Entered March 18 1864
Value $ 164 Duty $ 41

Entry made by Alfred Baker of Spirits per *Denbigh* from Havana.

Baker	12 Kegs & Bbls	Rum	$ 72.25	75		
by	23 Demijohns	Gin	80.50	84		
Skuse	2 "	Rum	5.00	5		
			157.75	164	25%	$ 41.00
			6.28			
			164.03			

606-607
Substitute for Preprinted Customs Form

No. 5
Entry of Merchandise
Importer R. S. Bunker
Vessel *Denbigh*
From Havana
Entered March 18 64
Value $ 99 Duty $ 17.45

Entry made by R. S. Bunker of goods per *Denbigh* from Havana.

R.S.B.	1 Box	Clothing	$ 57.25	$ 60	@ 15%	$ 9.00

Martin	1 "	Shirts	12.00	13	"	1.95
		Sigars	25.00	26	25	6.50
			94.25			$ 17.45
		Chg & Com	4.50			
			98.75			

608-609
Substitute for Preprinted Customs Form

No. 6
Entry of Merchandise
Importer James Scott
Vessel *Denbigh*
From Havana
Entered March 18 64
Value $ 194 Duty $ 29.10

Entry made by James Scott of Merchandise per Str. *Denbigh* from Havana.

1 Trunk	Flax mfs		$ 46.00	$ 48	15%	
	Cotton "		43.75	45		
	Silk "		24.00	25		
	Shoes	15 prs	38.50	40		
			186.87	194	15%	$ 29.10
	Chgs & Com		7.44			
			194.31			

611-612
Substitute for Preprinted Customs Form

No. 26
Entry of Merchandise
Importer Jms Ashby
Vessel *Denbigh*
From Havana
Entered May 3 64
Value $ 83 Duty $ 12.45

Entry of Merchandise imported by Jms. Ashby on board Str. *Denbigh* from Havana.

1 Pkg.	Clothing	$ 26.00	$ 27		
	Flax mfs	28.22	30		
	Cotton "	16.00	17		
	Shoes "	9.00	9		
	chags & Com	4.20	83	15%	$ 12.45
		83.42			

613
Invoice

Copy
Jms. Ashby, Invoice

1 Pce	Linen 32 yds		$ 10.00
29 Yards	organdie	35¢	10.15
60 "	Muslins	23¢	13.80
10 Yds	Linen	60¢	6.00
	Cotton thread &c		12.12
2 doz pr	Stockings		10.00
	shoes 6 prs		11.00
			$ 73.17
1	lot Linen	$ 10	10.00
			$ 83.17

614-615
Substitute for Preprinted Customs Form

No. 27
Entry of Merchandise
Importer W Waring
Vessel *Denbigh*
From Havana
Entered May 3 64
Value $ 26 Duty $ 3.90

Entry of Merchandise by M. Waring per *Denbigh* 30 April, ent. 2nd May, 64.
Wearing apparel $ 25.86 $ 26.00 15% $ 3.90

616-617
Substitute for Preprinted Customs Form

No. 24
Entry of Merchandise
Importer T. M. LeBarron
Vessel *Denbigh*
From Havana
Entered May 3 1864

Entry of Merchandise made by T. M. LeBarron (?) pr Str. *Denbigh*, Godfrey, from Havana, arrived 30 Apl

T.L.B.	1 Cas(e)	Cotton mfs.	$ 24.00	26		

		Wool "	39.00	39		
		Flax "	17.00	18		
		Shoes	15.00	17		
			92.50	100	15%	$ 15.00
		Chgs & Com	7.00			
			$ 99.50			

618-619
Substitute for Preprinted Customs Form

No. 25
Entry of Merchandise
Importer G. R. Tuttle
Vessel *Denbigh*
From Havana
Entered May 3   64
Value $ 159   Duty $ 22.70

Entry of Merchandise imported by G. R. Tuttle by Str. *Denbigh* from Havana.

1 Trunk Contg.					
	Tea 17 lbs	$21.88	23	10 (%)	$ 2.10
	Cotton mfs	69.04		15	10.80
		62.00			9.60
		6.37			22.70
		159.29			

620-621
Substitute for Preprinted Customs Form

No. 18
Entry of Merchandise
Importer Tho T. A. Lyon
Vessel *Denbigh*
From Havana
Entered May 3 1864
Value $ 21   Duty $ 3.15

Entry of Merchandise imported by T. T. A. Lyon per Str. *Denbigh* from Havana.
1 PKg   Cottons   with Chgs & Com 1.50 $ 20.64
Cotton mfs $ 21   15(%) $ 3.15

622
Invoice

Captn A. M. Godfrey To J. W. Dever Dr.

	T. P. Lyon			
200 lbs.	Coffee	22¢	44.00	21¢
1 piece	Eng. Calico pink		4.20	
1 "	" " purple		4.20	
5 doz	Cakes Windsor Soap	1.62½	8.91	
	Export duty, Launchage, cartage &c		1.80	
	Commn 2½%		1.53	$ 64.64
	E&OE.			
	Habana April 26, 1864			
	(signed) J. W. Dever			

623-624
Substitute for Preprinted Customs Form

No. 19
Entry of Merchandise
Importer W. B. Seawell
Vessel *Denbigh*
From Havana
Entered May 3 1864
Value $ 35 Duty $ 5.25

Entry of Merchandise imported by W. B. Seawell in the Str. *Denbigh* from Havana.

1 Pkge	Cotton prints	31.25	$ 32		
	Shoes 3 prs	2.70	3		
	Chr & Comm	1.44	35	@ 15%	$ 5.25
		35.39			

625-626
Substitute for Preprinted Customs Form

No. 20
Entry of Merchandise
Importer N. J. Delano
Vessel *Denbigh*
From Havana
Entered May 3 1864
Value $ 108 Duty $ 15.95

Entry of Merchandise imported by N. J. Delano pr. St. *Denbigh* from Harvard.

2 Boxes contg.					
	Writing paper	$ 25.00	$ 26	15%	$ 3.90

	Hats	15.00	15		2.25
	Stationary	15.25	16		2.40
	Tea 3 lbs	4.50	5	10 (%)	.50
	Cutlery	18.00	19	15 (%)	2.85
	Pins	17.26	18		2.10
	Files	9.00	9		1.35
	Chgs & Com 3.80 & .36	4.16	108		$ 15.95
		108.17			

627-628
Substitute for Preprinted Customs Form

No. 21
Entry of Merchandise
Importer G. G. Garner
Vessel *Denbigh*
From Havana
Entered May 3 1864
Value $ 54 Duty $ 7.70

Entry of Merchandise imported by Geo. G. Garner in the Br. St. *Denbigh* from Havana.

Indigo 4 lbs	$ 4.00	4	@ 5%	$ .20
Macaroni	6.75	7	15 (%)	1.05
Mackerel	17.50	19		2.85
Mustard	14.00	15		2.25
Soap 60 lbs	7.50	9		1.35
	49.75	53		7.70
	4.10			
	53.85			

629-630
Substitute for Preprinted Customs Form

No. 22
Entry of Merchandise
Importer Bal. Tardy
Vessel *Denbigh*
From Havana
Entered May 3 64
Value $ 191 Duty $ 28.65

Entry of Merchandise imported by W. B. Hamilton on board Str. *Denbigh* from Havana 30 Apl 64.

1 PKg.	Silk diaper	$ 122.00	127		
	Shoes 19 pr	40.87	42		
	Cottons	21.00	22		

	Chgs & Com	7.32	191	15%	$ 28.65
		191.19			

631
Invoice

Captn. A. M. Godfrey

To J. W. Dever Dr.

	Mrs. St. John			
2 Pieces	Russia diaper 60 yds	@45¢	$ 27.00	
2	Corsets	" $ 4	8.00	
3	Black belts	" 1.25	3.75	
1	White do		1.25	
1 Doz	Cakes toilet soap		1.75	
1 Gr(oss)	shoe strings		.60	
2 Lbs	Green Tea	@ 1.25	2.50	
	Launch		.50	
	Commn 2½%		1.12	$ 46.47
	E&OE			
	Habana April 26th /64			
(duty)	$ 6.75 (signed) J. W. Dever			

633-634
Substitute for Preprinted Customs Form

No. 23
Entry of Merchandise
Importer Tho St. John
Vessel *Denbigh*
From Havana
Entered May 3 1864
Value $ 47 Duty $ 6.90

Entry of Merchandize imported by T. St. John on board Str. *Denbigh* from Havana.

1 PKge					
	Tea 2 lbs	$ 2.50	3	10%	$ .30
	Wearing apparel	42.35	44	15 (%)	6.60
	Chges & Com	1.62			$ 6.90
		46.47			

635
Invoice

Memorandum of Cloths shipped by C. S. Ramsay to Mr. W. B. Hamilton per Steamer "*Denbigh*" for Mobile.

???				
W. B. Hamilton	1	Package Contg		
from C. S. Ry.	2	Fancy Silk dressed 36 varas	1.52	54.00
	1	Black Silk Dress 12 "	2 $	24.00
	2	Fancy summer dresses 44 "	1 $	44.00
	6 Pairs	shoes		19.50
	7 "	Kid gloves	2 $	14.00
	6 "	" "	1.20	7.20
	2 Pieces	Swiss Muslin	7.12	15.00
		For sundry trimmings		6.87
				$ 184.57
	1	little package with 2 Pair gloves black		2.50
				$ 187.07
		Havana April 26, 1864		4.12
Including charges				$ 191.19
& Comm		C. G. Ramsay		

636
Invoice

Invoice of Sundries shipped by Rafael Perez Sta Ma on board of the British Str *Denbigh* Godfrey master bound to Matamoros by order for account and risk and consigned to Major Ths M. Le Baron.[71]

Maj Ths le B		1 case cont'g			$ 1.00
	6/4 tin cans	French sardines			~~1.31½~~
	2 cardboard	prunes of 2 lbs each			~~1.75~~
	6 boxes	guava jelly			~~1.50~~
	1 box	vermicelli			3.50
	1 doz	silk Hose			13.00
	1 do	cotton do			5.00
	2¼ varas	black cloth	@ $ 5		11.25
	3	yds cassimere	@ " 2		6.00
	1	pattern silk vest		$ 2.25	
	1½ vara	black serge		1.87½	
	1½ do	moare		1.12½	
	2½ do	lustrina		.62½	
	1 do	Entretela (interlining)		.50	
	12	buttons		.37½	6.75
	14 yds	black alpaca	@ $ 1½		15.75
	30 do	calico	@ 20¢ yd		6.00

[71] Maj. Thomas M. Le Baron began the war as quartermaster of the 33rd Mississippi Infantry Regiment moving up to the same post in his brigade. Clearly this was an order for his family. The 1860 Mobile City Directory recorded him as a resident. See also the Le Baron and Son receipt for investment in the runner *Phoenix* shown in the introduction to this volume.

	6 pairs	Ladies Gaiters	@ 2½ $		15.00
	½ doz	bottles Cologne water			6.00
	2	Quinon Loteriae de cartones			4.25
					$ 98.06½
		Charges			
		Shipping expenses & boat hire			2.00
		???????			$ 100.06½
		Havana 26 April 1864			
		Rafael Perez Sta Ma			

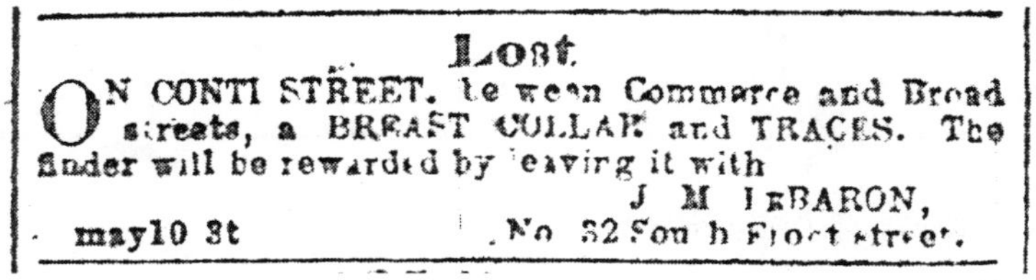
Lost.
ON CONTI STREET, between Commerce and Broad streets, a BREAST COLLAR and TRACES. The finder will be rewarded by leaving it with
J M LEBARON,
may10 3t No 32 South Front street.

Figure 61. *Mobile Register* newspaper ad (11 May 1864) placed by J. M. Le Baron, likely a relative of Maj. Le Baron mentioned in the above invoice.

637-640
Preprinted Customs Form

No. 27
Entry of Merchandise
Importer H O Brewer & Co
Vessel *Denbigh*
From Havana
Entered May 4 1864
Value $ 2763 Duty $ 420.60

Agent's Oath
(signed) Benj Donaldson
Sworn before me 4 day of May 1864

Mdse. Entered 4 May 1864 Ship Entered 30 April 1864
Entry of Merchandise imported into the Port of Mobile, District of Mobile, by H. O. Brewer & Co. in the Br. Str. *Denbigh*, Godfrey Master, from Havana.

Marks	No. of Packages	Contents	Quantity	Value in Foreign Currency	10	15	20	Duties
B	10 Cases	Cotton Cards	50 doz	$ 635.00		658		
	2 "	Quinine	100 oz	200.00		210		
	30 Coils	Rope	3100 lbs	310.00		327		
	6 cases	Cotton mfs		240.00		253		
		Shoes	720 prs	730.00		769		
		Ker. Oil	100 Gals	98.50		103		
	5 Cases	Candles	250 lbs	67.50		71		

	5 Boxes	Cod fish	1000 lbs	90.00		94		
	10 demijn	Honey	50 Gals	30.00		32		
	1 Box	Matches		37.50		39		$ 391.20
	6 Blls	Sugar	1192 lbs	92.18			97	
	4 Boxes	Pickles		40.00			42	27.80
	6 Bales	Oakum	300 lbs	15.00	16			1.60
		Shoes thread		48.75		52		$ 420.60
				2624.43	16	2608	139	
		Shippg Chags	& Com	138.42				
				2762.85				

641-642
Preprinted Customs Form

No. 10
Entry of Merchandise
Importer Flash Hartwell & Co
Vessel *Mary*
From Havana
Entered May 3 1864
Value $ 395 Duty $ 70.95

Owner's Oath
(signed) Wm Hartwell

Mdse. Entered May 3d 1864 Ship Entered 30 April 1864
Entry of Merchandise imported into the Port of Mobile, District of Mobile, by Flash Hartwell & Co in the Br. Str. *Mary* (error ?), ______ Master, from Havana.

No. of Packages	Contents	Quantity	Value in Foreign Currency	15%	20%	Duties
50 Kits	Mackerel		$ 100.00	104		$ 15.60
10 Boxes	Codfish		30.00	31		4.65
1 Box	Files (Saw)		25.00	26		3.90
1 Can	Camphor Refined	lbs 250 @ 90¢	250.00		234	46.80
			380.00	161	234	$ 70.95
	Chgs & Com		15.20			
			395.20			

643-644
Preprinted Customs Form

No. 35
Entry of Merchandise
Importer W. A. Smith
Vessel *Denbigh*
From Havana
Entered May 19 1864
Value $ 68 Duty $ 10.20

Owner's Oath
(signed) W. A. Smith
Sworn before me 19 day of May 1864

Mdse. Entered 19 May 1864 Ship Entered 18 May 1864
Entry of Merchandise imported into the Port of Mobile, District of Mobile, by W. A. Smith in the Br. Str. *Denbigh*, Godfrey Master, from Havana.

No. of Packages	Contents	Quantity	Value in Foreign Currency	15%	Duties
1 Pkge	Wearing apparel		$ 45.48	47	$ 7.05
	Shoes	4 pairs	8.00	8	1.20
1 Bdle	Iron mfs		12.00	13	1.95
			65.48	68	10.20
	Chgs & Com		2.60		
			68.08		

645a
Invoice

Note discrepancy in adding up totals.

Bot. for Mrs. Wm. A. Smith.

2 ps.	Blk. Braw.	$ 2	4.00
10 Varas	" Alpaca	.50	5.00
12 Varas	Linen Lawn	3/-	4.50
1 ps	cross boad (?) Nansook		5.50
16 Varas	Dark Cold. Linen	50¢	8.00
18 "	Checkd Linen	31¢	5.58
1 Doz	stockings		5.00
2 "	Spool Thread asstd. (assorted)	1.62½	3.25
1 " Skn. (Skein)	Sewing Silk		2.40
9 Varas	Cambric		2.25
2 pr.	Gaiters	@ $ 2.75	5.50
2 "	Slippers	10/-	2.50
	Cab & Porterage		2.00
			55.48

	Havana May 13th 1864		
4	**Scythe Blades**	$ 3.00	12.00
			67.48
	C.R.V.		3.35
			10.05
			16.30

645b
Invoice
Denbigh

No	????		
4	Chil.(drens) Shoes	$ 1	4.00
4	Ladies Do	$ 1	4.00
80 yds	Cotton Shirts	30¢	24.00
32 yds	Do Do	35¢	11.20
1 "	M. Kellie g (?)	$ 10	10.00
18 yds	Muslin	75¢	13.50
1 Doz	Hdfs	$ 3	3.00
56 yds	Calico	25¢	14.00
			83.70
	with all chgs		

648-649
Preprinted Customs Form

No. 30
Entry of Merchandise
Importer H. O. Brewer & Co
Vessel *Denbigh*
From Havana
Entered May 4 1864
Value $ 1070 Duty $ 160.50

Agent's Oath
(signed) Benj Donaldson

Mdse. Entered 4 May 1864 Ship Entered 30 April 1864
Entry of Merchandise imported into the Port of Mobile, District of Mobile, by __________ in the Br. Str. *Denbigh* Godfrey Master, from Havana.

Marks	No. of Packages	Contents	Quantity	Value in Foreign Currency		15%	Duties
G.	1 Box	Hats		$ 144.00		150	
		Quinine	113 oz.	226.00		240	

		Cotton Cards	40 doz	500.00		527	
		Calf Skins	4 "	140.00		149	
				1010.00		$ 1070	15% $ 160.50
		Chgs & Com		59.65			
				$ 1069.65	$ 1070		

651-652
Preprinted Customs Form

No. 32
Entry of Merchandise
Importer A. Luis
Vessel *Denbigh*
From Havana
Entered May 4 64
Value $ 84 Duty $ 12.60

Owner's Oath
(signed) A. Luis

Mdse. Entered May 4 1864 Ship Entered April 30 1864
Entry of Merchandise imported into the Port of Mobile, District of Mobile, by A. Luis in the Br. Str. *Denbigh*, Master, from Havana.

Marks	No. of Packages	Contents	Quantity	Value in Foreign Currency			Duties
Mrs. Luis	one PKge	Shoes	pr 8	$ 8.00	10		
		Cottons		71.70	74		
		Chgs & Com		4.00	$ 84	@ 15%	$ 12.60
				83.70			

655-656
Preprinted Customs Form

No. 31
Entry of Merchandise
Importer J. W. G. Innerarity
Vessel *Denbigh*
From Havana
Entered May 4 '64
Value $ 532 Duty $ 82.50

Owner's Oath
(signed) J. W. G. Innerarity

Entry of Merchandise, Ship Entered April 30
Imported into the Port and District of Mobile, by J. W. G. Innerarity in the Br. St. *Denbigh* Godfrey
Master, from Havana

Columns to be Filled by the Importer. Appraised Value, Subject to Duty at the Rate of

Packages	Packages and Contents	Quantities	In Foreign Currency Invoice Cost	10	15	20	Amount of Duty
6 Boxes	Flax mfs.		$ 226.10		245		$ 36.75
	Cotton mfs		127.35		137		20.55
	Writing paper & stationery		22.60		24		3.60
	~~Spirits, soap &c~~ Ker. Oil	20 Gals	16.25		18		2.70
	Tea	10 lbs	25.00	27			2.70
1 Box	Sugar (white)	282 lbs	36.02			39	7.80
	Soap (French, &c Toilet)		38.50			42	8.40
			491.82	27	424	81	$ 82.50
	Shippg Chgs &c 14.72						
	Comm @ 5% 25.30		40.02				
			$ 531.84				

657
Invoice

Invoice of Sundries shipped by J. W. Devers on board the Steamship *Denbigh*, for acct of Said ship. (This wording implied trade on behalf of the ship's owner's, and a very substantial shipment it was. Perhaps these goods were to be offered to retail stores. It seemed too complicated to sell item by item to the public.)

50 Doz	Cotton Cards	@ 12.50	625.00	
100 ozs	Quinine	" 2 $	200.00	
30 Coils	**Rope 3100 lbs**	" 10¢	310.00	
20 pcs	Bleached Muslin	" 7 $	140.00	
50 doz	Women's shoes	" 13 $	650.00	
20 Cans	Kerosene Oil 100 Gals	" 75¢	75.00	
10 dz	bluchers Copper Tap shoes	" 8 $	80.00	
4 Sks (Sacks)	Coffee 698 lbs	" 21¢	146.58	
1000 lbs	Codfish	" 9¢	90.00	
10 Demijohns	Honey	" 3 $	30.00	
1 Bx (Box) 50 Gro	Matches	" 75¢	37.50	
10 Cases	Spool Cotton 200 dz	@ 50¢	100.00	
3 Bbls	White Sugar 583 lbs	" 8½¢	49.55	
3 "	Brown " 609 "	" 7¢	42.63	
10 Bxs	astd Pickles	" 4 $	40.00	
5 "	Olive Oil	" 4.70	23.50	
10 "	Candles 250 lbs	" 27¢	67.50	
4 Bbls	Pork	" 20 $	84.00	
65 Pkgs	White Shoe Thread	" 75¢	48.75	
6	Bales Oakum 300 lbs	" 5¢	15.00	$ 2855.01
	Charges			

	Launchage		50.00	
	Export Duty		28.55	
	Comms 2½%		71.37	149.92
				$ 3004.93
	E & E			
	Havana April 26th 1864			

660a and b
Accounting notes by H. O. Brewer & Co.

Note: These scraps of paper provided a nice behind the scenes look at the mechanics of the trade. There was a hint that Capt. **Godfrey was trading on his own account.**

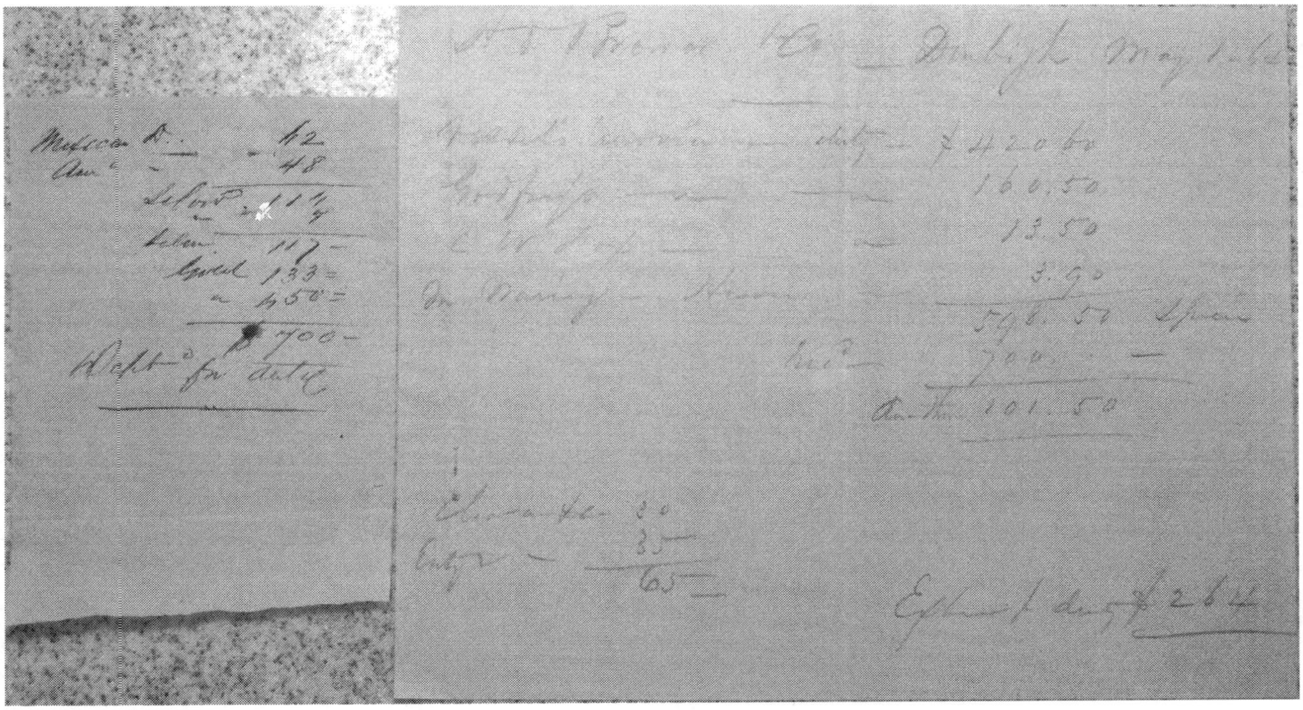

Figure 62. Accounting notes of H. O. Brewer & Co.

(left)

Mexican D(ollar)	62
Am. "	48
below	110
"	7
below	117
Gold	133 =
a	450 =
Deb to for date	700

(right)
H. O. Brewer & Co. *Denbigh* May 1, 64

Vessel invoice (ship owner's account)	duty	$ 420.60	
Godfrey's invoice (trade on his own account)	"	160.50	
C. W. Fox	"	13.50	
Mr. Waring – Hesser (?)	"	3.90	
		598.50	Specie
	Gold	700.00	
	(?)	101.50	
Char &c. 30			
Entry 35			
65			
Export & duty	$ 264		

661
Invoice

Invoice Sundries shipped by J. W. Devers per Steamship *Denbigh* for sale acct of A. M. Godfrey.

4 Doz	Soft Hats	36 $	144.00	
13 oz	French Quinine	2 $	26.00	
100 "	Pelletier Do[72]	2 $	200.00	
6¼ Casks	Alcohol 188 Gs	66¢	118.18	
40 Doz	Cotton Cards	12.50	500.00	
4 "	Calfskins	35 $	140.00	
10 Casks	Brandy	15 $	150.00	
				$ 1278.18
	Charges			
	Launch Hire		24.00	
	Export Duty		18.00	
	Comms 2½%		30.95	
				73.95
				$ 1352.13
	Less alcohol 118.18			
	Brandy 150.00			
	268.18			
	Havana April 26th 1864			

---

[72] Quinine was isolated in 1820 by the French chemists J. B. Caventou and P. J. Pelletier.

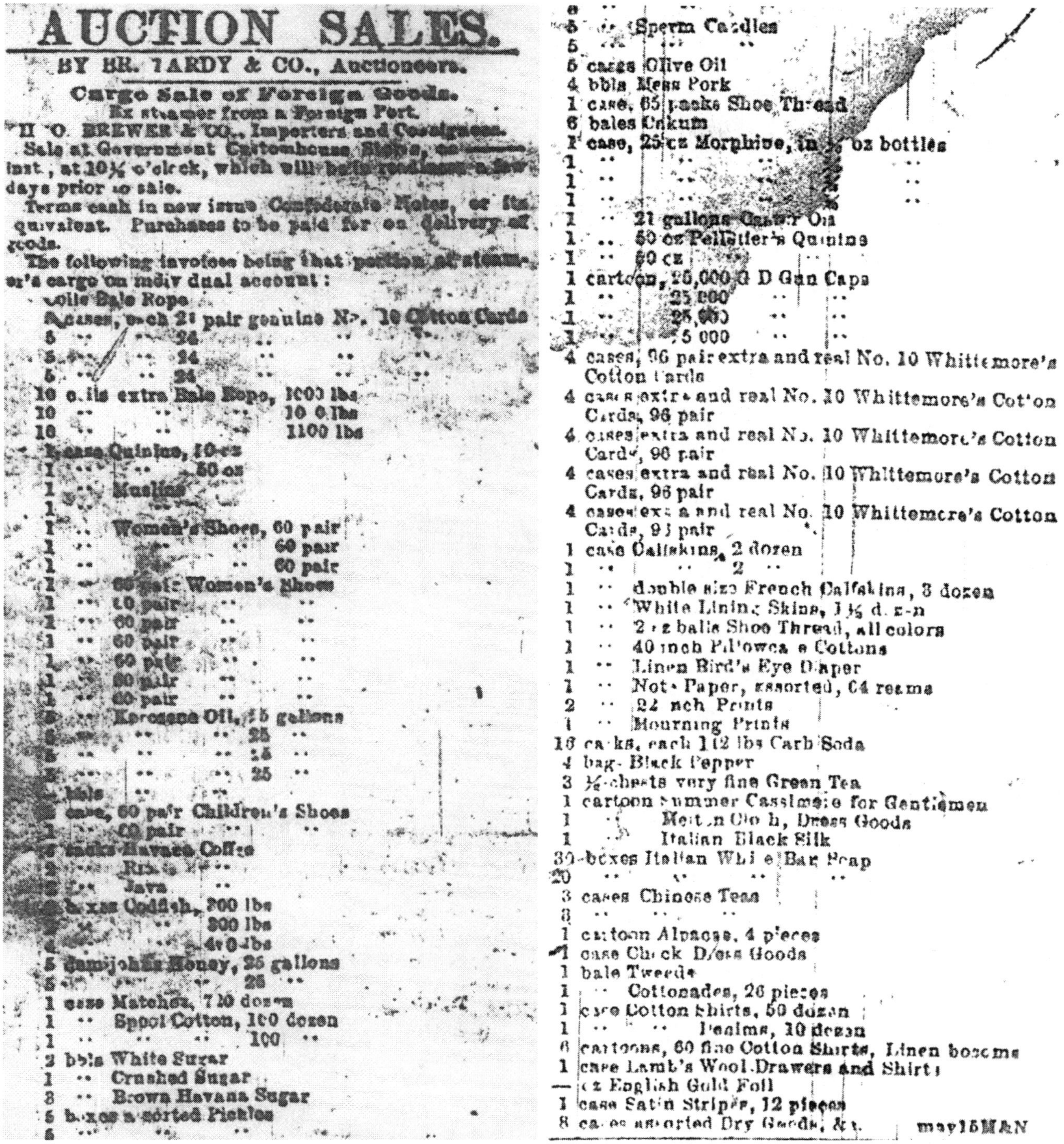

AUCTION SALES.

BY BR. TARDY & CO., Auctioneers.

Cargo Sale of Foreign Goods.

Ex steamer from a Foreign Port.

H. O. BREWER & CO., Importers and Consignees.

Sale at Government Customhouse Stores, on ... inst., at 10½ o'clock, which will be ... a few days prior to sale.

Terms cash in new issue Confederate Notes, or its equivalent. Purchases to be paid for on delivery of goods.

The following invoices being that portion of steamer's cargo on individual account:

- ... coils Bale Rope
- ... cases, each 24 pair genuine No. 10 Cotton Cards
- 5 .. 24 .. ..
- 5 .. 24 .. ..
- 5 .. 24 .. ..
- 10 coils extra Bale Rope, 1000 lbs
- 10 .. .. 1000 lbs
- 10 .. .. 1100 lbs
- 1 case Quinine, 10 oz
- 1 .. .. 50 oz
- 1 .. Muslins
- 1 ..
- 1 .. Women's Shoes, 60 pair
- 1 .. 60 pair
- 1 .. 60 pair
- 1 .. 60 pair Women's Shoes
- 1 .. 60 pair ..
- 1 .. 60 pair ..
- 1 .. 60 pair ..
- 1 .. 60 pair ..
- 1 .. 60 pair ..
- 1 .. 60 pair
- ... Kerosene Oil, 25 gallons
- ... . 25 ..
- ... . 25 ..
- ... . 25 ..
- ... bbls ..
- ... case, 60 pair Children's Shoes
- 1 .. 60 pair .. ..
- ... sacks Havana Coffee
- 2 .. Rio ..
- 2 .. Java ..
- ... boxes Codfish, 300 lbs
- ... .. 300 lbs
- ... .. 400 lbs
- 5 Demijohns Honey, 25 gallons
- 5 .. .. 25 ..
- 1 case Matches, 720 dozen
- 1 .. Spool Cotton, 100 dozen
- 1 .. .. 100 ..
- 2 bbls White Sugar
- 1 .. Crushed Sugar
- 3 .. Brown Havana Sugar
- 5 boxes assorted Pickles
- 5 .. ..
- 5 .. Sperm Candles
- 5 .. ..
- 5 cases Olive Oil
- 4 bbls Mess Pork
- 1 case, 65 packs Shoe Thread
- 6 bales Oakum
- 1 case, 25 oz Morphine, in ½ oz bottles
- 1 .. .. ..
- 1 .. .. ..
- 1 .. .. ..
- 1 .. 21 gallons Castor Oil
- 1 .. 50 oz Pelletier's Quinine
- 1 .. 50 oz ..
- 1 cartoon, 25,000 G D Gun Caps
- 1 .. 25,000 .. ..
- 1 .. 25,000 .. ..
- 1 .. 25,000 .. ..
- 4 cases, 96 pair extra and real No. 10 Whittemore's Cotton Cards
- 4 cases extra and real No. 10 Whittemore's Cotton Cards, 96 pair
- 4 cases extra and real No. 10 Whittemore's Cotton Cards, 96 pair
- 4 cases extra and real No. 10 Whittemore's Cotton Cards, 96 pair
- 4 cases extra and real No. 10 Whittemore's Cotton Cards, 96 pair
- 1 case Calfskins, 2 dozen
- 1 .. .. 2 ..
- 1 .. double size French Calfskins, 3 dozen
- 1 .. White Lining Skins, 1½ dozen
- 1 .. 2 oz balls Shoe Thread, all colors
- 1 .. 40 inch Pillowcase Cottons
- 1 .. Linen Bird's Eye Diaper
- 1 .. Note Paper, assorted, 64 reams
- 2 .. 22 inch Prints
- 1 .. Mourning Prints
- 16 casks, each 112 lbs Carb Soda
- 4 bags Black Pepper
- 3 ½ chests very fine Green Tea
- 1 cartoon Summer Cassimere for Gentlemen
- 1 .. Melton Cloth, Dress Goods
- 1 .. Italian Black Silk
- 30 boxes Italian White Bar Soap
- 20 .. ..
- 3 cases Chinese Teas
- 3 .. .. ..
- 1 cartoon Alpacas, 4 pieces
- 1 case Check Dress Goods
- 1 bale Tweeds
- 1 .. Cottonades, 26 pieces
- 1 case Cotton Shirts, 50 dozen
- 1 .. .. Pealms, 10 dozen
- 6 cartoons, 60 fine Cotton Shirts, Linen bosoms
- 1 case Lamb's Wool Drawers and Shirts
- — 1 case English Gold Foil
- 1 case Satin Stripes, 12 pieces
- 8 cases assorted Dry Goods, &c.

may15MAN

Figure 63. Items and quantities in this sale ad can be matched to the manifests above. See for instance three lots totaling 3100 lbs. of bale rope and four lots totaling 100,000 percussion caps for guns (*Mobile Advertiser and Register* May 21, 1864).

662-663
Preprinted Customs Form

No. 28
Entry of Merchandise
Importer C. W. Fox
Vessel *Denbigh*
From Havana
Entered May 3 1864
Value $ 90 Duty $ 13.50

Mdse. Entered 3d May 1864 Ship Entered _______
Entry of Merchandise imported into the Port of Mobile, District of Mobile, by C. W. Fox in the Br. Str. *Denbigh* ________ Master, from Havana

Marks	No. of Packages	Contents	Value in Foreign Currency	15%		Duty
C. W. Fox	1 Box	Boots & shoes 2 prs	$ 25.50	27		
		Wool mfs	25.00	26		
		Wearing appl (apparel)	36.62	37		
			87.12	$ 90	15%	$ 13.50
		Chges Comm	2.80			
			$ 89.92			

Denbigh Customs Manifests, May 1864 2 of 2, Transcripts

665-666
Preprinted Customs Form

No. 34
Entry of Merchandise
Importer Richd. H. Redwood
Vessel *Denbigh*
From Havana
Entered May 20 1864
Value $ 82 Duty $ 12.15

Owner's Oath
(signed) Richd. H. Redwood

Mdse. Entered ______ 18__ Ship Entered 18 May 1864
Entry of Merchandise imported into the Port of Mobile, District of Mobile, by Richd H. Redwood in the Br. Str. *Denbigh* Godfrey Master, from Havana

No. of Packages	Contents	Quantity	Value in Foreign Currency	10%	15%	Duties
18 Pkgs	Linen & Flax mfs		$ 21.50		22	$ 3.30
	Cotton mfs		49.80		53	7.95
	Shoes	4 prs	3.60		4	.60
	Tea	2 lbs	2.50	3		.30
			77.40	3	79	$ 12.15
	Chgs & Com		4.26			
			$ 81.66			

667
Invoice

Captn. A. M. Godfrey

To J. W. Dever Dr.

½ pcs	Linen Shirting	19 Yds	6.75	
1 "	Blea(ched) Cotton	48 "	7.25	
1 "	heavy " "	28 "	7.25	
1 "	Linen Sheeting	35 "	9.50	
1 "	English Calico	30 "	6.50	
12 Varas	" "		2.70	

12 Yds	**Mosquito Netting**	87½¢	10.50	
2 Dozen	Spools Cotton	1.75	3.50	
2	Silk Handkfs	75	1.50	
6	Linen tape ?? Do		2.75	
6 Pairs	Lady's Cotton Hose		2.10	
4 "	½ "		1.00	
4 Skeins	Silk		1.00	
2	Muslin Dresses		9.00	
4 Pairs	Children's Shoes	90	3.60	
150 lbs	Coffee ??	21	31.50	
2 Lbs	Green & Blk Tea	1.25	2.50	
	Export duty on Coffee		.30	
	Boxing Cartage & launch		1.50	
	Commission 2½%		2.76	$ 113.46
	E E			
	Havana May 13th 1864			

669-670
Preprinted Customs Form

No. 35
Entry of Merchandise
Importer Mrs. J. Mulford
Vessel *Denbigh*
From Havana
Entered May 20 1864
Value $ 104 Duty $ 15.60

Agent's Oath
(signed) J. L. Harris

Mdse. Entered 20 May 1864 Ship Entered 18 May 1864
Entry of Merchandise imported into the Port of Mobile, District of Mobile, by Mrs. J. Mulford in the Br. Str. *Denbigh*, Godfrey Master, from Havana

Marks	No. of Packages	Contents	Quantity	Value in Foreign Currency	15%	Duties
A J J J. M.	1 PKge	Lenin		$ 12.00	13	$ 1.95
		Cotton mfs		46.65	49	7.35
		Gloves Kid		6.00	6	.90
		Shoes	12 Pairs	29.90	32	4.80
		Needles		4.25	4	.60
				98.80	104	@ 15% $ 15.60
		Chges & Com		5.30		
				$ 104.10		

672a
Invoice

Note: Interesting notation to distinguish on which voyage this cargo arrived. Mrs. Mulford's merchandise was split between two voyages, perhaps to minimize chances of loss by capture.

Last trip. *Denbigh*, a J. I.

1 Dz	Hdfs. Linen	$ 8.00	8.00
25 Yds	Cotton Goods	30¢	7.50
15 "	Flannel	75¢	11.25
78 "	Calico	35¢	11.70
3½ Dz	Cotton Hose	$ 4.25 Ea	14.80
4 Pr	Gloves Kid	$ 1.25	6.00
2 Dz	L. Hdfs	$ 3	6.00
2 "	Hose Child's	$ 3	6.00
4 "	Thread	$ 1.50 Ea.	6.00
1 Dz	Soap	$ 2	2.00
1 "	Pins	.75	.75
7 Pr	Shoes	$ 1 Ea.	7.00
5 "	Gaiters	$ 3. Ea.	15.00
1 Gro(ss)	Shoe Strings	$ 1	1.00
			103.10
	Mrs. J. Mulford, Lagrange, Ga.		
	delivered to Harris		

672b
Invoice

Note: This invoice was difficult to read. The documents numbered 669-670, 672a, 672b, and 672c all went together. No. 670 is a summation of the two invoices. No. 672c was an Oath of Agent form signed by J. L. Harris.

Mrs. J. Mulford, Lagrange, Ga.

Linen Hdfs	4 doz		$ 18.00
Calicos	25 yd	25¢	6.25
Cotton	78 "		19.50
" Hose		25¢ a pair	20.90
Kid Gloves	4 pair		6.00
??? ???? &c			4.25
shoes	12 pairs		22.00
Shoe Strings	???		7.90
			98.80
	Chges & Comm		5.30
			$ 104.10

673-674
Preprinted Customs Form

No. 36
Entry of Merchandise
Importer Mrs J. Herty
Vessel *Denbigh*
From Havana
Entered May 21st 1864
Value $ 65 Duty $ 9.75

Agent's Oath
(signed) Mr. Harris

Mdse. Entered May 20 1864 Ship Entered April 30 1864
Entry of Merchandise imported into the Port of Mobile, District of Mobile, by Mrs. J. Herty in the Br. Str. *Denbigh*, Godfrey Master, from Havana

No. of Packages	Contents	Quantity	Value in Foreign Currency	15%		Duties
1 PKge	Wearing Apparel		$ 20.00	21		
	Cotton mfs		42.00	44		
			$ 65.25	65	15%	9.75
	Chgs & Coms		3.25			
			$ 65.25			

675
Invoice and Letter of Instructions

Mobile May 21,1864

Mr. Colsson,
Will please deliver Mr. Harris the package pr "*Denbigh*" (last trip) for Mrs. J. Herty, to my care @
N. H. Brown

Milledjorith (M Midjonith ? illegible), Ga.
Vests. (?) Hon, Harris &c Wearing. Aprl. 20
Cotton mfs, Thread, hose. 42
62

676-677
Preprinted Customs Form

No. 37
Entry of Merchandise

Importer Mr. Brainard
Vessel *Denbigh*
From Havana
Entered May 20 1864
Value $ 144 Duty $ 21.60

Owner's Oath
(signed) J. M. Brainard

Mdse. Entered 20 May 1864 Ship Entered 18th May 1864
Entry of Merchandise imported into the Port of Mobile, District of Mobile, by Mr. Brainard in the Br. Str. *Denbigh*, Godfrey Master, from Havana

Marks	No. of Packages	Contents	Value in Foreign Currency	15%	Duties
Br. B.	1 Box	Flax mfs.	$ 78.70	82	$ 12.30
		Cotton mfs.	27.50	29	4.35
		Clothing ready made	10.00	11	1.65
		Wool mfs.	7.00	7	1.05
		Silk mfs.	14.25	15	2.25
			137.45	144	$ 21.60
		Chgs & Com	6.51		
			$ 143.96		

678-679
Invoice

Captn. A. M. Godfrey to J. W. Dever Dr.

	Mr. J. M. Brainard			
25 Yds	brown Linen	@ 45¢	11.25	
25 "	blue check	" "	11.25	
3 Dozen	bond d linen Hdkfs	" 4.25	12.75	
3 "	" " "	" "	12.75	
40 Yds	blue check Linen	" 45¢	18.00	
30 "	Brown "	" 35¢	10.50	
2	**Corsets 21 inches**	" 4.25	8.50	
1	**" 19 "**		4.25	
1	**" 22 "**		4.25	
1 Dozen	**Corset laces**		3.50	
4 "	Spool Cotton	" 1.75	7.00	
2 "	**Singer's machine needles**		3.00	
3	Silk Parasols	" 3.75	11.25	
4 Pr	Silk Gloves No 7	" 75¢	3.00	
5 Yds	brown Cambric	" 20¢	1.00	
	Amt forward		$ 122.45	
	Amt brot forward		$122.45	
3 Yds	Green Cambric	@ 20¢	.60	

3 "	Drab "	" "	.60	
2 "	blue cloth double width	3.00	7.00	
4	Coarse Combs		1.25	
2	hair brushes		~~2.50~~	
1 Lb	bluing (none)			
6	Scrubbing brushes		~~3.25~~	
	Boxing, Cartage, & Launch		3.00	
	Commission 2½%		3.51	$ 143.76
	E. E.	14.40		
	Havana May 13, 1864	7.20		
	(added notes indicated 21.60 – duty)	21.60		

680-681
Preprinted Customs Form

No. 39
Entry of Merchandise
Importer M. A. Quarles
Vessel *Denbigh*
From Havana
Entered May 21 1864
Value $ 124 Duty $ 18.60

Owner's Oath
(signed) Mrs. A. Quarles

Mdse. Entered 19 May 1864 Ship Entered 18 May 1864
Entry of Merchandise imported into the Port of Mobile, District of Mobile, by M. A. Quarles in the Br. Str. *Denbigh*, Godfrey Master, from Havana

No. of Packages	Contents	Value in Foreign Currency	15%	Duties
1 PKge	Clothing ready made	$ 57.25	60	
	Silk mfs	12.00	13	
	Linens	22.00	23	
	~~Shoes~~ mfs of Leather	27.25	28	
		118.50	$ 124	15% $ 18.60
	Chgs & Com.	5.52		
		$ 124.02		

682-683
Preprinted Customs Form

No. 38
Entry of Merchandise

Importer Geo R. Tuttle
Vessel *Denbigh*
From Havana
Entered May 20th 1864
Value $ 150   Duty $ 22.60

Owner's Oath
(signed) Geo. R. Tuttle

Mdse. Entered May 20th 1864   Ship Entered 18 May 1864
Entry of Merchandise imported into the Port of Mobile, District of Mobile, by G. R. Tuttle in the Br. Str. *Denbigh*, Godfrey Master, from Havana

No. of Packages	Contents	Value in Foreign Currency	15%	20%	Duties
1 Case	Flax mfs	$ 8.25			
	Cotton Flax	79.60	91		$ 13.65
	~~Straw Hats~~ Cotton	39.40	40		6.00
	~~Soap~~ Straw Hats	8.50	9		1.35
	~~Silk ribbons~~ Soap	1.75		2	.40
	Silk ribbons	7.25	8		1.20
	Chgs & Com.	5.79	148	2	$ 22.60
		149.54			

684
Invoice

Capt. A. M. Godfrey
To J. W. Dever Dr.

	W. A. Quarles		
1 Doz	linen Shirts	@ 1.50	$ 18.00
½ " prs	drawers	1.50	9.00
1	Yellow Silk Sash		23.50
1 Doz	Gents socks		3.00
½ "	Shirt Collars		2.25
12 Yds	Dress silk		12.00
1	Vest		1.50
1 Bolt	Linen 38 Yds	50¢	19.00
1 doz.	Gents Hdkfs		3.00
2 prs	gaiters		6.50
1 pr	Do.		5.00
2	Calf skins		12.00
1 side	Sole leather		3.75
	Boxing, Carting & launch		2.50
	Comn 2½%		3.02
			$ 124.02
	E. E. Havana May 13th /64		
	12.40		

	6.20		
	(added note – duty) 18.60		

685 and 1249
Invoice

Capt. A. M. Godfrey to J. W. Dever dr

	Geo. R. Tuttle			
1 Piece	Blue Linen check 30 yds	@ 45	$ 13.50	
15 Yds	brown " drilling	" 45	6.75	
1 Piece	Linen 38 Varas	" "	17.10	
7 Doz	?? Socks ?? No. 7½		4.20	
4	Black Belt Ribbons	" 1.00	4.00	
1 Doz	Linen Socks 7½		4.25	
2	Fancy belt Ribbons	" 1.00	2.00	
1 Doz skeins	Black Silk		1.25	
6 " spools	" Cotton	" 1.75	10.40	
6	Patterns linen lawn		6.75	
1 Doz Balls	White knitting Cord		.75	
1 "	Cards hocks & Eyes		1.00	
20 Yds	Pillow Case linen	@55¢	11.00	
2 Pair	Black lace mits •		.75	
26 Yards	fine Swiss		8.50	
7 Varas	Calico	" 30¢		
	Amt fd (forward)		93.95	
	Amt brot fd		$ 93.95	
6 Boxes	Hair pins		.89	
2	Patterns Calico 10 Varas	@ 30¢	3.00	
2	" Merino Pink & Blue		3.75	
1 Doz	Towels		6.25	
1 Pc	brown linen Crash 30 vs	@ 45¢	13.50	
1 Doz	skeins while flax		1.00	
9	Gents undershirts	@ 1.00	9.00	
4	Gross Shoe Strings	" 60¢	2.40	
1	**Panama hat**		8.50	
1 Dozen	Toilet Soap		1.75	
	Cartage boxing & launch		2.00	
	Commission 2½%		3.64	$ 149.44
	E. E.			
	Havana May 13th 1864			
	(note added – duty) 22.50			

687-688
Preprinted Customs Form

No. 40
Entry of Merchandise
Importer A. S. White
Vessel *Denbigh*
From Havana
Entered May 21 1864
Value $ 70 Duty $ 10.50

Owner's Oath
(signed) A. S. White

Mdse. Entered May 21 1864 Ship Entered May 18 1864
Entry of Merchandise imported into the Port of Mobile, District of Mobile, by A. S. White in the Br. Str. *Denbigh*, Godfrey Master, from Havana

No. of Packages	Contents	Value in Foreign Currency	15%	Duties
1 Case	Cotton mfs	$ 67.30	.70	$ 10.50
	Chgs & Comm	2.70		
		$ 70.00		

689
Invoice

Capt. A. M. Godfrey
To J. W. Dever Dr.

	Mrs. A. S. White		
2 doz	White Cotton ladies Hose		8.00
2 doz	Spool Cotton 300 yds.		3.30
12 "	Hair Pins		2.00
13 yds.	Linen	40¢	5.20
4 oz	Worsted Zephyr (Thread)		3.30
2 oz	do " "		1.75
4 pairs	Corsets	4.25	17.00
12 papers	Pins		1.25
2 oz	Blk. Sewing Silk	30¢	.60
1 doz	White Embroidering Cotton		7.50
1 "	Red do "		7.50
7 yds	Black Silk	1.00	7.00
250 Skeins	**Embroidery Silk**	½¢	2.50
	Boxing, Cartage & Launch		1.00
	Commission 2½%		1.70
			70.00
	E. E.		
	Havana May 13th /64		

	(added note – duty) 10.50		

690-691
Preprinted Customs Form

No. 41
Entry of Merchandise
Importer Thos. Hogg
Vessel *Denbigh*
From Havana
Entered May 21 1864
Value $ 86 Duty $ 12.45

Owner's Oath
(signed) Thos. Hogg

Mdse. Entered May 21, 1864 Ship Entered May 18, 1864
Entry of Merchandise imported into the Port of Mobile, District of Mobile, by Thos. Hogg in the Br. Str. *Denbigh*, Godfrey Master, from Havana

No. of Packages	Contents	Quantity	Value in Foreign Currency	10%	15%	20%	Duties
1 Pkge	Flannels		12.50		14		2.10
	Cotton mfs		36.75		38		5.70
	Shoes	pr 9	18.50		19		2.85
	Tea	lbs 10	11.50	12			1.20
	Sugar	lbs 25	3.12			3	.60
			82.07	12	71	3	$ 12.45
	Chges & Com		4.00				
			$ 86.37				

692
Invoice

Mr. ~~J. Ekston~~ Thos Hogg *Denbigh*

6 pr	Shoes	$ 1.25	7.50
1 "	Gaiters	$ 5	5.00
1 Doz	Hdfs Silk	$ 8	8.00
8 yds	Muslin	50¢	4.00
6 "	Flannel	75¢	4.50
3 Doz	Stockings	$ 4 ea	12.00
2 Pair	Silk Gloves	$ 1 ea	2.00
16 yds	Muslin	50¢	8.00
2 pr	Ladies Gaiters	$ 3.00 ea	6.00
2 Doz	Spool Tread	1.25	3.50

1 "	Pins	75	.75
25 yds	Cotton	25¢	6.50
25 oz	Sugar	12½¢	3.12
10 oz	Tea	1.50	11.50
	Com & Chgs		82.37
	Coffee 6.50		4.00
			86.00
	(added note – duty 12.90)		

693
Invoice

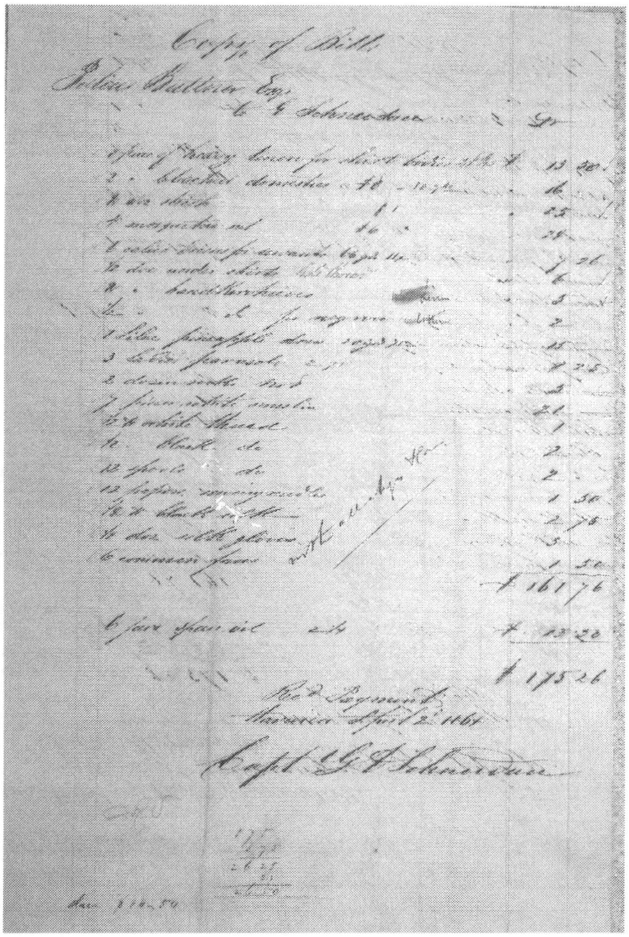

Figure 64. Invoice for sundries to Julius Buttner.

Copy of Bill
Julius Buttner Esq.

To G. Schneider Dr.

1 piece	**of heavy linen for shirt bodies** 2 yds (?)		13.50
2 "	bleached domestics 80 yds	@ $ 8	16.00
2 doz	shirts	$ 1	25.00

4	mosquito net	$ 6	24.00
6 calico	pieces for servants 66 yds	11¢	7.26
½ doz	under shirts lisle (?) thread		6.00
2 "	handkercheives white Linen		5.00
½ "	do for negroes " Cotton		2.00
1	Lilac pineapple dress 20 yds	75¢	15.00
3	ladies parasols	2.75	8.25
2 dozen	silk nod (?)		5.00
7 pieces	white muslin		21.00
½ ??	white thread		1.00
½	black do		2.00
12 spools	do		2.00
12 papers	sewing needles		1.50
½ ??	black silk		2.75
¼ doz	silk gloves		3.00
6	??? ???		1.50
	with all chges & Com.		$ 161.76
6	jars ??? oil 2¼		13.50
			$ 175.26
	Recd Payment		
	Havana April 2d 1864		
	(signed) Capt G. ?. Schneider		
	(duty 26.50) due $ 10.50		

694-695
Preprinted Customs Form

No. 42
Entry of Merchandise
Importer Julius Buttner
Vessel *Denbigh*
From Havana
Entered May 21 1864
Value $ 176 Duty $ 26.40

Owner's Oath
(signed) Julius Buttner

Mdse. Entered 21 May, 1864 Ship Entered May 18, 1864
Entry of Merchandise imported into the Port of Mobile, District of Mobile, by Julius Buttner in the Br. Str. *Denbigh*, Godfrey Master, from Havana

No. of Packages	Contents	Value in Foreign Currency	15%	Duties
1 Case	Linens	18.50	19	2.85
	Cotton mfs	92.25	97	14.55
	Clothing ready made	43.75	45	6.75
6 Jars	**Sp.(anish) Olive Oil** Gals 8	13.50	15	2.25

		168.00	176	$ 26.40
	Chgs & Com	7.52		
		$ 175.52		

697-698
Preprinted Customs Form

No. 43
Entry of Merchandise
Importer Mr. LeBaron
Vessel *Denbigh*
From Havana
Entered May 21 1864
Value $ 91 Duty $ 13.65

Owner's Oath
(signed) J. M. LeBaron

Mdse. Entered May 21, 1864 Ship Entered May 18, 1864
Entry of Merchandise imported into the Port of Mobile, District of Mobile, by J. M. LeBaron in the Br. Str. *Denbigh*, Godfrey Master, from Havana

No. of Packages	Contents	Value in Foreign Currency	15%	Duties
1 Box	Flannels	$ 14.50	15	$ 2.25
	Flax mfs	43.00	45	6.75
	Cotton mfs	17.18	18	2.70
4 Cans	Castor oil	12.50	13	1.95
		87.18	91	$ 13.65
	Chges & Com	4.00		
		$ 91.18		

699-700
Preprinted Customs Form

No. 44
Entry of Merchandise
Importer L. F. Zantzinger
Vessel *Denbigh*
From Havana
Entered May 21 1864
Value $ 460 Duty $ 71.95

Owner's Oath
(signed) L. F. Zantzinger

Mdse. Entered 21 May, 1864 Ship Entered May 18, 1864
Entry of Merchandise imported into the Port of Mobile, District of Mobile, by L. F. Zantzinger in the Br. Str. *Denbigh,* Godfrey Master, from Havana

Marks	No. of Packages	Contents	Value in Foreign Currency	10%	15%	20%	Duties
Z	19 Pkges.	Tea lbs 25	$ 27.00	28			2.80
"		Salted Fish	16.10	28	17		2.55
L H		Castor oil Gals 5	12.20		13		1.95
Z.		Shoes prs 20	32.25		34		5.10
		Hats & Caps	100.25		104		15.60
		Flax mfs	90.18		94		14.10
		Cotton mfs	37.00		38		5.70
		Wool mfs	47.00		49		7.35
		Sugar	81.22		349	84	16.80
			443.20			84	$ 71.95
		Chges & Com	17.72				
			$ 460.92				

701
Invoice

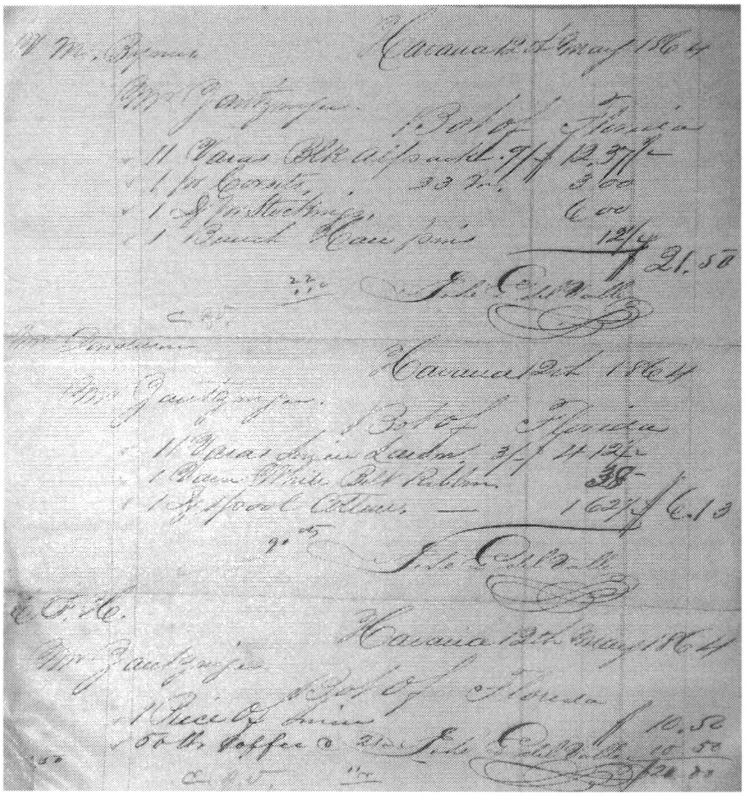
Havana 12th May 1864
$21.50
Havana 12th 1864
$6.10
Havana 12th May 1864
10.50

Figure 65. Invoice with small orders for three people.

V. M. Byrne		Havana 12th May 1864	
Mr. Zantzinger	Bot (Bought) of Florida (Store)		
11 Varas	Blk Alpacka 9/	$ 12.37½	
1 pr	Corsets 23 In.	3.00	
1 Dz pr	Stockings	6.00	
1 Bunch	Hair pins	.12¼	
			$ 21.50
	(signed) ?? G. (?) del Valle		
Mrs. Donaldson		Havana 12th May 1864	
Mr. Zantzinger	Bot of Florida		
11	Varas Linen Lawn 3/	$ 4.12½	
1	Vara White Belt Ribbon	.38	
1	Dz spool Cotton "	1.62½	$ 6.13
	(signed) ?? G. (?) del Valle		
E. O. E.			
		Havana 12th May 1864	
Mr. Zantzinger	Bot of Florida		
1	Piece of Linen	$ 10.50	
50	lbs Coffee @ 21¢	10.50	
		$ 21.00	
	(signed) ?? G. (?) del Valle		

702
Invoice

For Maj. Mohler			
		Havana 12th May 1864	
Mr. Zantzinger	Bot of Florida		
1 Dz	Fine (?) Chds; (Hose or Shoes?)	$10.00	
1 Dz	Socks,	5.00	
3 pr	Drawers 12/	4.50	
			$19.50
	(signed) ?? G. (?) del Valle		
Mr. Clisstu (?)			
		Havana May 12th 1864	
Mr. Zantzinger	Bot of Florida		
1 Piece	of Linen	$ 9.50	
	(signed) ?? G. (?) del Valle		
Mr. B. Hamilton			
		Havana May 12 /64	
Mr. Zantzinger	Bot of Florida		
1 Piece	of Fine Kersey (?)	$ 19.00	
2 Doz	½ Hose, No. 11, $ 5	10.00	
1 pc	of Linen for Pillow Cases	10.50	
			$ 39.50
	75 lbs Coffee 21¢ 15.75		

	3 lbs green tea @ 2 $ 6.00		
	21.75		21.75
			$ 60.25
	(signed) Jose G. (?) del Valle		
	(added note – duty?) 6.90		

703-704
Preprinted Customs Form

No. 51
Entry of Merchandise
Importer R. J. Cocke
Vessel *Denbigh*
From Havana
Entered May 26 64
Value $ 104 Duty $ 15.60

Owner's Oath
(signed) R. J. Cocke

Mdse. Entered ________18__ Ship Entered May 18th, 1864
Entry of Merchandise imported into the Port of Mobile, District of Mobile, by R. J. Cocke in the Br. Str. *Denbigh*, Godfrey Master, from Havana

No. of Packages	Contents	Quantity	Value in Foreign Currency		Duties
1 Box	**Quinine**	50 oz	$ 100.00		
	Chgs & Com		3.50		
			103.52	Quinine $ 104 15%	$ 15.60

705-706
Substitute for Preprinted Customs Form

No. 50
Entry of Merchandise
Importer E. H. Cummins
Vessel *Denbigh*
From Havana
Entered May 26 64
Value $ 87 Duty $ 13.05

Entry of Mds made E. H. Cummins
Pr. Br. Str. *Denbigh* from Havana May 18th, 1864

1 Pakge	Shoes	$ 15.00	$ 15%	16	$ 2.40
	Wool mfs	34.25	"	36	5.40

	Clothing ready made	34.00	"	35	5.25
	Chrs & Com	4.00		87	$ 13.05
		$ 87.25			

707
Invoice

Memorandum of cost and expenses on Sundry articles bought for Maj. E. H. Cummins, A. A. Gen'l, District of the Gulf, Mobile, Ala.[73]

6 prs	Shoes	$ 15.00
4 yds	Blue Cloth ??? suit	10.25
18 "	White " " "	24.00
	Hosiery ??? clothing ???	34.00
		$ 83.25
	Consignee Acct y (and) charges	2.50
	??? "	1.50
		87.50
	(added note – duty) $ 15.25	

709-710
Substitute for Preprinted Customs Form

No. 49
Entry of Merchandise
Importer Sands & Co.
Vessel *Denbigh*
From Havana
Entered May 26 64
Value $ 61 Duty $ 9.15

Entry of Mds made by Sands & Co. (?) pr Str *Denbigh* from Havana, May 18th, 1864

Mark						
Sands & Co. (?)	1 Pkge	Cotton mfs	$ 43.60	$ 46	15%	$ 6.90
		Worsted Silk & wool	13.40	15	"	2.35
			57.20	61		$ 9.15
		Chgs & com	3.40			
			$ 60.60			

711
Invoice

[73] A signal officer and staff officer, Edmond H. Cummins wrote a history of the Confederate Signal Corps after the war.

Invoice of Sunds (Sundries) shipped by M. A. Herrera & Co. on board of Brit Str *Denbigh*, Godfrey, Mr (Master) for Mobile, by order for acct & risk of & consigned to Messrs Sands & Co.

Sands & Co	1 Pkge etc			
Mobile		**20 Varas**	**Blk Alpaca ready for 2 dresses**	$ 12.40
		1 pce	dark Calico 53 yds " 2 $	13.20
		1 "	do do 48 " " 2 "	12.00
		1 "	Bleached Cotton, 34 " "	9.40
		1 doz	Socks No 9½ silks	7.40
		2 ps	Kid Gloves (Black) @ 10 $	2.40
				$ 57.20
			Boat hire & ship'g expenses	2.00
				$ 59.20
			Commission 2½ %	1.40
			E&O E	60.60
			Habana 13 May 1864	
			(signed) M. A. Herrera & Co.	
			(added note – duty) 9.00	

712
Invoice

Captn A. M. Godfrey
To J. W. Dever Dr.

	R. J. Cocke		
50 Oz	French Quinine @ $ 2	$ 100.00	
	Cartage & Launch	1.00	
	Commission 2½%	2.52	$ 103.52
		Net	~~10.30~~
	E. E.		~~113.82~~
	Havana May 13th 1864	Pd on a/	~~96.00~~
			~~12.82~~
	(added note – duty) $15.60		

714
Invoice

Mr. Hagan *Denbigh*

	1 Box		
1 Doz	Stockings	$ 4	$ 4.00
4 pair	Kid Gloves	$ 1	4.00
1 Pr	Linen 30 yds	50¢	15.00
4 "	Ladies Gaiters	$ 2.50	10.00
10 oz	Tea	$ 1.50	15.00
	Box	75¢	.75

			48.75
	to W. Thompson		
	15	10	$ 1.50
	34	15	5.10
	49		6.60
			(duty)

715-717
Preprinted Customs Form

No. 48
Entry of Merchandise
Importer Richd. H. Redwood
Vessel *Denbigh*
From Havana
Entered May 20 1864
Value $ 93 Duty $ 13.95

Owner's Oath
(signed) S. S. Webb

(No. 48, May 25, '64)

Entry of Merchandise, Ship Entered May 18, 1864
Imported into the Port and District of Mobile, by S. S. Webb in the Br. Str. *Denbigh* Godfrey
Master, from Havana

Packages	Packages and Contents	In Foreign Currency	15%	Amount of Duty
2 Bdles	Iron mfs	$ 36.00	37	$ 5.55
1 "	Cotton mfs	10.50	11	1.65
1 Bll	**glue** 183 lbs	42.42	45	6.75
		88.92	93	$ 13.95
	Chgs & Com	3.68		
		$ 92.60		

718a
Invoice

Havana

To L. F. Z.

2 Kits	Mackerel	$ 3.00
1 bll	**Potatoes**[74]	4.00
1	Cheese	3.36
1 Box	Codfish	10.50
		$ 20.86
	Recpt	
	Zantzinger	
	(added note – duty) 2.55	

718b

Scratch sheet summarizing duties on multiple shipments

Colomb	$ 1.65	Byron Donaldson & Co.	5.40
Skuse	15.00	Byron "	6.60
A. Leavins	2.55	Lyon	4.80
Geo White	1.20	Chistu (?)	1.50
Mohler	3.00		18.30
W. B. Hamilton	6.90		55.70
E. T. Hillen	1.65		74.00
D. W. Goodman	.80		
S. J. Mullany	11.70		
J. T. Lyon	5.25		
Wm Donaldson	.90		
V. M. Burns	3.30		
	55.70		

719a

Invoice

Colomb

To L. F. Z. (Zantzinger)

6	pairs boys shoes	@ 1.75	$ 10.50
12	lbs Coffee	@ .21	2.50
			$ 13.00
	Recp.		
	Zantzinger		
	(added note – duty) 1.65		

---

[74] Possibly seed potatoes. The farmers around Galveston Bay specifically requested that Capt. William Watson of the runner *Rob Roy* bring in urgently needed seed potatoes.

719b
Invoice

Mr. Skuse

Bot of L. F. Z.

S	40	hats	@ 1.25	50.00
1 Case	29	Caps	" 1.25	36.25
	7 doz	Socks	" 2.00	14.00
				$ 100.25
		Recpt		
		Zantzinger		

720
Invoice

H. J. Mullany Havana May 12, 1864
Mr. Zantzinger

Bot of Florida

26 Yards	Custom Kashmere	37½	$ 9.75
11 piece	of Linen	14	14.00
1 "	" " Fine	19	19.00
26 Varas	Muslin	20	5.20
1 Dz	Ladies Hose		6.00
14½ Varas	Flannel	4/	7.25
16 Varas	Delaine[75]	3/	6.00
10½ Varas	poplin	6/	7.87
			$ 75.07
	(signed) Jose G. del Valle		2.81
			77.88
	(added note – duty?) 11.70		

721
Invoice

Lyon	200 lbs	Crushed Sugar	@ 12	$ 24.00
Byrnes	329 lbs	palo Sugar	@ 10	$ 32.90

---

[75] Light woolen or wool and cotton dress fabric.

722a
Invoice

Lee H. Havana 13 May 1864
Mr. Zantzinger
Bot of Sta Maria
5 Gals Castor oil Box & Co $ 12.20
(added note) duty due $1.80

722b
Invoice

Donaldson	2 pr	Kid Cong Gaiters	4½	9.40
Byrnes	4 "	do	2.75	10.99
Chester	1 "	do	2.50	2.50
				21.90
Burqet	5 lbs	blk tea	@ 1.75	8.75
	14 lbs	**Chocolate**	@ 40¢	5.60
				14.35
.		(added note – duty) 5.40		

723a
Invoice

J. T. Lyon
To L. F. Z. Dr.

200 lbs	Crushed Sugar	@ 12¢	24.00
4 lbs	Green tea	@ $ 2	8.00
1	Round Cheese		3.36
300 lbs	Coffee	@ 21	63.00
	Recd paymt		98.36
	Zantzinger		

723b (translated from Spanish)
Invoice

Sr. A. P. Mullany
A Castro de Belaunde Debe

1 Dozen	assorted spools of thread	a $ 1.75	$ 1.75	
2 (lot)	embroidery thread	.50	1.00	

3 (lot)	hair pins	.02	.06	
	???		$ 2.81	
	Habana Mayo 13 1864			
	Recipp (?) de Castro de Belaunde			
	(signed) Pedro de Baros			

724a
Invoice

D. W. G. Havana 13th May 1864
Mr. Zantzinger Bot of Florida

2	White **Belt Ribbon**	3/	.75	
4	Blk " "	3/	1.50	
2	Blue	4/	1.00	
2	Pink	4/	1.00	
				$ 4.25
	(signed) Jose G. del Valle			

724b

Geo White Havana 12th May 64
Mr. Zantzinger Bot of Florida

2 pr	Corsets	$ 3	6.00	
1 lb	Eng(lish) tea		1.75	
34 lb	Coffee		7.25	
			$ 15.00	
	(signed) Jose G. del Valle			
	(added note – duty) 1.20			

725-726
Preprinted Customs Form

No. 47
Entry of Merchandise
Importer W. H. Jenifer (?)
Vessel *Denbigh*
From Havana
Entered May 25 1864
Value $ 46 Duty $ 6.55

Owner's Oath
(signed) W. H. Jenifer (?)

Mdse. Entered _________18__ Ship Entered May 18th 1864
Entry of Merchandise imported into the Port of Mobile, District of Mobile, by Mr. W. H. Jenifer (?) in the Br. Str. *Denbigh*, Godfrey Master, from Havana

No. of Packages	Contents	Value in Foreign Currency	10%	15%	Duties
1 Box	Cotton mfs	$ 21.12		22	$ 3.30
	Flax mfs	4.43		5	.75
	Shoes	10.50		12	1.80
	Tea 5 lb	6.12	7	39	.70
		42.17	7		$ 6.55
	Chgs & Com	3.44			
		$ 45.60			

727a
Invoice

Havana May 13th 1864

Luke J. Whitfield

To T. L. Carter Dr.

8 yds	Linen	@ 40¢	3.20
3 pair	Corsets	@ 1.25	3.75
1	Hat straw		4.00
2 pair	Shoes		2.00
100 lbs	Loaf Sugar		12.50
50 lbs	Coffee		5.00
			$ 41.45
	less Com & Exp, duty in Coffee[76]		2.00
	Received Payment T. L. Carter		

729a
Invoice

W. H. Jenifer

15	Yds Cotton for Shirts	25	5.62
6½	" dinnem (denim)	4.00	2.93
6	Linen hdchfs		1.50
1 Doz	Cotton Stockings 9		4.00
1 pr	Gloves		.75
12 yds	Cloth	7.00	10.00
4 prs	Boys Shoes	1.50	6.00

[76] Fees paid in kind.

	Shoe strings		.75
2	Blk hats		4.50
2½ lbs	Green tea	1.25	3.12
2½ "	Blk	"	3.12
	Charges		1.75
	Commission 2½%		1.69
			45.73

730-731
Substitute for Preprinted Customs Form

No. 46
Entry of Merchandise
Importer Luke Whitfiled
Vessel *Denbigh*
From Havana
Entered May 25 '64
Value $ 27 Duty $ 4.80

Entry of Mds made by Luke Whitfield per Str. *Denbigh* from Havana, May 18 '64

1 Box	Flax mfs	$ 12.95	14	15%	$ 2.10
	Sugar 100 lbs	11.00	13	20%	2.60
		23.95			4.70
	Chgs & Com	3.00			
		26.95			

733
Invoice

Capt. A. M. Godfrey
To J. W. Dever Dr.

	S. S. Webb[77]			
1 doz	**Spades**		13.00	
1 do	**Shovels**		13.00	
50 lb	**Rivets (iron)**	@ 20	10.00	
1 Doz	ladies Cotton hose		3.50	
4 "	Spools Cotton	1.75	7.00	
	Cartage & launch		1.00	
	Commission 2½%		1.18	43.92
	E E			
	Havana May 13 /64			
	1 7.35 led (?) 1 Bbl Glue 183	24¢	42.42	

[77] S. S. Webb & Co., a firm of cotton merchants in Mobile.

	6.60 Glue with chges &c		1.50	43.92
	13.95			92.60

734-735
Preprinted Customs Form

No. 45
Entry of Merchandise
Importer Mrs. C. Hayes
Vessel *Denbigh*
From Havana
Entered May 23 '64
Value $ 49 Duty $ 6.55

Agent's Oath
(signed) Walter Thompson

Mdse. Entered 23d May 1864 Ship Entered 18 May 1864
Entry of Merchandise imported into the Port of Mobile, District of Mobile, by Mrs. C. Hayes in the Br. Str. *Denbigh*, Godfrey Master, from Havana

No. of Packages	Contents	Value in Foreign Currency	10%	15%	Duties
1 Pkge	Tea 10 lbs	$ 15.00	16		$ 1.60
	Shoes	14.00		15	2.25
	Clothing ready made	17.00		18	2.70
		46.00	16	33	6.55
	Chgs & Com	2.55			
		$ 48.55			

736
Invoice

Captn A. M. Godfrey

To J. W. Dever dr

	N. H. Brown			
1 Piece	white Cotton 36 varas		$ 7.25	
1 Bolt	white flannel 30 "	@ 62½¢		
2 Dozen	linen towels	" 6 25/100	12.50	
1 " pair	Lady's hose 7½		5.50	
50 Lbs	white Sugar	" 12½¢	6.25	
	Export duty on Sugar			
	Boxing, Cartage & launch		1.00	
	Commission 2½%		1.52	52.77
	Sundries for Mrs. Anzi (?) cotton mfs			11.00

	E. E.			63.77
	Habana May 13th /64			
	(added note – duty) 9.60			
	1.65 Mrs. Anzi	@ 15 pr ??		

737-738
Substitute for Preprinted Customs Form

No. 52
Entry of Merchandise
Importer N. H. Brown
Vessel *Denbigh*
From Havana
Entered May 26 1864
Value $ 64 Duty $ 9.90

Entry of Mds. Made by N. H. Brown pr. Br. Str. *Denbigh* from Havana, May 18th 1864

1 PKge	Cotton mfs	$ 36.25	15%	$ 38	$ 5.70
1 Box	Sugar	6.25	20%	6	1.20
1 PKge	Flannel	11.75	15%	20	3.00
		60.25		$ 64	$ 9.90
		2.52			
		$ 63.77			

739
Invoice

Capt. A. M. Godfrey to J. W. Dever Dr

12 Varas	Organdy Muslin	25	3.00
1 dozen balls	white Cord		.75
8 Gross	Porcelain buttons		1.25
11 Yds	Calico	25	2.75
1 Lb.	flax thread		.75
50 "	Coffee	22	11.00
1 pr	Cotton Cards		2.00
			$ 21.50
	E. E. Havana May 13 1864		11.00
			11.50

740-741
Substitute for Preprinted Customs Form

No. 53
Entry of Merchandise
Importer Thos. St. John
Vessel *Denbigh*
From Havana
Entered May 26 1864
Value $ 12 Duty $ 1.80

Entry of mds made by Thomas St. John pr B. Str *Denbigh* from Havana, May 18th 1864
1 Bdle Calicos, with all chges & Com $ 11.50
Cotton mfs $ 12 ___15% $ 1.80

742
Invoice

Denbigh
Mr. Passe (?) St. John
3 Pair Gaiters $ 5 $ 15.00
(added note – duty) 2.25

743-744
Substitute for Preprinted Customs Form

No. 54
Entry of Merchandise
Importer Richd. H. Redwood
Vessel *Denbigh*
From Havana
Entered May 27 '64
Value $ 15 Duty $ 2.25

Entry of Mds made by A. L. St. John
Pr B. Str *Denbigh* from Havana, May 1864
1 PKge Shoes with chgs & Com 3 prs $ 15.00
Mfs of leather $ 15 ___ 15% __ $ 2.25

745-746
Substitute for Preprinted Customs Form

No. 35
Entry of Merchandise
Importer Richd. H. Redwood

Vessel <u>*Denbigh*</u>
From <u>Havana</u>
Entered <u>May 27 '64</u>
Value $ <u>50</u> Duty $ <u>7.50</u>

Entry of mds made by M. C. Eslava pr B Str *Denbigh* from Havana, May 18th 1864
1 Bdle Silk thread with Chge & Com $ 50
Silk mfs $ 50 ___ 15% ___ $ 7.50

747
Invoice

Denbigh 1 Package
Dr. Richd La Feaso (?)

1 **Parasol**			$ 5.00
4 pr Gloves	$ 1.25		<u>5.00</u>
			10.00

(duty) 1.50

748
Invoice

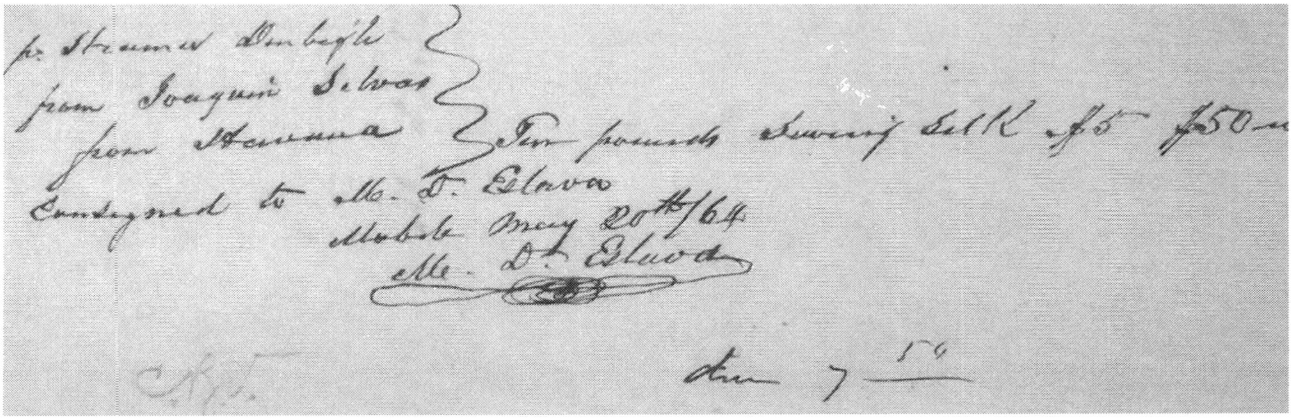

Figure 66. Invoice for sewing silk.

Pr Steamer *Denbigh*
From Joaquin Eslava
From Havana
Ten pounds Sewing Silk $ 5 $ 50.00
Consigned to M. D. Eslava
Mobile May 20th /64
M. D. Eslava
due 7.50

749-750
Substitute for Preprinted Customs Form

No. <u>56</u>
Entry of Merchandise
Importer <u>R. L. Fearn</u>
Vessel <u>*Denbigh*</u>
From <u>Havana</u>
Entered <u>May 27 '64</u>
Value $ <u>10</u> Duty $ <u>1.50</u>

Entry Mds made by R. L. Fearn pr Str. *Denbigh* from Havana, 18th May 1864

1 PKge	one parasol	$ 5	15%	$ 6		
	4 prs Gloves	4	"	<u>4</u>		
	Chges & Com	<u>1</u>		$ 10	15%	$ 1.50
		10				

751-752
Invoice (translation from Spanish)

Note the round about letter delivery route through Matamoros and the personally transmitted instructions to representative in Cuba.

(Opposite side cover: No. 34, Mr. Wm. H. Williamson, added note – duty 11.85.)

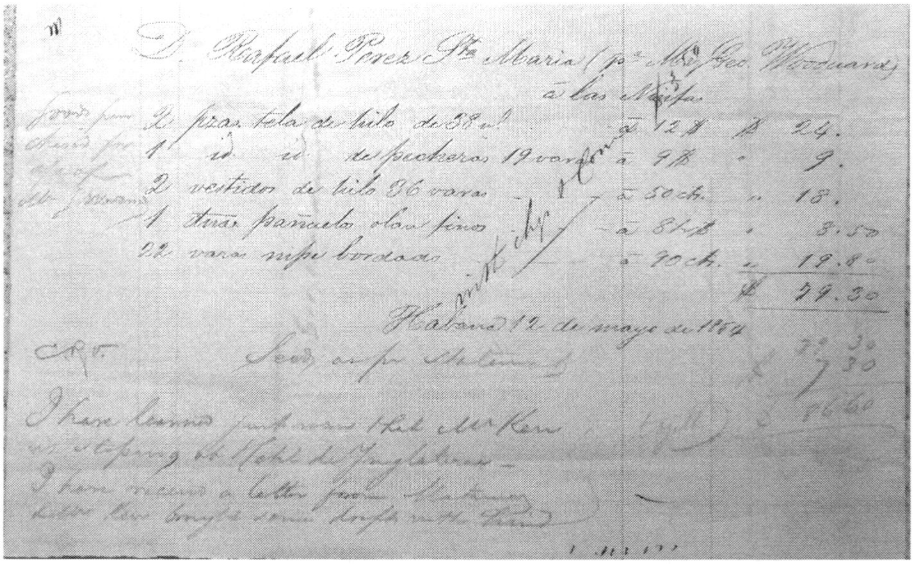
D. Rafael Perez Sta Maria (pr Mr Geo Woodward)
2 ... tela de hilo ... à 12 $ 24.
1 ... à 9 $ 9.
2 vestidos de hilo 36 varas à 50 cts. 18.
1 ... pañuelo ... à 8½ $ 8.50
22 varas ... bordado à 90 cts. 19.80
$ 79.30
Habana 12 de mayo de 1864
I have learned ... that Mr Kerr ... Hotel de Inglaterra –
I have received a letter from Matamoros ...

Figure 67. Invoice in Spanish for fabric with added instructions in English.

D. Rafael Perez Sta Maria (pr Mr. Geo. Woodward)

2 pieces	linen cloth 38 varas	@ 12 $	$ 24.00
1 piece	**fabric for shirt fronts** 19 varas	@ 9 $	9.00
2	dresses (?) of linen 36 varas	@ 50 cts.	18.00
1 dozen	handkerchiefs fine Dutch linen	@ 8½ $	8.50
22 varas	**embroidered nipa[78] cloth**	@ 90 cts.	19.80
			$ 79.30
	(with chgs & Com $ 3.50)		
			79.30
	Send as pr Matamoros		7.30
		together	$ 86.60

(Added notes, in English, penciled in margin and at bottom.) Goods per ??? and for a/c of Mr. J. Woodward. I have learned just now that Mr. Ken is stopping at Hotel de Inglaterra. I have received a letter from Matamoros & Mr. Ken brought some drafts with him.

753-754
Substitute for Preprinted Customs Form

No. 57
Entry of Merchandise
Importer Geo. Woodward
Vessel *Denbigh*
From Havana
Entered May 28 '64
Value $ 79 Duty $ 11.85

Entry of Mds made by Geo. Woodward pr Br. Str *Denbigh* from Havana, May 18th 1864
1 Pkge Lenin $ 75.80
Chgs & Com 3.50
79.30 Flax mfs $ 79 ___ 15% ___ $ 11.85

755
Invoice

1 Demijohn	Molasses	5 Gals	1.75
1 Sack	Sugar	50 lbs	3.75
3 Pieces	cold. (colored) calicos	92 yds 25¢	22.90
			28.40
		Chgs Com	1.50
			$ 29.90
	(added note – duty) 4.80		

78 Nipa – a type of palm.

756-757
Substitute for Preprinted Customs Form

No. 58
Entry of Merchandise
Importer James Robertson
Vessel *Denbigh*
From Havana
Entered May 28 '64
Value $ 30 Duty $ 4.80

Entry of Mds made by Jas. Robertson pr Str. *Denbigh* from Havana, May 18th 1864

1 Demijohn	Molasses	5 gals	$ 1.75	20%	2	$ .40
1 Sack	Sugar	50 lbs	3.75	20%	4	.80
1 Pkge	Calicos		22.90	15%	24	3.60
					30	$ 4.80

759
Invoice

Memorandum of Articles shipped by C. G. Ramsay per Steamer "*Denbigh*" to F. J. Hilton (?) Mobile

F J Hilton, Mobile				
1 Bundle cntg				
1 Piece	white Linen		10.50	
20 yds	white flannel		10.00	
1 Piece	Valona (?) Lawn		5.50	
1 "	Linen Lawn		13.00	
15 yds	Black Alpaca	@ $ 1.12½	16.87	
1	French corset		3.00	
3 Pieces	Ribbon	@ $ 1.12	3.00	
3 "	violet Ribbon		4.50	
1 Doz	Spool Thread		1.62	
55 yds	French Muslin	@ 20¢	11.00	
6 Pieces	Linen tape	@ 30¢	1.80	
½ Doz	packages hair pins		.75	
12 "	Pearl Buttons		.60	
12 "	shoe strings		.40	
1 "	Lace strings		.12	
2 "	Skeins working cotton		.80	
22 yds	Diaper	@ 50¢	11.00	94.46
~~1 Package~~	~~entg 1 Bottle essence of ???~~			~~.40~~
				$ 94.86
	Havana May 13, 1864			

	C. G. Ramsay			
	(added note – duty) Due $ 14.50			

760-761
Preprinted Customs Form

No. 59
Entry of Merchandise
Importer F. Hilton
Vessel *Denbigh*
From Havana
Entered May 28 64
Value $ 97 Duty $ 14.55

Owner's Oath
(signed) Fred. J. Hilton

Mdse. Entered ________18__ Ship Entered May 18th, 1864
Entry of Merchandise imported into the Port of Mobile, District of Mobile, by F. Hilton in the Br. Str. *Denbigh*, Godfrey Master, from Havana

No. of Packages	Contents	Value in Foreign Currency	15%	Duties
1 Bdle.	Flax mfs	66.59	69	
	Wool mfs	26.87	28	
		93.46	97	$ 14.55
		3.85		
		97.31		

Denbigh Customs Manifests, June 1864 1 of 2, Transcripts

Denbigh Voyage No. 6, Havana-Mobile-Havana
Havana, last date document prepared there, 4 June 1864 so the ship sailed soon thereafter.
Mobile, date ship entered (port and reported arrival to C.S. Customs) was 7 June 1864.
Mobile departure, cotton export manifests dated 14 June 1864 so ship sailed soon thereafter. (421 bales cotton, 218,890 lbs., $ 124,764, 57¢ per lb.)

774-776
Preprinted Customs Form

No. 1
Entry of Merchandise
Importer Mrs. M. Myers
Vessel *Denbigh*
From Havana
Entered 1 June '64
Value $ 200.~~50~~ Duty $ 33.50

Agent's Oath
(signed) Sidney Smith
Mrs. M. Myers the owner
Sworn before me, this 1st day of June 1864

Mdse. Entered 1sT. June 1864 Ship Entered May 18 1864
Entry of Merchandise imported into the Port of Mobile, District of Mobile, by R. S. Bunker in the Br. Str. *Denbigh* Godfrey Master, from Havana

No. of Packages	Contents	Value in Foreign Currency	10%	15%	20%	Duties
2 Blls	Sugar lbs 451	$ 37.45			40	$ 8.00
1 Box	Soap lbs 100	27.00			29	5.80
1 "	Pickles	10.00			11	2.20
1 Bdle	Shoes prs 38	66.50		71		10.65
2 Boxes	Candles lbs 72	34.56		37		5.55
		175.51		108	80	
	Charges & Com	12.50				
		188.01				
	Cheese with Chgs & Com lbs 20	12.50	13			1.30
		200.51	13	108	80	$33.50

777
Invoice

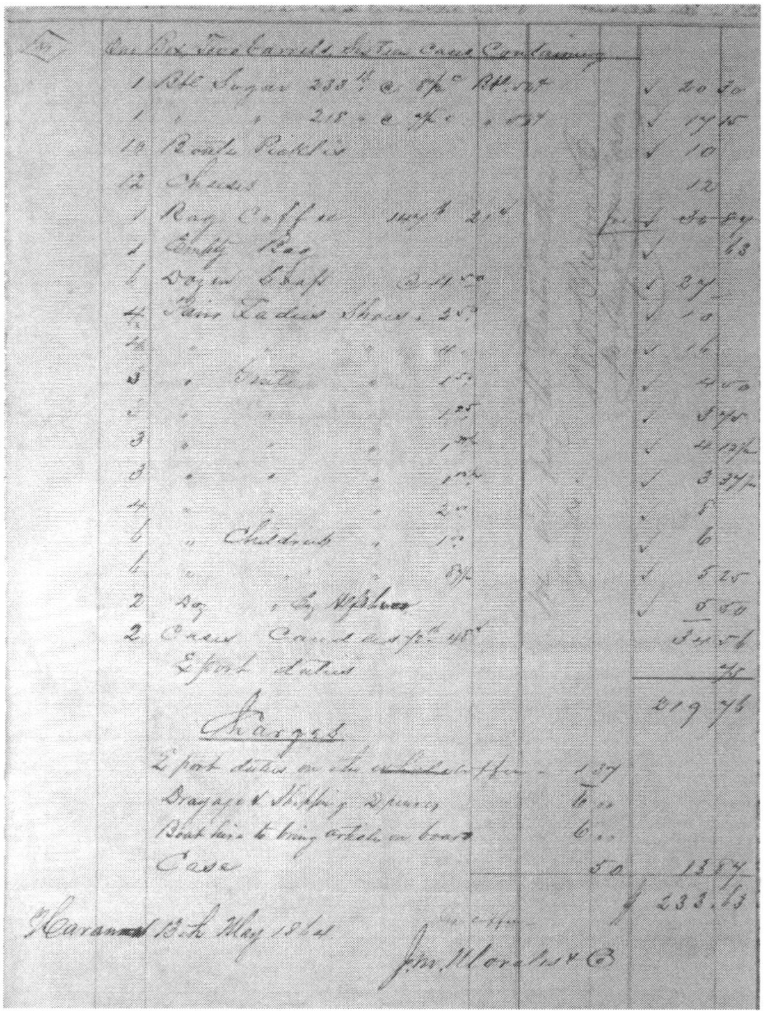

Figure 68. Invoice for large order including two barrels of sugar.

One Box, Two Barrels & Sixteen Cases Containing

M	1 Bbl	Sugar	233 lb @ 8½¢ Bbl .50¢		20.30
	1 "	"	218 " @ 7½¢ " 50¢		17.15
	10 Bottles	Pickles			10.00
	12	Cheeses			12.00
	1 Bag	Coffee	147 lb 21¢	free	~~36.84~~
	1 Empty	Bag			.63
	6 Dozen	Soap	@ 4.50		27.00
	4 Pairs	Ladies Shoes	" 2.50		10.00
	4 "	" "	4.00		16.00
	3 "	Gents "	1.50		4.50
	3 "	" "	1.25		3.75
	3 "	" "	1.37½		4.12½
	3 "	" "	1.12½		3.37½

	4 "	" "	2.00		8.00
	6 "	Children's "	1.00		6.00
	6 "	" "	87½		5.25
	2 Doz	" Eng Hlfshoes (Halfshoes)			5.50
	2 Cases	Candles	72 lb 48¢		34.56
		Export duties			.75
		Charges			219.76
		Export duties on the whole Coffee		1.37	
		Drayage & Shipping Expenses		6.00	
		Boat hire to bring articles on board		6.00	
		Case		.50	13.84
					$ 233.63
		Havana 13th May 1864	less coffee		
			J. M. Morales & Co.		
	Reverse side: We will pay the Duties on these Goods. H. O. Brewer & Co. pr Benj. Donaldson				

778
Small form: Oath of Importers or Agents.

Signed: Sydney Smith
Note below form: Mrs. Myers

779-782
Preprinted Customs Form

No. 2
Entry of Merchandise
Importer L. F. Zantzinger
Vessel *Denbigh*
From Havana
Entered June 1, 1864
Value $ 1016.~~69~~ Duty $ 152.40

Owner's Oath
(signed) L. F. Zantzinger

Mdse. Entered _____ 18___ Ship Entered May 18 1864
Entry of Merchandise imported into the Port of Mobile, District of Mobile, by L. F. Zantzinger in the Br. Str. *Denbigh* Godfrey Master, from Havana

No. of Packages	Contents			15%	Duties
5 Cases	Boots & Shoes 252 Pairs	£ 120 14 9	584.37	599	$ 89.85
1 Bag	Slippers 60 Pairs	9 0 0	43.56	44	6.60

3 Bales	Clothing ready made	75 0 0	363.00	373	55.95
		204 14 9	990.93	$1016	$152.40
	Com. 2½%	5 2 4	24.76		
		£ 209 17 1	$ 1015.69		
	Penciled note added: Major Barnwell has this invoice				

783a
Invoice

Steamer *Denbigh*

To Captn. Bevan Dr.

1864
May 13th

To No. 1 Box				
" 41 Pairs Strong Blucher boots	at 6/0	12	6	0
To No. 2 Box				
" 5 Pairs Strong Bluchers boots	" 6/0	1	10	0
" 23 pairs deck (?) Boots	" 19/3	22	2	9
To Case No. 3				
" 52 pairs of Calf Skin Shoes	" 7/0	18	4	0
" 3 pairs Strong Bluchers boots	" 6/0	0	18	0
" 26 pairs Calf Skin Bluchers	" 6/0	7	16	0
To Case No. 4				
" 54 pairs Calf hide Spring Boots	" 13/0	35	2	0
To Case No. 5				
" 24 Pairs Calf Bluchers	" 6/0	7	4	0
" 24 Pairs Calf hide Spring Boots	" 13/0	15	12	0
Wm Barnwell		£ 120	14	9

784b
Invoice

Note: Perhaps this and the previous order were for a merchant's stock.

Steamer *Denbigh*

To Captn. Bevan Dr.

1864
May 13th

To Bale No. 1					
12	Rugs	at 5/6	£ 3	6	0
To Bale No. 2					
" 12	fine coats	" 36/9	21	12	0
" 44 pairs	braces	" 1/3	2	15	0
" 97	Neckties	" 1/3	6	1	3

" 12 Pairs	duck trousers	" 3/6	2	2	0
" 17	Surge Jackets	" 14/6	12	6	6
" 3	Surge pants	" 10/0	1	10	0
" 35	Blue Surge Shirts	" 6/3	10	18	9
To Bale No. 3					
" 12	blue flannel Suits	" 27/0	16	4	0
To Bag No. 4					
" 66 pairs	canvas Slippers	3/0	9	0	0
			£ 85	15	0
Wm Barnwell					

785
Consumption Entry

Note: One wonders what a "consumption entry" might have been. This was one of very few invoices containing that term.

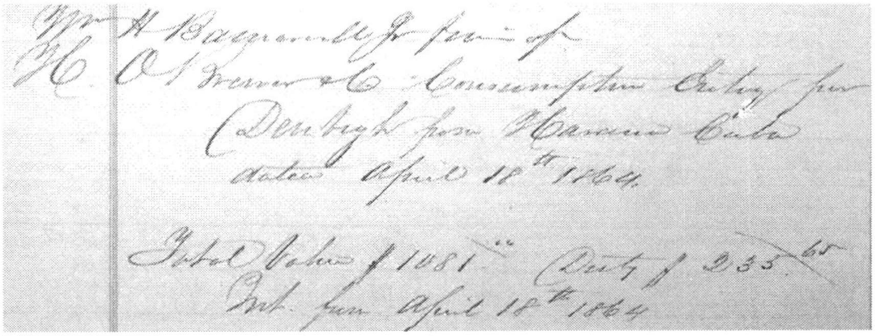

Figure 69. Consumption entry document.

Mr. Wm H. Barnwell Jr ??? ???
H. O. Brewer & Co **Consumption Entry** per
Denbigh from Havana Cuba
Dated April 18th 1864.
Total Value $ 1081.00 Duty $ 235.65
??? from April 18th 1864

787
Preprinted Customs Form

No. 4
Entry of Merchandise
Importer Richd. H. Redwood
Vessel *Denbigh*
From Havana
Entered June 1 '64

Value $ 166.12 Duty $ 24

Owner's Oath
Geo Cleveland
Sworn before me, this 1st day of June 1864

Mdse. Entered _____ 18___ Ship Entered May 18 1864
Entry of Merchandise imported into the Port of Mobile, District of Mobile, by Geo. Cleveland in the Br. Str. *Denbigh* Godfrey Master, from Havana

No. of Packages	Contents	Value in Foreign Currency	10%	15%	20%	Duties
	Cotton mfs	28.75		30		4.50
	Flax mfs	60.39		64		9.60
	Clothing ready made	18.00		19		2.35
	Hosiery	15.60		16		2.40
	Shoes	14.75		16		2.40
	Oil	2.50		3		.45
	Tea lbs 10	17.50	18			1.80
		$ 157.49	18	148		$ 24.00
	Chgs & Com	8.65				
		$ 166.14				

791
Invoice

Havana May 12 1864

Mr. Cleveland
Mr. Zantzinger

Bot of Florida

2 doz	Hand stitched Hdkfs	$ 3	6.00	
1 dz	Gents Hdkfs		3.00	
3 dz	tape Border Do	$ 3	9.00	
3 dz	Ladies Hose	4.20	12.60	
18 yds	Mull (?) Muslin		6.00	
2 pr	Mitts (Mittens ?)	4/---	1.00	
1 dz pr	Socks		3.00	
4 yds	fine **Marseilles**[79]	50¢	2.00	
12 Varas	Drilling	50¢	6.00	
1 dz	Towels		6.50	
1 dz	Napkins		3.00	
24 Varas	Linen Lawn	35¢	8.40	
1 pc	Jaconet Muslin		.5.00	
4 pc	Corsets	$ 3	12.00	
5 Varas	fine Linen	50¢	2.50	
1 pc	Linen for Underclothing		9.50	
1pc	Linen Shirting		14.00	

79 Heavy cotton fabric with a raised pattern. Use: bedspreads.

1 pc	" for Pillow Cases		9.50	
2¼ Varas	Linen Cambric		1.12	
1 dz	Black Thread		.75	
15 Varas	Calico 2½ patterns (?)		1.87	$ 122.74
1 pr	Ladies Slippers		1.50	
2 pr	Manella Gaiters	2.50	5.00	
2 pr	Walking Shoes	2.12	2.24	
1 pc	English (?) Gaiters		4.00	14.75
75 lbs	Coffee	21¢	15.75	
10 lbs	Tea	1.75	17.50	
72 ??	Salad Oil		2.50	
	Lighterage		2.00	
	Commissions &c		6.65	
	4½ ft freight at £ 30		16.87	61.27

793-794
Substitute for Preprinted Customs Form

No. 3
Entry of Merchandise
Importer R. W. Hallett
Vessel *Denbigh*
From Havana
Entered June 1st 1864
Value $ 24 Duty $ 3.60

Entry of Mdze by R. W. Hallett
In the Br. Str. *Denbigh*, Godfrey Master from Havana, 18th May 1864

One Box	**Chocolate** lbs 25	$ 18.75	19	15%	$ 2.85
1 Bdle	Cotton mfs	4.15	5	"	.75
		$ 22.90	24		$ 2.60
	Chges & Com	1.00			
		$ 23.90			

795a and 796
Invoice

one Bag	Coffee 200 lbs @ 20½¢	$ 41.00
one Box cont'g	25 lbs Chocolate @ 75¢	18.75
one Bundle "	7 yards Swiss muslin	3.15
2 Spools	Black silk	1.00
	Less Coffee chges & com	$ 63.90

(Reverse side of 795a)
Chges & Com 24.50 3.75 duty

795b
Small form: Oath of Importers or Agents.

Signed: Geo Cleveland

797
Invoice

Note: Invoice in Spanish with partial English translation in left margin written later in pencil.

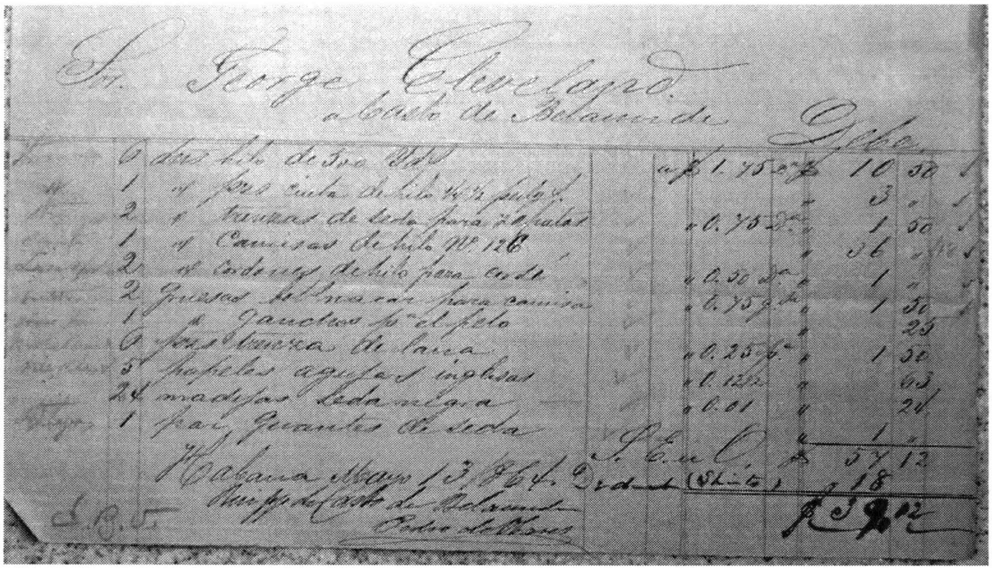

Figure 70. Invoice in Spanish with partial English translation added.

Por George Cleveland
a Costo de Belamide (?) Debe

threads	6 dns	hilo de 500 Yds	a $ 1.75 Da	$ 10.50
???	1 " prs	cuita de hilo ¼ ½ pulgs		3.00
Strings	2 "	trenzas de seda para zapatas	0.75 Da	1.50
Shirts	1 "	Caurisas de hilo No 126		36.00
???	2 "	Cordanes de hilo para conde (?)	0.50 Da	1.00
button	2 gruesas	bott nacar para caurisa	0.75 g. Da	1.50
Hair pins	1 "	ganchos pa el pelo		.25
???	6 prs	trenza de lana	0.25 pa	1.50
needles	5 papeles	agufars inglesas	0.12½	.63

	24	madefas seda nigra	0.01	.24
???	1	par guantes de seda		1.00
			S. E. u O.	$ 57.12
		Havana Mayo 13 1864 Deduct (Shirts)		18.00
		Duiss de Casto de Delaunda (?)		$ 39.12
		Pedro de Obases (?)		

798-801
Preprinted Customs Form

No. 5
Entry of Merchandise
Importer **D. H. Maury** (Commanding general of Mobile's defenses.)
Vessel *Denbigh*
From Havana
Entered 3d June 1864
Value $ 552 Duty $ 82.80

Owner's Oath
(signed) Dabney H Maury
Sworn before me, this 3d day of June 1864

Mdse. Entered _____ 18__ Ship Entered May 18 1864
Entry of Merchandise imported into the Port of Mobile, District of Mobile, by D. H. Maury in the Br. Str. *Denbigh* Godfrey Master, from Havana

No. of Packages	Contents	Value in Foreign Currency	10%	15%	20%	Duties
2 Pkges	Clothing ready made	$ 187.69		196		
1 Trunk	Cotton mfs	110.00		115		
"	Cloth, & wool mfs	127.09		133		
3 Pkges	Linen	28.00		29		
	Cotton mfs	42.75		44		
	Hosiery (Cotton)	12.50		15		
	Shoes 8 prs	18.00		26		
		526.03		$ 552	15%	$ 82.80
	Chges & Com	26.25				
		552.28				

802
Invoice

Memorandum of Articles shipped to Genl. D. H. Maury pr Steamer *Denbigh*

Genl D. H. Maury		
from C. G. R. No. 1	1 Package cntg	

2	Straw Hats for Ladies	
1	" " " a boy	
	also Bonnet trimmings	
" No. 2	1 Package cntg	
	Jaconet Cambric, Black Silk	
	Dress Shoes – Velvet Ribbon	
	Nansook Muslin – Working Cotton	
	Dress combs – Organdie Dress	
	Black Dress – shoe laces	
	Corset laces – **slates** -- Bonnet	
	Ribbon, Silk Belts – white	
	Cord – Towels ??	187.69
"	1 Bbl cntg	
5 lb	whole Pepper	1.25
5 "	ground "	2.50
6 Jars	English Mutton	3.50
2 lb	Joinglass (?)	4.00
12 Jars	Vanilla Essences	6.00
12	Vanilla Beans	3.60
Jars	Pickles 12	8.50
30 lb	Lump Sugar	4.50
30 "	Coffee	6.60
1 Kit	Mackerel	3.00
		$ 231.14
	Havana April 26, 1864	
	C. G. Ramsay[80]	
1 Box Brandy will be shipped per Steamer *Mary* costing $ 25.00		

Figure 71. Gen. D. H. Maury, Mobile commander.

Dabney Herndon Maury (May 21, 1822 – January 11, 1900) was an officer in the United States Army, instructor at West Point, author of military training books, and a major general in the Confederate States Army during the Civil War... He entered the Confederate Army as a colonel, serving as an Adjutant General,

[80] It seems that C. G. Ramsay was an agent of the Confederate Government in Havana.

then was Chief of Staff under General Earl Van Dorn. Following the Battle of Pea Ridge, he was promoted to the rank of brigadier general and assigned to field command. Maury led a division at the Battle of Corinth, and was appointed major general in November 1862. He participated in army operations around Vicksburg, Mississippi, and in the defense of Mobile, Alabama. In the latter military campaign, Maury commanded the Department of the Gulf.

803
Invoice

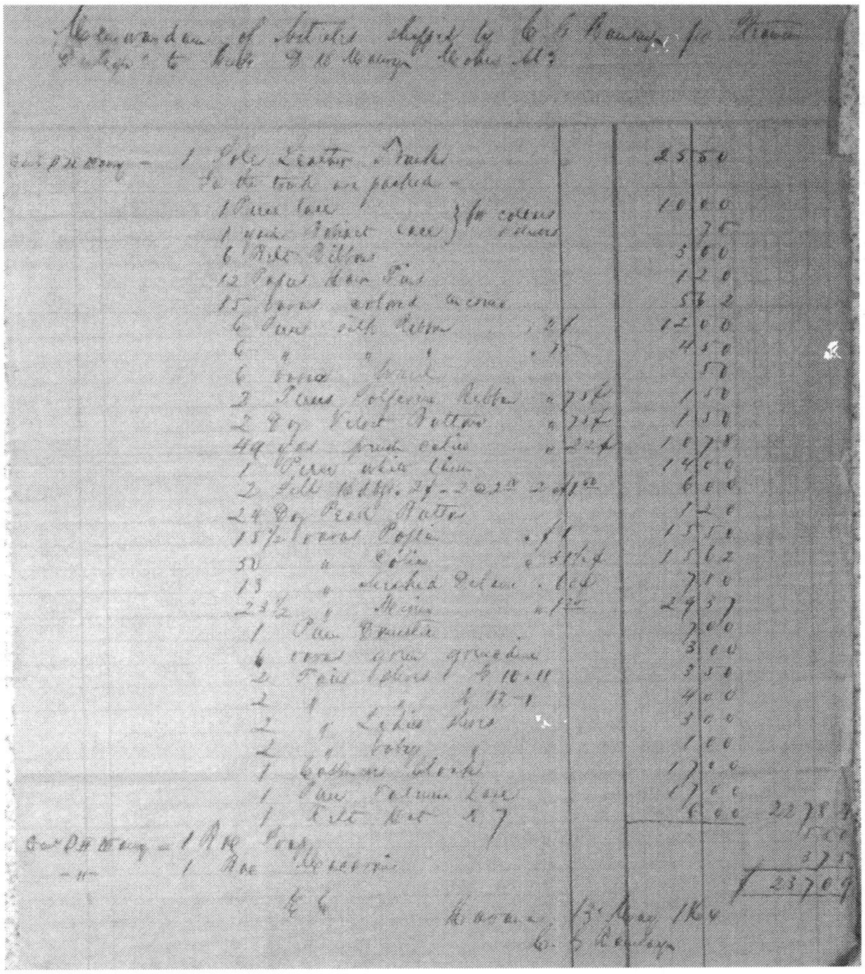

Figure 72. Invoice of goods ordered for Gen. Maury's family.

Memorandum of Articles shipped by C. G. Ramsay per Steamer *Denbigh* to Genl D H Maury Mobile Al:

Genl D H Maury	1 Sole Leather Trunk		25.50	
	In the trunk are packed			
1 Piece	lace		10.00	
1 yard	Bolinet (?) lace for collars & sleeves		.75	
6	Belt Ribbons		3.00	
12	Papers Hair Pins		1.20	

15 varas	colored ???		5.62	
6 varas	silk Ribbon	.21	12.00	
6 "	" "	.75	4.50	
6 varas	Waul (?)		.50	
2 Pieces	Pol??? Ribbon	75¢	1.50	
2 doz	Velvet Buttons	75¢	1.50	
49 yds	French calico	22¢	10.78	
1 Piece	white linen		14.00	
2	Silk Hdkfs 2¢ -- 2 @ 2.50 2 @ $1.50		6.00	
24 Doz	Peach (?) Buttons		1.20	
15½ varas	Poplin	$ 1	15.50	
50 "	calico	31½¢	15.62	
13 "	checked Delawn (?)	60¢	7.80	
23½ "	Merino	1.25	29.37	
1 Piece	Domestic		7.00	
6 varas	green grenadine (?)		3.00	
2 Pairs	shoes No. 10 - 11		3.50	
2 " "	No. 13 – 1		4.00	
2 "	Ladies shoes		3.00	
2 "	baby "		1.00	
1	Cashmere block		17.00	
1 Piece	Valencia Lace		17.00	
1 Felt	Hat No. 7		6.00	227.84
Genl D H Maury	1 Box Soap			5.50
"	1 Box **Macaroni**			3.75
				$ 237.09
	Havana 13th May 1864			
	C. G. Ramsay			

804
Invoice

Note: A sheet combining several orders and calculations of customs duties.

J. E. Morales (?)
1 Box containing

Tea	$ 10		10	1.00
Black pepper	2		15	18.45
Clothing &c	123		20	.40
	$ 135			$ 19.85
Paid				

Col. Garner 1 Box contg

Sugar	9	20%	1.80
Sherry wine	13	25	3.25
Tea	3	10	.30
	26		$ 5.35

Sugar & oil 7¢	14	15	2.10
			$ 7.45
Duty Paid			

Genl. Maury
1 Pkge

Cotton, Wool, & Flax mfs &c	225	15%	$ 33.75
	75		
	150		
	188	15%	50.70
	338		
Duties due			86.00

805-809
Preprinted Customs Form

No. 6
Entry of Merchandise
Importer H. O. Brewer & Co
Vessel *Denbigh*
From Havana
Entered June 3d 1864
Value $ 1265   Duty $ 185.10

Agent's Oath
(signed) Benj. Donaldson
Sworn before me, this 3d day of June 1864

Mdse. Entered _____ 18__   Ship Entered May 18 1864
Entry of Merchandise imported into the Port of Mobile, District of Mobile, by H. O. Brewer & Co. in the Br. Str. *Denbigh* Godfrey Master, from Havana

No. of Packages	Contents	Value in Foreign Currency	10%	15%	20%	Duties
20 Bales	Gunny Cloth	864.00		394		$ 134.90
10 Coils	Manila Rope lb 1807	268.67		278		41.70
20 Bales	Oakum 1000	90.00	93			9.30
		1,222.67	93	1172		$ 185.10
	Chges & Com	42.71				
		$ 1,265.38				

Note: Items 1 and 2 were cotton baling supplies.

810
Invoice

20 Bales	Gunny Cloth
20 "	Oakum
11 Bags	Coffee
1807 lb	Manila 7 pkgs

812
Invoice

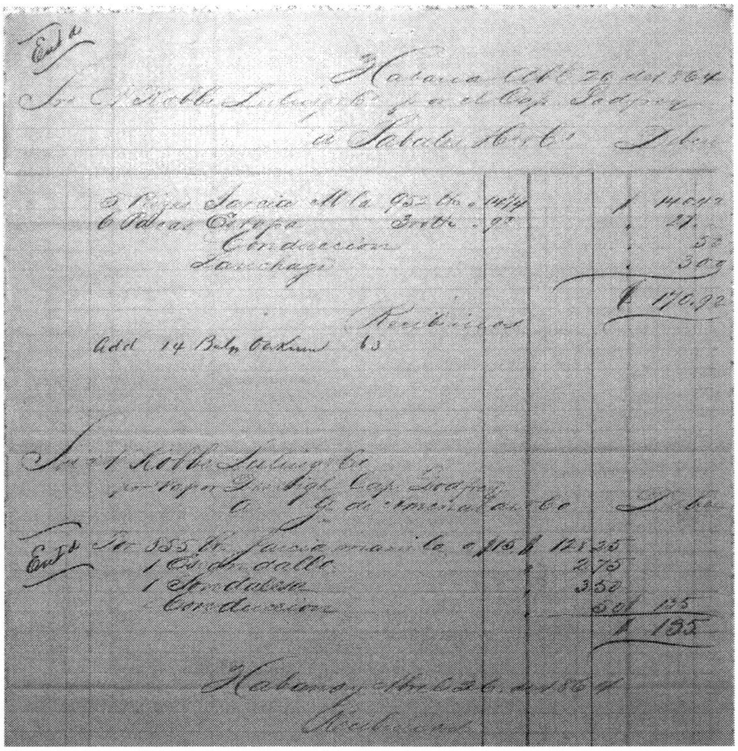

Figure 73. Invoice for Kobbe Luling & Co.

Habana Abl 26 dr 1864
Srs A Kobbe Luling & Co por el Cap. Godfrey
A Sabates H & Co Debes

5 Piezas	Jarcia Mla	952 lbs @ 14¾	$ 140.42
6 Pacas	Estopa	300 lbs @ 9¢	27.00
	Conduccion		.50
	Lanchage		3.00
			$ 170.92
		Recibimos	
	Add 14 Bales Oakum 63		

Srs A Kobbe Luling & Co.
Por Vapor *Denbigh* Cap Godfrey

	A G. de Amenabas & Co		Debes
Por 855 lbs	Jarcia manila	a $ 15	$ 128.25
1	Escandalla		2.75
1	Sondalesa		3.50
	Conduccion		.50
			135.00
	Habana Abril 26 de 1864		
		Recibimos	

813
Invoice

Note: These supplies were intended for baling cotton. Similar orders for gunny cloth and rope for baling cotton were common at Galveston late in the war.

Invoice of 10 Bales Gunny cloth shipped by A. Kobbe Luling & Co on board the Brit Str *Denbigh* Godfrey Mr bound to Mobile for account & risk of whom it may concern.

10 Bales	Gunny Cloth each 360 yds		
	3600 yds @ 12¢ pr. Yd		$ 4320.00
	Charges		
	Outward depot duty on 3888 varas		
	@ 2¢ $ 77.76 3 / ¢ No	$ 2.91	
	Launch hire	$ 5.25	
	Petties &tc	$ 2.12	10.28
			$ 442.28
	Commn 2½%		11.06
	E. & O. E.		$ 453.30
	Havana April 26 1864		
	A. Kobbe Luling & Co.		
	(signed) ??????		

814
Invoice

Invoice of 10 Bales Gunny cloth shipped by A. Kobbe Luling & Co on board the Brit Str *Denbigh* Godfrey Mr bound to Mobile for account & risk of whom it may concern.

10 Bales	Gunny Cloth each 360 yards		
	3600 yds @ 12¢		$ 4320.00
	Charges		
	Launch hire	$ 5.25	
	Petties &tc	$ 2.12	7.37

			$ 439.37
	Commn 2½%		11.00
	E. & O. E.		$ 450.37
	Havana May 13th 1864		
	A. Kobbe Luling & Co.		
	(signed) ??????		

815-818
Preprinted Customs Form

No. 7
Entry of Merchandise
Importer H. O. Brewer & Co.
Vessel *Denbigh*
From Havana
Entered 3d June 1864
Value $ 863 Duty $ 129.45

Agent's Oath
(signed) Benj. Donaldson
H. O. Brewer & Co., the owner
Sworn before me this 3d day of June 1864

Mdse. Entered _____ 18___ Ship Entered May 18 1864
Entry of Merchandise imported into the Port of Mobile, District of Mobile, by H. O. Brewer & Co. in the Br. Str. *Denbigh* Godfrey Master, from Havana

Marks	No. of Packages	Contents	Value in Foreign Currency	10%	15%	Duties
J. Scott	1 Box	Shoes 7 Prs	12.75		14	$ 2.10
		Cotton mfs	38.75		41	6.15
W. R. Smith	1 Box	Iron mfs	20.00		21	3.15
J. A. Murray	2 Bdles	Sheet iron Iron mfs lbs 1218	74.58		78	11.70
D. LeBaron	3 Coils	Manilla Rope 3083	531.96		558	83.70
No. 7	1 Bdle	Leather hose	144.00		151	22.65
			822.04		$863	$ 129.45
			41.10			
			$ 863.14			

819
Invoice

Mr. J. Scott

1 Pair	Boots	$ 3	3.00
6 Pr	Shoes	1.95	10.25

1 "	Gaiters	2.50	2.50
2 Doz	Stockings	4.00 Ea	8.00
5 yds	Linen	50¢	2.50
1 Doz	Silk Hdkfs		9.00
½ "	Stockg (Stockings)	3	1.50
1 "	???	2	2.00
1 Pc	Calico	28 yds 25¢	7.00
1 "	Cotton Goods	23 yds 25¢	5.75
			51.50
		Chg & Com	2.04
			53.54
		~~Mr. Hilton~~	
	8.35	H.O. Brewer & Co	

820
Invoice

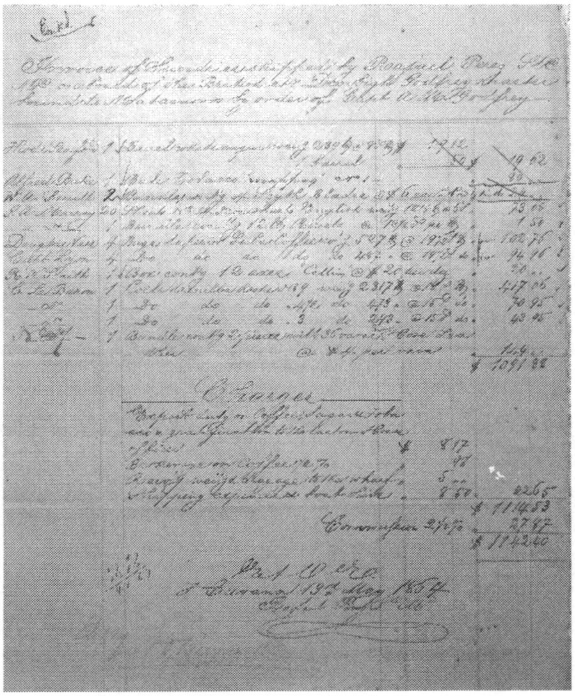

Figure 74. Invoice showing commercial orders for multiple individuals.

Invoice of Sundries shipped by Rafael Perez Sta Ma on board of the British str *Denbigh* Godfrey Master bound to **Matamoros** (false destination) by order of Capt. A. M. Godfrey.

Thods Sanford	1 Barrel	white sugar wei'g (weighing) 239 lbs	@ 8 P Lb ~~19.12~~	
		1 barrel	~~50¢~~	~~19.62~~
Alfred Batie	1 Bale	Tobacco "wrapping" No 1		~~80.00~~
W. A. Smith	2 Bundles cont'g	4 Scyth Blades	@ $ 6 ea Piece	~~24.00~~
J. A. Murray	20 Sheets	No 13 Iron sheets English wei'g 1219 lbs	@ 6 P	73.08
Do	1 Bundle cont'g	12 lbs Rivets	@ 12½ P pr lb	1.50

Douglas Vass	4 Bags	Superior Cuba Coffee w'g 1218 lb	@ 19½	102.75
Capt Lyon	4 Do	do do do do do 487 lbs	@ 19½	94.96
R. W. Smith	1 Box cont'g	12 axes "Collins"	@ $ 20 per doz	20.00
C. LeBaron	1 Coil	Manilla Rope No 9 wei'g 2317 lbs	@ 18 P	417.06
Do	1 Do	do do " 4½ do 473 "	@ 15 P	70.95
Do	1 Do	do do " 3 do 293 "	@ 15 P	43.95
No 7	1 Bundle cont'g	2 pieces with 36 varas Gum Hose Leather	@ $ 4/vara	144.00
				$ 1091.88
		Charges		
		Havana 13th May 1864		
		Rafael Perez Sta Ma		
	41.67 (duty)			
		Paid by H. O. Brewer & Co.		

822-824
Preprinted Customs Form

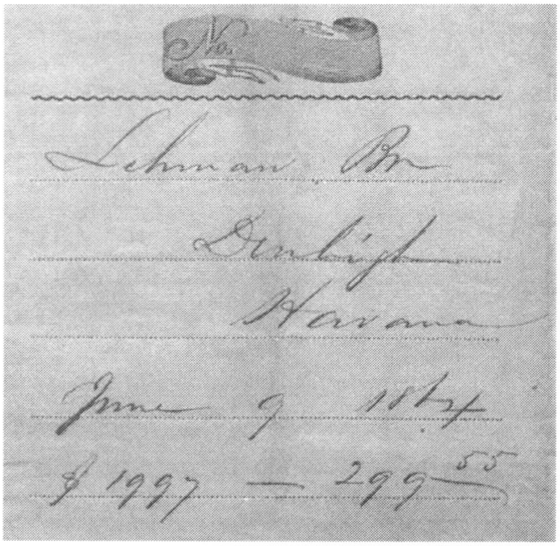
No.
Lehman Br
Denbigh
Havana
June 9 1864
$ 1997 — 299 55

Emanuel & Mayer Lehman

Figure 75. Customs form for Lehman Brothers.

No. ___
Entry of Merchandise
Importer **Lehman Br**[81]

---

[81] In 1844, 23-year-old Henry Lehman, the son of a Jewish cattle merchant, emigrated to the United States from Rimpar, Bavaria. He settled in Montgomery, Alabama, where he opened a dry-goods store, "H. Lehman". In 1847, following the arrival of his brother Emanuel Lehman, the firm became "H. Lehman and Bro." With the arrival of their youngest brother, Mayer Lehman, in 1850, the firm changed its name again and "Lehman Brothers" was founded.

During the 1850s, capitalizing on cotton's importance and high market value, the three brothers began to routinely accept raw cotton from customers as payment for merchandise, eventually beginning a second business trading in cotton. Within a few years this business grew to become the most significant part of their operation. Following Henry's death from yellow fever in 1855, the remaining brothers continued to focus on their commodities-trading/brokerage operations.

By 1858, the center of cotton trading had shifted from the South to New York City, where factors and commission houses were based. Lehman opened its first branch office in New York City's Manhattan borough, and 32-year-old

Vessel *Denbigh*
From Havana
Entered June 9 1864
Value $ 1997 Duty $ 299.55

Owner's Oath
(signed) M Lehman
Sworn before me, this 9th day of June 1864
J. C. Coleman Dy Collector

Mdse. Entered _____ 18__ Ship Entered June 7 18__
Entry of Merchandise imported into the Port of Mobile, District of Mobile, by Lehman Brs in the Br. Str. *Denbigh* Godfrey Master, from Havana

Marks	No. of Packages	Contents	Value in Foreign Currency	10%	15%	20%	Duties
T H	9 Cases	Cotton & Wool Cards	$ 1920.00				
		Chges & Com	76.80				
			1996.80				
			Iron mfs not sfd		1997	15%	$ 299.55

825a
Invoice

Lehman Brothers
Bot of Thomas Henry

T H	4 Cases	80 Doz Cotton Cards	$ 7.25	580.00
	1 "	20 " Wool "	7.00	140.00
				$ 720.00
		April 25th 1864		
		chgs & Com		28.80
				$ 748.80
		Ex dy Appr 112.35		

825b
Invoice

Havana May 28th 1864

Messrs Lehman & Bro
Bot of Thomas Henry

T H	4 Cases	Cotton Cards 60 doz each 240 Doz	$ 5	$ 1200.00

Emanuel relocated there to run the office. The firm's headquarters were eventually moved to New York City, where it helped found the New York Cotton Exchange in 1870. The firm later became the famous Wall Street firm that folded in 2008.

		Chgs & Com		48.00
				1248.00
		Ex dy Appr 187.20		

826
Preprinted Customs Form

No. 33
Entry of Merchandise
Importer J. L. Harris
Vessel *Denbigh*
From Havana
Entered June 10th 1864
Value $ 176 Duty $ 26.40

Owner's Oath
(signed) J. L. Harris
Sworn before me, this 10th day of June 1864

Mdse. Entered 10th June 1864 Ship Entered 7th June 1864
Entry of Merchandise imported into the Port of Mobile, District of Mobile, by J. L. Harris in the Br. Str. *Denbigh* Godfrey Master, from Havana

No. of Packages	Contents	Value in Foreign Currency	10%	15%	20%	Duties
1 Box	Cotton mfs	$ 61.00		64		$ 9.60
	Silk mfs	55.20		58		8.70
	Linens	51.10		54		8.10
		167.30		176		$ 26.00
	Chgs & Com	8.20				
		$ 175.50				

829a
Invoice

List of goods shipped by C. G. Ramsay Esq. On Steamer *Denbigh* for J. M. Muldon

J M Muldon	1 Sack	Coffee 181 lbs	21¢ free	$ 38.00
"	1 Bbl	White sugar 285 "	8	22.00
"	1 doz bottles	English Mustard		5.00
3 Packages	1 " "	Olive Oil		5.00
	1 lb	Indigo		2.00
	5 "	Carbonate Soda	20¢	1.00
	2 Doz	~~Toilet~~ Soap ???	$ 1.75	3.50
	13 Varas	White linen Lawn	@ 50¢	6.50
	6	Silk Pocket Hkchfs	$ 1.25	7.50

	16 Varas	figured Linen	40	6..40
	1 Pc.	India Mull 22.00	50	11.00
	1	Gold Pen & Hdle		4.25
	20 v	Blue **pineapple Silk**[82]	@ 90	18.00
	1	pine apple dress Silk		15.00
				$ 145.96
		Havana June 10 1864		38.01
				$ 107.95
		Chg & Com		3.50
		C. G. Ramsay		111.45
24 20	4.80			
87 15	13.05	Wool mfs		
	17.85	Fan. Trimmings $ 16.63		
	2.70			
	20.55 (duty)			

829b
Invoice

C. G. Ramsay Esq — Duplicate
To J. W. Dever Dr
Judge W G Jones — W. G. J.

1 Bundle	6½ Varas	White Muslin	40	2.60
	6½ "	Swiss "	37½	2.43
	2 pieces	fine blchd Domestic 40 yds	25	10.00
	13 Varas	Blue Delain	45	5.85
	13 "	Dark brown Calico	30	3.90
	2 prs	" Kid Gloves	137½	2.75
				$ 27.53
		Havana June 1 1864		
		4.20 (duty)		

831b
Invoice

J. L. Harris
1 Box Cont.
Cotton $ 61, Silk $ 55.2, Linen 17.01
$ 174.5½ R(eales)
Comiss adding 27.30
Denbigh

[82] Highly desirable fabric made of fibers extracted by hand from pineapple leaves and exported from the Philippines.

831c
Invoice

J Robertson

2 pieces	Linen	$ 16.50
3 doz	stockings	9.00
4 pieces	calicoes	9.25
		34.75

831a and 832
Invoice

Captn A. M. Godfrey to J. W. Dever Dr.
Wm T. Marshall

½ Yds	Black Alpaca	1.12½	8.43
1 Dz	Skeins Black Sewing Silk		3.00
31 Yds	Purple Linen for dress	37½	11.62
15 "	Black & White "	"	5.62
15 "	**Mourning** "		5.62
2 Pieces	White "	9.00	18.00
3	**Hoop Skirts**	2.59	7.50
2	French Corsetts 20 inch	3.50	7.00
1 Bunch	Shoe Strings		3.00
20 Yds	Mosquito Bobinet	40	8.00
2	Black Parasols	2.50	5.00
1 Dz	Corset Lace		3.00
2	Black Belts	50	1.00
2	Extra Fine Combs		1.25
			$ 89.54

	Amt Carried over			$ 89.54
1	Dressing Comb		.75	
2	Small tuck "	75	1.50	
1 Pr	Heel Slippers # 3½	1.50	3.00	
3 "	" " 3	1.50	3.00	
	Cartage & Launch		1.00	
	Commission 2½%		2.43	10.18
				$ 99.72
	Havana June 2nd 1864			
	J. W. Dever			
	43.94 (duty)			

833a-c
Three short forms: Oath of Importers or Agents

Signed: Wm. T. Marshall, Tho. C. McDowell, and H. L. Harris

834a-c
Three short forms: Oath of Importers or Agents

Signed: James M Muldon and Geo. A. Tuthill. The third is not signed but had the following notes:

1 fine Linen Hkchs &c	22.65
Cottons stockings	28.00
Cotton mfs	4.20
	$ 54.85

835a
Short form: Oath of Importers or Agents

Signed: 9 June 1864 Wm. G. Jones

835b
Invoice

C. G. Ramsey Esq. Duplicate
To J. W. Dever Dr
G A Tuthill G. A. Tuthill
1 Bundle

2 pieces	Robnett for bars (?) 53 yds	@ 45	$ 21.85
6 pair	Ladies Hose # 9½	$ 6	3.00
1½ doz	" " # 9	$ 6	9.00
6 pair	Children " " 8½	$ 4	2.00
1 oz	Chiny ??? Lephys		.50
1 "	Run (?) " "		.50
2	Jackonet Worked Bands (?)	1.50	3.00
3 each	White Col'd.& Black Belts	.75	6.75
1 doz	Hem Stchd (Stitched) Hkchfs		6.00
			$ 54.60
			2.00
	Havana June 1st 1864		57.00
	8.55 (duty)		

835c
Invoice

Goods imported by A. Peres per steamer *Mary* from Havana

100 lb.	Coffee	20.00
2 pieces	linen	30.00
3 lb	medicines	1.00
		$ 51.00
	Charges	6.00
		$ 57.00
	Mobile June 4 1864	
	A Peres	
	Less charges on coff(ee)	
	duties not paid	
	$ 5.10	

836
Invoice

Mr. McDowell
To the Florida Store

2½ doz	linen handkfs		$ 7.00
4 doz	ladies handkfs		15.00
10 vs	fine linen at	50¢	5.00
22 "	French calico at		2.20
32	barege at	37½¢	12.00
32	Muslin delaine at	37¢	12.00
10	cashmere at	1.12½	11.25
10 prs	**ladies silk hose**		15.00
12 papers	needles		1.20
15 Skeins	of black sewing Silk		3.00
2 pr.	ladies Gaiters		5.00
½	**ream paper**		1.25
	including all charges & Com		$ 92.10
	Havana May 28 1864		
	Received payment.		
$ 13.80 (duty)	Vicente ??? ???		

838
Invoice

C. G. Ramsey Esq. To J. W. Dever Dr Duplicate
J. Emanuel

J Emanuel	150 lbs	White Sugar	8¢	12.00
	2 Doz prs	Children's Hose	2.50	5.00
		including all charges		$ 17.00
		Havana June 1st 1864		
	3.35 (duty)			

839
Invoice

C. G. Ramsay Esq. Duplicate
To J. W. Dever Dr.
R. W. Hallett

R W Hallet				
1 Bundle	½ Doz	Silk Scks (Socks) for Infant		5.50
	13½ Varas	Linen Lawn	40	5.40
	2 prs	Infants Slippers	75	1.50
	1 "	" Shoes		.60
				$ 13.00
		Havana June 1st 1864		
		$ 7.50 (duty)		

840
Invoice

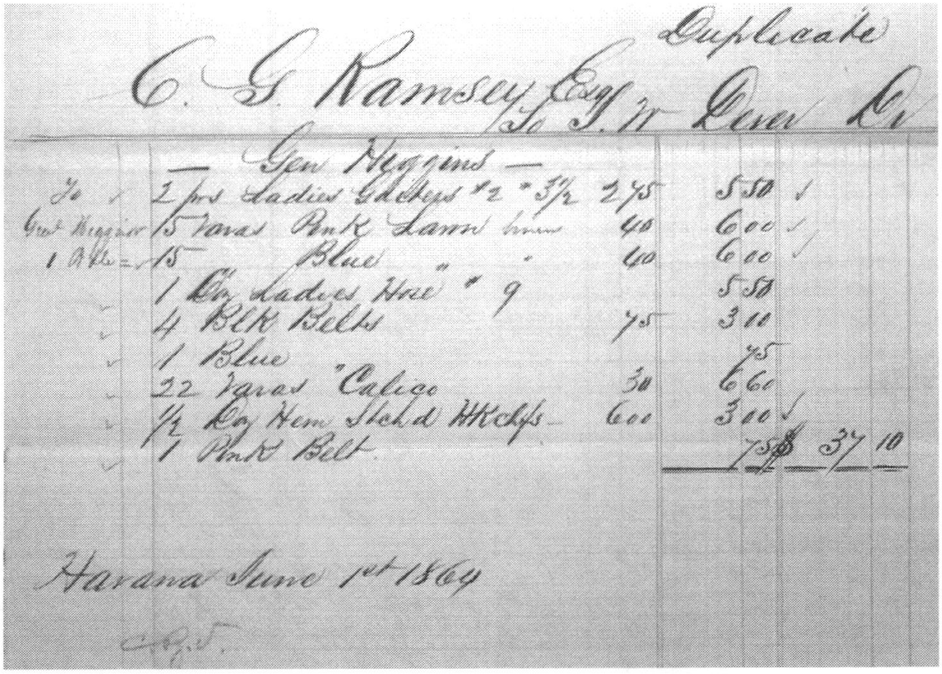
Duplicate
C. G. Ramsey Esq
To J. W. Dever Dr
— Gen Higgins —
To 2 prs Ladies Gaiters #2 #5½ 2.75 5.50
Genl Higgins 15 Varas Pink Lawn linen 40 6.00
1 Bdle = 15 Blue " " 40 6.00
1 Doz Ladies Hose #9 5.50
4 Blk Belts 75 3.00
1 Blue 75
22 Varas Calico 30 6.60
½ Doz Hem Stchd Hdkfs 6.00 3.00
1 Pink Belt 75 $37.10
Havana June 1st 1864
C.G.S.

Figure 76. Invoice for Gen. Edward Higgins, Commander of Fort Morgan.

C. G. Ramey Esq   Duplicate

To J. W. Dever   Dr

Gen Higgins

To	2 prs	Ladies Gaiters # 2 # 3½	2.75	5.50
Genl Higgins	15 Varas	Pink Lawn linen	40	6.00
1 Bdle	15	Blue " "	40	6.00
	1 Doz	Ladies Hose # 9		5.50
	4	Blk Belts	75	3.00
	1	Blue "		.75
	22 Varas	Calico	30	6.60
	½ Doz	Hem Stchd Hkchfs	6.00	3.00
	1	Pink Belt		.75
				$ 37.10
		Havana June 1st 1864		

841-842
Substitute for Preprinted Customs Form

No. 31
Entry of Merchandise
Importer A. Peres
Vessel *Denbigh*
From Havana
Entered June 9th 1864
Value $ 35   Duty $ 5.25

Entry of Mdse by A. Peres
In the Br. Str. *Denbigh*, Godfrey Master, from Havana, 7th June 1864

1 Pkge	Flax mfs linens	$ 31		
	Chges & Com	4	Flax mfs $ 35 15%	$ 5.25
		35		

843-844
Substitute for Preprinted Customs Form

No. 30
Entry of Merchandise
Importer J. Emanuel
Vessel *Denbigh*
From Havana
Entered June 9th 1864
Value $ 17 Duty $ 3.15

Entry of Mdse by J. Emmanuel
In the Br. Str *Denbigh*, Godfrey Master, from Havana, 7th June 1864.

1 Bdle	Hosiery	$ 5.00	5	15%	$ .75
1 Bll	Sugar white 150 lbs	11.00	12	20%	2.40
	Chges & Com	1.20			$ 3.15
		17.20			

845-846
Substitute for Preprinted Customs Form

No. 29
Entry of Merchandise
Importer R. W. Hallett
Vessel *Denbigh*
From Havana
Entered June 9th 1864
Value $ 50 Duty $ 7.50

Entry of Mdse by R. W. Hallett
In the Br. Str *Denbigh*, Godfrey Master, from Havana, 7th June 1864.

R. W. H./Higgins	1 Bdle	Flax mfs	$ 20.40	21	15%	$ 3.05
R. W. H.	1 Bdle	Cotton mfs	14.00	15	"	2.25
		Chgs & Com	13.10	14	"	2.10
			$ 47.50	50		7.40
			2.60			
			$ 50.10			

847-848
Substitute for Preprinted Customs Form

No. 28
Entry of Merchandise
Importer Geo A. Tuthill
Vessel *Denbigh*
From Havana
Entered June 9th 1864
Value $ 57 Duty $ 8.55

Entry of Mdse by Geo. A. Tuthill
In the Br. Str *Denbigh*, Godfrey Master, from Havana, 7th June 1864.

1 Bdle	Cotton mfs	$ 48.60	50	15%	$ 7.50
	Flax "	6.00	7	"	1.05
		$ 54.60			$ 8.55
	Chge & Com	2.35			
		$ 56.95			

849-850
Substitute for Preprinted Customs Form

No. 27
Entry of Merchandise
Importer W. T. Marshall
Vessel *Denbigh*
From Havana
Entered June 9th 1864
Value $ 100 Duty $ 15

Entry of Mdse by W. T. Marshall
In the Br. Str *Denbigh*, Godfrey Master, from Havana, 7th June 1864.

1 Pkge	Flax mfs	$ 40.86	$ 42	15%	$ 6.30
	Shoes	7.50	8	"	1.20
	Combs	3.50	4	"	.60
	Cotton mfs	43.94	46	"	6.90
		95.80	100		15.00
	Chges & Com	4.00			
		$ 99.80			

851-852
Substitute for Preprinted Customs Form

No. 22
Entry of Merchandise
Importer James Robertson
Vessel *Denbigh*

From Havana
Entered June 9th 1864
Value $ 37 Duty $ 5.55

Entry of Mdse by James Robertson
In the Br. Str *Denbigh*, Godfrey Master, from Havana, 7th June 1864.

1 Pkge	Flax mfs	$ 16.50	17	15%	$ 2.55
	Cotton mfs	18.25	20	"	3.00
		$ 34.75	37		$ 5.55
		2.00			
		$ 36.75			

853-854
Substitute for Preprinted Customs Form

No. 23
Entry of Merchandise
Importer Robert Otis
Vessel *Denbigh*
From Havana
Entered June 9th 1864
Value $ 58 Duty $ 8.70

Entry of Mdse by Robert Otis
In the Br. Str *Denbigh*, Godfrey Master, from Havana, 7th June 1864.

1 Box	Linen	$ 22.65	23	15%	$ 3.45
	Cotton mfs	28.00	30	"	4.50
	Hosiery	4.20	5	"	.75
		$ 54.85	58		$ 8.70
	Chges & Com	3.35			
		$ 58.20			

855-856
Substitute for Preprinted Customs Form

No. 26
Entry of Merchandise
Importer W. G. Jones
Vessel *Denbigh*
From Havana
Entered June 9th 1864
Value $ 28 Duty $ 4.20

Entry of Mdse by Wm. G. Jones

In the Br. Str *Denbigh*, Godfrey Master, from Havana, 7th June 1864.

1 Pkge	Cotton mfs, with chges & com	$ 27.53	Cotton mfs $ 28	15%	$ 4.20

857-858
Substitute for Preprinted Customs Form

No. 24
Entry of Merchandise
Importer James M. Muldon
Vessel *Denbigh*
From Havana
Entered June 9th 1864
Value $ 128 Duty $ 20.20

Entry of Mdse by J. Emmanuel
In the Br. Str *Denbigh*, Godfrey Master, from Havana, 7th June 1864.

1 Pkge	wool mfs	$ 16.63	17	15%	$ 2.55
	Flax mfs	34.25	36	"	5.40
2 Boxes	olive oil	14.50	15	"	2.25
	Silk mfs	33.00	34	"	5.10
1 lb	**Indigo**	2.00	2	5%	.10
1 Bll	Sugar white lb 285	22.80	24	20%	4.80
		123.18	$ 128		20.20
	Chges & Com	5.00			
		$ 138.18			

860-862
Preprinted Customs Form

No. 36
Entry of Merchandise
Importer John Scott
Vessel *Denbigh*
From Havana
Entered June 10th 1864
Value $ 28 Duty $ 4

Owner's Oath
(signed) John Scott
Sworn before me, this 10th day of June 1864

Mdse. Entered 10th June 1864 Ship Entered 7th June 1864
Entry of Merchandise imported into the Port of Mobile, District of Mobile, by John Scott in the B. Str. *Denbigh* Godfrey Master, from Havana

No. of Packages	Contents	Value in Foreign Currency	10%	15%	20%	Duties
1 Box	Olive Oil	$ 5		6		.90
1 Keg	Olives	4		4		.60
one	cheese	4	4			.40
1 Box	Pickles	12		14		2.10
		25	4	24		4.00
	Chgs & Com	3				
		28				

863a
Invoice

Capt A. M. Godfrey
To J. W. Dever Dr
J. C. Denis

2 Bolts	Domestic	$ 7.25	14.50
4 Doz	White Cotton Hose	6.50	26.00
3	Ladies Lawn Hkchfs	3.00	9.00
	Comm 2½%		1.23
			$ 50.73
	Habana June 1st 1864		
	J. W. Dever		
	7.65 (duty)		

863b
Short form: Oath of Importers or Agents

Signed: John J. Sage

865
Invoice

Mr Sage

12 yds	Linen	50¢	6.00
1	Calico	???	(blank)
1	P White Cotton	$ 3	3.00
7 Pr	Shoes	???	10.00
1 Doz	Hdfs	???	3.00
1 "	???	$ 2	2.00
14 Yds	Canvas	50¢	7.00

56 yds	Calico	22¢	11.20
48 "	Linen	30¢	14.40
			59.60
	9.65 plata (silver)		3.00
	5 papel (paper)		62.60
	$ 9.45 (duty)		

Note: Invoice on scrap of paper, written in smudged pencil and difficult to read.

866
Two short forms: Oath of Importers or Agents

Signed: P. Ch. Emanuel (?) for J. C. Denis (?) and John Scott

---

868-869
Substitute for Preprinted Customs Form

No. 34
Entry of Merchandise
Importer John J. Lazo
Vessel *Denbigh*
From Havana
Entered June 10th 1864
Value $ 63 Duty $ 9.45

Entry of Mdse by John J. Lazo
In the Br. Str *Denbigh*, Godfrey Master, from Havana, 7th June 1864.

1 Pkge	Flax mfs	$ 32.40	34	15%	$ 5.10
	Cotton	17.20	18	"	2.70
	Shoes 7 prs	10.00	11	"	1.65
		59.60	$ 63		$ 9.45
		3.00			
		$ 62.60			

870-871
Substitute for Preprinted Customs Form

No. 35
Entry of Merchandise
Importer J. C. Denis
Vessel *Denbigh*
From Havana

Entered June 10th 1864
Value $ 51 Duty $ 7.65

Entry of Mdse by J. C. Denis
In the Br. Str *Denbigh*, Godfrey Master, from Havana, 7th June 1864.

1 Pkge	Cotton mfs	$ 49.00			
	Chges & Com	1.73	Cotton mfs $ 51	15%	$ 7.65
		$ 50.73			

872-874
Preprinted Customs Form

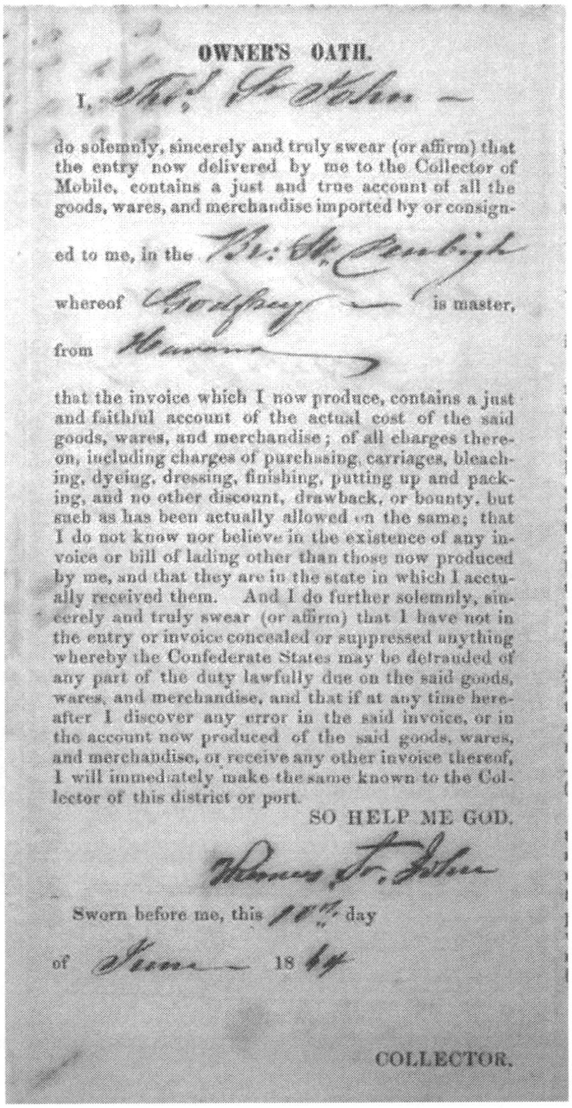

OWNER'S OATH.

I, Thos. St. John

do solemnly, sincerely and truly swear (or affirm) that the entry now delivered by me to the Collector of Mobile, contains a just and true account of all the goods, wares, and merchandise imported by or consigned to me, in the Br: Str. Denbigh whereof Godfrey is master, from Havana that the invoice which I now produce, contains a just and faithful account of the actual cost of the said goods, wares, and merchandise; of all charges thereon, including charges of purchasing, carriages, bleaching, dyeing, dressing, finishing, putting up and packing, and no other discount, drawback, or bounty, but such as has been actually allowed on the same; that I do not know nor believe in the existence of any invoice or bill of lading other than those now produced by me, and that they are in the state in which I actually received them. And I do further solemnly, sincerely and truly swear (or affirm) that I have not in the entry or invoice concealed or suppressed anything whereby the Confederate States may be defrauded of any part of the duty lawfully due on the said goods, wares, and merchandise, and that if at any time hereafter I discover any error in the said invoice, or in the account now produced of the said goods, wares, and merchandise, or receive any other invoice thereof, I will immediately make the same known to the Collector of this district or port.

SO HELP ME GOD.

Thomas St. John

Sworn before me, this 10th day of June 1864

COLLECTOR.

Figure 77. File contained an added short form with revised Owner's Oath.

No. 39
Entry of Merchandise
Importer Ths. St. John
Vessel *Denbigh*
From Havana
Entered June 10th 1864
Value $ 37 Duty $ 5.55

Owner's Oath
(signed) Thomas St. John
Sworn before me, this 10th day of June 1864

Mdse. Entered 10th June 1864 Ship Entered June 7th 1864
Entry of Merchandise imported into the Port of Mobile, District of Mobile, by Ths. St. John in the Br. Str. *Denbigh* Godfrey Master, from Havana

No. of Packages	Contents	Value in Foreign Currency	10%	15%	20%	Duties
2 Pkges	Flax mfs	$ 17.38		18		$ 2.70
	Wool mfs	6.00		6		.90
	Cutlery	12.25		13		1.95
		35.63		37		$ 5.55
	Chges & Com	1.30				
		$ 36.93				

875
Invoice

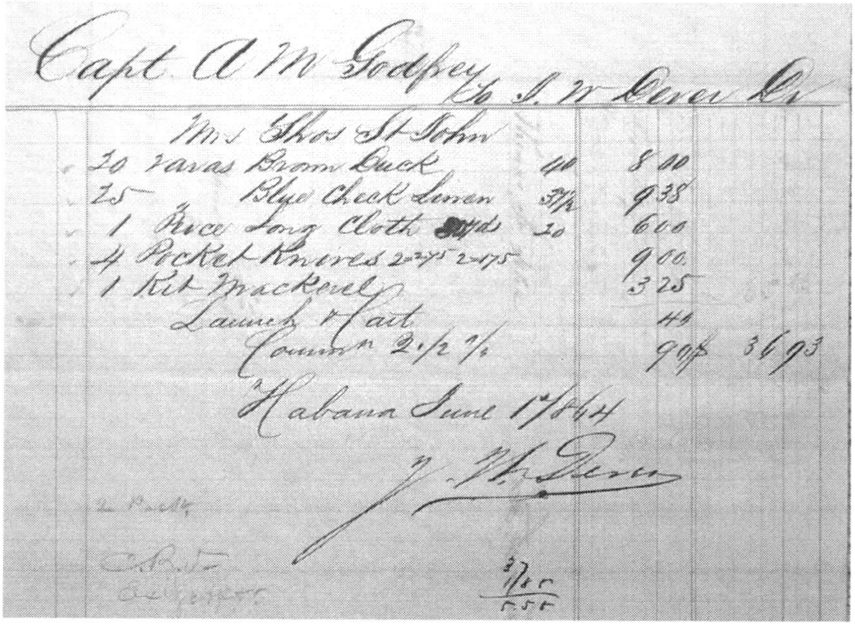
Capt A M Godfrey
To J. W. Deven Dr
Mrs Thos St John
20 varas Brown Duck 40 8 00
25 Blue Check Linen 37½ 9 38
1 Piece Long Cloth yds 20 6 00
4 Pocket Knives 2.25 2.75 9 00
1 Kit Mackerel 3 25
Launch & Cart 40
Comm 2½% 90 36 93
Habana June 1/864
J. W. Deven

Figure 78. Invoice of small order for Mrs. Thomas St. John. A pocket knife was found on the *Denbigh*.

Capt A. M. Godfrey

To J. W. Dever Dr

Mrs. Thos. St. John

20 Varas	Brown Duck	40	8.00
25 "	Blue Check Linen	37½	9.38
1 Piece	Long Cloth 30 yds	20	6.00
4	**Pocket Knives** 2=2.75 2=1.75		9.00
1 Kit	Mackerel		3.35
	Launch & Cart.		.40
	Commn 2½%		.90
			$ 36.93
	Habana June 1st 1864		
	J. W. Dever		
	5.55 (duty)		

876-877
Substitute for Preprinted Customs Form

No. 38
Entry of Merchandise
Importer J. Waldaner
Vessel *Denbigh*
From Havana
Entered June 10th 1864
Value $ 112 Duty $ 16.80

Entry of Mdse by J. Waldaner
In the Br. Str *Denbigh*, Godfrey Master, from Havana, 7th June 1864.

Three Pkges	Cotton mfs	$ 48.00	50	15%	$ 7.50
	Linens	58.95	62	"	9.30
	Chges & Com	5.30	112	"	$ 16.80
		112.25			

878a
Invoice

Note: Written in nearly illegible pencil.

Denbigh
Mr. Waldaner

3 Packgs ???	$ 106.95
Cotton ??? ???	5.30
	112.25
16.80 (duty)	

878b
A short form: Oath of Importers or Agents

Signed: J. Waldaner

879-880
Substitute for Preprinted Customs Form

No. 37
Entry of Merchandise
Importer J. N. Shawhan
Vessel *Denbigh*
From Havana
Entered June 10th 1864
Value $ 51 Duty $ 7.65

Entry of Mdse by J. N. Shawhan
In the Br. Str *Denbigh*, Godfrey Master, from Havana, 7th June 1864.

1 Box	wool mfs	$ 11.25	12	15%	$ 1.80
	Cotton "	15.00	16		2.40
	Flax "	22.50	23		3.45
		$ 48.75	$ 51		$ 7.65
	Chges & Com	2.50			
		$ 51.25			

881a-b
Two short forms: Oath of Importers or Agents

Signed: Thomas St. John and J. N. Shawhan

881c
Invoice

Mr. Shawhan
1 Box

Cloak		11.25
Cotton & Linen		41.25
		52.50
		- 3.20
		49.30
Box & Hire	$ 1	1.00
		$ 50.30
$ 7.50 (duty)		

Denbigh Customs Manifests, June 1864 2 of 2, Transcripts

Denbigh Voyage No. 6, Havana-Mobile-Havana
Havana, last date document prepared there, 4 June 1864 so the ship sailed soon thereafter.
Mobile, date ship entered (port and reported arrival to C.S. Customs) was 7 June 1864.
Mobile departure, cotton export manifests dated 14 June 1864 so ship sailed soon thereafter. (421 bales cotton, 218,890 lbs., $124,764, 57¢ per lb.)

885-887
Preprinted Customs Form

No. 41
Entry of Merchandise
Importer J. C. Hodges
Vessel *Denbigh*
From Havana
Entered June 10th 1864
Value $ 64 Duty $ 9.65

Owner's Oath
(signed) Jno. C. Hodges
Sworn before me, this 10th day of June 1864

Mdse. Entered 10th June 1864 Ship Entered June 7th 1864
Entry of Merchandise imported into the Port of Mobile, District of Mobile, by Jno. C. Hodges in the Br. Str. *Denbigh* Godfrey Master, from Havana

No. of Packages	Contents	Value in Foreign Currency	10%	15%	20%	Duties
1 Pkge	Flannel	$ 37.90		39		$ 5.85
	Shoes prs 7	15.50		16		2.40
	Indigo lbs 2	3.50	4			.40
	Castille Soap " 15	4.65			5	1.00
		61.55	4	55	5	$ 9.65
	Chges & Com	2.51				
		$ 64.12				

888a
A short form: Oath of Importers or Agents

Signed: Jno. C. Hodges

888b
Invoice

Capt A. M. Godfrey
To J. W. Dever Dr
John C Hodges

20 Varas	fine Flannel	55	11.00
18 Yds	figured fine Delaine	62½	11.25
1 Dz	Skeins Red hookg (hooking) Cotton		
2	Blk Belt Ribbons	65	1.30
1 pr	**Suspenders**		1.50
1 1/3 Yds	Casimer for Pants		5.50
2 Dz	Toilet Soap	2.00	4.00
5 lbs	Castile Soap	13	.65
2 lbs	Indigo	1.75	3.50
6	Tooth Brushes		???
1 Gros	**Shoe Strings**		.60
2	Woolen over Shirts	3.00	6.00
3 prs	Fine Blk Gaiters #1 & 1½	2.75	8.25
2 prs	Morocco Shoes debe	1.50	3.00
2 prs	Blck Slippers	13½	2.75
2	**porcelain Wash bowls**	75	1.50
	Cartage & Launch & Commission		2.57
			$ 65.62
	J. W. Dever		1.50
	$ 9.60 (duty)		64.12

890-891
Invoice

Note: Large quantities indicate possible merchant's order.

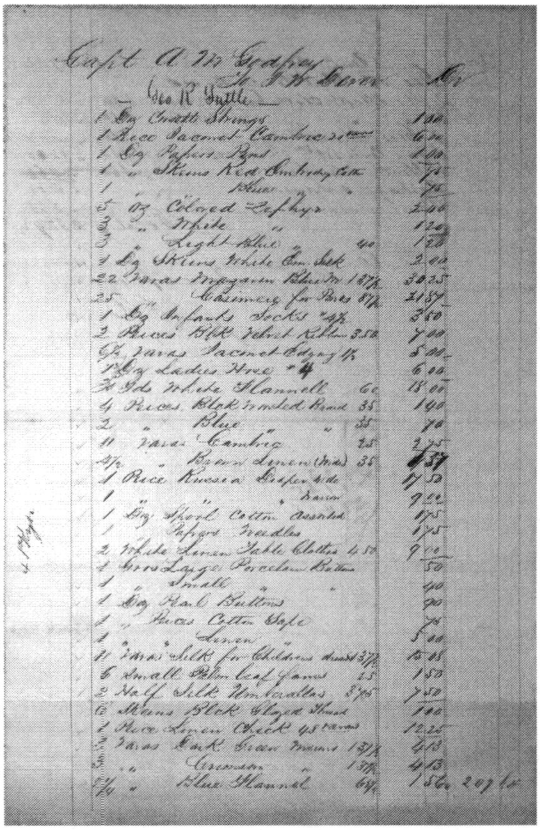

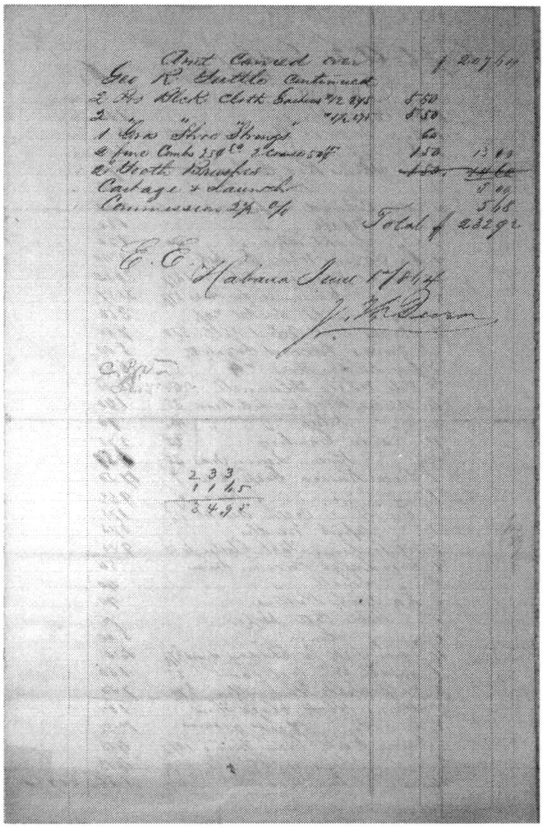

Figure 79. Invoice of large order for George R. Tuttle.

Capt A. M. Godfrey

To J. W. Dever Dr

Geo. R. Tuttle

1 Dz	**Corset Strings**		1.00	
1 Piece	Jaconet Cambric 20 varas		6.00	
1 Dz	Papers Pens		1.00	
1 "	Skeins Red Embroidery Cotton		.75	
1 "	" Blue " "		.75	
5 Oz	Colored Zephyr		2.00	
3 "	White "		1.20	
3 "	Light Blue "	40	1.20	
1 Dz	Skeins White Em.(broidery) Silk		2.00	
22 Varas	Mazarin Blu M.	1.37½	30.25	
25 "	Casimere for Pants	87½	21.87	
1 Dz	Infants Socks #4½		3.50	
2 Pieces	Blk Velvet Ribbon	3.50	7.00	
6½ varas	Jacont Edging	1½	5.00	
7½ Dz	Ladies Hose #4		6.00	
30 Yds	White Flannel	60	18.00	
4 Pieces	Blck Worsted Braid	35	1.40	
2 "	Blue " "	35	.70	
11 Varas	Cambric	25	2.75	
4½ "	Brown Linen (Wide)	35	4.57	

1 Piece	Russia Diaper wide		7.50	
1 "	" " Narrow		9.00	
1 Dz	Spool Cotton Assorted		1.75	
1 "	Papers Needles		1.75	
2	**White Linen Table Clothes**	4.50	9.00	
1 Gros	Large Porcelain Buttons		.50	
1 "	Small " "		.40	
1 Dz	Pearl Buttons		.90	
1 "	Pieces Cotton Tape		.75	
1 "	" Linen "		5.00	
11 Varas	Silk for Children's dresses	37½	15.08	
6	Small Palm leaf fans	25	1.50	
2	Half Silk Umbrellas	3.75	7.50	
6	Skeins Blck Glzd Thread		1.00	
1 Piece	Linen Check 48 varas		12.25	
3 Varas	Dark Green Merino	1.37½	4.13	
3 "	Crimson "	1.37½	4.13	
2¼ "	Blue Flannel	62½	<u>1.56</u>	207.64

	Amt Carried over			$ 207.64
	Geo. R. Tuttle Continued			
2 Prs	Black Cloth Gaiters #12	2.75	5.50	
2 "	" " " #1½	2.75	5.50	
1 Gros	Shoe Strings		.60	
2	fine Combs 25¢ 50 2 coarse 50¢ 100		1.50	13.00
2	Tooth Brushes		~~1.50~~	~~44.60~~
	Cartage & Launch			5.00
	Commission 2½%			5.68
	E. E.		Total	$ 232.92
	Havana June 1st 1864			
	34.95 (duty) J. W. Dever			

892
Preprinted Customs Form

No. <u>42</u>
Entry of Merchandise
Importer <u>Geo. R. Tuttle</u>
Vessel <u>*Denbigh*</u>
From <u>Havana</u>
Entered <u>June 10th 1864</u>
Value $ <u>228</u> Duty $ <u>34.20</u>

Owner's Oath
(signed) Geo. R. Tuttle
Sworn before me, this <u>11th</u> day of <u>June</u> 18<u>64</u>

Mdse. Entered 11th June 1864 Ship Entered June 7th 1864
Entry of Merchandise imported into the Port of Mobile, District of Mobile, by Geo. R. Tuttle in the Br. Str. *Denbigh* Godfrey Master, from Havana

No. of Packages	Contents	Value in Foreign Currency	10%	15%	20%	Duties
4 Boxes	Containing					
	Cotton Mfs	$ 34.50		37		$ 5.55
	Flax "	64.65		67		10.05
	Wool "	89.97		94		14.10
	Shoes	13.00		14		2.10
	Umbrellas	15.00		16		2.40
		$ 217.12		228		$ 34.20
	Chges & Com	10.68				
		$ 227.80				

895
(Two short forms: Oath of Importers or Agents)

Signed: Geo R Tuttle and **Thomas C. Healy**[83]

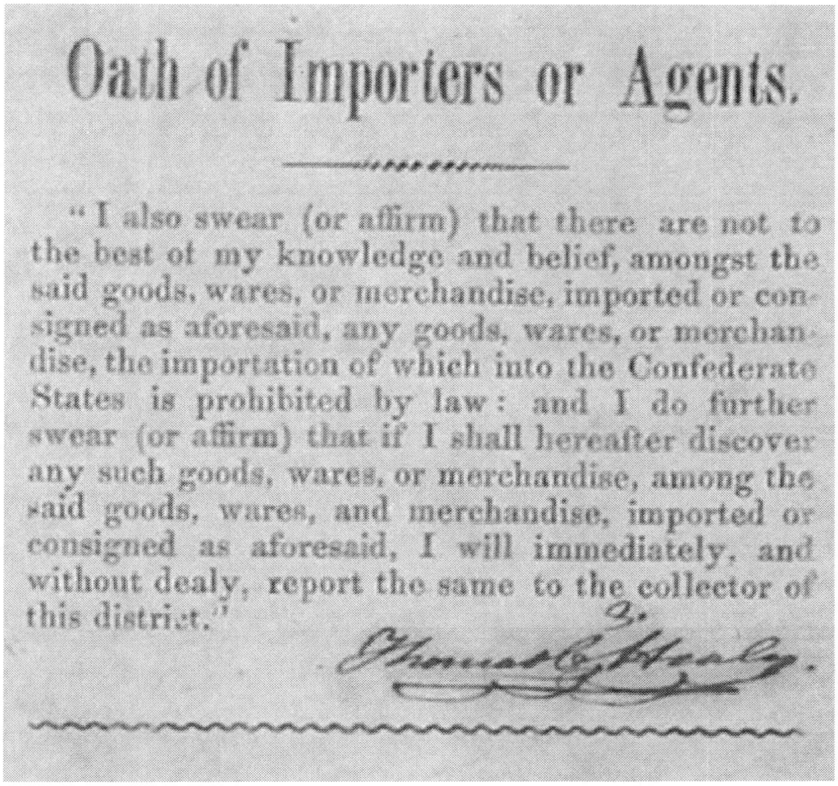

Oath of Importers or Agents.

"I also swear (or affirm) that there are not to the best of my knowledge and belief, amongst the said goods, wares, or merchandise, imported or consigned as aforesaid, any goods, wares, or merchandise, the importation of which into the Confederate States is prohibited by law: and I do further swear (or affirm) that if I shall hereafter discover any such goods, wares, or merchandise, among the said goods, wares, and merchandise, imported or consigned as aforesaid, I will immediately, and without dealy, report the same to the collector of this district."

Thomas C. Healy.

Figure 80. Owner's Oath signed by Thomas C. Healy, artist who painted the *Denbigh* portrait.

[83] Thomas C. Healy was the artist who painted the *Denbigh*'s portrait.

896-897
Substitute for Preprinted Customs Form

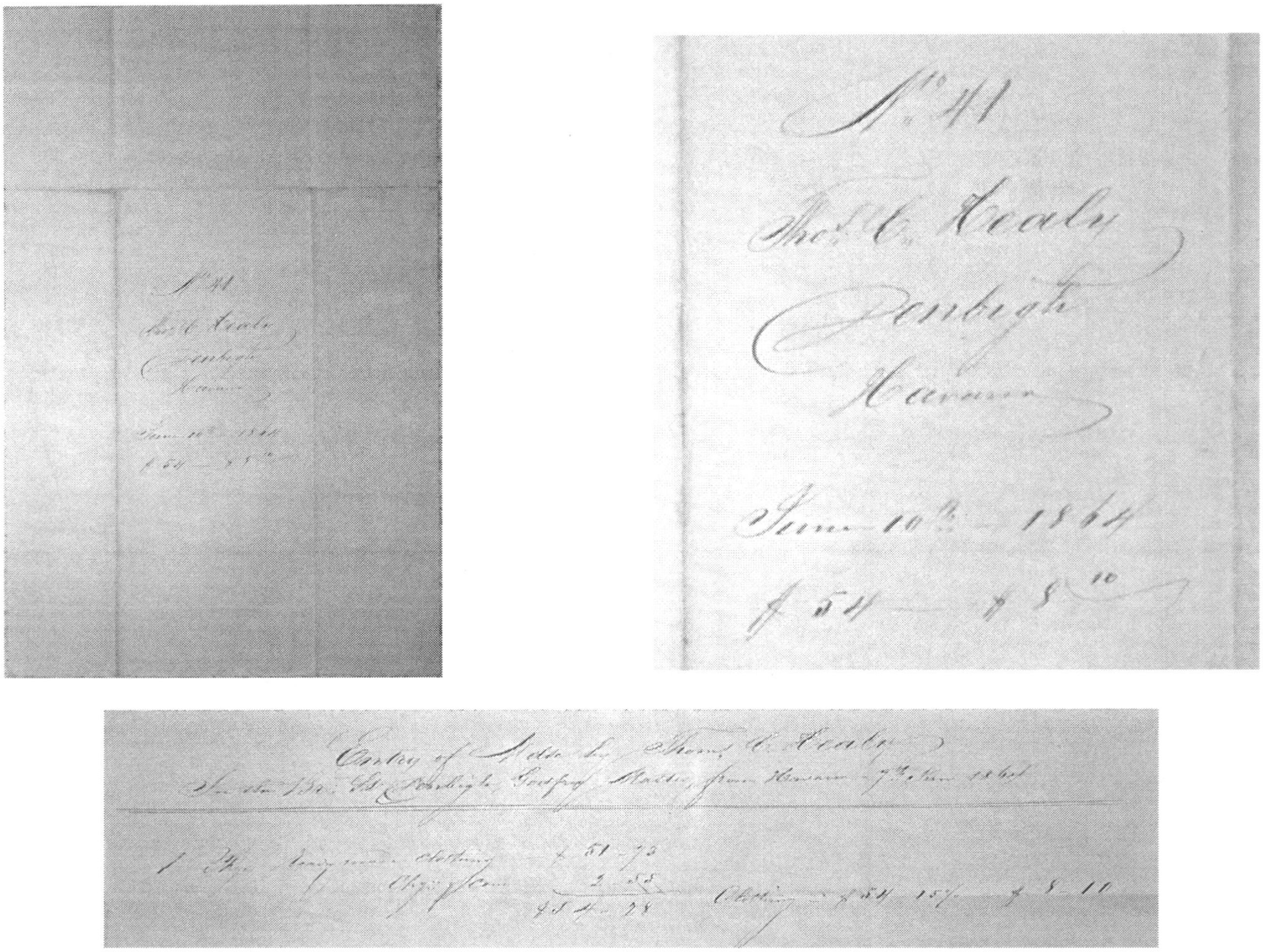

Figure 81. Substitute for preprinted customs form by Thomas C. Healy for readymade clothing.

No. 41
Entry of Merchandise
Importer **Thos. C. Healy**
Vessel *Denbigh*
From Havana
Entered June 10th 1864
Value $ 54 Duty $ 8.10

Entry of Mdse by **Thomas C. Healy**
In the Br. Str *Denbigh*, Godfrey Master, from Havana, 7th June 1864

1 Pkge	Ready made Clothing	$ 51.73				
	Chges & Com	2.55				
		$ 54.28	Clothing	$ 54	15%	$ 8.10

898
Invoice

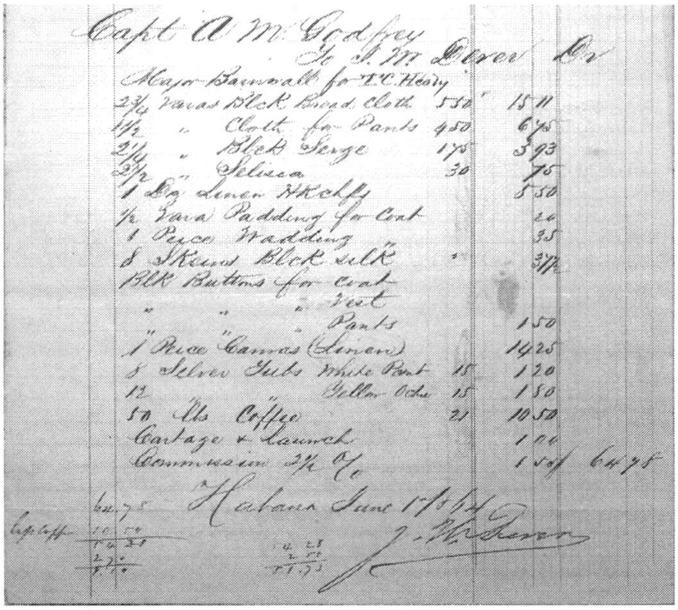

Figure 82. Invoice of sundries for Thomas C. Healy including canvas and paints.

Note: Invoice includes painting supplies, possibly the very canvas and paints used for the *Denbigh* painting.

Capt A. M. Godfrey

To J. W. Dever Dr

Major Barnwell for **T. C. Healy**

2¾ Varas	Blck Broad Cloth	5.50	15.11	
1½ "	Cloth for Pants	4.50	6.75	
2¼ "	Blck Serge	1.75	3.93	
2½ "	Silesia	.30	.75	
1 Dz	Linen Hkchfs		5.50	
½ Vara	Padding for Coat		.20	
1 Piece	Wadding "		.35	
8 Skeins	Blck silk		.37½	
	Blk Buttons for Coat			
	" " " Vest			
	" " " Pants		1.50	
1 Piece	**Canvas (Linen)**		14.25	
8	**Silver Tubs (tubes?) White Paint**	.15	1.20	
12	**" " Yellow Ochre**	.15	1.80	
50 lbs	Coffee	.21	10.50	
	Cartage & Launch		1.00	
	Commission 2½%		1.55	$ 64.78
	Havana June 1st 1864			

	J. W. Dever			
less Coffee	54.28 51.73			

900-902
Preprinted Customs Form

No. 43
Entry of Merchandise
Importer W. H. Williamson
Vessel *Denbigh*
From Havana
Entered June 10th 1864
Value $ 279 Duty $ 41.85

Owner's Oath
(signed) W. H. Williamson
Sworn before me, this 10th day of June 1864

Mdse. Entered 10th June 1864 Ship Entered June 7th 1864
Entry of Merchandise imported into the Port of Mobile, District of Mobile, by W. H. Williamson in the Br. Str. *Denbigh* Godfrey Master, from Havana

Marks	No. of Packages	Contents	Value in Foreign Currency	10%	15%	20%	Duties
W.	10 Pkges	Ready made clothing	$ 172.50		183		$ 27.45
		Flax mfs	63.85		68		10.20
		Shoes & Boots prs 7	25.00		28		4.20
			261.35		279		$ 48.85
		Shipping Chges & Comm	17.83				
			$ 279.18				

905
Invoice

clothing	172.50
Linens, Hkfs &c	63.85
7 prs Shoes & Boots	25.00
	261.35
Chges	5.00
Comm 5%	12.83
	17.83

904a
Invoice

Str *Denbigh*

(Illegible pencil notes on a scrap of paper. Reverse side of invoice in Frame 905. Duty recalculated at 41.85, with detailed notes, apparently resolving a disagreement with the original calculations. Likely the first customs collector did not realize that the commission was 5%, twice the usual rate. The commission and charges were not to be included in figuring the duty.)

904b
A short form: Oath of Importers or Agents

Signed: W. H. Williamson

907-909
Preprinted Customs Form

No. 44
Entry of Merchandise
Importer Thos. T. A. Lyon
Vessel *Denbigh*
From Havana
Entered June 10th 1864
Value $ 87 Duty $ 13.05

Owner's Oath
(signed) Thos T. A. Lyon
Sworn before me, this 10th day of June 1864

Mdse. Entered 10th June 1864 Ship Entered June 7th 1864
Entry of Merchandise imported into the Port of Mobile, District of Mobile, by Thos. T. A. Lyon in the Br. Str. *Denbigh* Godfrey Master, from Havana

Marks	No. of Packages	Contents	Value in Foreign Currency	10%	15%	20%	Duties
R P	7 Blls	**Copperas**[84] lbs 2240	$ 89.60				
		Chgs & Com	9.05				
			$ 98.05				
		Less 300 lbs short	12.04				
			$ 86.61		$ 87	15%	$ 13.05

---

84 Iron (II) sulfate or ferrous sulfate is the chemical compound with the formula (FeSO4), known since ancient times as copperas. Used in ink and in the second half of the 19th century, also used as a photographic developer for collodion process images.

910a
Invoice

Note the false destination at a neutral port, perhaps an attempt to lend the appearance of legality to the voyage in the event of capture.

Invoice of 7 Barrels Copperas shipped by Rafael Perez Sta Ma (Santa Maria) on board of the British Steamship *Denbigh* Godfrey, Master, bound to **Nassau** by order, for acct, & risk of Mr. Ths T. A. Lyon and to his consignment.

R P	7 Barrels Copperas wei'g nett 2240 lbs	@ 4¢/lb	~~$ 89.60~~
		$ 86.61	
	Charges		
	Export duty in bond out on Copperas	.40	
	Shipping expenses & lighterage	4.25	
	Cooperage	87½	
	Permits in the Custom House & seal		
		1.12½	6.65
			$ 96.25
	Commission 2½%		2.40
	Havana 31st May 1864		$ 98.65
	Rafael Perez Sta Ma		
	The above 7 Barrels Copperas was weighed by me and only weighed 1939 lbs being 301 lbs short @ 4¢	value	12.04
	June 10 '64 Thos T A Lyon		$86.61
	$ 13.05 (duty)		

910b
A short form: Oath of Importers or Agents

Signed: Thos T A Lyon

911-913
Preprinted Customs Form

No. 46
Entry of Merchandise
Importer William Otis
Vessel *Denbigh*
From Havana
Entered June 10th 1864
Value $ 931 Duty $ 139.65

Owner's Oath
(signed) William Otis
Sworn before me, this 10th day of June 1864

(signed) J. C. Colsson
Dep Collector

Mdse. Entered 10th June 1864 Ship Entered June 7th 1864
Entry of Merchandise imported into the Port of Mobile, District of Mobile, by William Otis in the Br. Str. *Denbigh* Godfrey Master, from Havana

No. of Packages	Contents	Value in Foreign Currency	10%	15%	20%	Duties
7 Coils	**Russia Hemp Rope** lbs 4292½	$ 901 2½				
	Chges & Com	291 ½				
		$ 930 4	Cordage & Rope	$931	15%	$ 139.65

914a
Invoice

Invoice of Cordage shipped by the Undersigned Per Br Str *Denbigh* Godfrey Mr bound to Mobile, by order of Messrs H. O. Brewer & Co. for act of Wm Otis Esqr. of said place.

W O #1	1 Coil	Russn Hemp Rope	7½ in Span	1154 lbs		
#2/4	3 "	" " "	6½ in 793 798 963	2554		
#5	1 "	" " "	4¼ in	334		
#6	1 "	" " "	3¼ in	192		
#7	1 "	Rattlins (ratlines)	18 Threads	58		
			lbs	4292 21¢	$ 901	2½
			Cartage to Wharf		1	4
		Charges			$ 902	6½
		Shipping & Launching			5	
					$ 907	6½
			Commission	2½%	22	5½
		E E			$ 930	4
		Havana 1st June 1864				
		??? Robertson Co				
		George ? Bell				

914b
A short form: Oath of Importers or Agents

Signed: William Otis

916-918
Preprinted Customs Form

No. 45
Entry of Merchandise
Importer N. W. Perry
Vessel *Denbigh*
From Havana
Entered June 10th 1864
Value $ 156 Duty $ 22.85

Owner's Oath
(signed) N. W. Perry
Sworn before me, this 10th day of June 1864

Mdse. Entered 10th June 1864 Ship Entered June 7th 1864
Entry of Merchandise imported into the Port of Mobile, District of Mobile, by N. W. Perry in the Br. Str. *Denbigh* Godfrey Master, from Havana

No. of Packages	Contents	Value in Foreign Currency	10%	15%	20%	Duties
3 Pkges	Containing					
	Flax mfs	$ 80.50		84		$ 12.60
	Cotton mfs	33.50		35		5.25
	Wool mfs	6.00		6		.90
	Shoes 8 Pairs	18.60		20		3.00
	Tea 8 lbs	10.00	11			1.10
		$ 148.60	11	145		$ 22.85
	Chgs & Com	7.03				
		$ 155.63				

919a-920
Invoice

Captn A. M. Godfrey to J. W. Dever Dr

	N. W. Perry			
1Piece	Bleached Shirting		$ 9.50	
1 "	Linen		13.00	
6	" Shirts		15.00	
6 prs	Men's Half Hose #10½		2.00	
2 "	Merino Drawers	3.00	6.00	
1 Dz	Hose #9		7.50	
1 "	" #8		5.00	
½ "	" #7		2.25	
1 "	Hkchfs		3.00	
1 "	" Ladies		6.00	
6 Spools	Thread		.87	
2 "	" Blck		.25	
1 Gros	Shirt Buttons		.63	

½ "	Pearl Buttons		.75	
1 Dz	Roles Tape		2.50	74.25
	(cont.)			

2 Skeins	Blck Silk		.50	
1 Pkg	Embroidery Cotton	.75	4.50	
1 Pr	Mitts		.75	
2	French Corsetts	3.50	7.00	
5½ Varas	Table Damask	1.50	8.25	
6 "	White Drilling	.75	4.50	
3 "	Dress Muslin	.50	1.50	
2	Dress Patterns 31 Varas	.37½	11.25	
2	" " 20 Varas	.37½	7.50	
6 Papers	Pins	.60	3.60	
8 lbs	Tea	1.25	10.00	
1 Pr	Gaiters #5		3.00	
2 "	Slippers #5	1.50	3.00	
1 "	Gaiters #3		3.00	
2 "	Misses Shoes #1	1.37½	2.75	
2 "	Boys Shoes	2.00	4.00	
	Cartage & Launch		2.50	
	Commission 2½%		3.79	$ 155.63
	Havana June 1st 1864			
	J. W. Dever			

919b
A short form: Oath of Importers or Agents

Signed: N. W. Perry

921-923
Preprinted Customs Form

No. 47
Entry of Merchandise
Importer Julius Hessee
Vessel *Denbigh*
From Havana
Entered June 11th 1864
Value $ 84 Duty $ 12.60

Owner's Oath
(signed) Julius Hessee
Sworn before me, this 11th day of June 1864

Mdse. Entered 11th June 1864 Ship Entered June 7th 1864
Entry of Merchandise imported into the Port of Mobile, District of Mobile, by Julius Hessee in the Br. Str. *Denbigh* Godfrey Master, from Havana

No. of Packages	Contents	Value in Foreign Currency	10%	15%	20%	Duties
2 Boxes	Ready made clothing	$ 79.15				
	Chges & Com	5.10				
		84.25	Clothing ready made	$ 84	15%	$ 13.60

925a
Invoice

Mr. Gardner
1 Packg
Wearing Appl $ 35
Including all charges
$ 5.55 (duty)

925b
Invoice

Maj. Hessee[85]
1 Case Contg
Wearing Appl 49.25
Box $1 Hire $ 1 &c including
12.90 (duty)

reverse, a note: Deposited $ 20 by Mr. Hessee

927
A short form: Oath of Importers or Agents

Signed: Julius Hessee

928-930
Preprinted Customs Form

[85] Maj. Julius Hessee, age 47, enlisted 1864 in the First Mobile Volunteers

No. 49
Entry of Merchandise
Importer C. J. Delano
Vessel *Denbigh*
From Havana
Entered June 11th 1864
Value $ 281 Duty $ 43.50

Agent's Oath
(signed) **C. J. Forstall**
Sworn before me, this 11th day of June 1864

Mdse. Entered 11th June 1864 Ship Entered June 7th 1864
Entry of Merchandise imported into the Port of Mobile, District of Mobile, by C. J. Delano in the Br. Str. *Denbigh* Godfrey Master, from Havana

No. of Packages	Contents	Value in Foreign Currency	10%	15%	20%	Duties
1 Pkge.	Ribbons	$ 46.00		48		$ 7.20
1 Trunk	Steel mfs (files, &c.)	87.75		92		13.80
	Cutlery	40.00		42		6.30
	Silk belts & Nests (?), Silk mfs	38.50		40		6.00
	Tea " lbs 10	15.00	16			1.60
	Camphor " 45	40.25			43	8.60
		267.50	16	222	43	43.50
	Shp & Charges & Com	13.25				
		$ 280.75				

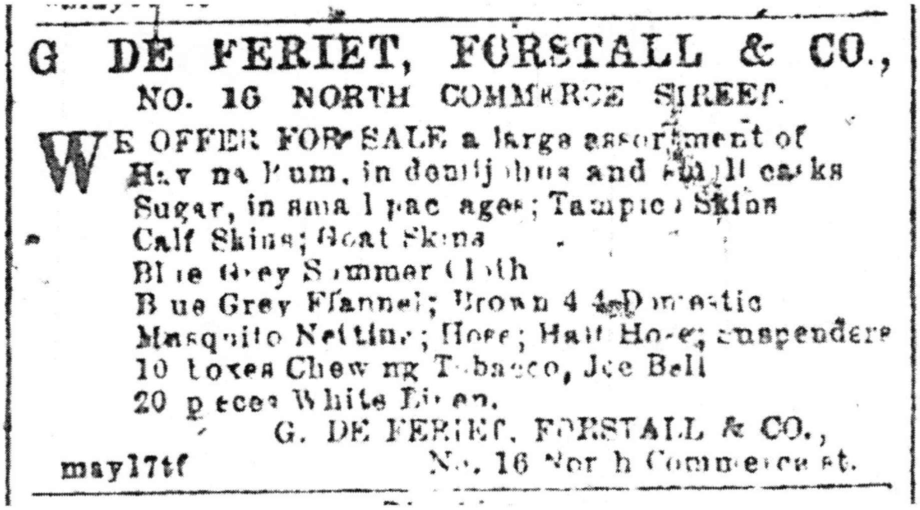
G DE FERIET, FORSTALL & CO.,
NO. 16 NORTH COMMERCE STREET.
WE OFFER FOR SALE a large assortment of
Havana Rum, in demijohns and small casks
Sugar, in small packages; Tampico Skins
Calf Skins; Goat Skins
Blue Grey Summer Cloth
Blue Grey Flannel; Brown 4-4 Domestic
Musquito Netting; Hose; Half Hose; suspenders
10 boxes Chewing Tobacco, Joe Bell
20 pieces White Linen.
G. DE FERIET, FORSTALL & CO.,
may17tf No. 16 North Commerce st.

Figure 83. Ad for sundries similar to above, offered by De Feriet, Forstall & Co. (Mobile Advertiser and Register May 18, 1864).

931
Invoice

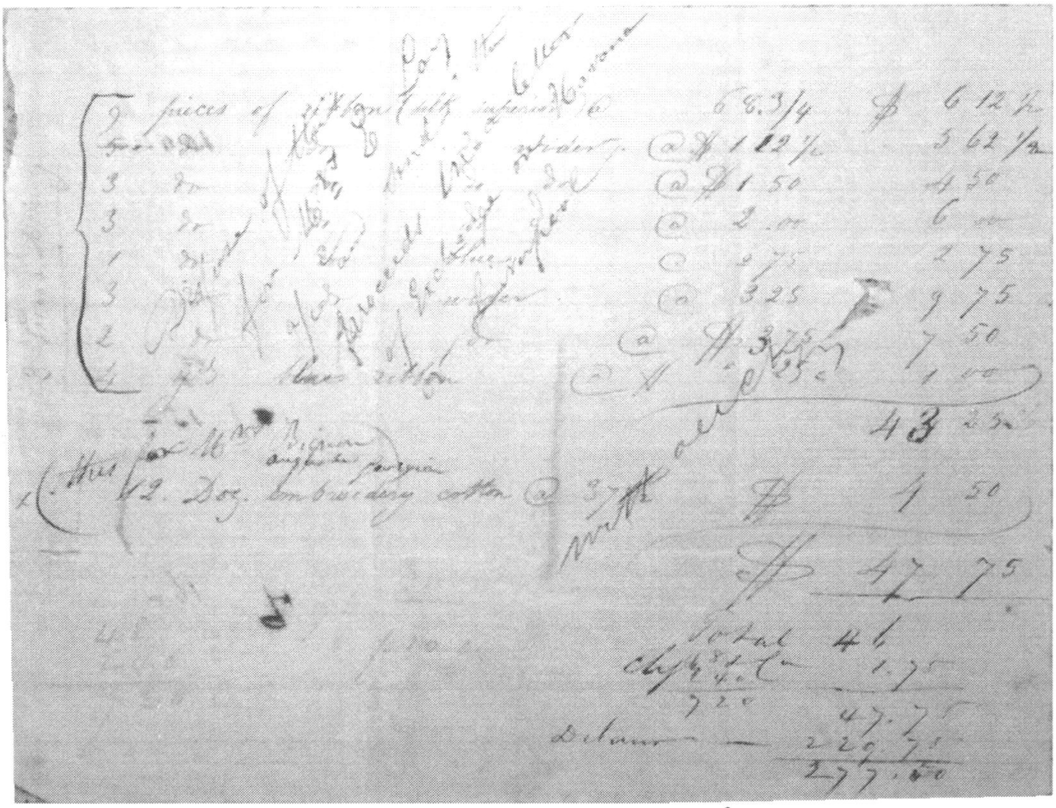

Figure 84. Invoice of order by Mrs. Bignon for silk ribbon and embroidery cotton.

(marginal note: 3 Pieces Missing)
(over-written note: Dispose of this for Mr. E. Lay a/cos (at cost?) & am and ??? proceeds in'd a letter of Exchange on Havana or Liverpool)

9 pieces	of ribbon (Silk Superior)	@ 68¾	$ 6.12½
5 Do	do do wider	@ $ 1.12½	5.62½
3 do	do do do	@ $ 1.50	4.50
3 do	do do do	@ 2.00	6.00
1 do	do blue	@ 2.75	2.75
3 do	do wider	@ 3.25	9.75
2 do	do do do	@ $ 3.75	7.50
4 yds	blue ribbon	@ 25¢	1.00
			43.25
	this for Mrs. Bignon		$ 4.50
	??? ???	with all chgs	$ 47.75
12 Doz	embroidery cotton	Total	46.00
		Chgs & Com	1.75
			47.75
		Delano	229.75
			277.50

933a
Invoice

Capt A. M. Godfrey

To J. W. Dever Dr

J. W.		~~A. J.~~ Mann			
	1 Piece	Russia Diaper 30 yds	35	10.50	
	1 "	Linen		10.00	
	9 Varas	fine Linen	50	4.50	
	1 Doz	Needles		1.75	
	½ "	Paper Pins		.80	
	4 Oz	White Split Zephyr		1.50	
	1 "	Pink "		.35	
	1 Doz pr	Stockings #7		4.25	
	9 Varas	Linen Lawn	40	3.60	
	1 Dz	Toilet Soap		2.00	
	1 Gro	Shoe Strings		.60	
		Cartage & Launch		.75	
		Commission 2½%		1.02	41.97
		Habana June 1st 1864			
		J. W. Dever			
		6.30 (duty)			

933b
A short form: Oath of Importers or Agents

Signed: Jno W. Mann

935-936
Substitute for Preprinted Customs Form

No. 48
Entry of Merchandise
Importer John W. Mann
Vessel *Denbigh*
From Havana
Entered June 11th 1864
Value $ 42 Duty $ 6.40

Entry of Mdse by John W. Mann
In the Br. Str *Denbigh*, Godfrey Master, from Havana, 7th June 1864

1 Pkge	Linens	$ 38.20	40	15%	$ 6.00
	Soap (French)	2.00	2	20%	.40
	Chges & com	1.77	42		$ 6.40
		$ 41.97			

937
Invoice

W. J. Delano (added note in pencil)
Mr. L. Lay
Dr to J H Barbot

2 doz	flat files	@ $ 5	$ 10.00
1 Gros	files Suco (?)	"	12.00
7 "	Screws assorted (?)	" 1	7.00
3 doz	tacks assorted	"	5.25
3 Gros	pill boxes	" 1.50	4.50
25 lbs	Camphor	.81	20.35
25 "	----------- (Powders/Br. Lustre)		10.00
2 doz	Bach (Black?) Hair dye		20.00
1 Gros	Carpenters pencil		5.00
3 doz	pack. Brad		6.50
1½ "	Augers assorted	@ 90¢	16.50
4	Crucibles		2.50
1 set	Chisels		6.00
10000	Needles	1.25	12.50
1 doz	ladies Silk netts		5.00
½ "	Hair do		3.50
12 pr	Ladies belts		24.00
1 doz	" buckles		6.00
2 lbs	**Nutmegs**		3.50
6 "	**Cloves**		3.00
10 "	Tea		15.00
10 "	**Allspice**		4.50
1 doz	penknives 404[86]		5.50
1 doz	do. 405		9.50
2 doz	Scissors		15.00
1	Trunk		4.25
	Drayage boat hire & C.& C.		3.00
			$ 239.75

939-941
Preprinted Customs Form

No. 50
Entry of Merchandise
Importer Mrs. Myers

[86] May refer to size and style. Penknives 404 and 405 can be found online today referring to a single-bladed pocketknife.

Vessel *Denbigh*
From Havana
Entered June 11th 1864
Value $ 127 Duty $ 20.45

Agent's Oath
Sidney Smith
Sworn before me, this 11th day of June 1864

Mdse. Entered 11th June 1864 Ship Entered June 7th 1864
Entry of Merchandise imported into the Port of Mobile, District of Mobile, by Sidney Smith Agent of Mrs. Myers in the Br. Str. *Denbigh* Godfrey Master, from Havana

No. of Packages	Contents	Value in Foreign Currency	10%	15%	20%	Duties
1 Pkge	Cheese lbs 40	$ 8.00	8			$ .80
1 Box	Candles " 25	10.00		11		1.65
1 Do	Paper	6.00		6		.90
1 Do	Shoes prs 20	60.00		63		9.45
1 Pkge	Hosiery	3.00		3		.45
1 Box	Pickles	9.00			9	1.80
1 Bll	Sugar lbs 242	22.28			24	4.80
	Soap	2.50			3	.60
		120.78	8	83	36	$ 20.45
	Chges & Com	6.10				
		$ 126.88				

942
Invoice

Invoice of 13 Packages Shipped on board the Brit Str *Denbigh* by Joseph Padia & Consigned to Mrs Julian Myers

Add d				
Mrs.				
J Myers	1 Bbl 242 lbs	Sugar	@ 9¢ & Bbl 50¢	$ 22.28
	1 Bag 138 "	Coffee	@ 21¢ & Bag 13¢ free	29.61
	1 Box 24 Jars	Pickles		9.00
	8	Dutch Cheeses	lbs 40	8.00
	25 lbs	Sperm (oil) candles		10.00
	2 Doz	Cakes Soap	" 25	2.50
	20 prs	Shoes	$ 3	60.00
	½ Ream	letter Paper		2.50
		Envelopes		3.50
	1 Doz	Ladies hose		3
		Charges		
		Pd Porterage & Boat Hire	1.50	
		Pd freight to Mobil pr *Denbigh*	63.00	64.50

	add	Comm 2½%		$ 214.89
		E&OE		
		Havana 1st June 1864		
		Jose Padia		
	Mr. Coleson: we will pay the Duties on these goods			
		H O Brewer & Co		
		pr Benj Donaldson		

Note the rare mention of charge for transport on the *Denbigh*.

943
A short form: Oath of Importers or Agents

Signed: Sidney Smith

944-946
Preprinted Customs Form

No. 51
Entry of Merchandise
Importer A. Godfrey (Capt. of *Denbigh*)
Vessel *Denbigh*
From Havana
Entered June 13th 1864
Value $ 946 Duty $ 159.70

Owner's Oath
(signed) A. M. Godfrey
Sworn before me, this 13th day of June 1864

Mdse. Entered 13th June 1864 Ship Entered June 7th 1864
Entry of Merchandise imported into the Port of Mobile, District of Mobile, by A. M. Godfrey in the Br. Str. *Denbigh* Godfrey Master, from Havana

Marks	No. of Packages	Contents	Value in Foreign Currency	10%	15%	20%	Duties
H. A. Bd	1 Pkge	Cotton mfs	$ 30.00		33		$ 4.95
J. M Bd	1 Do	Flax mfs	38.00		41		6.15
"	1 Coil	Rope	87.29		96		14.40
A. M. Gy	Boxes	Flax mfs.	184.56		202		30.30
"		Cotton mfs.	158.55		173		25.95
"		Wool mfs.	14.52		16		2.40
"		Umbrellas	26.75		29		4.35
"	8 Boxes	Sugar (white) lbs 3487	261.52			286	57.20

H. B.	2 "	Sugar (white) " 851 (by Barnwell)	63.82			70	14.00
			865.01		$ 990	356	$ 159.70
		Boxes & shippg chges & $ 49.59					
		Impt. Duty on Sugar 8.75	58.34				
			923.35				
		Com 2½%	23.08				
			$ 946.43				

947
Invoice

Invoice of Sugar & Coffee shipped by Rafael Perez Sta Ma on board of the British Str *Denbigh* Godfrey master bound to Nassau by order for a/c & risk of Mr. A. M. Godfrey & to his consignment:

HB	10 Sacks	Cuba Coffee wei'g nett	1316 lbs @19½¢ lb	$ 256.62
			10 Sacks @ 62½¢	6.25
HB	2 Boxes	refining white sugar wei'g	851 lbs @ 7½¢ lb	63.82
			2 Boxes @ $ 3.10	6.20
AMG	8 Do	do do do wei'g	3487 lbs @ 7½¢ lb	261.52
			8 Boxes @ $ 3.10	24.80
				$ 619.21
		Charges		
		Export & duty on Coffee	$ 2.90	
		Do do on Sugar	8.75	
		Brokerage ½% on Coffee	1.31	
		Do do ½% on Sugar	1.78	
		Storage on Sugar @ 40¢ pr box	4.00	
		Recv'g W'g @ 5¢ pr box	.50	
		Shipping expenses	2.50	
		Lighterage	8.50	30.24
				$ 649.45
			Commission 2½%	16.25
				$ 665.70
		(illegible signature)		
		Havana 31 May 1864		
		Rafael Perez Sta Ma		
		$ 14.80 (duty)		

948a
Invoice

Capt A. M. Godfrey

To J. W. Dever Dr

	Jas M Brainard			
2 Pieces	Linen for Shirts	$ 14.59	29.00	
2	Calf Skins French	3.00	6.00	
2 Yds	Blck Merino	1.50	3.00	
1 Coil	Manila Rope 5½ 602 lbs	14½	87.29	
1 Bbl	Mess Port		24.00	free
	Cartage & Launch		1.00	
	Commission 2½%		3.75	154.04
	Havana June 1, 1864			
	J. W. Dever			

(Marginal note.) Mess H. O. Brewer & Co will please pay the duties on this Bill & charge them to Your Obt Sevt A. M. Godfrey. (Note close association of Godfrey and Brewer.)

948b
Invoice

Harriet A. Brainard	$ 4.95	
J. M. Brainard	6.15	
Do	14.40	$ 25.50
A Barnwell Major – Paid by him	$ 14.00	
A M Godfrey		120.00
Done by Godfrey		$ 145.50

949a (Reverse side of 948a)
Invoice

Note: Reverse side of invoice had a list of articles lightly written in pencil. The paper for invoice 948a above was perhaps a reused shopping list for acquisition in Havana. There were no prices so it was unlikely to be an invoice.

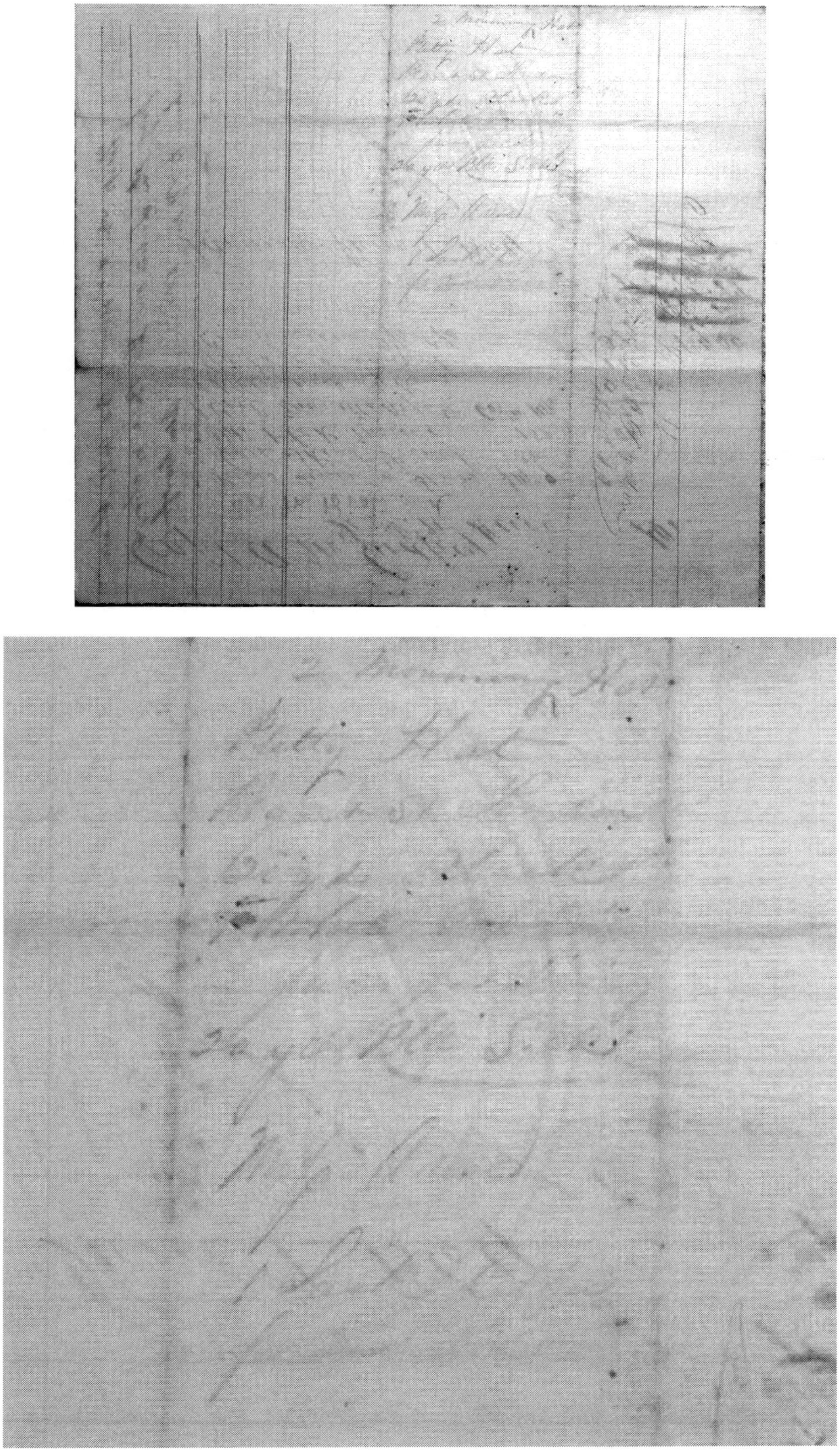

Figure 85. Shopping list for purchases in Havana.

2 Mourning Hose
Pretty Hat (Note: Surely written or requested by a woman!)
Regent St. London (Note: Referring to a style or origin?)
60 yds Black
??? ????
2 pairs (?) ???
20 yds Blk Silk
Miss's hose (?)
1 Sack Coffee

Pd ???
(Plus illegible marginal note.)

949b
Reverse side of Frame 948b

(Listing of costs by category, exact articles not specified.)

Flax	384.38
Cotton	158.55
Wool	14.52
Umbrellas	26.75

950a
Invoice

Capt A. M. Godfrey
To J. W. Dever Dr

	Harriet A Brainard		
32 Yds	White Swiss Muslin	15.00	
12 Boxes	Hair Pins	1.50	
6	Undershirts for Ladies 2.25	13.50	
	Commission 2½%	.75	$ 30.75
	Havana June 1st 1864		
	J. W. Dever		

(Marginal note.) Mesrs H. O. Brewer & Co will please pay the duties on this Bill & charge same to Your Obt Srvt (signed) A. M. Godfrey

950b
A short form: Oath of Importers or Agents

Signed: A. M. Godfrey

951
Invoice

Note: Large quantities in this invoice may suggest a commercial buyer or store for resale to the public.

Captain Godfrey
From the Florida Store

281 vs	Organdie at	20¢	56.30
	cotton mfs		
218 varas	Color linen Stripes	21¢	45.78
51 "	" " "	20¢	11.73
66 "	Ging(ham) barege	22¢	14.52
7	ladies Umbrellas	2.00	14.00
2	" parasols	3.00	6.00
85 vs	linen Cambric	18	15.30
2 pcs	White Linen	6.00 ea	13.00
6 "	" "	4.00	24.00
2 "	" " Cotton	3.00	6.00
1 Doz	Ladies Corsets		20.00
5 doz	ladies Handkf hand stitched	2.25	11.25
6 doz	" " "	2.75	16.50
2 pcs	White Nansook	5.00	10.00
6 doz	Linen handkfs	1.50	9.00
2 pcs	White Linen		17.00
6 doz	Cotton Handkfs		9.00
3 pcs	Swiss Muslin	3.50	10.50
1 "	" "		3.25
3 "	" "	4.00	12.00
5	ladies fans	.75	3.75
3 "	" " Mourning		3.00
6 doz	Gents Cotton Socks	1.00	9.00
2 "	" Col'd Hdkfs		2.50
6 "	" Brown cotton Socks		12.00
6 "	Ladies Cotton Hose 3		18.00
2 pcs	Linen checks		11.00
	Havana June 1 1864		$ 384.38
	Received payment		
	Vicente J ???		
	10 Boxes Sugar ___ lbs		

(Marginal note.) H. O. Brewer & Co Will please pay the duties on the ??? ??? ??? A. M. Godfrey

---

952-954
Preprinted Customs Form

No. 52
Entry of Merchandise
Importer W. J. Delano

Vessel *Denbigh*
From Havana
Entered June 13th 1864
Value $ 201   Duty $ 30.40

Owner's Oath
(signed) W. J. Delano
Sworn before me, this 13th day of June 1864

Mdse. Entered 13th June 1864   Ship Entered June 7th 1864
Entry of Merchandise imported into the Port of Mobile, District of Mobile, by W. J. Delano in the Br. Str. *Denbigh*   Godfrey Master, from Havana

No. of Packages	Contents	Value in Foreign Currency		10%	15%	20%	Duties
1 Trunk	Containing						
	Sul. Morphine Oz. 4	$ 16.25	$ 16.25		17		$ 2.55
	Medicinal preparations	64.50	62.00		64		9.60
	Bor.(ic) Acid	5.00	5.00	5			.50
	Camphor lbs 10	9.50	9.50			10	2.00
	Iron mfs, not Specified	66.60	61.20		64		9.60
	Paper (writing)	17.39	17.39		18		2.70
		179.24		5	163	10	
		7.25	171.34				
		$ 186.49					
		22.00	22.00		23		3.45
	Add Wearing apprl	208.49	193.34	5	186	10	30.40
	Less ??? not put in box 5.40	Chgs & Com	7.25				
	1 lb chloroform 2.50	7.90	$ 200.59				
		$ 200.59					

956a
A short form: Oath of Importers or Agents

Signed: W. J. Delano

Note: A second version of the short form.

956b
Invoice

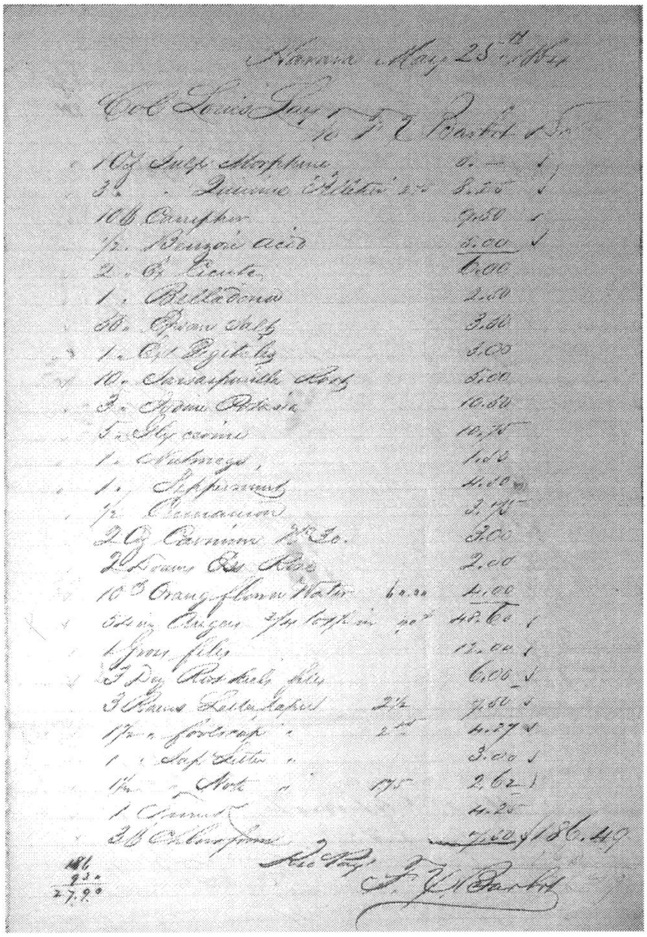

Figure 86. Invoice for medicines and sundries.

Col Louis Lay Havana May 25th 1864

To F Y Barbot Dr

1 Oz	Sulp Morphine		8.00	
3 "	Quinine Pelletion (?)	2.75	8.25	
10 lb	Camphor		9.50	
½ "	Benzoic Acid		5.00	
2 "	Ex(tract?) Cicuta[87]		6.00	
1 "	Belladona		2.50	
50 "	Epsom Salts		3.50	
1 "	Ex Digitalis		3.00	
10 "	Sarsaparilla Root		5.00	
3 "	Iodine Potsia		10.50	
5 "	Glycerine		10.75	
1 "	Nutmegs		1.50	
1 "	Peppermint		4.50	
½	Cinnamon		3.75	
2 Oz	Carmin (Carmine ?[88]) No 30		3.00	

[87] Highly poisonous herb, Water Hemlock. In this period Cicuta may have been used as an anesthetic (*Kings American Dispensatory*, 1898, Felter and Lloyd). The extract was also thought to cure rabies (*A Modern Herbal*).

2 Drams	Ess Rose		2.00	
10 lb	Orange flower Water	60.00	4.00	
54 in	Augers 3.4 / 7½	90¢	48.60	
1 Gross	files		12.00	
3 Doz	Rat tails files		6.00	
3 Reams	Letter paper	2½	7.50	
1½ "	fools cap "	2.45	4.27	
1 "	Sup(erior) Letter "		3.00	
1½ "	" Note "	1.75	2.62	
1	Trunk		4.25	
3 lbs	Chloroform		7.50	$ 186.49
	Rec Pay			160.00
	F. Y. Barbot			26.49
	27.90 (duty)			

---

957 (reverse side of 956b)

less			
½ dz	???	5.40	$ 186.49
1 lb	Chlorfm	8.50	
		7.90	--- 7.90
			178.59
	Wearing Apparel		22.00
			200.59
	$ 30.15 (duty)		

958-960
Preprinted Customs Form

No. 53
Entry of Merchandise
Importer O. S. Iglehart
Vessel *Denbigh*
From Havana
Entered June 13th 1864
Value $ 103   Duty $ 15.45

Owner's Oath
(signed) O. S. Iglehart
Sworn before me, this 13th day of June 1864

Mdse. Entered 13th June 1864   Ship Entered June 7th 1864

---

88 Carmine dye made from the insect cochineal was used medicinally to treat whooping-cough, neuralgia and other medical conditions as well as to color tinctures and ointments.

Entry of Merchandise imported into the Port of Mobile, District of Mobile, by O. S. Iglehart in the Br. Str. *Denbigh* Godfrey Master, from Havana

No. of Packages	Contents	Value in Foreign Currency	10%	15%	20%	Duties
1 Case	Ready made Clothing	$ 98.00		103		$ 15.45
	Chgs & Com	5.00				
		103.00				

961a
Invoice

Note: Nearly illegible pencil written scrap of paper, a make-shift invoice.

Str *Denbigh*
1 Box ?????
With all Chgs & Com 103
Mah ???
G. Mohr.
$ 15.45

961b
A short form: Oath of Importers or Agents

Signed: O S Iglehart

963
Preprinted Customs Form

No. 54
Entry of Merchandise
Importer L. F. Zantzinger
Vessel *Denbigh*
From Havana
Entered June 13th 1864
Value $ 310 Duty $ 46.50

Owner's Oath
(signed) L. F. Zantzinger
Sworn before me, this 13th day of June 1864

Mdse. Entered 13th June 1864 Ship Entered June 7th 1864

Entry of Merchandise imported into the Port of Mobile, District of Mobile, by A. M. Godfrey in the Br. Str. *Denbigh* Godfrey Master, from Havana

No. of Packages	Contents	Value in Foreign Currency	10%	15%	20%	Duties
22	Small Pkges containing					
	Sugar Lead lbs 169	$ 47.32		49		$ 7.35
	Oil Ru: Gals 10	9.50		10		1.50
	Flannel	6.00		6		.90
	Wool mfs.	2.00		2		.30
	Flax mfs.	63.74		66		9.90
	Silk mfs.	15.90		17		2.55
	Clothing (ready made)	5.00		6		.90
	Hosiery (Cotton)	29.00		30		4.50
	Shoes prs 22	45.00		47		7.05
	Cotton mfs, colored & white	65.97		69		10.35
	Needles	6.60		8		1.20
		296.63				
	Chges & Com	13.20				
		$ 309.83		310	15%	$46.50

966a
Invoice

Mr. Geo Cleveland

From the Florida

1	boy patent Leather Gaiter	2.00
1	ladies Gaiter	2.00
1	do do	2.50
3	do do at 2.50	7.50
1 doz	Children's Socks	3.00
1 package	pins	.50
4 pcs.	tape	1.00
4	black belt ribbon	1.00
2 pr	black silk gloves	1.50
		$ 22.50
	Havana June 1 1864	
	3.45 (duty)	

966b
Invoice

T. L. Owen

From the Florida

11 varas	linen Cambric at 37½¢	4.12 ½
11 "	French calico	2.20

11 "	"	2.20
1 pc	fine Jaconet	6.00
20 varas	linen toweling	6.00
1	corset	3.00
2½ doz	ladies cotton hose	10.00
4	ladies belts	1.00
3 doz	Skeins working cotton	1.20
(added note)	5 gals Kerosene Oil	$ 35.72½
	Havana June	4.00
	6.00 (duty)	39.72½

968a
Invoice

Mrs. C. V M. Waring
From the Florida

3 varas	Swiss muslin	1.20
½ doz	ladies cotton hose	2.50
2 pcs	Velvet ribbon	4.25
	voisted (?) to working	.50
1 package	white cotton	.40
1	do do Red	.40
4	ladies handkfs	2.50
~~6½ varas~~	~~blue ribbon at 73¢~~	~~4.89½~~
1	pen knife	1.50
1 bot(tle)	**pomade**	~~1.00~~
		$ 24.32½
	Havana June 1 1864	4.87½
		$ 19.45

968b
Invoice

Wm B. Seawell
From the Florida

13 varas	French calico	$ 2.60
12	Skeins of black sewing Silk	2.40
1 package	working cotton	.40
2 pr	boy Socks	1.50
11 Yds	Linen checks	2.75
1 pc	???	5.50
6 bunches	Red cotton	2.40
		$ 17.55
	Havana June 1 1864	
	2.70 (duty)	

969a
Invoice

G. M. Parker
From the Florida

½ doz.	socks	$ 1.50
½ doz.	ladies handkfs	3.50
½ doz	Gents	5.00
1 doz	ladies cotton hose	5.00
		$ 15.00
	2.25 (duty)	

969b
Invoice

E. F. Hellen
From the Florida

13 vs.	French calico at 20¢	$ 2.60
3 doz.	Spool thread	4.87½
3 doz.	papers of needles	3.50
no 1 1 Bot	**Mrs Allen's restorative**[89]	1.50
no 3	(blank)	.50
	Havana June 1 1864	$ 13.07½

970a
Invoice

Lee Hamelten
From the Florida

1 doz	Socks	$ 3.00
½ doz	ladies hose	2.50
2 pr	Leather Shoes	3.50
		$ .9.00
	1.65 (duty)	

970b
Invoice

A T Mullaney
From the Florida

5 doz.	cotton socks at $3	$ 15.00

[89] Hair product? Mrs. S. A. Allen's Hair Restorer was produced in New York.

2 doz	White Spool thread	3.25
1 doz	Skeins Working cotton	.40
½ doz	Gents handkfs	2.50
½ doz	ladies handkfs	3.50
2	ladies boots	5.00
2	Children's boots	3.50
		$ 33.15
	Havana June 1 1864	
	4.95 (duty)	

970c
Invoice

Augt Bullemer
From the Florida

52 varas	French calico	at 20¢	$ 10.40
40 "	"	at 20	8.00
4	ladies Gaiters		3.50
1	Gents Gaiters		3.50
1 pc.	White linen		10.50
			$ 42.40
	Havana June 1 1864		
	6.45 (duty)		

971a
Invoice

D E Huger
From the Florida

12 vs	White flannel	at 50¢	$ 6.00
1 pc.	fine Jaconet		6.00
5 varas	nansook		1.87½
1 doz	Turkish towel		5.00
16 varas	linen Cambric	at 37¢	6.00
2	black belts		.50
			$ 25.87½
	Havana June 1 1864		
	3.90 (duty)		

971b
Invoice

Havana 31 May 64

Invoice of sundry articles contained in a Box marked, Mrs Oskar Aichel, Anderson C. H. (Court House?), S.C.

2 pair	Ladies & 3 p. Children's shoes	$ 5.00
2 pieces	of ~~linen~~ & cotton goods	3.00
12 pair	Ladies & Children stockings	2.00
1	**Baby doll**[90]	~~.50~~
		$ 10.50
	Oskar Aichel	
	1.55 (duty)	

971c
Invoice

Note: An indecipherable scrap of paper. The first side showed a shipment including one trunk and 20 bags of coffee, perhaps of 40 lbs. each, shipped to J. N. Shannan.

[90] One of the artifacts found at the *Denbigh* wreck was a porcelain doll's leg.

Figure 87. Two-sided informal invoices.

Spear (?)
1 Bbl
129 lbs **Sugar Lead.**[91]
@ 28¢ $ 47.32
7.05 (duty)

973a
Invoice

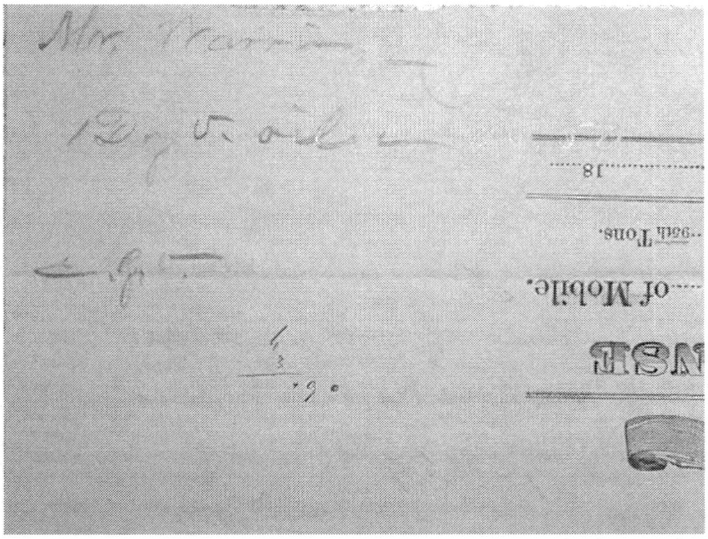

Figure 88. Invoice on torn off scrap of unused, out-of-date (?) printed form.

[91] Lead (II) acetate is a chemical compound, a white crystalline substance with a sweetish taste. It is made by treating lead (II) oxide with acetic acid. Like other lead compounds, it is toxic. Lead acetate is soluble in water and glycerin. Lead (II) acetate is also known as lead acetate, lead diacetate, plumbous acetate, sugar of lead, lead sugar, salt of Saturn, and Goulard's powder (after Thomas Goulard). Historical use included as a sweetener and as a treatment for poison ivy.

Mr. Warring
1 Doz O.(live) Oil $ 5.50
.90 (duty)

973b
Invoice

Note: Listing of duty on many small orders with names of buyers.

Paid by Zantzinger

T. D Owen	$ 6.00	Sugar for
M. Waring	.90	Donation 240 lbs
Do	3.00	
W B Seawell	2.70	
Spear	7.65	
D E Huger	3.90	
G M Parker	2.25	
J Hessee (?)	1.05	
Labuyan (?)	1.85	
O Aichel	1.55	
E T Hellen	1.95	
L. Hamilton	1.35	
G. Cleveland	3.45	Conway (?) $ 15
T. J. Mullany	4.95	
A Benthmat (?)	6.45	
	48.40	
	1.50	
	49.90	

975a
Invoice

Mr. for Mrs Hessee
A las Ninfas (store)

1 par	de mitones negro	a 50 cts	$ .50
2½ varas	seda maurici	a $ 1.50	3.75
4 varas	granadina negra	a 75 cts	3.00
			$ 7.25
	Habana 1 de Junio 1864		
	1.05 (duty)		

975b
A short form: Oath of Importers or Agents

(signed) L. F. Zantzinger

976-978
Preprinted Customs Form

No. 55
Entry of Merchandise
Importer W. J. Hughes
Vessel *Denbigh*
From Havana
Entered June 14th 1864
Value $ 107 Duty $ 15.45

Owner's Oath
(signed) L. F. Zantzinger
Sworn before me, this 14th day of June 1864

Mdse. Entered 14th June 1864 Ship Entered June 7th 1864
Entry of Merchandise imported into the Port of Mobile, District of Mobile, by W. J. Hughes in the Br. Str. *Denbigh* Godfrey Master, from Havana

No. of Packages	Contents	Value in Foreign Currency	10%	15%	20%	Duties
1 Pkge	Paper	$ 28.35		29		$ 4.35
1 "	Mfs. of Wood, **(card boards)**	5.25		6		.90
2 boxes	Medicinal preparations @ 15%	57.90		60		9.00
1 "	Acct. Aw'd (?)	10.50	12			1.20
		102.00	12	95		$15.45
	Chges & Com	5.35				
		$ 107.35				

979a
Invoice

Invoice of sundry Goods shipped by F. J Barbot on Steamer *Denbigh* & consigned to W. Ja Hughes for my account.

5 lbs	Hypo.	$ 2.65
100	Card boards	5.25
150	Sh paper (writing)	28.35
1 lb	Cotton	12.60
1 "	B. Potash	12.60
3 oz	T. of Zinc	2.40
1 lb	T. of Potash	12.60
3 oz	of T Ammonium	2.40
1 lb	Cyanide	1.60
10 "	Sulp of Iron	3.15

20 "	Acetic acid	10.50
10 "	Collodiva (?)	13.25
	with Mfu & Chges	$ 107.35
	Havana June 1 1864	
	F J Bardot	

979b
Invoice

B Labuzan (?)
From the Florida

1 pc	White linen	10.50
2	merino undershirts	2.00
		$ 12.50
	Havana May 1 1864	

979c
A short form: Oath of Importers or Agents

Signed: M J Hughes

981-983
Preprinted Customs Form

No. 58
Entry of Merchandise
Importer H. O. Brewer & Co
Vessel *Denbigh*
From Havana
Entered June 16th 1864
Value $ 434   Duty $ 65.10

Agent's Oath
(signed) H. O. Brewer & Co., owners
Sworn before me, this 16th day of June 1864

Mdse. Entered 16th June 1864   Ship Entered June 7th 1864
Entry of Merchandise imported into the Port of Mobile, District of Mobile, by H. O. Brewer & Co. in the Br. Str. *Denbigh* Godfrey Master, from Havana

Marks	No. of Packages	Contents	Value in Foreign Currency	10%	15%	20%	Duties
Geo. Tolson	1 Trunk	Wearing apparel	$ 45.00		47		$ 7.05
"		Cottons, Mafs.	52.00		54		8.10
"		Flax	108.40		112		16.80
"		Shoes prs 5	15.00		16		2.40

Isaac Scott	2 pkges	Medicinal preparations	34.00		35		5.25
"		Ready made clothing	50.75		52		7.80
T. S. Spear	1 Pkge	Brass mfs	89.09		92		13.80
Mrs. Wigfall[92]	1 Pkge	Cotton mfs	24.50		26		3.90
			418.74		434		$65.10
		Chges & Com	15.25				
			433.99				

Figure 89. Mrs. Wigfall.

984a
Invoice

LA BOTICA SUECA

DE FEDERICO HELLBERG

Calle de Sn Ygnacio No 32

entre Obispo y O'Reilly

Figure 90. Invoice for medicine with printed letterhead.

92 Charlotte Maria Cross Wigfall, the wife of Confederate Senator from Texas, Louis Wigfall.

La Botica Sueca de Federico Hellberg
Sr D Isaac Scott

Habana y May 13th 1864 Debe

5 Ounces	Sulphate Quinine (best French)	4.00	20.00
16 Do	Laudanum	.25	4.00
16 Do	Paregoric	12½	2.00
2 Drams	Sulphate Morphine	.01	2.00
16 Ounces	Calomel (Sublimated)	.15	2.50
	Rhubarb root		1.00
	Chloroform		1.00
	Sweet Spirits of Nitre		2.00
	Suma		$ 34.50
	Reciped (?)		
	(signed) Fedco Hellberg		

984b
Invoice

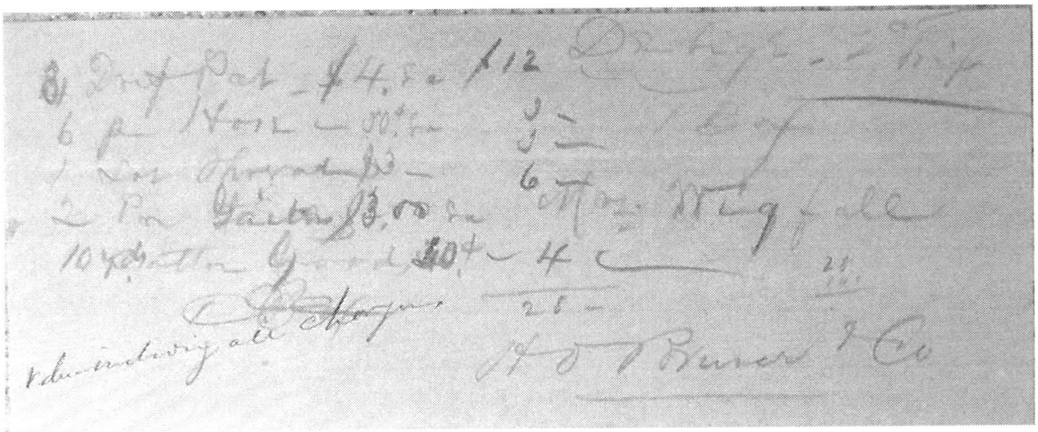

Figure 91. Invoice of order for Mrs. Wigfall.

Denbigh 2nd trip (referring to a shipment delivered to the Customs House on a previous voyage being processed after a longer delay than usual.)

1 Box
Mrs. Wigfall

3	Dress Pat(ern)	$ 4 ea	$ 12
6 pr	Hose	50¢	3
1 doz	Thread	$ 3	3
2 Pr	Gaiters	$ 3.00	6
10 yds	Cotton Goods	30¢	4
due	including all	charges	28
	H O Brewer & Co		

987a
Invoice

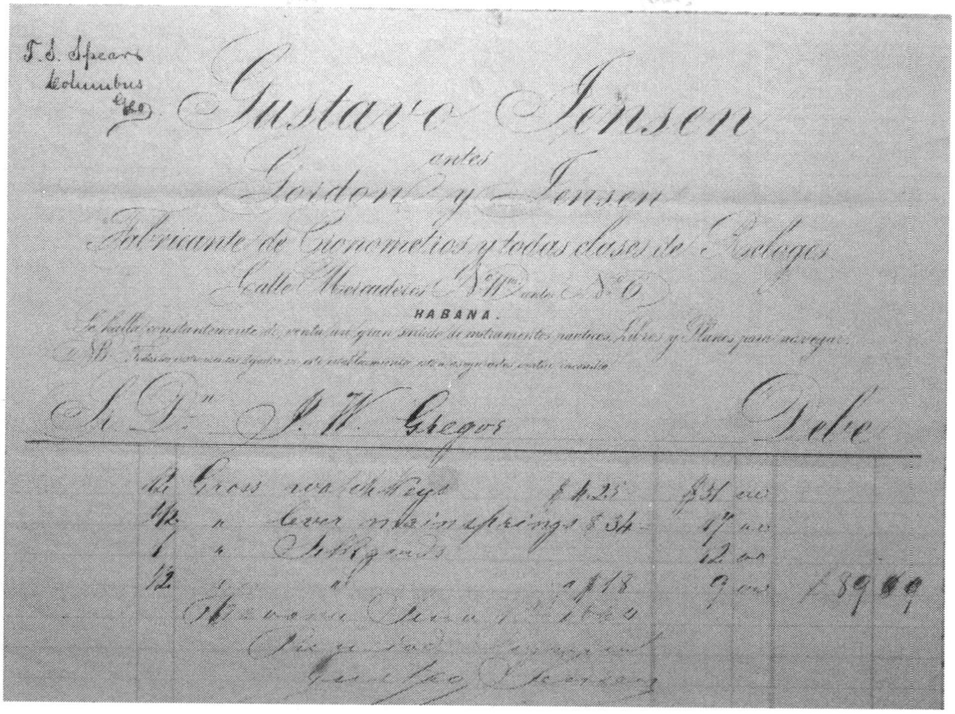

Figure 92. Invoice for watch parts.

T. S. Spear
Columbus Geo.

Gustavo Jensen
Antes
Gordon y Jensen
Fabricante de Cronometros y todas clases de Reloges
Calle Mercaderes No. 11(a) antes No. 6
Habana

Se halla constantemente de venta un gran surtido de instrumentos nauticos, Libros y Planos para navegar.
NB : Todos los instrumentos dejados en este establecimiento estan asegniada contra incendio.

Sr. Dn. J. W. Gregos				Debe
12 Gross	**watch keys**	$ 4.25	$ 51.00	
½ "	**lever main springs**	$ 34	17.00	
1 "	???		12.00	
½ "	"	a $ 18	9.00	$ 89.00
	Havana Junio 1st 1864			
	Received Payment			
	Gustavo Jensen			

987b
Invoice

Mrs. Geo Tolsom
One trunk Contg

Cottons 42, Linens 118, Hosiery 10, Shoes 15
With all Chgs & Com. Valued at $ ____ $ 231 ?? ____ ____
Duty $ 34.65

988a (Reverse side of 987 a)

To be sent by ~~Donaldson~~ for H O Brewer & Co

990-992
Preprinted Customs Form

Note commercial quantities.

No. 57
Entry of Merchandise
Importer H. O. Brewer
Vessel *Denbigh*
From Havana
Entered June 14th 1864
Value $ 6,450 Duty $ 956.30

Agent's Oath
(signed) H. O. Brewer & Co
Benj Donaldson
Sworn before me, this ___ day of June 1864
J. C. Colsson dep Collector

Mdse. Entered 14th June 1864 Ship Entered June 7th 1864
Entry of Merchandise imported into the Port of Mobile, District of Mobile, by H. O. Brewer & Co in the Br. Str. *Denbigh* Godfrey Master, from Havana

Marks	No. of Packages	Contents	Value in Foreign Currency	5%	10%	15%	20%	Duties
A	1 Box	Indigo lbs 270	$ 327.60	342				$ 17.10
N	2 Ahds.	**Hops** " 240	96.00		100			10.00
"	38 Blls	Copperas " 19,526	421.04			439		65.85
c	5 "	Blue Stone " 1766	388.52			405		60.75
N	10 Bales	Rope " 2792	272.22			283		42.45
"	7 Boxes	Fish oil Gals 60	190.00			197		29.55
"	4 Casks	Glue lbs 1465	322.30			336		50.40
"	69 pcs.	Striped Cottons	563.04			587		88.05
TM/I	3 Bales	Flannel	1725.00			1795		269.25
M	2 Bales	Flax mfs. (drilling)	1131.20			1177		176.55
N	45 Cans	White lead paint	84.37			88		13.20

"	20 Kegs	Nails lbs 2000	135.00			141		21.15
PYO	6 Boxes	Camphor refined " 672	537.60				560	112.00
			6193.89	342	100	5448	560	$ 956.30
		Charges & Com	256.54					
			$ 6450.43					

993
Invoice

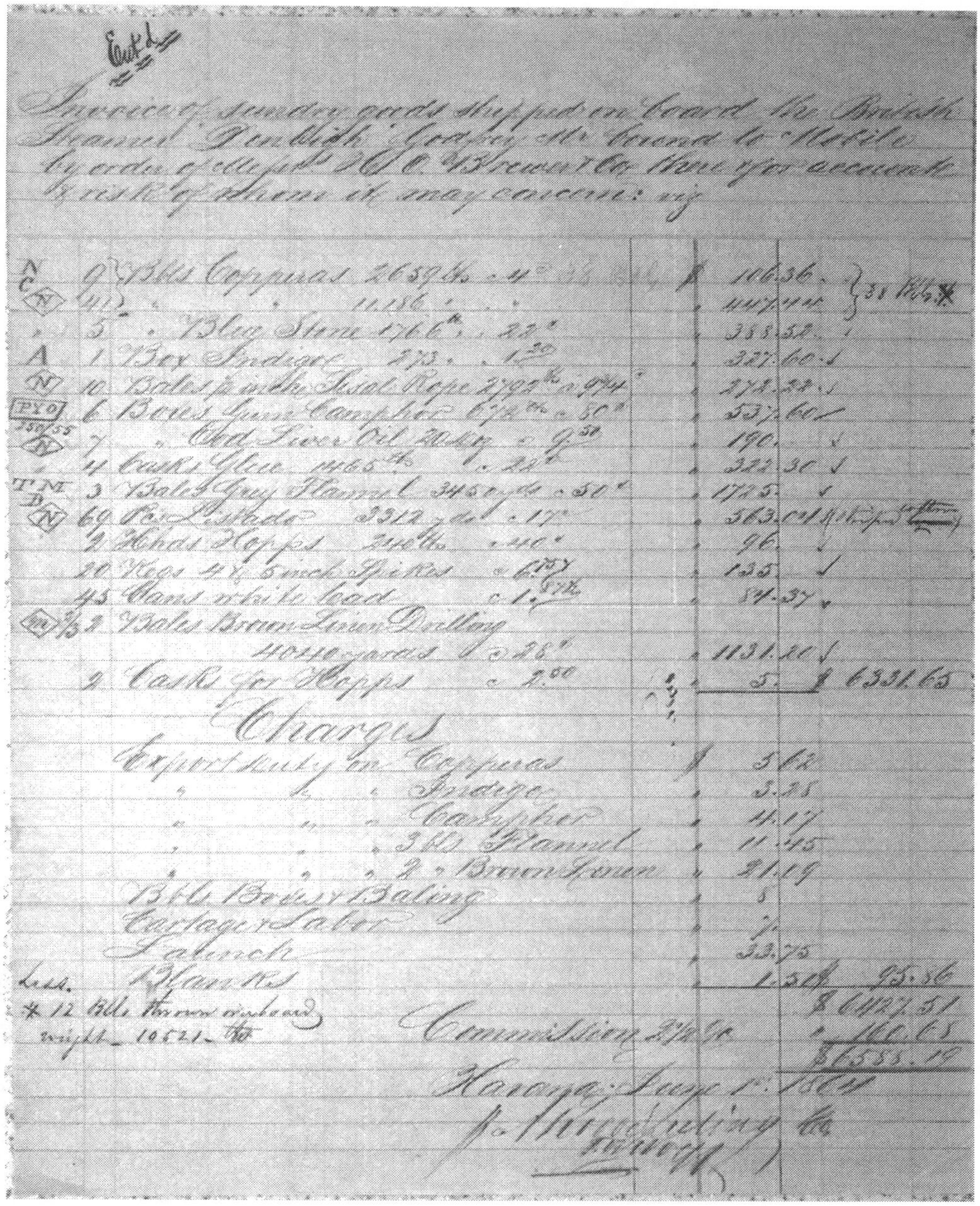

Invoice of sundry goods shipped on board the British Steamer ... bound to Mobile ... & risk of whom it may concern: viz

9 Bbls Copperas 2659 lbs	106.36	
41 " " 11,186	447.44	
5 " Blue Stone 1766 lbs	353.52	
1 Box Indigo 273	327.60	
10 Bales ... Rope	272.22	
6 Boxes Gum Camphor 672 lbs @ 80	537.60	
7 " Cod Liver Oil	190.	
4 Casks Glue 1465 lbs	322.30	
3 Bales Grey Flannel 345 yds @ 50	172.5	
69 Pcs ... 3312 yds @ 17	563.04	
2 Hhds Hopps 240 lbs @ 40	96.	
20 Kegs ... Spikes @ 6.75	135.	
45 Cans white lead	54.37	
32 Bales Brown Linen Drilling 4040 yards @ 28	1131.20	
2 Casks for Hopps @ 2.50	5.	$ 6331.65
Charges		
Export duty on Copperas	5.62	
" " " Indigo	3.25	
" " " Camphor	4.17	
" " " 3 B. Flannel	11.45	
" " " 2 " Brown Linen	21.19	
Bbls Boxes & Baling	5	
Cartage & Labor	7	
Launch	33.75	
...	1.50	95.56
		$ 6427.51
Commission 2½ %		160.68
		$ 6588.19

Less.
* 12 Bbls thrown overboard
weight 10521 lbs

Havana June 1st 1864

Figure 93. Invoice for unusually large commercial order.

(added note) Ent'd

Invoice of sundry goods shipped on board the British Steamer *Denbigh* Godfrey Mr bound to Mobile by order of Messrs H. O. Brewer & Co there & for account & risk of whom it may concern: viz

N/C	9 Bbls	Copperas 2659 lbs @ 4¢ 38 Bbls	$ 106.36	
N	41 "	" 11,186 " "	447.44	
"	5 "	Blue Stone 1766 lbs " 22¢	388.52	
A	1 Box	Indigo 273 " " 1.20	327.60	
N	10 Bales	½ inch Sisal Rope 2792 lbs @ 9¾¢	272.22	
PYO	6 Boxes	Gum Camphor 672 lbs @ 80¢	537.60	
250/55 N	7 "	Cod Liver Oil 20 Doz @ 9.50	190.00	
"	4 Casks	Glue 1465 lbs @ 22¢	322.30	
TM/D	3 Bales	Grey Flannel 3450 yds @ 50¢	1725.00	
N	69 Pc's	Listado[93] 3312 yds @ 17¢	563.04	striped cotton
	2 Hohds	**Hopps** 240 lbs @ 40¢	96.00	
	20 Kegs	4 ? 5 inch Spikes @ 6.75	135.00	
	45 Cans	white lead @ 1.87½	84.37	
M 2/3	2 Bales	Brown Linen Drilling 4044 yards @ 28¢	1121.20	
	2 Casks	for Hopps @ 2.50	5.00	$ 6331.65
		Charges		
		Export Duty on Copperas	$ 5.62	
		" " " Indigo	3.28	
		" " " Camphor	4.17	
		" " " 3 bls Flannel	11.45	
		" " " 2 " Brown Linen	21.09	
		Bbls Boxes & Baling	8.00	
		Cartage & Labor	7.00	
(added		Launch	33.75	
note)		Blanks	1.50	$ 95.86
Less	# 12 Blls	**thrown overboard**[94] Commission 2½%		$ 6427.51
	weight	10521 lbs		160.68
				$ 6588.19
		Havana June 1st 1864		
		??? Luling Co.		
		???		

995a
A short form: Oath of Importers or Agents

Signed: Benj Donaldson

995b
A short form: Oath of Importers or Agents

Signed: S. J. Douglas

[93] Striped (fabric).
[94] Probably indicates a problem on the voyage such as pursuit by blockader, storm, or grounding.

996-997
Substitute for Preprinted Customs Form

No. 56
Entry of Merchandise
Importer S. J. Douglas
Vessel *Denbigh*
From Havana
Entered June 14th 1864
Value $ 79 Duty $ 11.85

Entry of Mdse by S. J. Douglas
In the Br Str *Denbigh*, Godfrey Master, from Havana, 7th June 1864

1 Pkge	Wool mfs	$ 25.50	26	15%	$ 3.90
	Cotton mfs	17.00	18	"	2.70
	Lenin	10.25	10	"	1.50
	Clothing (ready made)	16.00	17	"	2.55
	Shoes	7.50	8	"	1.20
		76.25	79		$ 11.85

998
Invoice

Invoice of goods shipped on board the Brt Steamer *Denbigh* **Capt. Joseph Radin** & consigned to Mr Saml J Douglas

2 pc	Sheeting & long (?) Cloth	80 varas	$ 25.50
1 "	Calico	40 "	17.00
10 yds	linen		7.50
2 pr	ladies shoes		7.50
2½	Cashmere		8.50
1	Black Handkerchief		1.75
1 pr	Rersanen (?) pants		8.00
12 dozen	Shirt buttons		1.00
	including comm		76.75
	Saml J. Douglas		
	11.70 (duty)		

Note: Probably an error in recording the *Denbigh*'s Captain as this was the only listing of this name.

7

Denbigh Customs Manifests, July 1864, Transcripts

Denbigh Voyage No. 6, Havana-Mobile-Havana
Havana, last date document prepared there, 4 June 1864 so the ship sailed soon thereafter.
Mobile, date ship entered (port and reported arrival to C.S. Customs) was 7 June 1864.
Mobile departure, cotton export manifests dated 14 June 1864 so ship sailed soon thereafter. (421 bales cotton, 218,890 lbs., $124,764, 57¢ per lb.)

347-351
Preprinted Customs Form

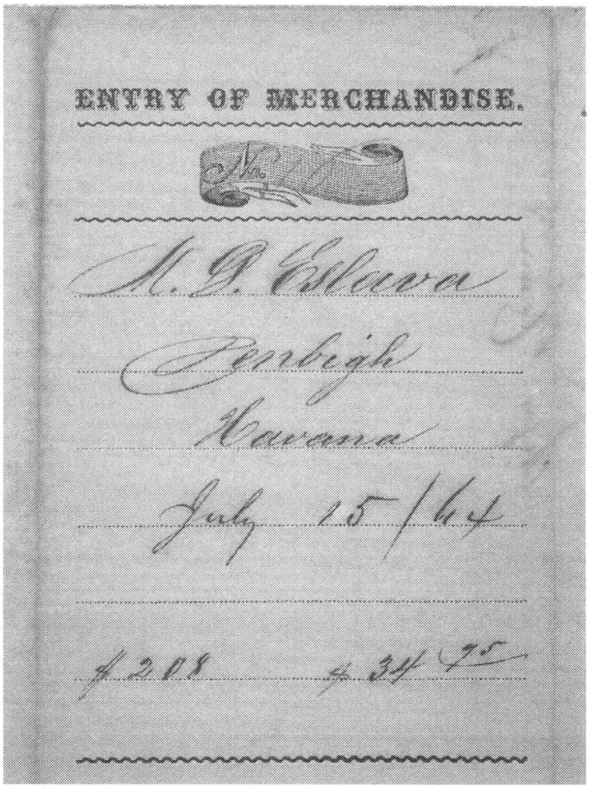
ENTRY OF MERCHANDISE.

No.

M. D. Eslava

Denbigh

Havana

July 15/64

$208 $34 75

Figure 94. Abstract block folded to outside of preprinted customs form.

351
Owner's Oath

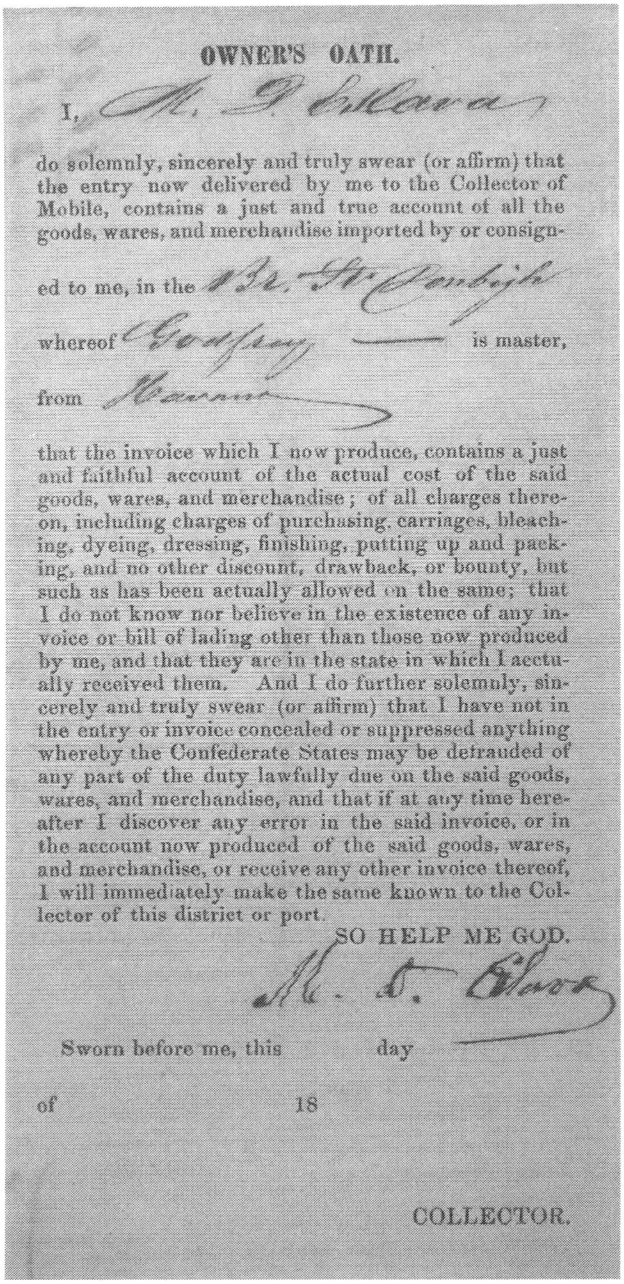

OWNER'S OATH.

I, M. D. Eslava

do solemnly, sincerely and truly swear (or affirm) that the entry now delivered by me to the Collector of Mobile, contains a just and true account of all the goods, wares, and merchandise imported by or consigned to me, in the Br. Str Denbigh

whereof Godfrey — is master,

from Havana

that the invoice which I now produce, contains a just and faithful account of the actual cost of the said goods, wares, and merchandise; of all charges thereon, including charges of purchasing, carriages, bleaching, dyeing, dressing, finishing, putting up and packing, and no other discount, drawback, or bounty, but such as has been actually allowed on the same; that I do not know nor believe in the existence of any invoice or bill of lading other than those now produced by me, and that they are in the state in which I actually received them. And I do further solemnly, sincerely and truly swear (or affirm) that I have not in the entry or invoice concealed or suppressed anything whereby the Confederate States may be defrauded of any part of the duty lawfully due on the said goods, wares, and merchandise, and that if at any time hereafter I discover any error in the said invoice, or in the account now produced of the said goods, wares, and merchandise, or receive any other invoice thereof, I will immediately make the same known to the Collector of this district or port.

SO HELP ME GOD.

M. D. Eslava

Sworn before me, this day

of 18

COLLECTOR.

Figure 95. Owner's oath section of preprinted customs form.

Owner's Oath
I, M. D. Eslava
… the entry now delivered by me to the Collector of Mobile, contains a just and true account of all the goods … imported by or consigned to me, in the Br. Str *Denbigh* whereof Godfrey is master, from Havana that the invoice which I now produce, contains … all charges of purchasing, … packing (etc). … that I have not … concealed … anything whereby the Confederate States may be defrauded … of the duty … due …

SO HELP ME GOD
(signed) M. D. Eslava …

No. 16
Entry of Merchandise
Importer M. D. Eslava
Vessel *Denbigh*
From Havana
Entered July 15/64
Value $ 208 Duty $ 34.75

Mdse. Entered ________18___ Ship Entered ~~May~~ June 7 1864
Entry of Merchandise imported into the Port of Mobile, District of Mobile, by M. D. Eslava in the Br. Str. *Denbigh* Godfrey Master, from Havana

Marks	No. of Packages	Contents	Value in Foreign Currency	10%	15%	20%	Duties
	1 Case	Brushes	$ 68.00			71	14.20
	1 "	Combs	132.00		137		20.55
		Chgs & Com	200.00		137	71	$ 34.75
			8.08				
			$ 208.08				

352
Invoice

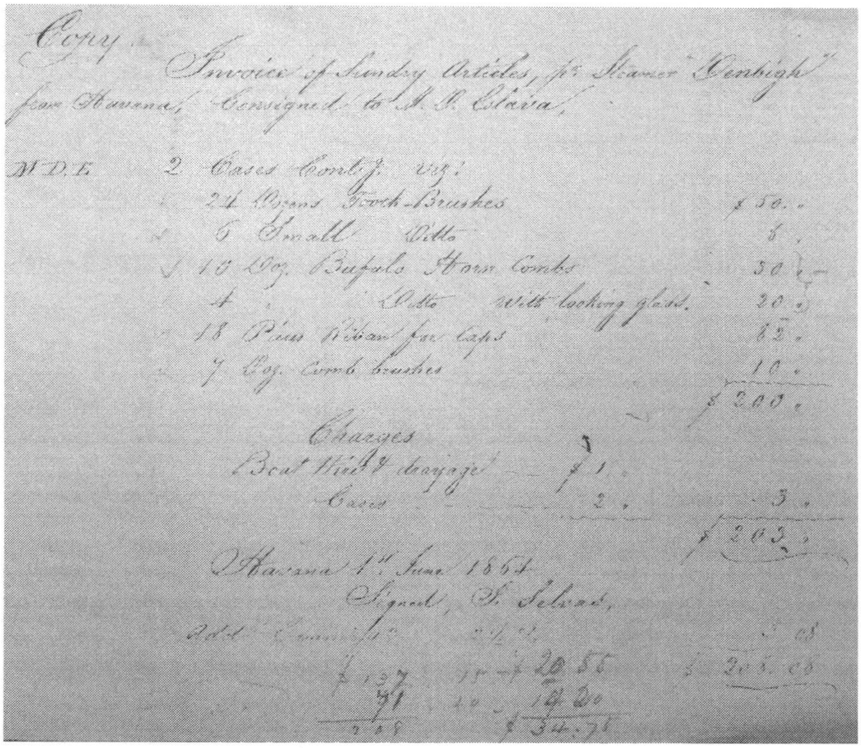
Copy.
Invoice of Sundry Articles, pr. Steamer "Denbigh" from Havana, Consigned to M. D. Eslava,

M.D.E. 2 Cases Contg. viz:
24 Dozns Tooth-Brushes $ 50.
6 Small Ditto 6.
10 Doz. Bufalo Horn Combs 30.
4 " Ditto with looking glass. 20.
18 Pieces Ribbon for caps 82.
7 Doz. Comb brushes 10.
$ 200.

Charges
Boat Hire & drayage $ 1.
Cases 2. 3.
$ 203.

Havana 1st June 1864
Signed, F. Selvas,
Add Commission 2½ % 5.08
$ 208.08
$ 137 15 $ 20.55
71 20 14.20
208 $ 34.75

Figure 96. Invoice for sundries including tooth brushes.

Copy

Invoice of Sundry Articles, pr Steamer *Denbigh* from Havana, Consigned to M. D. Eslava.

M. D. E.	2 Cases	Contg viz	
	24 Dozens	**Tooth Brushes**	$ 50
	6	Small Ditto	8
	10 Doz.	Buffalo Horn Combs	30
	4 "	Ditto with looking glass	20
	18 Pieces	Ribbon for Caps	82
	7 Doz.	Comb brushes	10
			$ 200
		Charges	
		Boat Hire & drayage $ 1	
		Cases $ 2	3
			$ 203
		Havana 1st June 1864	
		Signed J. Selvas	
		add Comissn. 2½	5.08
		$ 34.75 (duty)	$ 208.08

353

A Note

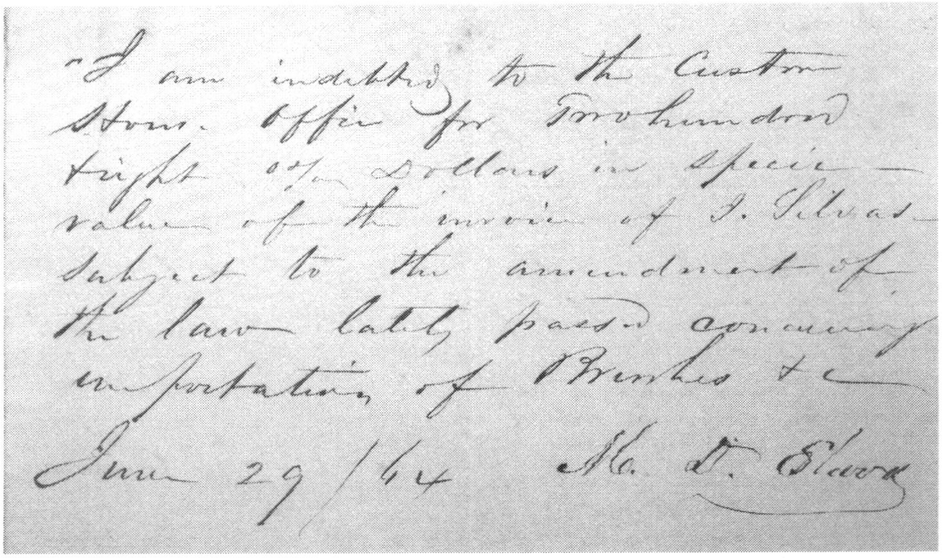

Figure 97. Note acknowledging debt for customs due.

I am indebted to the Custom House Office for Two hundred & eight 00/100 Dollars in specie – value of the invoice of J. Silvas – subject to the amendment of the law lately passed concerning importation of brushes &c

June 29/64 (signed) M. D. Eslava

354-356
Preprinted Customs Form

No. 15
Entry of Merchandise
Importer A. Dacovich
Vessel *Denbigh*
From Havana
Entered June 14th 1864
Value $ 31 Duty $ 7.75

Owner's Oath
(signed) A. Dacovich
Sworn before me, this 14th day of June 1864

Mdse. Entered 14th July 1864 Ship Entered 7th June 1864
Entry of Merchandise imported into the Port of Mobile, District of Mobile, by A. Dacovich in the Br. Str. *Denbigh* Godfrey Master, from Havana

Marks	No. of Packages	Contents	Value in Foreign Currency	10%	15%	25%	Duties
A Dacovich	2 Baskets	Champagne	$ 16.00			17	4.25
Col. Jennifer (?)	2 Boxes	Claret	13.00			14	3.50
			29.00			$ 31	$ 7.75
		Chgs & Com	2.25				
			$ 31.25				

357-360
Preprinted Customs Form

No. 14
Entry of Merchandise
Importer John Hutcheson
Vessel *Denbigh*
From Havana
Entered June 14th 1864
Value $ 53 Duty $ 13.25

Owner's Oath
(signed) Jno. C. Hodges
Sworn before me, this 10th day of June 1864

Mdse. Entered 14th July 1864 Ship Entered May 1st 1864
Entry of Merchandise imported into the Port of Mobile, District of Mobile, by John Hutchison in the Br. Str. *Denbigh* Godfrey Master, from Havana

Marks	No. of Packages	Contents	Value in Foreign Currency	10%	15%	25%	Duties

	18 Demijohns	Rum Gals 81	$ 32.00			34	8.50
	4 Do	Gin " 18	12.00			13	3.25
		Sigars 400	6.00			6	1.50
			50.00			$ 53	$ 13.25
		Chgs & Com	2.55				
			52.55				

361
Invoice

J Hutchinson	18 Demijohns	Rum	$ 32.00
	4 Do	Gin	12.00
	400	Segars	6.00
			50.00
	Chgs & Com		2.55
			52.55
	13.25 (duty)		

Note: Reuse of an old form torn into small scraps.

362
Affidavit Grandfathering Prohibited Goods

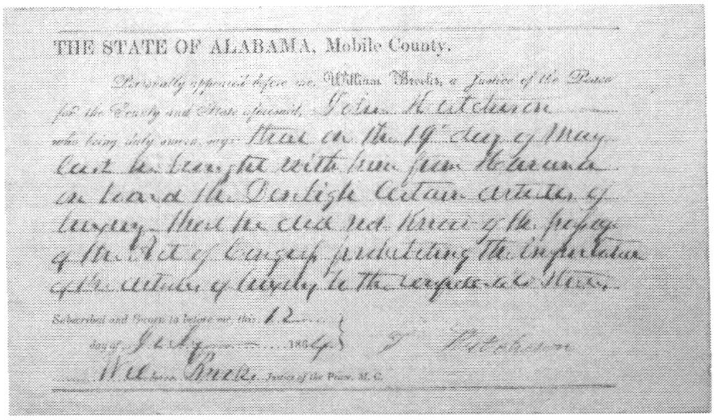

Figure 98. Form for approving importation of luxury goods forbidden by change in law.

The State of Alabama, Mobile County.

Personally appeared before me, William Brooks, a Justice of the Peace for the County and State aforesaid, John Hutcheson who being duly sworn says: that on the 19 day of May last he brought with him from Havana on board the *Denbigh* certain articles of luxury that he did not know of the passage of the Act of Congress prohibiting the importation of the articles of luxury to the Confederate States.

Subscribed and sworn before me, this 12

day of July 1864 (signed) J. Hutcheson

William Brooks Justice of the Peace, M. C.

363
Same oath, form and dates: John O'Brien his Mark +

364
Same oath, form and dates: William Lytel

365
Same oath, form and dates: James Bragan his Mark X

366
Same oath, form and dates: Edmond Wright

367-369
Preprinted Customs Form

No. 13
Entry of Merchandise
Importer D. Nichols
Vessel *Denbigh*
From Havana
Entered June 12th 1864
Value $ 12 Duty $ 3.00

Owner's Oath
(signed) D. Nichols
Sworn before me, this 12th day of June 1864
(signed) J. C. Coleson Dep. Collector

Mdse. Entered 12th July 1864 Ship Entered May 1st 1864
Entry of Merchandise imported into the Port of Mobile, District of Mobile, by D. Nichols in the Br. Str. *Denbigh* Godfrey Master, from Havana

Marks	No. of Packages	Contents	Value in Foreign Currency	10%	15%	25%	Duties
	2 Kegs	Rum 130 Gals.	$ 8.00			9	$ 2.25
	1 Demjhs	Gin 4½ Gals	3.00			3	.75
			11.00			12	$ 3.00
		Chgs & Com	1.00				
			12.00				

374-375, 1246
Preprinted Customs Form

No. 10
Entry of Merchandise
Importer H O Brewer & Co
Vessel *Denbigh*
From Havana
Entered June 16th 1864
Value $ 547 Duty $ 86.00

Owner's Oath
(signed) Benj. Donaldson
Sworn before me, this 16th day of June 1864

Mdse. Entered ________18___ Ship Entered June 7 1864
Entry of Merchandise imported into the Port of Mobile, District of Mobile, by H. O. Brewer & Co in the Br. Str. *Denbigh* Godfrey Master, from Havana

Marks	No. of Packages	Contents	Value in Foreign Currency	10%	15%	20%	Duties
	2 Cases	Quinine oz. 300	$ 450.00		465		$ 70.20
	2 "	Sugar Brown lbs 955	76.40			79	15.80
			526.40			79	$ 86.00
		Chgs & Com	21.05				
			$ 547.45				

370
Preprinted Customs Form

Mdse. Entered 16th July 1864 Ship Entered 7th June 1864
Entry of Merchandise imported into the Port of Mobile, District of Mobile, by Benj. Donaldson in the Br. Str. *Denbigh* Godfrey Master, from Havana

Marks	No. of Packages	Contents	Value in Foreign Currency	10%	15%	20%	Duties
N	1 Bll	Flour of Sulphur lbs 24	$ 19.52	20			$ 2.00
L B	20 Boxes	Extract of Logwood 500	50.00	52			5.20
M	5 "	Tin, in plates	65.00	68	26		6.80
	25 gross	Metallic pins	25.00		125		3.90
N	50 Boxes	Mustard	120.00		43		18.75
	1 Box	Paper & Envelopes (Mfs of)	41.50		437		6.45
H	1 "	Calf Shins doz 12	420.00		70		65.55
L B	10 Kegs	Bi Car. Soda lbs 1120	67.00		61		10.50
N	5 Blls	Salts (Epsom) " 1069	58.79		27		9.15
"	1 Box	Oil (Coal) Gals 35	26.25		94		4.05

"	5 Blls	Alum lbs 1500	90.00			83	14.10
B	1 Box	Copana Balsam " 100	80.00			19	16.60
		Sugar (White) " 150	18.00	140	883	102	3.80
			1081.26				$ 166.85
		Chgs & Com	43.25				
			$ 1,124.51				

372
Invoice

Benjamin Donaldson
To J. H. Dever Dr.

	25 Gross	**Gillot[95] Pens**		@ 1 $	25.00
L B 1/10	10 Kegs	Bi Carb Soda	1120 lbs	" 6¢	67.20
N 1/5	5 Bbls	Epsom Salts	1069 "	" 5½¢	58.79
N 6/10	5 "	Alumn	1500 "	" 6¢	90.00
N /11	1 "	Flour Sulphur	244 "	8¢	19.52
L B	20 Boxes	Extract Logwood	500 "	10¢	50.00
N	50 " 20 doz	English Mustard	240 Bott	50¢	120.00
N	1 " 10 Reams	Letter Paper		" 2.75	27.50
	3000	Envelopes		" 3.00	9.00
	2000	Do		" 2.50	5.00
N	1 Box 3 Tin Cans & 1 Demijohn 35 Galls	Coal Oil		" 75¢	26.25
M	5 " B L X	Tin Plates		" 13¢	65.00
B	1 " 100 lbs	Balsam Capaiva[96]		" 80¢	80.00
H	1 " 12 dz	Calf Skins		" 35.00	420.00
					$ 1063.26
		Charges			
	Export duty on	Bi Carb Soda		3.50	
	" " "	Logwood		1.50	
	" " "	Tin Plate		.87	
	" " "	Copana		1.25	
	" " "	Calf Skins		2.50	
		Boxes & Barrels		4.00	
		Cartage & Labor		4.00	
		Launch hire		19.50	
		Blanks		1.00	38.12
					$ 1101.38
	150 lbs	Sugar	@ 12¢	18.00	91.50
	350 lbs	Coffee	" 21¢	73.50	
					$ 1192.88
	Havana June 1st 1864	J. W. Dever			

[95] Joseph Gillot & Sons Steel Pens (pen nibs) company.
[96] balsam capivi – an oleoresin used in varnishes and ointments.

373
Short form

Oath of Benj. Donaldson, an agent of H. O. Brewer & Co, Mobile.

376
Preprinted Customs Form

No. 10
Entry of Merchandise
Importer A. M. Godfrey
Vessel *Denbigh*
From Havana
Entered June 6th 1864
Value $ 365 Duty $ 78.65

Owner's Oath
(signed) Bej. Donaldson

Mdse. Entered ______18__ Ship Entered May __1864
Entry of Merchandise imported into the Port of Mobile, District of Mobile, by A. M. Godfrey in the Brit. Str. *Denbigh* Godfrey Master, from Havana

Marks	No. of Packages	Contents	Value in Foreign Currency	10%	15%	25%	Duties
G	6 Blls	Alcohol 188 Gals	$ 118.18			124	31.00
"	10 Kegs	Brandy 120 "	150.00			157	39.25
B	1 Bale	Leaf tobacco 110 lbs	80.00	84			8.40
			348.18	84		281	$ 78.65
		Exp. duty on tobacco 1.95					
		Shpg Chgs & Com 15.22	17.17				
			$ 365.35				

379
Invoice

For a/c of A. M. Godfrey

6 Bll	Alcohol	188 Gals @ 66¢	$ 118.18
10 ½ Blls	Brandy	120 Gals	150.00
			$ 268.18

	Chgs & Com		12.72
			$ 280.90
	For a/c of Batre		
1 Bale of	leaf Tobacco		80.00
	Exp duty, Chgs & Com		4.45
			$ 84.45

381-383
Preprinted Customs Form

No. 9
Entry of Merchandise
Importer John Scott
Vessel *Denbigh*
From Havana
Entered June 14th 1864
Value $ 19 Duty $ 4.75

Owner's Oath
(signed) John Scott
Sworn before me, this 14th day of June 1864

Mdse. Entered _____ 18__ Ship Entered June 7 1864
Entry of Merchandise imported into the Port of Mobile, District of Mobile, by John Scott in the Br. Str. *Denbigh* Godfrey Master, from Havana

Marks	No. of Packages	Contents	Value in Foreign Currency	10%	15%	25%	Duties
	One Box	Containing					
		Sardines	$ 2.00			2	$ .50
		Comfits	2.00			2	.50
		Sigars 400	12.00			13	3.25
	1 Dmj	Gin 3 Gals	1.50			2	.50
			17.50			19	$ 4.75
		Chgs & Com	1.00				
			18.50				

384
Invoice

Gin 3 Gals	1.50
Sardines	2.00
Preserves	2.00
Sigars	12.00
	17.50

385-387
Preprinted Customs Form

No. 8
Entry of Merchandise
Importer N. H. Williamson
Vessel *Denbigh*
From Havana
Entered July 2d 1864
Value $ 64 Duty $ 14.85

Owner's Oath
(signed) W. H. Williamson

Mdse. Entered 2d July 1864 Ship Entered 7th June 1864
Entry of Merchandise imported into the Port of Mobile, District of Mobile, by W. H. Williamson in the Br. Str. *Denbigh* Godfrey Master, from Havana

Marks	No. of Packages	Contents	Value in Foreign Currency	10%	15%	25%	Duties
	1 Keg	Whiskey Gals 8	$ 16.00			17	$ 4.25
	1 Bl	Ale 7 doz.	18.00		19		2.85
		Segars 1000	30.00			31	7.75
			$ 64.00		19	48	14.85
		Chgs & Com	3.00				
			67.00				

388-390
Preprinted Customs Form

No. 9
Entry of Merchandise
Importer G. G. Garner
Vessel *Denbigh*
From Havana
Entered June 15th 1864
Value $ 209 Duty $ 31.35

Owner's Oath
(signed) Geo G Garner

Mdse. Entered ______18___ Ship Entered ______18___
Entry of Merchandise imported into the Port of Mobile, District of Mobile, by W. H. Williamson in the Br. Str. *Denbigh* Godfrey Master, from Havana

Marks	No. of Packages	Contents	Value in Foreign Currency	10%	15%	25%	Duties
G.G.G.	4 Pkges	Flax mfs, Linen	$ 32.85		34		$ 5.10
		Wool mfs. (Buttons, ???)	28.43		30		4.50
		Cotton mfs	4.90		5		.75
G.G.G.	2 Bdls	wool mfs	51.50		54		8.10
		Flax mfs (& Silk)	15.50		17		2.55
		Cotton mfs	54.92		58		8.70
		Shoes	10.10		11		1.65
		Chges & Com	11.00		209		$ 31.35
			$ 209.20				

391
Invoice

Memorandum of Entry shipped by C G Ramsay per Steamer *Denbigh* to Col G G Garner to Mobile

Col G G Garner from CGR

	1 Bundle contg			
20 yds	White flannel	50¢	10.00	
1 Doz	Socks		3.25	
13 yds	French Merino	1.75	22.75	
½ Doz	Lille Thread Undershirts		7.00	
14 yds	Lawn ???	35¢	4.90	
3 Pairs	shoes	3.30	10.50	58.40
	1 Bundle contg			
26 varas	checked Lawn	25¢	6.50	
9 "	Swiss Muslin	50¢	4.50	
15 "	blue merino	1.25	18.75	
1 Piece	fine cotton		5.25	
6	Madras Hdkfs	30¢	1.80	
2 Doz	??? stockings	3¼	6.50	
½ "	Cravats		3.50	
95½ varas	??? calico	21¢	23.87	
1 ???	??? Thread		1.75	
1 "	**Gold Lace**	25¢	3.00	
1 Bunch	Black		1.50	76.92
+	one separate package	1 $	142.32	7.00
	7 varas ??? Silk			

392-393
Substitute for Preprinted Customs Form

No. 11
Entry of Merchandise
Importer Geo. Wesborn
Vessel *Denbigh*
From Havana
Entered June 8th 1864
Value $ 44 Duty $ 11.00

Entry of Mdse by Geo. Wesborn in the Br. Str. *Denbigh*, Godfrey Mr from Havana, 7th June 1864

1 Case	Sigars 1000	$ 42	44 25%	$ 11
	Chges & Com	2		
		$ 44		

394
Invoice

8 Gals whiskey	$ 32
1 Bbl ale	18
1000 Hundred (sic) cigars	45
	$ 95

Mobile June 15 1864
We will deposit the above amount in Specie adding the duty.
H. O. Brewer & Co.

395
Invoice

Bill of Pharmacy

Capt A. M. Godfrey
For E. B. Gould

To J. W. Dever Dr

7 lbs	pure Bergamot Oil[97]	@ 5 $	35.00
2 lbs	" Oil Lemon	@ 3.75	7.50
1 oz	??? Rose (?)	@ 8.00	8.00
4 oz	Neroli Oil[98]	@ 3.50	14.00
2 oz	Musk in grain	@ 19	38.00
25 lbs	Tin Foil	@ 75¢	18.75
1 "	Ext. Colocynth[99]	2.75	2.75

---

[97] Oil from citrus fruit; a fragrant yellow-green essential oil; use – perfumes.
[98] Plant oil similar in scent to bergamot produced from the blossom of the bitter orange tree.

2 lbs	Gum Opium	8.25	16.50
2	??? Extract	5.50	11.00
			151.50
	Cartage & Launch		1.00
	Com 2½%		3.81
			$ 156.31
	Habana June 17th 1864		
		J. W. Dever	

396
Affidavit Regarding Prohibited Goods

Note: This statement was required due to a new law banning of luxury and other imports.

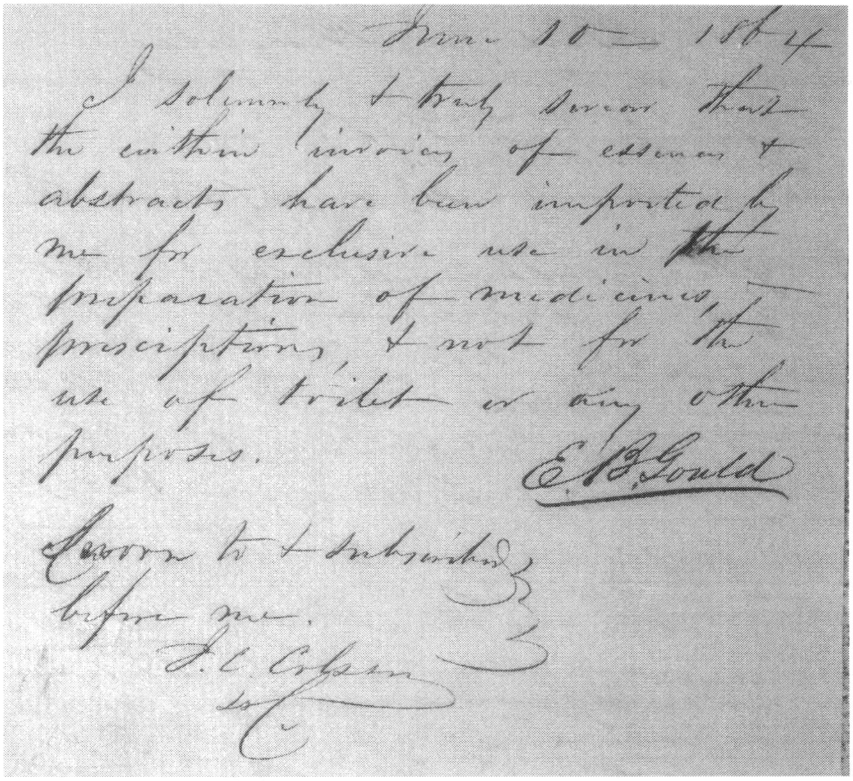
June 10 1864
I solemnly & truly swear that the within invoice of essences & abstracts have been imported by me for exclusive use in the preparation of medicines, prescriptions, & not for the use of toilet or any other purposes.
E. B. Gould
Sworn to & Subscribed before me.

Figure 99. Special oath regarding medicinal purpose of goods.

June 10 1864

I solemnly & truly swear that the within invoice of essences & abstracts have been imported by me for exclusive use in the preparation of medicines, prescriptions, & not for the use of toilet or any other purposes.

(signed) E. B. Gould

Sworn to & Subscribed
Before me.

---

[99] A spongy bitter yellow fruit about the size of a lemon but speckled with green; use – laxative.

(signed) J. C. Colsson
DC (Deputy Collector)

397
A short form: Oath of Importers or Agents

(signed) E. B. Gould

398-399
Substitute for Preprinted Customs Form

No. 12
Entry of Merchandise
Importer E. B. Gould
Vessel *Denbigh*
From Havana
Entered June 10th 1864
Value $ 156 Duty $ 26.45

Entry of Mdse by E. B. Gould (Druggist) In the Br Str *Denbigh*, from Havana, 7th June 1864.

4 Boxes	Extracts of ??? for medicinal preparations	$ 78.25	80	20%	$ 16.00
2 lbs	Gum opium	16.50	17	15%	2.55
2 oz	Musk in grain	38.00	40	"	6.00
25 lbs	Tin Foil	18.75	19	10%	1.90
		151.50	$ 156		$ 26.45
	Chges & Com	4.81			
		156.31			

Note on reverse side: Duty unpaid.

401
Invoice

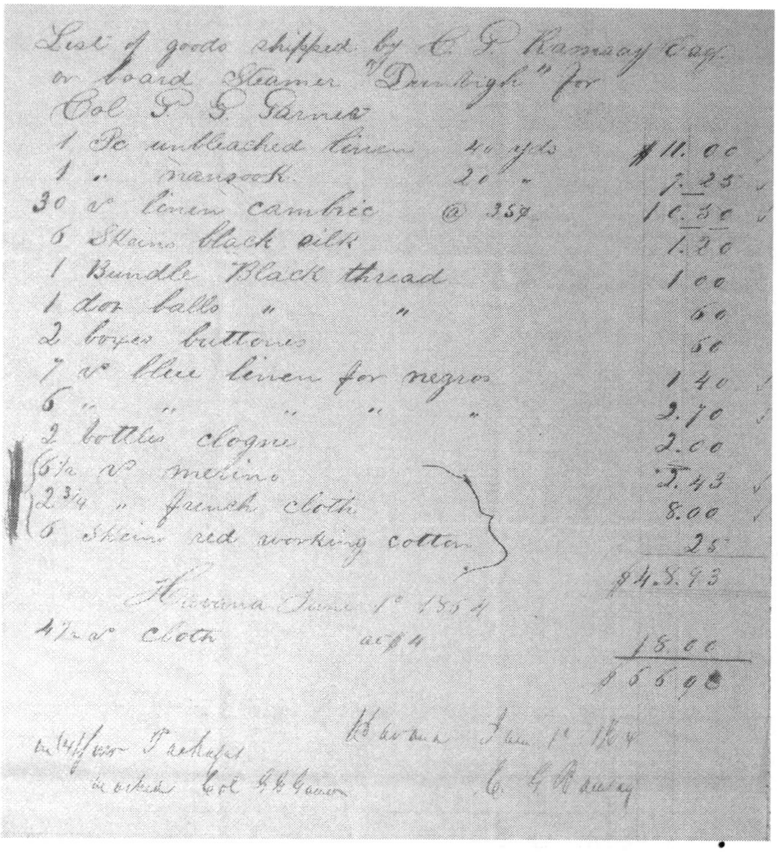

Figure 100. Invoice of sundries for the family of Col. G. G. Garner.

List of goods shipped by C. G. Ramsay Esq. on board Steamer *Denbigh* for Col G. G. Garner

1 Pc	unbleached linen	40 yds	$ 11.00
1 "	nansook[100]	20 "	7.25
30 v(aras)	linen cambric	@ 35¢	10.50
6 Skeins	black silk		1.20
1 Bundle	Black thread		1.00
1 doz balls	" "		.60
2 boxes	button		.60
7 v	blue linen for negros		1.40
6 "	" " " "		2.70
2 bottles	cologne		2.00
6½ v	merino		2.43
2¾ v	French cloth		8.00
6 Skeins	red working cotton		.25
			$ 48.93
	Havana June 1st 1864		
4½ v	cloth	at $ 4	18.00
			66.93
in (4) four Packages	Havana June 1st 1864		
Marked Col G G Garner	(signed) C. G. Ramsay		

[100] Type of muslin.

402
Preprinted Customs Form

No. 7
Entry of Merchandise
Importer Henry Gillman
Vessel *Denbigh*
From Havana
Entered June 14 64
Value $ 67 Duty $ 10.05

Owner's Oath
(signed) Henry Gillman
Sworn before me, this 14 day of July 1864

Mdse. Entered July 14 1864 Ship Entered May 18 1864
Entry of Merchandise imported into the Port of Mobile, District of Mobile, by Henry Gillman in the Br. Str. *Denbigh* Godfrey Master, from Havana

Marks	No. of Packages	Contents	Value in Foreign Currency	10%	15%	25%	Duties
	1 Pkge	Clothing ready made	$ 37.25		39		$ 5.85
		Cotton prints	27.32		28		4.20
			64.57		$ 67		$ 10.05
		Chgs & Com	2.60				
			67.17				

403
Invoice

H. Gillman

1	Felt Hat	$ 2.00
1 pr	Gaiters	3.00
4 vrs	Cloth 3	12.00
1½ vs	blue cloth	4.50
4	Shirts linen	6.00
2	under shirts	2.00
½	linen HDKfs	1.50
2 pr	drawers	2.00
02	Blk cravats	1.50
1	Skin	2.75
	Calicos & dry goods	27.32
	Chges & Com	2.00
		66.17
	with Ch & Com	

408-410
Preprinted Customs Form

No. 6
Entry of Merchandise
Importer F. B. Darcy
Vessel *Denbigh*
From Havana
Entered July 6 64
Value $ 80 Duty $ 12.10

Agent's Oath
(signed) Geo G. Brown

Mdse. Entered ______18___ Ship Entered ______18___
Entry of Merchandise imported into the Port of Mobile, District of Mobile, by F. B. Darcy in the Br. Str. *Denbigh* Godfrey Master, from Havana

Marks	No. of Packages	Contents	Value in Foreign Currency	5%	15%	25%	Duties
F B D	2 Pkges	Indigo 1 lb	$ 2.00	2			$ .10
		Cloth mfs.	32.62		34		5.10
		Flax mfs.	23.30		24		3.60
		Boots	10.75 2.25		14		2.10
		Gold mfs, for officers in the army	5.00			6	1.20
			75.92	2	72	6	$ 12.10
		Chgs & Com	4.26				
			$ 80.18				

409
Short Form

Oath of Importers or Agents
G. J. Brown (signed)

412
Invoice

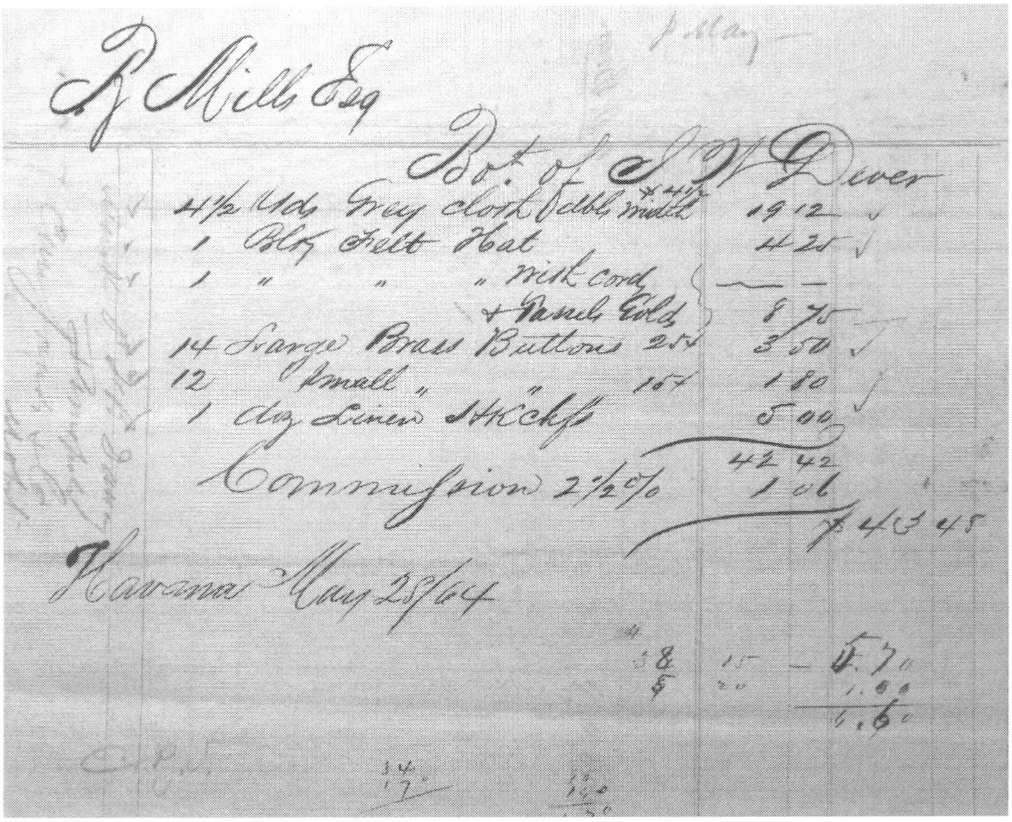
R. Mills Esq
Bot. of J W Dever
4½ Yds Grey cloth dble width $4½ 19 12
1 Blk Felt Hat 4 25
1 " " " with cords & Tassels Gold 8 75
14 Large Brass Buttons 25¢ 3 50
12 Small " " 15¢ 1 80
1 doz Linen HKchfs 5 00
42 42
Commission 2½% 1 06
$43 48
Havana May 28/64

Figure 101. Invoice for sundries bought in Havana by R. Mills.

Note: R. Mills name appeared in Galveston records in association with R. & D. G. Mills company.

R. Mills Esq 1 May

Bot. of J. W. Dever

4½ Yds	Grey cloth dble width	$ 4½	19.12	
1	Blk Felt Hat		4.25	
1	" " " with cords & Tassels Gold		8.75	
14	Large Brass Buttons	25¢	3.50	
12	Small " "	15¢	1.80	
1 doz	Linen HKchfs		5.00	
			42.42	
	Commission 2½%		1.06	
				$ 43.48
	Havana May 28/64			
	6.60 (duty)			
mark for Dr F B Darcy				
Demopoli ??? & Co				
Mobile				

413
Invoice

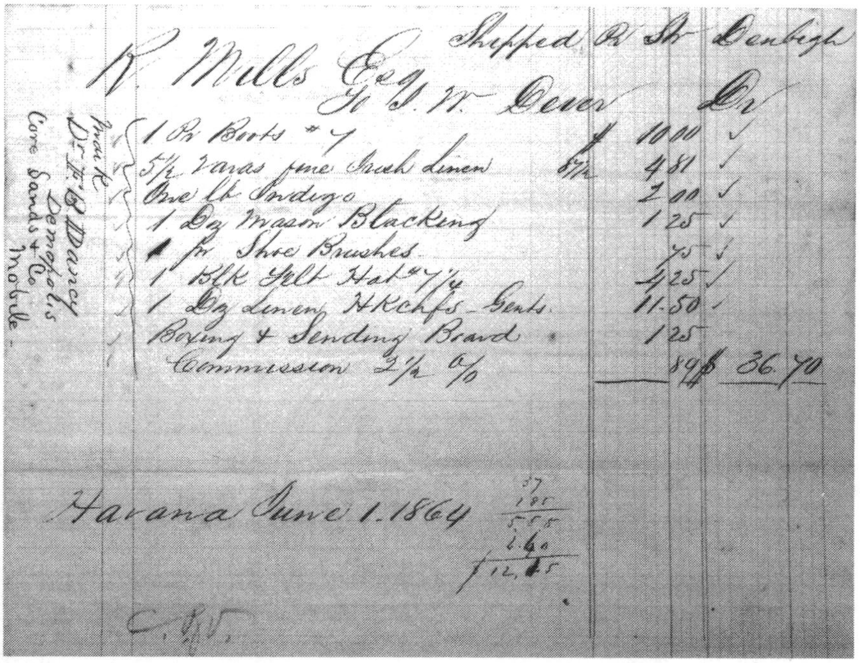

R Mills Esq — Shipped pr Str Denbigh
To J. W. Dever Dr

1 Pr Boots #7 — 10 00
5½ varas fine Irish Linen 37½ — 4 81
One lb Indigo — 2 00
1 Doz Mason Blacking — 1 25
1 pr Shoe Brushes — 75
1 Blk Felt Hat #7¼ — 4 25
1 Doz Linen HKchfs Gents — 11 50
Boxing & Sending Board — 1 25
Commission 2½ % — 89 $ 36.70

Havana June 1. 1864

mark Dr F B Darcy Demopolis Core Sands & Co Mobile

Figure 102. Invoice for goods bought in Havana by R. Mills.

R. Mills Esq Shipped pr Str *Denbigh*

To J. W. Dever Dr

1 Pr	Boots #7		$ 10.00	
5½ Varas	Fine Irish Linen	37½	4.81	
One lb	Indigo		2.00	
1 Doz	Mason Blacking		1.25	
1 pr	Shoe Brushes		.75	
1	Blk Felt Hat #7¼		4.25	
1 Doz	Linen HKchfs Gents		11.50	
	Boxing & Sending (on) Board		1.25	
	Commission 2½%		.89	$ 36.70
	Havana June 1, 1864			
	(Duty) $ 12.15			
mark for Dr F B Darcy				
Demopolis Core Sands & Co				
Mobile				

414-416
Preprinted Customs Form

No. 5
Entry of Merchandise
Importer J. B. Gladney
Vessel *Denbigh*
From Havana
Entered July 5th 1864
Value $ 56 Duty $ 9.05

Agent's Oath
(signed) Charles Walsh
J. B. Gladney, owner
Sworn before me, this 5th day of June 1864

Mdse. Entered _______18___ Ship Entered May 18 1864
Entry of Merchandise imported into the Port of Mobile, District of Mobile, by J. B. Gladney in the Br. Str. *Denbigh* Godfrey Master, from Havana

Marks	No. of Packages	Contents	Value in Foreign Currency	15%	20%	25%	Duties
	Pkge	Containing					
		Flannel clothing	$ 35.50	37			$ 5.55
		Soap	2.00		2		.40
		Mustard	1.50	2			.30
		Sardines	1.80			2	.50
		Preserved fruit paste	1.50			2	.50
		Sugar	2.50		3		.60
		Silk mfs	7.50	8			1.20
			52.30	47	5	4	9.05
		Chgs & Com	4.15				
			$ 56.45				

417
Invoice

~~G. G. Steerer~~ (?) J. B. Gladney

2 prs	boots	$ 4 8	8.00
		from New Orleans	
18 "	Socks	25¢	4.50
7 yds	grey cloth & trimmings	$ 2	14.00
	$ 1 6 6.75 6.25		1.00
	Silk Hkfs, neck ties & Cottons		7.50
25 lbs	white Sugar	10¢	2.50
6 Boxes	Sardines	30¢	1.80
6 "	guava	25¢	1.50
3 bottles	Mustard	50¢	1.50
1 Doz	Soap	$ 2	2.00
25 lbs	Coffee		52.30
	Chgs & Com		4.15

			$ 56.45

418-420
Preprinted Customs Form

No. 5
Entry of Merchandise
Importer A. Perez
Vessel *Denbigh*
From Havana
Entered July 2 '64
Value $ 41 Duty $ 10.25

Owner's Oath
(signed) A. Perez
Sworn before me, this 2nd day of July 1864

Mdse. Entered ____18__ Ship Entered May 18 1864
Entry of Merchandise imported into the Port of Mobile, District of Mobile, by A. Perez in the Br. Str. *Denbigh* Godfrey Master, from Havana

Marks	No. of Packages	Contents	Value in Foreign Currency	10%	15%	25%	Duties
	500	Segars	$ 40.00				
		Chgs & Com	1.37	Segars	$ 41	25%	$ 1025
			$ 41.37				

421-422
Invoice and Affidavit

500 Segars	$ @ $ 40.00
Chgs & Com	1.37
	41.37

11.25 (duty)

(reverse side of above)
Affidavit Grandfathering Prohibited Goods

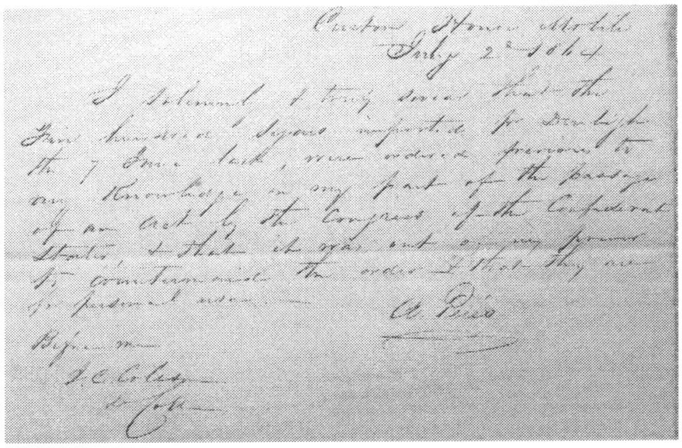

Figure 103. Affidavit to grandfather import of cigars, newly prohibited luxury goods.

Custom House Mobile
July 2d 1864

I Solemnly & truly Swear that the Five hundred Segars imported pr. *Denbigh* the 7 June last, were ordered previous to any Knowledge on my part of the passage of an Act by the Congress of the Confederate States, & that it was out of my power to countermand the order & that they are for personal use.

(signed) A. Perez

Before me
(signed) J. C. Colsson
D Coll

423-425
Preprinted Customs Form

No. 4
Entry of Merchandise
Importer Julian Myers
Vessel *Denbigh*
From Havana
Entered July 2d 1864
Value $ 217 Duty $ 71.05

Owner's Oath
(signed) Julian Myers
Sworn before me, this 2d day of July 1864

Mdse. Entered ____18__ Ship Entered May 18 1864

Entry of Merchandise imported into the Port of Mobile, District of Mobile, by Julian Myers in the Br. Str. *Denbigh* Godfrey Master, from Havana

No. of Packages	Contents	Value in Foreign Currency	10%	15%	25%	Duties
4 Boxes	Comfits	$ 17.00			18	$ 4.50
1 "	Preserves assorted	27.50			29	7.25
8 "	Wine, (Claret) 8 doz	82.00			87	21.75
5 "	Brandy 5 doz	67.00			70	17.50
2 Bdls	Segars 2000	65.00			69	17.25
1 Pkgs	Cologne water	13.00		14		2.80
		271.50		14	273	$ 71.05
	Chges & Com $ 8.12					
	Com 2½ 7.00	15.12				
		$ 286.62				

426

Affidavit Grandfathering Prohibited Goods

Custom House Mobile Dist.
July 2d 1864

I Solemnly & truly Swear that the articles in the within invoice, imported pr Str *Denbigh* from Havana had been ordered by me previous to the passage of the Act of Congress prohibiting the importation of certain articles of luxury & it was out of my power to countermand the order, owing to risks of communication & time, and that they are for personal use exclusively.

Before me

Note: Written on the reverse side of invoice, filed with customs form but not signed.

428

Invoice

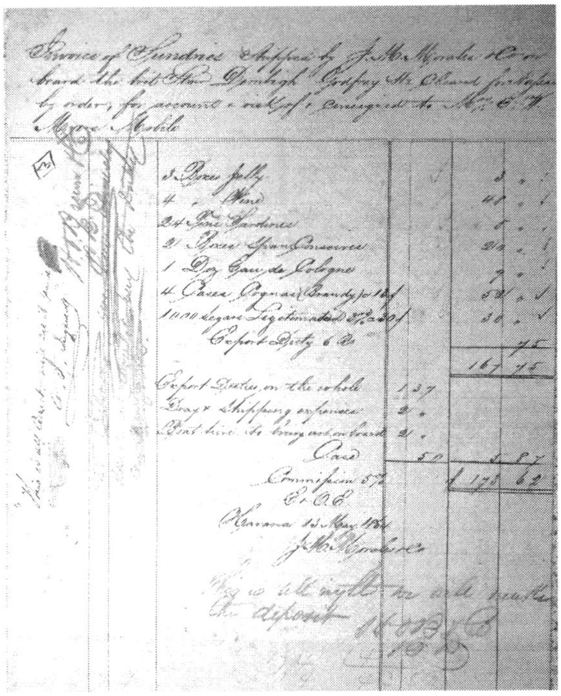

Figure 104. Invoice of goods for Mrs. E. W. Myers.

Invoice of Sundries Shipped by J. M. Morales & Co on board the brit Stmr *Denbigh* Godfrey Mr. Cleared for **Nassau** by order, for account & risk of a consigned to Mrs. E. W. Myers Mobile

M	3 Boxes	Jelly		3.00
	4 "	Wine		48.00
	24 Tins	Sardines		5.00
	2 Boxes	Span. Conserves		20.00
	1 Doz	Eau de Cologne		9.00
	4 Cases	Cognac (Brandy) @ 13?		52.00
	1000	Legitimada 3rd @ 30?		30.00
		Export Duty 6 Rs		.75
				167.75
		Export Duties on the whole	1.37	
		Dray. & Shipping expenses	2.00	
		Boat hire to bring art. On board	2.00	
		Case	.50	5.87
		Commission 5%		$ 173.62
		Havana 13 May 1864		
		J. M. Morales & Co		
		this is all right we will make the deposit		
		H O B & Co		
		B D		
		(from margin) This is all correct. Will see it paid		
		A. J. ??? H O Brewer & Co		
		B D		

427
Invoice

Invoice of 8 Packages Shipped on board the Brit Str *Denbigh* by Joseph Padin & Consigned Mrs Julian Myers.

Added				
Mrs	1 Box	Sweet Meats		10.00
J Myers	12 Boxes	Jelly 2 lbs each		4.00
	12 Bottles	Cognac		15.00
	2 Boxes	Sherry		24.00
	2 "	Claret		10.00
	5 Galls	Whiskey not received		~~16.00~~
	4 Bottles	Bay Rum		4.00
	1000	Segars		35.00
	24 Tins	Sardines ¼ boxes		2.50
				104.50
		Charges		
		Pd Portage & Boat hire	1.50	
		Freight to Mobile pr *Denbigh*	~~64.50~~	~~66.00~~
				~~$ 186.50~~
		E&OE		
		and to be deposited in coin		$ 133.25
		Jose Padin		
		We will deposit the duty &c on this		
		H O Brewer & Co		
		Benj Donaldson		

432
Affidavit

(Same oath as above, regarding ordering prior to new law, written on back of invoice.)

433-435
Preprinted Customs Form

Note: This customs form showed Capt. Godfrey's work bringing in small orders of individuals.

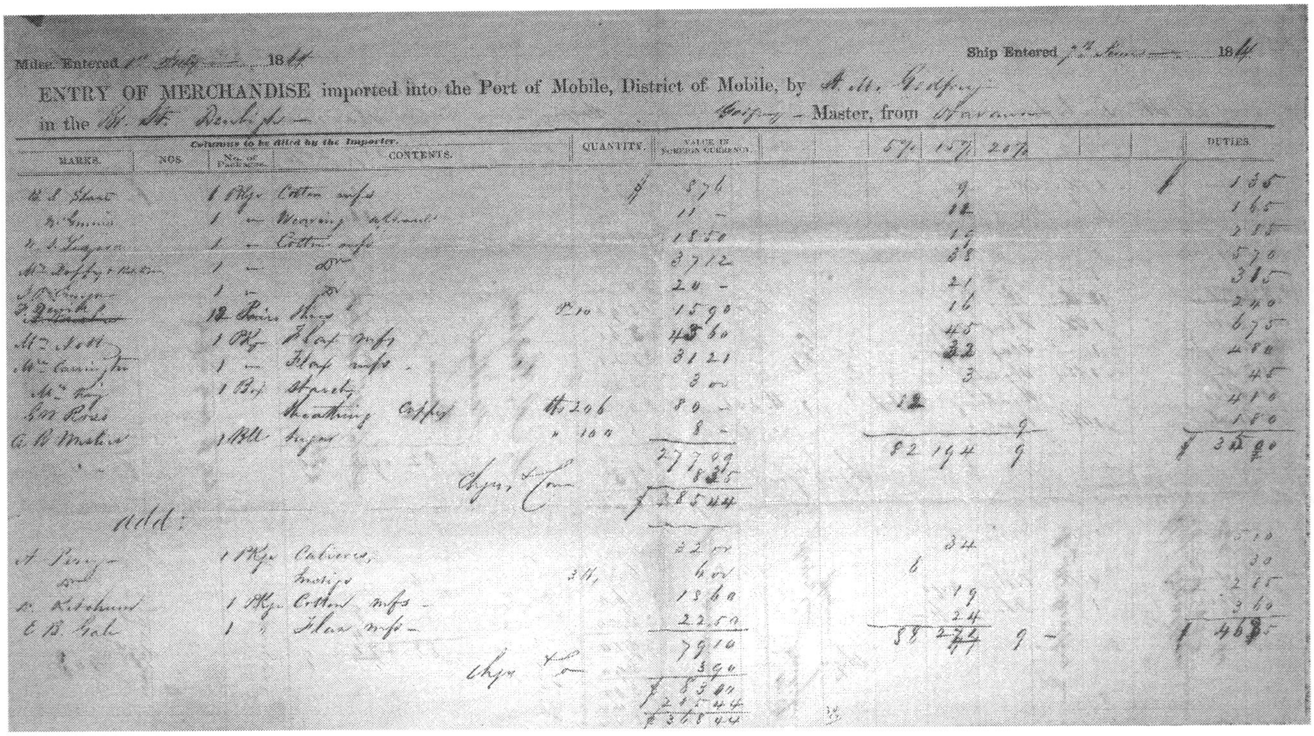

Mdse. Entered 1st July 1864 Ship Entered 7th June 1864

ENTRY OF MERCHANDISE imported into the Port of Mobile, District of Mobile, by A. M. Godfrey
in the Br. St. Denbigh — Godfrey — Master, from Havana

MARKS.	NOS.	No. of Packages.	CONTENTS.	QUANTITY.	VALUE IN FOREIGN CURRENCY.	5%	15%	20%	DUTIES.
W. S. Stark		1 Pkge	Cotton mfs		576		9		135
B. Greene		1 —	Wearing apparel		11 —		12		165
W. S. [illegible]		1 —	Cotton mfs		1850		15		225
Mc Duffy & [illegible]		1 —	Do		3712		38		570
[illegible]		1 —	Do		20 —		21		315
[illegible]		12 Pairs	Shoes	£10	1590		16		240
Mc Nott		1 Pkg	Flax mfs		4560		45		675
Wm Carrington		1 —	Flax mfs		3121		32		480
Mc [illegible]		1 Box	Sundries		300		3		45
G. M. Ross			Sheathing Copper	lbs 206	80 —	12			410
A. W. Mather		1 Bbl	Sugar	" 100	8 —			9	180
					27709	82	194	9	$ 3520
			Chgs & Com		835				
					$ 28544				
add:									
A. Perry		1 Pkge	Calicoes,		2200		34		510
do			Sundries	3 lb	600	6			30
W. Ketchum		1 Pkge	Cotton mfs —		1360		19		285
E. B. Gale		1	Flax mfs —		2250		24		360
					7910	58	277	9 —	$ 4685
			Chgs & Com		390				
					$ 8300				
					28544				
					$ 36844				

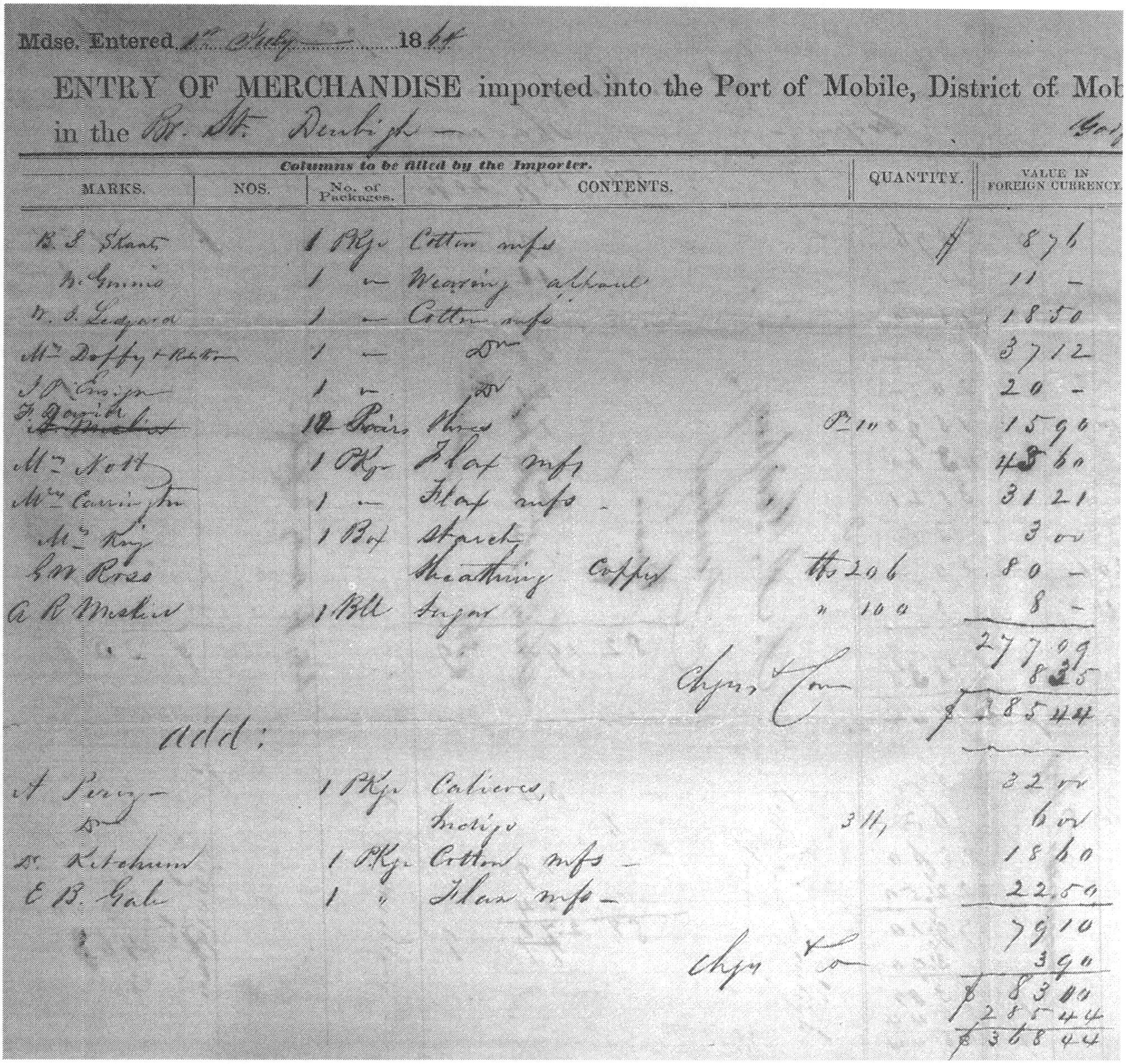

Mdse. Entered 1st July 1864

ENTRY OF MERCHANDISE imported into the Port of Mobile, District of Mob

in the Br. St. Denbigh —

Columns to be filled by the Importer.

MARKS.	NOS.	No. of Packages.	CONTENTS.	QUANTITY.	VALUE IN FOREIGN CURRENCY.
B. S. Stant		1 Pkg	Cotton mfs	$	8 76
McGinnis		1 —	Wearing apparel		11 —
W. S. Ledyard		1 —	Cotton mfs		18 50
Mr Duffy & Ralston		1 —	Do		37 12
J. R. Ensign		1 —	Do		20 —
F. Daniels		10 Pairs	Shoes	Pr 10	15 90
Mr Nott		1 Pkg	Flax mfs		43 60
Mrs Carrington		1 —	Flax mfs —		31 21
Mr King		1 Box	Starch		3 00
G. M. Rose			Sheathing Copper	lbs 206	80 —
A. R. Maskin		1 Bbl	Sugar	" 100	8 —
					277 99
			Chgs & Com		8 35
					$ 285 44
add:					
A. Perry		1 Pkg	Calicoes,		32 00
Do			Indigo	3 lb	6 00
Dr. Ketchum		1 Pkg	Cotton mfs —		18 60
E. B. Gale		1 "	Flax mfs —		22 50
					79 10
			Chgs & Com		3 90
					$ 83 00
					285 44
					$ 368 44

Figure 105. Customs form illustrating Capt. Godfrey bringing in small orders for a number of people.

No. 2
Entry of Merchandise
Importer A. M. Godfrey
Vessel *Denbigh*
From Havana
Entered July 1st 1864
Value $ 368 Duty $ 46.85

Agent's Oath
(signed) Benj Donaldson
Sworn before me, this 1st day of July 1864

Mdse. Entered 1st July 1864 Ship Entered 7th June 1864
Entry of Merchandise imported into the Port of Mobile, District of Mobile, by A. M. Godfrey in the Br. Str. *Denbigh* Godfrey Master, from Havana

Marks	No. of Packages	Contents	Value in Foreign Currency	10%	15%	20%	Duties
B. S. Skants	1 Pkge	Cotton mfs	$ 8.76		9		$ 1.35
N. Ginnis	1 "	Wearing apparel	11.00		12		1.65
N. J. Leyard	1 "	Cotton mfs	18.50		19		2.85
Mrs Duffy & Relations	1 "	Do	37.12		38		5.70
J P Ensign	1 "	Do	20.00		21		3.15
F. David ~~A. Mislen~~	10 Pairs	Shoes pr 10	15.90		16		2.40
Mrs Nott	1 Pkge	Flax mfs	43.60		45		6.75
Mrs Carrington	1 "	Flax mfs	31.21		32		4.80
Mrs King	1 Box	Starch	3.00		3		.45
G N Ross		**Sheathing Copper lbs 206**	80.00	82			4.10
A R Mislen	1 Bll	Sugar " 100	8.00			9	1.80
			277.09	82	194	9	$ 35.00
		Chges & Com	8.35				
			$ 285.44				
Add							
A. Perez	1 Pkge	Calicoes	32.00		34		5.10
Do		Indigo 3 lbs	6.00	6			.30
Dr. Ketch	1 Pkge	Cotton mfs	18.60		19		2.85
E B Gale	1 "	Flax mfs	22.50		24		3.60
			79.10	88	271	9	$ 46.85
		Chges & Com	3.90				
			$ 83.00				
			285.44				
			$ 368.44				

437
Invoice

Capt A. M. Godfrey
To J. Dever Dr
A. Mesler

199 lbs	White Sugar	8¢	8.00	
25 "	Coffee	21	5.25	
	Cartage & Launch	40	.40	
	Commission 2½%	34	.34	$ 13.99
	Habana June 1st 1864			
	J. M. Dever			
	1.60 (duty)			

438
Invoice

Capt A. M. Godfrey
To J. Dever Dr
Wm Carrington

1 piece	Bleached Cotton		7.50	
1 Bolt	Calico 30 Varas	25	7.50	
12 Yds	Linen	45	5.40	
1 Doz	Spool Cotton		1.75	
1 Piece	Toweling		10.25	
	Commission 2½%		.81	$ 33.21
	Havana June 1st 1864			
	J. W. Dever			
	4.95 (duty)			

439
Invoice
Havana May 31 /64
H D McGinnis
To E W McGinnes

40 Yds	muslin 5	20¢	8.00
1 Doz	Ladies Hose		4.00
			$ 12.00
	Paid 1.80 (duty)		

441
Invoice

W. J Leyard

1	Dress Pattern	18.75
1	Cotton Goods	.50
		19.25
	Str *Denbigh*	
	2.85 (duty)	

442
Invoice

Capt. A. M. Godfrey

To J. W. Dever Dr.

B. S. Skaats

1 Doz	Cotton Hose #9		5.00	
3 "	Embroidery Cotton #7.8.9	.75	2.25	
2 Yds	Linen Cambric	.65	1.30	
	Commission 2½%		.21	8.76
				11.00
				2.26
	Habana June 1st 1864			
	J. W. Dever			
	1.35 (duty) Paid			

443
Invoice

Capt. A. M. Godfrey

To J. W. Dever Dr.

Mrs Nott

2 Doz	Towels	6.00	12.00	
22 Varas	unbleached Cotton	.30	6.60	
1 Doz	Skeins Blck Cotton		1.25	
2 "	White Cotton	1.75	3.50	
1 "	Gents Hkchfs	5.00	5.00	
1 "	Ladies Hose #9		6.50	
2 lbs	Chloroform	2.50	5.00	
1	Hair Brush		~~1.50~~	not recd
1 Box	Castile Soap		.75	
1	Felt Hat #7		5.00	
1 Bbl	Ale		~~20.00~~	not sent
	Cartage & Launch		.75	
	Commission 2½%		1.19	65.44
	Havana June 1st 1864		???	20.00
				45.00
	6.45 (duty)			

444-445
Invoice and letter

Note: This page was the last of a personal letter from P. Duffy, probably in Havana, to his wife in Mobile. The invoice and a post script, partly on the reverse side, were shown here complete with idiosyncratic spelling. The rest of letter was not preserved in the customs file, and this part was present because of the requirement to include an invoice showing costs of goods shipped.

their best respects no more
from yours Aff Husband
P. Duffy

For Mrs Roberson

One piece Linen	$	10.50
One piece Cotton	"	7.00
One piece cross bar Muslin	"	5.62
One Corset . - - - -	"	3.00
One piece Moscito bar Stof	"	5.50
One dozin of Stoking -	"	4.00
Half dozin stoks - -	"	1.50
		$ 37.12

For Mrs Doffy

2½ Yds linen inserting	$	1.50
2 Embroider linen	"	.50
1 Doz shirt bottons	"	.75
1 Pair Galeters	"	2.50
1 Corset -	"	2 50
		$ 7.75

The Corsets of this place I
dont think they soot you
because they made short as
the fashion of the country —

Next time you want such
article as those that I have
sent to you I hope you will
send Johny Pennell or
somebody else that under
stand it better than I
do. — P. Doffy. —

Figure 106. Invoice and note from P. Duffy to his wife regarding corsets.

	For Mrs Roberson	
One piece	Linen	$ 10.50
One piece	Cotton	7.00
One piece	cross bar Muslin	5.62
One	Corset	3.00
One piece	Mosquito bar Staf	5.50
One dozen	of Stoking	4.00
Half dozen	sto'ks	1.50
		$ 37.12
	For Mrs Duffy	
2½ Yds	linen inserting	$ 1.50
2	Embroider linen	.50
1 Doz	Shirt buttons	.75
1 Pair	Gaiters	2.50
1	Corset	2.50
		$ 7.75

… their best respects. No more from yours, Aff(ectionate) Husband, P. Duffy

(PS) The Corsets of this place I don't think they soot you because they made short as the fashion of the country. Next time you want such articles as those that I have sent to you, I hope you will send Johny Pennell or somebody else that understand it better than I do. P. Duffy

---

446
Invoice

Dr. Ketkum (Ketchum?)
Dry goods cottons, hosiery 18.00
.60
18.60

$2.85 (duty)

447
Invoice

Note that documentation of invoice cost was often quite informal and scrawled on the merest scrap of paper.

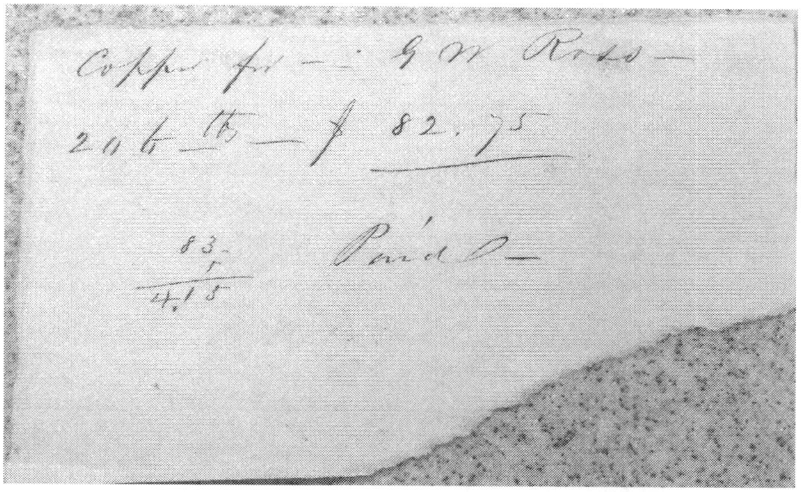
Copper for – G W Ross –
206 lbs – $ 82.75
83
5
4.15
Paid –

Figure 107. Informal invoice for copper.

Copper for	G W Ross
206 lbs	$ 82.75
4.15 (duty)	Paid

450
Invoice

Havana Apl 8 1864

E B Gayle

Bot of J. W. Dever

1 doz	White Cotton Hose	5.50
1 "	do Children	4.50
15 yds	Linen @ 50¢	7.50
1 doz	fine Hose Ladies	5.50
	Coms 2½%	.50
		$ 23.50
	Recd by J. W. Dever	
	$ 3.00 Paid	
	Correct Zantzinger	

451
Invoice

F K David
12 Prs Shoes $ 16.90

453
Invoice

G. P. E.
Linen & Cotton $ 20.00
1.00
$ 21.00
3.05 (duty)
J. P. Ensign Williamson

454-460
Preprinted Customs Form

Note: This shipment arrived in Mobile on the *Denbigh*'s April trip. The correspondence and arrangements for clearing customs involved notifying the owner in Macon, Georgia and took until early July. The records showed that most shipments cleared much more promptly, probably by local Mobile purchasers or agents.

No. 7
Importer Isaac Scott
Vessel *Denbigh*
From Havana
Entered July 2d 1864
Value $ 76 Duty $ 12.20

Oath of Consignee, Importer or Agent
Isaac Scott of Macon Ga owner
(signed) Chs Fonda
Sworn to, this 2d day of May 1864
Before me J. C. Colsson
Depty. Collector

Entry of Merchandise Ship Entered April 14 '64
Imported into the Port and District of Mobile, by Isaac Scott in the Br. Str. *Denbigh* Godfrey Mater, from Havana

Packages	Packages and Contents	In Foreign Currency Invoice Value	Appraised Value, Duty Rate			
			10	15	20	Duty
One	Shoes 6 prs	19.00		20		$ 3.00
trunk	Calicoes	38.00		40		6.00
	Tooth brushes	6.60				1.40
	Cologne Water	4.00			7	1.80
	~~Comfits~~ Do	4.00			9	~~1.00~~
		71.60		60	16	$ 12.20
	Trunk &c	4.30				
		$ 75.90				

461-463
Preprinted Customs Form

No. 17
Entry of Merchandise
Importer J. G Stewart
Vessel *Mary*
From Havana
Entered July 20 64
Value $ 16 Duty $ 3.85

Owner's Oath
(signed) James G. Stewart
Sworn before me, this 29th day of July 1864

Mdse. Entered ______18___ Ship Entered May 18 18___
Entry of Merchandise imported into the Port of Mobile, District of Mobile, by J. G. Stewart in the Br. Str. *Mary* Peat Master, from Havana

No. of Packages	Contents	Value in Foreign Currency	10%	15%	25%	Duties
1 Case	Comfits, Whiskey, Brandy	$ 9.25			10	$ 2.50
1 Case	Gin, ~~Whiskey, Br~~	4.75			5	1.25
	Cheese	1.00	1			.10
	Chgs & Com	1.00	1		15	$ 3.85
		16.00				

464-465
Invoice and Affidavit regarding importation of banned items, specifically alcohol.

Mr. Jas (James) G. Stewart ??
Pr J. W. Dever

1 doz	Jelly	3.00
2 bottles	**brandy**	2.75
1	English cheese	1.00
1 Case	**Gin**	4.75
6 bottles	**whiskey**	3.50
	chges	1.00
	with chgs & Com	$ 16.00
	Havana May 28th 1864	
	Paid	
	J. W. Dever by J. B	

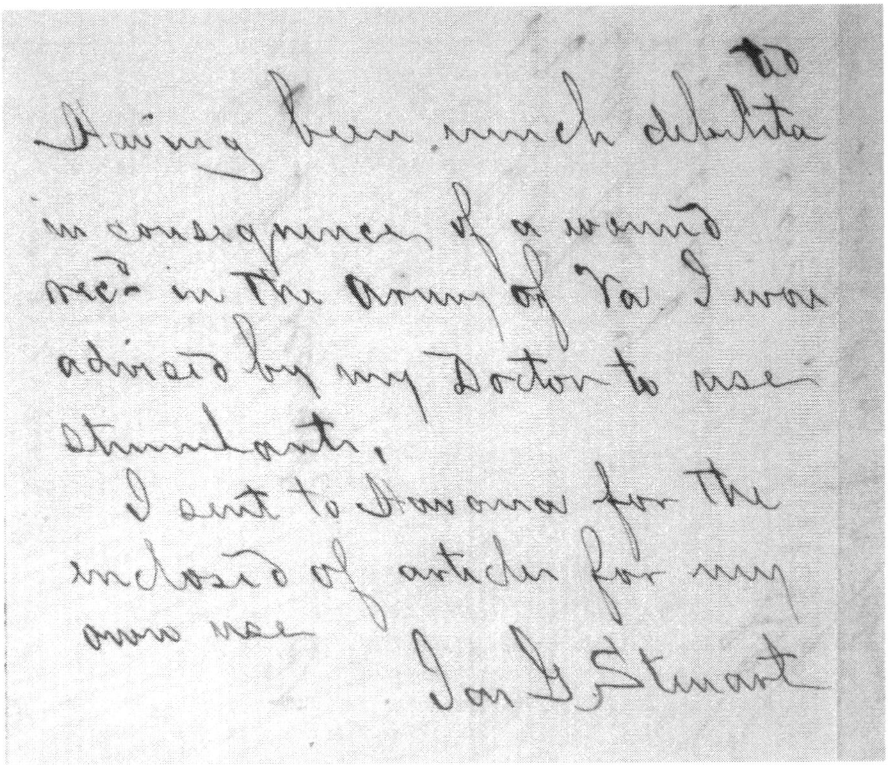
Having been much debilitated
in consequence of a wound
recd in the Army of Va. I was
advised by my Doctor to use
stimulants,
I sent to Havana for the
enclosed of articles for my
own use
Jas G Stewart

Figure 108. Affidavit regarding stimulants imported under doctor's orders.

(reverse side of invoice)

Having been much debilitated in consequence of a wound recd in the Army of Va. I was advised by my Doctor to use stimulants.

I sent to Havana for the enclosed of articles for my own use.

Jas G Stewart

8

Denbigh Customs Manifests, August 1864, Transcripts

Denbigh Voyage No. 6, Havana-Mobile-Havana
Havana, last date document prepared there, 4 June 1864 so the ship sailed soon thereafter.
Mobile, date ship entered (port and reported arrival to C.S. Customs) was 7 June 1864.
Mobile departure, cotton export manifests dated 14 June 1864 so ship sailed soon thereafter. (421 bales cotton, 218,890 lbs., $124,764, 57¢ per lb.)

Denbigh Voyage No. 7, Havana-Mobile-Havana
No records for the Havana-Mobile leg of the seventh voyage were preserved in the NARA files. Other records told of the *Denbigh's* last departure from Mobile. She was the last runner out, early in August 1864 when Admiral Farragut captured Fort Morgan at the bay's mouth. The *Denbigh's* subsequent runs were Havana-Galveston-Havana. The detailed customs records, like those shown herein, for those runs have not turned up.

1003-1007
Preprinted Customs Form

No. 1
Entry of Merchandise
Importer R. S. Bunker
Vessel *Denbigh*
From Havana
Entered Aug 3 64
Value $ 31 Duty $ 5.00

Owner's Oath
(signed) Robert S. Banks

Mdse. Entered ______18___ Ship Entered May 18 1864
Entry of Merchandise imported into the Port of Mobile, District of Mobile, by R. S. Bunker in the Br. Str. *Denbigh* Godfrey Master, from Havana

Marks	No. of Packages	Contents	Value in Foreign Currency	10%	15%	25%	Duties
		Tea	$ 3.00	3			$ .30
		Oil &c, Soda, &c	21.65		23		3.45
		Spirits	5.00			5	1.25
			29.65	3	23	5	$ 5.00
		Chges & Co	1.50				
			$ 31.15				

1008
Invoice

Per *Denbigh*
Invoice of Merchandise imported from Havana per *Denbigh* from Havana – Mobile 18 May 1864

3 lbs	Green & Black Tea	3.00
5 lbs	Starch	.50
	Cream Tartar, Soda, Sugar Maple &c	3.65
	Sundry Articles as per mem(o)	12.00
1 doz	Sweet oil $ 5. Drayage .50	5.35
	Duties & Ship Charges	$ 30.00
	Robert S. Bunker	

1009-1011
Preprinted Customs Form

No. 2
Entry of Merchandise
Importer Bn. Tardy
Vessel *Denbigh*
From Havana
Entered Aug 3 64
Value $ 94 Duty $ 20.35

Owner's Oath
(signed) Bn Tardy
Sworn before me, this 3 day of August 1864

Mdse. Entered ______18___ Ship Entered May 18 1864
Entry of Merchandise imported into the Port of Mobile, District of Mobile, by B. Tardy in the Br. Str. *Denbigh* Godfrey Master, from Havana

No. of Packages	Contents	Value in Foreign Currency	10%	15%	20%	25%	Duties
1 Pkge	Tea 5 lbs	$ 7.50	8				.80
1 "	Honey & 1 Chocolate	7.00		8			1.20
1 Box	Sugar & 1 Pickles	21.45			23		4.60
1 Pkge	Cigars (paper)	5.00				5	1.25
2 Boxes	Claret					50	12.50
1 Cask	Do 62 Gals	49.00	8	8	23	55	$ 20.35
		89.95					
	Chgs & Co	4.00					
		$ 93.95					

1012
Invoice

B. Tardy

1 Cask	Claret		$ 40.00	
1 Demijo	honey		3.25	
1 Pkge	Pork		23.00	free
1 "	Gelatin		4.75	Deduct Com
1???	Chocolate		3.75	
1 Bdle	Pr (?) Sugar	21?cP (?)	17.20	
12 lbs	Tea	1.25	7.00	only part
1 "	Coffee	14?c22 (?)	21.46	free
1 Box	Pickles		3.25	
???	Butter	32oz (?)		all ???
				???
1 Bl	???		18.40	
2 bts	Claret	4½	9.00	
5 pck	Cigarettes		5.00	
(Denbigh)				

Note: Written hastily in pencil. Much of this invoice was illegible.

1014
Invoice

Claret	2 Boxes		$ 9.00	
Do	1 Cask		40.00	
Cigarettes			5.00	
Sugar	1 Box	215 lbs	17.20	
Pickles			4.25	
Chocolate			3.25	
Honey			3.75	
	1 Bll	Potatoes	18.40	free
Tea		$ 6	7.50	
			$ 89.95	
		Chgs	4.00	
			$ 93.95	

1016
Preprinted Customs Form

No. 3
Entry of Merchandise
Importer J. C. Nott
Vessel *Denbigh*
From Havana
Entered August 3 1864
Value $ 39 Duty $ 6.70
~~$ 43~~ ~~$ 7.30~~

Owner's Oath
(signed) J. C. Nott
Sworn before me, this 3d day of August 1864
J. C. Coleson Depy Collector

Mdse. Entered ______18___ Ship Entered May 18 1864
Entry of Merchandise imported into the Port of Mobile, District of Mobile, by J. C. Nott in the Br. Str. *Denbigh* Godfrey Master, from Havana

No. of Packages	Contents	Value in Foreign Currency	15%	20%	25%	Duties
	Medical preparations	$ 5.00	5			.75
	Merino, &c	22.00	23			3.45
	Brooms & Brushes	4.25		5		1.00
	Brandy	6.00			6	1.50
		37.25	28	5	6	6.70
	Chges & Com	2.08				
		$ 39.33				

1019
Invoice

Capt. A. M. Godfrey to J. W. Dever Dr.
Mr. Nott

2 Large	Scrubbing brushes	@ 60¢	1.20	
2 Small	do do	.30	.60	
1	White washing do		.75	
1	Hair broom		1.40	
2 Lbs	**Chloroform**	@ 1.75	3.50	not recd
2 oz	finest Quinine	@ 2.75	5.50	
1 Box	French brandy		6.00	
1 Varas	merino for Coat	" 2.75	16.50	
3 do	Serge	" 2.00	6.00	
	~~Silk & Lining 18 buttons~~		1.00	
	Cartage, boxing & Launch		1.00	
	Commission 2½%		1.08	$ 44.73
	E. E.			
	Havana May 13th 1864			

9

Denbigh Customs Manifests, Oct.–Dec. 1864, Transcripts

Denbigh Voyage No. 6, Havana-Mobile-Havana
Havana, last date document prepared there, 4 June 1864 so the ship sailed soon thereafter.
Mobile, date ship entered (port and reported arrival to C.S. Customs) was 7 June 1864.
Mobile departure, cotton export manifests dated 14 June 1864 so ship sailed soon thereafter. (421 bales cotton, 218,890 lbs., $124,764, 57¢ per lb.) No *Denbigh* manifests in Sept.

1023
Preprinted Customs Form

No. 3
Entry of Merchandise
Importer R. Bartow[101]
Vessel *Denbigh*
From Havana
Entered Oct 25 1864
Value $ 34 Duty $ 5.10

Agent's Oath
(signed) J. Cavanagh
Sworn before me, this 25 day of Oct 1864

Mdse. Entered ______18___ Ship Entered May 18 1864
Entry of Merchandise imported into the Port of Mobile, District of Mobile, by **R. Bartow** in the Br. Str. *Denbigh* Godfrey Master, from Havana

No. of Packages	Contents	Value in Foreign Currency	10%	15%	25%	Duties
1 Box	Ready made Clothing,					
	Boots &c					
	with chges & Com	$ 34.40	$ 34	Duty 15%		$ 5.10

[101] Relation not established, but the Bartows were a prominent planter family in Georgia that included Gen. Francis Bartow killed at the First Battle of Manassas and a delegate to the Confederate constitutional convention.

Part II

Prewar and Early War Examples for Comparison

10

Prewar Mobile Customs Manifests, Nov. 1860

Note: The prewar customs records for imports to Mobile provided a stark contrast to those of Dec. through Aug. 1864 when the *Denbigh* ran the blockade there. The large orders of merchants predominated in the prewar period and the private orders of the *Denbigh* records were distinctly different. Assuming the *Denbigh* also carried inbound military supplies for the government, documentation for such did not appear in the customs house records.

Also here we presented the documents and forms that comprised sets of ship's papers so often referred to in historic descriptions of voyages. The ship's papers during the Civil War lacked consul's certificate and bills of lading that commonly appeared in the prewar period.

This section was a departure from the usual practice herein of transcribing the documents completely. Some were abbreviated and paraphrased being labeled "Summary."

1313-1315
Preprinted Customs Form

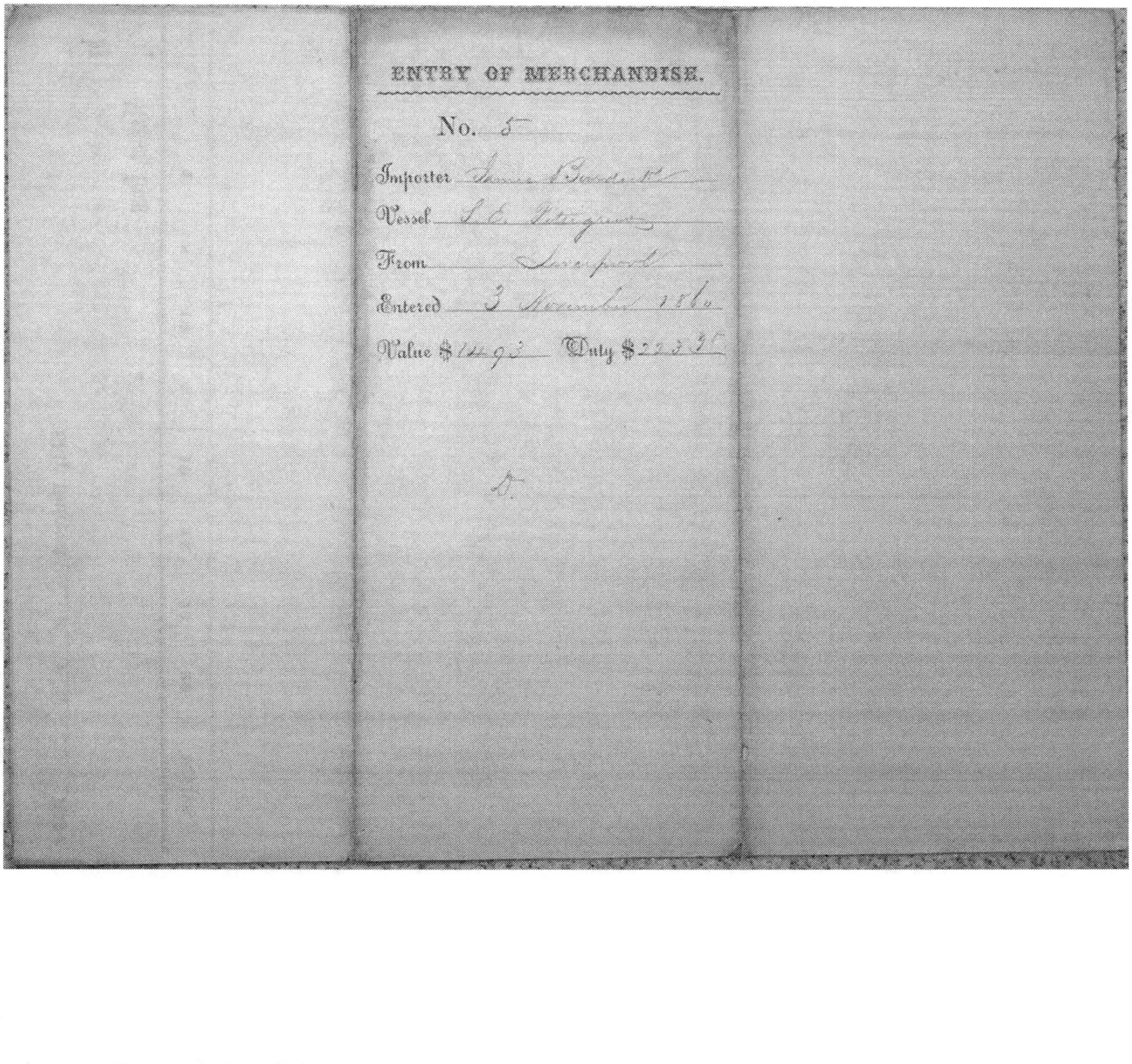

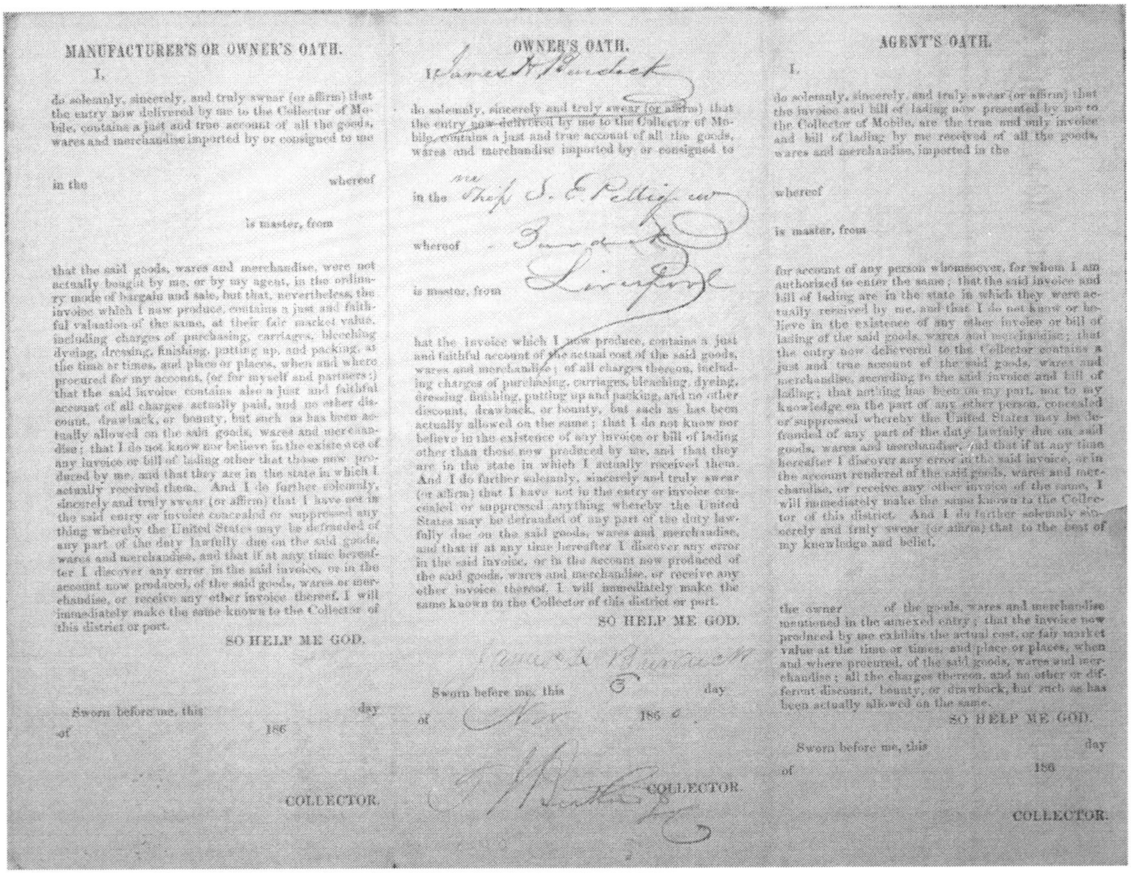

MANUFACTURER'S OR OWNER'S OATH.

I,

do solemnly, sincerely, and truly swear (or affirm) that the entry now delivered by me to the Collector of Mobile, contains a just and true account of all the goods, wares and merchandise imported by or consigned to me

in the whereof

is master, from

that the said goods, wares and merchandise, were not actually bought by me, or by my agent, in the ordinary mode of bargain and sale, but that, nevertheless, the invoice which I now produce, contains a just and faithful valuation of the same, at their fair market value, including charges of purchasing, carriages, bleaching, dyeing, dressing, finishing, putting up, and packing, at the time or times, and place or places, when and where procured for my account, (or for myself and partners;) that the said invoice contains also a just and faithful account of all charges actually paid, and no other discount, drawback, or bounty, but such as has been actually allowed on the said goods, wares and merchandise; that I do not know nor believe in the existence of any invoice or bill of lading other that those now produced by me, and that they are in the state in which I actually received them. And I do further solemnly, sincerely and truly swear (or affirm) that I have not in the said entry or invoice concealed or suppressed any thing whereby the United States may be defrauded of any part of the duty lawfully due on the said goods, wares and merchandise, and that if at any time hereafter I discover any error in the said invoice, or in the account now produced, of the said goods, wares or merchandise, or receive any other invoice thereof, I will immediately make the same known to the Collector of this district or port.

SO HELP ME GOD.

Sworn before me, this day

of 186

COLLECTOR.

OWNER'S OATH.

I,

do solemnly, sincerely and truly swear (or affirm) that the entry now delivered by me to the Collector of Mobile, contains a just and true account of all the goods, wares and merchandise imported by or consigned to

in the

whereof

is master, from

hat the invoice which I now produce, contains a just and faithful account of the actual cost of the said goods, wares and merchandise; of all charges thereon, including charges of purchasing, carriages, bleaching, dyeing, dressing, finishing, putting up and packing, and no other discount, drawback, or bounty, but such as has been actually allowed on the same; that I do not know nor believe in the existence of any invoice or bill of lading other than those now produced by me, and that they are in the state in which I actually received them. And I do further solemnly, sincerely and truly swear (or affirm) that I have not in the entry or invoice concealed or suppressed anything whereby the United States may be defrauded of any part of the duty lawfully due on the said goods, wares and merchandise, and that if at any time hereafter I discover any error in the said invoice, or in the account now produced of the said goods, wares and merchandise, or receive any other invoice thereof, I will immediately make the same known to the Collector of this district or port.

SO HELP ME GOD.

Sworn before me, this day

of 186

COLLECTOR.

AGENT'S OATH.

I,

do solemnly, sincerely, and truly swear (or affirm) that the invoice and bill of lading now presented by me to the Collector of Mobile, are the true and only invoice and bill of lading by me received of all the goods, wares and merchandise, imported in the

whereof

is master, from

for account of any person whomsoever, for whom I am authorized to enter the same; that the said invoice and bill of lading are in the state in which they were actually received by me, and that I do not know or believe in the existence of any other invoice or bill of lading of the said goods, wares and merchandise; that the entry now delivered to the Collector contains a just and true account of the said goods, wares and merchandise, according to the said invoice and bill of lading; that nothing has been on my part, nor to my knowledge on the part of any other person, concealed or suppressed whereby the United States may be defrauded of any part of the duty lawfully due on said goods, wares and merchandise, and that if at any time hereafter I discover any error in the said invoice, or in the account rendered of the said goods, wares and merchandise, or receive any other invoice of the same, I will immediately make the same known to the Collector of this district. And I do further solemnly sincerely and truly swear (or affirm) that to the best of my knowledge and belief,

the owner of the goods, wares and merchandise mentioned in the annexed entry; that the invoice now produced by me exhibits the actual cost, or fair market value at the time or times, and place or places, when and where procured, of the said goods, wares and merchandise; all the charges thereon, and no other or different discount, bounty, or drawback, but such as has been actually allowed on the same.

SO HELP ME GOD.

Sworn before me, this day

of 186

COLLECTOR.

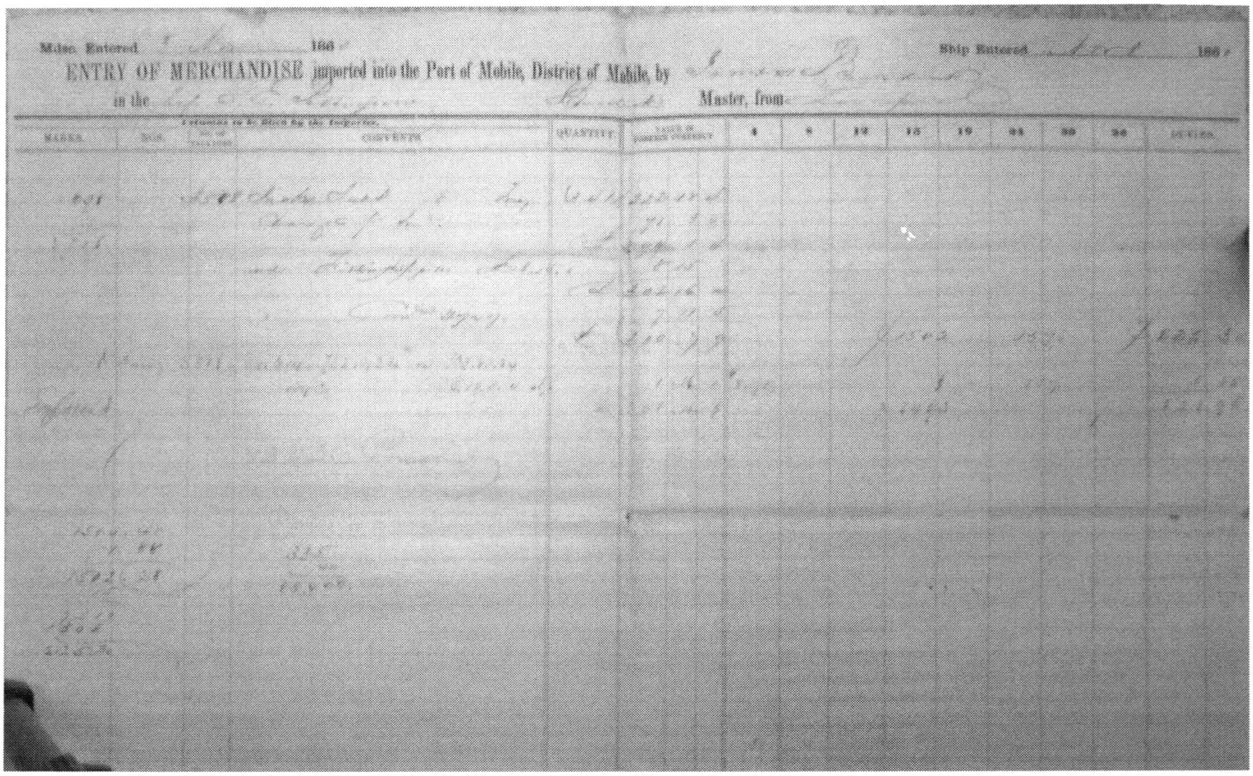

Mdse. Entered 186 Ship Entered 186

ENTRY OF MERCHANDISE imported into the Port of Mobile, District of Mobile, by

in the Master, from

Figure 109. Example of prewar customs form for a cargo of salt from Liverpool.

No. 5
Entry of Merchandise
Importer James Burdeck
Vessel *S. E. Pettigrew*
From Liverpool
Entered 3 November 1860
Value $ 1493 Duty $ 223.95

Owner's Oath
James H Burdeck
Sworn before me, this 3d day of Nov 1860
T. J. Burton Collector

Mdse. Entered 3 Nov 1860 Ship Entered Nov 1 1860
Entry of Merchandise imported into the Port of Mobile, District of Mobile, by James Burdick in the Ship *S. E. Pettigrew* Burdick Master, from Liverpool

Marks	No. of Packages	Contents	Value in Foreign Currency				Duties
001	3508 Sacks	Salt 6 Tons 341	£ 222 8 4				
		Charges for Ins.	71 3 0				
			£ 294 1 4				
		Forwarding £5/ p 100	8 15 0				
			£ 302 16 4				
		" Comn 2½%	7 11 5				
			£ 310 7 9		$1502	15%	$225.30
	Rtamy (?)3516	?? 414 752.4.21 ?? 335.0s.14					
		Dept. 5.19.3.4 aby	1. 16. 0	$8.71	8	15%	1.25
	England		£ 308. 11. 9		$ 1493		224.95
		13436 Burdick					

1316
Invoice

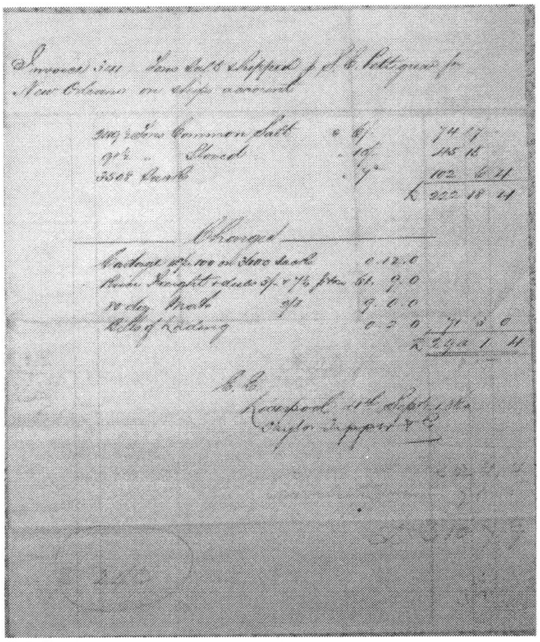

Figure 110. Invoice for cargo of salt.

Invoice 341 Tons Salt shipped p(er) *S. E. Pettigrew* for New Orleans on ships account

249½ Tons	Common Salt	@ 6/	74	17	0
91½ "		" 10/	45	15	0
3508 Sacks		" 7¢	102	6	4
			£ 222	18	4
	Charges				
Cartage 4¢	pr 100 on 3600 Sacks	0.12.0			
River Freight	& dues 3/. & 7¼ Stone	61.9.0			
80 doz	Mats 2/3	9.0.0			
Bills of Lading		0.2.0	71	3	0
			£ 294	1	4
	Filling		8	15	
	E.E.				
	Liverpool 4th Sept. 1860				
	Taylor Tipper & Co.				
			02	16	4
	Com 2½%		7	11	5
			£ 310	7	9
$ 240					

1317-1319
Preprinted Customs Form

No. 29
Importer Barnet Brs & Co

Vessel *Cumberland*
From Lpool
Entered 15 November 1860
Value $ 2149   Duty $ 515.76

Owner's Oath
L Scranton
Consigned to Barnes Bros & Co
Sworn before me, this 15 day of Nov 1860
T. J. Burton Collector

Mdse. Entered 15 Nov 1860   Ship Entered Nov 1860
Entry of Merchandise imported into the Port of Mobile, District of Mobile, by Barney Rots (?) & Co in the Ship *Cumberland* Merrill Master, from Liverpool

Marks	No. of Packages	Contents	Value in Foreign Currency		Duties
443					
442/444	3 Casks	Cutlery	£ 422 3 5		
		Cmms & dry	21 16 2		
			£ 443 19 7	$ 2149	$ 515.76
England		adal. Comn			

1320
Bill of Lading

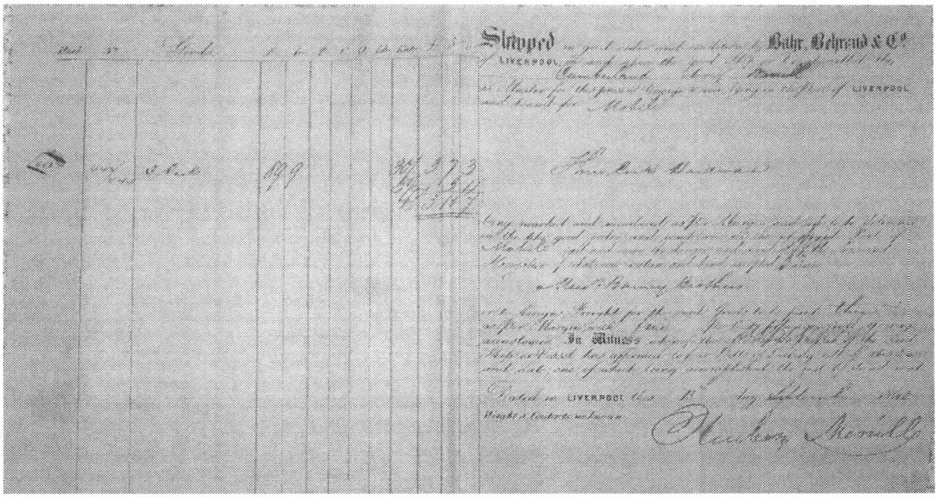

Figure 111. Bill of lading for cargo of hardware.

Mark	No.	Goods	F.	In.	T.	C.	Q.	Lbs	Rate	£	s	d
443	442/444	3 Casks	89	9					30/.	3	7	3
									50/S (?)		3	4
									£	3	10	7

Shipped in good order and condition by Bahr, Behrend & Co.[102] of Liverpool and upon the good Ship or Vessel called the *Cumberland* whereof Merrill is Master for this present Voyage, & now lying in the Port of Liverpool, and bound for Mobile.

Three Casks Hardware

Being marked and numbered as Per Margin, and are to be delivered in the like good order and condition at the afore said Port of Mobile (all and every the danger and accidents (overwritten "fire") in the Seas and Navigation of whatsoever nature and kind excepted ?? unto

Messrs Barney Brothers

Or to Assignees, Freight for the said Goods to be paid them as per Margin with five Per Cent primage and overage accustomed. In Witness whereof the Master (unintelligible overwriting) or person of the said ship or Vessel has affirmed to four Bills of Lading all of this tenor and date, one of which being accomplished, the rest to stand void.

Dated in Liverpool this 13th day September 1860
Weight & Contents unknown (signed) Henley Merrill

1321-1323
Invoice

[102] Still in business, freight forwarders based in Liverpool (www.bahrbehrend.co.uk).

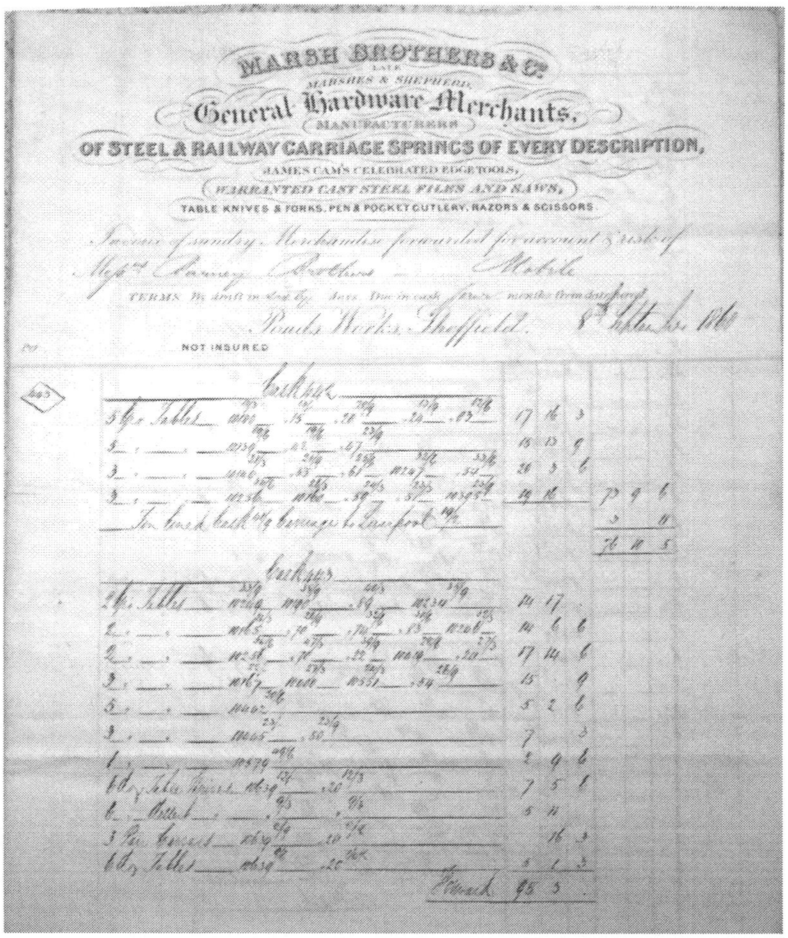
MARSH BROTHERS & Co.
LATE
MARSHES & SHEPHERD,
General Hardware Merchants,
MANUFACTURERS
OF STEEL & RAILWAY CARRIAGE SPRINGS OF EVERY DESCRIPTION,
JAMES CAM'S CELEBRATED EDGE TOOLS,
WARRANTED CAST STEEL FILES AND SAWS,
TABLE KNIVES & FORKS, PEN & POCKET CUTLERY, RAZORS & SCISSORS.
Invoice of sundry Merchandise forwarded for account & risk of
Mobile
TERMS
Sheffield.
NOT INSURED

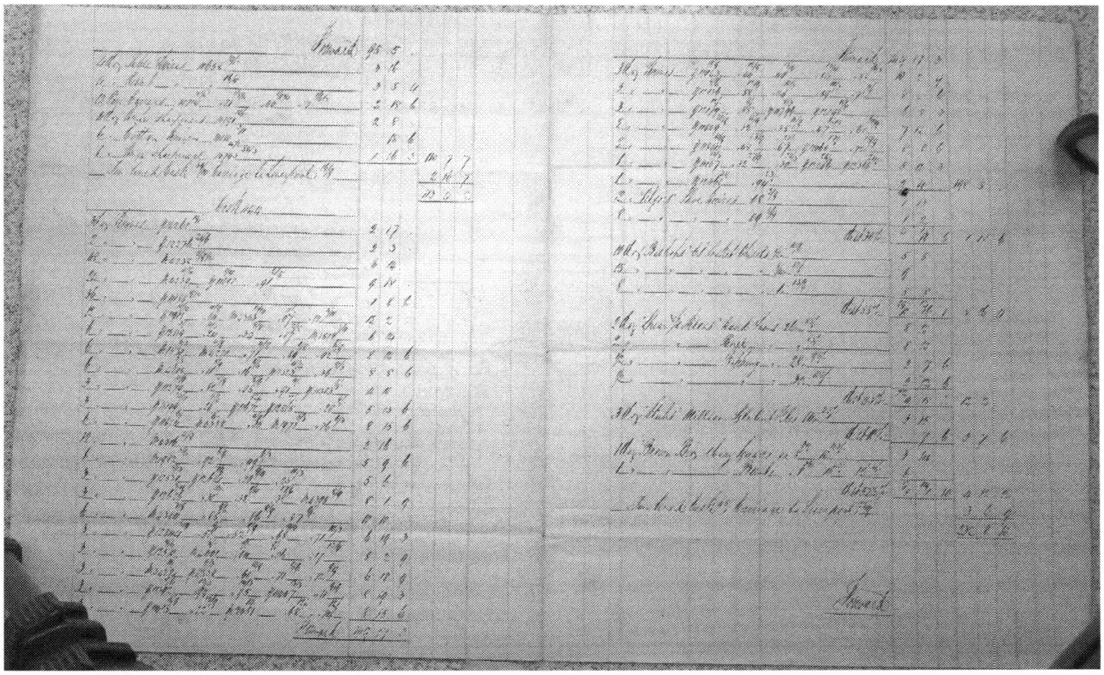

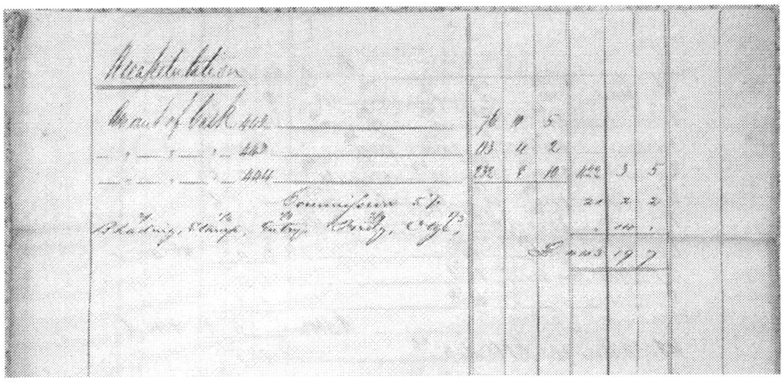

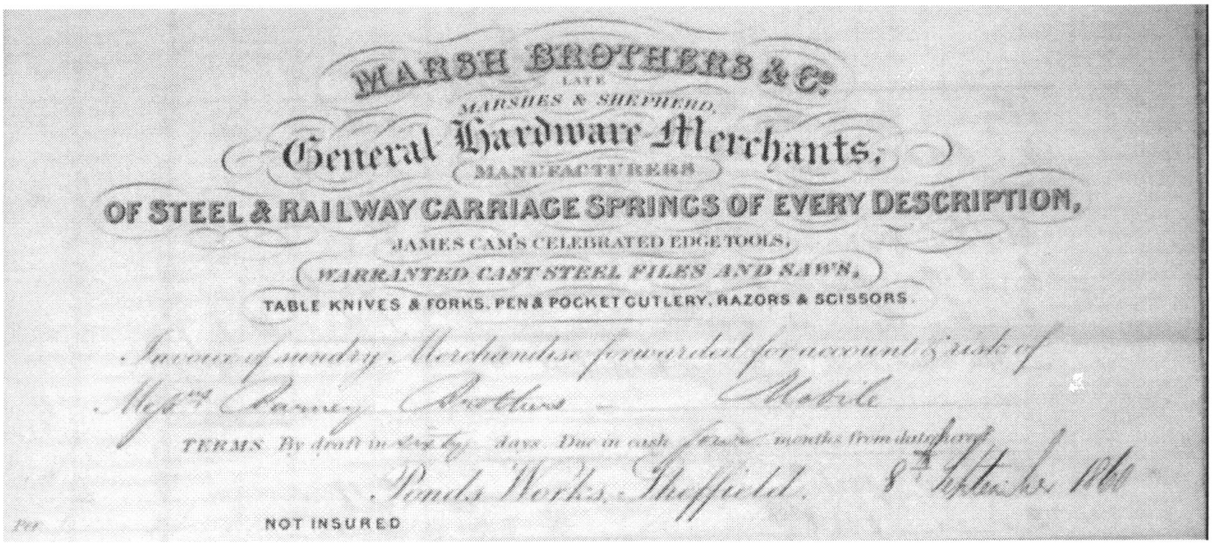
MARSH BROTHERS & Co.
LATE
MARSHES & SHEPHERD,
General Hardware Merchants,
MANUFACTURERS
OF STEEL & RAILWAY CARRIAGE SPRINGS OF EVERY DESCRIPTION,
JAMES CAM'S CELEBRATED EDGE TOOLS,
WARRANTED CAST STEEL FILES AND SAWS,
TABLE KNIVES & FORKS. PEN & POCKET CUTLERY, RAZORS & SCISSORS.
TERMS. By draft in days. Due in cash months from date hereof.
NOT INSURED

Figure 112. Invoice for cargo of cutlery.

Summary:[103] The cutlery invoice was highly detailed and used an abbreviated notation hard to decipher. Parts only were transcribed here.

Marsh Brothers & Co.
Late
Marshes & Shepherd.
General Hardware Merchants.
(Manufacturers)
Of Steel & Railway Carriage Springs of Every Description
James Cam's Celebrated Edge Tools.
Warranted Cast Steel Files and Saws,
Table Knives & forks, Pen & Pocket Cutlery, Razors & Scissors.
Invoice of sundry Merchandise forwarded for account & risk of
Messrs. Barney Brothers, Mobile
Terms: By draft in sixty days. Due in cash four months from date hereon.
Ponds Works, Sheffield 8th September 1860

Per _________ Not Insured

Cask 442
Four lots described as Tables

[103] In this section some documents were summarized rather than transcribed completely.

Tin lined Cask 41/9 Carriage to Liverpool 19/2
Cask Subtotal 76 10 5

Cask 443
Seven lots described as Tables
6 doz Table knives
6 " dessert "
6 doz Tables
3 Pair Carvers
6 doz Tables
4 doz Table knives
4 doz dessert "
12 Pair Carvers
4 doz knife sharpeners
6 " Cotton knives[104]
1 " knife sharpeners
Tin lined Cask 39/10 Carriage to Liverpool 16/9
Cask Subtotal 113 4 2

Cask 444
29 lots – knives
Subtotal 198 5
12 doz "Algors" Shoe knives
8 " " " "
Subtotal 1 18 6
10 doz "Bishops" bS Socket Chisels ½ in
15 " " " " " ¾ in
8 " " " " " 1 in
Subtotal 8 16 11
2 doz "Spear & Jacksons" Hand Saws 26 in
2 " " Panel " "
½ " " Ripping " 28 in
½ " " " " 30 in
Subtotal 12 2
3 doz "Stubs" Mill saw Sgle Cut Files 14 in
Subtotal 3 7 6
1 doz "Brown Bros" tbouy (?) Squares 8 and 10 in
1 " " " Biruls (?) 8, 10, 12 in
Subtotal 4 12 2
Tin lined Cask 45/- Carriage to Liverpool 21/9
Subtotal 3 6 9
Cask subtotal 232 8 10

Recapitulation

Amount of Cask 442	76	10	5			
" " " 443	113	4	2			
" " " 444	232	8	10	442	3	5
Commission 5%				21	2	2
B Lading 2/-, Stamp 1/6, Entry 1/6, Fordg. 3/9				-	14	-
				£ 443	19	7

[104] Blunt ended blade used to cut into and sample cotton bales.

1324-1326
Preprinted Customs Form

No. 26
Importer T. P. Officer
Vessel *Cumberland*
From Liverpool
Entered 8 Nov 1860
Value $ 506 Duty $ 121.48

Agent's Oath
T. P. Officer
W. Stow & Co. (?) owner
Sworn before me, this 8 day of Nov 1860
T. J. Burton Collector

Mdse. Entered 8 Nov 1860 Ship Entered 31 Octr 1860
Entry of Merchandise imported into the Port of Mobile, District of Mobile, by T P Officer in the Ship *Cumberland* Merrill Master, from Liverpool

Marks Nos.	No. of Packages	Contents	Value in Foreign Currency				Duties
S&C/M							
1?10.12.	11	Casks, &					
11&12	2	Pkgs. Chains & H & Hinges 60	£ 82 10 4				
	6	bags nails lbs 600	17 3 9				
			£ 99 14 1				
		Chgs 1/18/6 & Com 2/19/10	4 18 4				
			104 12 5	$ 506.37			
				Nails	$ 87	24%	$ 20.88
England				Iron mfs ??	419		100.56
					$ 506		$ 121.44

1327-1333
Invoice

Outside of folder inscribed:
J P Shaw & Co
Pr *Cumberland*

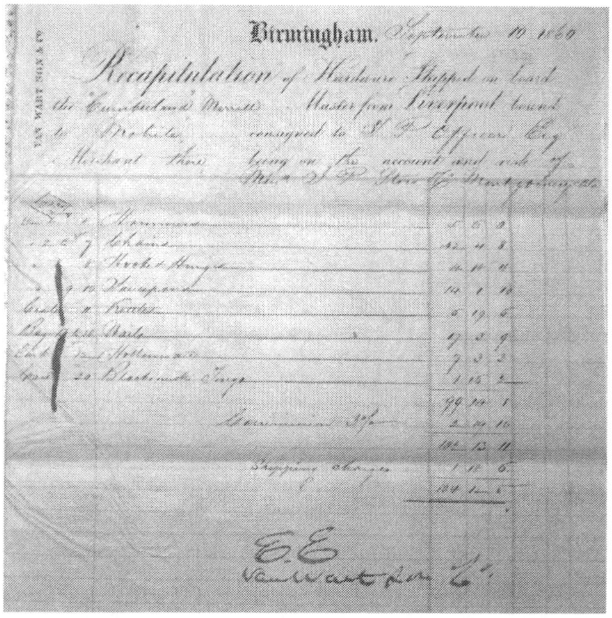

Figure 113. Invoice for cargo of hardware. Page 1 of 6 pages in set.

Van Wart Son & Co. (margin) September 10 1860

Birmingham.

Recapitulation of Hardware Shipped on board the *Cumberland* Merrill Master from Liverpool bound to Mobile consigned to T P Officer Esq Merchant there being on the account and risk of Messr J. P. Stow & Co Montgomery

S & Co/r v				
Cask 1	Hammers	5	6	0
" 2 to 7	Chains	42	4	8
" 8	Hooks & Hinges	4	18	11
" 9, 10	Saucepans	14	1	10
Crate 11	Kettles	6	19	6
Bag ?? to 18	Nails	17	3	9
Cask 12	Hollowware[105]	7	3	3
Case 20	Blacksmith's Tongs	1	16	2
		99	14	1
	Commission 3%	2	19	10
		102	13	11
	Shipping charges	1	18	6
		104	12	5
	E.E			
	Van Wart Son Co			

[105] A term that referred to table service items such as sugar bowls, creamers, coffee pots, teapots, soup tureens, hot food covers, water pitchers, platters, butter pat plates, and other metal items that went with the china on a table. It did not include flatware. Hollow ware was constructed to last a long time. It differed from some other silver plated items in being made with thicker walls and more layers of silver plate.

1329
Invoice

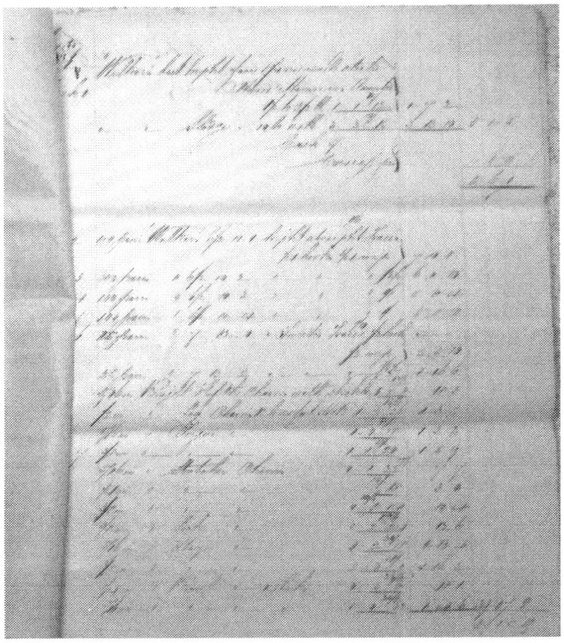

Figure 114. Invoice for cargo of harness equipment. Page 2 of 6.

	Walkers best bright face & panvwell (?) steel						
Cask 1	Hand Hammers Assortd						
	20/						
	½ to 2½ lb 1 1 12	1	7	2			
	19/						
	" " Sledges " 10 to 14 lb 3 3 15	3	13	10	5	1	0
	Cask 1						
	Carriage fee					5	0
					5	6	0
	1/6						
	100 pairs Walkers 6½ 10 1 bright straight Traces						
	¼ hooks ¾ rings	7	10	0			
	100 pairs " 6½ 10 2 " " " 1/2½	6	0	10			
	100 pairs " 6½ 10 3 " " " 1/1	5	8	4			
	100 pairs " 6½ 10 4 " " " 1/	5	0	0			
	25 prs " 7 12 1 " Twisted Traces 1/10 ½ hook ½ anss (?)	2	5	10			
	25 prs " 7 12 2 " Twisted Traces 1/10½ " 1/5½	1	16	6			
	5/16 in Bright Fifth Chains with shackle 1-0-8 14/.		18	3			
	½ in " Log Chains 12 hks feet H&R 1-2. 26 13/6	1	3	5			
	5/16 in " Tongue " 1-0. 18 20/.	1	3	3			
7	3/8 in " " " 1 1- 20 18/.	1	5	9			
	5/16 in " Stretcher Chains 0-1-22 14/.		7	7			
	¼ in " " " 18 19/.		3	0			
	3/8 in " " " 0-2-14 16/6		10	4			
	3/8 in " Lock " 0-2-24 17/6		12	6			
	5/16 in " Stay " 1-2-18 20/.	1	13	4			
	3/8 in " " " 2-0-1 18/.	1	16	2			

	¼ in " Breast " 14 links 0-3-6 22/6		18	1			
	5/16 in " " " " 1-0-22 20/6	1	4	6	39	17	8
					39	17	8

1330
Invoice

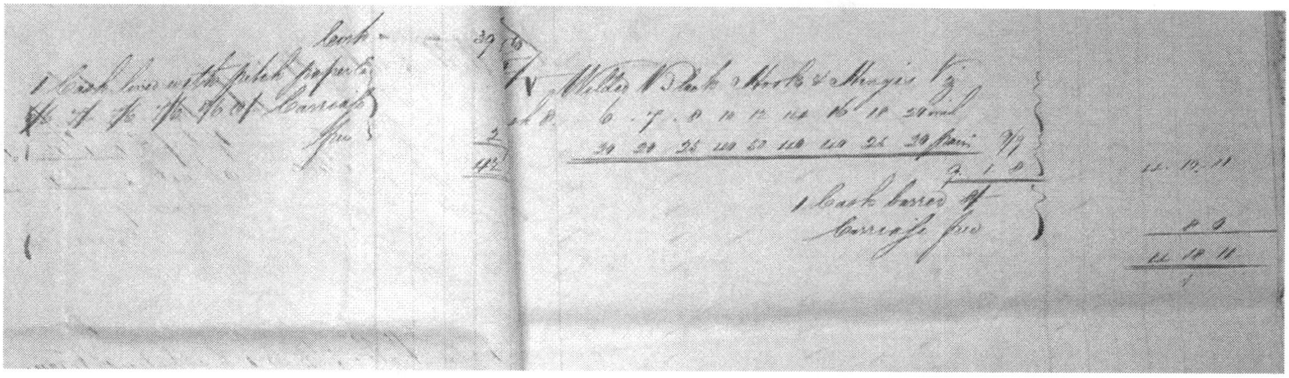

Figure 115. Invoice for cargo of hooks and hinges. Page 3 of 6.

(reverse side of 1329)
1 Cask lined with pitch paper & Coms 39 ???
6/6 7/. 7/6 7/6 8/6 10/. Carriage fee 2 ???
42 ???

(page 2)

	Welded Black Hooks & Hinges Vz						
Cask 8	6 7 0 10 12 14 16 18 20 mil						
	20 20 25 40 50 40 40 26 20 pain		9/9				
		9	1	8	4	10	11
	1 Cask barer 8/-						
	Carriage fee					8	0
					4	18	11

1131
Invoice

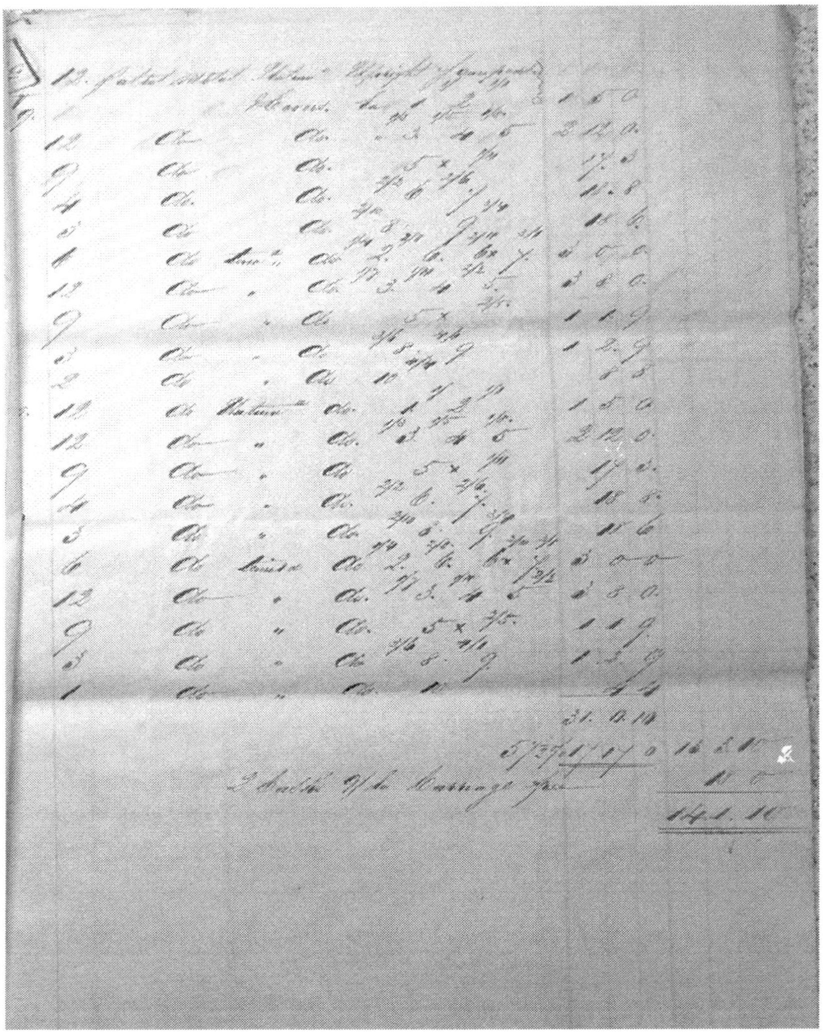

Figure 116. Invoice for cargo of patent metal utensils. Page 4 of 6.

Summary: A difficult-to-decipher invoice for 20 lots of various Patent Metal Utensils (?). Packed in "2 Casks 9/? Carriage fee 18 0. Total £ 14.1.10."

1132
Invoice

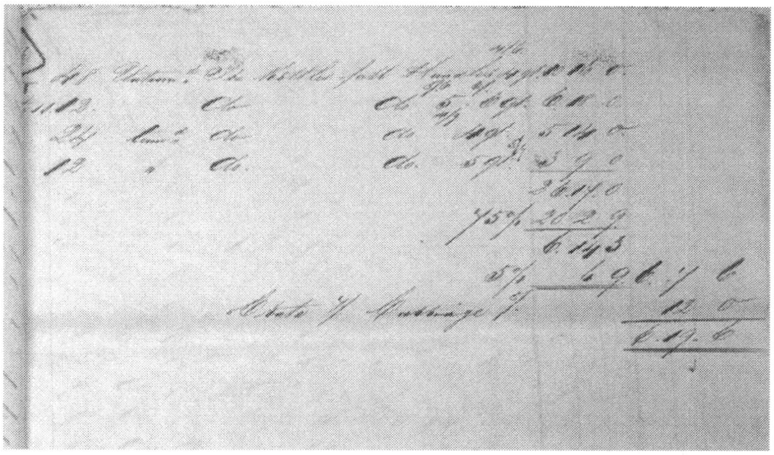

Figure 117. Invoice for cargo of kettles. Page 5 of 6.

Summary: A difficult to interpret invoice for kettles with fall handles including 4 lots, totaling 86 items in a crate for a total cost of £ 6.19.6.

1133
Invoice

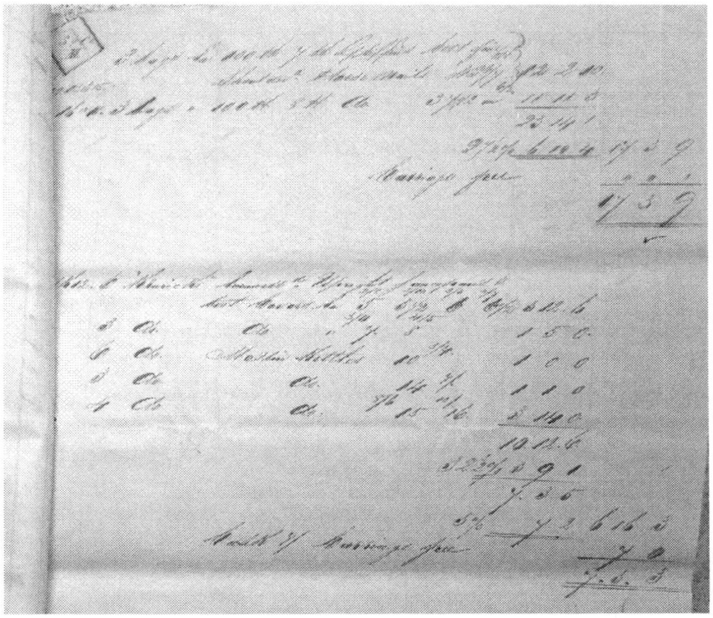

Figure 118. Invoice for cargo of hardware. Page 6 of 6.

S & Co./M							
Bag 13 to 15	3 bags Ea 100 lbs 7 lb Griffins best fine Shouldered Horse nails 42 6/7 5/0	12	2	10			
Bag 16 to 18	3 bags " 100 bls 8 lb do. 37 1/2 6/2	11	11	3			
		23	14	1			
	24½% (discount)	6	10	4	17	3	9
	Carriage free				"	"	"
					17	3	9

?? ?? TO 12	6 "Kensicks" Enameled Upright fancy ?? & best Covers Ea 5 5½ 6 6½ @ 12.6 3/11 4/5	3	12	6			
	3 do. do. " 7 8	1	5	0			
	6 do. Maslin Kettles 10 3/4	1	0	0			
	3 do. do. 14 7/.	1	1	0			
	4 do. do. 15 8/6 16 10/.	3	14	0			
		10	12	6			
	32½%	3	9	1			
		7	3	5			
	5%		7	2	6	16	3
	Cask 4/ Carriage fee					7	0
					7	3	3

1134
Invoice

"Dirks" (?) Blacksmiths Tongs Assorted Vs

3	4	5 lb		18/6					
1	2	1 Dzen	1	3	6	1	13	5	
			Case 2/9						
			Carriage fee				2	9	
						1	16	2	

1135a
Bill of Lading

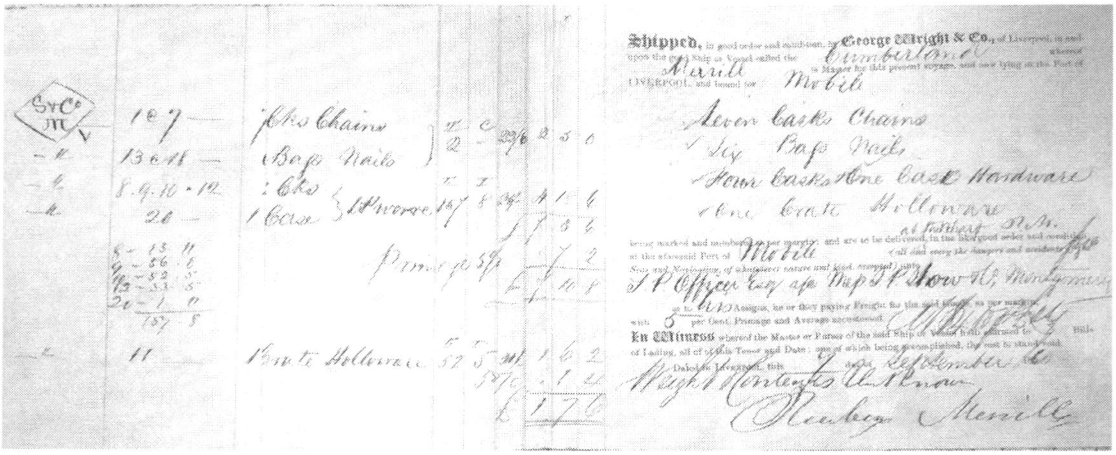
Shipped, in good order and condition, by George Wright & Co. of Liverpool
Cumberland
Merrill
Mobile
Seven Casks Chains
Six Bags Nails
Four Casks One Case Hardware
One Crate Holloware
Mobile

Figure 119. Bill of lading for cargo of hardware.

Shipped, in good order and condition, by George Wright & Co., of Liverpool, in and upon the good Ship or Vessel called the *Cumberland* whereof Merrill is Master for this present voyage, and now lying in the Port of Liverpool, and bound for Mobile

Seven Casks Chains
Six Bags Nails
Four Casks & One Case Hardware
One Crate Hollowware

N. M.

Being marked and numbered as per margin; and are to be delivered, at the Wharf, in the like good order and condition at the aforesaid Port of Mobile (all and every dangers and accidents (overwritten: fire) of the Seas and Navigation, of whatsoever nature and kind, excepted) unto

T. P. Officer Esq a/c Mess. S. P. Stow & Co., Montgomery

or to his Assigns, he or they paying Freight for the said Goods, as per margin, with 5 per Cent. Primage and Average accustomed. At $ 4.00 p £ ?? In Witness whereof the Master or Purser of the said Ship or Vessel hath affirmed to 3 (?) Bills of Lading, all of of (stet) this Tenor and Date; one of which being accomplished, the rest to stand void.

Dated in Liverpool, this 7 day of September 185_ (overwritten: 60)

Weight & Contents Unknown

(signed) Newbey(?) Merrill

Note: Left side of form, not transcribed, shows accounting details and total £ 176 for shipment with 5% fee.

1135b
Owner's Oath

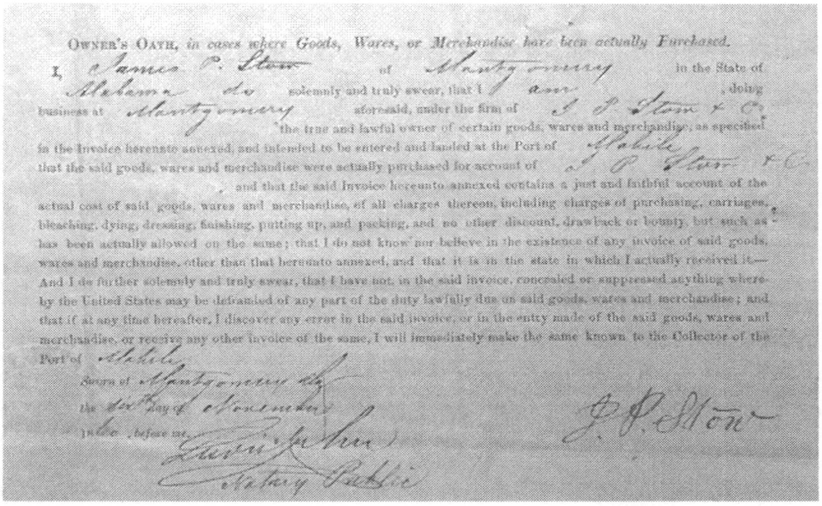

OWNER'S OATH, *in cases where Goods, Wares, or Merchandise have been actually Purchased.*

I, James P. Stow of Montgomery in the State of Alabama do solemnly and truly swear, that I am, doing business at Montgomery aforesaid, under the firm of J. P. Stow & Co the true and lawful owner of certain goods, wares and merchandise, as specified in the Invoice hereunto annexed, and intended to be entered and landed at the Port of Mobile that the said goods, wares and merchandise were actually purchased for account of J. P. Stow & Co, and that the said Invoice hereunto annexed contains a just and faithful account of the actual cost of said goods, wares and merchandise, of all charges thereon, including charges of purchasing, carriages, bleaching, dying, dressing, finishing, putting up, and packing, and no other discount, drawback or bounty, but such as has been actually allowed on the same; that I do not know nor believe in the existence of any invoice of said goods, wares and merchandise, other than that hereunto annexed, and that it is in the state in which I actually received it— And I do further solemnly and truly swear, that I have not, in the said invoice, concealed or suppressed anything whereby the United States may be defrauded of any part of the duty lawfully due on said goods, wares and merchandise; and that if at any time hereafter, I discover any error in the said invoice, or in the entry made of the said goods, wares and merchandise, or receive any other invoice of the same, I will immediately make the same known to the Collector of the Port of Mobile

Sworn at Montgomery the ... day of November ... before me,

Notary Public

J. P. Stow

Figure 120. Owner's Oath by James P. Stow of Montgomery for cargo of hardware.

Summary: A form with the Owner's Oath:

Owner's Oath, in cases where Goods, Wares, or Merchandise have been actually Purchased.
I, James P. Stow of Montgomery in the State of Alabama do solemnly and truly swear, that I am, doing business at Montgomery aforesaid, under the firm of J. P. Stow & Co. the true and lawful owner … landed at the Port of Mobile …

Sworn at Montgomery Ala
The sixth day of November
1860, before me, (signed) Lewis Cahn (?), Notary Public

(signed) J. P. Stow

1336
Affidavit naming agent

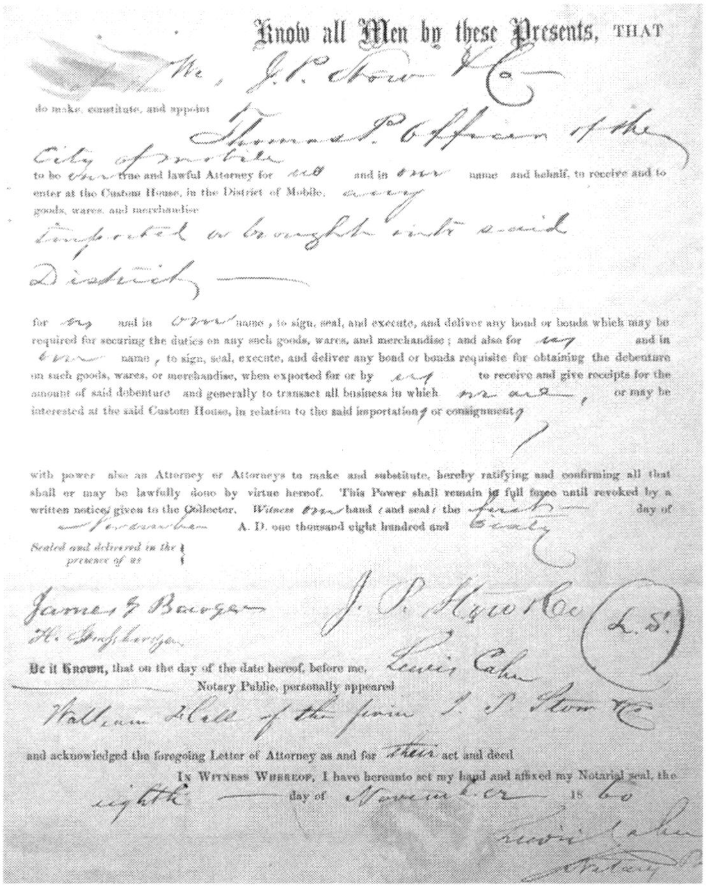

Know all Men by these Presents, THAT We, J. P. Stow & Co do make, constitute, and appoint Thomas P. Officer of the City of Mobile to be our true and lawful Attorney for us and in our name and behalf, to receive and to enter at the Custom House, in the District of Mobile, every goods, wares, and merchandise imported or brought into said District —

for us and in our name, to sign, seal, and execute, and deliver any bond or bonds which may be required for securing the duties on any such goods, wares, and merchandise; and also for us and in our name, to sign, seal, execute, and deliver any bond or bonds requisite for obtaining the debenture on such goods, wares, or merchandise, when exported for or by us to receive and give receipts for the amount of said debenture and generally to transact all business in which we are, or may be interested at the said Custom House, in relation to the said importations or consignments

with power also as Attorney or Attorneys to make and substitute, hereby ratifying and confirming all that shall or may be lawfully done by virtue hereof. This Power shall remain in full force until revoked by a written notice given to the Collector. *Witness* our hand and seal the first day of November A. D. one thousand eight hundred and sixty

Sealed and delivered in the presence of us

James G. Barger
H. [illegible]

J. P. Stow & Co (L.S.)

Be it Known, that on the day of the date hereof, before me, Lewis Cahn Notary Public, personally appeared William Hall of the firm J. P. Stow & Co and acknowledged the foregoing Letter of Attorney as and for their act and deed

In Witness Whereof, I have hereunto set my hand and affixed my Notarial seal, the eighth day of November 1860

Lewis Cahn
Notary P.

Figure 121. Affidavit naming agent for customs matter.

Summary: Thomas P. Officer of the City of Mobile was appointed to handle customs matters in Mobile on behalf of J. P. Stow & Co. by means of this notarized letter. (Not transcribed.)

1337
Owner's Oath

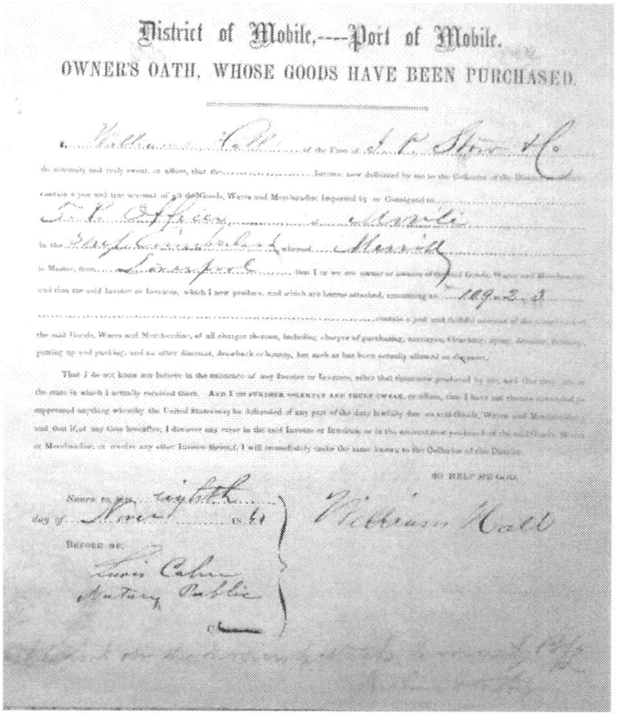
District of Mobile,---Port of Mobile.
OWNER'S OATH, WHOSE GOODS HAVE BEEN PURCHASED.

Figure 122. Owner's oath for cargo of hardware.

Summary: William Hall of J. P. Stow & Co. signed the Owner's Oath for imported goods valued at £ 109.2.5.

1338-1339
Invoice

Summary: Duplicate Van Wart Son & Co. invoice for chains and hardware.

1340
Preprinted Customs Form

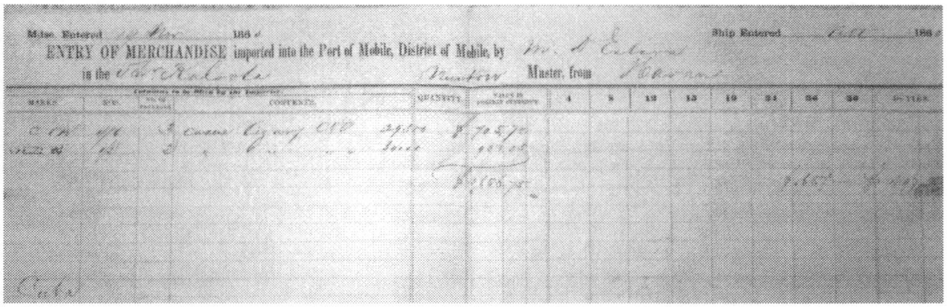
ENTRY OF MERCHANDISE imported into the Port of Mobile, District of Mobile, by

Figure 123. Customs form for cargo of cigars.

No. 45
Entry of Merchandise
Importer M D Eslava
Vessel *Kaloola*
From Havana
Entered 19 Nov '60
Value $ 1657 Duty $ 497.10

Agent's Oath
M. D. Eslava
Gautherin Le More & Cruzat
Sworn before me, this 19 day of Nov 1860
T. J. Butler D(eputy) Collector

Mdse. Entered 19 Nov 1860 Ship Entered Nov 1860
Entry of Merchandise imported into the Port of Mobile, District of Mobile, by M. D. Eslava in the Schr. *Kaloola* Newton Master, from Havana

Marks	Nos.	No. of Packages	Contents	Value in Foreign Currency	30%	Duties.
C&W	4/6	3 cases	Cigars C&O 29500	$ 705.70		
MD R	1/2	2 "	" " " 30000	951.05		
Cuba				$ 1656.75	$ 1657	$ 497.??

1341
Bill of Lading in Spanish

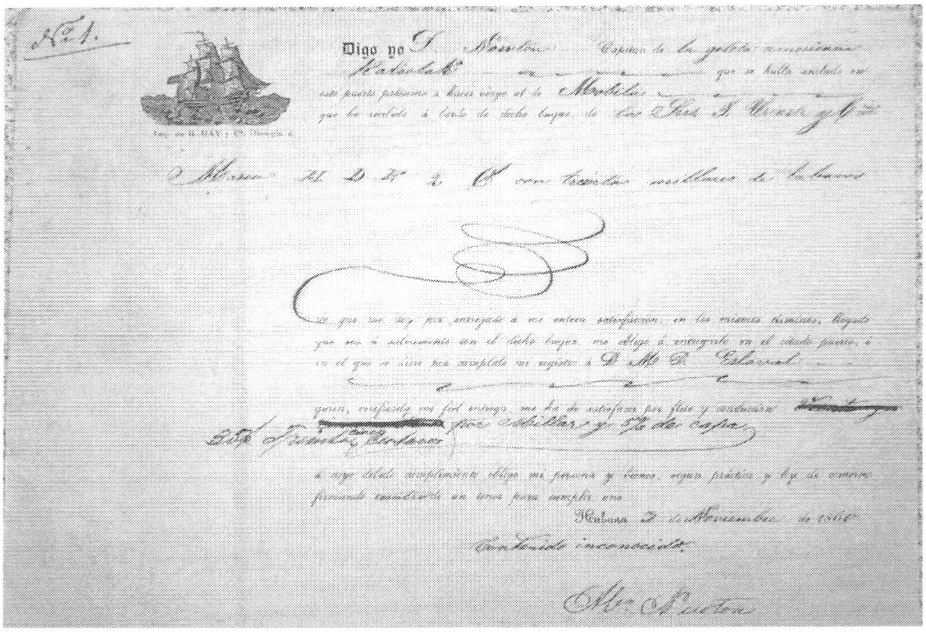
Nº 1.
Digo yo D. Newton
Mobila
Habana 2 de Noviembre de 1860
Contenido inconocido.

Figure 124. Bill of lading in Spanish for cargo of 30,000 cigars.

No. 1
Digo yo D. Newton Capitan de la galeta americana *Kalsolak* que se halla anclado en este puerto proesimo a hacer viage al de Mobila que he recigido a bordo de dicho buque, de los Sres. T. Uriarte y Cina.

Marca M D E 2 C/ con treinta millares de tabacos

De que me doy per entregado a me entera satisfaccion, en los mismos terminos, llegado que sea a sulvamento con el dicho buque, me obligo a entregarlo en el citado puerto, o en el que se diero por cumplido mi registro a D. M. D. Eslava quien, verificada mi fiel entrega, me ha de satisfacer por flete y conduccion por Millar y 5% de casa 35k Treinta cinco centavos a cuyo debido cumplimiento obligo mi persona y bienes, segun practica y ley de comercio firmando cuatro de un tenor para cumplir uno.

Habana 3 de Noviembre de 1860

Contenido inconocido.

(signed) ??? Newton

1343
Consul's Certificate

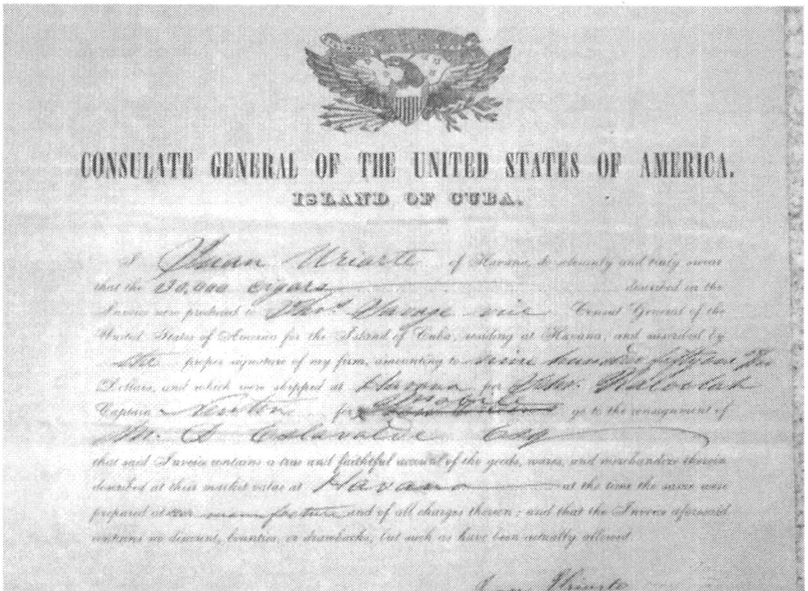
CONSULATE GENERAL OF THE UNITED STATES OF AMERICA.
ISLAND OF CUBA.

Figure 125. Consul's certificate for cargo of cigars.

Consulate General of the United States of America
Island of Cuba.

I Juan Uriarte of Havana, do solemnly and truly swear that the 30,000 cigars described in the Invoice now produced to Thos Salvage Vice Consul General of the United States of America for the Island of Cuba, residing in Havana, and subscribed by the proper signature of my firm, amounting to nine hundred fifty one 05/100 Dollars, and which were shipped at Havana per Schr. *Kaloolah* Captain Newton for Mobile go to the consignment of M. D. Eslavalde[106] Esq that said Invoice contains a true and faithful account of the goods, wares, and merchandize therein described at their market value at Havana at the time the same were prepared at our manufacture and of all charges thereon; and that the Invoice aforesaid contains no discount, bounties, or drawbacks, but such as have been actually allowed.

(signed) Juan Uriarte

Sworn to, and subscribed before me, at Havana, the third day of November A. D. 1860, and of the Independence of the United States the ____; and further certify that I am satisfied that Juan Uriarte who subscribes to the foregoing oath, is the person he represents himself to be that he is a credible person; and that the statements made by him under said oath are true.

(signed) Thos. Savage
U.S. Vice Consul

1345 (attached to 1344)
Invoice

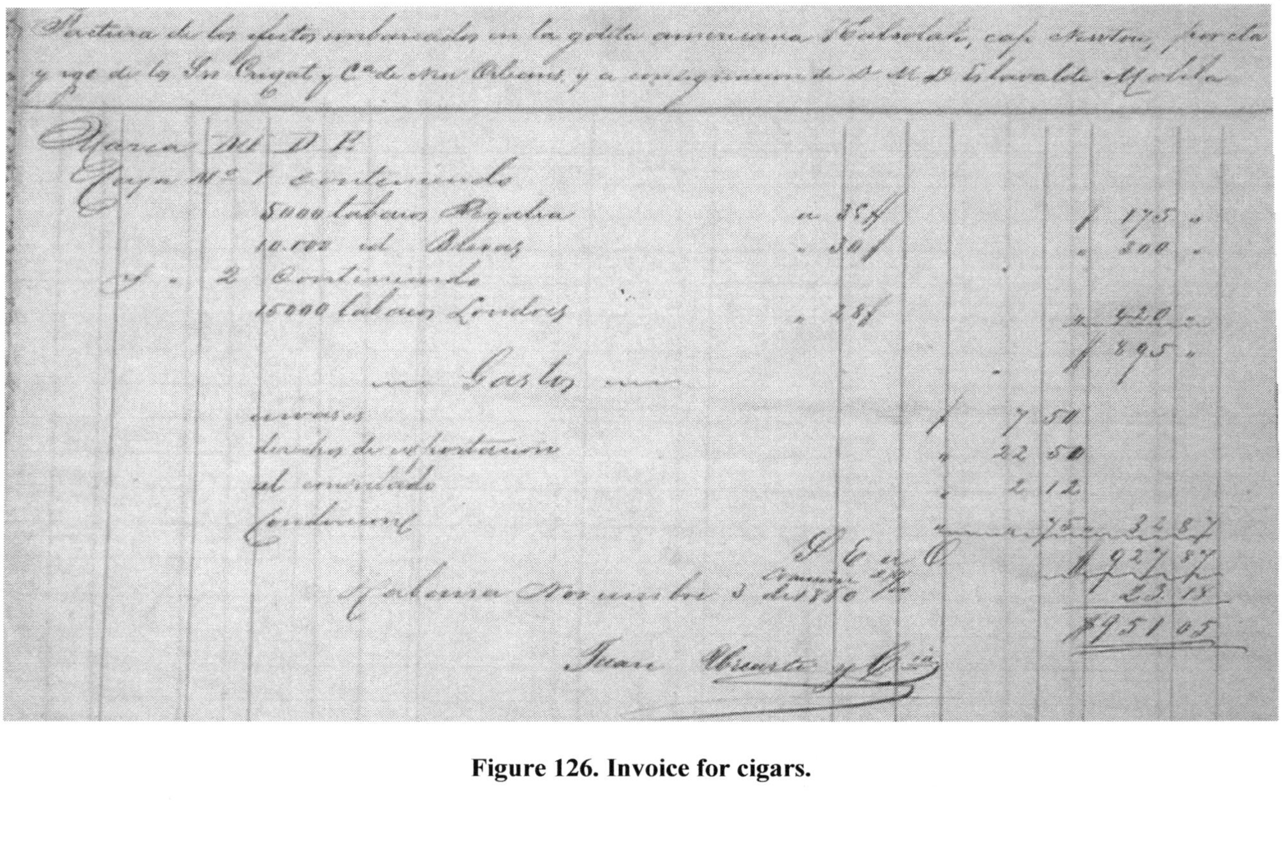
5000 tabacos Regalia @ 35 $ 175
10.000 id 30 300
15000 tabacos Londres 28 420
$ 895
Gastos
$ 7 50
22 50
2 12
32 87
$ 927 87
23 18
$951 05
Juan Uriarte y Cia

Figure 126. Invoice for cigars.

---

106 Note the longer version of M. D. Eslava, a name that often appeared in these documents.

Factura de los fictos imbarcados en la goleta america *Kuloolak*, cap Newton, poreta y ago de los Srs Cruzat y Ca de New Orleans, y a consignamento de **D(on) M D Eslavalde** Mobila

Mfarca MDE			
Casa No 1	conteniendo		
	5000 tabacos Regalia a 35 $		$ 175.00
	10,000 id (?) Brevas a 30 $		300.00
id " 2	Continiendo		
	15000 tabacos Londres a 28 $		420.00
			$ 895.00
	Gartos		
	arvases (?)	$ 7.50	
	derechos de ueportacion	22.50	
	al consulado	2.12	
	Condivion	.75	32.87
	S E a O (?)		$ 927.87
	Commsn 2½ /00		23.18
	Havana Noviembre 3 de 1860		$ 951.05
	(signed) Juan Uriarte y Cin.		

1347
Bill of Lading

No 4
Shipped in good order and well conditioned by Gautherin Le More & Cruzat, in and upon the good Amc Brig called the *Kalloolah* whereof Newton is Master, for this present voyage and now lying in the port of Havana, and bound for Mobile. To say

3. Three Cases containing together twenty nine thousand and five Hundred Segars.
2. Two Cases containing together twenty six thousand & four Hundred fifty Segars.
2. Two bags tobacco, weighg 14,@

Being marked and numbered as in the Margin and to be delivered in the like good Order and Condition, at the aforesaid Port of Mobile all and every the Dangers and Accidents of the Seas and Navigation of whatever Nature or kind excepted, unto M. D. Eslava Esqre. or to his Assigns he or they paying Freight for the said goods, at the rate of thirty five cents pr thousand segars & one Dollar twenty five cents pr bag tobacco. with 5% Primage and Average accustomed. In Witness Whereof, the Master or Purser of the said vessel has affirmed to four Bills of Lading all of this Tenor and Date; One of which being accomplished the others to stand void.

Dated Havana the Nove 3d 1860

(signed) ??? Newton

1348
Consul's Certificate

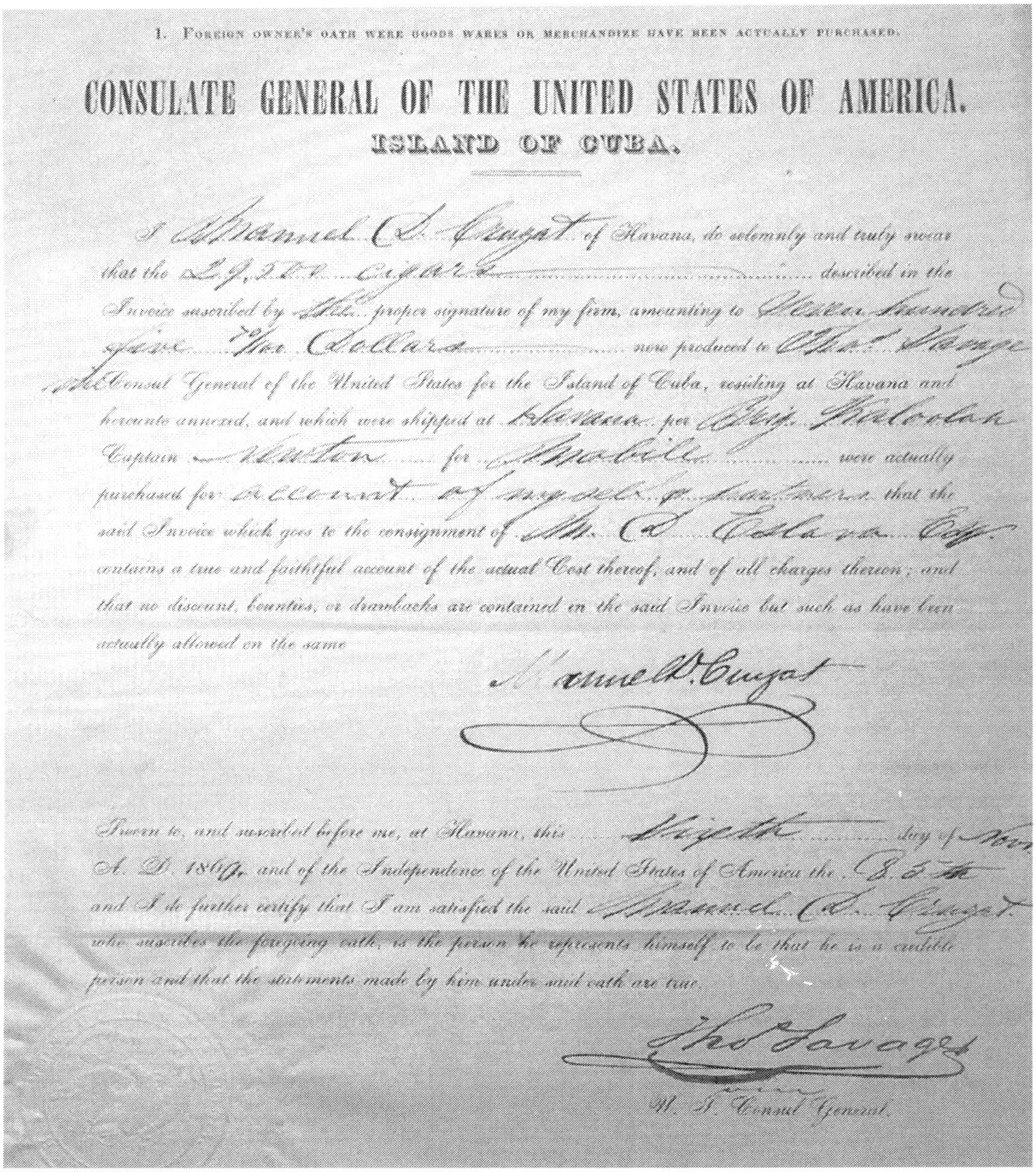

1. Foreign owner's oath were goods wares or merchandize have been actually purchased.

CONSULATE GENERAL OF THE UNITED STATES OF AMERICA.

ISLAND OF CUBA.

I Manuel D. Cruzat of Havana, do solemnly and truly swear that the 29,000 cigars ...... described in the Invoice subscribed by the proper signature of my firm, amounting to Seven hundred five 70/100 Dollars ...... now produced to Thos. Savage the Consul General of the United States for the Island of Cuba, residing at Havana and hereunto annexed, and which were shipped at Havana per Brig Kaloolah Captain Newton ...... for Mobile ...... were actually purchased for account of myself & partners that the said Invoice which goes to the consignment of M. D. Eslava Esq. contains a true and faithful account of the actual Cost thereof, and of all charges thereon; and that no discount, bounties, or drawbacks are contained in the said Invoice but such as have been actually allowed on the same

Manuel D. Cruzat

Sworn to, and subscribed before me, at Havana, this Eighth ...... day of Nov A. D. 1860, and of the Independence of the United States of America the 85th and I do further certify that I am satisfied the said Manuel D. Cruzat who subscribes the foregoing oath, is the person he represents himself to be that he is a credible person and that the statements made by him under said oath are true.

Thos Savage

V. S. Consul General.

Figure 127. Consul's certificate for cargo of cigars.

Summary: U.S. Consul's form verifying shipment on the *Kaloolah* by Manuel D. Cruzat of 29,000 cigars, $ 705.70, to Mobile consigned to M. D. Eslava, document dated 8 Nov 1860, Signed Thos Savage, Vice Consul General.

1349 (attached to 1348)
Invoice

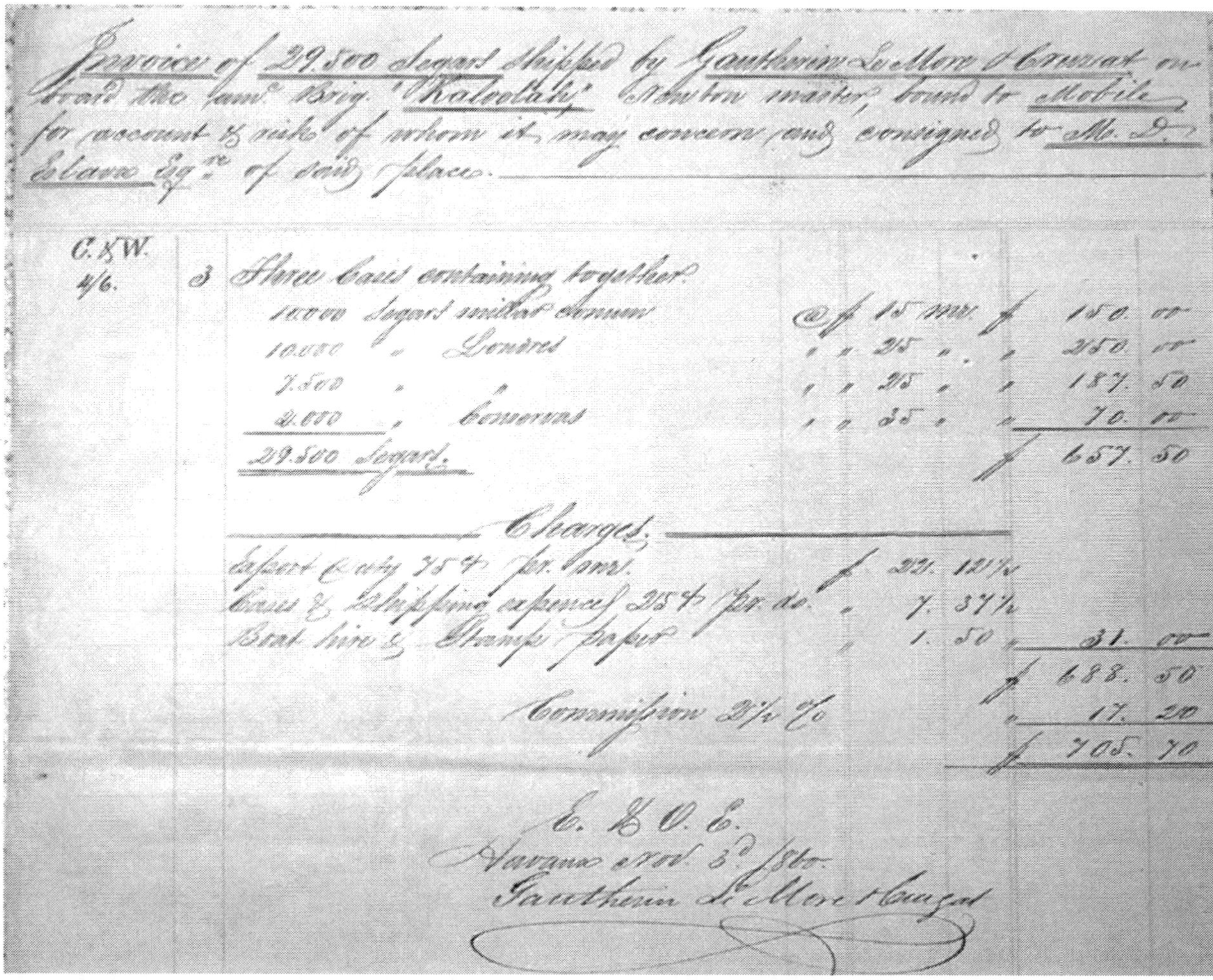

Figure 128. Invoice for cargo of cigars.

Invoice of 29,500 Segars shipped by Gautherin Le More & Cruzat on board the amc. (American) Brig *Kaloolah*, Newton master, bound to Mobile for account & risk of whom it may concern and consigned to M. D. Eslava Esqre of said place.

C&W				
4/6	3	Three Cases containing together		
		10,000 Segars millar common	@ $ 15 mr	$ 150.00
		10,000 " Londres	" " 25 "	250.00
		7,500 " "	" " 25 "	187.50
		2,000 " Conservas	" " 35 "	70.00
		29,500		$ 657.50
		Charges		
		Export Duty 75¢ pr. Mr.	$ 22.12½	
		Cases & shipping expenses 25¢ pr. do.	7.37½	
		Boat hire & Stamp paper	1.50	31.00
				$ 688.50
		Commission 2½%		17.20
		E. & O. E.		$ 705.70
		Havana Nov. 3d 1860		
		Gautherin Le More & Cruzat		

1350-1352
Preprinted Customs Form

No. 24
Importer J. Lunas & Co
Vessel *Kaloola*
From Havana
Entered 13 Sept 1860
Value $ 2612 Duty $ 626.88

Agent's Oath
Jas. Sands & Sands & Co (?)
Mendoza (owner)
Sworn before me, this 3 day of Sept 1860
(signed) T. J. Butler D(eputy) Collector

Mdse. Entered 13 Sept 1860 Ship Entered 8 Sept 1860
Entry of Merchandise imported into the Port of Mobile, District of Mobile, by Sands & Co in the Schr *Kaloola* Santer (?) Master, from Havana

Marks	Nos.	No. of Packages	Contents	Value in Foreign Currency	24	Duties
JM.	1/23	23 Boxes	Brn Sugar 9,981	$ 492.00		
MP.	1/79	79 "	" " 38,154	1692.58		
		102	Boxes 48,135	331.50		
				$ 2516.08		
			Charges	149.04		
				$ 2665.12		
			Com	66.63		
Cuba				$ 2731.75	$2732@24%	$655.68
			Less 2396 @ 5%	119.80	120 __ 24%	28.80
						$626.88

1353
Invoice

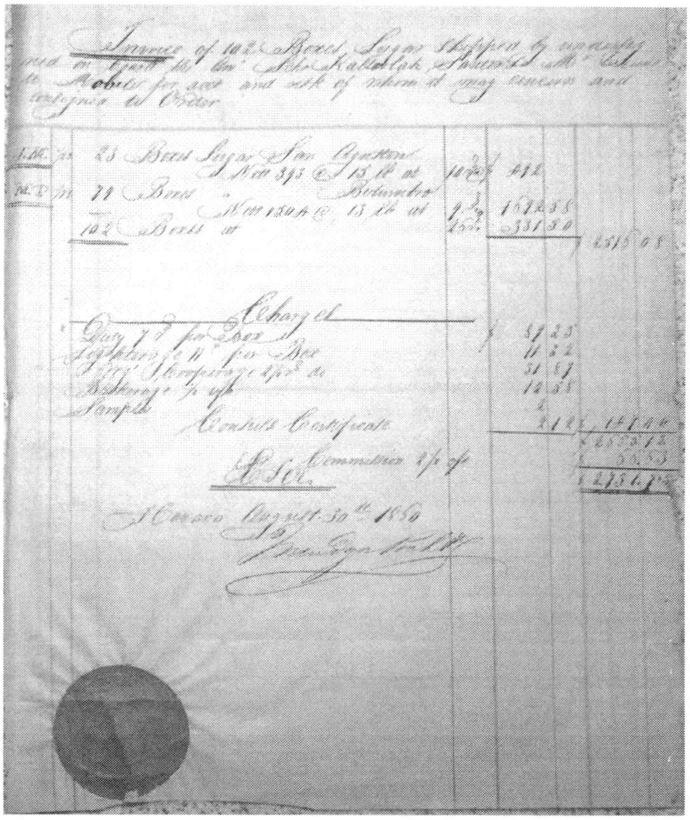

Figure 129. Invoice for cargo of sugar.

Invoice of 102 Boxes Sugar Shipped by undersigned on board the Am Schr *Kaloolah* James S Mr ?? to Mobile for acct and risk of whom it may concern and consigned to Order

J.M.	1/23	23 Boxes	Sugar San Agustin Nett 393 @ 15 lb	at 10¢	492.00	
M.P.	1/79	79 Boxes	" Bolumbro Nett 150 @ 13 lb	at 9¢	1692.58	
		102 Boxes	at	26¢	331.50	$ 2516.08
			Charges			
			Duty 7¢ per Box			
			Lighterage 11¢ per Box			
			Wg Cooperage 2½¢ do			
			Brokerage ½%			
			Samples			
			Consul's Certificate			
			Commissions 2½%			
			E&OE			
			Havana August 30th 1860			
			(signed) Mendoza Poch & Co			

1354a
Invoice (attached to U.S. Consul's certificate.)

Summary: J. A. Mendoza shiped 102 Boxes of Sugar to Mobile per Schn. *Kaloolah*, purchased for the account of himself and partners and consigned to Order. 30th Aug 1860, (signed) Thos. Savage Vice Consul General.

1354b

(Calculation of discount or partial loss of shipment or perhaps payment in kind for transport by schooner. Unclear.)

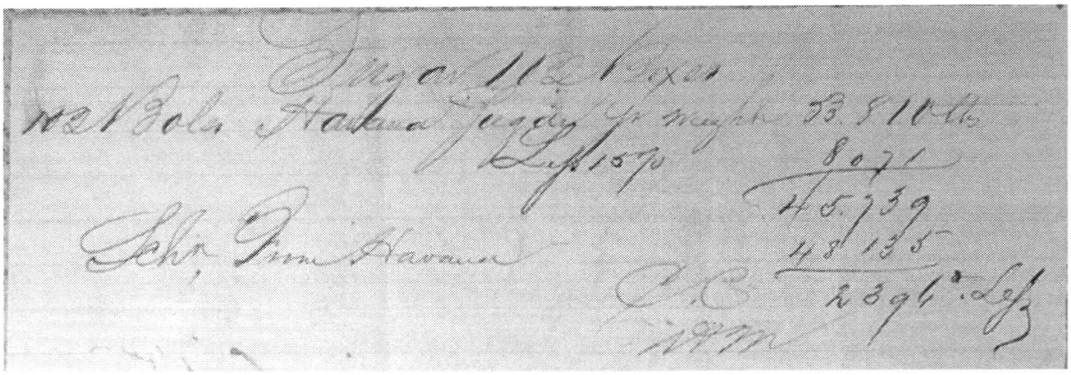

Figure 130. Calculation of discount concerning partial loss of sugar cargo during transport.

Sugar 102 Boxes

102 Boxes Havana Sugar Gr Weight	53,810 lbs
Less 15%	8,071
	45,739
Schn From Havana	48,135
C C	2,396 lb Less
?? M	

1356
Bill of Lading

JM 1/23
MP 1/79 102

Shipped in good order and well conditioned by Mendoza Poch & Co. in and upon the good Amn Schr called the *Kalloolah* whereof Senter is Master, for this present voyage and now lying in the port of Havana, and bound for Mobile. To say

One hundred and two boxes Sugar and one package Samples.

Being marked and numbered as in the Margin and to be delivered in the like good Order and Condition, at the aforesaid Port of Mobile all and every the Dangers and Accidents of the Seas and Navigation of whatever

Nature or kind excepted, unto Order or to --- Assigns he or they paying Freight for the said goods, One dollar per box the rate of thirty five cents pr thousand segars & one Dollar twenty five cents pr bag tobacco. with and Primage and Average accustomed. In Witness Whereof, the Master or Purser of the said vessel has affirmed to four Bills of Lading all of this Tenor and Date; One of which being accomplished the others to stand void.

Dated Havana the 30th August 1860
Weight & ??? unknown (signed) B A Senter

1357-1358
Preprinted Customs Form

No. 23
Importer M D Eslava
Vessel *Kaloola*
From Havana
Entered 10 Sept 1860
Value $ 472 Duty $ 65.48

Owner's Oath
M. D. Eslava
Sworn before me, this 10 day of Sept 1860
T. J. Butler Collector

Mdse. Entered 10 Sept 1860 Ship Entered 8 September 1860
Entry of Merchandise imported into the Port of Mobile, District of Mobile, by M. D. Eslava in the Schr *Kaloolah* Senter Master, from Havana

Marks	No. of Packages	Contents	Value in Foreign Currency			Duties
	8 pieces	Mahogany	$ 170.00	a 8%		
	6 "	Cedar	126.00	" 8%		
			$ 296.00			
		Shg & Expt Dues &c	41.63			
			$ 337.63			
		Com	8.44			
			$ 346.07	a 8%		
	33 cases	Com Sp red Wine doz 33	$ 99.00			
		Com 2½%	2.48			
			$ 101.48			
			24.35			
			$ 125.83	30 %		
Cuba				$ 346	8%	$ 27.68
				$ 126	30%	37.80
				$ 472		$ 65.48

1360a
Invoice

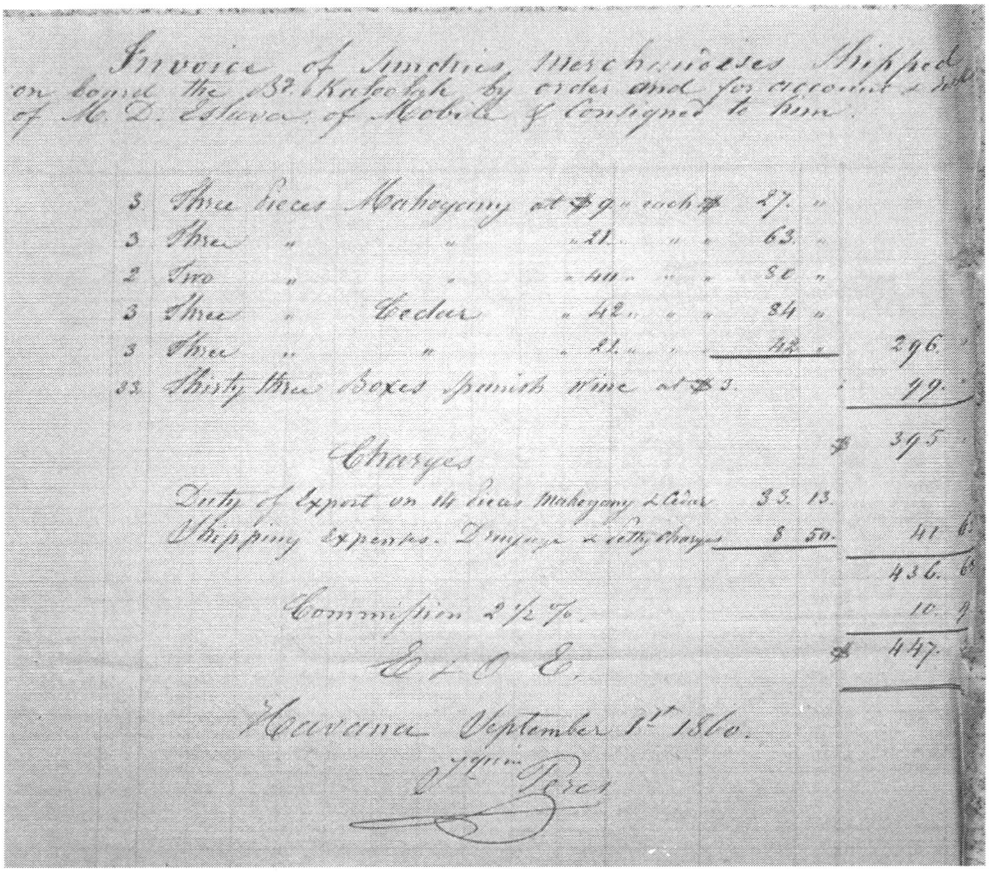

Figure 131. Invoice for cargo of exotic wood and Spanish wine.

Invoice of Sundries Merchandise Shipped on board the Bg. (Brig) *Kaloolah* by order and for account & risks of M. D. Eslava of Mobile & Consigned to him.

3 Three Pieces	Mahogany	at $ 9 each	$ 27.00	
3 Three "	"	21 "	63.00	
2 Two "	"	40 "	80.00	
3 Three "	Cedar	42 "	84.00	
3 Three "	"	21 "	42.00	296.00
33 Thirty Three Boxes	Spanish Wine	at $ 3		99.00
				$ 395.00
	Charges			
Duty of Export on	14 Pieces Mahogany & Cedar		33.13	
Shipping Expenses	Drayage & Jetty charges		8.50	41.63
				436.63
	Commission 2½%			10.92
	E & O E			$ 447.55
	Havana September 1st 1860			
	(signed) ??? Peres			

1360b
Statement of cargo weight

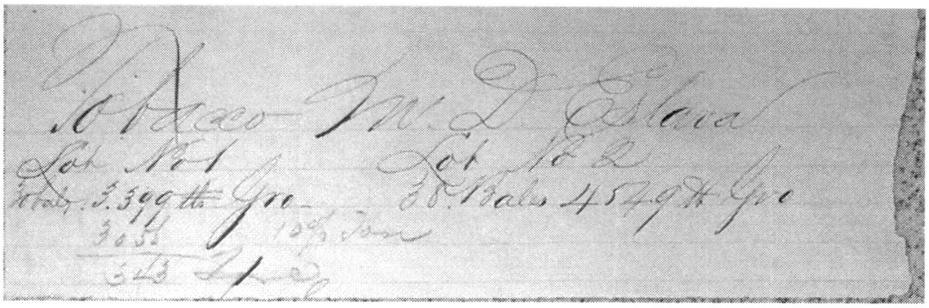

Figure 132. Statement of weight for cargo of tobacco.

Tobacco M. D. Eslava

Lot	No 1	Lot No 2
30 bales	3300 lbs Gro	38 Bales 4549 lbs Gro
	3055 10% ???	
	343 ???	

1361
Invoice

Invoice of 2 barrels wine shipped by Gautherin Le More & Cruzat on board the Amern Schr *Kaloolah* Senter Mr by order & for a/c & risks of & consigned to M. D. Eslava Esqre of said place

2 Barrels	Dry Malaga wine @ $11 each		$ 22.00
	Charges		
	Shipping	$ .50	
	Boat hire & stamps	1.25	1.75
			$ 23.75
	Commission 2½%		.60
			$ 24.35
	E&O.E.		
	Havana September first 1860		
	Gautherin Le More & Cruzat		
	30%		

1362-1364
Preprinted Customs Form

No. 34

Importer Dade Huxthal (?) & Co
Vessel *Cumberland*
From L'pool
Entered 28 Nov '60
Value $ 3860 Duty $ 902.01

Owner's Oath
Jno. R. Ketchum (agent)
Dade Huxthal (?) & Co
Sworn before me, this 28 day of Nov 1860
T. J. Butler Collector

Mdse. Entered Nov 1860 Ship Entered 31 Oct 1860
Entry of Merchandise imported into the Port of Mobile, District of Mobile, by Dade Huxthal & Co in the Ship *Cumberland* Merrill Master, from Liverpool

Marks	Nos.	No. of Packages	Contents	Value in Foreign Currency			Duties
DH&Co							
DH&Co/H	1	1 Cask	Cutlery	69 17 1	add Com		
DH&Co/W	2	1 Case	do	150 7 0	" "		
R/143	1	1 "	do	107 15 0	" "		
DH&Co/V	1507 8/30	1 Cask	& 23 Bags Nails 17.2.25	61 5 2			
	1536 1533 1576 1481	16 Casks	& 5 Bales Havana				
	1588/9	2 Casks		307 13 8			
	1591/3	3 Casks			421.16.4		
	1590	1 Case		43 7 10	17.3.6		
	1580	1 Bale	Thread	9 9 8			
			Com	17 3 6			
			Sh Charges	4 3 4			
			Sh ar	10 2 2			
				£ 781 4 5			
			add Coms 2½% 327.19.1	16 8 0			
England				£ 797 12 5	$ 3860.49		
			??? case		$ 233.00	15%	33.45
			??? Flax mfs		48.00	"	7.20
			Iron mfs not etd		3589.00	24	861.36
					3860.00		902.01

1365-1367
Preprinted Customs Form

No. 6
Importer A Ruiz
Vessel *Harriet Lewis*
From Havana

Entered 7 Nov '60
Value $ 240 Duty $ 19.20

Owner's Oath
Antonio Ruiz
Sworn before me, this 7 day of Nov 1860
T. J. Butler Collector

Mdse. Entered 7 Nov 1860 Ship Entered 7 Nov 1860
Entry of Merchandise imported into the Port of Mobile, District of Mobile, by Barney Rots (?) & Co in the Schr *Harriet Lewis* Master, from Havana

No. of Packages	Contents	Value in Foreign Currency	8	Duties
70 ~~M~~	**Oranges**	$ 280.00		
	Other green fruit	52.50		
		$ 332.50		
	Chg & Com	16.62		
		$ 349.12		
	Rotted	149.00		
Havana		$ ~~269.12~~	240	$ 19.20

1368
Invoice

Captn Estes (?) Schooner *Harriet Lewis*
To M. L. Perry Dbt

70000 oranges	at $ 4.	$ 280.00
150 bananas	at 0.25 ea	37.50
de nose (?) platano	at 2 $	8.00
14 doz pineapples	at 50¢	7.00
Havana 27th Oct (?) 1860		$ 332.50

Rt. Payment MS Perez (?)

1369-1371
Preprinted Customs Form

No. 38
Importer O. Masange & Co
Vessel *Cumberland*
From Liverpool
Entered 28 November 1860
Value $ 3457 Duty $ 802.14

Owner's Oath

A J Mullany (agent)
O Masange & Co (consignee)
Sworn before me, this 28 day of Nov 1860
T. J. Butler Collector

Mdse. Entered 28 Nov 1860 Ship Entered 31 Oct 1860
Entry of Merchandise imported into the Port of Mobile, District of Mobile, by O Mazange & Co in the Ship *Cumberland* Merrill Master, from Liverpool

Marks	No. of Packages	Contents	Value in Foreign Currency						
OM & Co	2 Casks	Saws, Chisels &c	£ 89	14	2				
		Com 2/4/10 Chgs 11/.	2	15	10				
			£ 92	10	0	$ 447.70			
						Percussion Caps	$ 270	15%	$ 40.50
OM & Co/v.	47 pkgs	chains, hoes &c	£ 493	12	9	Tinned Saddlery	36	"	5.40
		percussion caps	53	4	6	Plated "	101	24%	24.24
	(17 Bgs)	nails lbs 1700	50	10	0	Brass mfs not spd	102	"	24.48
		Chgs	9	2	10	Nails	260	"	62.40
		Coms	15	3	3	Iron mfs not spd	2688	"	645.12
			£ 621	13	4		$3457		$802.14
England		Total	£ 714	13	4	$ 3008.87			
						$ 3456.57			

1372
Invoice

Sept. 11, 1860

Birmingham.

Recapitulation of Hardware Shipped on board the *Cumberland* Master from Liverpool bound to Mobile consigned to Mes O. Mazange & Co Merchants these being on their account and risk

OM&Co/V				
Cask 1693	Chain	£ 27	10	6
1696 1667	Hammers	14	7	9
1665	Mills	15	2	1
1675 1677	Saucepans	21	3	6
1679	Hoes	8	2	4
		6	10	6
(etc)	Hooks & Hinges & Hoes	57	10	11
	Chain	2	2	3
	Traces	66	11	6
	Nails	50	10	0
	Traces	7	19	5
	Fry pans	10	12	3
		-	13	6
	Vices	12	2	0
	do	55	14	1
	Sundries	15	10	10
	Rat traps	8	17	6

	Sundries	28	6	0
	do	37	5	8
	do	53	4	5
	do	20	8	4
	do	37	14	1
	do	20	7	9
		£ 597	7	3

1373
Invoice

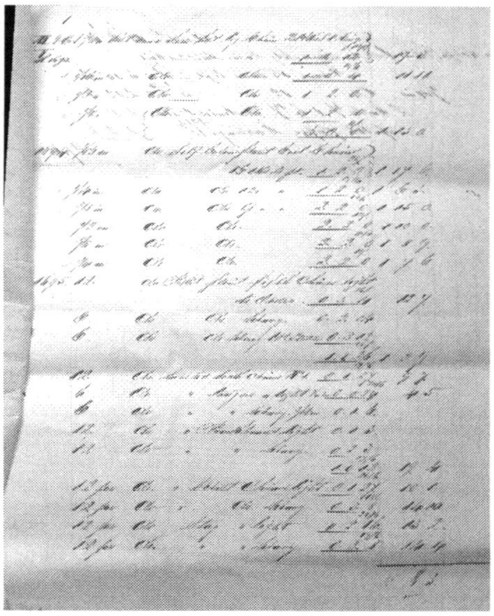

Figure 133. Page two of multi-page invoice for chains.

Summary: Page 2 showing detailed specifications for chains in frame 1370:
log chain 2HKs (hooks?) & 1 Ring – 7/16, ½, 5/8
" Self Colored (?) Strait Coil Chains -- 3/16, 16 lks (links) to ft; ¼, 12 lks to ft. 3/8, 9 lks to ft; ½ , 5/8, ¾
" Brit Strait fifth Chain light to Sides (?)
And 11 other varieties of chains, (writing and abbreviations illegible).

1374a
Invoice

Summary: Three more varieties of chain.

1374b (page 2)

Summary: 140 "Attends" (?) bat (?) face & pane With Steeld Hand Hammers assd (assorted)
41 " Sledge "

3 "Ye old ???" Indian **Cain Mills** wh (with ?) 2 Handles 9.4.0

3	"	"	3.18.0	
3	"	" & Wheels (5)	30. 3.0	
			43. 5.0	
		67½%	29. 3.11	14.1.1
Contg. 10 Wheels				1.1.1
				15.2.1

1375
Invoice

Summary: Two cases, each with Five varieties (sizes ?), 52 quantity, Patent Metal tinned Saucepans & Covers Two varieties (sizes ?), 4 quantity, fall handle Kettles sub totaling 12.15.7

(New case) Eight varieties (sizes ?), 79 quantity, Saucepans & Covers
Two varieties (sizes ?), 5 quantity, fall handle Kettles sub totaling 44.7.8

	55% 24.8.2	19.19.6
3 Cases 8/. Ea Carriage free		1. 4.6
		21.3.6

1376
Invoice

Summary: 5 Doz. J L & Co, Jass & Star hoes (4 varieties or sizes?), £ 8.2.4.

1377
Invoice

Summary: Two casks with Welded black hooks & hinges assd. from 8–30 in., even numbered sizes advances, 147 total. Total cost with casks 6.10.6

50 doz ??? ½ bit Carolina hoes		31. 5. 0	
	47½%	14. 16.10	16. 8. 2
25 doz Cis. Brit back hoes		12. 3. 9	
25 doz " "		12. 16. 3	
25 doz " "		14. 1. 3	39. 1. 2
			£ 57. 10. 14 tot

1378
Invoice

Summary: Best round Stan. Brit Log Chain 2 hooks 1 ring, various sizes; round Self Color Strait link Coil Chain, various sizes; round Brit Strait fifth Chains light to ???; same heavy; same ??? Stretchers (?); same twisted link Chain light; twisted tongue light; same heavy; Backbands (?) light; same heavy; 12 pr. Breast Chains light; same heavy; 12 pr. Stay Chains light; same heavy; 1 cask extra hoop c& lined with pitch paper 18/3; Carriage 1. 8. 6; totaling £ 21. 2. 3.

1379
Invoice

(This page much more readable than those above and so transcribed as example for the set.)

Cask 1713	50 pairs 6½ feet 10 link No 4 best round Iron bright straight Traces wh (with) rings 9/4	1	18	7			
	25 pairs 6½ feet 10 link No 1 " " 1/1 wh hooks	1	7	1			
	25 pairs " " " 2 " " 11¢ " "	1	2	11			
	50 pairs " " " 1 " " 1/1 " Rings	2	14	2			
1714	100 pairs " " " 3 " " 9¾¢ " hooks	4	1	3			
1715	150 pairs " " " 3 " " 9¾¢ " Rings	6	1	11			
" 18	3 Casks Ea 100 pair 6½ ft 10 link 2 " " 11¢ " "	13	15	0			
1719	150 pair 6½ feet 10 link 2 " " 11¢ " hook	6	17	6			
1720	100 pair " " 1 " " 1/1 " "	5	8	4			
" 23	3 Casks Ea 100 pairs 6 ½ ft 10 link No 1 " 1/1 " Rings	16	5	0	59	11	9
	2 Casks lined with pitch paper 9/6						
	1 do 6/6 9/. 4 7/6 3 7/. Carriage 54/3				6	19	9
				£	66	11	6

1380
Invoice

Summary: 16 bags of 100 lbs. each – Griffins 6 lb., 7 lb., 8 lb., and 9 lb. best fine Shouldered Horse nails plus a 100 lb. cask (?) Griffins same 10 lb. – 50 10 0 after 25% discount.

(1.) 25 pr No 1 Griffins 6½ ft 10 link brit Strait traces (with) rings
(2.) 25 pr No 2 " 7 ft 10 link " rings
(3.) 25 pr No 2 " 7 ft 10 link " hooks
(4.) 25 pr No 1 " 7 ft 12 link " hooks
Totaling £ 7 19 5

1381
Invoice

Summary: 18 doz. good quality, short handled **frying pans** in three sizes for £ 10 12 3 after 65% discount

1 Doz. good quality, bright bowled, long handled frying pans for 13/6.

1382
Invoice

Summary: 20 bright, cotter key vices with associated items for £ 12 2 0 after 37½% discount.

1383
Invoice

Summary: Items specified but per item prices dropped from table.

2 doz yds	Iron Jack chain 12		7	6			
	75%		5	7		1	11
2 doz yds	Brass " " 14 and 16	1	10	0			
	67½%	1	1	3		9	9
100 ft	**Iron Wove Web** 18 Mesh 18 in	1	3	6			
200 ft	" " 18 Mesh 24 in	3	2	6			
50 ft	" " 2 Mesh 24 in		10	5			
50 ft	" " 6 Mesh 24 in		7	8			
50 ft	" " 10 Mesh 24 in		7	8			
50 ft	" " 2 Mesh 36 in		15	8			
1 doz	**Corkscrews** 2300 (catalog or model no.?)	1	14	9			
3 doz	" " 9549	1	4	0			
5 gro	C S polished sewing **awls** asod (assorted) large		11	3			
5 gro	" Pol **Pegging**[107] " " "		13	9			
2 doz	Outside plated **Port Brdls** 833		17	0			
3 doz	" " loose ring twisted mouth snaffles	2	17	0	14	5	2
	Case @ 10/6						
	Carriage 3/6					14	0
				£	15	10	10

1384-1385a

[107] Stabbing Awl, Pegging Awl, Sail maker's Awl, or Pricker. The stabbing awl was used to make holes in sails, which were then finished with a grommet, and sometimes in making shoes or boots. It was round or oval.

Invoice

Summary: Items specified but per item prices dropped from this table to facilitate space.

3 doz	spring round jaw **rat traps**	4	19	0			
	72½%	3	11	9	1	7	3
2 doz	Bender traps no teeth	1	14	0			
1 doz	" " "	5	4	3	6	18	3
	Cask & Carriage					12	0
					8	17	6
1 doz	patnd **door springs** 12 16 20 in.	5	3	0			
	82½%	4	4	0		18	0
6	"Chestermans" patent metallic measuring tapes[108] 80 100 ft	6	12	0			
	20%	1	6	5	5	5	7
3 pair	Brass C Sticks 9 in.		10	10½			
2 pair	do 10 in.		4	10			
6 pr	" Chamber Candlesticks	1	13	0			
3 doz	Outside plated 2 ring part bitts lbk (?) curbs		18	5			
1 doz	do 4 ring do	3	12	0			
3 each	66 80 ft brass case folding handle measuring tapes &c	1	7	6			
3 "	50 66 ft leather case do		7	10			
3 "	66 100 ft ass skin do		6	10			
3 doz	Outside plated plain mouth ???		5	7			
6 cases	patd Elastic steel K & B Spence's (?) lock 2 pc latch	1	16	0			
6 cases	plated do 2 pc lock with leathers (?) complete	2	2	0			
	Contd	15	17	11	6	3	7
	Contd	15	17	11	6	3	7
12 cases	Cleated (?) Spurs (?) 10 in. leathers 6 pr	2	8	0			
24 "	tinned Spurs 2 pr	2	17	0	21	2	11
	Cases Carriage					19	6
				£	28	6	0

1385b

Summary: Strong sqr spring bolts var. sizes; brass night locks, brass locks, brass night Battling (?), brit **shoe pincers**, hole (?) chain & crew (?) eyes, brass bolts, hinges, outside plated hinges, patented Basting Spoons (?), (continued)

1386a

[108] James Chesterman invented the spring retractable measuring tape in about 1829. His company was ultimately bought by Stanley.

Invoice

Note: **Gun parts**

Summary: (continued) patd. (patented?) loose ring bradoons,[109] Carpenter's patented lock keys for No. 60 lock, patented staples, sqr. welded head stamp thread brass screws, brown Japd. (japanned – tinned) trunk locks brass bushed, ??? squares marked both sides, 5 gross gun nipples assd., 1 doz. ??? flint gun locks assd., 2½ doz. single cotter gun locks, 1 doz. swivel & cotter skeleton pan flash, 1 doz. finest forward action percussion lock, 6 pair swivel back action steel insides lock, 3 pair forward action insides lock, 3 pr. forward action not steel same, 3 pr. back action same, 6 pr. skeleton pans swivel & cotter flint gun locks assd., 1½ doz. Pr. ??? stirrups.

1386b

Summary: 5 lots totaling 450,000 percussion caps of various kinds, more stirrups, gun parts as above in similar quantities (continued).

1387a
Invoice

(1386b continued) 6 lots, totaling 500 ft. of "iron wove wire" various mesh and widths.

1387b
Invoice

Summary: Brass knobs, 48 pr. various kinds Rogers Warranted flatgoods,[110] one doz. 6 to 12 in. strong sqr. Spring bolts, Van Warts warranted Italy goods, brass night cocks (?), brass lock, shoe pincers. Cont.

1388a
Invoice

Summary: Twelve doz., various sizes, Tinned Mullen bits; 15 gro. iron pressed table spoons, 3 patterns; 6 doz. 3 lb. Japanned Bradoons (bits); 6 doz. 3 lb. plated same; 6 doz. 4 lb. Japanned Mullen bits; 3 doz. tumbler bushed padlocks assd. 12 kinds; 36 lock and master key tumbler bushed padlocks; 1 doz. Carpenters rim lock keys for No 60 locks; 12 doz. iron squares marked both sides; trunk locks; total £ 37.14.0.

1388b
Invoice

[109] A horse's bit: a small snaffle used in double bridles.
[110] A term used to designate woolen or cotton knitted underwear as distinguished from Jersey or ribbed underwear.

Summary: **Rat traps**, 10 pair brass candle sticks, 9 measuring tapes, 6 pair round brass chamber candlesticks, 2 doz. part bitts, 3 doz. snaffle (bits), 5 gro. Sewing awls, 5 gro. pegging awls, 6 cases patd elastic steel B&B **spurs** each 2 prs., 6 cases plated same, 24 cases tinned spurs, 12 cases spurs with leathers, total £ 20.7.9

1389
Preprinted Customs Form

Note: **A ship-load of coffee.** Customs documents sometimes showed monetary exchange rates used as in this case.

Free (of duty)
No. ___
Importer Geo. Westfield & Bro.
Vessel *Zephyr*
From Rio de Janeiro
Entered 8 Nov 1860
Value $ 62,397.32 Duty $ free
62,400

Owner's Oath
G. Westfield
Sworn before me, this 8 day of Nov 1860
T. J. Butler Collector

Free

Mdse. Entered ___ Ship Entered Nov 1860
Entry of Merchandise imported into the Port of Mobile, District of Mobile, by G. Westfield & Bro in the Br Bark *Zephyr* McMurtry Master, from Rio de Janeiro, Brazil

Marks	Nos.	No. of Packages	Contents	Value in Foreign Currency		
			609			
WA 1/28	800	3407 Bags	Coffee Arr 17.035	Ra. 111	296	000
WB 29/44	800		Charges	10	226	160
WC 45/67	800		Comm &c	3	272	040
WD 68/83	1027			Reis 124	794	200
			lbs 551,593			
			at 2000 Reis to the Sp.(anish) Dollar	**is $ 62,397**		

1394
Invoice

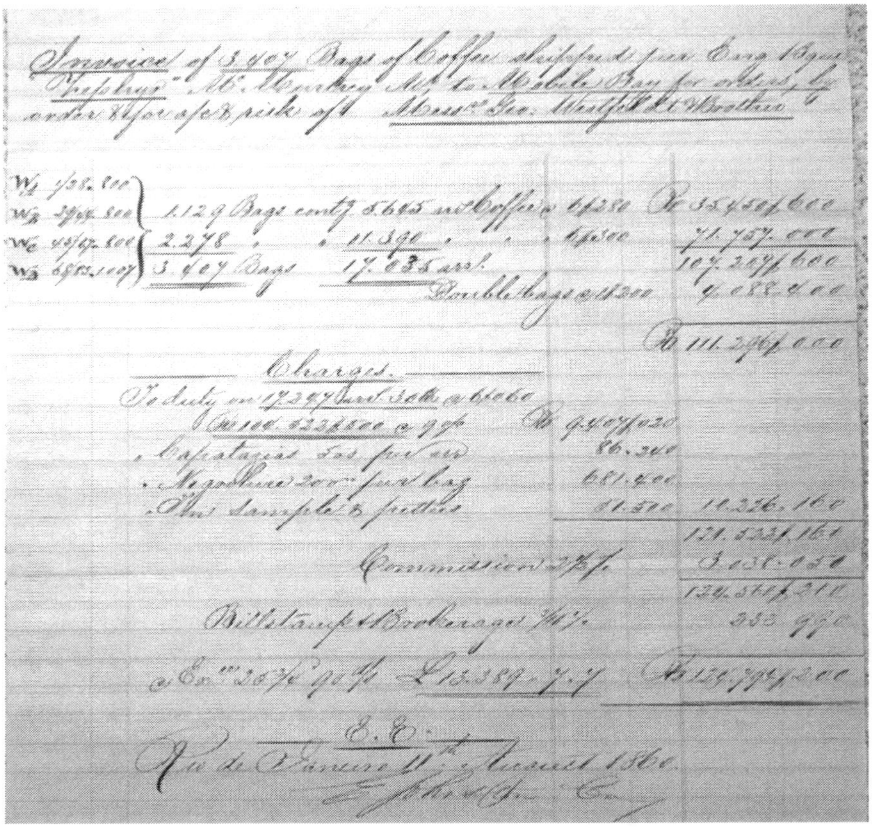

Figure 134. Invoice for ship load of coffee.

Invoice of 3407 Bags of Coffee shipped per Eng Barque *Zephyr* Mc Murtry Mr to Mobile Bay for orders by order & for a/c & risk of Messrs. Geo. Westfield & Brother

WA 1/28 800				
WB 29/44 800	1,129 Bags contg	5,645 arr Coffee @	6?280	~~Rs~~ 35.450$600
WC 45/67 800	2,278 " "	11,390 " "	6?300	71.757.000
WD 68/83 1007	3,407 Bags	17,035 arro		107.204$600
		Double bags @	1?200	4.088.400
				~~Rs~~111.296$000
	Charges			
	To duty on 17.24.7 arro 30 lbs @ 6?060			
	~~Rs~~ 104.522$500 @ 9%		~~Rs~~9.407$020	
	Cafrtazias 5 rs per arr		86.240	
	Negro hire 200 per bag		681.400	
	Tins Sample & petties		51.500	10.226.160
				121.522$160
		Commission 2½%		3.038.050
				124.560$210
	Bill stamp & Brokerage 3/16%			233.990
	@ Exce 25¾ 90% £ 13.389.7.7			~~Rs~~124.794$200
	E. E.			
	Rio de Janeiro 11th August 1860			
	(signed) E Johnston Co			

1393
Consul's Certificate

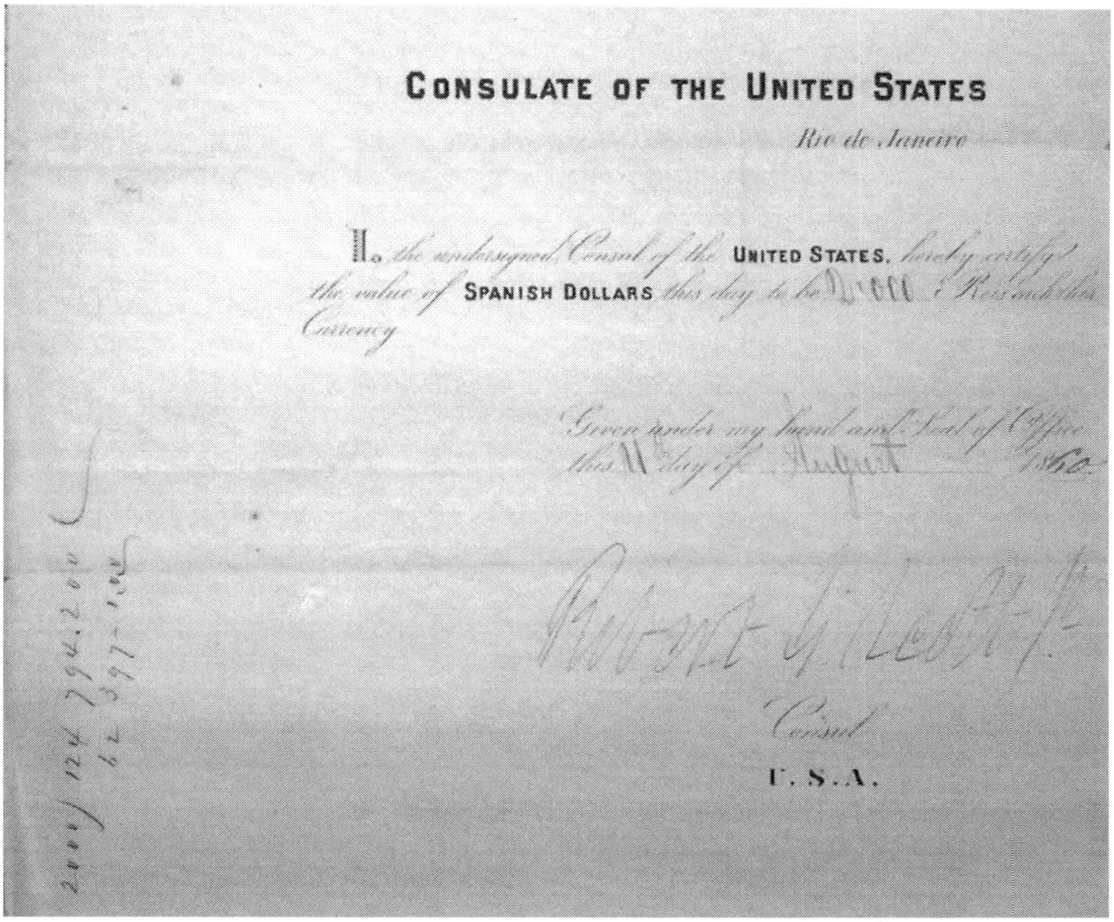
CONSULATE OF THE UNITED STATES
Rio de Janeiro

I, the undersigned Consul of the UNITED STATES, hereby certify the value of SPANISH DOLLARS this day to be 2,000 Reis each this Currency

Given under my hand and Seal of Office this 11 day of August 1860

Robert G. Scott Jr.
Consul
U.S.A.

2000/124 794.200
62 397-100

Figure 135. Simplified version of Consul's certificate form verifying exchange rate.

Consulate of the United States
Rio de Janeiro

I, the undersigned Consul of the United States, hereby certify **the value of Spanish Dollars this day to be <u>2,000</u> Reis each this Currency**

Given under my hand and Seal of Office
this 11th day of August 1860.
(signed) Robert G. Scott Jr.
Consul
U.S.A.

2000/124 794.200
62 397-100

1392
Bill of Lading

Summary: EJ& Co. (ornate initials printed on form). Standard boiler plate bill of lading in good condition, 3,407 bags of **coffee** at five arrobas each (about 25 lbs.), on the *Zephyr* for Mobile Bay, ordered by Geo. Westfeldt Esq. paying freight "as per charter party. (signed) Thomas McMurtry" (the captain signed and acknowledged the number of bags but declined to vouch for the weight).

1395
Preprinted Customs Form

No. 12
Importer Campbell & Co
Vessel *Cumberland*
From L'pool
Entered 1 Nov 1860
Value $ 53 Duty $ 12.72

Agent's Oath
W. Shepherd agent
H. King (owner)
Sworn before me, this __ day of Nov 1860
T. J. Butler Collector

Mdse. Entered 7 Nov 1860 Ship Entered 31 Octr 1860
Entry of Merchandise imported into the Port of Mobile, District of Mobile, by Campbell & Co (a/c H. King) in the Ship *Cumberland* Merrill Master, from Liverpool

Marks	Nos.	No. of Packages	Contents	Value in Foreign Currency			24	Duties
RHH	5	1 Cask	Trace Chain, Iron	£ 10	17	4		
			Chgs		3	8		
				£ 11	1	0	$ 53	$ 12.72
England								

1398
Owner's Oath

Summary: Owner's oath re U.S. Customs (signed) Hezekiah King, sworn 22d Oct 1860. Collector's signature indecipherable, probably in New York.

1399
Invoice

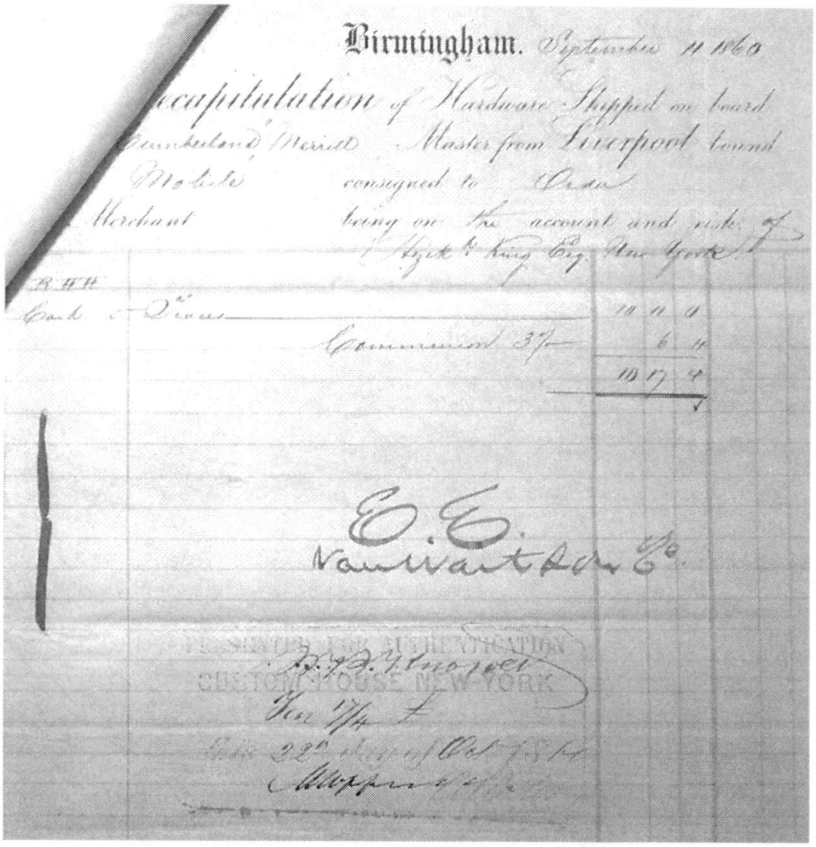

Birmingham. September 11 1860

Recapitulation of Hardware Shipped on board Cumberland Merrill Master from Liverpool bound Mobile consigned to Order Merchant being on the account and risk of Hezek King Esq New York

R H H

Cask 5 Traces — 10 11 0

Commission 3% — 6 4

10 17 4

E. E.

Van Wart Son & Co.

PRESENTED FOR AUTHENTICATION CUSTOM HOUSE NEW-YORK

Figure 136. Invoice for cask of trace chains.

Summary: Birmingham, September 11, 1860. Recapitulation of a one cask, order of traces by Hezek. King, Esq, New York. Purchased from Van Wart Son Co. The commission was 3%. Total £ 10.17.4. This invoice had a stamp at the bottom of the page saying “Presented for authentication, Custom House New York this 22d day of Oct 1860” and over-signed by the Collector.

1400
Bill of Lading

Summary: Bill of lading for one cask of hardware shipped by John Trippett & Brother, at Liverpool, dated in Liverpool 15th Sept 1860 and signed by Capt. Newberry (?) Merrill of the *Cumberland*. The Trippett company seemingly was forwarding agents who took delivery from the seller in Birmingham and saw to getting the cask on board ship bound for Mobile.

1401a (reverse side of 1400 above)

Summary: Short inscription about papers and invoice shipped and signed by J. Tippett and beneath, after arrival in New York, signed by Hezekiah King.

1401b
Invoice

Summary: Detailed invoice describing the hardware – ? pair, ¼ (¼ inch?), best round iron 6½ x 10 x 1 brit. (British) straight traces lbh. (?) rings for £ 10 in a **cask with pitch paper** (better sealed from salt air to protect from rust?) for 11/ and carriage free.

1402
Letter

Note: A duplicate set of papers and invoices sent by post as a letter from the supplier to H. King in New York. Mailing via a different ship, duplicate records was a way of assuring contact with overseas clients.

Figure 137. Letter transmitting duplicate paperwork for hardware order.

Per Steamer *Persia*
Hezekiah King Esq
86 John St
Invs of RHH #5 New York

1403
Invoice

Letterhead:
N.B. – It is particularly requested that
all communications may be addressed
to our agents, Messrs. Irving Van Wart
and Co., 12, Platt Street, New York.

Shrubbery & Lawn Garden Iron Works, Duplicate
Wolverhampton, September 7 1860
Dade Hunxthal (?) Co Mobile
Bot. of G. B. Thorneycroft & Co.

Summary of detailed specifications and prices: Over 77 tons of iron and steel in a variety of forms and sizes at a cost of £ 676.14.3. Kinds included bar, rod, sheet, and plate. Due to heavy usage of symbols and abbreviations it was difficult to understand the details specified.

1404
Invoice (Reverse side 1403)

The annexed ??? forwarded by J. Trippett & Bros. Liverpool pr shipt. To your address by first class vessel on you're a/c and instr.

Summary: Listing of charges for a total invoice of £ 686.7.10.

1405
Preprinted Customs Form

No. 33
Importer Dade Hunxthal & Co
Vessel *Cumberland*
From L'pool
Entered 28 Nov 1860
Value $ 4232 Duty $ 910.83

Owner's Oath
Jno R Ketchum
Sworn before me, this 25 day of Nov 1860
T. J. Butler Collector

Mdse. Entered 28 Nov 1860 Ship Entered Nov 1860
Entry of Merchandise imported into the Port of Mobile, District of Mobile, by Dade Hunxthal & Co in the Ship *Cumberland* Merrill Master, from Liverpool

Marks	No. of Packages	Contents	Quantity	Value in Foreign Currency			12	15	24	Duties
hun	2628	Bars Iron	55.0.3.9	£ 440	6	8	Rod iron	$ 660	24%	$ 158.40
	312 Bales	" Rod	12.0.0.0	134	15	6	Bar iron	2165	24%	519.60
DH&C	88	Sheets	4.19.1.5	47	19	3	Sheet do	260	"	62.40
	5	plates "	5.2.7	2	12	10		237	"	56.88
	200 Bdls	Hoop	5.0.0.0	51	0	0	Cast Steel &c (Bars)	765	12%	91.80
				£ 676	14	3	Other Steel	145	15%	21.75
			Sh Chgs	10	2	2		$ 4232		$ 910.83
			Com	16	14	10				
				£ 703	11	3				
	Less	2½ on	£ 686.16.5	17	3	5				
				£ 686	7	10	$ 3322.12			$ 797.28
DH&Co										
42/48	7 Cases	Cast Steel Bar	2.7.2.22	£ 124	0	2				
58/68	2 Bdls	German " "	1.2.1.20	33	12	10	765			91.80
49/57	9 "	Blister " "	14.1.4	27	1	8				21.75
				£ 184	14	8				
			Cases Carriage & C	7	17	11	$ 765	145	3322	$ 910.83
				£ 192	12	7				
			Less disct	9	4	9				
				183	7	10				
			+ Coms 2½%	4	11	8				
				£ 187	19	6	$ 909.80			
England										

1408
Bill of Lading

Summary: Bill of lading dated 10 Sept 1860 for goods "Shipped in good order and condition by Naylor, Vickers & Co." including 7 Cases and 30 bundles bar steel. Form with boiler plate legal language signed by Newberry Merrill (Capt. of the *Cumberland*) specifying weight unknown. The weights were written on the form as follows:

			Tons	Cwt	Qrs	Lbs
DH &Co	42/48	7 Cases	2	7	2	22
	49/78	30 Bdls	1	16	0	9
			4	3	3	3

1409-1410
Invoice

Figure 138. Invoice for steel on letterhead of Naylor and Vickers.

A beautifully ornate letterhead:

River Don Works, Sheffield. August 28, 1860
Messrs Dade Hamthal of Mobile *Cumberland* to Mobile
Bought of Naylor, Vickers & Co
Manufacturers of all kinds of Steel & Files

Summary: Page 1 of a multi-page invoice containing 4 cases of the total 7 case and 30 bundle order. Square steel bars in sizes from ½–1½ inch, packed about 8 per case (smaller sizes) or about 4 per case (larger sizes). Length not given.

1411
Invoice

Summary: Page two of same invoice with 3 cases and 30 bundles of steel bars of various dimensions. This page had notations of bar lengths including 3 and 6 ft. and another case with "…bars of about the usual length." The cases contained cast steel bars and the bundles were specified as blister steel and German steel. The total cost was £ 183 7 10 after a 5% discount and the shipment was specified "Not Insured."

1412
Bill of Lading

Summary: Bill of lading by John Trippett & Brother, of Liverpool, goods on the *Cumberland*, form dated 8 Sept 1860, ordered by and shipped to Dade & Hunxthall (?) & Co. in Mobile and signed by Newberry Merrill, ship's captain. Shipment consisting of iron in 2628 bars, 31 bdls., 88 sheets, 5 plates, 200 bdls. hoops. And weighing 80.17.2.21.

1414
Preprinted Customs Form

No. 39
Importer J. Gibson & Co
Vessel *Addison*
From New Castle
Entered 1 Oct '60
Value $ 126 Duty $ 18.90

Agent's Oath
Douglas Campbell, agent
J D Spear & Co, owner
Sworn befcre me, this 25 day of Nov 1860
T. J. Butler Collector

Mdse. Entered 1 Nov 1860 Ship Entered 30 Oct 1860
Entry of Merchandise imported into the Port of Mobile, District of Mobile, by John Gibson in the Ship *Addison* Pike Master, from New Castle

No. of Packages	Contents	Value in Foreign Currency						Duties
10 ~~M~~	Fire brick	£ 25	0	0				
	Chgs & Com	1	0	0				
		£ 26	0	0	$ 125.84	$ 126	15%	$ 18.90
England								

1417
Bill of Lading

Summary: Bill of Lading form by Joseph Cowen Esq. in good order aboard the *Addison*, Capt. W. Pike for Mobile (Bay) 10,000 common size fire bricks by order of Mr. J. D. Spear,[111] 12 South Common Street, Mobile, Ala., freight cost 21 shillings/ton of 20 cwt., dated 18th Aug 1860, signed W. L. Pike who noted he was not responsible for breakage. Terms written on blank right half of form: **32 tons of brick** to be discharged (unloaded from the vessel) at the rate of not less than 50 tons/working day or pay $50/day demurrage. Reverse side signed by Isaac Spear.

1419
Consul's Certificate

Summary: Joseph Cowen, Manufacturer and seller's certificate issued by U.S. Consul re a cargo of fire bricks, 25 pounds (Sterling) consigned to Messrs. Mead & Bell in Mobile. Signed by Jos. Cowen and Robert Plummer J.P. "I, Herbert Davy, Vice-Consul of the United States of America at Newcastle-upon-Tyne, do certify and make known to whom these presents shall come, that Robert Plummer Esqr before whom the foregoing affidavit of Joseph Cowen hath been made, is a Justice of the Peace, duly authorized to administer Oaths and Affirmations; that I believe the deponent is worthy of credit, and qualified to verify the annexed Invoice." Dated 1st Sept 1860.

1420
Consul's Certificate

(page 2 of 1419)

Blaisdon Brun (?)
Newcastle on Tyne
August 24th 1860

Invoice of Fire Bricks shipped Pr *Adison* Capt for Mobile and
No 236 Consulate of the United States,
Newcastle-on-Tyne, 1st Sept 1860

Mr. J. Cowen Dr.
To / Certificate to Deposition to invoice $ 2
Received the above, Herbert Davy

1421
Invoice

Blaisdon Brun (?)
Newcastle on Tyne
August 24th 1860

---

[111] J. D. Spear & Co. was a large Mobile foundry.

Invoice of Fire Bricks shipped Pr *Adison* Capt. for Mobile and consigned to Mess. Mead & Bell, Cliff Street New York for a/c of Jos. Cowen & Co.

		£	s	d
COWEN	10,000 Com.(Common) Size **Fire Bricks** @50/	25	0	0
	(signed) Jos. Cowen			

1422-1424
Preprinted Customs Form

No. 3
Importer H. O. Brewer & Co
Vessel *Wm Woodberry*
From L'pool
Entered 7 Nov 1860
Value $ 1238 Duty $ 185.70

Agent's Oath
T. K. Emanuel, agent
Dean Bros., owner
Sworn before me, this 7 day of Nov 1860
T. J. Butler Collector

Mdse. Entered 7 Nov 1860 Ship Entered 30 Octr 1860
Entry of Merchandise imported into the Port of Mobile, District of Mobile, by H O Brewer & Co in the Ship *Wm Woodberry* M Lelland Master, from Liverpool

No. of Packages	Contents	Quantity	Value in Foreign Currency			15	24	Duties
3045 Sacks	Com(mon) **Salt** & Sacks ?/6	304½	£ 184	12	1			
	Charges	304.10.0.0	69	3	3			
	Com		6	6	10			
			£ 260	2	2	$ 1259	15%	$ 188.85
3045 @	214 651.630.	290.18.0.14						
	Less	13.11.3.14	4	8	2	21		3.15
		304.10.0.0	£ 255	14	0	$ 1238		$ 185.70
England	11636 Bushels							

1425
Consul's Certificate
161
I, the undersigned Consul of the United States of America, for the Port of Liverpool and its dependencies, do certify and make known to whom these presents shall come, that

Henry Wilding

Before whom the annexed affidavit of Edward Lloyd Hath been made is Vice Consul duly authorized to administer Oaths and Affirmations; that the deponent is in my opinion worthy of credit and qualified to verify the annexed Invoice; and that the said affidavit was administered in the presence of E. A. Turner

Given from under my Hand and Seal of Office at Liverpool,
the 27th day of August
and year one thousand eight hundred and sixty
(signed) Beverley Tucker
(signed) Bn H Wilding
Vice Consul

1426
Consul's Certificate

Summary: Oath of owner of goods shipped on *William Woodberry*. This was a U.S. Consul's form, verifying the invoice for £ 260 2 2. The owner was Edward Lloyd of Liverpool, manager at Liverpool of Dean Brothers.

1427
Invoice

Note: 200 lbs. per sack @ 2000 lb/ton.

Invoice of 304½ Tons Common White Salt in 3045 Half bleached sacks shipped by Dean Brothers on board the *Willm. Woodberry* McLelland, Master for Mobile & consd. to Messrs. Meeker, Knoac (?) & Co. for sale.

304½ Tons Common White Salt	@ 6/8				98	19	3
3045 Half bleached sacks	" 6¾				85	12	10
					184	12	1
Charges							
River freight on 304½ Tons	@ 3/0	45	13	6			
Filling sacks at works 3035	" 5/0	7	12	3			
Dock & Town Dues	" 2/4	9	4	0			
25 Dozen Petersburgh Mats	" 4/6	5	12	6			
Certificate 11/6 B/Lading	2/0		13	6			
Entry 1/6 Cartage	6/0		7	6	69	3	3
Commission @ 2½% on		£ 253	15	4	253	15	4
					6	6	10
E&OE					£ 260	2	2
Liverpool 25th August 1860							
pprp. (?) Dean Brothers							
(signed) Edw Lloyd							

1430
Bill of Lading

Summary: Bill of Lading by Taylor, Tipper, & Co. signed by ship's captain, S. B. McLellan on 27th Aug 1860, and with an interesting note, "half profit (on sale of goods) if any for freight."

1432-1434
Preprinted Customs Form

No. 2
Importer P. C. Merryman
Vessel *Enoch Talbot*
From Liverpool
Entered 1 Nov 1860
Value $ 1498 Duty $ 224.70

Agent's Oath
P. C. Merryman, agent
Warren & Thayer, owners
Sworn before me, this __ day of Nov 1860
T. J. Butler Collector

Mdse. Entered Nov 1 1860 Ship Entered 29 Octr 1860
Entry of Merchandise imported into the Port of Mobile, District of Mobile, by P. C. Merryman in the Ship *Enoch Talbot* Merryman Master, from Liverpool

No. of Packages	Contents	Quantity	Value in Foreign Currency			15	Duties
3585 Sacks	Salt & sacks abt 6 ???	Tons 358½	£ 217	6	10	3560 – 214--	761,840 (lbs?)
	Less		5	8	8		
			£ 211	18	2	340.2.0.16	
	Charges & Comm		88	9	10	358.10.0.0	
			£ 292	18	0	Less 18.7.3.12	
	add Dist. Disallowed	£ 5. 8. 8					
	putting on board 5/- per 100	8. 19. 3				13604 16/56 Bushels	
	& Com	7.2	14	15	1		
			£ 307	13	1		
	Com on £ 292. 18. 0		7	6	5		
			£ 314	19	6	$ 1524.48	
	Delay (?)		5	11	4	26.92	
			£ 309	8	2	$ 1497.56	
England						$ 1498 @ 15%	$ 224.70

1435
Invoice

Invoice of Common Salt shipped by Warren & Thayer p. ship *Enock Talbot*, P.C. Merryman, Master, for Mobile, consigned to Capt. P. C. Merryman for sale and returns, for account and risk of Warren & Thayer.

358½ Tons	Common Salt	@ 6/6				116	10	3
	3585 Sacks	@ 6¾ d (?)				100	16	7
						217	6	10
		Less 2½%				5	8	8
						211	18	2
	Charges							
	Dock & Town dues & export duty		10	18	2			
	River freight		53	15	6			
	Bagging & filling		8	1	4			
	40 Doz. Mats @ 3/9		7	10	0			
	Cartage of Sacks			12	4			
	Insurance on £ 350 @ 40/- % & policy		7	10	0			
	Bills of Lading			2	6	88	9	10
						£ 300	8	0
	Coms 2% 1/6							
	E.E.							
	Liverpool, 24 Augt. 1860							
	Warren &Thayer							

1436
Bill of Lading

Summary: Bill of Lading by Warren & Thayer form signed by ship's Captain, P. C. Merryman on 24 Aug 1860, specifying the exchange rate of $4.80 per Pound Sterling, and Capt. Merryman paying freight at the rate of half the profits.

1437-1439
Preprinted Customs Form

No. __
Importer Jones & Watts
Vessel *Cumberland*
From L'pool
Entered 1 Nov 1860
Value $ 844 Duty $ 202.56

Agent's Oath
Js. Shepherd, agent

Jones & Watts, owner
Sworn before me, this __ day of Nov 1860
T. J. Butler Collector

Mdse. Entered 1 Nov 1860 Ship Entered 31 Oct 1860
Entry of Merchandise imported into the Port of Mobile, District of Mobile, by H O Brewer & Co in the Ship *Cumberland* Merrill Master, from Liverpool

Marks	No. of Packages	Contents	Value in Foreign Currency			15	24	Duties
J&W	28/38 11 Casks	Hardware Chgs & Com	£ 174	8	5	$ 844.20	844	$ 202.56
England								

1440
Invoice

Summary: First page of Van Wart Son & Co. recapitulation of a packet of papers and invoices dated Sept. 3, 1860 regarding a shipment of hardware in eleven casks, hoes were the specified items, total £ 174.8.5. An order for Jones & Watts firm of Selma, Alabama.

1441
Invoice

Summary: Invoice and specs for Casks 28–32, 130 dozen of "Perk's Polished Planters Hoes," stamped and labeled to order, cost total £ 94.2.6; Casks 33–34, 50 dozen No. 2 and No. 3 "Cluells" (?) Oval Eye half brit planters hoes, totaling £ 30.10.3.

1442
Invoice

J&W/V							
Cask 35	10 doz.	000x00	7½ in Ericson Oval Eye ½ brit hoes No 38535	7/0	3	10	0
	15 doz.	00x0	do. 8 in	7/6	5	12	6
	10 doz.	0x1	do. 8½	8/3	4	2	6
" 36	10 doz.	000x00	7½ in Oval brit back do 38554	9/0	4	10	0
	15 doz.	00x0	8 in do "	9/2	7	6	3
	10 doz.	0x1	8½ in do "	10/6	5	5	0
" 37	25 doz.		"Powel's" iron Hoes 00 No 124 E	4/4	5	8	4
" 38	25 doz.		do 0 "	4/10	6	0	10

			2 Casks 7/6.1 Ea 6/6 7/0 Carriage free		1	8	6
				£	43	3	11

1443
Bill of Lading

Summary: Bill of lading of shipment of hardware by George Wright & Co. of Liverpool to Mess. Campbell & Co. a/c Mess Jones & Watts of Selma who pay 5% primage (£ 4.4.2) and Average accustomed, delivered at the wharf in Mobile. Signed by Newberry Merrill who noted "Contents Unknown" probably meaning that he did not personally verify or inspect the casks' contents.

1448
Preprinted Customs Form

No. 37
Importer W H Ketchum
Vessel *Minnesota*
From Liverpool
Entered 30 Nov 1860
Value $ 1157 Duty $ 276.24

Owner's Oath
W H Ketchum, owner
Sworn before me, this 30 day of Nov 1860
T. J. Butler Collector

Mdse. Entered 30 Nov 1860 Ship Entered 30 Octr 1860
Entry of Merchandise imported into the Port of Mobile, District of Mobile, by W H Ketchum in the Ship *Minnesota* Deshon Master, from Liverpool

Marks	No. of Packages	Contents	Value in Foreign Currency			15	24	Duties
MRT	4 bales	**Carpets**	Fr 6,035.70					
		Coms 2½%	150.89					
			Fr 6,186.59				$ 1,151	$ 276.24
France	HLC							

1451-1452
Delivery Instructions

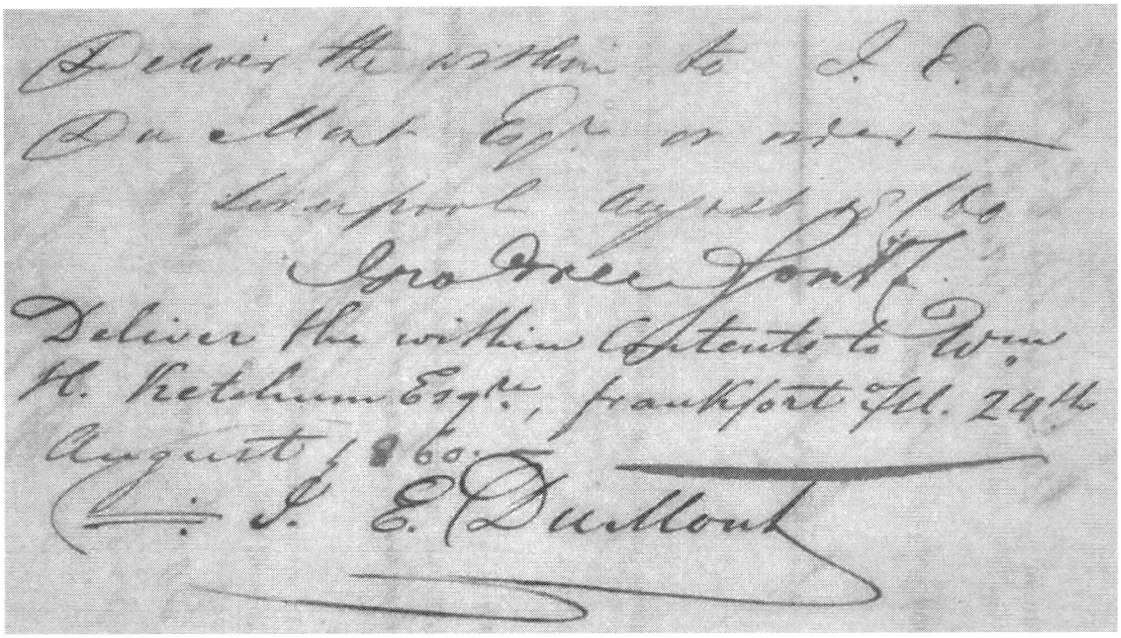

Figure 139. Delivery instructions for cargo of carpets.

Deliver the within to J. E. Du Mont Esqr as order –
Liverpool August 18/60
Geo Green Son & Co.
Deliver the within Contents to Wm H Ketchum Esqre., Frankfort Jul. 24th
August 1860.
(signed) J. E. Ducllout (?)

1452
Bill of Lading

Summary: Bill of lading of four bales of carpets on board the *Minnesota* at the rate of 30 shillings per ton and 5% primage payable in Mobile, signed by the captain, F. B. Deshon who also noted Contents Unknown.

1453
Invoice

Note: Document in French provided great detail describing carpets. Perhaps the buyer in Mobile specified the design details desired.

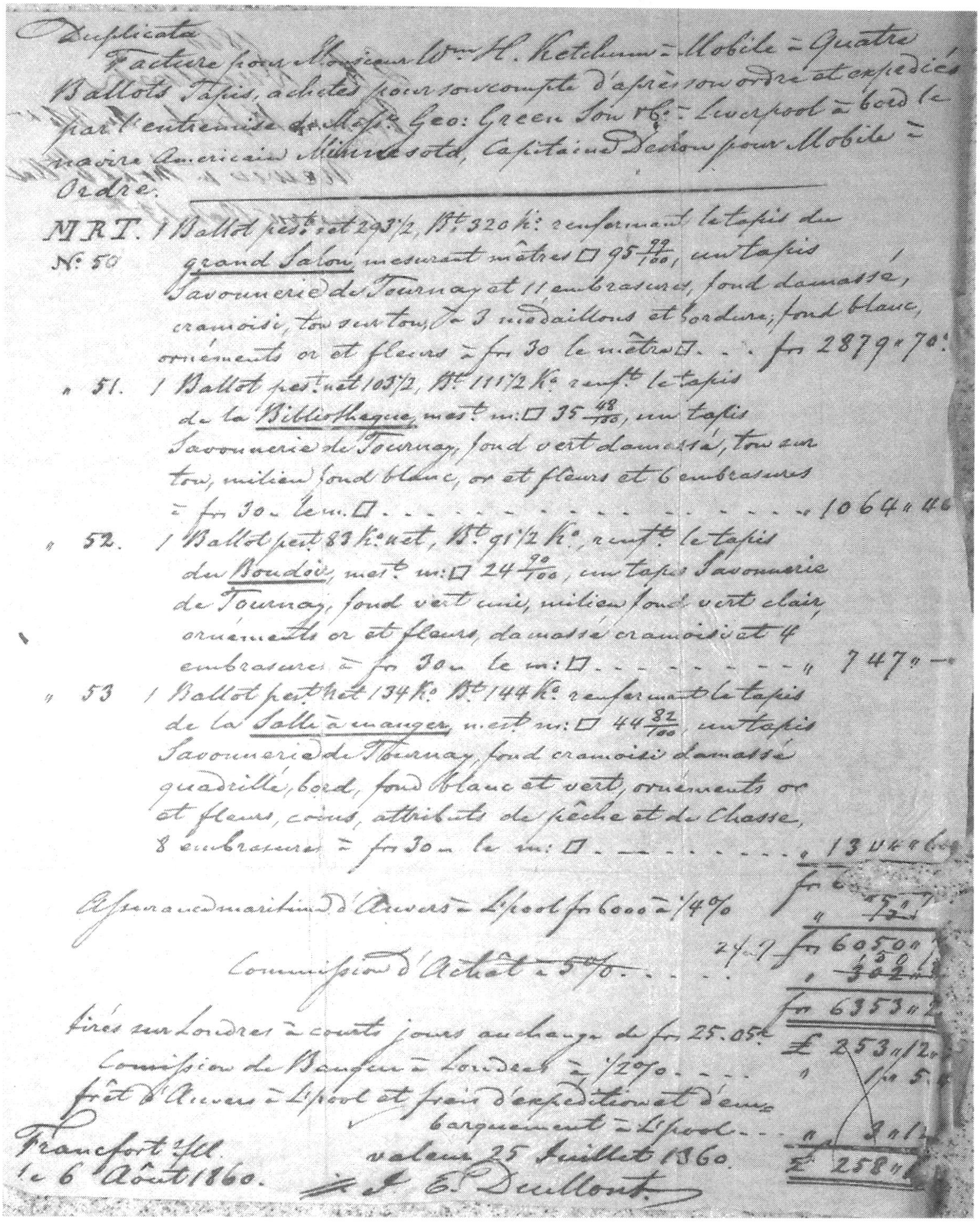
Duplicata
Facture pour Monsieur Wm H. Ketchum à Mobile = Quatre Ballots Tapis, achetés pour son compte d'après son ordre et expédiés par l'entremise de Mess. Geo: Green Son & Co. Liverpool à bord le navire Americain Minnesota, Capitaine Dedow pour Mobile = Ordre.

MRT. N: 50 — 1 Ballot pes. net 293/2, Bt 320 k: renfermant le tapis du grand Salon mesurant mètres □ 95 99/100, un tapis Savonnerie de Tournay et 11 embrasures, fond damassé, cramoisi, ton sur ton, à 3 médaillons et bordure; fond blanc, ornements or et fleurs à frs 30 le mètre □ . . . frs 2879 " 70

" 51. 1 Ballot pes. net 103/2, Bt 111/2 K. renft le tapis de la Bibliothèque, mes. m: □ 35 48/100, un tapis Savonnerie de Tournay, fond vert damassé, ton sur ton, milieu fond blanc, or et fleurs et 6 embrasures à frs 30 le m. □ . . . . . " 1064 " 40

" 52. 1 Ballot pes. 83 k: net, Bt 91/2 K., renft le tapis du Boudoir, mes. m: □ 24 90/100, un tapis Savonnerie de Tournay, fond vert uni, milieu fond vert clair, ornements or et fleurs, damassé cramoisi et 4 embrasures à frs 30 le m: □ . . . . " 747 " —

" 53 1 Ballot pes. net 134 K. Bt 144 K. renfermant le tapis de la Salle à manger, mes. m: □ 44 82/100, un tapis Savonnerie de Tournay, fond cramoisi damassé quadrillé, bord, fond blanc et vert, ornements or et fleurs, coins, attributs de pêche et de chasse, 8 embrasures à frs 30 le m: □ . . . . " 1344 " 60

frs 6[illegible]

Assurance maritime d'Anvers à L'pool frs 6000 à 1/4% . . . " 15 "

frs 6050 "

Commission d'Achat à 5% . . . . 24.7 . . . " 302 "

frs 6353 "

tirés sur Londres à courts jours au change de frs 25.05 . . . £ 253 " 12 "

Commission de Banquier à Londres à 1/2% . . . " [illegible] 5 [illegible]

frêt d'Anvers à L'pool et frais d'expédition et d'embarquement à L'pool . . . " 3 " [illegible]

valeur 25 Juillet 1860. £ 258 " [illegible]

Francfort s/M. le 6 Août 1860.

p.p. J. E. Dullont

Figure 140. Invoice for shipment of carpets.

Summary: An invoice showing details of 4 bales of carpets for a cost of about £ 258 being shipped from Tornay, Belgium where they were made, to Antwerp (?) to London to Liverpool to Mobile. Notations added at the bottom indicated part of the transaction involved banking in Frankfurt, an interesting trail of international trade and banking. Described at length in French:

Bale No. 50 – Carpet, "Savonnerie de Tournay"[112] for "grand Salon," 95 99/100 square meters, Fr 2879.
Bale No. 51 – Carpet for "Bibliotheque," 35 48/100 square meters, Fr 1064.
Bale No. 52 – Carpet for "Boudoir," 24 90/100 square meters, Fr 747.
Bale No. 53 – Carpet for "Salle a manger," 44 82/100 square meters, Fr 1344.

(The following translation of the invoice provided by the late Dr. Lee Johnson, Austin, Texas.)

Duplicate
Note/document for Mr. Wm. H. Ketchum – Mobile – Four bundles of carpets bought for (this) account as per his order through the good offices of M. Geo. Green, Liverpool; (these goods) are aboard the American ship *Minnesota* – Captain Deslou – (destination) Mobile.

Order
MRT 50. 1 bundle net weight 293½: British 320 K with carpet for **Grand Drawing-Room** measuring 95.99 sq. meters: Savonnerie-style Tournai (Belg.) rug (having) 11 edge-binding hoops, damask background/foundation colored 'crimson-flush' (as well as) blue, (with) golden ornamentation and flowers. At 30 Francs per square meter = Fr. 2879.70

51. 1 bundle net weight 105½: British 111½ K (containing) **Library** rug measuring 35.48 sq. meters: Savonnerie-style Tournai (Belg.) rug with green background and white middle, gold decorations (with) flowers and an edge-binding of 6 hoops.
At 30 Francs per square meter = Fr. 1064.46

52. 1 bundle weighing 82 K net, British 91½ K (labeled) **Bedroom** carpet measuring 24.90 square meters: Savonnerie-style rug (made in) Tournai (Belg.), green and light-green background, gold ornamentation and flowers, crimson-flush damask with 4-hoop edge-binding.
At 30 Francs per square meter .... Fr. 747.00

53. 1 bundle net weight 134 K: British 144 K, described as **Dining Room** carper measuring 44.82 square meters: Savonnerie-style from Tournai (Belg.), crimson-flush background ruled in squares, edged, blue and green background, gold ornamentation plus flowers, small patches of cloth, symbols of fish and the hunt, 8-hoop edge binding.
At 30 Franks per square meter .... Fr. 1344.60

Maritime Insurance, from Anvers (Antwerp) to Liverpool for 6000 at ¼% (subt) Fr. 6050. ??

Commission for Making Purchases at 5% (subt) Fr. 6353.??

(Passage with banking jargon, translation unclear.) ??? in London, short-rated when changing to Francs (?) at 25.05 (per £) (subt) £ 252.12.?

---

[112] The Savonnerie manufactory was the most prestigious European manufactory of knotted-pile carpets, enjoying its greatest period ca. 1650–1685; the cachet of its name was casually applied to many knotted-pile carpets made elsewhere. Until 1768, the products of the manufactory remained exclusively the property of the Crown, and Savonnerie carpets were among the grandest of French diplomatic gifts.

The carpets were made of wool with some silk in the small details, knotted using the Ghiordes knot, at about ninety knots to the square inch. Some early carpets broadly imitated Persian models, but the Savonnerie style soon settled into more purely French designs, pictorial or armorial framed medallions, densely-massed flowers in bouquets or leafy rinceaux against deep blue, black or deep brown grounds, within multiple borders.

Banking Commission at London at ½%   £ 1.5.4

For Freight from Anvers (Antwerp) to Liverpool and for expediting an embarkation at Liverpool   £ 3.12.?

value, 25 July 1860   (tot) £ 258.??.??

Frankfort ???
6th of August 1860

1454-1456
Preprinted Customs Form

No. 23
Importer M. Carmelich
Vessel *Cumberland*
From L'pool
Entered Octr 1860
Value $ 233   Duty $ 55.92

Agent's Oath
W ???, agent
M. Carmelich, owner
(signed) C. G. ???
Sworn before me, this __ day of Nov 1860
T. J. Butler Collector

Mdse. Entered 6 Nov 1860   Ship Entered 31 Octr 1860
Entry of Merchandise imported into the Port of Mobile, District of Mobile, by M. Carmelich in the Ship *Cumberland*   Merrill Master, from Liverpool

Marks	No. of Packages	Contents	Value in Foreign Currency			24	Duties
CC	10 Hhd (hogshead)[113]	porter[114]	£ 45				
		Charges & Com	3	2	4		
England			£ 48	2	4	$ 233	$ 55.92

1457
Consul's Certificate fronted the glued together set of Cargo Papers

113 A hogshead of beer or ale was 54 gallons (250 L if old beer/ale gallons, 245 L if imperial).
114 Heavy, dark-brown ale made with malt browned by drying at a high temperature.

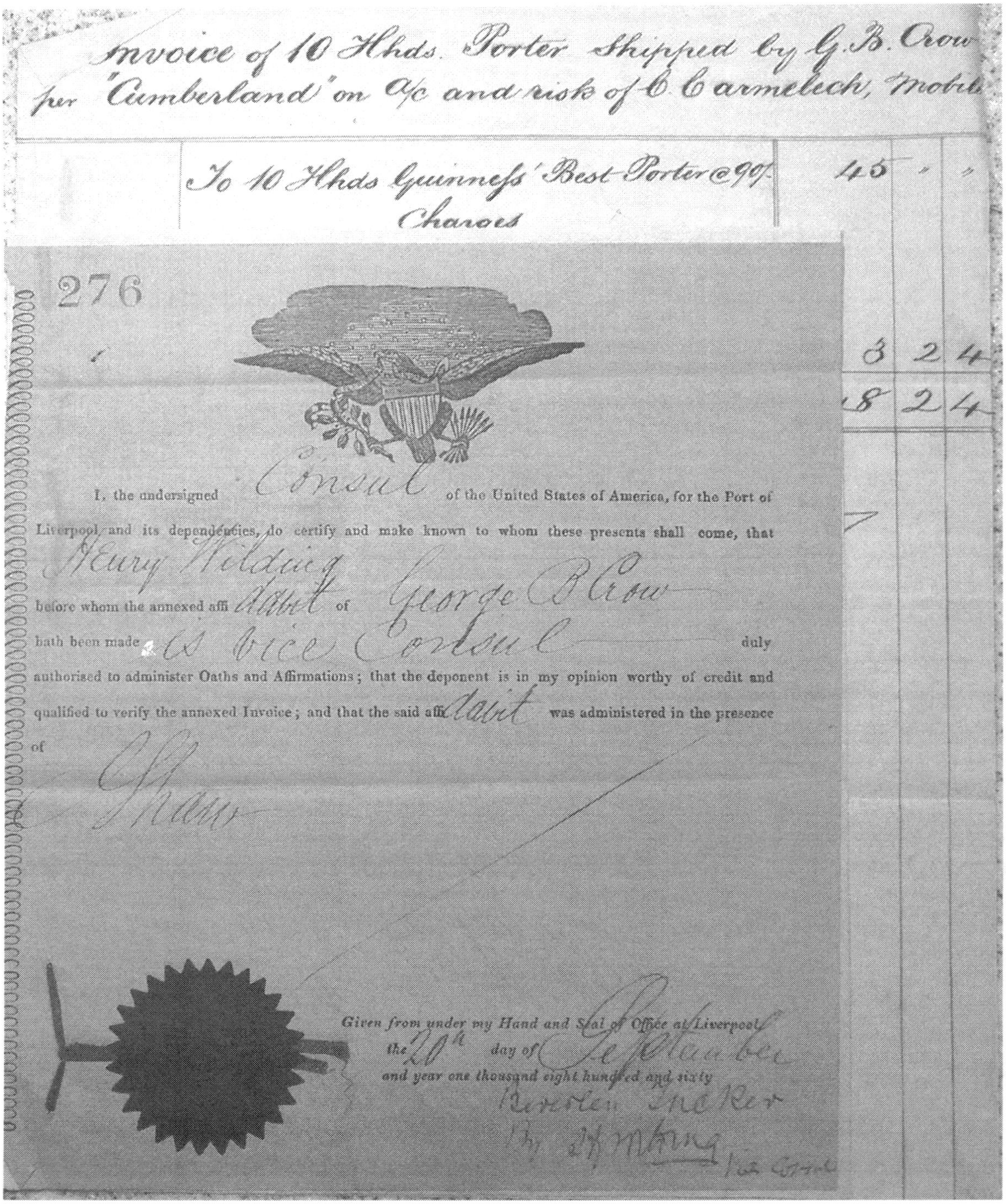

Invoice of 10 Hhds. Porter Shipped by G. B. Crow per "Cumberland" on A/c and risk of C. Carmelich, Mobile

To 10 Hhds Guinness' Best Porter @ 90/- 45 " "
Charges

3 2 4
8 2 4

276

I, the undersigned Consul of the United States of America, for the Port of Liverpool and its dependencies, do certify and make known to whom these presents shall come, that Henry Wilding before whom the annexed affidavit of George B Crow hath been made as Vice Consul duly authorised to administer Oaths and Affirmations; that the deponent is in my opinion worthy of credit and qualified to verify the annexed Invoice; and that the said affidavit was administered in the presence of C Shaw

Given from under my Hand and Seal of Office at Liverpool the 20th day of September and year one thousand eight hundred and sixty

Beverley Tucker
By [illegible]
Vice Consul

Figure 141. Consul's certificate for cargo of porter.

Summary: U.S. Consul's certificate and supporting documents attesting to the shipment, signed 20 Sept 1860 by Beverley Tucker.

1458
Consul's Certificate

Summary: Second page of consul's certificate containing the oath of the shipping merchant, George B. Crow, concerning the value of the cargo, £ 48.2.4.

1459
Invoice

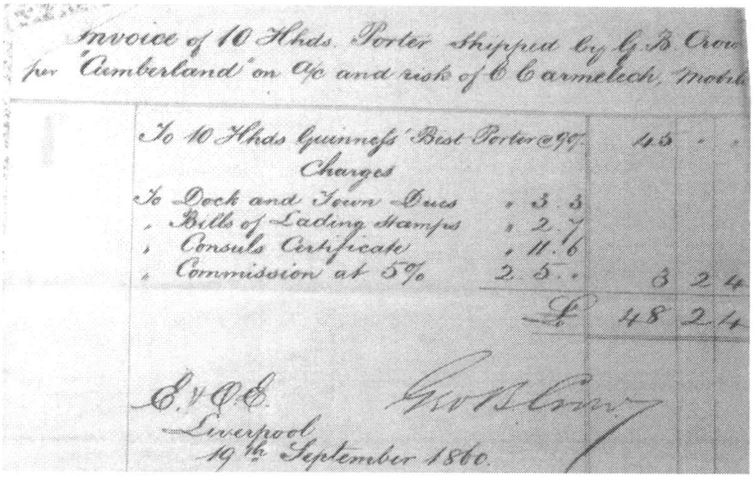

Invoice of 10 Hhds. Porter Shipped by G. B. Crow per "Cumberland" on a/c and risk of C Carmelich, Mobile

To 10 Hhds Guinness' Best Porter @ 90/			45	.	.
Charges					
To Dock and Town Dues	. 3	. 3			
" Bills of Lading Stamps	. 2	. 7			
" Consuls Certificate	. 11	. 6			
" Commission at 5%	2. 5	. .	3	2	4
£			48	2	4

E&OE Geo B Crow
Liverpool
19th September 1860.

Figure 142. Invoice for 10 hogsheads of porter.

Invoice of 10 Hhds (hogsheads) Porter Shipped by G. B. Crow per *Cumberland* on a/c and risk of C. Carmelich, Mobile.

To 10 Hhds **Guinness'** Best Porter @ 90/0				45	0	0
Charges						
To dock and Town Dues		3	3			
" Bills of Lading Stamps		2	7			
" Consuls Certificate		11	6			
" Commission at 5%	2	5	0	3	2	4
				£ 48	2	4
E.&O.E. (signed) Geo B. Crow						
Liverpool						
19th September 1860						

1460-1462
Preprinted Customs Form

No. 15
Importer J. C. Gwin
Vessel *Cumberland*
From L'pool
Entered 1 Nov '60

Value $ 945 Duty $ 226.80

Owner's Oath
W ???, agent
J. C. Gwin & Co, owner
(signed) J. C. Gwin
Sworn before me, this 1 day of Nov 1860
T. J. Butler Collector

Mdse. Entered 1 Nov 1860 Ship Entered 31 Octr 1860
Entry of Merchandise imported into the Port of Mobile, District of Mobile, by J. C. Gwin & Co in the Ship *Cumberland* Merrill Master, from Liverpool

No. of Packages	Contents	Value in Foreign Currency			24	Duties
90 Bdls	Sheet iron 5.11.1.25	52	11	0		
600 do	Hoop do 15.0.0.0	135	5	0		
	20.11.1.25	£ 187	16	0		
	Com	4	12	11		
		£ 192	9	11		
	Sh. Chg	2	14	9		
		£ 195	4	8	$ 945	$ 226.80
	Sheet iron				$ 336	$ 87.84
	Hoops				579	138.96
					$ 945	$ 226.80
England						

1463
Bill of Lading

Figure 143. Decorative illustrations on a bill of lading form.

Summary: Bill of lading from seller Joshua Scholefield & Sons, Birmingham, for the cargo of iron shipped to J. C. Gwin & Co, Mobile and dated 14 Sept 1860 in Liverpool.

1465
Invoice

Summary: Invoice with details of sizes and weights of Staffordshire sheet iron and "Elephant" hoop iron. The hoop iron ranged in sizes from ¾ in. to 1½ in. wide in 1/8th in. progression. The sheets of iron were all 6.0 x 26. ranging from 12 G to 24. (Possibly 6 ft. x 26 inches; G may designate a thickness grade.)

1466
Invoice

Summary: Invoice form specifying shipping charges by Joshua Scholefield & Sons to J. C. Gwin & Co. for the cargo of 20½ tons of iron sheets and hoops.

1468
Bill of Lading sent by Letter

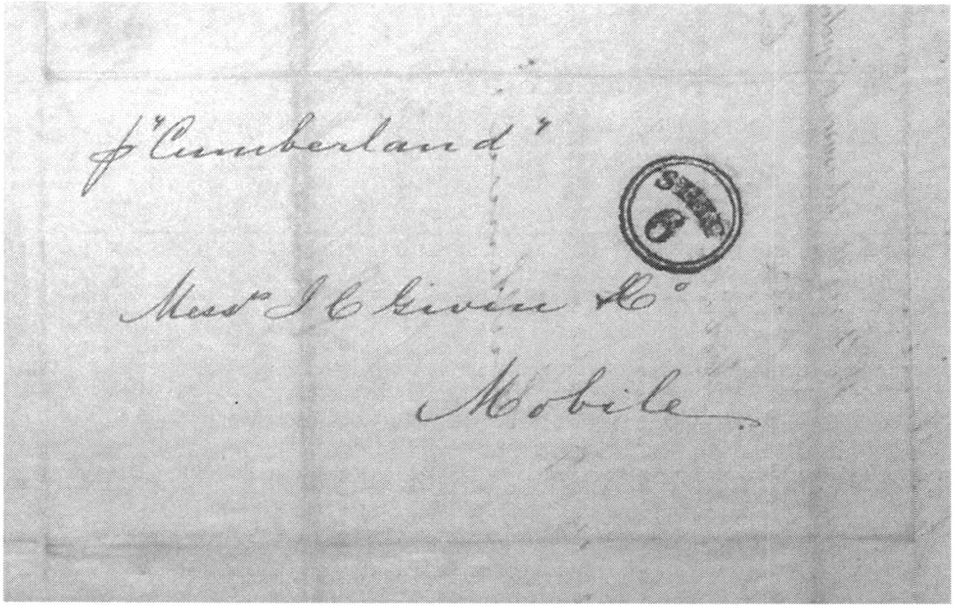

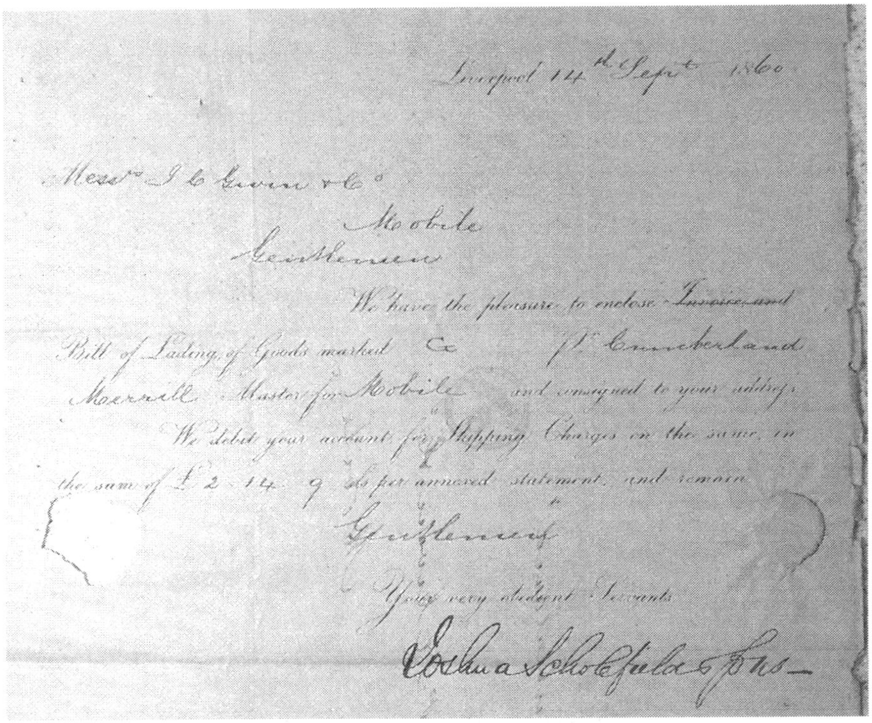
Liverpool 14th Sept 1860

Messrs J C Gwin & Co
Mobile
Gentlemen
We have the pleasure to enclose ~~Invoices and~~ Bill of Lading of Goods marked G pr. Cumberland Merrill Master for Mobile and consigned to your address.
We debit your account for Shipping Charges on the same, in the sum of £ 2.14.9 as per annexed statement, and remain
Gentlemen
Your very obedient Servants
Joshua Scholefield & Sons

Figure 144. Cover letter transmitting bill of lading.

Liverpool 14th Sept 1860

Messrs J C Gwin & Co

Mobile

Gentlemen

We have the pleasure to enclose ~~Invoices and~~ Bill of Lading of Goods marked G pr. *Cumberland* Merrill Master for Mobile and consigned to your address.

We debit your account for Shipping Charges on the same, in the sum of £ 2.14.9 as per annexed statement, and remain,

Gentlemen

Your very obedient Servants,

Joshua Scholefield & Sons

1469

Bill of Lading

Summary: Bill of lading by John Trippett & Brother of Liverpool for two casks of hardware shipped to O. Mazange & Co. in Mobile dated 15 Sept 1860.

1470
Invoice

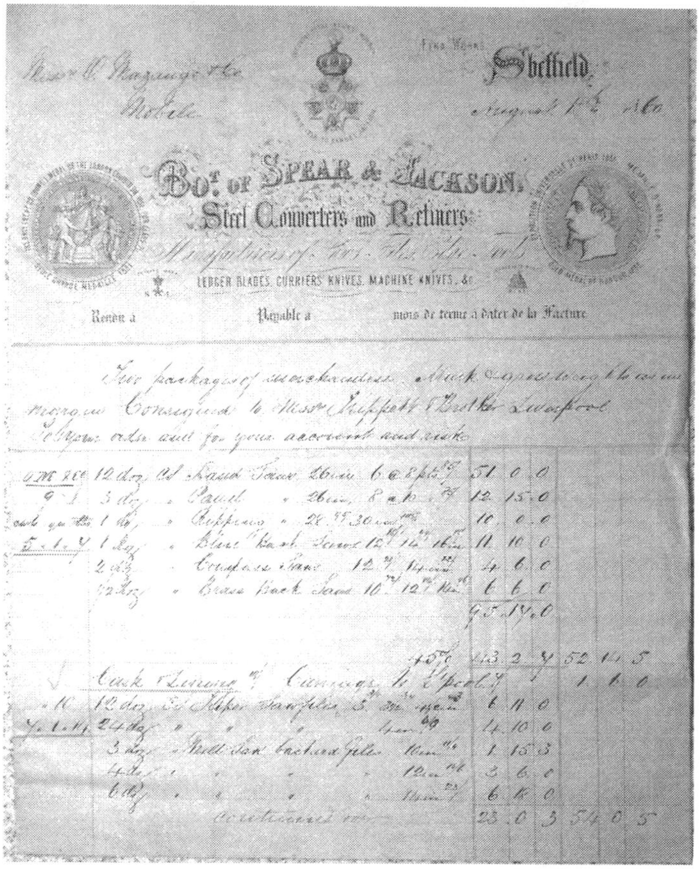

Etna Works, Sheffield.

Messrs O. Mazange & Co
Mobile

August 1[illegible] 1860

Bo^t. of Spear & Jackson,
Steel Converters and Refiners,
Manufacturers of Saws, Files, Edge Tools,
Ledger Blades, Curriers' Knives, Machine Knives, &c.

S. J.

Rendu à Payable à mois de terme à dater de la Facture.

Two packages of merchandise [illegible] Consigned to Messrs [illegible] & Brother Liverpool
To your order and for your account and risk

O M & Co	12 doz. C.S. Hand Saws 26 in. 6 @ 8 pts.	51	0	0		
	3 doz. " Panel " 26 in. 8 a 10	12	15	0		
	1 do. " Ripping " 28 & 30 in.	10	0	0		
	1 doz. " Blue Back Saws 12, 14, 16 in.	11	10	0		
	2 doz. " Compass Saws 12, 14 in.	4	6	0		
	½ doz. " Brass Back Saws 10, 12, 14 in.	6	6	0		
		95	17	0		
	45%	43	2	7	52	14	5
	Cask & Lining & Carriage to L'pool				1	6	0
	12 doz. [illegible] Saw files [illegible]	6	11	0		
	24 doz. " " " [illegible]	4	10	0		
	3 doz. Mill Saw [illegible] files 10 in.	1	15	3		
	4 doz. " " " 12 in.	3	6	0		
	6 doz. " " " 14 in.	6	16	0		
	continued [illegible]	23	0	3	54	0	5

Messrs O. Mazange & Co
Mobile

Ætna Works,
Sheffield.
August 1[illegible] 1860

Bo^t. of Spear & Jackson,
Steel Converters and Refiners,
Manufacturers of Saws, Files, Edge Tools,
Ledger Blades, Curriers' Knives, Machine Knives, &c.

S. J.

Rendu à Payable à mois de terme à dater de la Facture.

Figure 145. Invoice for saws and files.

Summary: Detailed invoice for two casks hardware consisting of various sizes of saws including hand, panel, ripping, blue back, compass, and brass back types, and of various sizes of files including taper saw files and mill saw bastard files.

1474
Invoice (second page of hardware invoice)

Summary: Invoice continues with drawing knives, mortice (sic) chisels, and carpenter adzes. With expenses and discounts the total invoice was £ 92.10.0 for 19½ doz. saws, 49 doz. files, and 12 doz. divided among the remaining types of tools.

1475
Bill of Lading

Summary: Bill of lading for cargo of hardware shipped to Mazange & Co. in Mobile by Brown, Shipley, & Co. of Liverpool dated 14 Sept 1860 and signed by the *Cumberland's* captain, Reuben Merrill (the first legible signature of first name) and including: 36 casks hardware, one case hollow ware, two cases hardware, four casks hollow ware, one case percussion caps, two bundles nails, 17 bags nails, and one bundle of pans. Freight: 30 shillings sterling per ton of 40 cu. ft. for hardware and caps and 25 shillings per ton of 40 cu. ft. for nails and hollow ware. Total shipping charges £ 24.7.6 as calculated case by case on the facing page. The document included a 6 pence impressed official (export?) stamp.

1476
Invoice

Summary: Invoice from F. W. Tillon of New Orleans to Brown Shipley & Co. regarding charges for loading and customs clearances in Liverpool on 64 packages for Mobile dated 11 Sept 1860 and totaling £ 9.2.10. Transshipped in New Orleans?

1478
Cover Letter

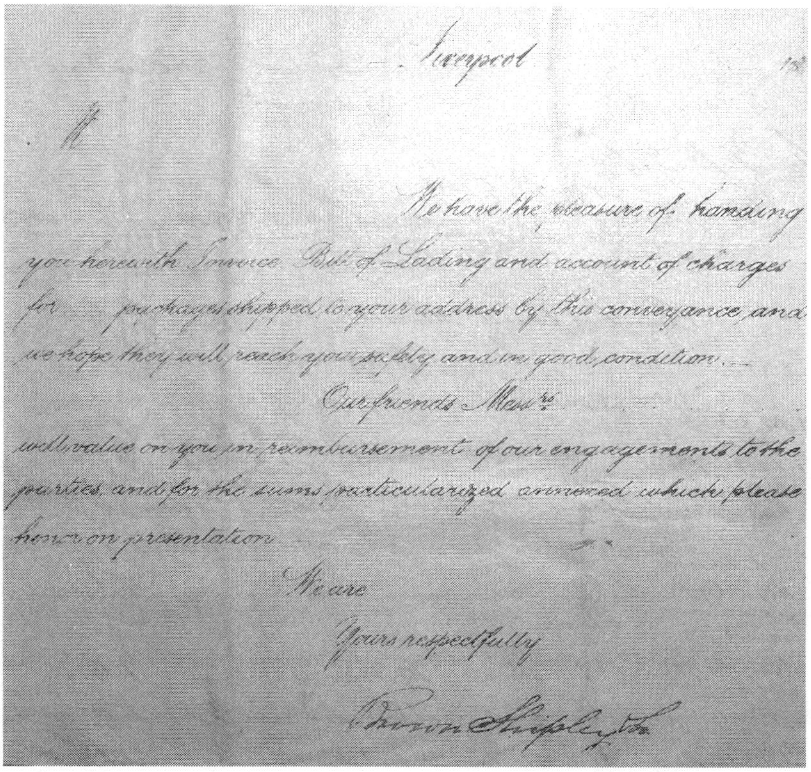

Liverpool 18

M

We have the pleasure of handing you herewith Invoice, Bill of Lading and account of charges for packages shipped to your address by this conveyance, and we hope they will reach you safely and in good condition. —

Our friends Messrs

will value on you in reimbursement of our engagements to the parties, and for the sums particularized annexed which please honor on presentation

We are

Yours respectfully

Brown Shipley & Co

Figure 146. Cover letter for hardware cargo documents.

Liverpool

We have the pleasure of handing you herewith Invoice, Bill of Lading and account of charges for ______ packages shipped to your address by this conveyance and we hope they will reach you safely and in good condition –

Our friends Messrs. ______

Will value on you in reimbursement of our engagements to the parties and for the sums particularized annexed which please honor on presentation.

We are

Yours respectfully

Brown Shipley & Co.

1481
Preprinted Customs Form

No. 4
Importer James, Williams & Co
Vessel *Wm. Woodberry*
From L'pool
Entered Nov 1860
Value $ 367 Duty $ 55.05

Agent's Oath
John Slaughter, agent

Garner, Williams & Co, owner
(signed) John Slaughter
Sworn before me, this __ day of Nov 1860
T. J. Butler Collector

Mdse. Entered 6 Nov 1860 Ship Entered 31 Octr 1860
Entry of Merchandise imported into the Port of Mobile, District of Mobile, by Garner, Williams & Co in the Ship *Wm. Woodberry* M Lelland Master, from Liverpool

Marks	No. of Packages	Contents	Value in Foreign Currency			15	Duties
GW/H&Co	1 Case	Flax thread	£ 73	14	4		
		Charges		5	8		
			£ 74	0	0		
		Coms 2½%	1	17	0		
England			£ 75	17	0	$ 367	$ 55.05

1485
Cover Letter

Summary: For shipment of a case linen thread made to order for Garner Williams & Co. by Jonn. Harris & Sons of Cockermouth, England.

1486
Invoice

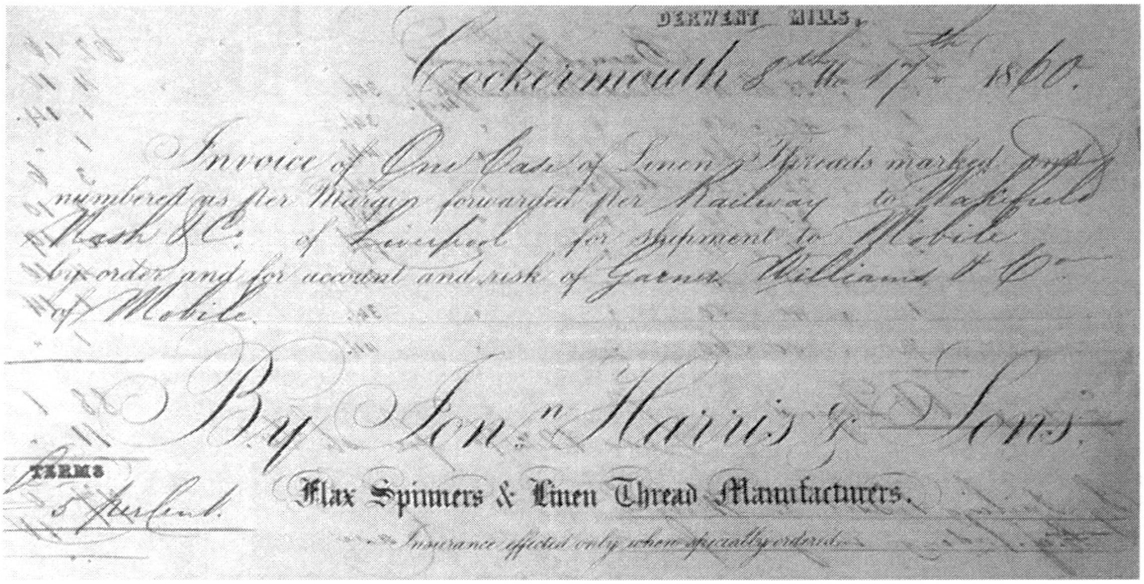
DERWENT MILLS,
Cockermouth 8th Mo 17th 1860.
Invoice of One Case of Linen Threads marked and numbered as per Margin forwarded per Railway to Wakefield Nash & Co. of Liverpool for shipment to Mobile by order and for account and risk of Garner Williams & Co of Mobile.
By Jonn. Harris & Sons,
Flax Spinners & Linen Thread Manufacturers.
Insurance effected only when specially ordered.
TERMS
5 per cent.

Figure 147. Letterhead of invoice for shipment of thread.

Derwent Mills
Cockermouth 8th Mo 17th 1860

Invoice of One case of Linen Threads marked and numbered as per Margin forwarded per Railway to Wakefield Nash & Co. of Liverpool for shipment to Mobile by order and for account and risk of Garner Williams & Co. of Mobile.

By Jonn. Harris & Sons,

Terms
£ 5 percent. Flax Spinners & Linen Thread Manufacturers,
Insurance effect only when specially ordered

Summary: Page one of invoice details 48 doz. thread described as "½ oz. line 14 oz." subtotaling £ 62.16.0.

1484
Invoice (reverse side of invoice 1486)

Summary: Thread invoice continued showing total 66 doz. Costing £ 73.14.4 with fees.

1488
Bill of Lading

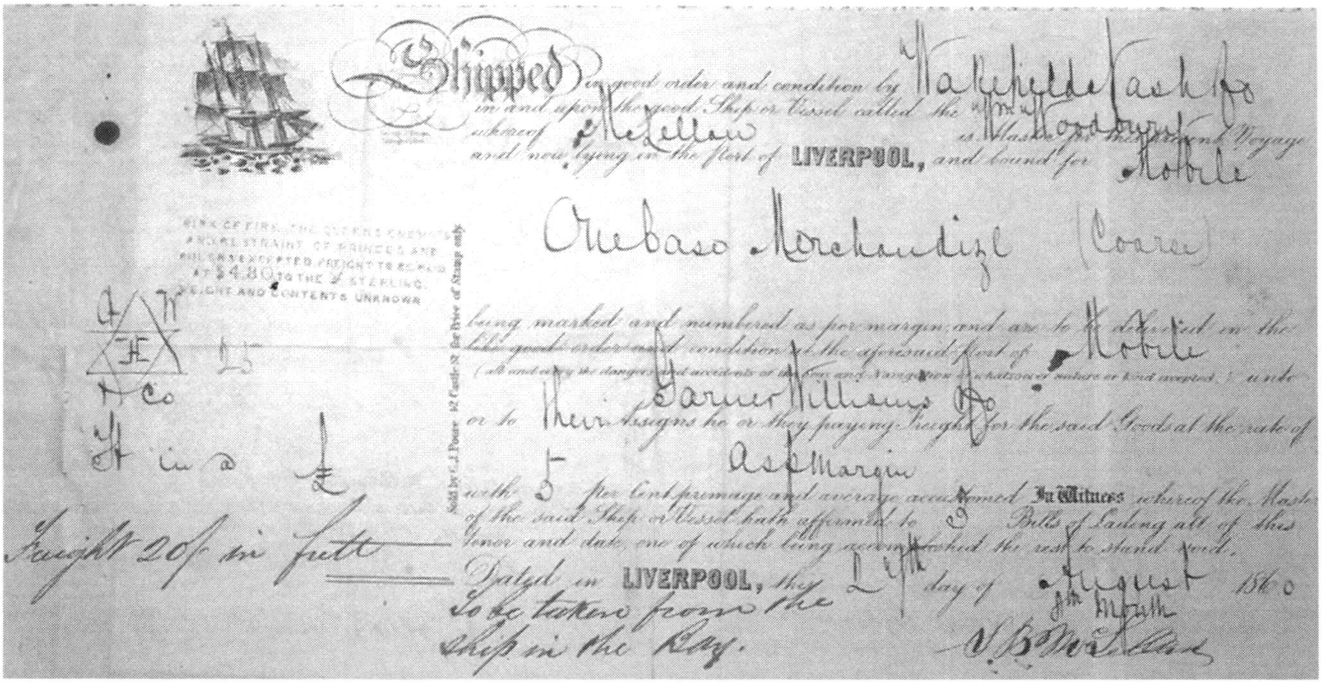
Shipped in good order and condition by Wakefield Nash & Co in and upon the good Ship or Vessel called the Wm Woodbury whereof J McLellan is Master for this present Voyage and now lying in the Port of LIVERPOOL, and bound for Mobile

One case Merchandize (Coarse)

being marked and numbered as per margin, and are to be delivered in the like good order and condition at the aforesaid Port of Mobile (all and every the dangers and accidents of the Seas and Navigation of whatsoever nature or kind excepted) unto Garner Williams & Co or to their Assigns he or they paying Freight for the said Goods at the rate of As p Margin with 5 per Cent primage and average accustomed. In Witness whereof the Master of the said Ship or Vessel hath affirmed to 3 Bills of Lading all of this tenor and date, one of which being accomplished the rest to stand void.

Dated in LIVERPOOL, the day of August 1860

Risk of fire, the Queen's enemies and restraint of princes and rulers excepted. Freight to be paid at $4.80 to the £ sterling. Weight and contents unknown.

Sold by C. J. Poole 1-2 Castle St. for Price of Stamp only

Freight 20/ in full

To be taken from the ship in the Bay.

Figure 148. Bill of lading for cargo of thread.

Summary: This bill of lading revealed two interesting factors about maritime trade. First the form itself was "Sold by C. J. Poole (?) 1-2 Castle St. for Price of Stamp only." Second was an added rubber stamp disclaiming liability saying, "Risk of Fire, the Queen's enemies and restraint of princes and rulers excepted. Freight to be paid at $4.80 to the £ Sterling. Weight and contents unknown." Signed by Capt. S. B. McLelland, 27 Aug 1860, who noted that this cargo was to be taken from the ship in the bay (by lighter) as opposed to at the wharf.

1491-1493
Preprinted Customs Form

No. 25
Importer Clark Stewart & Bibb
Vessel *Cumberland*
From L'pool
Entered 8 Nov '60
Value $ 2058 Duty $ 491.76

Agent's Oath
T. P. Officer, agent
Clark Stewart & Bibb, owner
(signed) T P Officer
Sworn before me, this 8 day of Nov 1860
T. J. Butler Collector

Mdse. Entered Nov 1860 Ship Entered 31 Octr 1860
Entry of Merchandise imported into the Port of Mobile, District of Mobile, by Clark Stewart & Bibb in the Ship *Cumberland* Merrill Master, from Liverpool

Marks	No. of Packages	Contents	Value in Foreign Currency			24	Duties
CSB M	3 Casks	Cutlery & Chgs	£ 274	0	5		
		Comm 2½%	6	7	6		
			£ 280	7	11	$ 1357	$ 325.68
CSB	6 Casks	Hardware Chgs & Com	£ 144	14	7	677	162.48
						24 @ 15%	3.60
England			£ 425	2	6	$ 2058	$ 491.76

1494
Invoice

Carlisle and Beeley Wood Works.
Sheffield. August 31st 1860
M
Bought of Wilson Hawksworth, Ellison & Co.

Figure 149. Letterhead of invoice for hardware.

Summary: Hardware "Bought of Wilson Hawksorth Ellison & Co."

Page 1, hardware details including 7 gross table cutlery, dozens of butcher knives, steels; John Wilson & Sons furriers, shoe, and butchers knives and steels; saws; Spear & Jackson saws; sheep shears; knives. Subtotal £ 73.17.3 for page 1.

Page 2, dozens of knives, scissors, mortise chisels, turning chisels, gouges, and socket chisels, screw drivers, spoke shaves, squares, Impd. (Imported) sliding T bevels; W. H. C. & Co. horse rasps, mill saw files, flat bastard files. Subtotal £ 200.1.11 for page 1 and 2.

Page 3, flat bastard, round bastard, taper saw, and flat smooth files. Total with fees £ 274.0.5.

1498
Bill of Lading

Summary: Two Bills of lading for the shipment of hardware above and dated 14 Sept 1869.

1500-1501
Owner's Oath

Summary: James R. Stewart signed two owner's oath forms regarding customs in Mobile for the two shipments above, dated 26 Oct 1860 and 9 Nov 1860.

1502-1506
Invoice

Summary: Detailed invoice for hardware bought of Van Wart Son & Co., Birmingham, England, by Clark Stewart & Bibb and shipped to Mobile. Items included chains for harnesses, japanned hat and coat hooks, tinned iron table and tea spoons, brass picture nails, corkscrews, pocket corkscrews, police handcuffs, one gross gun nipples, and locks and keys. Total £ 144 14 7.

1507-1509
Preprinted Customs Form

No. 44
Importer R. Westfeldt
Vessel *Kaloola*
From Havana
Entered 17 Nov 1860
Value $ 3819 Duty $ 1145.70

Owner's Oath
R. Westfeldt, owner
(signed) R. Westfeldt
Sworn before me, this 17 day of Nov 1860
T. J. Butler Collector

Mdse. Entered 17 Nov 1860 Ship Entered 31 Octr 1860
Entry of Merchandise imported into the Port of Mobile, District of Mobile, by R. Westfeldt in the Schr *Kaloola* Newton Master, from Liverpool

Marks	No. of Packages	Contents	Value in Foreign Currency	30	Duties
RW	12 Cases	Cigars C & Com 156.6 m	$ 3819.43	$ 3819	$ 1145.70
Cuba					

1518
Bill of Lading

Note: This one seemed to be misfiled and was mixed into a subsequent file's papers. The quantity of cigars was quite a contrast to the few hundred per order typical of the cargo carried by the *Denbigh* in 1864.

Summary: Bill of lading by Patrick & Co. for 156,600 cigars bound to Mobile. Freight rate 35¢ per thousand to be paid by the receiving party, R. Westfeldt.

1510-1511
Invoice

Summary: Detailed invoice for 156,600 Cuban cigars, in dozens of varied types and sizes, shipped by Patrick & Co. to R. Westfeldt in Mobile. Total with fees $ 3819.43 and dated 3 Nov 1860.

1512-1514
Preprinted Customs Form

No. 48
Importer J. Aubo (?)
Vessel *Kaloola*
From Havana
Entered 28 Nov '60
Value $ 75 Duty $ 22.50

Owner's Oath
J. Aubo, owner
(signed) J. Aubo
Sworn before me, this 28 day of Nov 1860
T. J. Butler Collector

Mdse. Entered 20 Nov 1860 Ship Entered Nov 1860
Entry of Merchandise imported into the Port of Mobile, District of Mobile, by J. Aubo in the Sch *Kaloola* Master, from Havana

Marks	No. of Packages	Contents	Value in Foreign Currency	30	Duties
	20 boxes	Segars Chrg & Cmm 2 ~~M~~	$ 50.00	$50	$ 15.00
	2 boxes	S. Meats (?) &c Chg & C	25.00	25	7.50
Cuba			$ 75.00		$ 22.50

1515-1517
Preprinted Customs Form

No. 36
Importer Walkington & Co.
Vessel *Cumberland*
From L'pool
Entered 29 Nov 1860
Value $ 2907 Duty $ 537.41

Owner's Oath
Jno McKendley, owner
Consigned to Walkington & Co.

(signed) Jno. McKindley
Sworn before me, this 29 day of Nov 1860
T. J. Butler Collector

Mdse. Entered ____ 1860 Ship Entered 31 Octr 1860
Entry of Merchandise imported into the Port of Mobile, District of Mobile, by Walkington & Co. in the Ship *Cumberland* Merrill Master, from Liverpool

Marks	No. of Packages	Contents	Value in Foreign Currency			15	19	24	Duties
L&U/M	8 Bales	Blankets	£ 334	4	2	1618			242.70
	4 Cases	Cotton prints	137	17	9			667	160.08
	2 do	??? Baize	38	2	8		185		35.15
	1 do	??? Cot. Hosiery	12	8	0	60			9.00
		Silk do	50	7	11			244	58.56
		Wool co	27	12	0			133	31.92
		Chgs & Coms incld	£ 600	12	6	$ 1678	185	1044	$537.11
England						$2907.03			

1519-1522
Invoice

Summary: Invoice Walkington & Co. to A & L Henry & Co. debit, details of shipment of various fabrics, blankets, table oil, baize, ladies' hose and gloves, merino vests, ladies' merino drawers, and towels. Total £ 600.12.6.

1523a
Bill of Lading

Summary: Bill of lading by Leech, Harrison & Forwood of Liverpool of 8 bales and 7 crates aboard the *Cumberland* to be delivered on the wharf at Mobile, dated 15 Sept 1860.

1523b
Invoice for Port Charges

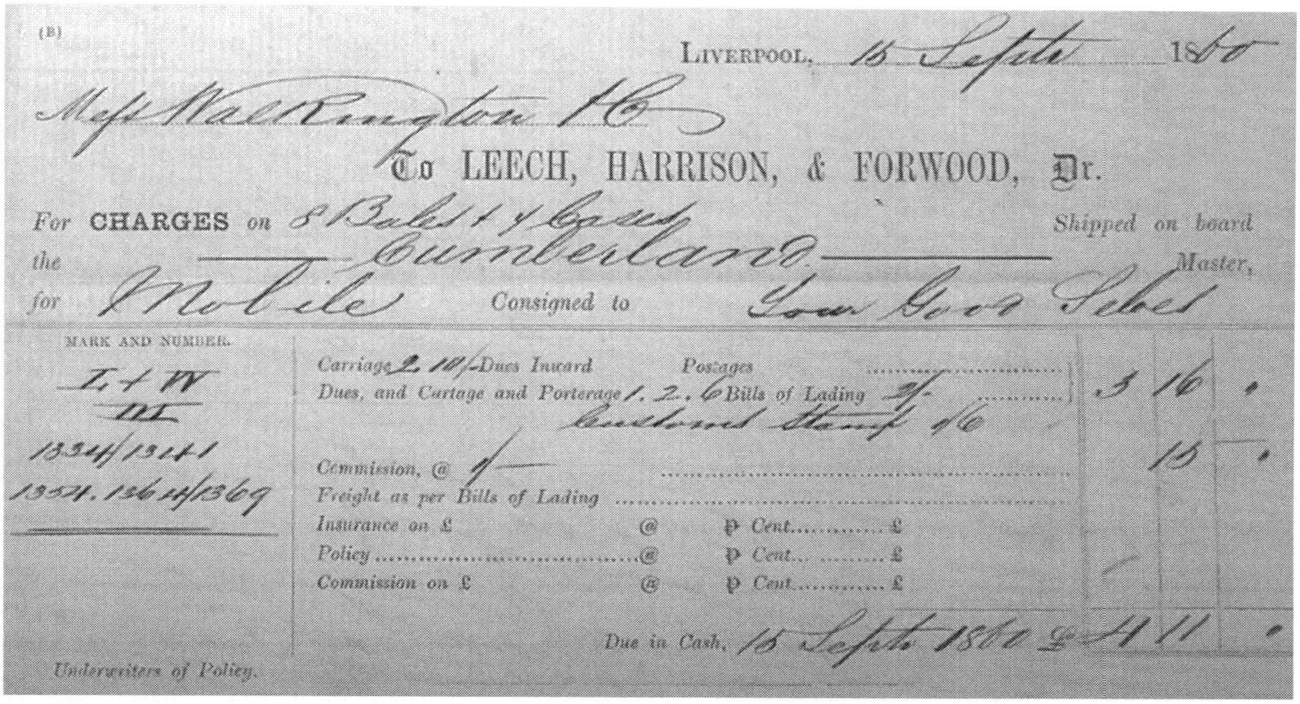
(B)
LIVERPOOL, 15 Septr 1860
Messrs Walkington & Co
To LEECH, HARRISON, & FORWOOD, Dr.
For CHARGES on 8 Bales & 4 Cases Shipped on board
the Cumberland Master,
for Mobile Consigned to Your Good Selves
MARK AND NUMBER.
Carriage 2. 10/- Dues Inward Postages
Dues, and Cartage and Porterage 1. 2. 6 Bills of Lading 2/- 3 16 .
Customs Stamp 1/6
Commission, @ 1/- 15 .
Freight as per Bills of Lading
Insurance on £ @ ₽ Cent £
Policy @ ₽ Cent £
Commission on £ @ ₽ Cent £
Due in Cash, 15 Septr 1860 £ 4 11 .
Underwriters of Policy.

Figure 150. Invoice for port charges.

Summary: Port charges and export stamp shown on a printed form.

1524-1526
Preprinted Customs Form

No. 4
Importer Hadom
Vessel St. Ship *Wasp*
From L'pool
Entered 7 Nov 1860
Value $ 1647 Duty $ 247.05

Agent's Oath
Henry A Lowel, agent
John & Thos. Johnson, owner
(signed) Henry A Lowel
Sworn before me, this 7th day of Nov 1860
T. J. Butler Collector

Mdse. Entered 7 Nov 1860 Ship Entered Nov 7 1860
Entry of Merchandise imported into the Port of Mobile, District of Mobile, by H. A. Lowe in the Br. Ship *Wasp* Storey Master, from Liverpool

Marks	No. of Packages	Contents	Value in Foreign Currency			15	Duties
	4268 Sacks	Salt Chgs 426.16.0.0	£ 322	11	0		
		36 doz mats 2/-	5	8	0		
		Tolling	10	14	0		
			£ 338	13	0		
		Coms 2½	8	9	4		
			£ 347	24	16	1680.05	
		less discount (?)				$ 1647	$ 247.05
England							

1527
Bill of Lading

Summary: Bill of lading by John & Thomas Johnson in Liverpool for Mobile signed weight & contents unknown by Capt. Thos. Storey of the *Wasp*, freight 5 shillings per ton to be paid in Mobile at $4.80 per £. Storey noted the cargo was to be taken from the ship's tackles in Mobile Bay as fast as the vessel discharges the same. Dated 18 Sept 1860.

1530-1531
Consul's Certificate

Summary: Consul's certificate no. 273 and dated 19 Sept 1860. On the second page the seller certified the sale price of the cargo shipped on the *Wasp*. Notice how the invoice for the cargo was attached by punched holes with ribbon running under the Consul's seal.

1532
Invoice

Invoice of 4268 Bags Common Salt Shipped by John & Thos Johnson of Liverpool per *Wasp*, Storey Master for Mobile & Consigned to Henry A. Howe Esq for Sale there & return on a/c of the Shippers. (So the Johnson company is taking on this trade themselves.)

Summary: Cost with fees £ 322.11.0 with added penciled amounts added in later making the total £ 347.2.4.

1533-1535
Preprinted Customs Form

No. 2
Importer A Philipi
Vessel B Shp *Culloden*
From Lpool
Entered 21 Nov 1860
Value $ 2171 Duty $ 521.04

Agent's Oath
A Philipi, agent
? Girardi, owner
(signed) A Philipi
Sworn before me, this 2 day of Nov 1860
T. J. Butler Collector

Mdse. Entered 2 Octor 1860 Ship Entered Octr 29 1860
Entry of Merchandise imported into the Port of Mobile, District of Mobile, by A Philify Charles Girardi in the Br. Ship *Culloden* Hartley Master, from Liverpool

Marks	No. of Packages	Contents	Value in Foreign Currency			24	Duties
C.G.	One Box	**Jewelry** Chgs & Coms	Frs. 1670	00	$ 2170.62	$ 2171	$ 521.04
France							
via England							•

1536
Power of Attorney for Customs Purposes

Summary: J. A. Girarde gave A. Philipi power of attorney to handle customs in Mobile regarding cargo on board the *Culloden*.

1537-1539
Invoice

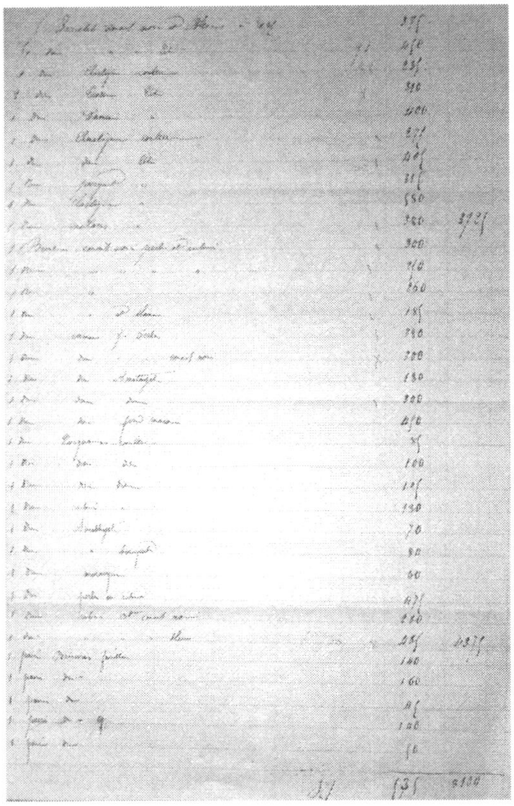

Figure 151. Invoice for shipment of jewelry from Paris.

Summary: Invoice with a detailed listing of jewelry shipped from Paris. Descriptions included enamel, pearls, ruby, emerald, jasper, amethyst, and turquoise in such items as bracelet, chain, medallion, buttons or balls, and necklace. A particularly interesting item was an aluminum broche. The invoice was in French in a cramped hand that was only readable with great difficulty. The author thanks Lee Johnson for his assistance with the script and the translation.

1540
Owner's Oath

Summary: Owner's oath form by Charles Girardi of Mobile for customs clearance testifying to value of the jewelry cargo dated 10 Nov 1860.

1541-1543
Preprinted Customs Form

Note: Ship captain's personal trade.

No. 3
Importer Harley

Vessel B. Ship *Culloden*
From Liverpool
Entered 29 Nov 1860
Value $ 63 Duty $ 15.12

Owner's Oath
G. Harley, owner
(signed) G. Harley
Sworn before me, this 29 day of Nov 1860
T. J. Butler Collector

Mdse. Entered 29 Nov 1860 Ship Entered 29 Oct 1860
Entry of Merchandise imported into the Port of Mobile, District of Mobile, by G. Harley in the Br. Ship *Culloden* Henley Master, from Liverpool

No. of Packages	Contents	Value in Foreign Currency			24	Duties
7 ???	Ale 6 oz -- 8 oz 2 ???	£ 12	12	0		
	Com &c		6	4		
		£ 12	18	4		
England					$ 63	$ 15.12

1544-1546
Preprinted Customs Form

No. 8
Importer Geo Haws
Vessel B. Ship *Calista Haws*
From Lpool
Entered 13 Nov 1860
Value $ 1480 Duty $ 222.00

Owner's Oath
Geo Haws, owner
(signed) George Haws
Sworn before me, this 13 day of Nov 1860
T. J. Butler Collector

Mdse. Entered 13 Nov 1860 Ship Entered Nov 1860
Entry of Merchandise imported into the Port of Mobile, District of Mobile, by Geo Haws in the Br. Ship *Calista Haws* Haws Master, from Liverpool

No. of Packages	Contents	Value in Foreign Currency			15		Duties
4050 Sacks	Salt Chs &c 3/9 (?)	£ 303	8	1			
	add Mats	5	0	0			

		£ 308	8	1			
	addl. Com Chs		11	6			
		308	19	7	806418 lb	14400 Bs. (Bushels)	
	Addl. Coms	2	3	9			
		£ 311	3	4	$ 1506.05	$ 1506	$ 225.90
3786 Sacks	Rctr (?) 18.19.3.10	5	9	2		26	3.90
		£ 305	14	2	1479.63	1480	$ 222.00
England							

1547
Bill of Lading

Summary: Bill of lading by Moran, Gallowy & Co. of 379 sacks, 379 tons common salt. ("Freight free, being Owners' (of the ship) property.")

1549-1550
Consul's Certificate

Summary: U.S. Consul's certificate issued at the port of Liverpool, stamped 275, and dated 19 Sept 1860. Page two showed the owners of the cargo as Robert Galloway, Moran Galloway & Co., and others of Liverpool. The firm was owner of the ship *Calista Haws*.

1551
Invoice

Summary: Invoice for the cargo of salt totaling with fees £ 303.8.1.

1552
Preprinted Customs Form

Free
No. ___
Importer W. H. Anderson
Vessel B. Ship *Wasp*
From Lpool
Entered 7 Nov 1860

Value $ 1990 Duty $ Free
Anatomical Preparations say 2000

Owner's Oath
The Medical College of Alabama, consignee
(signed) Wm H. Anderson
Sworn before me, this 7 day of Nov 1860
T. J. Butler Collector

Mdse. Entered 7 Nov 1860 Ship Entered 7 Nov 1860
Entry of Merchandise imported into the Port of Mobile, District of Mobile, by **The Medical College of Alabama** in the Br. Ship *Wasp* Storey Master, from Liverpool

No. of Packages	Contents	Value in Foreign Currency			24	Duties
17 Cases	**Chemical &c**	Fr 10,700	0	0	$ 1990	Free
	Anatomical Preparations					
England						

1556
Bill of Lading

Summary: Bill of lading by Ewes (?) & Macey, aboard the *Wasp* for delivery in Mobile to Dr. W. F. Anderson, Medical College of Alabama, Mobile. Seventeen cases to be taken from the ship's tackle in the bay within 48 hours of the ship being at the customhouse. Signed 18 Sept 1860, Thos. Storey, captain of the *Wasp* and endorsed by him weight and contents unknown. Freight 25 shillings per ton totaling £ 7.11.4 at the exchange rate of $4.80 per pound Sterling.

1557
Consul's Certificate

Summary: Consul's certificate numbered 297 dated 25 Sept 1860 by Henry Wilding, vice consul, and signed by Beverley Tucker.

1559
Invoice

Summary: Invoice for 400 tons of common salt and 4000 sacks on board ship *Ben Nevis*, Cumming master for Mobile for sale there on acct. of ship's owners. Total with fees £ 309.8.6 dated 25 Sept 1860, Farnsworth & Jordan. Interestingly, this invoice had a £ 100 addition error with later corrections marked.

1560

Note on back of packet of documents for salt cargo dated 25 Sept 1860 in Liverpool and showing the "Rcd." Date of 18 Octr 1860. **A sailing date close to the 25th gave a passage time Liverpool to Mobile of under 23 days for this voyage of the *Ben Nevis*.**

1561-1563
Preprinted Customs Form

No. 1
Importer D. Wheeler & Co
Vessel Br. Ship *Culloden*
From Lpool
Entered 1 Nov 1860
Value $ 1890 Duty $ 283.50

Agent's Oath
Geo. W. Owen, agt (agent)
John Jardine & Son, owner
(signed) Geo. W. Owen
Sworn before me, this 7 day of Nov 1860
T. J. Butler Collector

Mdse. Entered Nov 1860 Ship Entered Octr 29 1860
Entry of Merchandise imported into the Port of Mobile, District of Mobile, by Doherty & Co in the Ship (Br) *Culloden* Harley Master, from Liverpool

No. of Packages	Contents	Value in Foreign Currency			15	Duties
4500 Sacks	Salt (Com) tons 450	£ 283	2	6	972,000 lbs	
42 Doz	Mats	11	0	0	tons 433.18.2.8	
	Charges pr Inc	80	18	4	Br. 17,356	
		£ 375	0	10		
	add Filling & 5/. Pr 100 d.	11	5	0		
		£ 386	5	10		
	" Coms 2½%	9	13	4		
		£ 395	19	2	$ 1916	$ 287.40
	Dfy (?) 16.1.1.20				26	3.90
England					$ 1890	$ 283.50

1565
Weigher's Certificate

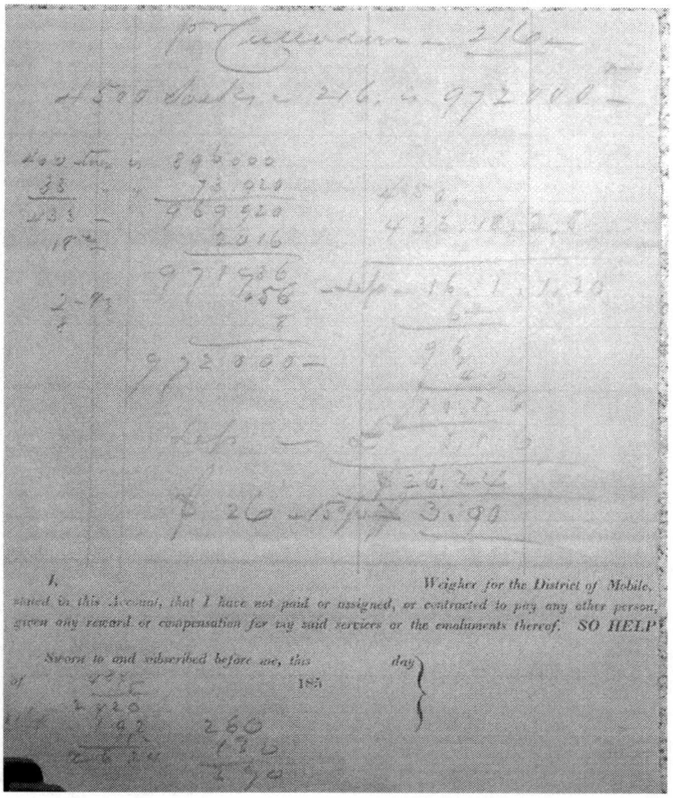
pr Culloden 216
4500 Sacks @ 216. = 972000

I, Weigher for the District of Mobile, ... stated in this Account, that I have not paid or assigned, or contracted to pay any other person, given any reward or compensation for my said services or the emoluments thereof. SO HELP

Sworn to and subscribed before me, this day of 185

Figure 152. Weigher's certificate for cargo of salt.

Summary: Certificate of the Weigher for the District of Mobile, 4500 sacks salt @ 216 was 972,000 lbs. showing calculations.

1566
Consul's Certificate

Summary: Consul's certificate dated 6th day of Sept 1860 and numbered 216.

1567
Consul's Certificat

Summary: Page 2 of consul's certificate for cargo of salt valued at £ 375.0.10 owned by John Jardine & Son of Liverpool loaded aboard the *Culloden* for Mobile dated 6 Sept 1860.

1568
Invoice

Summary: Invoice for cargo of salt on board the *Culloden* dated 5 Sept 1860 valued at £ 375.0.10 with fees.

1569-1571
Preprinted Customs Form

No. 17
Importer R. Westfeldt
Vessel *Cumberland*
From Lpool
Entered 1 Nov 1860
Value $ 449 Duty $ 107.76

Agent's Oath
J. H E Blossom, owner
(signed) R. Westfeldt
Sworn before me, this 1 day of Nov 1860
T. J. Butler Collector

Mdse. Entered 1 Nov 1860 Ship Entered 31 Octr 1860
Entry of Merchandise imported into the Port of Mobile, District of Mobile, by R. Westfeldt in the Ship *Cumberland* Merrill Master, from Liverpool

Marks	No. of Packages	Contents	Value in Foreign Currency			24	Duties
Ross & Co	Ten Cases	Sauces	£ 89	18	0		
W& C.	Ten Cases	"	2	18	0		
		2½% Comm	92	16	0	$ 449.15	$ 107.76
England							

1572a
Power of Attorney for Customs

Summary: Certificate by J. H. E. Blossom of New York assigning to Reinholdt Westfeldt of Mobile his power of attorney for customs transactions regarding cargo on the *Cumberland* dated 25th Octr 1860 and 5 Nov 1860.

1572b
Bill of Lading

Summary: Bill of lading by Benjamin Ackerley of Liverpool aboard the *Cumberland* for Mobile, 20 cases of **sauce**. Dated in Liverpool 6 Sept 1860.

1573
Invoice

Invoice for 20 boxes of sauce from **Lea & Perrins**. Total £ 92.16.0 with fees. Dated 24 Aug 1860.

1574
Owner's Oath

Summary: Form for H. E. Blossom of New York, owner's oath regarding imported cargo of sauce in the District of Mobile dated 5 Nov 1860.

1575
Invoice

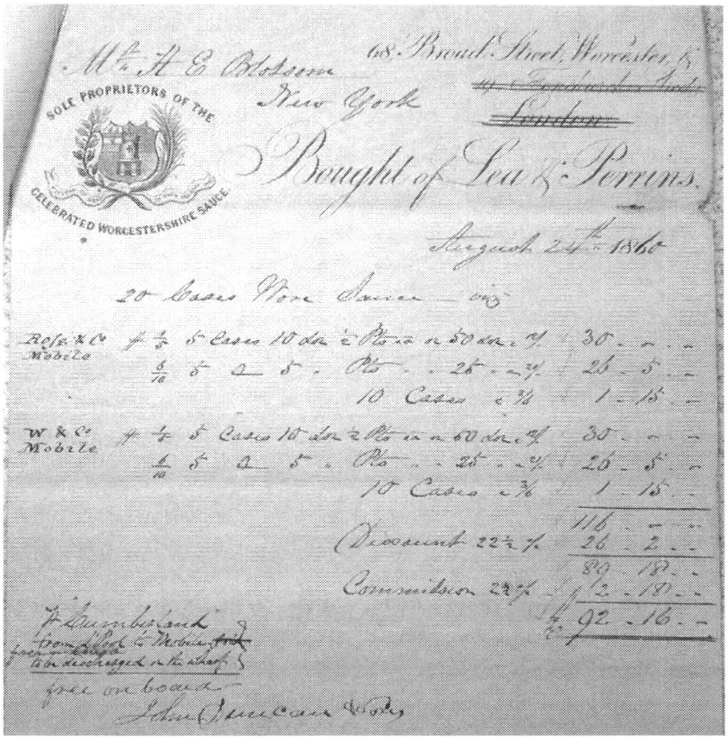

Mr. H. E. Blossom
New York

68 Broad Street, Worcester, & ~~[illegible]~~
~~London~~

SOLE PROPRIETORS OF THE CELEBRATED WORCESTERSHIRE SAUCE

Bought of Lea & Perrins.

August 24th 1860

20 Cases Worc Sauce viz

R&Co Mobile	5 Cases 10 doz ½ Pts in a 50 doz. [illegible]	30 . - . -
	5 do 5 . Pts . . 25 . [illegible]	26 . 5 . -
	10 Cases [illegible]	1 . 15 . -
W & Co Mobile	5 Cases 10 doz ½ Pts in a 60 doz. [illegible]	30 . - . -
	5 do 5 . Pts . . 25 . [illegible]	26 . 5 . -
	10 Cases [illegible]	1 . 15 . -
		116 . - . -
	Discount 22½ %	26 . 2 . -
		89 . 18 . -
	Commission 2½ %	2 . 18 . -
		92 . 16 . -

Cumberland
from L'pool to Mobile
to be discharged on the wharf
free on board
John Duncan [illegible]

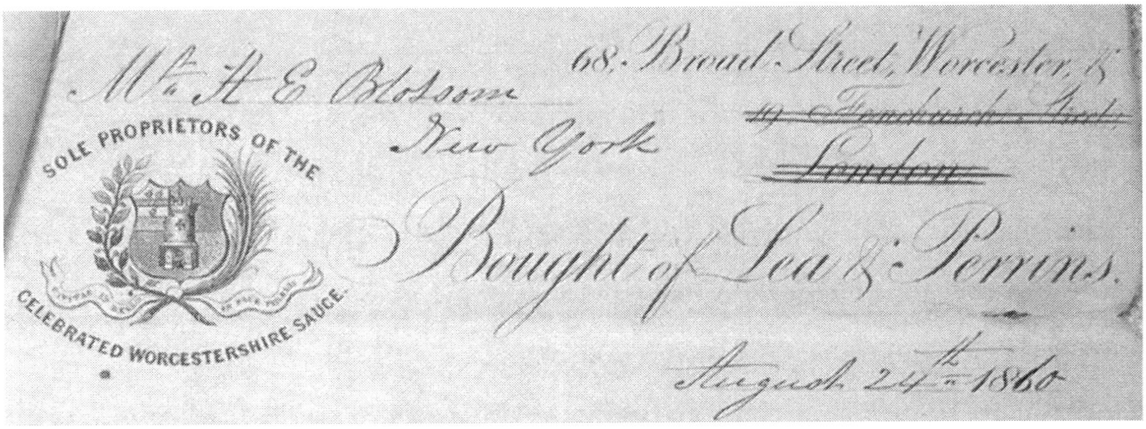
Mr. H. E. Blossom
New York
68, Broad Street, Worcester, &
~~11 Fenchurch Street~~
~~London~~
SOLE PROPRIETORS OF THE CELEBRATED WORCESTERSHIRE SAUCE.
Bought of Lea & Perrins.
August 24th 1860

Figure 153. Invoice for Worcestershire sauce from Lea & Perrins.

Summary: Invoice on **Lea & Perrins** printed form for **Worcestershire Sauce** dated 24 Aug 1860 to H. E. Blossom, New York.

1579-1581
Preprinted Customs Form

No. 28
Importer Haynes & Walther
Vessel *Cumberland*
From L'pool
Entered 8 Nov 1860
Value $ 421 Duty $ 101.04

Agent's Oath
Blood, Wolfe & Co, owner
(signed) H. E. Walthew
Sworn before me, this 8th day of Nov 1860
T. J. Butler Collector

Mdse. Entered Nov 8 1860 Ship Entered Oct 31 1860
Entry of Merchandise imported into the Port of Mobile, District of Mobile, by Haynes & Walther in the Ship *Cumberland* Merrill Master, from Liverpool

No. of Packages	Contents	Value in Foreign Currency			24	Duties
25 Casks	**Ale** – pints doz 175	£ 39	7	6		
30 "	**porter** " doz 210	45	10	0		
		£ 84	17	6		
	Com 2½%	2	2	6		
		£ 87	0	0	$ 421	$ 101.04
England						

1582
Bill of Lading

Summary: Bill of lading from Blood, Wolfe & Co. on board the *Cumberland* for Mobile, 55 Brls. of bottled beer, "Containing the legal Quantity." Measurement in margin "55 Brls @ 6 feet – 9 inch, Case of Stowboards,[115] Measuring 371 feet 3 inch @ 15/- per ton." Signed by the *Cumberland*'s captain Ruben Merrill with his note "Ship not accountable for leakage unless arising form improper stowage."

1584
Consul's Certificate

Note: Typical packet of papers attached to consul's certificate.

Summary: Page 1 of consul's certificate No. 254 for the cargo of beer, for Frederick Blood of Blood Wolfe of Liverpool, owners, dated 14 Sept 1860.

1586
Invoice

Summary: Invoice for beer made with letter press on onion skin, mostly illegible.

1587
Record of Cargo Unloaded

Note: An unusual kind of document not often seen in the present files.

[115] Interesting nautical term from context meaning the boards used in packing and stabilizing barrels in the hold of a ship.

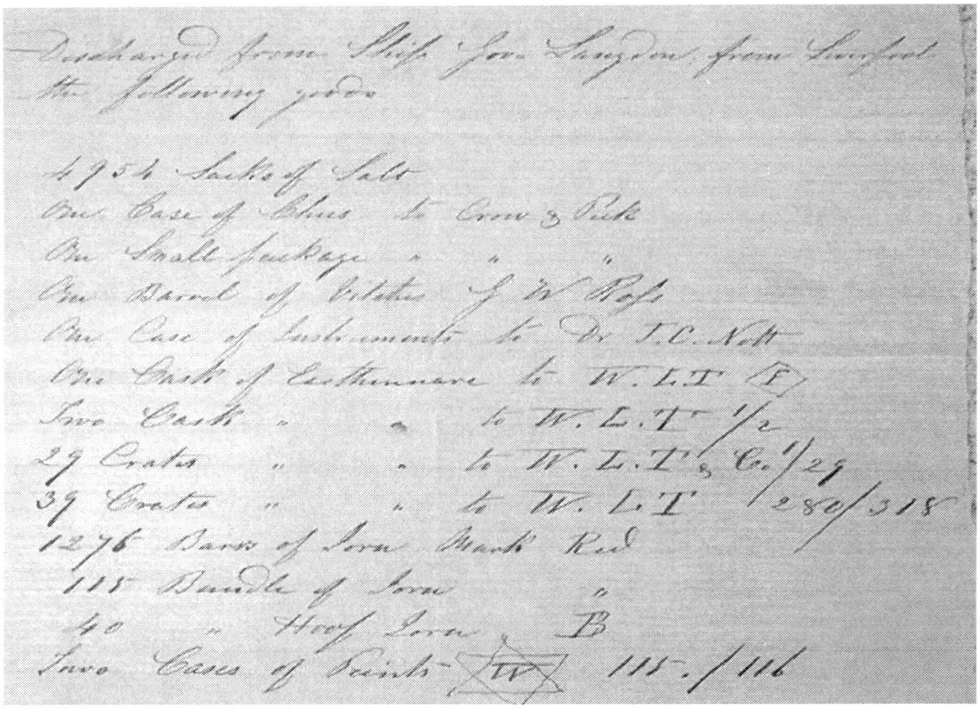

Figure 154. Record of cargo unloaded.

Discharged from Ship *Gov. Langdon* from Liverpool the following goods.

4954 Sacks of Salt
One Case of Clues to Crow & Peck
One Small package " " "
One Barrel of ??? T (?) W Ross
One Case of Instruments to Dr J. C. Nott
One Cask of Earthenware to W. LT F
Two Cask " " to W. L. T 1/2
29 Crates " " to W. L. T & Co 1/29
39 Crates " " to W. LT 280/318
1276 Bars of Iron Mark Red
115 Bundle of Iron "
40 " Hoof Iron B
Two Cases of Prints W 115/116

1588-1589

No. 30
Importer J. Hesse
Vessel *Cumberland*
From Lpool
Entered 20 Nov 1860
Value $ 835 Duty $ 200.40
Anatomical Preparations say 2000

Agent's Oath
Wyman Moses & Romly (?)
(signed) Julius Hesse
Sworn before me, this 18 day of Nov 1860
T. J. Butler Collector

Mdse. Entered 18 Nov 1860 Ship Entered 7 Nov 1860
Entry of Merchandise imported into the Port of Mobile, District of Mobile, by J. Hessen & Co. in the Ship *Cumberland* Merrill Master, from Liverpool

Marks	No. of Packages	Contents	Value in Foreign Currency			24	Duties
W (White)	400 Bundles	**Axe iron** 20 Tons	£ 165	15	1		
		Com	4	5	0		
		Charges	2	10	0		
			£ 172	10	0		
		addl Comsn Chgs		1	3		
	England		£ 172	11	3	$ 835	$ 200.40

1590
Invoice

Figure 155. Invoice for cargo of 20 tons of iron.

Note: The product was described as Stitt & Coy's Best (sideways U shaped) Iron.

Summary: Wyman Moses & Co. of Montgomery, Alabama bought of Stitt Brothers Iron & General Metal Merchants of Liverpool 20 tons of iron shipped on the *Cumberland* care of Julius Hesse of Mobile. Invoice dated 5 Sept 1860.

1591a
Bill of Lading, part

by STITT BROTHERS, of LIVERPOOL, in and upon
Cumberland
is Master for this present Voyage, and now
bound for Mobile viz.

Figure 156. Part of a bill of lading showing shape of ax iron.

Note: The symbol of a sideways U must have designated a particular type of ax iron. Perhaps it meant it had been made by folding larger piece of iron intended, when finished, to form the handle socket.

Summary: Bill of lading by Stitt Brothers of Liverpool of cargo of best ax iron on board the *Cumberland* bound for Mobile and Wyman Moses & Co. of Montgomery, Alabama and dated 5 Sept 1860.

1591b
Owner's Oath

Summary: Form for owner's oath regarding the cargo of ax iron signed by A. J. Moses, Montgomery, Alabama and dated 7 Nov. 1860.

1593-1594
Preprinted Customs Form

No. 18
Importer S. Twelves
Vessel *Cumberland*
From Liverpool
Entered 2 Nov 1860
Value $ 308 Duty $ 73.92

Owner's Oath
Stephen Twelves, owner
(signed) Stephen Twelves
Sworn before me, this 20 day of Nov 1860
T. J. Butler Collector

Mdse. Entered 2 Nov 1860 Ship Entered 7 Nov 1860
Entry of Merchandise imported into the Port of Mobile, District of Mobile, by S. Twelves in the Ship *Cumberland* Merrill Master, from Liverpool

Marks	No. of Packages	Contents	Value in Foreign Currency			24	Duties
ST	30 casks	Ale Pts 190 Doz	£ 62	0	0		
		Coms	1	11	0		
England			£ 63	11	0	$ 308	$ 73.92

1595a
Bill of Lading

Summary: Bill of lading by Ihlers & Bell of Liverpool of cargo of ale aboard the *Cumberland* for Mobile shipped to Stephen Twelves and dated 7 Sept. 1860.

1595b
Invoice

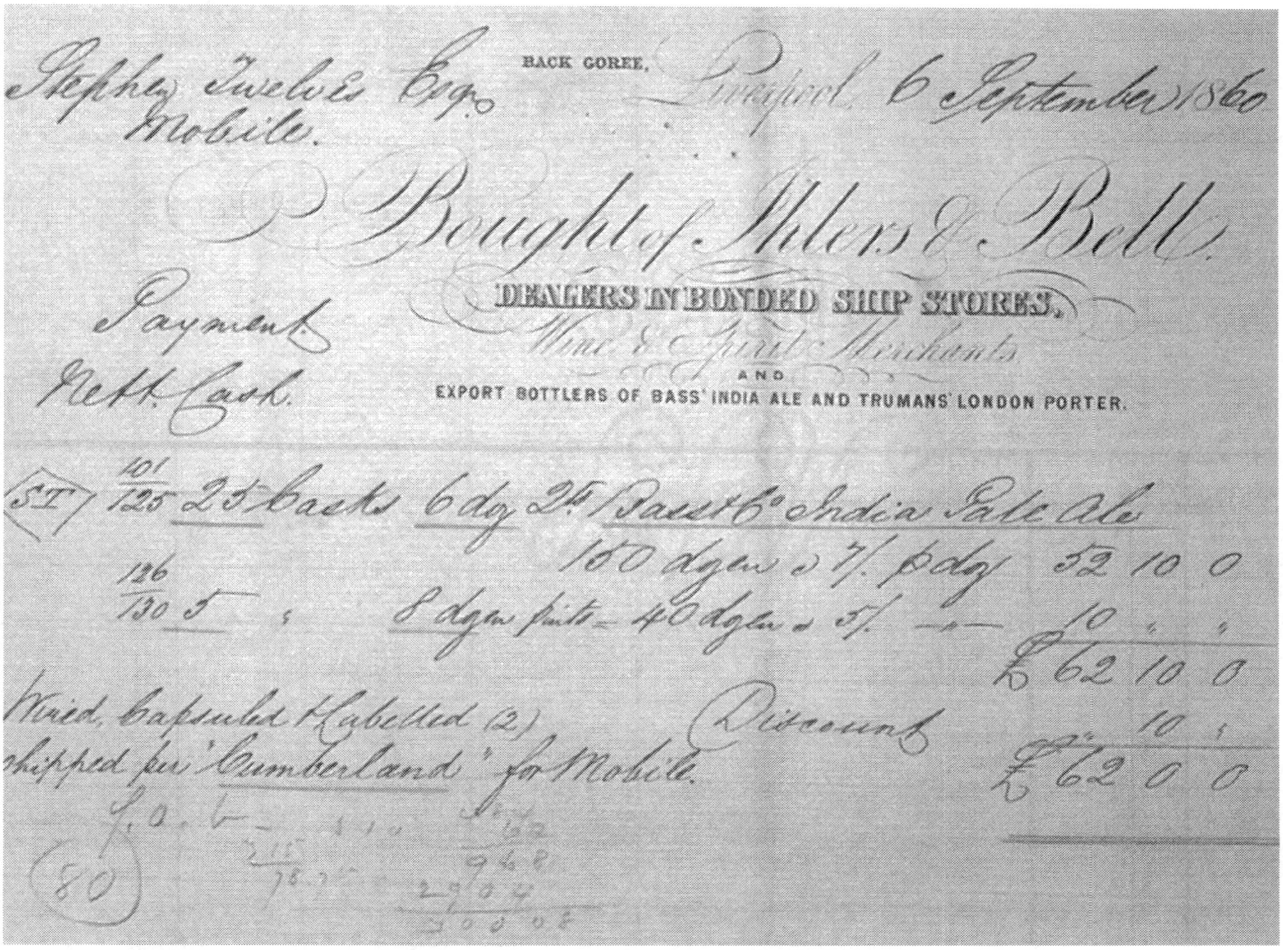
Stephen Twelves Esq.
Mobile.
BACK GOREE, Liverpool 6 September 1860
Bought of Ihlers & Bell
DEALERS IN BONDED SHIP STORES,
Wine & Spirit Merchants
AND
EXPORT BOTTLERS OF BASS' INDIA ALE AND TRUMANS' LONDON PORTER.
Payment
Nett Cash.
ST 101/125 25 Casks 6 doz Pts Bass & Co India Pale Ale
150 dozen @ 7/ p doz 52 10 0
126/130 5 " 8 dozen pints – 40 dozen @ 5/ – 10 " "
£ 62 10 0
Wired, Capsuled & Labelled (2) Discount 10 "
shipped per "Cumberland" for Mobile. £ 62 0 0

Figure 157. Invoice for cargo of India pale ale.

Summary: Invoice for cargo of ale shipped to Stephen Twelves, Mobile by Ihlers & Bell Dealers in Bonded Ship Stores, Wine & Spirit Merchants and Export Bottlers of Bass' India Ale and Truman's London Porter. The cargo consisted of 25 casks of 6 doz. quarts of Bass & Co. India Pale Ale totaling 150 doz. @ 7/. Per doz. and 5 casks of 8 doz. pints totaling 40 doz. @ 5/. per doz., "wired, capsuled & labeled," total £ 62.

1596-1598
Consul's Certificate

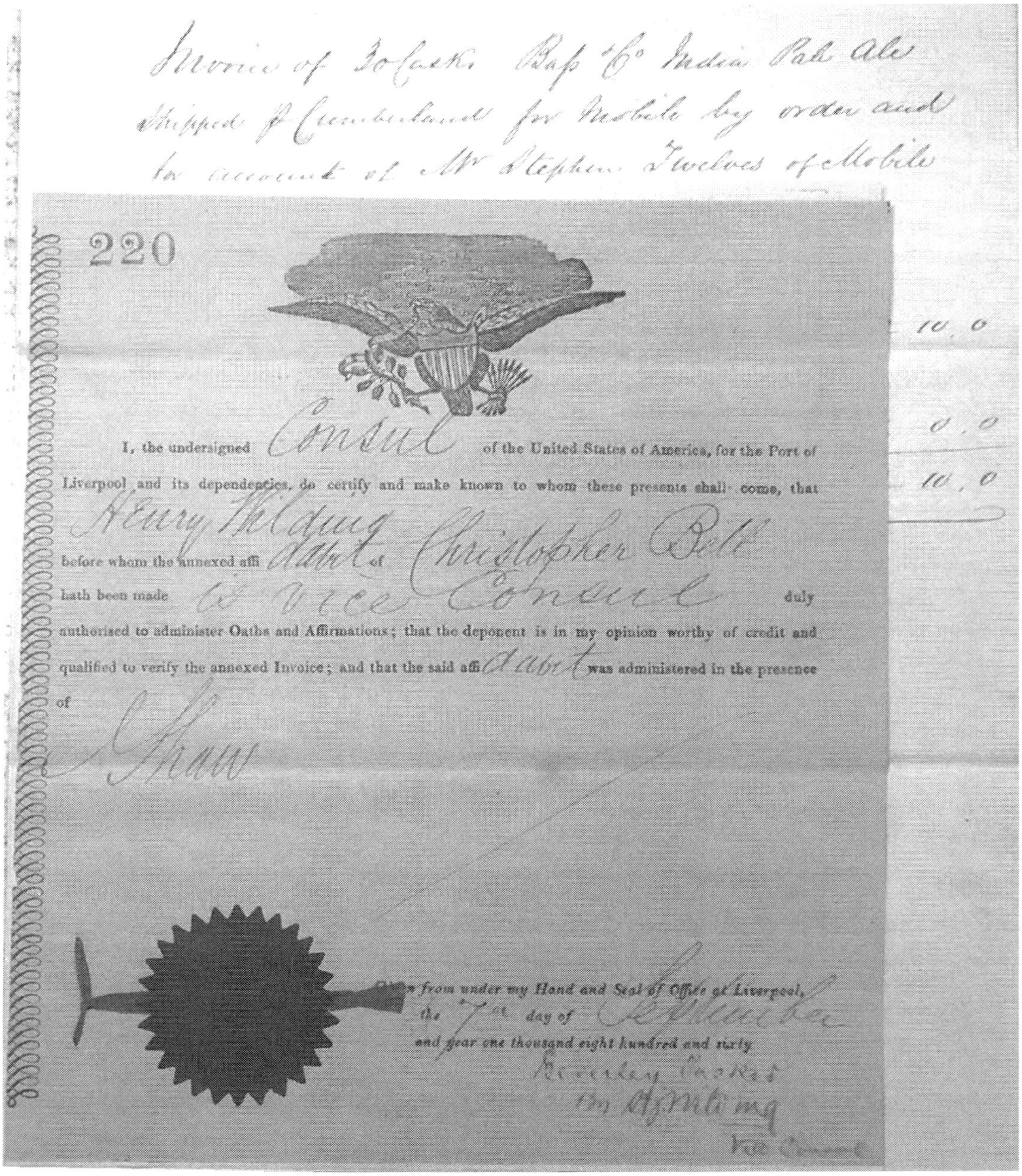
Invoice of 30 casks Bass & Co India Pale Ale shipped p Cumberland for Mobile by order and for account of Mr Stephen Twelves of Mobile

220

I, the undersigned Consul of the United States of America, for the Port of Liverpool and its dependencies, do certify and make known to whom these presents shall come, that Henry Wilding before whom the annexed affidavit of Christopher Bell hath been made is Vice Consul duly authorised to administer Oaths and Affirmations; that the deponent is in my opinion worthy of credit and qualified to verify the annexed Invoice; and that the said affidavit was administered in the presence of

J Shaw

Given from under my Hand and Seal of Office at Liverpool, the 7th day of September and year one thousand eight hundred and sixty

Beverley Tucker
Pr H Wilding
Vice Consul

Figure 158. Consul's certificate for shipment of ale.

Summary: U.S. Consul's certificate Number 220 dated 7 Sept 1860 for cargo of ale and set of documents to accompany the consul's certificate.

1599-1600
Preprinted Customs Form

No. 7
Importer Pollok (?) & Hofton (?) & Co.
Vessel Br. Ship *Ben Nevis*
From Lpool
Entered 9 Nov 1860
Value $ 1556 Duty $ 233.40

Agent's Oath
Edward Sessoms (?), agent
Pollok Hofton & Co. (?), owner
(signed) Edward Sessoms
Sworn before me, this 9 day of Nov 1860
T. J .Butler Collector

Mdse. Entered Nov 1860 Ship Entered 7 Nov 1860
Entry of Merchandise imported into the Port of Mobile, District of Mobile, by J. Hessen & Co. in the Ship (Br.) *Ben Nevis* Commings (?) Master, from Liverpool

No. of Packages	Contents	Value in Foreign Currency				15	Duties
4000 Sacks	Salt Tons 400	£ 236	13	4	Av 213		
	Charges pr invoice	72	15	2			
		£ 329	8	6			
	add ??? 5/. Pr 100 £	10	0	0			
	" Coms	7	19	6			
		£ 327	8	0		$ 1585	$ 237.75
Tons	Defg (?) 19.12.3.12						
380.7.0.16	@ 6/.	5	17	6		29	4.35
15,214 Bshls		£ 321	10	6		$ 1556	$ 233.40
852,000 lbs							
England							

1601-1602
Preprinted Customs Form

No. 16
Daniels Elgin & Co.
Vessel *Cumberland*
From Lpool
Entered 1 Nov 1860
Value $ 2558 Duty $ 413.70

Owner's Oath
A. M. Elgin for Daniels Elgin & Co., owner
(signed) A. M. Elgin
Sworn before me, this 1 day of Nov 1860
T. J. Butler Collector

Mdse. Entered 1 Nov 1860 Ship Entered 31 Oct 1860
Entry of Merchandise imported into the Port of Mobile, District of Mobile, by Daniels Elgin & Co in the Ship *Cumberland* Merrill Master, from Liverpool

Marks	No. of Packages	Contents	Value in Foreign Currency			15	Duties
DE/M	7 Cases	Flax mfs	£ 554	11	4		
		Charges 4/.	1	8	0		
Ireland			£ 555	19	4		
via		Comsn	13	18	10		
England			£ 569	18	2	$ 2758	$ 413.70

1604-1606
Invoice

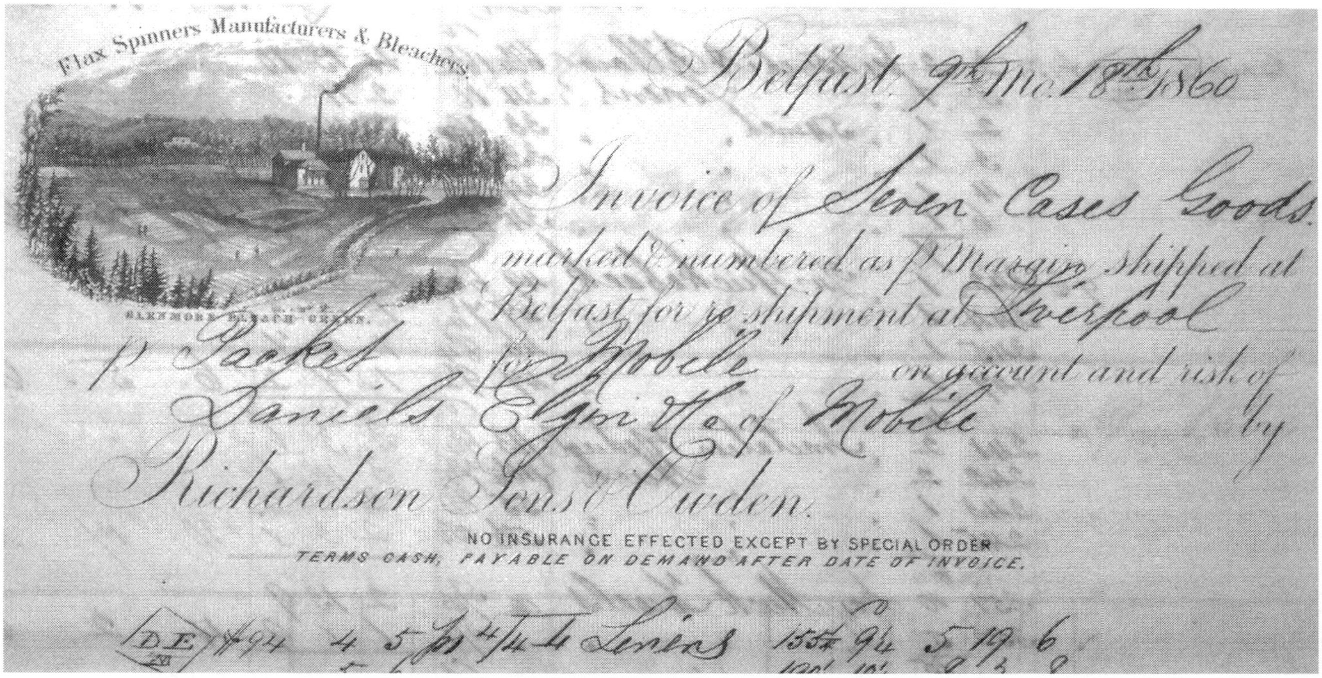

Flax Spinners Manufacturers & Bleachers.

GLENMORE BLEACH GREEN.

Belfast. 9th Mo. 18th 1860

Invoice of Seven Cases Goods marked & numbered as p Margin shipped at Belfast for re shipment at Liverpool p Packet for Mobile on account and risk of Daniels Elgin & Co of Mobile by Richardson Sons & Owden.

NO INSURANCE EFFECTED EXCEPT BY SPECIAL ORDER
TERMS CASH, PAYABLE ON DEMAND AFTER DATE OF INVOICE.

D.E #94 4 5 pi 4/4 Linens 155¼ 9¼ 5 19 6

Figure 159. Invoice for shipment of Irish linen.

Summary: Invoice for linen manufactured goods by Richardson Sons & Owden shipped 18 Sept 1860 at Belfast for reshipment at Liverpool for Daniels Elgin & Co. of Mobile. Cargo consisted of sheeting, napkins, handkerchiefs, diapers, etc. and table linens mostly damask or double damask[116] some specified as snow drop pattern.

1607
Bill of Lading

Summary: Bill of lading by Wakefield Nash & Co. in Liverpool aboard the *Cumberland* for Mobile regarding a cargo of seven cases of merchandise dated 18 Sept 1860.

1610-1611
Preprinted Customs Form

No. 19
Importer Ennis Dougherty & Co.
Vessel *Cumberland*
From Liverpool
Entered 3 Nov 1860
Value $ 738 Duty $ 174.32

Agent's Oath
(? Document damaged), agent
Ennis Dourgherty, owner
(signed) J Stephens
Sworn before me, this 3 day of Nov 1860
T. J. Butler Collector

Note: Reverse side not included because of document damage.

1615
Bill of Lading

Summary: Bill of lading by John Trippett & Brother of Liverpool aboard the *Cumberland* bound for the Mobile wharf, a cargo of hardware in 3 casks, 2 cases, and 25 anvils for Campbell & Co., dated 15 Sept 1860.

[116] Damask – a type of weaving that can be applied to linen as well as silk and cotton. A pattern was formed by the weaving of the fibers and gives the fabric a three-dimensional look on a two dimensional surface. The damask pattern was woven into the front side of the fabric and had a shiny lustrous finish. The backside of the damask cloth looked dull and two-dimensional. Damask weaves came in two weights, a single damask weave and a double damask weave. A double damask tablecloth would have a higher value because of the work involved making this quality design.

1613
Invoice

Summary: Invoice for hardware purchased by Richard Hill & Co. of Birmingham for the account and risk of Messrs. Campbell & Co., Mobile, Ala.: Chains for harness, hammers, anvils, and two punches reading "Ennis Daughtery & Co."

1614
Invoice

Summary: Page two of hardware invoice: 31 **double barrel guns** of 7 varieties with interesting detailed descriptions but ink smeared and nearly illegible. For example saying in part, "fine Double Guns Laminated Steel Barrels real Manton (?) Strikes … ." Other examples specified "Silver thumb piece," "Dolphin Cocks," "neatly Engd (Engraved) Locks," and "Ebony rod." Altogether very fancy weapons. Total £ 151.16.6.

11

Prewar Examples, Various Dates

Here we included a sample of interesting prewar documents from 1860 for comparison with wartime documents.

1824-1825
Preprinted Customs Form

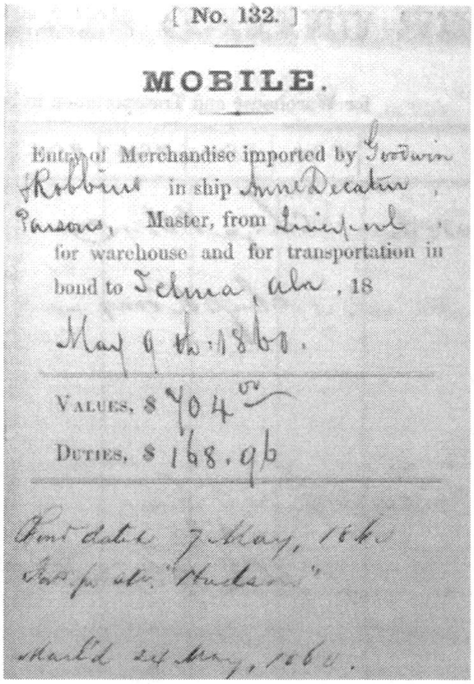

[No. 132.]

MOBILE.

Entry of Merchandise imported by Goodwin & Robbins in ship Anne Decatur, Parsons, Master, from Liverpool for warehouse and for transportation in bond to Selma, Ala, 18 May 9th 1860.

Values, $ 704.00

Duties, $ 168.96

Bond dated 7 May, 1860
Sent per str. "Hudson"

Mail'd 24 May, 1860.

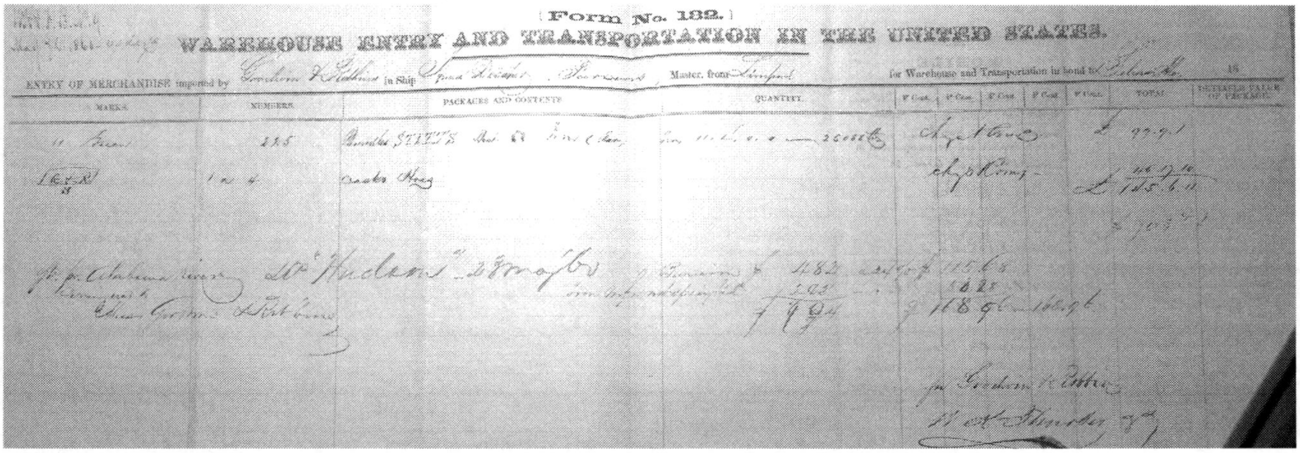

[Form No. 132.]

WAREHOUSE ENTRY AND TRANSPORTATION IN THE UNITED STATES.

ENTRY OF MERCHANDISE imported by Goodwin & Robbins in Ship Anne Decatur, Parsons, Master, from Liverpool for Warehouse and Transportation in bond to Selma, Ala. 18

MARKS	NUMBERS	PACKAGES AND CONTENTS	QUANTITY		TOTAL

per Str. Hudson 28 May 60

for Goodwin & Robbins

Figure 160. Customs form for cargo of iron and hoes.

Summary: Merchandise shipped on the *Anne Decatur*, Parsons Master, from Liverpool to Mobile and shipped on, in bond, to Goodwin & Robbins in Selma, Ala., dated 9 May 1860 totaling $ 704.00 with duties calculated at $ 168.96. Merchandise consisted of 225 bundles of bar iron, 25,088 lbs. and 4 casks of hoes.

1826-1827
Preprinted Customs Form

Summary: Imported by Thos. J. Riley on board the *Cumberland*, Reuben Merrell Master, from Liverpool, entered Mobile 31 Oct 1860, total $ 1077, duty $ 204.63, for a cargo of 63,400 slates (roofing).

1828
Bill of Lading

Summary: Bill of lading for slates, 90¼ tons, freight rate 15 shillings per ton, "to be taken from alongside ship (meaning at anchor by liter) within five days after arrival in Mobile Bay." Shipped by John K. Gilliat & Co. at the consignee's risk and expense.

1829
Invoice

Summary: Invoice for cargo of "First Bangor Slates" 36,700 16 x 10 @ 76/- (Sterling) per thousand and 26,700 16 x 8 @ 58/- per thousand. Bangor Slates were fine quality dark blue roofing slates that form what was considered a practically indestructible roof.

1830
Preprinted Customs Form

Summary: Cargo imported to Mobile by Theo. Guesnard, Jr. aboard the Schooner *Kaloola*, Newton Mr., from Havana, entered 20 Nov 1860, total $ 1240 and duty $ 372.00.

1831
Bill of Lading

Summary: Bill of lading for 5 cases of 57,000 cigars @ 35 cents per thousand dated in Havana 3 Nov 1860.

1832
Invoice

Summary: Invoice specifying numbers and types of cigars. Many of the cigar invoices with details like type names were very hard to read so this legible one presented a good opportunity for an example of Cuban cigars. The invoice was in Spanish. The *Denbigh* Project solicits translation and discussion by cigar aficionados regarding these cigar types. The invoice read in part:

10,000	Meda. negalia Telegafo Submarinos	17¢	170.00
6,200	Conchas " "	16	99.20
16,900	Conchas No me olvides	23	342.70
500	Principes prensados Noriega	20	10.00
5,000	Cilindrado reg. de Noriega	25	125.00
4,500	Principes prensado "	20	90.00
600	Conchas Telegrafo Submarino	16	9.60
5,000	Meda reg. Pruebesa	17	85.00
100	Conchas No me olvides	23	2.30
2,600	" Telegrafo Submarino	16	41.60
6,000	Londres P. de Gales	24	144.00
1,000	Regalia " "	30	30.00
600	Conchas Telegrafo	16	7.60
57,000			$ 1,159.00

1833-1834
Preprinted Customs Form

Summary: Entry of Merchandise to Mobile by Thos. Henry & Co. aboard the *Cumberland* from Liverpool, ship entered 31 Oct 1860, cargo entered 8 Nov 1860, valued at $ 2077 and duty of $ 498.48, cargo manufactured in England and France consisting porcelain and pottery.

1835-1838
Invoice

Summary: Eight page invoice detailing porcelain, pottery, crystal, flatware, and costume jewelry purchased by J. Glaenzer & Versepuy Jr. of Paris dated 1 Sept 1860 in Paris for account and risk of Messrs. Henry & Co. of Mobile shipped at Liverpool. Examples: tea sets, coffee sets, 24 attached spittoons, 88 Greek sugars, and 2 ordinary toilet sets composed of 1 ewer & basin, brush tray, 1 covered chamber (pot), 1 soap (dish), 1 mug at £ 8.16.0 each, 6 gross coffee spoon tin (plated) & iron at £ 5.25.0, ½ gross gilt scarf pins @ $15.00.

1839-1841
Invoice

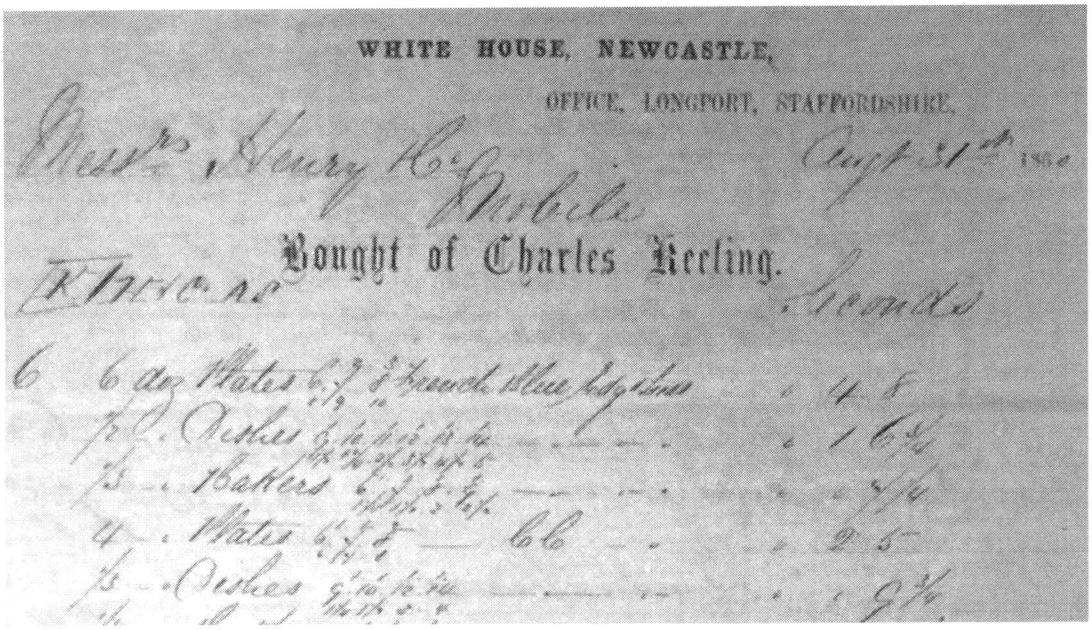
WHITE HOUSE, NEWCASTLE,
OFFICE, LONGPORT, STAFFORDSHIRE.
Messrs Henry & Co
Mobile
Aug 31st 1860
Bought of Charles Keeling.
Seconds

Figure 161. Invoice for Staffordshire pottery.

Summary: Four page invoice detailing 5 crates of pottery bought by Henry & Co. from Charles Keeling dated 31 Aug 1865 in Longport, Staffordshire. Items on 2 pages were specified as seconds. Invoice totaled £ 126.10.2.

1843-1844
Invoice

Messrs Henry & Co
Mobile
Tunstall Aug 14th 1860
Bo of Thos Goodfellow
MANUFACTURER of EARTHENWARE &c.
Erie White Granite

Figure 162. Invoice for Erie white granite pottery.

Summary: Two page invoice for 10 crates of pottery, mostly Erie White Granite type, Tho. Goodfellow sold to Henry & Co. dated 16 Aug 1860 and totaling £ 47.14.2.

1845-1846
Preprinted Customs Form

Summary: Customs form for a cargo of green fruit aboard the Schr. *Yankee Blade*, Gray Mr., from Matanzas, Cuba to Mobile, imported by Mark Gray, merchandise entered 22 Nov 1860, value $ 200 and duty $ 16.00.

1847
Invoice

Brig *Yankee Blade*

To M. Cudina ???

60000 oranges at 3½ $ (per) thousand	$ 210.00
150 bunch bananas at 20 cent	30.00
90 dozens pine apples at 40 "	36.00
	$ 276.00
Matanzas 14th November 1860	
Received by M. Cudina	
Left 17 Nov	

1848-1849
Preprinted Customs Form

No. 40
Vessel *Addison*
From New Castle
Entered 6 Nov 1860
Value $ 8651 Duty $ 2076.24

Summary: Customs form for cargo of railroad rails aboard the Ship *Addison*, W. F. Pike Mr, for John Gibson & Co. in Mobile, ship entered 31 Oct 1860, cargo entered 6 Nov 1860 consisting of 1275 (rail road) rails each 5/5, weight 294.11.3.14 , 5000 fishing pieces, 18 pkgs. bolts & nuts, totaling $ 2076.24.

1850
Bill of Lading

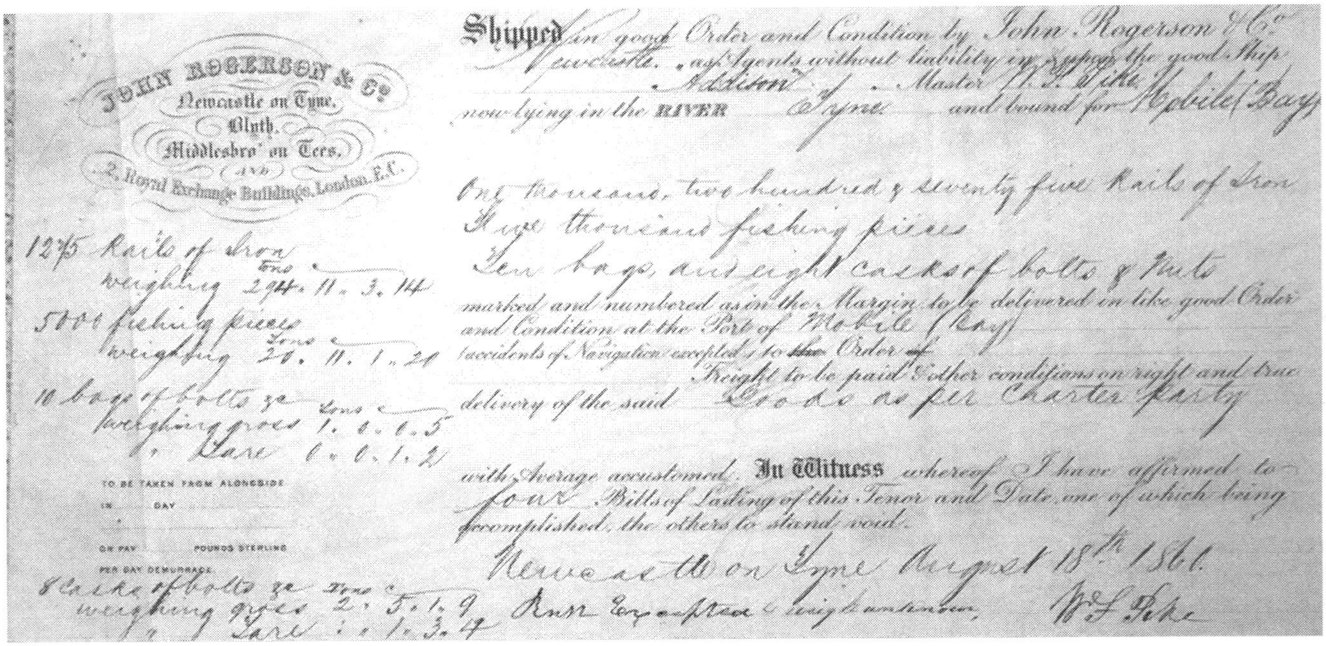
JOHN ROGERSON & Co.
Newcastle on Tyne,
Blyth,
Middlesbro' on Tees,
and
2, Royal Exchange Buildings, London, E.C.

1275 Rails of Iron
weighing Tons 294. 11. 3. 14
5000 fishing pieces
weighing Tons 20. 11. 1. 20
10 bags of bolts &c
weighing gross Tons 1. 0. 0. 5
Tare 0. 0. 1. 2

TO BE TAKEN FROM ALONGSIDE
IN DAY
OR PAY POUNDS STERLING
PER DAY DEMURRAGE.

8 casks of bolts &c
weighing gross Tons 2. 5. 1. 9
Tare 0. 1. 3. 4

Shipped in good Order and Condition by John Rogerson & Co. Newcastle. as Agents without liability on & upon the good Ship Addison of . Master W. L. Pike now lying in the RIVER Tyne and bound for Mobile (Bay)

One thousand, two hundred & seventy five Rails of Iron
Five thousand fishing pieces
Ten bags, and eight casks of bolts & Nuts

marked and numbered as in the Margin to be delivered in like good Order and Condition at the Port of Mobile (Bay) (accidents of Navigation excepted) to the Order of
Freight to be paid & other conditions on right and true delivery of the said Goods as per Charter Party

with Average accustomed. In Witness whereof I have affirmed to four Bills of Lading of this Tenor and Date, one of which being accomplished, the others to stand void.

Newcastle on Tyne August 18th 1860
Rust excepted [illegible] W L Pike

Figure 163. Bill of lading for railroad rails.

Summary: Bill of lading detailing shipment of rails etc. dated 18 Aug 1860.

1851-1853
Consul's Certificate

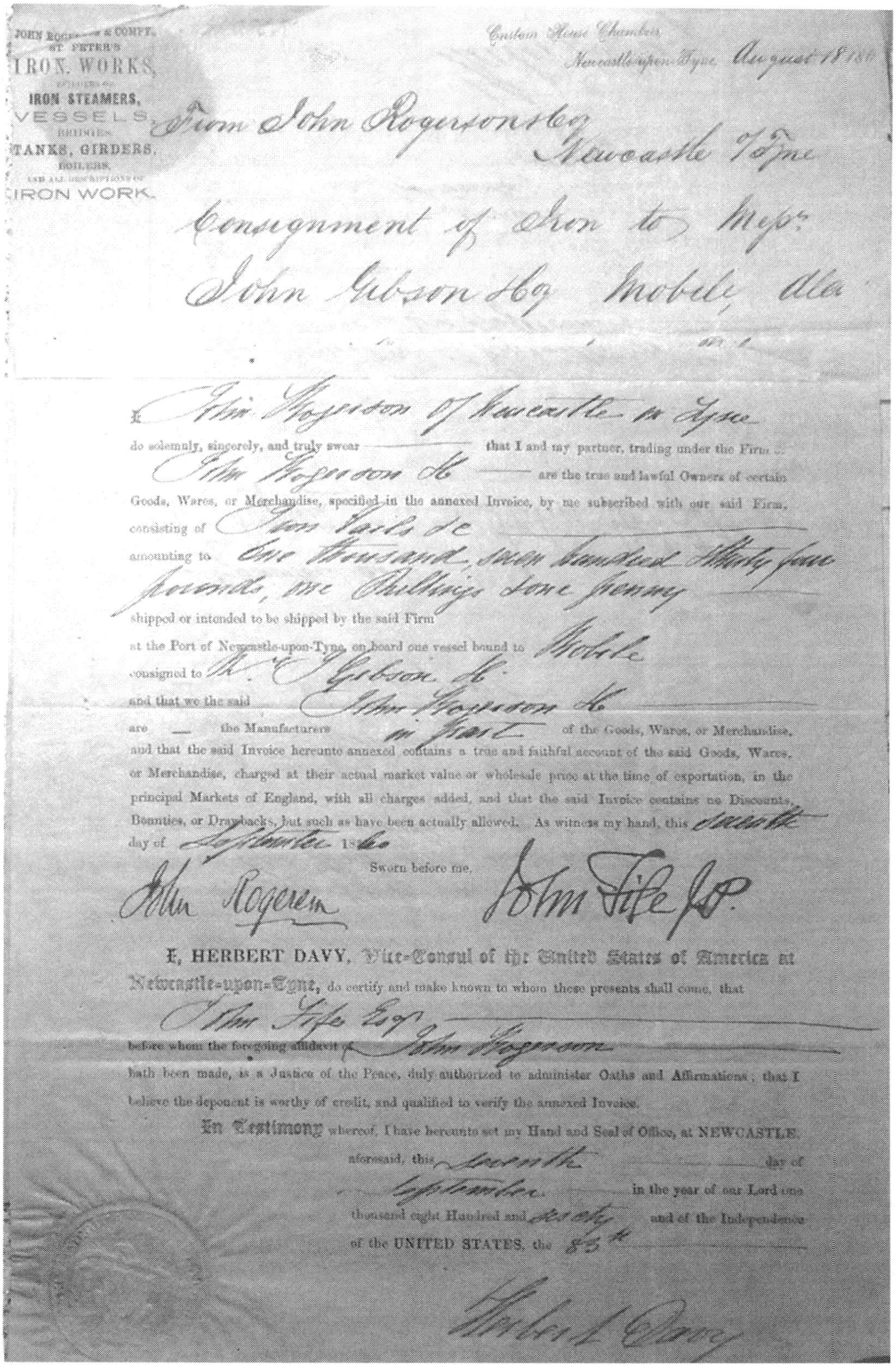

JOHN ROGERSON & COMPY.
ST PETER'S
IRON WORKS,
BUILDERS OF
IRON STEAMERS,
VESSELS,
BRIDGES,
TANKS, GIRDERS,
BOILERS,
AND ALL DESCRIPTIONS OF
IRON WORK.

Custom House Chambers
Newcastle upon Tyne August 1860

From John Rogerson & Co
Newcastle o Tyne

Consignment of Iron to Messrs
John Gibson & Co Mobile, Ala

I John Rogerson of Newcastle on Tyne do solemnly, sincerely, and truly swear that I and my partner, trading under the Firm of John Rogerson & Co are the true and lawful Owners of certain Goods, Wares, or Merchandise, specified in the annexed Invoice, by me subscribed with our said Firm, consisting of Iron Rails &c amounting to One thousand seven hundred Thirty four pounds, one Shilling & one penny shipped or intended to be shipped by the said Firm at the Port of Newcastle-upon-Tyne, on board one vessel bound to Mobile consigned to Mr. J Gibson & Co and that we the said John Rogerson & Co are — the Manufacturers in part of the Goods, Wares, or Merchandise, and that the said Invoice hereunto annexed contains a true and faithful account of the said Goods, Wares, or Merchandise, charged at their actual market value or wholesale price at the time of exportation, in the principal Markets of England, with all charges added, and that the said Invoice contains no Discounts, Bounties, or Drawbacks, but such as have been actually allowed. As witness my hand, this seventh day of September 1860

Sworn before me,

John Rogerson

John Fife J.P.

I, HERBERT DAVY, Vice-Consul of the United States of America at Newcastle-upon-Tyne, do certify and make known to whom these presents shall come, that John Fife Esq before whom the foregoing affidavit of John Rogerson hath been made, is a Justice of the Peace, duly authorized to administer Oaths and Affirmations; that I believe the deponent is worthy of credit, and qualified to verify the annexed Invoice.

In Testimony whereof, I have hereunto set my Hand and Seal of Office, at NEWCASTLE, aforesaid, this seventh day of September in the year of our Lord one thousand eight Hundred and sixty and of the Independence of the UNITED STATES, the 85th

Herbert Davy

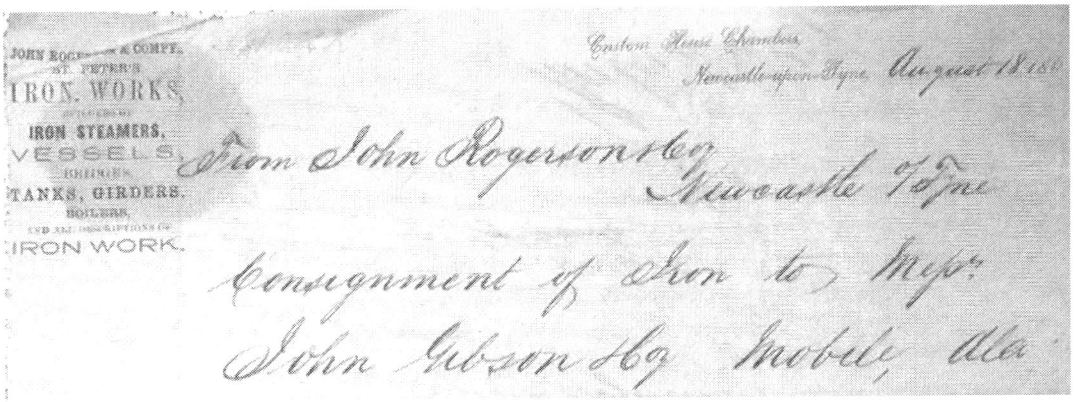
IRON WORKS,
IRON STEAMERS,
VESSELS,
TANKS, GIRDERS,
IRON WORK.

Custom House Chambers
Newcastle-upon-Tyne August 18

From John Rogerson & Co
Newcastle Tyne

Consignment of Iron to Messrs
John Gibson & Co Mobile Ala

Figure 164. Consul's certificate for cargo of railroad iron.

Summary: Multi-page U.S. Consul's certificate (Herbert Davy, Vice-Consul at Newcastle upon Tyne) on form printed with the letterhead of the supplier, John Roberson & Co.

1854-1855
Preprinted Customs Form

No. 43
Importer A Roig (?)
Vessel *Fanny Fern*
From Havana
Entered 20 Nov 1860
Value $ 200   Duty $ 16.00

Summary: Custom form for cargo of green fruit from Havana to Mobile on board the Schr. *Fanny Fern*. Correction on the form indicated that part of the cargo ($ 122 worth) did not survive the voyage, probably due to spoilage.

1856
Invoice

Summary: Invoice for cargo of fruit sold to Capt. J. B. Briggs by M. S. Perez signed in Havana and dated 13 Nov 1860 consisting of 52,000 oranges, 380 ??? quinces, and 22 doz. pineapples.

1857-1858
Preprinted Customs Form

No. 8
Importer Julius Hesse & Co

Vessel <u>*Genl Washington*</u>
From <u>Liverpool</u>
Entered <u>1 Aug 1860</u>
Value $ <u>1417</u> Duty $ <u>212.55</u>

Summary: Cargo of 422 plates **plough steel**[117], weighing 17.2.0.14 or just over 17 tons.

1859
Bill of Lading

Summary: Bill of lading for one cask of earthenware aboard the *Genl. Washington*, Richardson Mr. Ordered by Henry & Mott of Mobile and to be delivered on the wharf in Mobile. Freight cost 12 shillings to be paid at the rate of $ 4.80 per £ Sterling. Dated 16 May 1860 in Liverpool and signed by J. B. Richardson.

1860a
Invoice

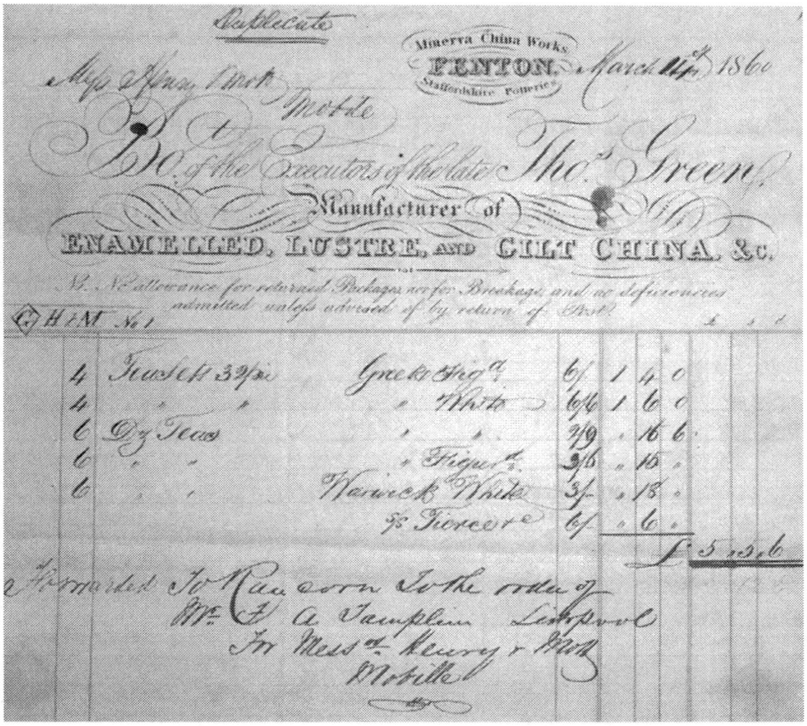
Duplicate

Minerva China Works
FENTON.
Staffordshire Potteries

Messrs Henry & Mott
Mobile

Bo. of the Executors of the late Thos. Green,
Manufacturer of
ENAMELLED, LUSTRE, AND GILT CHINA, &c.
N.B. No allowance for returned Packages nor for Breakage and no deficiencies admitted unless advised of by return of Post.

Figure 165. Invoice for Staffordshire tea sets.

117 "'Plough'-Steel Wire. The term 'plough,' given in England to steel wire of high quality, was derived from the fact that such wire is used for the construction of ropes used for ploughing purposes. It is to be hoped that the term will not be used in this country (U.S.), as it tends to confusion of terms. Plough steel is known here in some steel-works as the quality of plate steel used for the mould-boards of ploughs, for which **a very ordinary grade** is good enough" (Kent, W. *The mechanical engineer's pocket-book*, 1903: 224).

Summary: Invoice from Minerva China Works, Fenton, Staffordshire Potteries to Henry & Mott for an order of tea sets:

4	Tea Sets 32 piece	Greek Fig(ure)d.	6/-	1	4	0			
4	" "	" White	6/6	1	6	0			
6	Doz Teas	" "	2/9	"	16	6			
6	" "	" Figurd.	3/6	"	15	"			
6	" "	Warwick White	3/-	"	18	"			
		s/s Tierce &c	6/-	"	6	"			
							£ 5	5	6

1860b-1861
Invoice

Note: Folded with outside addressed like a letter.

Figure 166. Invoice for shipping expenses sent by letter.

Summary: By separate letter (that went via New York) the shipping expenses charged by Mark A. Tamplin, the forwarder in Liverpool, were explained in detail and quoted here:

Per *Genl Washington*

1 C(as)k (marked) G H&M			
Carriage	£ 0	5	9
DR Chgs 5 Cartage 1/ dR 2/-		3	5
Forwarding Commission		1	0
Customs **Stamp** & Bd (bond?)		2	6
		12	8

By a new law each shipper had to furnish a stamped customs Bd (bond?) hence the additional charge.

1862
Preprinted Customs Form

No. 16
Importer Gelbke Bros
Vessel *Ticonderoga*
From L'pool
Entered 10 Sep 1860
Value $ 126 Duty $ 29.04

1863
Invoice

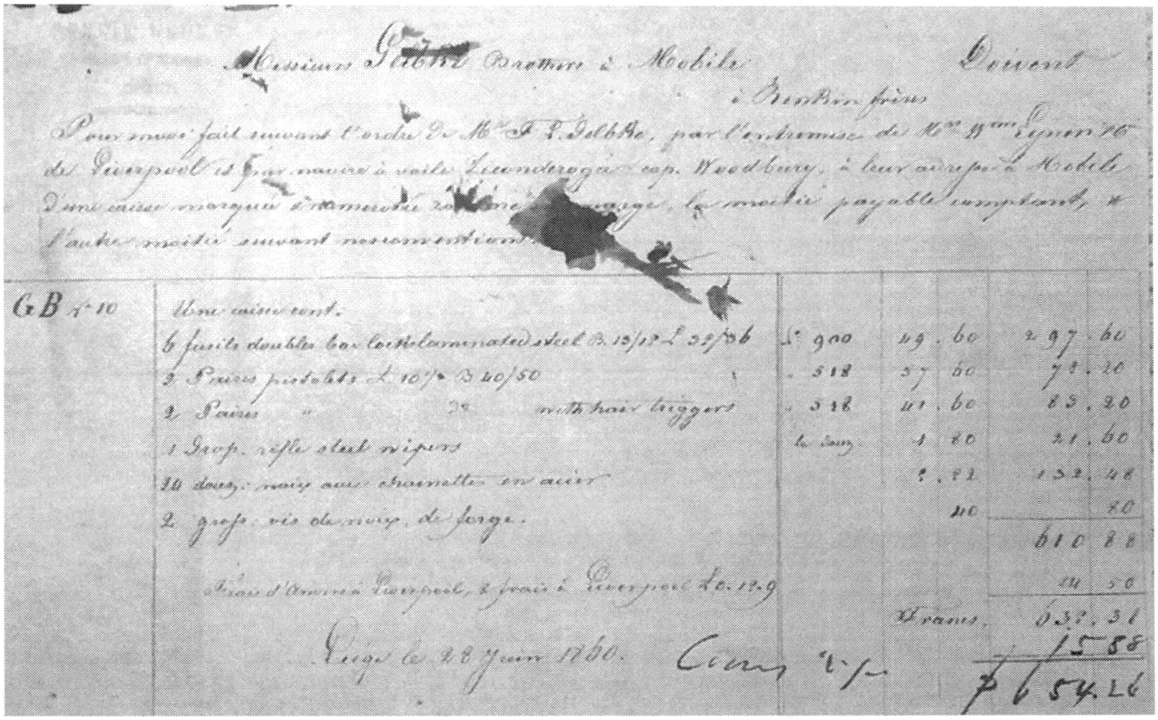

Figure 167. Invoice for high quality firearms from Liege, Belgium.

Summary: Invoice for firearms to F. L. Gelbke Bros. of Mobile from Reuben frères in Liege, Belgium, 28 June 1860 totaling 654.26 Francs. Shipped via Liverpool. Interesting entries: 6 double barrel shot guns, laminated steel, B 13/18 L 35/36 ea 49.60 francs; 2 pairs pistols, L 10½ B 40/50, ea pair 37.60 francs; 2 pair pistols same sizes but with hair triggers, ea pair 41.60 francs.

By coincidence the internet revealed the recent sale of a pair of Gelbke Brothers pistols in a case with all the accompanying tools. The ornate pistols were shown and the photos reproduced here with the seller's permission.

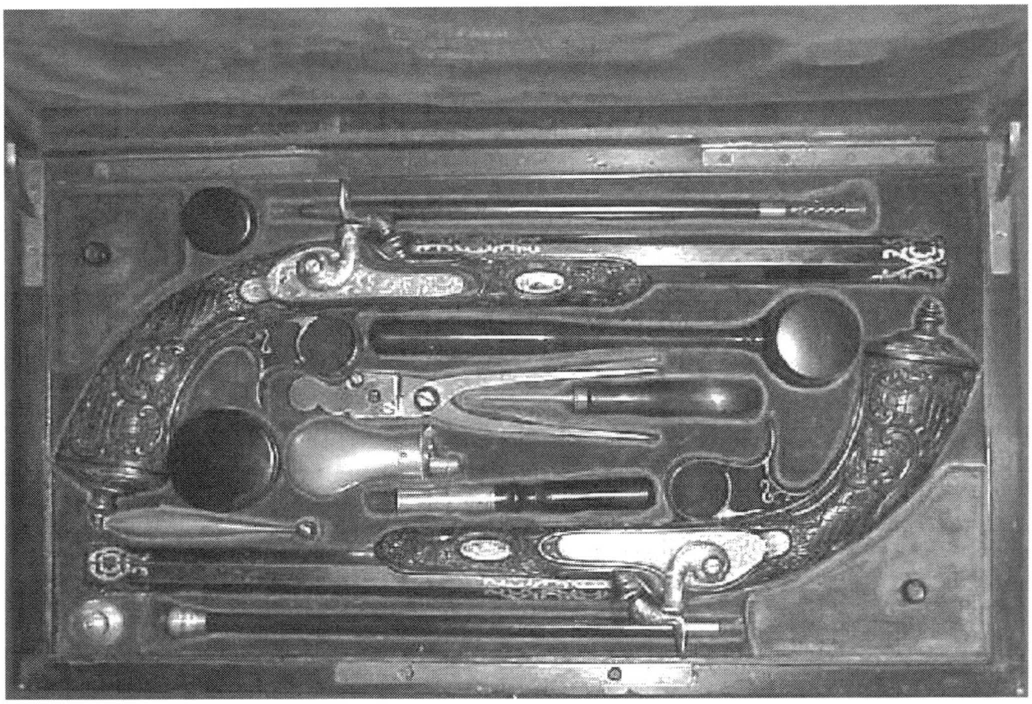

Figure 168. Example of similar, conceivably the same, weapons sold recently.

Described by a modern dealer: "A French made set of dueling pistols made for Gelbke & Brother, Mobile, Alabama. Highly decorated with gold, engraved, elaborate carved ebony grips. An attractive and complete set in excellent condition."

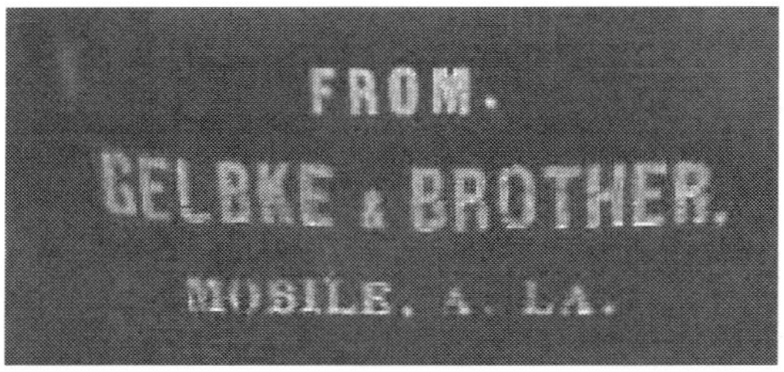

Figure 169. Gelbke & Brother label.

Label inside case lid. Note the error in rendering ALA., abbreviation for Alabama, perhaps in confusion by a non-English speaker who made the box at the gun maker's establishment in Belgium.

1864a
Bill of Lading

Summary: Bill of lading for one case going to Gelbke Brothers in Mobile shipped aboard the *Ticonderoga*, Woodburry Master, dated 4 July 1860 in Liverpool, freight 10/- including **primage** or fee for special care in handling the shipment aboard ship.

1864b
Invoice

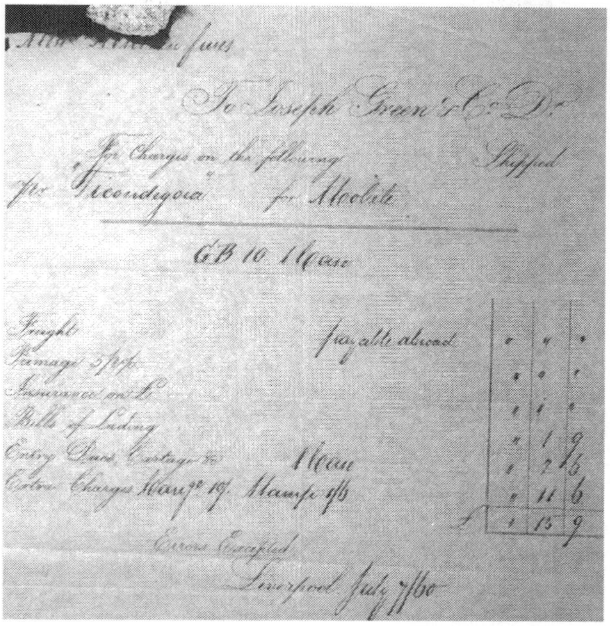
To Joseph Green & Co. Dr
For Charges on the following Shipped
for Mobile
Freight payable abroad
Primage
Insurance on £
Bills of Lading
Entry, Dues, Cartage &c
Extra Charges
£ 15 9
Errors Excepted
Liverpool July 7/60

Figure 170. Invoice for costs of transshipping.

Summary: Invoice to Reuben frères in the amount of 15/9 for transshipping dated 7 July 1860 in Liverpool by forwarder Joseph Green & Co.

1866-1867
Preprinted Customs Form

No. 5
Importer J. T. Soule
Vessel *Uncle Toby*
From L'pool
Entered 5 Octr '60
Value $ 1540 Duty $ 231.00

Summary: Cargo of salt, about 393 tons in 3940 sacks, master of ship was the importer, duty 15%.

1868
Invoice

Summary: Invoice for cargo of salt dated 20 Aug 1860 and totaling £ 320.15.9.

1869
Bill of Lading

Summary: Bill of lading for salt dated 25 Aug 1860.

1871-1872
Preprinted Customs Form

No. 28
Importer O. Mazange & Co.
Vessel *Minnesota*
From Lpool
Entered 10 Octr 60
Value $ 4530 Duty $ 917.76

Owner's Oath
(signed) A. J. Mullany, owner
Sworn to, this 10 day of October 1860
T. J. Butler Collector

Mdse. Entered 10 Octr 1860 Ship Entered 9 Octr 1860
Entry of Merchandise imported into the Port and District of Mobile, by O. Mazange & Co in the ship *Minnesota* Deshon Master, from Liverpool

Summary: 8 casks **anvils**; 17 bags nails; 33 casks mills, hooks & hinges, traces &c, hoes, pickaxes, vices, pans &c, perc(ussion) caps &c; 3 Bdls. **wheels**; 1 bdl. pans; 8 cases cast steel bars.

1873
Bill of Lading

Summary: Bill of lading for 8 casks hardware by John Trippett & Brother of Liverpool, forwarder, signed 10th August 1860 by F. B. Deshon, Master, shipping charges £ 2.15.2 including 2/8 primage for delivery on the wharf at Mobile.

1874-1875
Invoice

Summary: Invoice from Corson, Denton, Burdekin, & Co. of Sheffield dated July 25, 1865 to O. Mazange & Co. for anvils.

1876-1877
Invoice

Summary: Invoice from Naylor, Vickers & Co. of Sheffield to O. Mazange & Co. for bar steel, cast steel, blister steel, and German steel totaling £ 274.12.0.

1878
Invoice

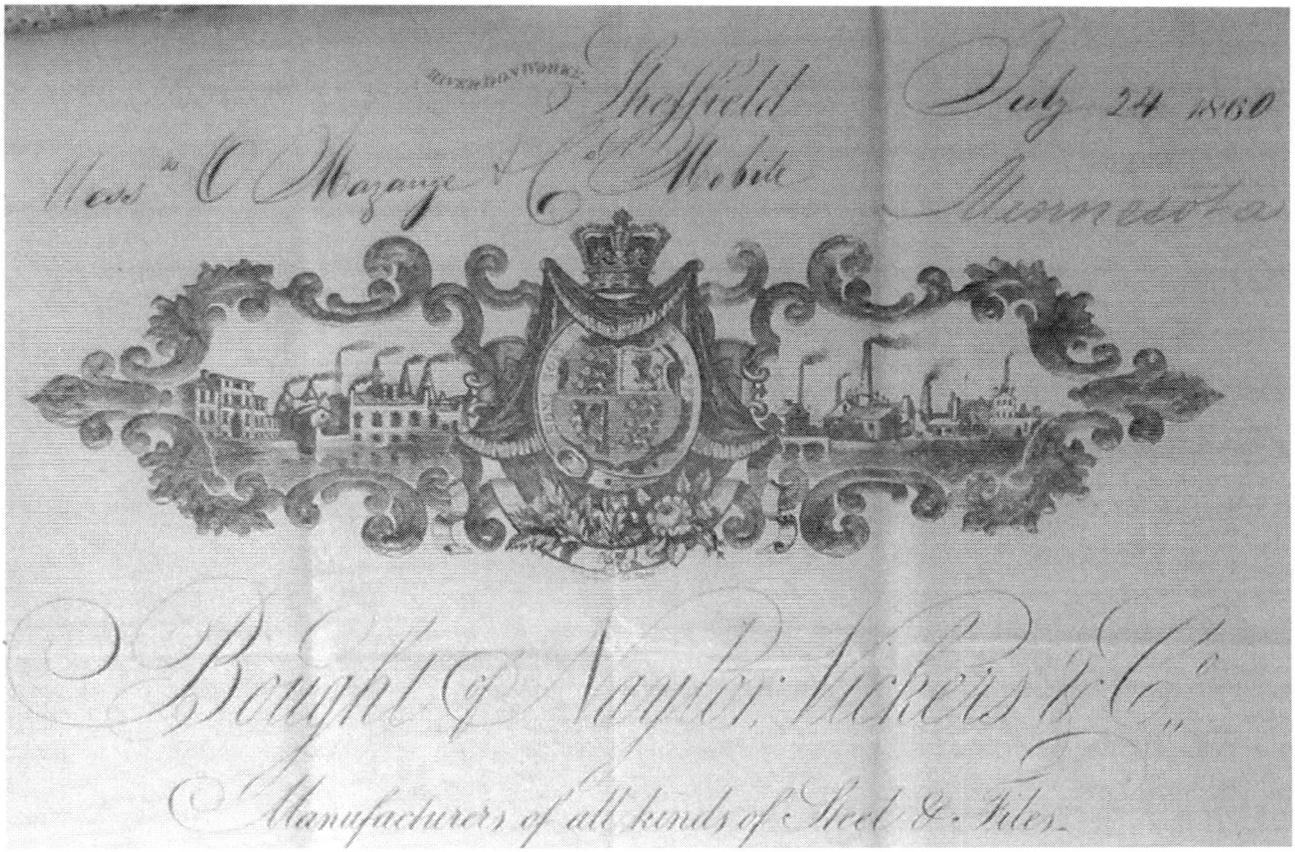
River Don Works
Sheffield July 24 1860
Mess.rs O Mazange & Co Mobile
Minnesota
Bought of Naylor Vickers & Co.
Manufacturers of all kinds of Steel & Files

Figure 171. Invoice from Naylor, Vickers, & Co. for steel.

Summary: Separate order for steel with same firms as above dated 24 July 1860 totaling £ 42.5.8.

1879
Bill of Lading

Summary: Bill of lading for steel in 4 cases sheet steel, and two cases and forty seven bundles of bar steel from Liverpool to the wharf at Mobile dated 27 July 1860 in Liverpool for total transport cost of £ 8.11.9 including primage. Capt. F. B. Deshon of the *Minnesota* signed and noted that seven of the bundles were received in rusty condition. Total weight of steel cargo 7.5.1.18 (tons, cwt., qrs., and lbs.).

1880-1882
Invoice

Summary: Invoice for costs of transshipping in New Orleans 54 packages shipped on board the *Minnesota* and addressed to O. Mazange &Co., Mobile. F. W. Tilton of New Orleans billed Brown Shipley & Co. of Liverpool for costs of £ 7.6.? (third numeral illegible) for transshipping in New Orleans, dated 10 August 1860. From the itemized list of costs it seemed the British consul in New Orleans facilitated the transshipping.

1883
Bill of Lading

Summary: Bill of lading further hard ware cargo shipped to Mazange & Co. on the *Minnesota* dated 10 August 1860 in Liverpool total cost of shipping £ 18.10.9. Cargo: 4 casks hollow ware, 29 casks hardware, 3 bundles wheels, 17 bags nails, and one bundle pans for delivery at the wharf in Mobile.

1884-1895
Invoice

Summary: Multi-page invoice detailing the hardware above from Van Wart Son & Co. dated Birmingham 9 August 1860. Interesting details: Z. Parkes corn mills with 1 handle, hopper, and fly wheel, 10 each at 50 shillings each totaling 6.19.9 discount, and costs included; Carolina hoes and grubbing hoes; 400 pairs traces, one size and description detail example – 6½ feet 10 link No. 4 best round iron polished straight traces; 48 Rogers warranted steelyards assorted 100–250 lb. in 50 lb. increments.

1896-1897
Preprinted Customs Form

No. 3
Importer Kop & Howland
Vessel Schr. *Break O Day*

From Ruatan[118]
Entered 12 May 1860
Value $ 570 Duty $ 44.00

Owner's Oath
(signed) J Peresi of Kopf & Howland, owner
Sworn to, this 12th day of May 1860
(signed) T. J. Butler Collector

Mdse. Entered 12 May 1860 Ship Entered May 11 1860
Entry of Merchandise imported into the Port and District of Mobile, by Kopp & Howland in the Sch. *Break O'Day* Deusy Master, from Ruatan

Packages	Contents	Value in Foreign Currency					Duties
	Coca Nuts	$ 37.92			$ 40	4%	$ 1.60
	Green fruit	606.38			530	8%	42.40
		$ 644.30			$ 570		$ 44.00
	For Chgs & Com	21.20					
		$ 665.50					
	Less rotted	95.25					
		$ 570.25					
Ruatan							

1898
Invoice

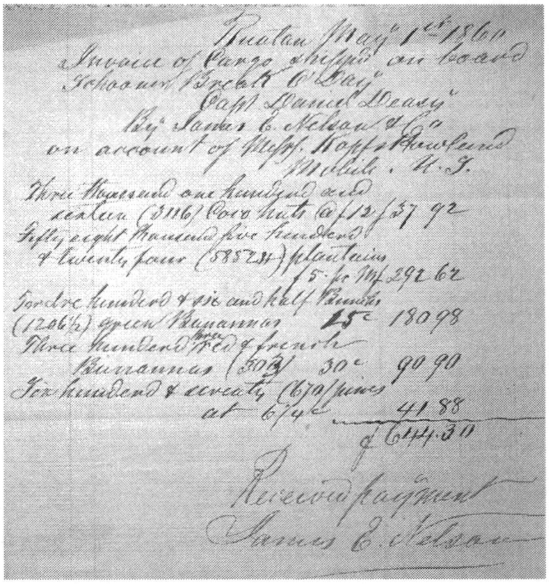
Ruatan May 1st 1860
Invoice of Cargo shipped on board
Schooner Break O'Day
Capt Daniel Deasy
By James E. Nelson & Co
on account of Messrs. Kopp & Howland
Mobile. U. S.
Three thousand one hundred and sixteen (3116) Coco Nuts @ $12 $37 92
Fifty eight thousand five hundred & twenty four (58524) plantains
$5 pr M $292 62
Twelve hundred & six and half [illegible] (1206½) green Bananas 15c 180 98
Three hundred three [illegible] & [illegible] Bananas (303) 30c 90 90
Six hundred & seventy (670) pines at 6¼c 41 88
$644.30
Received payment
James E. Nelson

Figure 172. Invoice for fresh fruit.

[118] One of the Bay Islands of Honduras.

Ruatan May 1st 1860

Invoice of Cargo shipped on board Schooner *Break O' Day*
Capt Daniel Deusay
By James E. Nelson & Co.
On account of Messrs. Kopp & Howland
Mobile, U.S.

Three thousand one hundred and Sixteen (3116) Coco Nuts @ ¢12/		37.92
Fifty eight thousand five hundred & twenty four (58524) plantains ¢5 pr M/		292.62
Twelve hundred & six and half Bushels (1206½) green Bananas	25¢	180.98
Three hundred three Red & French Bananas (303) 30¢		90.90
Six hundred & seventy (670) pieces at 6¼¢		41.88
		$ 644.30

Received payment
James E. Nelson

1899-1900
Preprinted Customs Form

No. 1
Importer The Mobile & Ohio RR Co
Vessel *Chicago*
From Cardiff
Entered 3 May 1860
Value $ 39531 Duty $ 9487.44

Owner's Oath
(signed) J. C. Colsson, Secretary of the Mobile & Ohio Railroad, owner
Sworn to, this 3 day of May 1860
T. J. Butler Collector

Mdse. Entered 3 May 1860 Ship Entered 18 April 1860
Entry of Merchandise imported into the Port and District of Mobile, by The Mobile & Ohio Railroad Co in the Ship *Chicago* Chase Master, from Cardiff

Summary: Cargo of 5,542 **rails** @ £ 6, 11,800 fishbars @ 10 (shillings?), and 23 casks bolts 23,650 @ £ 22. Total tons 263.5.0.26.

1901-1902
Preprinted Customs Form

No. 1
Importer D. Jones
Vessel Br ship *Maitland*
From Ascension[119]
Entered 3 May 1860
Value $ 21 Duty $ 5.04

Owner's Oath
(signed) David Jones, owner
Sworn to, this Third day of May 1860
(signed) T. J. Butler Collector

Mdse. Entered 3 May 1860 Ship Entered 20 April 1860
Entry of Merchandise imported into the Port and District of Mobile, by Kopp & Howland in the Br Ship *Maitland* Jones Master, from Ascension

Packages	Contents	Value in Foreign Currency				24	Duties
	Common Coal (gas) 10/6 tons 8	£ 4	4	0			
	Chgs & Com 5%		4	2			
		£ 4	8	2	$ 21.32	$ 21	$ 5.04
Ascension							

1901c and d
Invoices

Summary: The two invoices did not match the customs form for reasons that were not clear. The invoices did give interesting details: 200 tubs 314 lbs. (each), total 62,800 lbs., 28 tons, **gas coal** transshipped in Ascension from St. Paul de Loanda (modern Luanda, Angola) aboard Br. Ship *Lord Harriston* (?), Halstead master. From the "gas coal" designation it seems Mobile may have had gas service by this date.

1904-1905
Preprinted Customs Form

[119] South Atlantic Island.

No. 26
Importer Le Baron (?) & Son
Vessel *James Rose*
From Matanzas
Entered May 1860
Value $ 1633 Duty $ 391.92

Mdse. Entered May 1860 Ship Entered May 25 1860
Entry of Merchandise imported into the Port and District of Mobile, by C. Le Baron & Son in the brig *James Rose* Dastays Master, from Matanzas

Summary: Cargo of Molasses 50 bbls. with 7418 gals. and 30 tierces with 2317 gals., for a total 9735 gals.

1906-1907
Preprinted Customs Form

Free
No.
Importer G. Westfeld & Bro
Vessel *J. G. Richardson*
From Rio de Janeiro
Entered 29 Dec 1860
Value $ 57740 Duty $ Free
Coffee 453644 lbs

Mdse. Entered Dec 29 1860 Ship Entered 29 Dec 1860
Entry of Merchandise imported into the Port and District of Mobile, by Geo Westfeldt in the Ship *J. G. Richardson* Wright Master, from Rio de Janeiro

Summary: Coffee in 3,000 bags of 50 lbs. each, total 15,020 lbs. costing 101,549,060 Rs. (reales) valued at $1 to 2,000 rs. This seemed to be an entire shipload of coffee and a big contrast to the small wartime shipments.

1908
Bill of Lading

Summary: Bill of lading for 3,004 bags coffee, 5 arrobas weight each. It seems the ship was charted to carry this cargo to Mobile and the cargo was per order and sailing from Rio, Sept. 1860 (no day given). Shipper in Rio was Edward Johnston & Co.

1910
Invoice

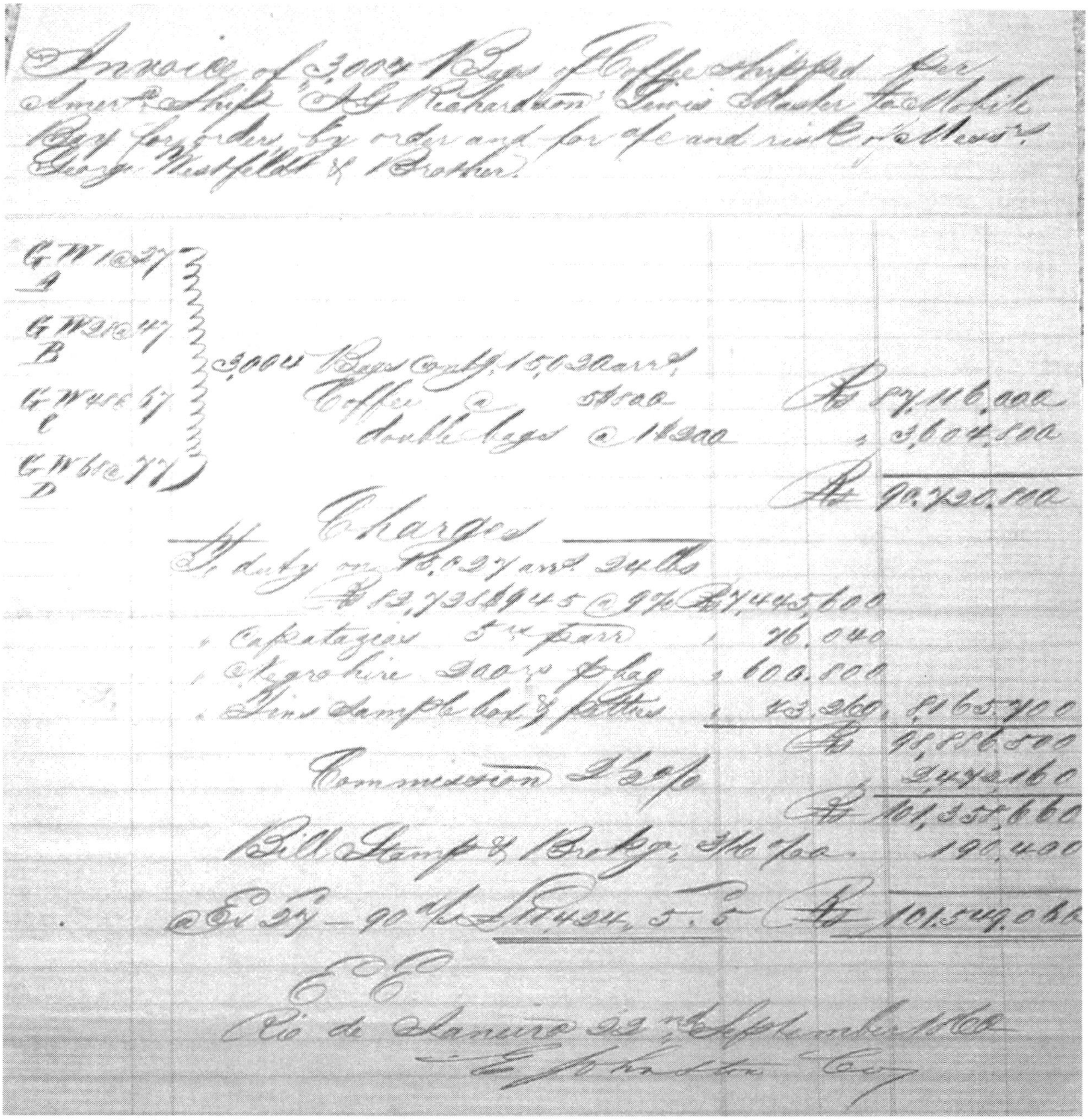

Invoice of 3,004 Bags of Coffee shipped per Amer. Ship "A. G. Richardson" Lewis Master to Mobile for order, by order and for a/c and risk of Messrs. George Westfeldt & Brother.

GW 1 @ 27 A
GW 31 @ 47 B
GW 48 @ 67 C
GW 68 @ 77 D

3,004 Bags cont. 15,0?? arr. Coffee @ 5$800		Rs 87,116,000
double bags @ 1$200		3,604,800
		Rs 90,720,800
Charges		
Duty on 15,027 arr. 24 lbs Rs 13,738$945 @ 9%	Rs 1,445,600	
Capatazias 5 rs p. arr.	76,040	
Negro hire 200 rs p. bag	600,800	
Lines, stamp, lab. & fatters	43,260	2,165,700
		Rs 92,886,500
Commission 2½%		2,442,160
		Rs 101,355,660
Bill Stamp & Brokge. 3/16%		190,400
@ Ex 27-90 ... £ 11,424. 5. 5		Rs 101,549,060

E. E.

Rio de Janeiro 22nd September 1860

E. Johnston & Co.

Figure 173. Invoice for shipload of coffee from Brazil.

Summary: Invoice for coffee dated 22 Sept 1860 signed by E. Johnston & Co. Interestingly, the ship's master was said to be Lewis indicating a mistake or a change in command before the end of the voyage since a different master was specified on the customs form filled out at Mobile.

1911-1912
Preprinted Customs Form

Free
No.
Importer A. Skolfield
Vessel *J. L. Dimmick*
From Genoa
Entered 20 Dec '60
Value $ 35 Duty $ Free

Mdse. Entered 20 Dec 1860 Ship Entered Dec 1860
Entry of Merchandise imported into the Port and District of Mobile, by A. Skolfield in the Ship *J. L. Dimmick* Master, from Genoa

Summary: One package containing a **marble lectern** costing 190 lira with charges.

Note: If the lectern was intended for a church one might identify this as dramatic foreshadowing considering all the funerals soon to be needed.

1913-1914
Preprinted Customs Form

No. 12
Importer A. L. Skolfield
Vessel *J. L. Dimmick*
From Genoa
Entered 20 Dec '60
Value $ 60 Duty $ 18.00

Owner's Oath
(signed) Alfred Skolfield, owner
Sworn to, this 20 day of Dec 1860
(signed) T. J. Butler Collector

Mdse. Entered 20 Dec 1860 Ship Entered Dec 1860
Entry of Merchandise imported into the Port and District of Mobile, by A Skolfield in the Ship *J. L. Dimmick* Skolfield Master, from Genoa

Summary: 3 cases **alabaster ornaments** costing 320.25 lira with charges. Cargo originally from Sardinia.

1916-1917
Preprinted Customs Form

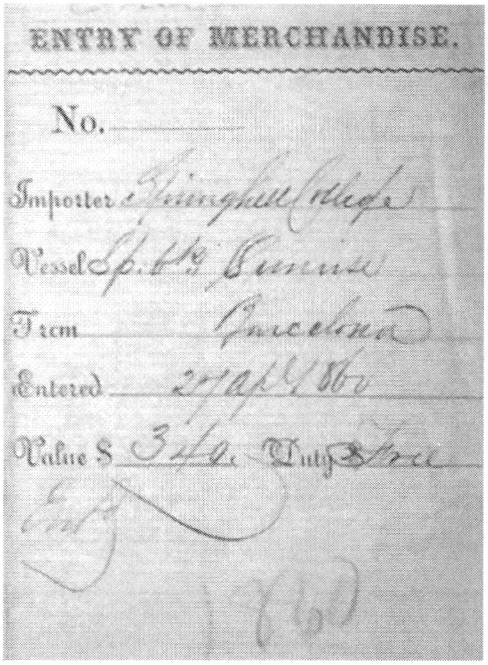

ENTRY OF MERCHANDISE.

No.

Importer Springhill College

Vessel Sp. bk Sunrise

From Barcelona

Entered 27 Apl 1860

Value $ 340 Duty $ Free

Figure 174. Customs form for shipment of books for Springhill College.

Free
No.
Importer Springdale College
Vessel Sp. (Spanish) bk (bark) *Sunrise*
From Barcelona
Entered 27 Apl 1860
Value $ 340 Duty $ Free

Owner's Oath
(signed) F Gautrelet, **president of the Springhill College**, owner
Sworn to, this 27 day of April 1860
(signed) T. J. Butler Collector

Mdse. Entered 12 May 1860 Ship Entered May 11 1860
Entry of Merchandise imported into the Port and District of Mobile, by The Springhill College in the Sp.(anish) Bark *Sunrise* Roig Master, from Barcelona

Summary: Customs form for **box of books**, 2710.00 Reales, $ 340.00.

1919-1920
Preprinted Customs Form

Summary: 128 bbls. chestnuts, 12 lbs. per bbl., 1648.20 "Lira of Sardinia," $ 306.58, imported by Geo. Hite aboard the Ship *H. H. Boody*, Badger Master, from Genoa. Customs form also noted Sardinia, perhaps an interim stop, ship entered 16 Jan 1860, and merchandise entered 21 Jan 1860.

1923
Invoice

Summary: Invoice for **chestnuts** dated 21 Nov 1859 in Genoa totaling 1648.20 lira.

1921a & b
Power of Attorney and Bill of Lading

Summary: Power of attorney from Santana Brothers of New Orleans, buyers of the chestnuts, appointing as their agent George Hite of Mobile, port of arrival of the cargo.

1922
Owner's Oath

Summary: Owner's oath recorded at Port of New Orleans for cargo of chestnuts signed by Joseph Lantana and dated 16 Jan 1860.

1923
Invoice

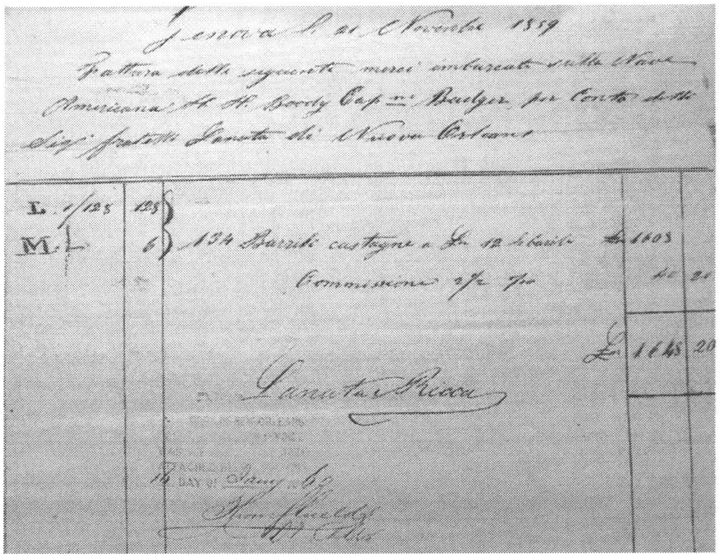
Genova li 21 Novembre 1859
Fattura delle seguenti merci imbarcate sulla Nave Americana H. H. Boody Cap.no Badger per Conto delli Sig.i fratelli Lanata di Nuova Orleans

L. 1/125	125	134 Barrili castagne a L. 12 il barile	L. 1608	
M.	6	Commissione 2½ %	40	20
			L. 1648	20

Lanata e Ricco

16 day of Jany 60

Figure 175. Invoice for shipment of chestnuts from Genoa.

Summary: Invoice for 134 barrels of chestnuts shipped from Genoa.

12

Early War Mobile Customs Manifests,

Various Ships and Dates

1617-1618
Preprinted Customs Form

No. ___
Importer Martin
Vessel Br schr *Wide Awake*
From Havana
Entered Jany. 1862
Value $ 692.00 Duty $ free

Owner's Oath
Martin, owner of cargo and master of ship
(signed) D. A. Martin
Sworn to, this 1 day of Jany 1862

Ship Entered 1 Jany 1862

Entry of Merchandise, imported into the Port and District of Mobile, by Martin in the Br. Schr *Wide Awake* Martin Master, from Havana

Packages	Contents	Value in Foreign Currency				15	Duties
3705 lbs.	**Pig Lead** lbs 3705	$ 277.87					Free
15 Bbls	Sulphur " 5250	354.50					
2	Swords	28.00					
	Charges	20.00					
		$ 692.37					

Note: Lead for making bullets was in critically short supply leading even to such measures as gleaning spent rounds from battlefields. Though somewhat later in date, the following newspaper article also illustrates the problem. Records from Fort Morgan show that the *Denbigh* had lead cargo at least once and some had been jettisoned during a grounding. Fort Morgan's artifact collection includes lead bars found in the dunes nearby.

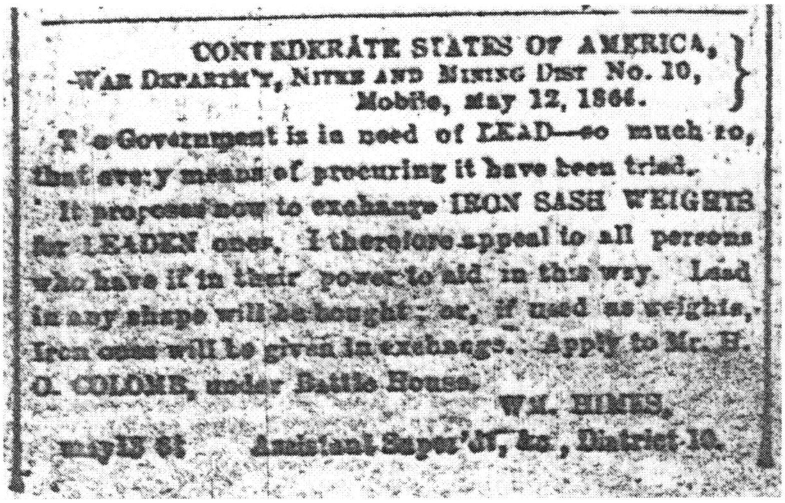

CONFEDERATE STATES OF AMERICA,
WAR DEPARTM'T, NITRE AND MINING DIST No. 10,
Mobile, May 12, 1864.

The Government is in need of LEAD—so much so, that every means of procuring it have been tried.

It proposes now to exchange IRON SASH WEIGHTS for LEADEN ones. I therefore appeal to all persons who have it in their power to aid in this way. Lead in any shape will be bought; or, if used as weights, Iron ones will be given in exchange. Apply to Mr. H. O. COLOMB, under Battle House.

WM. HIMES,
may13 6t Assistant Super'dt, &c., District 10.

Figure 176. Newspaper appeal for lead.

Government notice about shortage of lead (*Mobile Register and Advertiser* May 16, 1864).

1619
Invoice

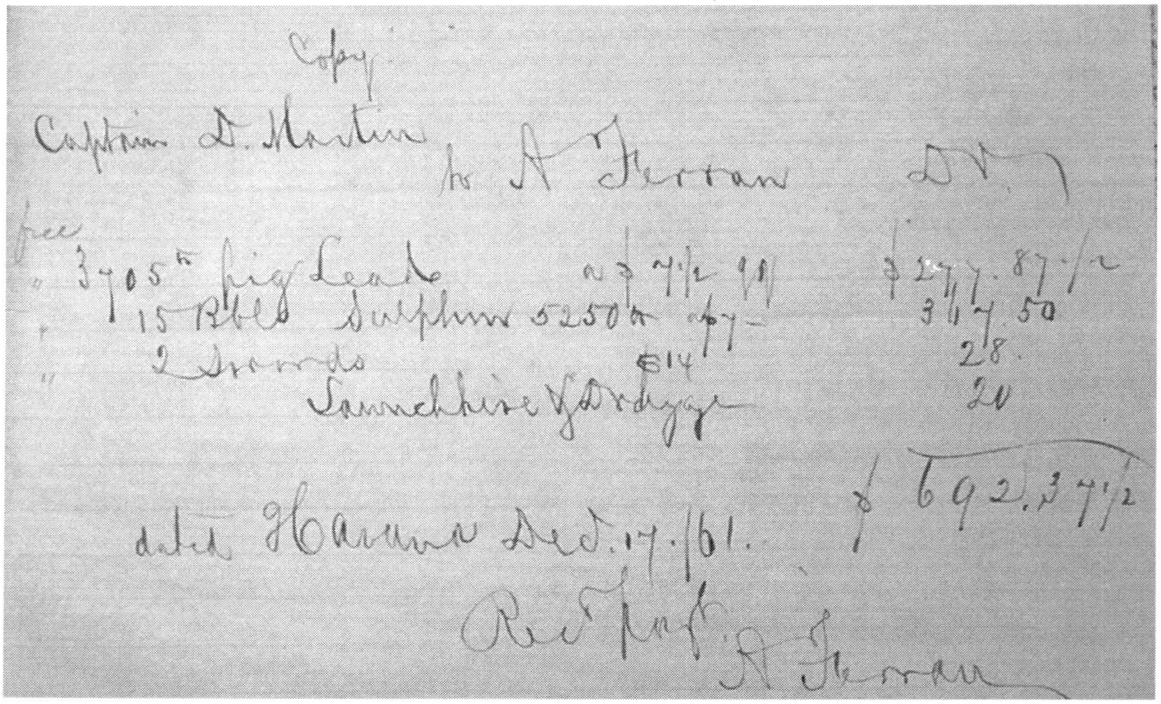

Copy

Captain D. Martin
to A. Terran Dr

3705 lb pig Lead @ $7½ $277.87½
15 Bbls Sulphur 5250 lb @ 7 367.50
2 Swords $14 28
Launchhire & Drayage 20

$692.37½

dated Havana Dec. 17. /61.

Rec'd Payt. A. Terran

Figure 177. Invoice for lead, sulfur, and swords.

Summary: Invoice for lead, sulfur, and swords bought from A. Terran in Havana at a cost of $ 692.37½.

1620-1621
Preprinted Customs Form

No. __
Importer Martin
Vessel Br. Schr *Wide Awake*
From Havana
Entered 1 Jany. 1862
Value $ 4484 Duty $ free

Owner's Oath
Martin, owner of cargo and master of ship
(signed) D. A. Martin
Sworn to, this 1 day of Jany 1862
T. J. Butler Collector

Ship Entered 1 January 1862
Entry of Merchandise imported into the Port and District of Mobile, by Martin in the Br. Schr *Wide Awake* Martin Master, from Havana

Packages	Contents	Value in Foreign Currency					Duties
148 bags	Coffee lbs 314,855	$ 4,247.00					free
	Bags	55.50					
	Charge	50.56					
	Brokage.	21.50					
		$ 4,374.56					
		109.36					
	Com	$ 4,483.92					

1622
Invoice

Summary: Invoice for cigars (7,000) and coffee (1 bag) on board the British Schooner *Clara* from Havana to Mobile on a/c and risk of T. (?) Guzman, Jr. of Mobile. Total $ 225.08, dated 14 Jan 62.

1623-1624
Preprinted Customs Form

No. No.1
Importer D. A. Martin
Vessel Br. Schr *Wide Awake*
From Havana

Entered 1 Jany 1862
Value $ 668 Duty $ 99.99

Owner's Oath
D. A. Martin, owner of cargo and master of ship
(signed) D. A. Martin
Sworn to, this 1 day of Jany 1862
T. J. Butler Collector

Ship Entered 1 January 1862

Entry of Merchandise imported into the Port and District of Mobile, by D. A. Martin in the British Schr *Wide Awake* Martin Master, from Havana

Marks	Packages	Contents	Value in Foreign Currency					Duties
L	3 Casks	Soda Ashe lbs 3,386	$ 169.30					
		add coms	4.23		$ 173,53			
	2 Boxes	**Leeches**	152.00					
		Add Coms 2½	3.80		155.80	*		
	2 ps.	Blue Broad Cloth 63.28 ea	204.07½					
		Com	5.35		219.51			
	10 Cases	Castile Soap lbs 1042	109.41					
		Com	2.73		112.14			
	10 Cases	Olive Oil Doz 10	55.00					
		Chgs	1.37		56.37			
	1 Cask	Claret Eng 59	27.00					
		Com	1.00		28.00			
					$ 745.35			
		Less 1 box not delivd.			78.00			
					$ 667.35			

*** Less 1 box Leeches thrown overboard $78. (Spoilage in transit?)**

1625-1627
Preprinted Customs Form

No. No.2
Importer D. A. Martin
Vessel Br. Schr *Wide Awake*
From Havana
Entered 3 Jany 1862
Value $ 76 Duty $ 11.40

Agent's Oath
D. A. Martin, Agent
Wm. McAliston Esq, Owner
(signed) D. A. Martin
Sworn to, this 1 day of Jany 1862
T. J. Butler Collector

Ship Entered 1 January '62

Entry of Merchandise imported into the Port and District of Mobile, by D. A. Martin in the Br. Schr *Wide Awake* Martin Master, from Havana

Packages	Contents	Value in Foreign Currency					Duties
Two boxes	**Leeches** 4000	$ 76.00			76	15%	$ 11.40

1628-1629
Preprinted Customs Form

No. No. 3
Importer Wm. Peck
Vessel Schr *Wm. Mallory*
From Havana
Entered 3 Jany 1862
Value $ 4437 Duty $ 609.65

Owner's Oath
William Peck
(signed) William Peck
Sworn to, this 3 day of Jany 1862
T. J. Butler Collector

Ship Entered January 1862

Entry of Merchandise imported into the Port and District of Mobile, by W. Peck & Co. in the Br. Schr *Wide Awake* (contradicts reverse side) Martin Master, from Havana

Packages	Contents	Value in Foreign Currency					Duties
Sundry Packages	??? (smeared)	$ 60				5%	3.00
"	Carbonate ??? &c	2,080				10%	208.00
"	Olive Oil, Leeches &c	1,392				15%	208.80
"	Soap, ??? &c	876				20%	175.20
"	Cigars	103				25%	25.75
	including chgs & Com	$ 4511					$ 620.75
	Less Leeches thrown overboard	74					11.10
		$ 4437					$ 609.65

1633-1634
Preprinted Customs Form

No. No 6
Importer M. D. Eslava
Vessel Br. Schr *Clara*
From Havana
Entered January 1862
Value $ 1183 Duty $ 233.95

Owner's Oath
(signed) M. D. Eslava
Sworn to, this 27th day of January 1862
T. J. Butler Collector

Ship Entered 27 January 1862

Entry of Merchandise imported into the Port and District of Mobile, by M D Eslava in the Br. Schr *Clara* Master, from Havana

Marks	Packages	Contents	Value in Foreign Currency			Duties
A	14 Pkgs.	Ker. (kerosene) oil Gals 430	280.08			
	10 "	Raisins lbs 175	17.50			
	10"	Sweet oil Doz 30	30.00			
	1 "	Cheese lbs 120	18.00			
	15 "	Soap lbs 1074	58.57			
	2 "	Starch	5.00			
	1 "	Paper	24.00			
	4 "	Ker. Oil Gal 160	100.00			
	4 "	Candles lbs 120	31.20			
	31,500	Segars & w pks Cigarettes	471.50			
	1 Box	Shoe thread	75.00			
	3, ¼ Casks	Red Wine $30 & charges & Com	72.21			
			$ 1,183.00			
		Cheese	18	10%		$ 1.80
		Oil &c	552	15%		82.80
		Raisins Soap	78	20%		15.60
		Wine	31	25%		7.75
		Cigars	504	25%		126.00
			$ 1183			$ 233.95

1635-1636
Preprinted Customs Form

No. No.7
Importer Jn W. Innerarity (?)
Vessel Br. Schr *Clara*
From Havana
Entered 27 Jany 1862
Value $ 16 Duty $ 4.00

Owner's Oath
Jno. Innerarity (?)
(signed) John W Innerarity
Sworn to, this 27th day of Jany 1862
T. J. Butler Collector

Ship Entered 27 Jany '62
Entry of Merchandise imported into the Port and District of Mobile, by Jn Innerarity in the Br. Schr *Clara* Master, from Havana

Packages	Contents	Value in Foreign Currency					Duties
1 Cask ¼	Red Wine 32 (gals ?)	$ 15					
	Chgs & C	1					
		$ 16			$ 16	25%	$ 4.00
1 Sack	Coffee						

1638-1639
Preprinted Customs Form

No. No. 8
Importer John Douglas
Vessel Br. Schr *Clara*
From Havana
Entered 27 Jany 1862
Value $ 108 Duty $ 16.20

Owner's Oath
D. A. Martin, owner of cargo and master of ship
(signed) John Douglas
Sworn to, this 27 day of Jany 1862
T. J. Butler Collector

Ship Entered 27 Jany 1862
Entry of Merchandise imported into the Port and District of Mobile, by Jn Douglas in the Br. Schr *Clara* Master, from Havana

Packages	Contents	Value in Foreign Currency					Duties
30 yds (?)	Calico @ 3½	$ 105.00					
	Coms	2.62					
		$ 107.62			$ 108	15%	$ 16.20

1640
Invoice

Summary: Invoice, 2 copies, for calico John Douglas bought of W. Douglas dated Jan 16th 1862 in Havana totaling $ 107.62 and 1 bag of coffee, duty free, costing $31.50.

1641-1642
Preprinted Customs Form

No. No. 9
Importer E. H. Weed
Vessel Br. Schr *Clara*
From Havana
Entered 27 Jany 1862
Value $ 57 Duty $ 13.10

Owner's Oath
Ed. H. Weed
(signed) Edward H. Weed
Sworn to, this 27 day of Jany 1862
T. J. Butler Collector

Ship Entered January 27/62

Entry of Merchandise imported into the Port and District of Mobile, by E. H. Weed in the Schr (Br) *Clara* Master, from Havana

Packages	Contents	Value in Foreign Currency					Duties
	Green fruit	$ 3.00					
1 Box	preserves	12.00					
	Cigars	22.50					
1¼ Cask	Red Wine	12.00					
1 Box	Oil (Ker.) (kerosene)	7.00					
		$ 56.50					
	fruit			3		10%	$ 0.30
	pres &c			47		25%	11.75
	Ker oil			7		15%	1.05
				$ 57			$ 13.10

1643-1644
Preprinted Customs Form

No. ___
Importer M D Eslava
Vessel Br. Schr *Clara*

From Havana
Entered 27 Jany 1862
Value $ 8169 Duty $ free

Owner's Oath
(signed) M. D. Eslava
Sworn to, this 27 day of Jany 1862
T. J. Butler Collector

Ship Entered Jany 27/62

Entry of Merchandise imported into the Port and District of Mobile, by M D Eslava in the Br. Schr *Clara* Rogers Master, from Havana

Packages	Contents	Value in Foreign Currency	Duties
30 Boxes	Gun powder 3000 (lbs)	$ 948.63	
20 "	" " 2000 (lbs)	633.45	
230 Bags	Coffee 37,260 (lbs)	6,457.06	
13 Bales	Leaf Tobneer (Tobacco?)	130.00	
		$ 8,169.14	Free

1646-1649
Preprinted Customs Form

Summary: Entry from New York, May 8, 1861 aboard Brig *East*, Spates Master, included dolls.

1651
Invoice

Summary: Sundries – 2/3 doz. Crying Dolls, $3.50 May have been a last large order of fancy goods from before the war but arriving after hostilities commenced. Ordered from Lathrop & Wilkinson, Importers and Dealers in Foreign and Domestic Fancy Goods, New York, N.Y.

1708-1709
Preprinted Customs Form

Note: The Oath blocks on the outside of customs form 1708 were not used, no signatures. Invoices accompanying the customs forms were mostly omitted by the author in the rest of this chapter.

No. ___
Importer H O Brewer & Co.
Vessel *Alice*
From Havana

Entered 10 Jany 63
Value $ 1270 Bushels Duty $ 25.40

Ship Entered ________

Entry of Merchandise imported into the Port and District of Mobile, by H O Brewer & Co. in the *Alice* Nelson (?) Master, from Havana

Packages	Contents	Value in Foreign Currency					Duties
342 Sacks	Salt 1270 Bushels	$ 513					
	(average 208 lbs ea.)						
	Salt (Common)	1270 Bushels	@ 24				$ 25.40

1710-1711
Preprinted Customs Form

No. ___
Importer M D Eslava
Vessel *Relief*
From Havana
Entered Feby 12
Value $ 705 Duty $ Free

(Oath blocks not used.)

Ship Entered ________

Entry of Merchandise imported into the Port and District of Mobile, by M D Eslava in the Schr *Relief* Master, from Havana

Packages	Contents	Value in Foreign Currency					Duties
15 Sacks	Coffee 2928 lbs	550					
	Lead, in pigs 4500 "	155					
		$ 705					
	Free						

1712-1713
Preprinted Customs Form

No. ___ Free goods
Importer T Lecerne & Co
Vessel *Laura Dudly*
From Havana
Entered ______
Value $_____ Duty $ _____

Owner's Oath
(signed) Julius Bithier (?)
Sworn to, this ___ day of _______ 18__
___________ Collector

Ship Entered _______

Entry of Merchandise imported into the Port and District of Mobile, by T Lecerne (?) & Co. in the *Laura Dudly* _______________ Master, from Havana

Packages	Contents		Value in Foreign Currency					Duties
	4100 lbs	Powder	$ 1452					
	2062 "	Coffee	392					
	2 Gross	Per.(cussion) Caps	36					
			1808					Free

1714-1715
Preprinted Customs Form

No. ___
Importer E H Weed
Vessel *Relief*
From Havana
Entered Feby 12 1863
Value $ 75 Duty $ 11.25

Owner's Oath
(signed) Edwd H. Weed

Ship Entered 6 Feb 1863

Entry of Merchandise imported into the Port and District of Mobile, by E. H. Weed in the Schr *Relief* Master, from Havana

Packages	Contents	Value in Foreign Currency			15		Duties
1 Box	Containing Sundry articles						
	of clothing with Chgs & Com	$ 75.00			75		$ 11.25

1717a
Invoice

M. D. Eslava

Invoiced		2642.63	
	Cigars	62.76	
			$ 2705.39
Deduct	Coffee & Lead	851.42	
	24 Sacks Salt	36.00	
	7 Boxes Soap	31.36	
	20 " Candles	145.00	
	2½ " Cast. (?) brass (?)	27.60	
	1 En. (?) pipe rum	13.00	
		1104.38	
		33.12	
			1137.50
			$ 1567.89

1717b
List of Salvaged Cargo from the *Relief*, Page 1

Mobile February 1 Discharged from Schooner *Relief* from Havana Capt. Smith.
1 Trunk to Hughes sent to ???
3 Sacks Coffee, 2 Sacks Salt, 1 Bag shot
1 Box Cheese, 1 Can Oil, 56 yds Calico
3 Kegs Rum, 1 Box Soap, 1 Can Oil (Delivered)
Sent to Government Warehouse
4 Barl. Oil
3 Casks ???
3 " Wine
13 Brl Chestnuts sent Warehouse (?)
2 Boxes Dry goods 1 Barl. ???
12 Sacks Coffee
1 Trunk of Cotton (goods?)
2 Boxes Soap 1 Damaged
18 Boxes Soap
5 Boxes Soap
1 " Candles
1 " Matches
1 " Leathers
76 Sacks Salt
3 Boxes Shot & 5 Bags
288 **Bars Lead** (signed) A. Stokes

1718
List of Salvaged Cargo from the *Relief*, Page 2

Title on reverse: “Return of Cargo Discharged from Schooner *Relief* from Havana. Capt. Smith.”

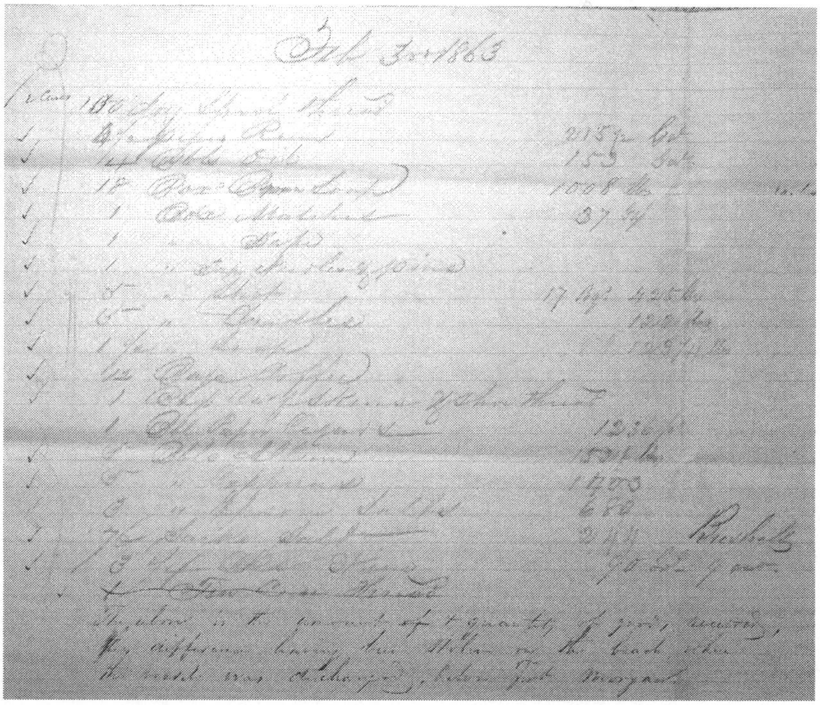

Figure 178. Salvaged cargo from the Schooner *Relief*.

		Feb 3rd 1863	
2 Cases	100 doz	Spool thread	
	4½ pipes	Rum	215½ Gal
	4 Bbls	Oil	153 Gal
	18 Boxes	Brown Soap	1008 lbs
	1 Box	Matches	37 Gal
	1 “	Tape (?)	
	1 “	Tape (?) Needles & pins	
	5 “	Shot 17 Bgs	425 lbs
	5 “	Candles	122 lbs
	1½ “	Soap	123¼ lbs
	12 Bags	Coffee	
	1 Box	Calf Shins & shoe thread	
	1 Bbl	Paper Cigars	1236 ps
	5 Bbls	Alum	1521 lbs
	5 “	???	1403 “
	3 “	Epsom Salts	680 “
	70 Sacks	Salt	244 Bushels
	3¼ Cks	Wine	90 Gal 9 ???
	~~1 Tin Case~~	~~Thread~~	
The above is the amount of & quantity of goods received, the difference being having been stolen on the beach, when the vessel was discharged, below Fort Morgan.			

Note: Just a year later the *Denbigh* grounded while outbound with cotton near the same place, leading to a salvage suit and extensive depositions about this kind of situation (To be published in a *Denbigh* Project book, Gerald Powell et al., in preparation).

1720
Invoice

Summary: Invoice for barrel of 2000 bundles, 36 bundles per $1, "El Comercis" paper cigars shipped by Rafael Perez Sta Mra aboard the "Confederate Schooner *Relief* Smith Master bound to Nassau (false destination)" consigned to M. D. Eslava Esq. for sale and valued at $ 62.76 with fees dated in Havana 15th Jan 1863.

1721-1722
Preprinted Customs Form

No. ___
Importer T. Lecesne (?) & Co.
Vessel Br. Sch *Emma*
From Beliz
Entered Feby 21
Value $ 499 Duty $ 75.65

Owner's Oath
J. Buttner of the firm of T. Lecesne (?) & Co, owner
(signed) Julius Buttner
Sworn to, this 21 day of Feby 1863
__________Collector (J. C. Colsson Depy signature smeared as though to erase.)

Ship Entered __________

Entry of Merchandise imported into the Port and District of Mobile, by T. Lecesne (?) & Co in the Br. Schr *Emma* Roach (?) Master, from Beliz, Honduras

Packages	Contents	Value in Foreign Currency	15	20	Duties
40 Kegs	Nails 4000 lbs	$ 240.00	250		37.50
20 Boxes	Common Soap 1000 "	70.00	74		11.10
10 "	Candles	75.00	79		11.85
10 "	Olive Oil	77.04	80		12.00
6 doz.	Brooms	15.00		16	3.00
		477.04			
	Comm 2½%	11.92			
	Shippg Chgs	10.00			
		$ 498.96		499	$ 75.65

1723
Invoice

Summary: This manifest was unusual having a note added later in pencil at the bottom. The *Emma's* cargo inbound to Mobile from Belize was specified in detail. At the bottom, the subsequent outbound cargo, 150 bales of cotton totaling 30,000 lbs., was recorded. The cotton's value at 40¢/lb. was $ 120,000 (Confederate $).

The heading of the invoice included extra information not usually provided, "Manifest of the British Schooner '*Emma*,' Roach Master 63 Tons, 7 Men, no Guns bound for New Orleans." **New Orleans fell May 1862 and so would have been a legal destination under the Union blockade. A clever ruse this.** The cargo included: coffee, salt, 8 barrels pork, 2 bales garlic, 24 cases gin, nails, soap, candles, oil, and 6 doz. brooms. Total value of the cargo as shipped from Belize was $ 2885.16 and dated 28 Jan 1863, signed by Capt. Richard Roach and Henry Shaw & Co. representative G. W. Holmes.

1724-1725
Preprinted Customs Form

No. 4
Importer R Roach
Vessel *Emma*
From Belize
Entered 21 Feby 63
Value $ 124 Duty $ 13.60

Ship Entered ____________

Entry of Merchandise imported into the Port and District of Mobile, by R Roach in the *Emma* Master, from Havana

Packages	Contents	Value in Foreign Currency					Duties
2 Pkgs	Tea 120 lbs	$ 100					$ 10.00
1 Drum	Redfish	24					3.60
		124					13.60

1726-1727
Preprinted Customs Form

No. 6 Specific duty
Importer M D Eslava
Vessel *Relief*
From Havana
Entered Feby 14 1863
~~Value~~ $ Bushels 244 Duty $ 4.88

Owner's Oath
M D Eslava, owner
(signed) M. D. Eslava
Sworn to, this 14 day of Feb 1863
J. C. Colsson Depy Collector

Ship Entered 6 Feby 1863

Entry of Merchandise imported into the Port and District of Mobile, by M D Eslava in the Br. Schr *Clara Rogers* Master, from Havana

Packages	Contents	Value in Foreign Currency					Duties
76 Sacks	Salt 244 Bshl	$ 114			Specific	Duty	
					244 Bushels	@ 2¢ per	$ 4.88

1728-1729
Preprinted Customs Form

No. ___
Importer T. Lecesne (?) & Co
Vessel *Emma*
From Belize
Entered 21 Feby 63
Value $ 708 Bushels Duty $ 14.16
Salt Sp. Duty

Ship Entered __________

Entry of Merchandise imported into the Port and District of Mobile, by T. Lecesne (?) in the *Emma* Master, from Havana

Packages	Contents	Value in Foreign Currency					Duties
197 Sacks	Salt 201 lbs or 708 Bushels	$ 445					
					798 Bushels	Salt @ 2	$ 14.16

1730-1731
Preprinted Customs Form

No. 5
Importer T Lecesne & Co.
Vessel *Laura Dudly*
From Havana
Entered 18 Mar 1863
Value $ 646 Duty $ 98.45

Owner's Oath
(signed) Julius Buttner

Sworn to, this __ day of ____ 18
_________Collector

Ship Entered ___________

Entry of Merchandise imported into the Port and District of Mobile, by T. Lecesne (?) & Co in the Sloop *Laura Dudly* _______________ Master, from Havana

Packages	Contents	Value in Foreign Currency					%	Duties
	Cotton Cards 20 doz	$ 400.00						
6 Boxes	Tin	81.00						
3 Bbls	Kerosene oil	75.30			Cotton Cards	$ 410	15	$ 61.50
6 cases	Gin 6 doz	55.50			Ker. Oil	77	"	11.55
10 Bags	Shot	18.12			Shot	19	"	2.85
		629.92			Tin	83	10	8.30
	Comm 2½ %	15.75			Spirits	57	25	14.25
		645.67				646		98.45

1732
Invoice

Summary: Invoice with detail of merchandise shipped in the *Laura Dudly* by F. H. Barbot to Lecesne & Co. (This example was the most legible version of the name.) The duty free items were not listed on the above customs form.

Invoice of Merchandise shipped pr Sloop *Laura Dudly* by F H Barbot for a/c of Owner, Consigned to Messrs Lecesne & Co. Mobile

168 Kegs	Powder 4000 lbs @	35	1400.00	
111 Sacks	Coffee 2062 "	19	391.78	
15 "	Salt	1.30	19.50	
1 Gross	Percussion Caps		24.00	
1 "	" "		12.00	
100 lbs	Rifle Powder		52.00	
10 Bags	Shot 5/8 5/4	1.81½	18.12	
3 Bbls	Kerosene Oil 125½ Gals @	60	75.30	
2 Boxes	**Tin 1c**	$ 12.50	25.00	
2 "	**" 1x**	13.50	27.00	
2 "	**" 1xx**	14.50	29.00	
20 Doz	Cotton Cards #10	20.00	400.00	
4 Bbls	Aguardeinte	7.50	30.00	
6 Cases	Gin 1 doz Ea. 35	4.25	25.50	
				$ 2529.20
	E&OE			
	Havana Feby 23, 1863			
	(signed) F H Barbot			

Note the different types (thicknesses?) of tin indicated.

1733-1734
Preprinted Customs Form

No. 6
Importer T Lecesne & Co
Vessel *Fashion*
From Havana
Entered 23 Mar 63
Value $ 951 Duty $ 192.25

Owner's Oath
(signed) Julius Buttner
Sworn to, this ___ day of _________ 18
Collector

Ship Entered ___*

Entry of Merchandise imported into the Port and District of Mobile, by T. Lecesne & Co in the Sloop *Fashion* Master, from Havana

Packages	Contents	Value in Foreign Currency					Duties
49 boxes	Brandy 47 10/12 doz	$ 287			296	25%	$ 74.00
98 "	Claret 96 11/12 "	194			200	"	50.00
74 "	oil olive 73 9/12 "	442			455	15%	68.25
		$ 923			951		$ 192.25
	Chgs & Comm	28					
		$ 951					

* Sunk by the blockading fleet in attempting to run in, March 7, 1863, portion of cargo saved. (Original note written just below the "Ship Entered" blank on the form.)

1735
Invoice

Note: An interesting and perhaps deceptive invoice with a false destination. The invoice covers the whole cargo including the portion lost with the ship.

Invoice of Sundry Merchandise shipped on board the Conf. schooner *Fashion* Northrup master bound to Jamaica & consigned to Messrs. J. Le Cesne Co. for account & risk of whom it may concern.

JLC	100 boxes	Old Brandy $ 6	$ 600.00	
	100 "	Claret " 2	200.00	
	100 "	Olive Oil " 6	600.00	
	40 Kegs	ea 43½ lbs		
	380 "	" 21¾ " = 10005 lbs Powder		
		@ $ 35 per 100 lbs	3501.75	
	143 Pigs	Lead weighing together		
		8508 lbs @ $ 5½ per 100 lbs	467.94	

				5369.69
		Charges		
		Duty (out of bond)	$ 37.74	
		Lighterage	57.00	
		Carriage to wharf	22.32	
		Petty expenses	8.75	125.81
				$ 5495.50
		Comm 2½%		127.38
		E&CE		$ 5632.88
		Havana 21st February 1863		
		Caro (?) Bros & Watson		
		(notes added in pencil with figures		
		on the portion saved from the wreck		
		as per Customs Form above.)		

1736-1737
Preprinted Customs Form

No. ___
Importer H O Brewer & Co.
Vessel *Sea Drift*
From Havana
Entered 16 Mar 63
Value $ B(ushels) 404 Duty $ 8.08

In this entry is consolidated
Salt pr Schr *Sea Drift*
" *Sun Flower*
" *Fashion*
making one entry for the whole

Mdse. Entered ____________ Ship Entered ____________
Entry of Merchandise imported into the Port of Mobile, District of Mobile, by H. O. Brewer & Co in the Schr *Sea Drift* ______________ Master, from Havana

Packages	Contents	Value in Foreign Currency					%	Duties
113 Sacks	Salt avg 200 lbs 22600	$ 226						
	Bushels 404 @ 2¢							$ 8.08

1738-1739
Preprinted Customs Form

No. 3
Importer Jos E Murrell
Vessel *Sea Drift*
From Havana
Entered Mar 14 63
Value $ 404 Duty $ 60.60

Owner's Oath
(signed) Jos E Murrell
Sworn to, this ___ day of ________ 18
Collector

Ship Entered ________
Entry of Merchandise imported into the Port and District of Mobile, by Jos E Murrell in the Schr *Sea Drift* Peacock Master, from Havana

Packages	Contents	Value in Foreign Currency					Duties
1000 Reams	wrapping paper with Comn &c	$ 403.70			$404	15%	$ 60.60
25 Bags	Salt petre 5,000 lbs	Free					

1740
Invoice

Summary: Invoice for salt peter shipped on the *Sea Drift* dated 20 Feb 1863 in Havana. Interesting note added to bottom in pencil stated that the estimated value was $ 1120.

1741-1742
Preprinted Customs Form

No. 4
Importer H O Brewer & Co
Vessel *Sea Drift*
From Havana
Entered Mar 63
Value $ 3111 Duty $ 483.60

Owner's Oath
(signed) A. J. Ingersoll
Sworn to, this ___ day of ________ 18
Collector

Ship Entered __________

Entry of Merchandise imported into the Port and District of Mobile, by ____________ in the Master, from ____________

Packages	Contents	Value in Foreign Currency					Duties
2 Baskets	+ 12 Cases Gin 20 doz flasks	$ 101.67					
12 Bbls	rum	90.00					
25 Cases	Brandy	100.00		Spirits	302	25%	$ 15.50
6 "	Tin 10%	81.00		Spices	26	20	5.20
4 Bbls	Soda Ash 10% 2000 lbs	90.00		Tin &c	291		29.10
15 Boxes	Soap 15"	98.64		Various	2492		373.80
2 Bags	Black pepper 20"	26.25			3111		$ 483.60
3 Cases	Cotton Cards						
6 Bales	gunny cloth						
1 Box	hats						
	Shoes & Gaiters						
12 Bbls	25,000 nails						
8 Pkgs	Cotton & Linen mfs. thread &c						
2 Bales	Sole Leather 10% $ 120						
25000	Needles, pins & combs						
2 boxes	Stationery						
1 Bbl	Castor oil						
1 Bdle	horsewhips						
1 Box	Quinine & Medicine 50 oz. subt	2,392					
		$ 3,110.56					

1743-1744
Invoice

Note: This was a merchant's order with large quantities of goods like prewar orders and a contrast to the later invoices from the *Denbigh* which were mostly quite small by comparison. Matamoros was a false destination. One item not covered on the customs form (because duty free?) was 2188 lbs. lead @ 6½¢ for total value of 133.00. Name of master changed after invoice originally written.

Invoice of goods pr Brit. Schr *Sea Drift* ~~Haywood Mr.~~ for Matamoros Peacock Mr.

50 bags	salt 10150 lb	62½	$ 63.43	
	Export duty & lighterage		12.00	75.43
	50 empty bags	@ 35¢		17.50
2 baskets of	gin 100 flasks	$ 5 doz	41.57	
	lighterage & cartage		10.50	52.17
12 barrels	rum	7½		90.00
3 cases	150 cavalry swords			375.00
1 "	120 pairs men's Brogans	16¢	160.00	
6 bales	gunny cloth 2168 yds	12¢	260.16	
3 cases	cotton cards 6 doz	$30	180.00	600.16
	Export duty & lighterage			20.00

100	men's hats	$ 15 doz.		125.00
50 ounces	quinine	$ 2.75 onzas		137.50
8 doz	ladies gaiters	$ 13		104.00
3 "	children's "	$ 8½	25.50	
5½ "	**ladies hoops**	$14	77.00	
4 bales	Manila rope 260 $ Ea	$26	104.00	
2128 lbs	**lead**	6¼¢	133.00	
6 cases	tin	$ 13½	81.00	420.50
12 brls	assorted nails	6¼¢	75.00	
25000	horse shoe nails	$ 2.75	68.75	
12 doz pairs	**spurs**	$ 2.75	33.00	
8 boxes	assorted shot	7½ $	60.00	
20 doz	Men's merino shirts	9 $	180.00	
6 bags	coffee 1136 lbs	18½	210.16	626.91
15 boxes	Castille soap 1644 lbs	6¢	98.64	
2 bags	pepper 175 lbs	15¢	26.25	
25 cases	cognac	$ 4	100.00	
12 "	gin	5 $	60.00	
2 bales	sole leather 24 hides	@ $ 5	120.00	
20000	(percussion ?) Caps	$ 2	40.00	444.89
30 pieces	calico 28 vrs (varas)	$ 3.50	105.00	
39 doz	handkerchieves	9 rs (reales?)	46.31	
6 "	do col (colored) ½ cotton	12 rs	9.00	
6 "	do white "	12 rs	9.00	
6 "	do do ladies	18 rs	12.75	
3 pieces	166 yds 155.52 vrs hunting drill	2 rs	38.88	
2 "	99¾ " 101.25 vrs white drill	3¼ rs	41.12	262.06
	carried over			$ 3351.12
1863	Brought forward			$ 3351.12
50 doz	spool thread		$ 43.75	
3 pieces	cotton goods	$ 5	15.00	58.75
25000	needles		20.31	
2 gross	buffalo comb	$ 12	24.00	
2 "	horn "	$ 15	30.00	
1 "	fine tooth "		18.00	
13 "	buckles	75¢	9.00	101.31
1 "	thimbles		3.00	
50 "	shirt buttons	25¢	12.50	
2 "	Caps	$ 12	24.00	
3 doz	pen holders	??	1.87	
14 "	gloves	$2	28.00	69.37
12 "	hair brushes	$ 2½	30.00	
12 packages	pins	50¢	6.00	
8 "	bone buttons	$ 1.50	12.00	
20 "	hair pins	5 rs	12.50	
30 gross	silk buttons	$ 1	30.00	90.50
2 "	tooth brushes	$ 7	14.00	
24 "	steel pens	75¢	18.00	
12 "	pencils	$ 1.75	21.00	
3 "	Carpenter's pencils	$ 4½	13.50	

2 "	Hooks & Eyes	$ 4½	9.00	75.50
1 barrel	Castor oil 44 gals	$ 2.20	96.80	
4 "	soda ash 2000 lbs	4½	90.00	
2 "	Epsom salt 800 lb	4½	36.00	
	Export duty 4.75			
	Cartage 3.50			
	Lighterage 3.50		11.75	234.55
	25 Bags	37¢		9.25
1 Bdle 25 Doz	horsewhips	73¢		18.75
	12 Enfield Rifles	**12 $**	**144.00**	
	1 Cannon & Carriage 6 pounder		**45.00**	
	12 Marine Cutlasses	$ 2.50	30.00	
	Cartridges & Canister (?)		12.00	
	Boat hire & C House official		37.00	268.00
	100 Cans Powder	87½	87.50	
	Shipping Expenses		4.25	91.75
	E&OE			$ 4,368.85
	Havana February 20th 1863 add com			
	(signed) Francois (?) Schnabelius			
		$ 4,368.85		
	Add Com	86.00		
		$ 4,454.85		

1745-1746
Preprinted Customs Form

No. ___ Free
Importer H O Brewer & Co
Vessel __________
From ___________
Entered ______
Value $ _____ Duty $ _____

Owner's Oath
(signed) A. J. Ingersoll
Sworn to, this ___ day of _________ 18
Collector

Ship Entered ___________
Entry of Merchandise imported into the Port and District of Mobile, by H. O. Brewer & Co. in the Br. Schr *Sea Drift* Peacock Master, from Havana

Packages	Contents	Value in Foreign Currency					Duties
150	Swords	$ 375					
2128 lbs	Lead	133					
1136 lbs	Coffee	210					
	Percussion Caps, Rifles, Powder	360					

1747-1748
Preprinted Customs Form

No. No. 1
Importer M. D. Eslava
Vessel *Joe Flanner (?)*
From Havana
Entered March 11
Value $ 4238   Duty $ 574.10
                                   153.75
                          Total $727.85

Owner's Oath
(signed) M. D. Eslava
Sworn to, this ___ day of ________ 18
Collector

Ship Entered __________

Entry of Merchandise imported into the Port and District of Mobile, by M. D. Eslava in the *Joe Flanner* (Schr) ____________________ Master, from Havana

Packages	Contents	Value in Foreign Currency	10	15	Duties
10 Casks	Soda Ash lbs 8304	$ 415.20			
	Cast Steel " 843	151.95			
30 Boxes	Tin in plates	405.00			
2 Bales	tanned skins	220.00			
15 Blls	Alum & Copperas lbs 4687	249.13			
5 "	Epsom Salts	56.80			
6 " & 5 Cases	Ker. Oil Gals 285	185.25			
28 Sacks	Shot lbs 2850	224.00			
1 Case	thread, needles, Tape, & pins	161.50			
		176.00			
		187.50			
	Iron & Iron mfs lbs 3372	521.18			
5 Bales	Rope " 1128	101.52			
7 Boxes	Soap " 3554	294.78			
7 "	Candles " 925	231.25			
1 Cases	Castor Oil Gals 21	51.60			
2 Jugs	**Quicksilver** lbs 184	110.40			
1 Trunk	Shoes	338.00			
		$ 4,101.06	1232		123.20
	Charges & Comm	136.70		3006	450.90
		$ 4,237.76			$ 574.10

1750
Invoice

Summary: Invoice detailing the merchandise titled A List of the Cargo with Weights & Measurements, of Schr *Joe Flanner*. A note added at top stated, "Pro forma Invoice by appraisement. **All the papers having been thrown overboard, vessel being chased by the enemy.**" A few items of interest enumerated here: 5 pipes wine, 10 1/8 casks alcohol, 49 sacks salt (158 bushels), 27 cases brandy, 321 pigs lead (4074 lbs.), 60 pkgs. shoe thread (90 lbs.), 1 lot garlic, 5 bbls. saltpeter, and 7000 cigars. By calculation the interesting facts emerged: shoe thread came in packages averaging 1.5 lb. each; pigs of lead averaged 12.7 lbs. each; and a sack of salt averaged 3.2 bushels.

Note: Under Prize Law, a ship with no papers was automatically open to seizure since the lack of papers was considered proof of an illegal voyage.

1752-1753
Preprinted Customs Form

No. 18
Importer H O Brewer & Co
Vessel ***Alice*** (Possibly an E.T.C. ship like the *Denbigh.*)
From Havana
Entered April 16 '63
Value $ 2132 Duty $ 483.50

Ship Entered April '63

Entry of Merchandise imported into the Port and District of Mobile, by H O Brewer & Co in the Br. Str. *Alice* Smith Master, from Havana

Packages	Contents	Value in Foreign Currency					Duties
1 Box	**Bank note paper** Sheets 12,000	$ 480			15		$ 74.25
2 Cases	**Sigars** 48 ~~M~~	1560				25	409.25
	Chgs & Comm & Export duty	92					$ 483.50
		$ 2132					

Note: The irony here was superb. Bankers and fat cigars just seemed to go together.

1754
Invoice

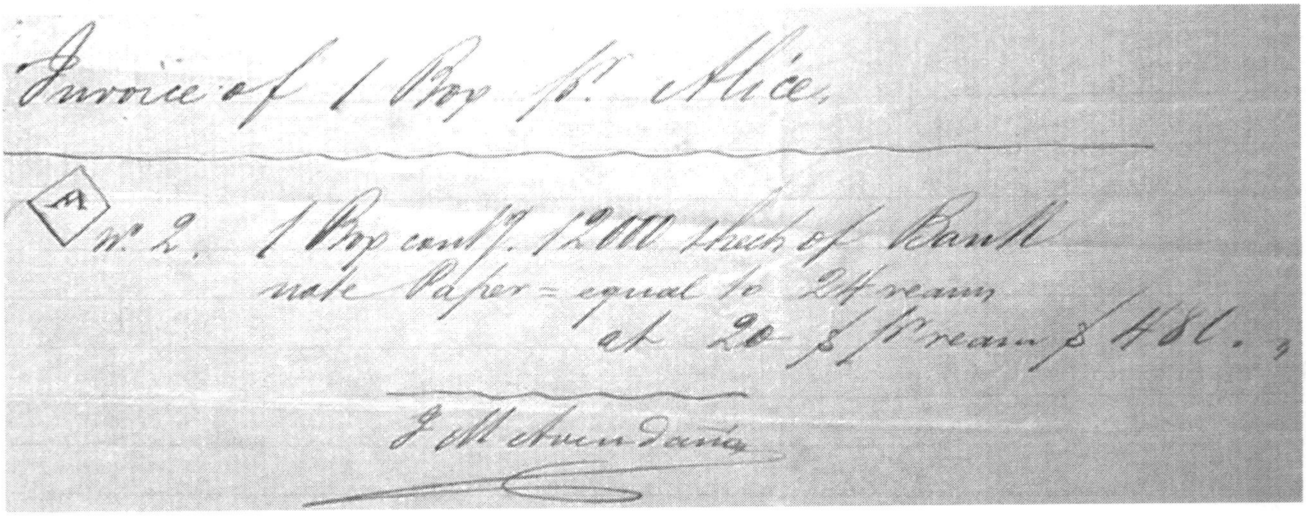

Invoice of 1 Box p. Alice

A No. 2. 1 Box cont. 1200 sheets of Bank note Paper = equal to 24 ream at 20 $ p. ream $ 480.

J M Arendaña

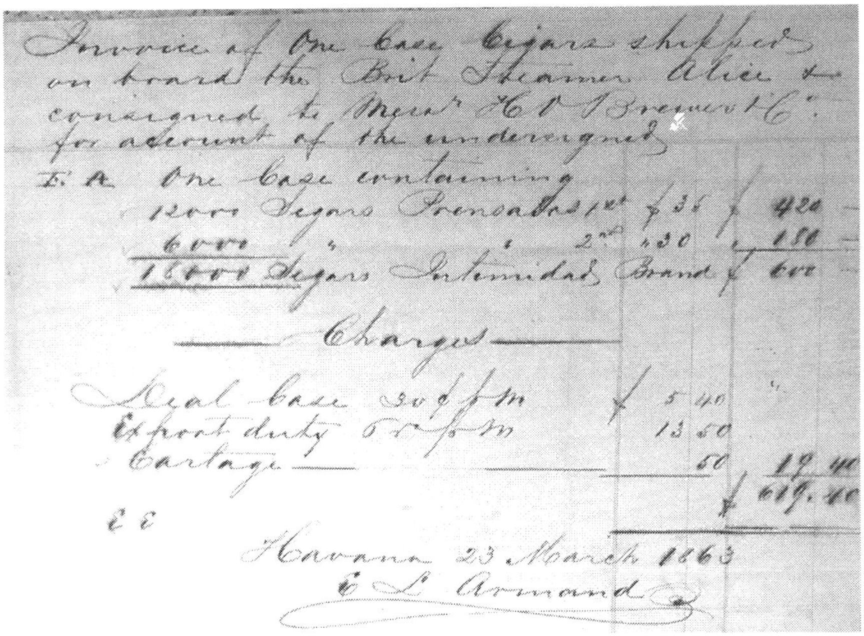

Invoice of One Case Cigars shipped on board the Brit Steamer Alice & consigned to Messrs H O Brewer & Co for account of the undersigned

E.A One Case containing

12000 Segars Prensados 1st	$ 35	$ 420	
6000 " " 2nd	30	180	
18000 Segars Intimidad Brand		$ 600	
Charges			
Deal case 30 c p M		$ 5 40	
Export duty 75 c p M		13 50	
Cartage		50	19 40
			$ 619.40

E E

Havana 23 March 1863
E L Armand

Figure 179. Two invoices for bank note paper and cigars.

Summary: Two invoices regarding the above. The cigar invoice was dated 23 Mar 1863 which would have been close to the sailing date. Many cigar invoices observed in these documents were nearly impossible to interpret because of unusual handwriting and unfamiliar names and abbreviations. In this case not so: 18,000 of the shipment were Intimidad Brand.

1755
Invoice

Summary: Second invoice for cigars. Note the specification as to how boxed and shipped.

Joseph Hernandez, Esqr

Sr. Ml. Delgado Esqr, ??? (probably Dr)

1863	17000	Londres size Sigars	@ $32	$ 544.00	
March 17	7000	" " "	32	224.00	
	6000	Cilendrados "	32	192.00	
	30000				$ 960
		Charges			
		Export duties @ 75$ per mil		$ 22.50	
		Cases & packing @ 25 " "		7.50	
		Drayage to the Wharf		1.00	
		Boating to Steamer		2.00	33
		Havana March 20th 1863			$ 993
		(signed) Ml Delgado			
N.B.	Case No. 1	Contains 170 Small boxes, contg each 100 Sigars in bundles of 50 Sigars each			
	Case No. 2	70 Small Boxes of 100 Segars in a single bundle & 60 Boxes contg each 100 Sigars & bundles of 25 Segars			

1757-1758
Substitute for Preprinted Customs Form

No. 16
Importer Chs Walsh
Vessel Str *Alice*
From Havana
Entered April 6 1863
Value $ 261 Duty $ 40.50

Summary: Two shipments of sundries belonging to Mr. Carroll and C. L. Burckmyer. Mr. Carroll – 35 lbs. tea, 80 yds drilling, 1000 needles, coffee, and cotton cards. C. L. Burckmyer – stationery, shoes, dry goods, needles & thread, **drapes**, shoes, gloves, hosiery etc. £ 27.4.11.

1759-1760
Substitute for Preprinted Customs Form

Note: Hand written substitute for customs form for goods shipped to C. L. Burkmyer apparently to fill an order by Mrs. Gregor who owed $232.39½ to Las Ninfas store in Havana for the purchases.

No. 15
Importer C L Burkmyer
Vessel Str *Alice*
From Havana
Entered 6 April '63

Value $ 137 Duty $ 20.55

Mrs. Gregor

To Las Ninfas Dr.

1 piece	fine Cotton		$ 8.50
1 "	thick linen		14.25
18 varas	German linen	@ 9 rs	20.25
1 doz	**towels**		6.50
1 "	" Turkish		3.50
1 "	" linen		7.00
1 "	table napkins		4.50
1 "	cotton stockings		10.00
1 "	" "		14.00
1 "	" "		6.00
26 varas	Holland linen	4 rs	13.00
22 "	Organdie muslin	3 rs	8.25
33 "	French Calico	3½ rs	14.43½
41 "	English ba?ge	50 cts	20.50
2	**Parasols**		12.10
11 varas	Organdie muslin	X 4 rs	X 5.50
10½ "	" "	X 2½ rs	X 3.28
1 piece	colored calico	$ 4¼	4.25
1 "	Linen		9.50
11 varas	French calico	2½ rs	3.43
3 pairs	Ladies ??? gaiters	$ 3.75	11.25
1 "	Boys pegged shoes		1.00
1 "	Girls Boots No. 12		1.00
1	Packing Trunk		3.50
	Carry over		$ 205.39½
	Br forward		$ 205.39½
5 lbs	Tea	@ 10 rs	6.50
	Drayage & Shipping		.50
			$ 212.39½
1 Sack	Coffee 150 lbs	19 cts	$ 20.50
	Less organdies		

1761a-1763
Substitute for Preprinted Customs Form

No. 13
Importer J. E. Merrell
Vessel *Alice*
From Havana
Entered Apl 3 63
Value $ 63.00 Duty $ 15.75

Summary: Invoice for 2000 Londres (London type) cigars.

No. 14
Importer J. A. Rice
Vessel *Alice*
From Havana
Entered April 6, 1863
Value $ 69 Duty $ 10.35

Summary: Hand written substitute for customs form for 7 pieces of cotton goods. The invoice accompanying included **"1 Silk Dress Pattern"** at a cost of $ 30. This seemed high for a pattern only. Perhaps the silk cloth was included.

1764-1765
Preprinted Customs Form

No. 19
Importer H O Brewer & Co
Vessel *Alice*
From Havana
Entered April 16 63
Value $ 21,807 Duty $ 3255

Owner's Oath
(signed) Benj. Donaldson, owner
Sworn to, this ___ day of ________ 18
Collector

Ship Entered ___________
Entry of Merchandise imported into the Port and District of Mobile, by H O Brewer & Co in the Br. Str *Alice* Smith Master, from Havana

Marks	Packages	Contents	Value in Foreign Currency	10	15	25	Duties
ΔΔ	118 Blls	Soda Ash lbs 31270	$ 1250. 6½	1302			
	45 "	Soda Ash " 19859	893. 5	929			
A H	4 Boxes	Tea " 172	163. 3	170			
	1 Case	Do " 337½	337. 4	350			
"	10 Carb.	Ammonia, with carboys &c " 900	129.	135			
"	4 Cases	Cheese " 464	109. 0½	113			$ 299.90
TPTB	11 Cases	Shoes & Boots	6975.		7254		
WF	68 Blls	Copperas lbs 21816	872. 5		907		
CVO	19 Bales	Blankets	3063.		3186		
O	14 Cases	Lawn, Muslins, & Cotton mfs	4378. 3		4554		
"	7 "	Thread	1050.		1092		
C	50 Boxes	Soap lbs 2500	187. 4		194		
"	5 Coils	Rope " 2038	193. 5		201		
C	1 Pkge	Shirts	21.		22		
	1 Cask	Oil lamp Gals 42	53.		55		2619.75
	200 Boxes	Brandy	750.			780	

	5 Blls	Whiskey " 207	311. 2					324	
	10 Casks	Rum	230.					239	335.75
			$ 20,968. 6						$ 3255.40

Note: The monetary notation used in the center column of the document was unusual in the customs manifests herein examined. Perhaps it was dollars and reales or pesos and reales, but it probably was not dollars and cents. In the four right columns where duties were calculated and reported, the cost was converted to dollars. Regarding the ammonia, a carboy was a large container made of glass, usually protected by a wooden casing and used to hold corrosive liquids.

1766-1767
Invoice

Summary: Invoice for above sundries aboard the *Alice* with false destination, Nassau, for account of the vessel and consigned to order. The invoice included arms but the customs form did not. The arms were duty free and so not listed on the form. Arms included the following: 330 kegs powder, 7500 lbs., $ 2625; 2 cases with 100 doz. soldier's shoes, $ 1475; and 2 cases with 100 Colt's Navy revolvers, $ 2500.

1768
Invoice

Summary: Invoice for 118 bbls. soda ash for $ 1369.2 shipped on the *Alice* and dated 21 Mar 1863. Note the false destination of Nassau.

1769-1770
Preprinted Customs Form

No.
Importer H O Brewer & Co
Vessel *Alice*
From Havana
Entered 16 April
Value $ 8653 Duty $ free

Summary: Separate customs form for the duty free arms included on invoice 1766-1767 above, plus an order of coffee for a total of $ 8653.

1771-1772
Invoice

Summary: "Invoice of Goods received pr. Schooner *Helena* belonging to Capt. Chas. Marian." Total $ 649.20. The large quantities of items may suggest a dry goods merchant's order. The total price was an order of magnitude higher than the family orders common elsewhere in these files. Perhaps the captain himself was bringing in this cargo on speculation for sale to stores or individuals.

1773-1774
Substitute for Preprinted Customs Form

Free goods
~~*Alice*~~ & *Eugenie*
April 30, 1864
$7,174

Free goods per *Alice* from Havana

300 Kegs Powder	75000 lbs	$ 2625
100 Revolvers		2500
11200 lbs Sulphur		616
12672 " Coffee		2313
602 Do		120
		$ 8174
(all above crossed out)	already made dup	
Per Str *Eugenie*		
20,000 lbs powder		$ 7000
Cartridge boxes		2000

Note: It appeared that a cargo was split between two vessels. Very rarely were there two shipments on different ships documented on a single invoice in this collection.

1775-1776
Preprinted Customs Form

No. 3
Importer Chs Marian
Vessel Helena
From Havana
Entered April 2 63
Value $ 765 Duty $ 122.95

Ship Entered ________
Entry of Merchandise imported into the Port and District of Mobile, by Chs Marian in the Br. Schr *Helena* Smith Master, from Havana

Packages	Contents	Value in Foreign Currency	10	15	25	Duties

1 Box	Tea lbs 20	$ 23.12						
3 Doz pr	shoes	27.00			Tea	$ 24	10%	$ 2.40
2 Doz	brooms & brushes	21.00			Brooms	22	20	4.40
10 PKkgs	thread, Prints & Cotton	584.32			Cigars & Sardines	83	25	20.75
4 ~~M~~	Cigars	74.00			Sundries	636	15	95.40
24	¼ boxes Sardines	6.00				765		$ 122.95
		$ 735.44						
		29.40						
		$ 764.84						

1777
Invoice

Statement of Cargo on board Schr. *Helena*

Summary: Total $ 3442.53 for what might have been a large merchant's order although the people involved were not named. Interesting items: 20 reams paper, 1 gross lamp chimneys, 3 bales rope and 2 bales gunny bagging (supplies for baling cotton), 10 gross matches, $ 77.53 worth of garden seeds, and 400 pigs lead 4556 lbs.

1779-1780
Preprinted Customs Form

No. 10
Importer H O Brewer & Co
Vessel *Isabel*
From Havana
Entered April 14 63
Value $ 4046 Duty $ 716.45

Ship Entered ____________

Entry of Merchandise imported into the Port and District of Mobile, by H O Brewer & Co in the Br. Schr *Isabel* Jefferson Master, from Havana

Packages	Contents	Value in Foreign Currency	10	15	25	Duties
5 Boxes	Soap lbs 461	$ 62.81		65		
2 Bales	Sole leather	114.00		117		11.70
4 Casks	Ale pints doz 28	57.00		59		
5 Cases	Calicos & Cotton mfs	560.00		576		105.00
2 Casks	Soda Ash lbs 1600	64.00	66			6.60
2 bales & 2 Cases	prints, thread &c	1214.93		1251		
1 Do	12 doz shirts cotton	684.00		704		293.25
12 Boxes	Gin	36.00			37	
25 Demijhs	Do	75.00			77	
14 pipes	Rum 1680 Gals	369.00			380	

25 Demijhs	Brandy	87.50					90	
16 Do	Anisette (?) & absynth	68.50					72	
50 boxes	Kirchinnasser (?)	250.00					258	
1 Case	Sigars 14,000	238.00					252	291.50
2 Boxes	Sugar	40.68				42		8.40
		$ 3,921.42			66	2814	1166	$ 724.45
Exp duty	& Chgs & Comms	124.63						716.45
		$ 4,046.05						

1781-1782
Invoice

Invoice of sundries shipped by Messrs Harrel (?) & Co on board of the English schooner *Isabel*, Jefferson Mr. bound to Matamoros for account of whom it may concern.

Summary: Details of items from customs form above. Interesting items: 14,000 Londres cigars, 3 doz. hoopskirts, and 5 bags salt. Total $ 4469.30.

1783-1784
Preprinted Customs Form

No. 28
Importer G D Rickarly (?)
Vessel *Neptune*
From Havana
Entered 27 Apl 63
Value $ 1126 Duty $ 168.90

Ship Entered ___________
Entry of Merchandise imported into the Port and District of Mobile, by G D Rickarly in the ___________ Master, from

Marks	Packages	Contents	Value in Foreign Currency			10	15	25	Duties
C&(?)	5 Cases	Hand Card 8 & 10	£ 220	3	1				
		on leather & on cloth				**Cotton cards**	$1126	15	$ 168.90
		Packing &c	6	15	1				
		Comm 2½%	5	16	4				
			£ 232	14	6	$ 1126.39			

Note: Shortage of cotton cards and wool cards was a choke point that severely inhibited home weaving of cloth. The tools had many teeth and were used to align the fibers before spinning. State and local governments made efforts to supply the cards in order for cloth and clothing to be made at home due to shortages and high cost of imported fabrics.

1785
Invoice

Summary: Invoice detailing 5 Cases of cotton cards purchased by order of Messrs. C. & H. Nelson, Liverpool, dated in Manchester 24 Jan 1863 and signed by J. & J. Bell and totaling £ 229.4.9.

1787-1788
Preprinted Customs Form

Free
No.
Importer J L Harris & Durand
Vessel *Fanny*
From Havana
Entered April 16 63
Value $ Duty $

Ship Entered ___________

Entry of Merchandise imported into the Port and District of Mobile, by _________ in the Master, from

Packages	Contents	Value in Foreign Currency			10	15	25	Duties
70 Bales	Jerked Beef lbs 10,486	707	6½					
3 Casks	Ham lbs 928	111	3½					
25 Cases	Pork lbs 10,992	1099	1½					
50 Blls	Mess Pork	750	0					
97 Pigs	Lead lbs 6,044	332	3½					
		$ 3000	6[120]					

1790a and b
Invoices

Summary: Two invoices in Spanish from Basset pharmacy, Havana, each for two carboys, one invoice for muriatic acid and one invoice for alcohol and (???) debit to J. Foster dated 5 Aug 1863 and totaling 11 and 32 pesos respectively. Notations on the invoices indicate peso and dollar were of equal value.

---

[120] At 8 reales per dollar, this sum may indicate the notation shown was dollars and reales. The lack of conversion might indicate parity between the Spanish dollar and the U.S. dollar. One puzzling aspect of the invoices herein was that rarely was conversion from U.S. to Confederate dollars shown. Yet it was hard to imagine the Havana merchants being willing to denominate their transactions in the rapidly fluctuating Confederate dollar.

1792-1793
Preprinted Customs Form

No. 1
Importer H O Brewer & Co
Vessel *A(lice) Vivian*
From Havana
Entered Aug 3 63
Value $ 8346 Duty $ 1251

Ship Entered ___________
Entry of Merchandise imported into the Port and District of Mobile, by H O Brewer & Co in the Str *A. Vivian* Abels Master, from Havana

Marks	Packages	Contents	Value in Foreign Currency	10	15	25	Duties
G W	20 Kegs	Olives	$ 20.00		23		
"	1 Case	Yeast powder	81.90		93		
"	55 Kits	Salted & pickled fish	165.50		189		
"	5 Blls	assorted family groceries in pkgs	191.50		199		
"	4 "	lard oil	296.25		338		
A V	1 Case	Combs assorted & corsets $477.75	988.25		1126		
"	7 Blls & 3 boxes	Empty vials, glass mfs	209.50		238		
G V	2 Cases & 1 Bll	Skins ??? & varnished	898.50		1020		
F E L	1 "	Quinine oz. 200	500.00		570		
B	2 Blls	Salts	71.90		87		
H	4 Cases	Ipecacuana lbs 50	700.00		800		
	2 "	Cans opium, Gum & powder lbs 198	1367.75		1560		
	7 Kegs	Iod. Potass 162 lbs	749.00		854		
	10 Cases	Calomel &c 150 lbs	925.00		1054		
	2 "	Rhubarb	150.00		171		
			7,312.05		$8,317	15%	$1,247.55
		Chgs & Com	292.48		29		4.35
			$ 7,604.53		8,346		1,251.90
		10% on Chgs & Com		29			

1794-1795
Preprinted Customs Form

No. 2
Importer H O Brewer & Co
Vessel *A Vivian*
From Havana
Entered Aug 3 63
Value $ 18,275 Duty $ 2,741.25

Ship Entered ___________

Entry of Merchandise imported into the Port and District of Mobile, by H O Brewer & Co in the Str *A. Vivian* Abels Master, from Havana

Marks	Packages	Contents	Value in Foreign Currency	10	15	25	Duties
M F	1 Box	Envelopes	$ 85.32		97		
H.O.B & Co	8 "	Paper & Stationery	1023.25		1,164		
G B	19 "	Cotton & Wool Cards	2119.50 47.00		2,470		
M F	1 "	Shirts & Wearing apparel	812.25		926		
D	8 "	Wool Hats	515.50		588		
G	19 Cases	Ladies & men's shoes	2041.31		2,328		
N	2 "	Flannels & wool mfs	879.25		1,004		
B	120 Kegs	**Cut nails** 12000 lbs	620.00		707		
P	52 Pkgs	Hardware	660.84		754		
A V	1 "	Pen Knives 24 doz	186.00		212		
P	2 Boxes	Harness	240.00		274		
A V	1 "	Braids, cotton & Silk	600.00		684		
"	4 Cases	Prints & Cotton mfs	1,994.06		2,273		
H	1 Box	Shoe Thread	139.25		158		
B + F	30 Bales	**Gunny bagging**	1458.00		1,663		
	213 Coils	**Rope**	2553.51		2,910		
			15,975.04		$ 18,212	15%	$ 2731.80
		Chgs & Comms	639.00		63		9.45
			$16,614.04		18,275		$ 2,741.25

Note: Rope and gunny cloth were materials for baling cotton and thus of great importance. They were a particular choke point in Houston and Galveston during the *Denbigh's* trips there later in the war.

1796-1802
Invoice

Invoice of Sundries shipped by the Undersigned by order of Geo Woodward Esq pr Confed Str *Alice Vivian*, Abels Mr for Mobile for acc & risk of Owners of said vessel & consigned to Messr H O Brewer & Co.

Summary: Detailed invoice for merchandise on seven pages. The heading provided vital information. The names *Alice*, *Vivian*, *A. Vivian* and here *Alice Vivian* either cleared up or maybe further confused the identification of one vessel. These names appeared several times in the documents. This document specified the ship was Confederate flagged, an unusual case since a neutral flag provided some cover, at least at the level of legal fiction. The heading seemed to this author to suggest this might have been the European Trading Co. vessel called the *Alice*. The *Denbigh* was also an E.T.C. ship.

Interesting items on the invoice: 8 gross playing cards of the following types, Steamboat & Monitor, Prince of Wales, Clubhouse Mogul Highlander, and Decatur; 37 gross pens of types reservoir, Commercial, and Senate; 18 bags black pepper; 18 doz. traveling shirts; 1 gross wooden pipes; 10 kegs bicarbonate soda; 30 boxes tin plates; 19 bbls. copperas; 10 bbls. Bourbon whiskey 425 gal. each; 50 boxes brandy; 2 boxes with 5 sets of 4 mule harness; traveling shirts of types plain, plaid, fancy, and striped; shoe makers tools inclung hammers, pincers, scrapers, knives, awl blades; 19 cases Champagne; 1 bbl. and 100 boxes claret;

100 boxes of gin; 50 kits mackerel; 3 teirces (35 gal. casks) 924 lbs. ham; 230 gals. coal oil; 1 doz. sets dominoes; 3 bbls., 900 lbs. borax; 5 bbls., 1227 lbs. saltpeter; 10 pkgs., 10 doz. iron pails; 5 pkgs., 5 doz. wood pails; 5 bbls., 1980 lbs. block tin; 2 bdls., 20 sheets zinc 282 lbs.; 20 bdles., 100 iron kettles 739 lbs.; 13 bdls. sheet iron 2420 lbs.; 5 tierces cod fish 640 lbs.; 10 bbls. sherry wine 200 gals.; red, white, and blue bunting 1417 varas; 55 gross various size screws; 25 tins white paint; 120 shoe brushes; 100 boxes gin; 30 bales gunny bagging 1080 yds.; 200 coils sisal rope 24,016 lbs.; large shipment of medicines –

4 cases each 50 lbs mercurial ointment (for treating venereal disease?)
4 " " 50 lbs Ipecacuana, rhubarb
2 " " 50 lbs rhubarb
2 " " 50 lbs cantharides
3 " " 50 lbs sod(a) of potass(ium)
1 " " 173 lbs gum opium
1 " " 25 lbs powdered opium
4 kegs each 112 lbs chlorate of potass(ium)
4 cases each 100 lbs calomel
6 " " 50 lbs blue mass

Merchants who supplied portions of the shipment: Currety Hassan & Co.; Carro; Dover; Gener; Louis Petit; Barcendiasan & Co.; Edward Pellyou & Co.; O. A. Heniedan (?) & Co.; Sabates; Louis Petit; P. A. Deefarges; La Central; Beckel Kermit & Co.; Scott & Lemis; Vegnier R & Co.; Jose de la Puente; Casto de Belamundi; Ortiz Carasa & Co.; J. W. Dever; Ligero Hermanos; A. Mahe; G. de Amenabas; Benjamin & Low; C Penot & Co.; Rottenam I. Finke.

Total $ 32,144.90, dated Havana 9 July 1863 and signed Vignier Robertson Co. and George Bell.

1803-1804
Preprinted Customs Form

No. 2
Importer H O Brewer & Co
Vessel *A. Vivian*
From Havana
Entered August 3 1863
Value $ 5224 Duty $ 900.80

Agent's Oath
(signed) B. Donaldson, owner
Sworn to, this 3 day of Aug 1863
Collector

Ship Entered ___________
Entry of Merchandise imported into the Port and District of Mobile, by H. O. Brewer & Co in the Steamer *A. Vivian* Abils Master, from Havana

Marks	Packages	Contents	Value in Foreign Currency			Added*	15	25	Duties
M F	1 Box	**Playing Cards**	$ 298.50			$ 328.35			
	18 Bags	Black pepper 2641 lbs	343.33			377.66			
JW D	50 Boxes	Castille Soap	192.00			211.20			
P	50 Pkgs	**Brooms**	125.00			137.50			

	1 Box	Brushes of all Kinds	378.25			416.07			
S	10 Blls	Whiskey 425 Gals	518.75			570.62			
	61 boxes	Brandy 61 doz.	275.00			302.50			
	3 Blls	Rum 160 Gals	63.00			69.30			
	11 Blls	Claret 660 Gals	158.00			173.80			
	100 Boxes	Do 100 doz	200.00			220.00			
	19 baskets	Champagne 36 "	158.00			173.80			
JJ Q	30 Boxes	Tin plates	315.00			346.50	$ 915	5%	$45.75
H +P	4 Blls	Borax 1169 lbs	323.70			356.07	971	10	97.10
P	3 "	Block Tin 1980 lbs	772.20			849.42	1531	20	306.20
	2 Bdls	Trav(eling) Shirt 282 lbs	23.97			26.36	1807	25	451.75
	2 Pieces	Tanned Leather	34.50			37.95	$ 5224		900.80
H	2 Cases	Cantharides	175.00			192.75			
			4354.20			233.75			
		Charges & Com	174.16			182.66			
			4528.36						
S	100 Boxes	Gin 100 doz	212.50			$ 5,206.01			
		Chg & Com	8.50			18.26			
			4749.36			$ 5,224.27			

*Hand written note added to form, "Added by importers."

1807
Preprinted Customs Form

Summary: Customs form, H. O. Brewer & Co. shipment from Havana aboard the *A. Vivian* consisted of duty free items: mess pork, salt peter, hams, coffee, total cost $ 2958.30.

1808-1809
Preprinted Customs Form

No. 8
Importer J J Morrison
Vessel *Fanny* (This may have been an E.T.C. ship like the *Denbigh.*)
From Havana
Entered August 20 1863
Value $ 264 Duty $ 57.75

Ship Entered August 15 1863

Entry of Merchandise imported into the Port and District of Mobile, by J. J. Morrison in the Str *Fanny* Morrison Master, from Havana

Packages	Contents	Value in Foreign Currency			10%	15	20	25	Duties
1 Box	Cheese & Tea	7.00			7				$ .70
1 Lot	Green print	27.25			29				2.90

6 Bottles	Sweet oil $3.50, 1 box starch $4.00	7.50				8			1.20
2 boxes	Mustard $4.50 Soap 7.70	12.20				13			1.95
1 Bll	Sugar $10, Pickles $3.00 Sardines 1.37	13.00 1.37					15		3.00
~~6 boxes~~	~~Sardines~~								
1 Pipe	Rum	26.00						27	6.75
1 Case	Sigars 6500	157.00						165	41.25
		252.32							$ 57.75
	Chgs & Com	12.55							
		263.87			36	21	15	192	

1810-1811
Preprinted Customs Form

No. 9
Importer J L Harris & Duram
Vessel *Fanny*
From Havana
Entered August 26 1863
Value $ 8047 Duty $ 1207.05

Owner's Oath
(signed) J. L. Harris, owner
Sworn to, this 3 day of Aug 1863
Collector

Ship Entered ___________
Entry of Merchandise imported into the Port and District of Mobile, by L. Duram & J. L. Harris in the *Fanny* ________________________ Master, from

Marks	Packages	Contents	Value in Foreign Currency			15%		Duties
F	3 Case	Letter or writing paper & Statem(ent paper)	$ 30 675	0 4		737		
"	3 "	Hosiery & Cotton mfs	845	2		883		
"	1 "	Linen Towels & flax mfs	506	2		529		
"	4 "	Calicoes & Cotton mfs	1240	0		1296		
"	5 pieces	Silk Mfs	216	6		227		
	15 cases	Shoes, Men's & Ladies'	2077	0		2171		
F S	1 "	Nitrate of Silver lbs 55	1114	7½		1165		
"	1 "	Powdered Ipecac Lbs 98	392	0		410		
"	8 "	Cod liver oil doz 8	66 55	0 0		127		
"	1 "	Cast Car. Iron	109	3		114		
"	1 Bll	Nitrate of Potash	61	5		64		
"	1 Cask	Vitriol Gum (?)	131	2		137		
B	20 Kegs	Bi carbonate of Soda	179	1½		187		
			7,790	1½		$8,047	15%	$1207.05

		Chgs & Com	346	4				
			$8,046	5½				

1813-1818
Invoice

Invoice of Sund(rie)s. Ship by M. A. Herrera & Co on board of the Confedt. Steamer *Fannie*, Morrison Mr for Nassau & P. for a/c & risk of whom it may concern & consigned to Order. Total $ 25,078 and 5 reales, dated Havana 8 Aug 1863 and signed M. A. Herrera & Co.

Summary: Detailed 6 page invoice for large quantities of sundries and including medicines and medical supplies for example: surgeon's silk and surgeon's needles (assorted), 5,000 vials, 10,000 corks (bottle stoppers), 600 men's glass syringes, 500 men's metal syringes, 200 female glass syringes, 17 doz. English lancets, 21,100 cigars, 1 gross cosmetic (small), 2 gross pkgs. hair powder, ½ gross hair oil hygenique, 2 gross cologne water, 50 pkges. hair pins, and 1 gross Bachelder's hair dye, 720 lbs. green tea, 776 lbs. black tea, 1459 varas flannel, 13 bales white wax 2468 lbs., 12 bales hops, 20 coils Richardson's Ky bale rope 1564 lbs.

1819-1821
Preprinted Customs Form

No. ___ Free
Importer C. G. Ramsey
Vessel Str *Alabama*
From Havana
Entered
Value $ 2611 Duty $ Free

Free Ship Entered ____________
Imported into the Port and District of Mobile, by _____ in the _______________ __Master, from

Packages	Contents	Value in Foreign Currency			15	25	Duties
329 Pigs	Lead 41,968 lbs[121]	2302.24					
1 Box	Percussion Caps	200.00					
		$ 2508.24					
	Coffee a/c of C. J. Brown	890.00					

Note: The above documents were a sample showing examples having particular interest for the *Denbigh* Project. The E.T.C., owner of the *Denbigh* and other runners, was organized in 1863.

[121] Average about 125 lbs. each.

13

The *Denbigh's* Mobile Outbound Cotton Cargoes

This chapter included blockade-running cotton export documents of two types. The purpose was to present just a bit of context for the outbound side of the trade. First we showed the transcripts of the *Denbigh's* customs forms for export cargoes. Second we presented a table gleaned form the monthly reports rendered by the Mobile collector of customs showing duties and other details on the ships and cargoes departing the port. All of the reports for the war period ending April 1863 found in the Confederate Treasury records (NARA–Washington and NARA–Atlanta) were combined in one large table. Also, at the end of the chapter we included transcripts of the complete monthly reports for the months in which the *Denbigh* sailed from Mobile to Havana excepting the first voyage (Jan. 1864) and the last voyage (Aug. 1864) which were missing.

The *Denbigh's* Mobile to Havana Customs Documents

In the case of the export documents, the forms were presented complete with all the wording that printed on the form as required by government regulations (. Each voyage departing Mobile generated a set of three forms: Entry of Cotton, General Manifest, and Special Manifest-Outward.

Voyage 1, January 16, 1864

ENTRY OF COTTON

laden for exportation by H. O. Brewer & Co. on board the St. Ship called *Denbigh*, MacNevin Master, bound for Havana made 16th Jany. 1864

Marks and Nos.	Number of Bales and description of Cotton	Quantity in Pounds	Rate of Duty	Amount of Export Duty	
				Dollars	Cents
Various	500 Bales Cotton	249,658	1/8¢		
				$311.	82

DISTRICT AND PORT OF MOBILE.

I, Benj. Donaldson do solemnly swear or affirm that the export entry now delivered by me to Collector of the District contains a true account and description of all the Cotton laden by me on board the Br St Ship *Denbigh* for exportation to Havana, together with the weight of said cotton as far as I can at this time ascertain the same.

I further swear (or affirm) that if at the time of making this entry I am unable to ascertain the actual weight of the cotton described therein, I will obtain from a duly authorized weigher a certificate of said weights in detail, and deposit the same with the Collector of this Port without delay.

SO HELP ME GOD.

(signed) Benj. Donaldson

Sworn to before me this Sixteenth day of Jany 1864.

(this copy not signed by Collector)

Collector.

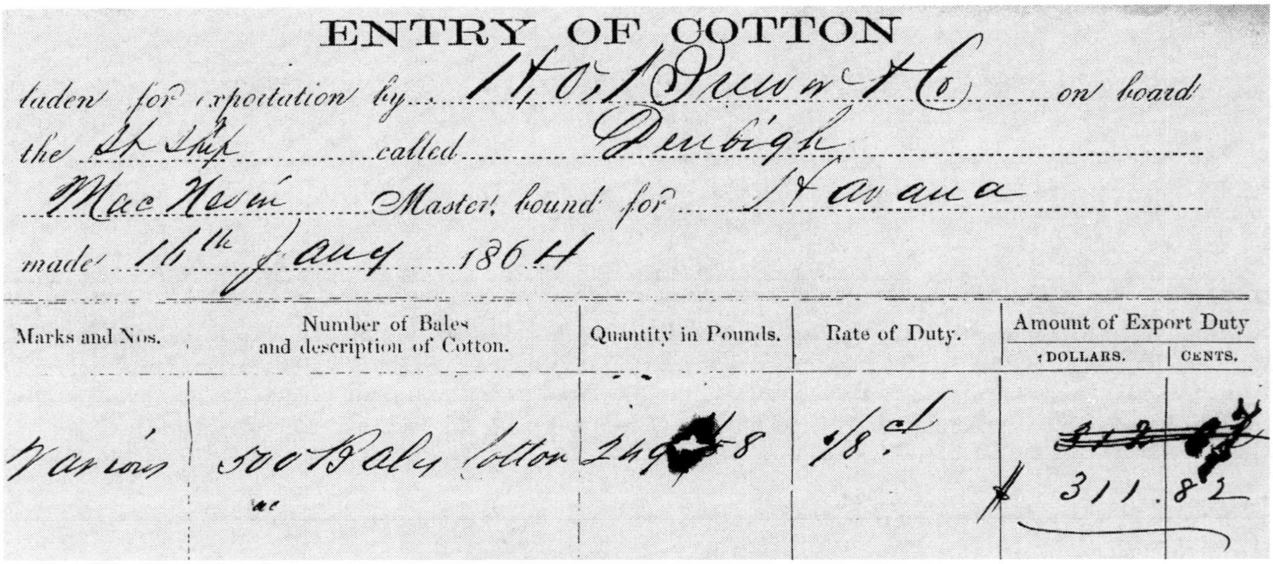

ENTRY OF COTTON

laden for exportation by H. O. Brewer & Co on board the St Ship called Denbigh MacNevin Master, bound for Havana made 16th Jany 1864

Marks and Nos.	Number of Bales and description of Cotton.	Quantity in Pounds.	Rate of Duty.	Amount of Export Duty DOLLARS.	CENTS.
Various	500 Bales Cotton	249[illegible]8	1/8 c	~~312~~ $ 311	~~07~~ 82

(Omitted blank middle section of these forms.)

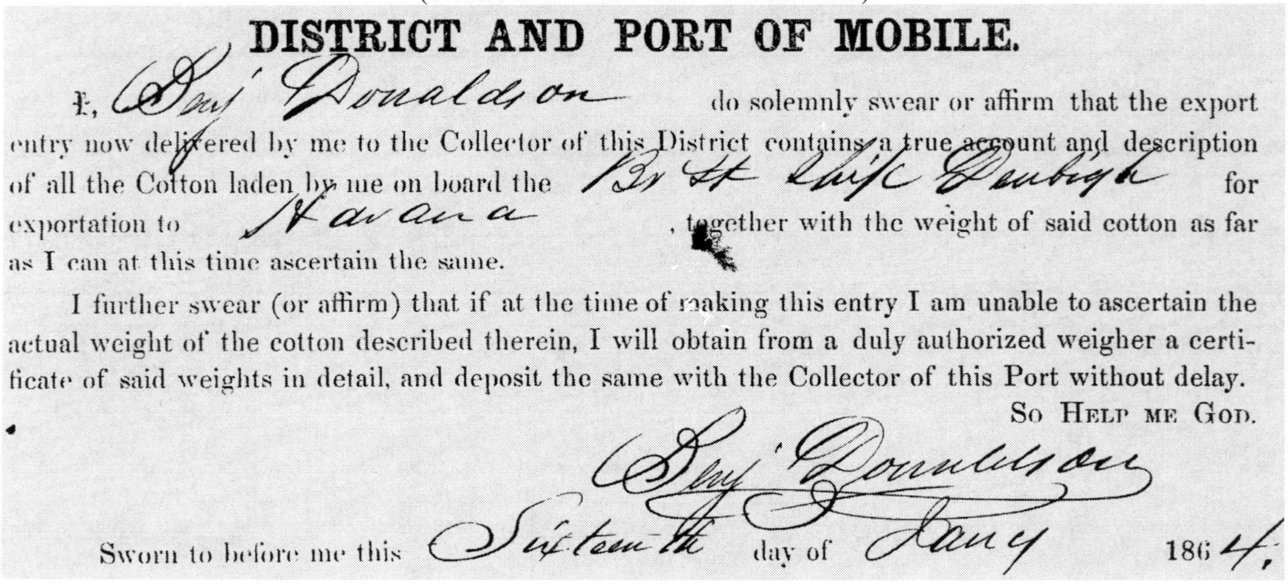

DISTRICT AND PORT OF MOBILE.

I, Benj Donaldson do solemnly swear or affirm that the export entry now delivered by me to the Collector of this District contains a true account and description of all the Cotton laden by me on board the Br St Ship Denbigh for exportation to Havana, together with the weight of said cotton as far as I can at this time ascertain the same.

I further swear (or affirm) that if at the time of making this entry I am unable to ascertain the actual weight of the cotton described therein, I will obtain from a duly authorized weigher a certificate of said weights in detail, and deposit the same with the Collector of this Port without delay.

So Help me God.

Benj Donaldson

Sworn to before me this Sixteenth day of Jany 1864.

Figure 180. Entry of Cotton form, 500 bales on the *Denbigh's* first voyage returning from Mobile to Havana.

Note that on her first voyage the *Denbigh* grounded near Fort Morgan while leaving Mobile Bay. The cotton cargo was unloaded on the beach to refloat the ship which then returned to port for minor repairs, reloading, and a later successful run back to Havana. This incident lead to a successful salvage claim by the fort's garrison who helped unload and save the ship and cotton. The litigation generated depositions by many of those involved representing the only first-hand accounts from the *Denbigh*. The court records are presented in a subsequent *Denbigh* Project book (Powel, Cordon, and Arnold, in preparation).

GENERAL MANIFEST.
Sold by Thos. S. Bidgood & Co., Booksellers, Mobile.

Report and Manifest of the Cargo laden at Port of Mobile, on board the Br St Ship *Denbigh* Mac Nevin Master, bound for Havana

MARKS AND NUMBERS	PACKAGES AND CONTENTS	QUANTITIES	VALUE	
			Dolls.	Cts.
Various	500 B/c	249,658	124,729	---

DISTRICT AND PORT OF MOBILE.

I, Frank Mac Nevin[122] Master and commander of the Br St Ship *Denbigh* bound from the Port of Mobile to Havana do solemnly, sincerely and truly swear, that the Manifest of the Cargo on board the said St Ship now delivered by me to the Collector of this District, and subscribed with my name, contains, according to the best of my knowledge and belief, a full, just and true account of all the Goods, Wares, or Merchandise shall be laden on board the said St Ship previous to her sailing, I will immediately report the same to the said Collector: I do also swear that I verily believe the duties on all Foreign Merchandise therein specified have been paid or secured according to law, and that no part thereof is intended to be relanded within the United States;[123] and that if by distress or other unavoidable accident, it should become necessary to reland the same, I will forthwith make a just and true report thereof to the Collector of the Customs of the District within which such distress or accident may happen. And I further swear, that the Merchandise is intended to be exported to Havana

Sworn to before me, this 16th
Day of Jany. 1864

SO HELP ME GOD.

(signed) F. M. Nevin

(this copy not signed by Collector)

Collector.

---

[122] On this document was the signature of Capt. Francis MacNevin in his own hand. Interestingly it seems he went by Frank and he signed F. M. Nevin as though the Mac was a separate middle name. The treatment of the name Mac as a middle rather than combined with the last name led to the varied forms that confused rendering of his name in other historic documents.

[123] This manifest form was left over from before secession. Often on other such forms United States was crossed out and Confederate States written above.

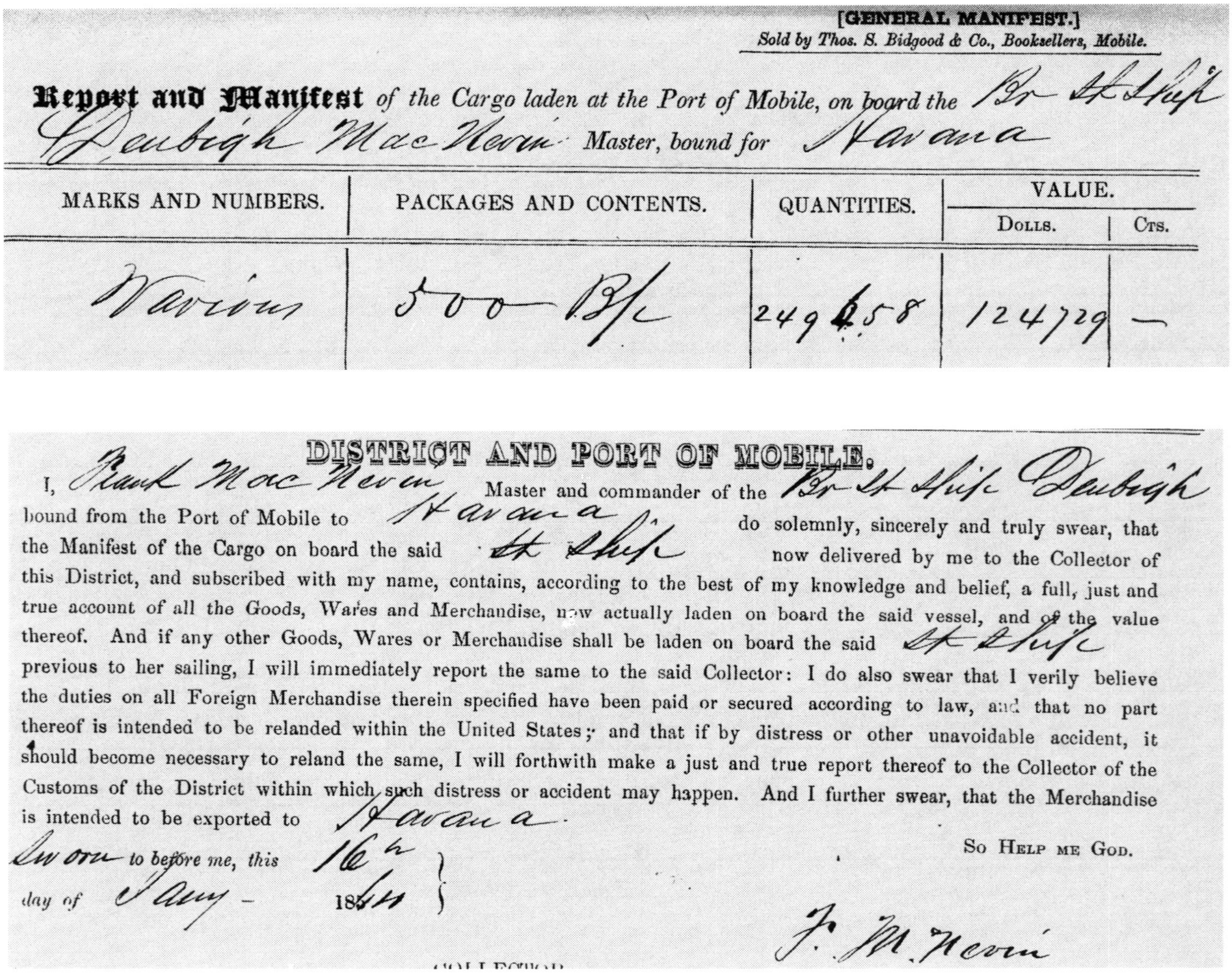

[GENERAL MANIFEST.]
Sold by Thos. S. Bidgood & Co., Booksellers, Mobile.

Report and Manifest *of the Cargo laden at the Port of Mobile, on board the* Br St Ship Denbigh MacNevin *Master, bound for* Havana

MARKS AND NUMBERS.	PACKAGES AND CONTENTS.	QUANTITIES.	VALUE. DOLLS.	CTS.
Various	500 B/c	249.58	124729	—

DISTRICT AND PORT OF MOBILE.

I, Frank MacNevin Master and commander of the Br St Ship Denbigh bound from the Port of Mobile to Havana do solemnly, sincerely and truly swear, that the Manifest of the Cargo on board the said St Ship now delivered by me to the Collector of this District, and subscribed with my name, contains, according to the best of my knowledge and belief, a full, just and true account of all the Goods, Wares and Merchandise, now actually laden on board the said vessel, and of the value thereof. And if any other Goods, Wares or Merchandise shall be laden on board the said St Ship previous to her sailing, I will immediately report the same to the said Collector: I do also swear that I verily believe the duties on all Foreign Merchandise therein specified have been paid or secured according to law, and that no part thereof is intended to be relanded within the United States; and that if by distress or other unavoidable accident, it should become necessary to reland the same, I will forthwith make a just and true report thereof to the Collector of the Customs of the District within which such distress or accident may happen. And I further swear, that the Merchandise is intended to be exported to Havana.

So Help me God.

Sworn *to before me, this* 16th *day of* Jany 1864

F. McNevin

Figure 181. Example of a *Denbigh* first voyage customs document filled out and signed by Captain McNevin Jan. 16, 1864. The Jan. 1864 set of customs documents relates to the cargo jettisoned near Fort Morgan in early February when the *Denbigh* grounded. The garrison of the fort helped save the cargo and received a salvage award of $25,000, about a fifth of the cargo's value.

SPECIAL MANIFEST – Outward.
Sold by Wm Strickland Bookseller and Stationer, 28 Dauphin Street, Mobile.

Manifest of all the Goods, Wares, Merchandise, and Specie, shipped by H O Brewer & Co. on board the British St Ship *Denbigh* whereof Mac Nevin is Master, bound for the port of Havana in Cuba

MARKS	NUMBERS	PACKAGES OR ARTICLES IN BULK	CONTENTS	VALUE AT THE PORT OF EXPORTATION					
				Value of Domestic Produce or Merchandise		Value of Foreign Produce or Merchandise		Total Amount	
				Dollars	Cents	Dollars	Cents	Dollars	Cents
Various	Various	500 Bales Cotton	249,658 lbs	124,729	00			126,729	00

DISTRICT OF MOBILE

I, Benj Donaldson do solemnly swear that the above Manifest contains a full, just, and true account of all the Goods, Wares, Merchandise, and Specie, of every kind, shipped by H O Brewer & Co. on board the above named vessel, and the quantities and values of each article are truly stated, according to their actual cost, or the values which they truly bear in this port at this time: And further swear, that the said Merchandise is truly intended to be exported to Havana

Sworn this 16th day January 185___ (overwritten 64)[124]

Before me, _______________ Collector. (signed) Benj Donaldson

(this copy not signed by Collector)

[124] Another left over form. This one was a ledger-sized sheet with an American Eagle and E Pluribus Unum engraving at the top.

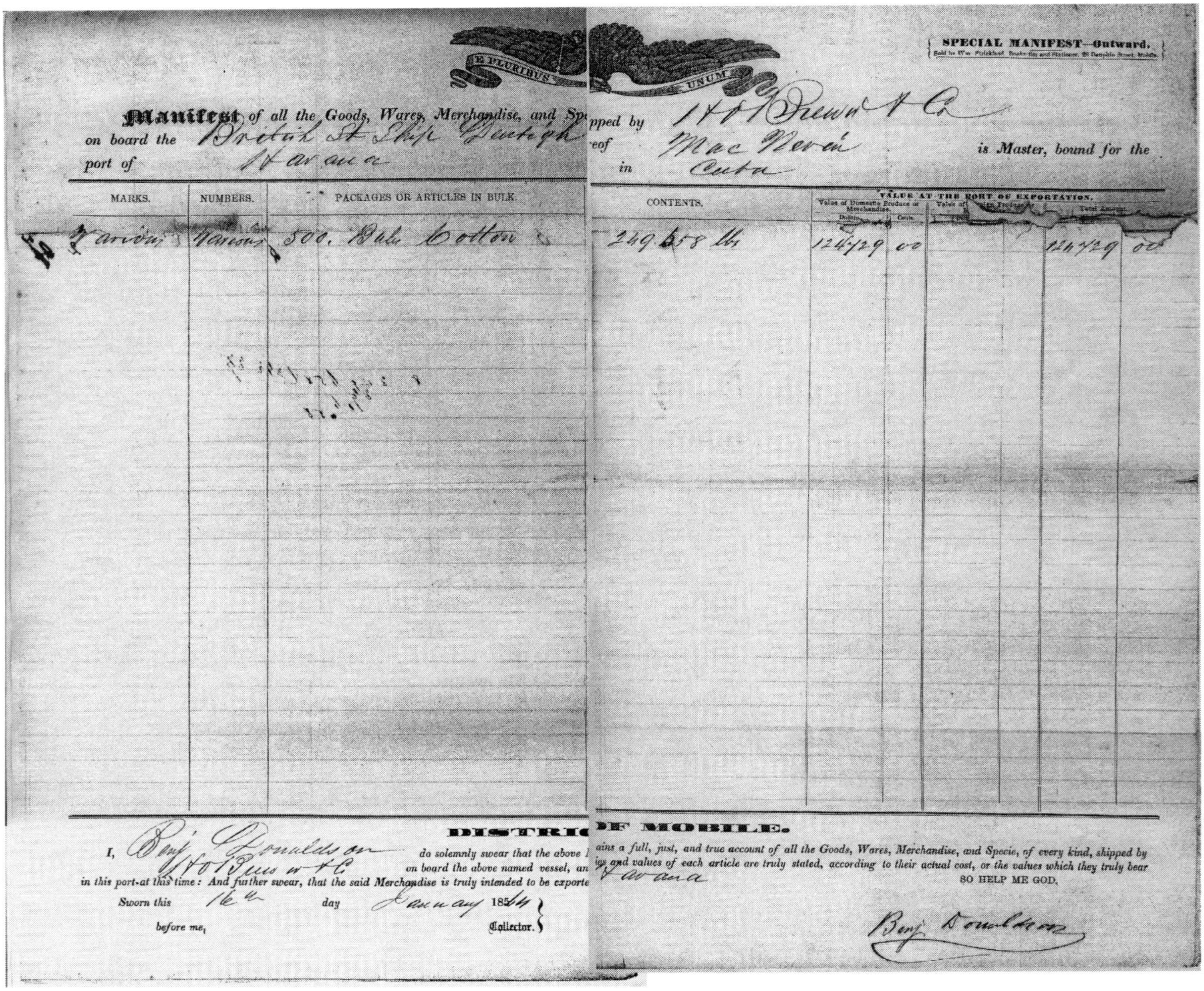

SPECIAL MANIFEST—Outward.

E PLURIBUS UNUM

Manifest of all the Goods, Wares, Merchandise, and Sp[ecie ship]pped by H O Brewer & Co on board the British St Ship Denbigh [wh]ereof Mac Nevin is Master, bound for the port of Havana in Cuba

MARKS.	NUMBERS.	PACKAGES OR ARTICLES IN BULK.	CONTENTS.	VALUE AT THE PORT OF EXPORTATION. Value of Domestic Produce or Merchandise. Dollars.	Cents.	Value of Foreign ...		Total Amount.	
Various	Various	500. Bale Cotton	249.658 lbs	124729	00			124729	00

DISTRIC[T] OF MOBILE.

I, Benj Donaldson do solemnly swear that the above [Manifest cont]ains a full, just, and true account of all the Goods, Wares, Merchandise, and Specie, of every kind, shipped by H O Brewer & Co on board the above named vessel, an[d that the quantit]ies and values of each article are truly stated, according to their actual cost, or the values which they truly bear in this port at this time: And further swear, that the said Merchandise is truly intended to be exporte[d to] Havana

SO HELP ME GOD.

Sworn this 16th day January 1864 before me, Collector.

Benj Donaldson

Figure 182. Special Manifest – Outward for the *Denbigh's* first 500 bale cargo.

Voyage 2, March 16, 1864

ENTRY OF COTTON

laden for exportation by H. O. Brewer & Co. on board the St. Ship called *Denbigh* McNevin Master, bound for Havana made 16th March 1864

Marks and Nos.	Number of Bales and description of Cotton	Quantity in Pounds	Rate of Duty	Amount of Export Duty	
				Dollars	Cents
Various	424 Bales Cotton	201,482	1/8¢	$251	85
		118			15
				252	

DISTRICT AND PORT OF MOBILE.

I, Benj. Donaldson do solemnly swear or affirm that the export entry now delivered by me to Collector of the District contains a true account and description of all the Cotton laden by me on board the Br St Ship *Denbigh* for exportation to Havana, together with the weight of said cotton as far as I can at this time ascertain the same.

I further swear (or affirm) that if at the time of making this entry I am unable to ascertain the actual weight of the cotton described therein, I will obtain from a duly authorized weigher a certificate of said weights in detail, and deposit the same with the Collector of this Port without delay.

SO HELP ME GOD.

(signed) Benj. Donaldson

Sworn to before me this 16th day of March 1864.

(this copy not signed by Collector)

Collector.

GENERAL MANIFEST.
Sold by Thos. S. Bidgood & Co., Booksellers, Mobile.

Report and Manifest of the Cargo laden at Port of Mobile, on board the Br St Ship *Denbigh* Mac Nevin Master, bound for Havana

MARKS AND NUMBERS	PACKAGES AND CONTENTS	QUANTITIES	VALUE	
			Dolls.	Cts.
Various	421 B Cotton	200,020	150,015	
	2 "	996	747	
	1 "	466	349	50
	424 B Cotton			
		201,482 lbs.	$151,111	50

DISTRICT AND PORT OF MOBILE.

I, McNevin Master and commander of the Br St Ship *Denbigh* bound from the Port of Mobile to Havana do solemnly, sincerely and truly swear, that the Manifest of the Cargo on board the said St Ship now delivered by me to the Collector of this District, and subscribed with my name, contains, according to the best of my knowledge and belief, a full, just and true account of all the Goods, Wares, or Merchandise shall be laden on board the said St Ship previous to her sailing, I will immediately report the same to the said Collector: I do also swear that I verily believe the duties on all Foreign Merchandise therein specified have been paid or secured according to law, and that no part thereof is intended to be relanded within the United States; and that if by distress or other unavoidable accident, it should become necessary to reland the same, I will forthwith make a just and true report thereof to the Collector of the Customs of the District within which such distress or accident may happen. And I further swear, that the Merchandise is intended to be exported to Havana

Sworn to before me, this 16th
Day of March 1864

SO HELP ME GOD.

(signed) F. M. Nevin

(this copy not signed by Collector)
Collector.

Note the Special Manifest form was missing from file. Instead there were two General Manifest forms, the second slightly altered as a substitute and signed by Benj. Donaldson. (See next page.) Probably there was a shortage of the Special Manifest forms.

GENERAL MANIFEST.
Sold by Thos. S. Bidgood & Co., Booksellers, Mobile.

Special[125]
~~Report and~~ Manifest of the Cargo laden at Port of Mobile, on board the Br St Ship *Denbigh* MacNevin Master, bound for Havana

MARKS AND NUMBERS	PACKAGES AND CONTENTS	QUANTITIES	VALUE	
			Dolls.	Cts.
Various	421 Bales Cotton	200,020	150,015	00
	2 "	996	747	
	1 "	466	349	50
	424 Bs Cotton	201,482	$ 151,111	50
		118		
		201,600		

DISTRICT AND PORT OF MOBILE.

I, B. Donaldson ~~Master and commander of the Br St Ship *Denbigh* bound from the Port of Mobile to~~ do solemnly, sincerely and truly swear, that the Manifest of the Cargo on board the said St Ship *Denbigh* now delivered by me to the Collector of this District, and subscribed with my name, contains, according to the best of my knowledge and belief, a full, just and true account of all the Goods, Wares, or Merchandise shall be laden on board the said St Ship *Denbigh* previous to her sailing, I will immediately report the same to the said Collector: I do also swear that I verily believe the duties on all Foreign Merchandise therein specified have been paid or secured according to law, and that no part thereof is intended to be relanded within the United States;[126] and that if by distress or other unavoidable accident, it should become necessary to reland the same, I will forthwith make a just and true report thereof to the Collector of the Customs of the District within which such distress or accident may happen. And I further swear, that the Merchandise is intended to be exported to Havana

Sworn to before me, this 16th
Day of March 1864

SO HELP ME GOD.

(signed) Benj. Donaldson

(this copy not signed by Collector)
Collector.

---

[125] Handwritten above strike out. This altered General Manifest form was substituted for the normal Special Manifest form.

[126] This manifest form was left over from before secession. Often on other such forms United States was crossed out and Confederate States hand written above the cross out.

Voyage 3, April 16, 1864

ENTRY OF COTTON

laden for exportation by H. O. Brewer & Co. on board the St. Ship called *Denbigh*, A. M. Godfrey Master, bound for Havana made 16th April 1864

Marks and Nos.	Number of Bales and description of Cotton	Quantity in Pounds	Rate of Duty	Amount of Export Duty	
				Dollars	Cents
Various	452 Bales Cotton	202,748	1/8¢	253	43
	20 " "	10,060	1/8	12	57
	472 Do.	212,808		$ 266	00

DISTRICT AND PORT OF MOBILE.

I, B Donaldson do solemnly swear or affirm that the export entry now delivered by me to Collector of the District contains a true account and description of all the Cotton laden by me on board the Br St Ship *Denbigh* for exportation to Havana, together with the weight of said cotton as far as I can at this time ascertain the same.

I further swear (or affirm) that if at the time of making this entry I am unable to ascertain the actual weight of the cotton described therein, I will obtain from a duly authorized weigher a certificate of said weights in detail, and deposit the same with the Collector of this Port without delay.

SO HELP ME GOD.

(signed) Benj. Donaldson

Sworn to before me this Sixteenth day of April 1864.

(signed) J. C. Coleson Dep(uty)

Collector.

GENERAL MANIFEST.
Sold by Thos. S. Bidgood & Co., Booksellers, Mobile.

Report and Manifest of the Cargo laden at Port of Mobile, on board the Br St Ship *Denbigh* A. M. Godfrey Master, bound for Havana

MARKS AND NUMBERS	PACKAGES AND CONTENTS	QUANTITIES	VALUE	
			Dolls.	Cts.
Various	447 Bs Cotton	200,254	150,190	50
"	4 do	2,014	1,510	50
"	1 do	480	360	00
	452 Bs Cotton	202,748	152,060	
	24 "	10,012	1,284	
	476 "	212,760	15,334	

DISTRICT AND PORT OF MOBILE.

I, A. M. Godfrey Master and commander of the Br St Ship *Denbigh* bound from the Port of Mobile to Havana do solemnly, sincerely and truly swear, that the Manifest of the Cargo on board the said St Ship now delivered by me to the Collector of this District, and subscribed with my name, contains, according to the best of my knowledge and belief, a full, just and true account of all the Goods, Wares, or Merchandise shall be laden on board the said St Ship *Denbigh* previous to her sailing, I will immediately report the same to the said Collector: I do also swear that I verily believe the duties on all Foreign Merchandise therein specified have been paid or secured according to law, and that no part thereof is intended to be relanded within the United States;[127] and that if by distress or other unavoidable accident, it should become necessary to reland the same, I will forthwith make a just and true report thereof to the Collector of the Customs of the District within which such distress or accident may happen. And I further swear, that the Merchandise is intended to be exported to Havana

Sworn to before me, this 16th
Day of April 1864

SO HELP ME GOD.

(signed) A. M. Godfrey[128]

(this copy not signed by Collector)
Collector.

---

[127] This manifest form was left over from before secession. Often on other such forms United States was crossed out and Confederate States written above.

[128] Note that this is Godfrey's first voyage as the *Denbigh's* captain.

GENERAL MANIFEST.
Sold by Thos. S. Bidgood & Co., Booksellers, Mobile.

Special[129]
~~Report and~~ Manifest of the Cargo laden at Port of Mobile, on board the Br St Ship *Denbigh* A. M. Godfrey Master, bound for Havana

MARKS AND NUMBERS	PACKAGES AND CONTENTS	QUANTITIES	VALUE	
			Dolls.	Cts.
Various	452 Bales Cotton	202,748	152,061	---
	20	10,012	1,284	---

DISTRICT AND PORT OF MOBILE.

I, B. Donaldson ~~Master and commander of the Br St Ship *Denbigh* bound from the Port of Mobile to~~ do solemnly, sincerely and truly swear, that the Manifest of the Cargo on board the said St Ship *Denbigh* now delivered by me to the Collector of this District, and subscribed with my name, contains, according to the best of my knowledge and belief, a full, just and true account of all the Goods, Wares, or Merchandise shall be laden on board the said St Ship *Denbigh* previous to her sailing, I will immediately report the same to the said Collector: I do also swear that I verily believe the duties on all Foreign Merchandise therein specified have been paid or secured according to law, and that no part thereof is intended to be relanded within the United States;[130] and that if by distress or other unavoidable accident, it should become necessary to reland the same, I will forthwith make a just and true report thereof to the Collector of the Customs of the District within which such distress or accident may happen. And I further swear, that the Merchandise is intended to be exported to Havana

Sworn to before me, this 16th
Day of April 1864

SO HELP ME GOD.

(signed) Benj. Donaldson

(this copy not signed by Collector)
Collector.

---

[129] Handwritten above strike out. This altered General Manifest form was substituted for the normal Special Manifest form.

[130] This manifest form was left over from before secession. Often on other such forms United States was crossed out and Confederate States written above.

Voyage 4, May 4, 1864

ENTRY OF COTTON

laden for exportation by H. O. Brewer & Co. on board the Steamship called *Denbigh* A. M. Godfrey Master, bound for Havana made 4th May1864

Marks and Nos.	Number of Bales and description of Cotton	Quantity in Pounds	Rate of Duty	Amount of Export Duty	
				Dollars	Cents
Various	445 Bs Cotton	210,992	1/8¢	263	74

DISTRICT AND PORT OF MOBILE.

I, __________ do solemnly swear or affirm that the export entry now delivered by me to Collector of the District contains a true account and description of all the Cotton laden by me on board the St Ship *Denbigh* for exportation to Havana, together with the weight of said cotton as far as I can at this time ascertain the same.

I further swear (or affirm) that if at the time of making this entry I am unable to ascertain the actual weight of the cotton described therein, I will obtain from a duly authorized weigher a certificate of said weights in detail, and deposit the same with the Collector of this Port without delay.

SO HELP ME GOD.

(signed) A. J. Dugusol (?)

Sworn to before me this Fourth day of May 1864.

(this copy not signed by Collector)

Collector.

GENERAL MANIFEST.
Sold by Thos. S. Bidgood & Co., Booksellers, Mobile.

Report and Manifest of the Cargo laden at Port of Mobile, on board the Br St Ship *Denbigh* "A. M. Godfrey" Master, bound for Havana

MARKS AND NUMBERS	PACKAGES AND CONTENTS	QUANTITIES	VALUE	
			Dolls.	Cts.
Various	445 Bales Cotton	210,992 Pounds	105,496	"
	20 Bbls Rosin[131]		100	"

DISTRICT AND PORT OF MOBILE.

I, A. M. Godfrey Master and commander of the St Ship *Denbigh* bound from the Port of Mobile to Havana do solemnly, sincerely and truly swear, that the Manifest of the Cargo on board the said St Ship now delivered by me to the Collector of this District, and subscribed with my name, contains, according to the best of my knowledge and belief, a full, just and true account of all the Goods, Wares, or Merchandise shall be laden on board the said St Ship previous to her sailing, I will immediately report the same to the said Collector: I do also swear that I verily believe the duties on all Foreign Merchandise therein specified have been paid or secured according to law, and that no part thereof is intended to be relanded with the United States; and that if by distress or other unavoidable accident, it should become necessary to reland the same, I will forthwith make a just and true report thereof to the Collector of the Customs of the District within which such distress or accident may happen. And I further swear, that the Merchandise is intended to be exported to Havana

Sworn to before me, this 4th
Day of May 1864

SO HELP ME GOD.

(signed) A. M. Godfrey

(this copy not signed by Collector)
Collector.

---

[131] The salvage lawsuit showed that there were also about twenty barrels of rosin and turpentine on board for the January voyage. Interestingly that part of the cargo did not show up on that January set of customs documents.

SPECIAL MANIFEST – Outward.
Sold by Wm Strickland Bookseller and Stationer, 28 Dauphin Street, Mobile.

Manifest of all the Goods, Wares, Merchandise, and Specie, shipped by H. O. Brewer & Co. on board the St Ship *Denbigh* whereof "A. M. Godfrey" is Master, bound for the port of Havana

MARKS	NUMBERS	PACKAGES OR ARTICLES IN BULK	CONTENTS	VALUE AT THE PORT OF EXPORTATION					
				Value of Domestic Produce or Merchandise		Value of Foreign Produce or Merchandise		Total Amount	
				Dollars	Cents	Dollars	Cents	Dollars	Cents
Various	Various	445 Bales Cotton	210,992 Pounds	105,496	"			105,496	00
		20 Bbls Rosin		100				100	

DISTRICT OF MOBILE

I, __________ do solemnly swear that the above Manifest contains a full, just, and true account of all the Goods, Wares, Merchandise, and Specie, of every kind, shipped by H. O. Brewer & Co. on board the above named vessel, and the quantities and values of each article are truly stated, according to their actual cost, or the values which they truly bear in this port at this time: And further swear, that the said Merchandise is truly intended to be exported to Havana

Sworn this 4th day May 185___ (overwritten 64)
Before me, _______________ Collector. (signed) A. J. Dugusol (?)
(this copy not signed by Collector)

Voyage 5, May 24, 1864

ENTRY OF COTTON

laden for exportation by H. O. Brewer & Co. on board the St Ship called *Denbigh* A. M. Godfrey Master, bound for Havana made 26th May 1864

Marks and Nos.	Number of Bales and description of Cotton	Quantity in Pounds	Rate of Duty	Amount of Export Duty	
				Dollars	Cents
Various	442 Bl Cotton	224,544	1/8¢	$ 280	68
	20 B				

DISTRICT AND PORT OF MOBILE.

I, Benj. Donaldson do solemnly swear or affirm that the export entry now delivered by me to Collector of the District contains a true account and description of all the Cotton laden by me on board the Br St Ship *Denbigh* for exportation to Havana, together with the weight of said cotton as far as I can at this time ascertain the same.

I further swear (or affirm) that if at the time of making this entry I am unable to ascertain the actual weight of the cotton described therein, I will obtain from a duly authorized weigher a certificate of said weights in detail, and deposit the same with the Collector of this Port without delay.

SO HELP ME GOD.

(signed) Benj. Donaldson

Sworn to before me this 26th day of May 1864.

(this copy not signed by Collector)

Collector.

GENERAL MANIFEST.
Sold by Thos. S. Bidgood & Co., Booksellers, Mobile.

Report and Manifest of the Cargo laden at Port of Mobile, on board the St Ship *Denbigh* A. M. Godfrey Master, bound for Havana

MARKS AND NUMBERS	PACKAGES AND CONTENTS	QUANTITIES	VALUE	
			Dolls.	Cts.
Various	442 Bales Cotton in 450 Packages	224,544	112,272	00
	20 Bbls Rosin[132]		200	00

DISTRICT AND PORT OF MOBILE.

I, A. M. Godfrey Master and commander of the St Ship *Denbigh* bound from the Port of Mobile to Havana do solemnly, sincerely and truly swear, that the Manifest of the Cargo on board the said St Ship now delivered by me to the Collector of this District, and subscribed with my name, contains, according to the best of my knowledge and belief, a full, just and true account of all the Goods, Wares, or Merchandise shall be laden on board the said St Ship previous to her sailing, I will immediately report the same to the said Collector: I do also swear that I verily believe the duties on all Foreign Merchandise therein specified have been paid or secured according to law, and that no part thereof is intended to be relanded within the United States; and that if by distress or other unavoidable accident, it should become necessary to reland the same, I will forthwith make a just and true report thereof to the Collector of the Customs of the District within which such distress or accident may happen. And I further swear, that the Merchandise is intended to be exported to Havana

Sworn to before me, this 26th
day of May 1864

SO HELP ME GOD.

(signed) A. M. Godfrey

(this copy not signed by Collector)
Collector.

---

[132] The salvage lawsuit showed that there were also about twenty barrels of rosin and turpentine on board for the January voyage. Interestingly that part of the cargo did not show up on the January set of customs documents.

SPECIAL MANIFEST – Outward.
Sold by Wm Strickland Bookseller and Stationer, 28 Dauphin Street, Mobile.

Manifest of all the Goods, Wares, Merchandise, and Specie, shipped by H. O. Brewer & Co. on board the St Ship *Denbigh* whereof A. M. Godfrey is Master, bound for the port of Havana in Cuba

MARKS	NUMBERS	PACKAGES OR ARTICLES IN BULK	CONTENTS	VALUE AT THE PORT OF EXPORTATION					
				Value of Domestic Produce or Merchandise		Value of Foreign Produce or Merchandise		Total Amount	
				Dollars	Cents	Dollars	Cents	Dollars	Cents
Various	Various	442 Bales Cotton in 450 Packages	222,544 lbs					112,272	00

DISTRICT OF MOBILE

I, Benj. Donaldson do solemnly swear that the above Manifest contains a full, just, and true account of all the Goods, Wares, Merchandise, and Specie, of every kind, shipped by H. O. Brewer & Co. on board the above named vessel, and the quantities and values of each article are truly stated, according to their actual cost, or the values which they truly bear in this port at this time: And further swear, that the said Merchandise is truly intended to be exported to Havana

Sworn this 26th day May 185__ (5__ overwritten 64)

Before me, _______________ Collector. (signed) Benj. Donaldson

(this copy not signed by Collector)

Voyage 6, June 14, 1864

ENTRY OF COTTON

laden for exportation by H. O. Brewer & Co. on board the Steam ship called *Denbigh* A. M. Godfrey Master, bound for Havana made 14th June 1864

Marks and Nos.	Number of Bales and description of Cotton	Quantity in Pounds	Rate of Duty	Amount of Export Duty	
				Dollars	Cents
Various	346 Bales Cotton	178,948	1/8¢	$ 223	68

DISTRICT AND PORT OF MOBILE.

I, Benj. Donaldson do solemnly swear or affirm that the export entry now delivered by me to Collector of the District contains a true account and description of all the Cotton laden by me on board the Steam ship *Denbigh* for exportation to Havana, together with the weight of said cotton as far as I can at this time ascertain the same.

I further swear (or affirm) that if at the time of making this entry I am unable to ascertain the actual weight of the cotton described therein, I will obtain from a duly authorized weigher a certificate of said weights in detail, and deposit the same with the Collector of this Port without delay.

SO HELP ME GOD.

(signed) Benj. Donaldson

Sworn to before me this 14th day of June 1864.

(this copy not signed by Collector)

Collector.

ENTRY OF COTTON

laden for exportation by John Scott on board the Steam Ship called *Denbigh* A. M. Godfrey Master, bound for Havana made 14th June1864

Marks and Nos.	Number of Bales and description of Cotton	Quantity in Pounds	Rate of Duty	Amount of Export Duty	
				Dollars	Cents
Various	75 Bales Cotton	39,942	1/8¢	$ 49	92

DISTRICT AND PORT OF MOBILE.

I, __________________ do solemnly swear or affirm that the export entry now delivered by me to Collector of the District contains a true account and description of all the Cotton laden by me on board the Steam Ship *Denbigh* for exportation to Havana, together with the weight of said cotton as far as I can at this time ascertain the same.

I further swear (or affirm) that if at the time of making this entry I am unable to ascertain the actual weight of the cotton described therein, I will obtain from a duly authorized weigher a certificate of said weights in detail, and deposit the same with the Collector of this Port without delay.

SO HELP ME GOD.

(signed) T. H. Mann

Sworn to before me this 14th day of June 1864.

(this copy not signed by Collector)

Collector.

GENERAL MANIFEST.
Sold by Thos. S. Bidgood & Co., Booksellers, Mobile.

Report and Manifest of the Cargo laden at Port of Mobile, on board the Steam Ship *Denbigh* A. M. Godfrey Master, bound for Havana

MARKS AND NUMBERS	PACKAGES AND CONTENTS	QUANTITIES	VALUE	
			Dolls.	Cts.
Various	75 Bales Cotton	39,942	22,766	94
"	346 " "	178,948	102,000	36
	421	218,890	124,767	30
		lbs		

DISTRICT AND PORT OF MOBILE.

I, A. M. Godfrey Master and commander of the Steam Ship *Denbigh* bound from the Port of Mobile to Havana do solemnly, sincerely and truly swear, that the Manifest of the Cargo on board the said Steam ship *Denbigh* now delivered by me to the Collector of this District, and subscribed with my name, contains, according to the best of my knowledge and belief, a full, just and true account of all the Goods, Wares, or Merchandise shall be laden on board the said Steamship previous to her sailing, I will immediately report the same to the said Collector: I do also swear that I verily believe the duties on all Foreign Merchandise therein specified have been paid or secured according to law, and that no part thereof is intended to be relanded within the United States; and that if by distress or other unavoidable accident, it should become necessary to reland the same, I will forthwith make a just and true report thereof to the Collector of the Customs of the District within which such distress or accident may happen. And I further swear, that the Merchandise is intended to be exported to Havana

Sworn to before me, this 14th
Day of June 185_ (overwritten 64)

SO HELP ME GOD.

(signed) A. M. Godfrey

(this copy not signed by Collector)
Collector.

SPECIAL MANIFEST – Outward.
Sold by Wm Strickland Bookseller and Stationer, 28 Dauphin Street, Mobile.

Manifest of all the Goods, Wares, Merchandise, and Specie, shipped by John Scott on board the Steam Ship *Denbigh* whereof A. M. Godfrey is Master, bound for the port of Havana in Island Cuba

MARKS	NUMBERS	PACKAGES OR ARTICLES IN BULK	CONTENTS	VALUE AT THE PORT OF EXPORTATION					
				Value of Domestic Produce or Merchandise		Value of Foreign Produce or Merchandise		Total Amount	
				Dollars	Cents	Dollars	Cents	Dollars	Cents
Various		75 Bales Cotton	39,942 Pounds	22,766	94			22,766	94

DISTRICT OF MOBILE

I, _____________do solemnly swear that the above Manifest contains a full, just, and true account of all the Goods, Wares, Merchandise, and Specie, of every kind, shipped by John Scott on board the above named vessel, and the quantities and values of each article are truly stated, according to their actual cost, or the values which they truly bear in this port at this time: And further swear, that the said Merchandise is truly intended to be exported to Havana

Sworn this 14th day June 185__ (overwritten 64) SO HELP ME GOD
Before me, ______________ Collector. (signed) T. H. Mann
(this copy not signed by Collector)

Forms for cotton export on the *Denbigh's* seventh and final voyage to Mobile were not in the NARA–Atlanta files. The ship departed in a rush as Fort Morgan was falling to Admiral Farragut in early August 1864. Perhaps the crisis accounts for incomplete records. Import documents for voyage seven were also missing.

Other Export Documents Providing Context for Blockade Running at Mobile

In this section presents several kinds of archival gleanings (NARA–Washington)[133] that provide added context for blockade running in Mobile. The Customs House reported weekly and monthly ship departures and particulars of the cotton cargoes. First we show a table combining the reports covering the period May 10, 1862 to Sept. 30, 1863. During that time 19,155 bales were exported, close to ten million pounds of cotton. Second we present a summary table of *Denbigh's* cotton cargoes outbound from Mobile. Third are the transcripts of the surviving monthly reports showing the *Denbigh.* Not all the monthly reports for the *Denbigh's* period of service, Jan.–Aug. 1864, were found, but for those three months we know which ships were running the blockade along with the *Denbigh.*

This section adds much basic data important in understanding Civil War blockade running at Mobile.

[133] RG 365, Treasury Dept. Collection of Confederate Records, Records of the Bureau of Customs.

Mobile Customs Reports

Export duties collected from 10th May 1862 to 30th Sept 1863 (Mobile)*

Date	Vessel	Cotton		Duty Received		
'62		Bales	Pounds	Coupons	Specie	Total Duty
May 10	*Swan* Steamer	982	531,164		$ 663.96	$ 663.96
"	Do	12	5,480		6.85	6.85
15	*Fashion* Sloop	60	43,440		41.80	41.80
28	*Clara* Schr*	89	42,418		53.02	53.02
Aug. 16	*Yorktown* Str	836	437,100		546.37	546.37
Sept. 1	*Phantom* Schr	75	38,250		47.80	47.80
"	*Shiloh* Schr	180	94,500		118.13	118.13
6	*Cuba* Str*	807	430,414		538.01	538.01
19	*Alice* Str	823	444,306		555.38	555.38
25	*M. R. Harris* Schr	30	15,076		18.85	18.85
"	*?? Ariel "*	34	17,190		21.50	21.50
27	*Jms Arthur "*	200	99,534		124.42	124.42
28	*Relief "*	75	43,254		54.07	54.07
31	*Baltic "*	110	54,672		68.34	68.34
Nov. 1	*Pelican "*	94	49,840		62.30	62.30
18	*M. R. Harris "*	32	15,124		18.90	18.90
Dec. 1	*Hortense "*	18	9,288	10	1.61	11.61
17	*Ray "*	70	36,076	44	5.09	45.09
'63						
Jan. 2	*Never Tell*	48	25,026	30	1.28	31.48
21	*Alice*	705	381,180	476	.48	476.48
23	*Joe Flanner*	700	51,789	64	.73	64.73
Feb. 1	*Atlantic*	24	11,350	14	.19	14.19
14	*Relief*	82	41,697	52	.12	52.12
19	*Mary Taylor*	158	79,406	99.25		99.25
26	*Stingaree*	190	95,499	118	1.37	119.37
Mch. 1	*Lealtad*	132	70,228	86	1.78	87.78
11	*Sea Drift*	120	48,850	60	1.06	61.06
12	*Alabama*	130	47,663	58	1.58	59.58
16	*Julian*	107	57,047	70	1.30	71.30
17	*Emma*	150	74,698	92	1.37	93.37
18	*Laura Dudley*	77	41,600	52		52.00
21	*Elvira Eager*	136	67, 954	84	.94	84.94
24	*Joe Flanner*	127	54,387	68		68.00
Apr. 9	*A. J. Hodge*	28	15,237	18	1.05	19.05
10	*Helena*	142	80,022	100		100.00
10	*Nita (Crescent)*	203	115,978	144	1.00	145.00
14	*Rapid*	22	11,610	14	.51	14.51
"	*Bright*	16	7981	10		10.00
"	*Rapid*	242	130,870	162	1.60	163.60
15	*Jane Adele*	20	9800	12	.25	12.25
"	*Magnolia*	19	10,633	12	1.30	13.30

"	*Genl Prim*	50	26,354	32	.94	32.94
16	*Alice*	701	359,036	448	.80	448.80
"	"	6	2494	2	1.12	3.12
18	*Wenona*	276	137,576	172		172.00
20	*Isabel*	200	100,882	126	.10	126.10
22	*Mississippian*	165	85,175	106	.47	106.47
"	*Hunter*	43	21,666	26	1.08	27.08
24	*Genl Buckner*	169	83,922	104	.90	104.90
May 1	*Neptune*	300	149,432	186	.79	186.79
1	*Maria*	75	40,832	50	1.04	51.04
6	*Elizabeth Morse*	281	141,446	176	.80	176.80
7	*Mischief*	36	18,704	23.33	.05	23.38
8	*Sea Lion*	272	157,086	194.66	1.67	196.33
8	*Ripple*	102	53,140	66	.42	66.42
12	*Fashion*	28	14,244	16	1.80	17.80
13	*Star*	167	83,314	104	.14	104.14
18	*Ruby*	252	128,474	160	.59	160.59
21	*Nita*	188	94,382	118		118.00
21	*Neptune*	296	152,502	190	.63	190.63
21	*Badger*	32	15,640	18.66	.89	19.55
June 9	*A. Vivian*	150				
"	"	663	348,427	435.33	.20	435.53
11	*Planter*	625	308,840	386	.05	386.05
12	*Kate Dale*	825	432,476	540	.60	540.60
13	*Fanny*	407	201,606	252		252.00
15	*Alabama*	657	334,412	418		418.00
16	*W. Bagorly*	886	428,544	535.33	.35	535.68
July 7	*Alice*	710	367,192	458.66	.34	459.00
16	*James Battle*	749	350,382	438		438.00
17	*Warrior*	444	219,928	274	.91	274.91
18	*Lizzie Davis*	402	200,046	249.40	.66	250.06
Aug. 8	*A. Vivian*	589	284,122	355.33		355.33
18	*Fanny*	197	95,666	120		120.00
20	*Alabama*	657	327,108	408.66	.22	408.88
8	*Vanguard*	50	23,056	28	.82	28.82
		19,155	9,715,737	$ 9,166.61	$ 2,978.69	$ 12,145.30

* Schr – Schooner, Str – Steamer. Whither column omitted because all sailed for Havana. The export duties payment method was specified as coupons or specie starting Dec. 1, 1863. The coupon substituted for hard currency for most of the payment and specie used to make up a small balance. Exactly what the coupon was is not explained. It probably related to an alternative method of payment involving cotton bonds. Four ships running to Mobile belonged to the European Trading Company (E.T.C.): the *Denbigh*, *Fanny*, *Alabama*, and *Crescent*. Several authorities attribute a confusing array of different ships to the E.T.C. also including the *Alice*, *Vulture*, *Vixen*, and *Virgin*. The full history of the E.T.C. and its ships is unclear, and the fact of several blockade running ships having some of the same names further confuses the situation. Several of the ships appear in the above listing for Mobile. The E.T.C. must have done very well indeed.

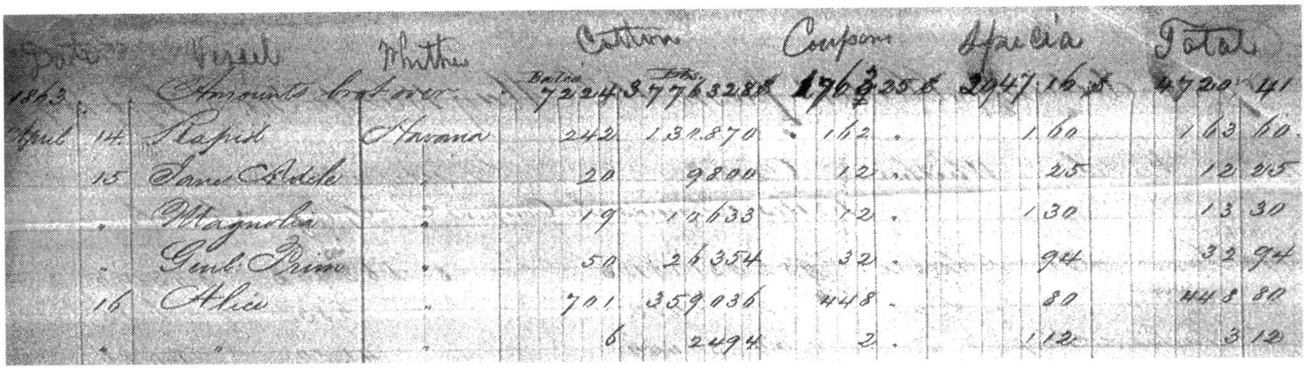

Figure 183. Top of page 2 of the table above, a hand written rather than printed report form, showing collection of export duties in Mobile. It includes, at the top, the subtotal carried forward from page 1 of the table. ***National Archives.***

Next we present a table showing only the entries regarding the *Denbigh.* The author constructed this table with data taken from several report forms and manifests.

Mobile Customs Export Extracts for the *Denbigh*

Date 1864	Exporter	Vessel	Bales Cotton	Pounds	Bales with Coupon*	Coin $	Total Duty $
Jan. 16	H. O. Brewer & Co.	*Denbigh*	500	249,658	?	?	311.82
Mar. 16	H. O. Brewer & Co.	"	424	201,402	252		252.00
Apr. 16	H. O. Brewer & Co.	"	472	212,808	266		266.00
May 4	H. O. Brewer & Co.	"	445	210,992	264		264.00
May 26	H. O. Brewer & Co.	"	442	224,544	280	0.68	280.68
June 14	H. O. Brewer & Co.	"	346	178,948	222	1.68	223.68
June 14	John Scott, Cotton Agent	"	75	39,942	50		50.00

* All sailings to Havana. "Bales with Coupon" probably refers to cotton provided by the Confederate government as required by the terms for redeeming the cotton bonds. The June 14 cargo seems to include 75 bales exported for the Confederate government. The weight per bale is interesting because later, on her runs to Galveston there was mention that special undersized bales were prepared for the *Denbigh* weighing about 400 lb. each. The current researcher thought perhaps this had to do with requirements for efficiently loading the narrow hull or the size of the hatches. The average weights of bales shipped from Mobile ranged from 451to 533 lbs., and the overall average was 488, close to the ideal standard 500 lb. bale. Other factors must have been at work regarding the Galveston bales weighing about 400 lbs.

Monthly Customs Reports, Mobile

The following transcripts were those that recorded the *Denbigh's* outbound voyages. The reports for Jan. and Aug. 1864 were missing from the archives. On the forms, the cargoes sent out by private parties and by the Confederate government were distinguished. Interestingly, export duties were not paid on the government's cotton, but duties were paid on its shipment in May. Perhaps customs regulations changed in the interim.

Abstract of duties collected on cotton exported from the district of Mobile during the month of March 1864*

Date	Exporter	Vessel	B/C	Pounds	Coupons	Coin	Total duty
Feb. 6	M. D. Esclava	*Donegal*	510	260,796	326		326.00
Mar. 1	S. Festrazzi	*Cecilia*	93	40,008	56		50.00
12	W. G. Ford	*Advance*	63	30,318	38		38.00
12	J. Tuit	*Thistle*	115	62,936	78	.67	78.67
16	R. Tuller	*Judson*	27	12,306	16		16.00
16	H. O. Brewer	*Denbigh*	424	201,602	252		252.00
Feb. 6	A. H. Brown, C.S. agent	*Donegal*	491	246,400			
Mar. 1	"	*Cecilia*	40	20,066			
12	"	*Advance*	30	15,386			
12	"	*Thistle*	115	61,354			
16	"	*Judson*	11	5,606	436		436
					1196	.67	1,196.67

Collector's Office
Mobile 31st March 1864

*The "Whither" column was omitted from the forms herein when all vessels were bound for Havana.

Abstract of duties collected on cotton exported from the Port of Mobile during the month of Apr. 1864

Date	Exporter	Vessel	Whither	B/C	Pounds	Cpn	Coin	Total
Apl. 1	J. Brittner	*Mary Virginia*	Honduras	140	68,782	$86	.00	$86.00
1	Do	*Belle*	Havana	87	35,354	44	.20	44.20
16	H. O. Brewer	*Denbigh*	"	472	212,808	266	.00	266.00
					316,944	396	.20	396.20

Collector's Office
Mobile Apr. 30th 1864
(signed) T. Sanford
Collr.

Abstract of duties collected on cotton exported from the Port of Mobile during the month of May 1864

Date	Exporter	Vessel	B/C	Pounds	Cpns	Coin	Total
May 1	M. D. Esclava	*Donegal*	567	267,164	334		334.00
"	A. H. Brown C.S. agent	"	512	240,438	300		300.00
7	Flash, Hartwell & Co.	*Mary*	671	345,232	430	1.54	431.54
7	H. O. Brewer	*Denbigh*	445	210,992	264		264.00
26	Do	do	442	224,544	280	.68	280.68
			2,637	1,288,370	$ 1,608	2.22	1,610.22

Collector's Office
Mobile, 31st May 1864
(signed) T. Sanford
Collr.

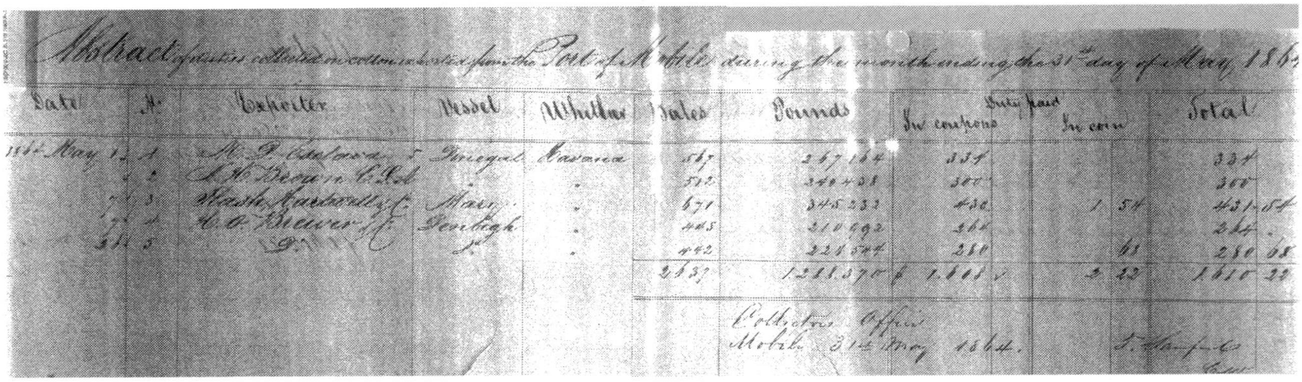

Abstract of duties collected on cotton exported from the Port of Mobile during the month ending the 31st day of May 1864

Date	No.	Exporter	Vessel	Whither	Bales	Pounds	Duty paid In coupons	In coin	Total
1864 May [illegible]	1	[illegible]	Donegal	Havana	567	267,164	334		334
"	2	A. H. Brown C. S. Agt	"	"	512	[illegible]	300		300
[illegible]	3	Flash, Hartwell & Co	Mary	"	671	345,233	430	1 54	431 54
[illegible]	4	H. O. Brewer & Co	Denbigh	"	445	210,992	264		264
31	5	Do	Do	"	442	221,544	280	[illegible]	280 68
					2637	[illegible]	1,608	2 22	1,610 22

Collector's Office
Mobile 31st May 1864.
T. Sanford
Collr.

Figure 184. Example of Monthly Abstract of Duties for Mobile, dated May 1864. ***National Archives.***

Abstract of duties collected on cotton exported from the Port of Mobile during the month ending the 30th June 1864

Date	Exporter	Vessel	B/C	Pounds	Cpn	Coin	Total
June 4	Flash, Hartwell & Co.	*Mary*	656	342,854	428	.57	$428.57
9	A. H. Brown C. S. agent	*Heroine*	272	122,846	154		154.00
14	H. O. Brewer	*Denbigh*	346	178,948	222	1.68	223.68
"	John Scott Cotton Agt.	"	75	39,942	50		50.00
					854	2.25	$ 856.25

Collr. Off. Dist. of Mobile
Montgomery, 1 July 1864
(signed) T. Sanford
Collr.

Wise in his landmark work, *Lifeline of the Confederacy*, has an historical sketch of some of the *Denbigh's* fellow runners listed on the above reports, The *Donegal* (ex-*Austin*, nine successful runs) was captured by the USS *Metacomet* June 6 while bound for Mobile. The *Mary Virginia* (also called the *Mary*, seven successful runs) was built by Laird and Sons (as was the *Denbigh*) in 1863 and was trapped in Mobile with the fall of the forts in early August. Taken for army service, the ship was captured at Gainesville, Alabama on April 12, 1865. The *Heroine* (five successful runs in the Atlantic and the Gulf) was also trapped at Mobile with the fall of the forts. The remaining ships were not covered by Wise. Since a blockade runner usually paid for herself with one successful round trip, the ships mentioned above, with multiple successful runs, were major money makers.

14

Conclusion

The first section of this book showed each of the *Denbigh's* customs documents for imports to Mobile on her voyages from Havana during the period Jan.–June 1864. These documents did not include cargo shipped in on behalf of the Confederate government, but rather merchandise shipped in by civilians. One would imagine that most such shipments would have been by merchants or other commercial middlemen. Surprisingly, many of the shipments were identified as orders by individual families for comparatively small amounts of money paid for just a few items. Careful reading of these documents provided an unrivaled insight into the exact items bought from Havana stores after a few years of shortages due to the blockade. Many of the family orders included some fabric for new cloths, a few pair of shoes, and a couple of modest treats. There were also a few examples of less obvious items like corsets, pocket knives, and dress patterns. The documents gave much detailed information on daily life, sometimes similar to things we might send for today, sometimes quite different.

The second part of the book showed prewar (fall of 1860) and early war import customs documents for comparison to the *Denbigh's* documents. These documents were most useful for comparison with the merchant orders brought in by the *Denbigh*. The merchant orders aboard the *Denbigh* were quite small compared to the prewar merchant orders. Also the wartime orders were mainly filled by Havana merchants as opposed to much larger prewar shipments direct from English manufacturers and merchants. Chapter 13 briefly covered the *Denbigh's* cotton exports form Mobile.

Archaeologists often hope to find answers to questions like "What was life like for the civilian population during the Civil War?" "What were those people up to and why?" The voluminous data form the *Denbigh's* Mobile import customs records allowed us to approach some pretty good answers to those questions. Many kinds of analysis of the data in these documents remain to be done, but those studies can follow later. Presenting the data with some commentary was a worthy purpose for the present book.

Printed in Dunstable, United Kingdom

91335481R00288